Doctors Academy

University Clinic

(For 2021 and 2022 Sittings)

R X X Ooi
S Z Y Ooi
R C Williams
S Enoch

DOCTORS ACADEMY
BETTER EDUCATION. BETTER HEALTH.

AASCE
The Academy for Advanced Scientific Communication in English

College of Physicians and Surgeons of Cardiff
Eruditio. Novatio. Excellentia. Misericordia.

Doctors Academy Publications

Doctors Academy Preparatory Guide

University Clinical Aptitude Test

(For 2021 and 2022 Sittings)

Dr Rucira Xiu Xian Ooi
Academic Foundation Doctor
University Hospital of Wales, Cardiff
NHS Wales, United Kingdom

Mr Setthasorn Zhi Yang Ooi
Medical Student, Cardiff University School of Medicine
Director, Medical School Interview Preparation Courses
Doctors Academy Group (Intl), Cardiff, United Kingdom

Miss Rebecca Charlene Williams
Lead Tutor and Director
Academy for Advanced Scientific Communication in English
Doctoral Fellow (PhD), Cardiff University, United Kingdom

Professor Stuart Enoch
Academic Lead, Higher Surgical and Postgraduate Studies
Director, Division of Advanced Medical Education
Doctors Academy Group (Intl), Cardiff, United Kingdom

DOCTORS ACADEMY
BETTER EDUCATION. BETTER HEALTH.

AASCE
The Academy for Advanced Scientific Communication in English

College of Physicians and Surgeons of Cardiff
Eruditio. Novatio. Excellentia. Misericordia.

Reprint of 1st Edition (2021), Doctors Academy Publications, Cardiff, United Kingdom

Reprint of 1st Edition	:	January 2021
Electronic Version published at	:	Doctors Academy, 189, Whitchurch Road, Cardiff, CF14 3JR, United Kingdom
Print version printed and published at	:	Abbey Bookbinding and Print Co., Unit 3, Gabalfa Workshops, Clos Menter, Cardiff CF14 3AY
ISBN	:	978-93-80573-70-0
Cover page Design	:	Sreekanth. S. S
Type setting	:	Viji Shaji
Contact	:	publishing@doctorsacademy.org.uk

CONTENTS COPYRIGHT AND DISCLAIMER

Acknowledgement:
Mrs Janine Carrigan
Academic Coordinator, Doctors Academy Educational Division
Content Developer, Doctors Academy Publications

PREFACE

The UCAT (University Clinical Aptitude Test) is an admissions test used by many medical and dental schools in the United Kingdom, Australia and New Zealand to assess a range of skills and thinking abilities in a prospective applicant. Among some of these skills is the ability to interpret data from tables and graphs, to make reasonable conclusions from abstract diagrams and text passages, and to reflect on the key qualities needed to become a doctor. It is essentially a test of aptitude rather than knowledge.

The UCAT is designed such that the difficulty of its questions is not due to the breadth of knowledge needed to answer them but, rather, since candidates must answer correctly in a few seconds. It is the constant time constraint that puts students under immense pressure during the two-hour live exam. It is advised that there is no need to revise any specific material in preparation for most of the exam. We would, however, suggest that students read the General Medical Council's Good Medical Practice as an appropriate guide to prepare them for the Situational Judgement Test section. We believe that, with early preparation and ample practice, students will eventually learn to recognise patterns and potential distractors that may be present in questions. This book will hopefully give students an insight into recognising the format in which questions are written. We have also prepared an introduction for each section with valuable 'tips and tricks' on shortcuts that will save students' time when they attempt questions.

With over 1200 questions, we hope that students find this book an essential "must-have" in their preparation for the UCAT entrance exam. This book allows all UCAT candidates the opportunity to refine and optimise their technique to answer questions effectively due to its wide range of exercises and levels of difficulty. This makes it the consummate preparation tool yet for all those who want to achieve a high score and maximise their chances of getting into the medical or dental school of their choice.

We sincerely hope that this book proves valuable in your preparation for the UCAT. We wish you all the very best.

- R X X Ooi, S Z Y Ooi, R C Williams, S Enoch

CONTENTS

CONTENTS (Continued)

CONTENTS (Continued)

CONTENTS (Continued)

CONTENTS (Continued)

CONTENTS (Continued)

CONTENTS (Continued)

General Information

About the UCAT

- It is an admissions test used by many medical and dental schools in the United Kingdom, Australia and New Zealand.
- It is used to assess a range of skills and thinking abilities in a prospective applicant.
- It is a test of aptitude rather than knowledge, which requires the candidate to reflect on the key qualities needed to become a doctor.
- A candidate's UCAT score is often used together with pre-university grades, personal statement, and performance in interview to determine the outcome of an application.
- Most students sit the UCAT prior to their application.
- Students can only sit the UCAT once per application cycle.

Format

- It is a two-hour computer-based test which consists of five separately timed sections in a multiple-choice format.
- Once the test is started, it cannot be paused for a break.
- Candidates sit either the standard UCAT or the UCATSEN (extended version) if they are entitled to extra time due to a documented medical condition or disability.
- Questions will appear in the order of:

Sections	Questions	UCAT	UCATSEN
Verbal Reasoning	44	21 minutes + 1 minute to read instructions	26 minutes 15 seconds + 1 minute 15 seconds to read instructions
Decision Making	29	31 minutes + 1 minute to read instructions	38 minutes 45 seconds + 1 minute 15 seconds to read instructions
Quantitative Reasoning	36	24 minutes + 1 minute to read instructions	30 minutes + 1 minute 15 seconds to read instructions
Abstract Reasoning	55	13 minutes + 1 minute to read instructions	16 minutes 15 seconds + 1 minute 15 seconds to read instructions
Situational Judgement	69	26 minutes + 1 minute to read instructions	32 minutes 30 seconds + 1 minute 15 seconds to read instructions

General Information (Continued)

Dates and Pricing

- The UCAT usually runs between July and October in the United Kingdom, with registration typically open in May.
- At the time of writing (January 2021), the fee for tests taken within the UK and the EU is £75, whilst the fee for tests taken outside the EU is £120. We would, however, advise that you check the UCAT website for the most updated information (https://www.ucat.ac.uk/ucat/dates-and-fees/).

Scores

- The UCAT is marked on the number of correct answers you give.
- There is **NO** negative marking for incorrect answers.
- The candidate's performance on one question does not influence the next question presented.
- Candidates will receive test results immediately after taking the test (before they leave the test centre).
- Candidates will also be able to access test results online via their Pearson VUE account.
- Candidates should allow 24 hours after their test for the results to be uploaded.
- The UCAT is scored out of 3,600. This is the accumulated score achieved in the Verbal Reasoning, Quantitative Reasoning, Abstract Reasoning and Decision Making sections.
- Candidates will receive a breakdown of scores from each of these four sections, scaled between a score of 300 and 900.
- For the Situational Judgement section, candidates will be awarded a band between Band 1 (i.e. the highest band) and Band 4 (i.e. the lowest band).
- Apart from the Decision Making section, where multiple-part questions are worth 2 marks, every other question is worth 1 mark.
- For more information on previous UCAT test statistics for the years 2015 – 2019, please refer to the next page titled 'UCAT Test Statistics 2015 – 2019'.
- A score of above 650 represents a good and average score.
- A score of above 700 represents a high score.
- A score of below 600 represents a low score.

Application

- To maximise your chances of getting into a UK medical or dental school,

look at individual university entry requirements to find out how much emphasis is placed on the UCAT score.
Keep in mind the deadline to submit your personal statement. It is advised that candidates take the exam 3–4 weeks before this deadline.
Should you attain a less competitive score, you will then have sufficient time to tailor your personal statement if you have to change your choice of university. This is because various universities use personal statements and UCAT scores differently.

Preparation

- A timeline for preparation is included at the start of each section in this book.
- Book your test through the Pearson VUE official website.
- After booking, you will receive a confirmation email for your chosen exam time, date and location.

On the Day

- Remember to print out the confirmation email and take it with you to the test centre.
- Candidates are also expected to bring photographic identification (e.g., passport or driving licence).
- Pens, pencils or a whiteboard marker will be provided.
- Be sure to arrive early and before your test starts.
- Most importantly, relax!

UCAT Test Statistics 2015 - 2019

After each year, scores are published by the UCAT Consortium.

These scores are demonstrated in deciles. Each decile represents 10% of candidates who sat the UCAT test in that particular year. This is to show candidates where they have been placed in relation to the rest of the cohort who took the test that year.

If a candidate attains a UCAT score in the 1st decile, this means that the candidate has scored in the bottom 10% of that cohort. A score in the 10th decile means that the candidate is in the top 10% of all the candidates who sat the UCAT exam that year.

General Information (Continued)

These scores are created by adding together the scores from all sections except Situational Judgement.

The table below shows the UCAT scores of candidates in the last five years:

Decile Rank	2015	2016	2017	2018	2019
10th	>2850	> 2160	> 2870	> 2820	> 2800
9th	2840	2150	2860	2810	2800
8th	2740	2060	2750	2690	2690
7th	2660	1990	2670	2610	2610
6th	2600	1940	2600	2550	2540
5th	2540	1890	2540	2490	2480
4th	2470	1850	2480	2420	2420
3rd	2410	1790	2420	2360	2360
2nd	2330	1730	2340	2280	2280
1st	2210	1640	2230	2160	2170

The table below shows the average score attained by candidates for each section in the last five years:

	2015	2016	2017	2018	2019
Verbal Reasoning	577	573	570	567	565
Quantitative Reasoning	685	690	695	658	662
Abstract Reasoning	640	630	629	637	638
Decision Making	629	Unscored	647	624	618
Total	2531	1893	2540	2485	2483
Average	633	631	635	621	620

General Information (Continued)

The table below shows the distribution of candidates' performance in the Situational Judgement section in the last five years:

	2015	2016	2017	2018	2019
Band 1	24%	26%	28%	21%	17%
Band 2	45%	44%	42%	34%	40%
Band 3	22%	22%	21%	32%	33%
Band 4	9%	9%	9%	13%	10%

Based on the data presented, Verbal Reasoning appears to be the most difficult section. Candidates attained an average score of 570 from 2015 to 2019. This is in comparison to Quantitative Reasoning where an average score of 678 was attained by candidates from 2015 to 2019.

In regard to Abstract Reasoning and Decision Making, scores appear to have a wider variation, with Abstract Reasoning scores ranging between 630 to 640 and Decision Making scores ranging between 620 to 630.

Unlike other sections, Situational Judgement is scored between Band 1 (highest) and Band 4 (lowest). From the data shown, most candidates scored Band 2 from 2015 to 2019.

Verbal Reasoning

FORMAT

In the exam, you have:

- 44 questions
- two types of questions
- 21 minutes
- +1 minute to read the instructions

In this section, there are:

- 75 scenarios (300 questions)

Objectives:

- To be able to comprehend written information.
- To be able to extrapolate the information required to logically answer a series of associated questions.

TYPES OF QUESTIONS

Type 1 | True/ False/ Can't Tell

- You will be presented with a statement and must decide whether, based on the information within the passage, it is true, false or cannot be known.
- **True** – The statement is true on account of the information provided in the passage.
- **False** – The statement is false on account of the information provided in the passage.
- **Can't Tell** – It cannot be known if the statement is true or false on the basis of the information provided in the passage.

Type 2 | Multiple Choice

- You will be given four statements and asked a question such as 'Which of the following statements is best supported by the information contained in the passage?' or 'According to the writer, which amongst the following assertions cannot be considered to be accurate?'
- You must select the correct statement.

TIPS AND TRICKS TO SCORE

Revision Tips

- Read the question and look for keywords.
- Practice speed reading passages (recommended twelve weeks before your test date) to improve your reading comprehension skills and ability to look for keywords.
- Learn to make inferences and understand arguments.
- Familiarise yourself with 'extreme' words and 'softer' words.
  - ⇒ Examples of 'softer' words: many, most, some, majority.
  - ⇒ Examples of 'extreme' words: never, none, always, the best.
- 'Soft' statements tend to be true.
- 'Extreme' statements tend to be false or can't tell.
- Learn how to spot passage adjustments by reading both the passage and statement carefully.
- Avoid using external knowledge.

Answering Techniques

- The Verbal Reasoning section of the test comprises 11 written passages, each of which is based on a topic of general interest and is not necessarily related to the field of medicine. They might be descriptive, informative, argumentative or analytical. You will be asked four questions on each passage, which means that you will be required to answer a total of 44 questions. You will be given 21 minutes to answer all of the questions, therefore, it is recommended that you spend approximately 30 seconds per question (or two minutes per passage).
- **Skim the passage**. Due to the tight time restrictions, you will not have time to read the passage in detail. You should aim to obtain the most important details and the information that enables you to answer the questions. You will often find that a question refers to a specific part of the passage. Locate this paragraph and focus on it more closely; you can ignore the phrases that do not help you to answer the questions. You should, however, be aware that you will encounter questions that require you to simultaneously consider information expressed in different parts of the passage. It will take you a little more time to answer these questions, but you would have saved valuable seconds by concentrating on particular sentences to respond to other questions.

TIPS AND TRICKS TO SCORE (Continued)

- **Do not apply the knowledge that you already possess.** You might find that you are familiar with the topic discussed in a passage. However, you must use only the information in the passage to answer the questions, and you should not respond based on your own knowledge. It is possible that the passage might contain details that you know to be incorrect, but you must answer the questions according to the information presented in that particular passage. Remember that the questions are tools to determine if you can interpret a given written passage.
- **Read the question carefully.** This is particularly vital for the multiple -choice questions. Look for keywords such as 'deduce', 'infer', 'corroborate', 'support', 'negate', 'accurate', 'agree', and 'disagree'. What is the question really asking? If it asks which statement can be deduced, inferred, corroborated or supported, you should find the statement that is true. If it asks with which statement the writer disagrees, select the one that is false.
- **Look for keywords.** The questions will contain keywords and, if you ignore or overlook them, the entire meaning of the assertion will change. Some common keywords are: 'might', 'could', 'only', 'if true', 'presumably', 'commonly', 'many', 'likely', 'unlikely', 'best' and 'cannot'. When you are preparing for the test, compile a list of keywords that you frequently encounter and consider what they really mean. For example, the word 'commonly' is not synonymous with the word 'always'. It can imply that something happens *often*, but it does not infer that it *always* happens.
- **Decipher what the information suggests.** Consider the phrase: 'This research shows that the majority of people who had a myocardial infarction have eaten fast food between four and six times each week for the last thirty years.' The question might be: 'Fast food causes heart attacks.' The correct answer is 'can't tell'. The phrase suggests that there could be a relationship between fast food and heart attacks, but it does not explicitly state that it is the definitive cause. In addition, it neither infers nor refutes that a heart attack is caused by another factor. These statements require you to apply logic and reasoning, a skills that, with practice, you can develop in order to approach these questions confidently in the test.
- **Use your own logic.** Think about the statement: 'The shampoo made by Hair Factory is not tested on animals.' This statement tells us that

TIPS AND TRICKS TO SCORE (Continued)

shampoo that is tested on animals cannot be produced by Hair Factory. Yet, we cannot assume that all shampoo that is not manufactured by Hair Factory is tested on animals; the statement does not preclude that other producers of shampoo do not test on animals. We also cannot surmise that all shampoo that is not tested on animals is made by Hair Factory since the statement does not allude to other companies.

- **Answer every question.** The UCAT is not negatively marked, and you cannot lose marks for selecting the wrong answer. You might not get the mark if you guess incorrectly, but you definitely will not get the mark if you leave the answer blank.

Verbal Reasoning is included in the test since it evaluates your suitability to the medical profession by requesting you to quickly understand a piece of information and decipher it in a useful manner. This skill is essential to a career in medicine. You will routinely be required to speak to patients and relatives. On occasions, it might prove difficult to interpret what they truly mean, but you must be able to comprehend correctly in order to make the right diagnosis or enact the most appropriate mode of treatment. You will also need to read research papers, infer the primary findings and, in some instances, apply them to your own clinical practice. The verbal reasoning component tests your capability to interpret information in a logical and rational manner in order to determine the accurate answer and/or outcome.

Question 1 - Food Allergy Knowledge and Attitudes

More than 10 percent of people in Europe have food allergies. When eating out, they rely on restaurant staff to provide suitable foods, but previous research points to major gaps in food allergy knowledge among restaurant staff. Moreover, most studies have not adequately addressed staff attitudes toward food allergies, nor which factors might determine food allergy knowledge and food allergy attitudes.

To improve understanding in this area, Loerbroks and colleagues conducted structured, face-to-face interviews with 295 staff members of restaurants in 15 randomly selected districts of Düsseldorf, Germany. They found that just 30 percent of the interviewees could correctly name three common food allergens, and 41 percent correctly answered five true-or-false statements about food allergies.

Most of the staff held positive attitudes regarding their and their colleagues' responsibility to help meet the needs of customers with food allergies. However, the interviewees generally held negative attitudes about serving such customers and had negative attitudes regarding the accuracy of customers' reports of their own food allergies.

Statistical analyses revealed factors that could influence food allergy knowledge and attitudes. For instance, higher food-allergy knowledge levels were found among managers, staff members with the highest school degree, staff at larger restaurants, and staff at restaurants with more comprehensive customer service. Female staff were more likely to believe customers' self-reports of food allergies. Notably, no links were found between prior food allergy training and food allergy knowledge.

Source: Adapted from Science Daily (https://www.sciencedaily.com/releases/2019/04/190424153711.htm).
The text used here is for educational purposes. The contents and the copyright belong to the aforementioned source.

1. Food allergies must be taken seriously because:
    A. the number of Europeans with one has increased.
    B. limited studies have been conducted on attitudes towards them.
    C. the public is completely reliant on the knowledge that restaurant staff possess.
    D. less than 50% of those interviewed have sufficient knowledge of food allergies.

2. Which amongst the following statements corroborates the information in the passage?
    A. Those who were interviewed understand their responsibility towards customers with food allergies.
    B. Those who were interviewed are supportive of customers with food allergies.
    C. Those working in restaurants in the UK are positive about supporting customers with food allergies.
    D. Those who were interviewed are entirely dependent on what the customer tells them about his or her food allergy.

3. The author suggests that existing studies on food allergies leave much to be desired.
    A. True
    B. False
    C. Can't Tell

4. This study has revealed that:
    A. only one in three restaurant workers in Germany is able to name three common food allergies.
    B. more than 181 interviewees had adequate knowledge of food allergies.
    C. every corner of society exhibits gendered distinctions.
    D. those with a sound educative background are more alert to concerns surrounding food allergies.

Question 2 - Part-Time Courses

Diploma Units Law and Practice (Legal Studies): This is the final academic stage towards becoming a qualified legal executive. Completion of the qualification will enable you to become a member of the Chartered Institute of Legal Executives (CILEx). The course is suitable for anyone in the final stages of being a qualified legal executive.

Professional Diploma in Accounting: AAT qualifications develop relevant and practical accounting and finance skills for life. If you are looking to improve your prospects and earning potential in an accounting environment, this course will help you achieve your goals. It is suitable if you are interested in finance and accountancy and want to be chartered in your industry.

IOSH Certificate in Managing: If you're a manager or supervisor, this course will help you to apply sound management principles to safety and health issues in your team as part of a total management strategy. As it is modular in nature, the course can be tailored to meet your individual business requirements. This course is for managers from any organisation or sector who need to manage efficiently and effectively in compliance with both their organisation's safety policy and current health and safety legislation.

City and Guilds Award in Employability (Level 2): Whether you're heading into the world of work or thinking about longer-term career development, this course will give you some of the basic skills you'll need. It will allow you to progress in education and/or employment, improve your job prospects, and provide you with appropriate life skills to become more independent.

Source: Adapted from Coleg Gwent (https://www.coleggwent.ac.uk/learning/part-time).
The text used here is for educational purposes. The contents and the copyright belong to the aforementioned source.

1. Legal Studies will not provide automatic membership to the professional body.
   A. True
   B. False
   C. Can't Tell

2. A Professional Diploma in Accounting will provide you with the opportunity to increase your salary.
   A. True
   B. False
   C. Can't Tell

3. The IOSH Certificate would not be appropriate for managers working in an office environment.
   A. True
   B. False
   C. Can't Tell

4. The City and Guilds Award in Employability will not prove advantageous for an individual who is keen to enhance his or her CV.
   A. True
   B. False
   C. Can't Tell

Question 3 - Warming Clips the Nightingale's Wings

Rising temperatures may be having a profound physical impact on one of the world's favourite songbirds. Researchers in Spain found that, over a 20-year period, nightingales had evolved smaller wingspans.

The scientists say this is linked to a changing climate in the region which has seen the early onset of spring and increased drought. They are concerned that this could affect the bird's ability to migrate in winter.

Farmed for its ability to sing, the nightingale has a very rich repertoire as it is able to produce over 1,000 different sounds, compared to just 340 by skylarks. Although common in many parts of Europe and Asia, the bird is mainly seen and heard in southern England.

Numbers here have declined markedly over the last half century, down 90%, with multiple factors to blame, including deer eating their preferred nesting sites, but also because of a changing climate.

Source: Adapted from The BBC (https://www.bbc.co.uk/news/science-environment-52111309).
The text used here is for educational purposes. The contents and the copyright belong to the aforementioned source.

1. Which amongst the following statements is supported by the information in the passage?
   A. The number of nightingales in parts of the UK has decreased over the last fifty years.
   B. Nightingales can be found in Spain.
   C. Skylarks are found in Europe.
   D. Nightingales can be found throughout the world.

2. The researchers to which reference is made in this passage studied the nightingale in its natural habitat.
   A. True
   B. False
   C. Can't Tell

3. Which of the following statements is not corroborated by the information in this passage?
   A. Nightingales are bred due to their ability to sing.
   B. The consequences of climate change are affecting the livelihood of the nightingale.
   C. The researchers mentioned in this passage have studied data from less than twenty years ago.
   D. Skylarks are less popular than nightingales.

4. Skylarks produce three times as many sounds as nightingales.
   A. True
   B. False
   C. Can't Tell

Question 4 - Excerpt from *Jane Eyre*

There was no possibility of taking a walk that day. We had been wandering, indeed, in the leafless shrubbery an hour in the morning; but since dinner (Mrs. Reed, when there was no company, dined early) the cold winter wind had brought with it clouds so sombre, and a rain so penetrating, that further outdoor exercise was now out of the question. I was glad of it; I never liked long walks, especially on chilly afternoons: dreadful to me was the coming home in the raw twilight, with nipped fingers and toes, and a heart saddened by the chidings of Bessie, the nurse, and humbled by the consciousness of my physical inferiority to Eliza, John, and Georgiana Reed.

The said Eliza, John, and Georgiana were now clustered round their mamma in the drawing-room: she lay reclined on a sofa by the fireside, and with her darlings about her (for the time neither quarrelling nor crying) looked perfectly happy. Me, she had dispensed from joining the group, saying, "She regretted to be under the necessity of keeping me at a distance; but that until she heard from Bessie, and could discover by her own observation that I was endeavouring in good earnest to acquire a more sociable and childlike disposition, a more attractive and sprightly manner – something lighter, franker, more natural, as it were – she really must exclude me from privileges intended only for contented, happy little children."

1. The narrator had enjoyed being outdoors on that particular day.
   A. True
   B. False
   C. Can't Tell

2. Which amongst the following statements does the passage corroborate?
   A. Eliza is Georgiana's only sister.
   B. The narrator is related to John.
   C. The narrator is often scolded.
   D. The narrator is younger than the other children.

3. Bessie is the person who would determine if the narrator had behaved as the other children.
   A. True
   B. False
   C. Can't Tell

4. The narrator has been told to:
   A. resemble other children.
   B. adopt different characteristics to other children.
   C. sit with the other children.
   D. stop arguing with the other children.

Question 5 - Excerpt from *Father Sergius*

Abbot Kasatsky submitted himself as to his chosen director. Here in the monastery, besides the feeling of ascendency over others that such a life gave him, he felt much as he had done in the world: he found satisfaction in attaining the greatest possible perfection outwardly as well as inwardly. As in the regiment he had been not merely an irreproachable officer but had even exceeded his duties and widened the borders of perfection, so also as a monk he tried to be perfect, and was always industrious, abstemious, submissive, and meek, as well as pure both in deed and in thought, and obedient. This last quality in particular made life far easier for him. If many of the demands of life in the monastery, which was near the capital and much frequented, did not please him and were temptations to him, they were all nullified by obedience: 'It is not for me to reason; my business is to do the task set me, whether it be standing beside the relics, singing in the choir, or making up accounts in the monastery guest-house.' All possibility of doubt about anything was silenced by obedience to the starets. Had it not been for this, he would have been oppressed by the length and monotony of the church services, the bustle of the many visitors, and the bad qualities of the other monks. As it was, he not only bore it all joyfully but found in it solace and support.

Source: Copyright © 1911 by Leo Tolstoy.

1. The abbot took care of his physical appearance.
   A. True
   B. False
   C. Can't Tell

2. The abbot's dutiful temperament meant that he:
   A. was able to compare himself to the other abbots in the monastery.
   B. dismissed any antipathetic sentiments.
   C. pleased those in charge of the monastery.
   D. encouraged many visitors to speak to him.

3. Which of the following statements is supported by the information in the passage?
   A. Abbot Kasatsky felt superior to the other monks in the monastery.
   B. Abbot Kasatsky served in the army.
   C. Abbot Kasatsky's faith prompted him to put up with things that he thought were tedious.
   D. Abbot Kasatsky was required to speak to many people who came to the monastery.

4. The monk was often able to achieve perfection; he had done so throughout his life.
   A. True
   B. False
   C. Can't Tell

Question 6 - Inulin in Food Products Could Be Bothering Your Stomach

Fibre is "the new protein," according to market research firms. But it could also be the new pain in your stomach. If you're like most Americans, you're trying to add more fibre to your diet. That's a good thing, because the average American gets only half the recommended amount of fibre each day. Manufacturers are responding to consumers' wishes by adding fibre to a plethora of foods and beverages, including cereals, energy bars, protein supplements, "healthier" cookies, diet ice cream and even bottled water.

One of the most prevalent fibre-boosting ingredients is inulin. Like any fibre, it can cause gas, bloating and abdominal pain if consumed too quickly or in large quantities. Many of my clients who have complained about digestive discomfort don't realise how much inulin they're consuming each day. Most of them have never even heard of it.

Inulin is a type of prebiotic, a substance that's used by the microorganisms in your digestive tract and positively influences health. At this point, there is evidence that three prebiotics can provide health benefits: inulin, also referred to as long-chain inulin; fructooligosaccharide (FOS), a short-chain inulin that's also called oligofructose; and galactooligosaccharide (GOS).

Source: Adapted from The Washington Post (https://www.washingtonpost.com/lifestyle/wellness/what-is-inulin-and-why-is-it-showing-up-in-so-many-food-products/2019/06/11/3ee3d4be-86ec-11e9-98c1-e945ae5db8fb_story.html?utm_term=.fc1d852ebdd4).
The text used here is for educational purposes. The contents and the copyright belong to the aforementioned source.

1. Insulin can cause gas, bloating and abdominal pain.
   A. True
   B. False
   C. Can't Tell

2. Which amongst the following is always true?
   A. Americans are trying to increase the amount of fibre they ingest.
   B. Certain foods contain more fibre than others.
   C. "Healthier" cookies are made up of more fibre than regular cookies.
   D. Inulin causes side-effects.

3. According to the information in the passage, inulin:
   A. cannot be digested by the human body.
   B. is not worth taking since the consequences outweigh the benefits.
   C. can replace fibre.
   D. should not be consumed in large quantities, and one should eat products that contain it slowly.

4. One in 6 Americans does not consume the recommended daily amount of fibre.
   A. True
   B. False
   C. Can't Tell

Question 7 - Florence Nightingale

Florence Nightingale was the superintendent of a private hospital for gentlewomen. She became a nurse, a disreputable occupation that rivalled scullery work on the social scale, and spent time with a Protestant institution near Düsseldorf and with the French Sisters of Charity in Paris. She was appointed superintendent of female nursing at Scutari and, crucially, gave her authority to select and dismiss staff.

She arrived in Scutari in November, with a group including 10 Irish Sisters of Mercy based in Bermondsey near London, and established headquarters in an abandoned Turkish army barracks which had been converted into a hospital. The stench from blocked sewers was overwhelming, and the place was so filthy that, as she wrote to Herbert, the vermin, if they had unity of purpose, could carry off the beds on their backs.

Over the next 18 months, she fought a mostly successful battle to introduce hygiene, reorganise kitchens and laundries, employ soldiers as orderlies, and obtain such basic items as blankets from the bureaucratic army commissariat. About 125 nurses served under her, including Irish laywomen. By May 1855, mortality from cholera and typhoid had halved.

While her lasting image is of a kindly lady with a lamp flitting from room to room in the glimmering gloom, an image based on a comment by Russell and a poem by Henry Longfellow, her main contribution was as a manager and organiser who did not brook opposition.

So when 15 Mercy sisters were sent from Ireland to Scutari without her agreement in December 1854, she initially refused to receive them. Eventually she accepted five at the Barrack hospital and sent the others to a new hospital at Koulali a few miles away. In September 1855, they took over the main hospital at Balaclava, outside her jurisdiction, and remained until the war ended.

Source: Adapted from The Irish Times (https://www.irishtimes.com/opinion/unshakeable-purpose-florence-nightingale-the-woman-who-revolutionised-nursing-1.4249703).
The text used here is for educational purposes. The contents and the copyright belong to the aforementioned source.

1. What conclusion can be drawn from the passage?
   A. Florence rejected the trainees as she had not initiated their enrolment.
   B. Florence was dedicated to welcoming any recruits enlisted.
   C. Florence initiated some antagonism within the staff under her supervision.
   D. Florence was deficient in the level of education to follow a more appropriate career.

2. Which of the following assertions is not supported by the information in the passage?
   A. Florence was efficacious in plummeting death levels.
   B. Florence was instrumental in the enhancement of sanitation.
   C. Florence was committed to developing and educating laywomen.
   D. Florence was committed to an occupation that was belittled.

3. It can be inferred from the passage that the author:
   A. deems that Florence had a negligible impact on the nursing vocation.
   B. considers the reputation of Florence to be wholly vindicated.
   C. believes that Florence was somewhat supercilious and formidable.
   D. implies that Florence has not obtained the acknowledgement she warrants.

4. Which of these statements can best be corroborated from the information contained in the passage?
   A. Florence instantly exhibited empathy to all who encountered her.
   B. Florence begrudged any usurping of her authority.
   C. Florence's parents did not encourage her to enrol in the nursing profession.
   D. Florence had a profound trepidation of rodents.

Question 8 - A Non-Invasive Way of Monitoring Diabetes

Saliva could be used instead of blood to monitor diabetes in a method proposed in research involving the University of Strathclyde. The test has been developed as an alternative to the current prevalent practice of monitoring blood glucose, which can be invasive, painful, and costly.

Lab tests of the saliva process had an accuracy rate of 95.2%. The research shows promising results for monitoring diabetes, which affects an estimated 425 million people worldwide – around half of them undiagnosed.

The research has been published in the journal *PLOS ONE*. It also involved partners at the Federal University of Uberlandia in Minas Gerais, Brazil, the University of Vale do Paraíba in Sao Paolo, Brazil and the University of Saskatchewan in Canada.

Source: Adapted from Science Daily (https://www.sciencedaily.com/releases/2020/04/200416135954.htm).
The text used here is for educational purposes. The contents and the copyright belong to the aforementioned source.

1. According to the information in the passage, saliva could be used in tests to monitor diabetes because:
   A. it is more reliable than blood.
   B. fifty percent of people with diabetes are unaware that they have the condition.
   C. it is easier to obtain than blood.
   D. it would prove advantageous for patients.

2. Which of the following assertions is not corroborated by the information in the passage?
   A. People with severe diabetes will benefit from this type of test.
   B. This research involved scholars in Brazil.
   C. Researchers in the UK were involved in this study.
   D. The test that relies on saliva is very accurate.

3. A quarter of the world's population has diabetes.
   A. True
   B. False
   C. Can't Tell

4. Which amongst the following statements is always true?
   A. Tests that use saliva will replace those that use blood.
   B. Such research is published in reliable journals.
   C. There are two universities in Brazil.
   D. Blood enables diabetes to be monitored effectively.

Question 9 - A Shock Response

Our immune system does a remarkable job of protecting us against the harmful effects of infectious agents that cause disease. However, every so often this defence mechanism can be made to turn on itself, triggering a violent, often fatal, reaction against its host. Understanding how the immune system can be prompted to behave in such a self-destructive manner can be traced to discoveries made by a Nobel Laureate in Physiology or Medicine.

Through a series of experiments, Charles Richet demonstrated that this adverse response, which he termed anaphylaxis, was far from being an accident or an aberration, as many scientists in the field had thought. Working with Paul Portier, Richet discovered that dogs that had received an injection of sea-anemone poison without any noticeable distress always went into shock and died quickly after receiving a weaker dose a set amount of days later. Instead of raising tolerance towards the toxin, as expected, the initial dose in fact made animals highly sensitive for a set period of time to even miniscule amounts of the poison. Systematically administering a number of poisons in this manner and examining the violent reactions led Richet to conclude that anaphylaxis behaves in a similar, but opposite, manner to immunity. For instance, reactions were specific to the poison in question, and transferring blood from an affected animal to a healthy one could provoke hypersensitivity to the toxin.

Source: Adapted from Nobel Prize (https://www.nobelprize.org/prizes/medicine/1913/speedread/).
The text used here is for educational purposes. The contents and the copyright belong to the aforementioned source.

1. Which amongst the following can be verified by the information offered in the passage?
   A. The immune system did not start to be studied recently.
   B. The Nobel Prize in Physiology or Medicine is awarded every year.
   C. Portier and Richet were awarded the Nobel Prize in Physiology or Medicine.
   D. Richet used only animals as experimental subjects.

2. Dogs died during Richet's research.
   A. True
   B. False
   C. Can't Tell

3. Which amongst the following assertions is corroborated by the information in the passage?
   A. Dogs are the only animal on which this research was conducted.
   B. Richet had to apply for ethical approval.
   C. Richet's findings led him to confute what other scientists had proposed.
   D. Richet administered poison into dogs only.

4. That an individual goes into anaphylactic shock:
   A. had been suspected for many years.
   B. poses a risk to his or her life.
   C. often occurs after he or she has been poisoned.
   D. can be alleviated with medicine.

Question 10 - CRISPR Might Be the Banana's Only Hope Against a Deadly Fungus

The race to engineer the next-generation banana is on. The Colombian government confirmed last month that a banana-killing fungus has invaded the Americas — the source of much of the world's banana supply. The invasion has given new urgency to efforts to create fruit that can withstand the scourge. Scientists are using a mix of approaches to save the banana.

A team in Australia has inserted a gene from wild bananas into the top commercial variety — known as the Cavendish — and is currently testing these modified bananas in field trials. Researchers are also turning to the powerful, precise gene-editing tool CRISPR to boost the Cavendish's resilience against the fungus, known as *Fusarium* wilt tropical race 4 (TR4).

Breeding TR4 resistance into the Cavendish using conventional methods is not possible because the variety is sterile and propagated by cloning. The variety accounts for 99% of global banana shipments.

Source: Adapted from Nature
(https://www.nature.com/articles/d41586-019-02770-7).

1. Which amongst the following statements can be verified by the information within the passage?
   A. We should be concerned that a fungus has invaded the Americas because a significant number of bananas are sold there.
   B. We should be concerned that a fungus has invaded the Americas because a significant number of bananas are grown there.
   C. We should be concerned that a fungus has invaded the Americas because extensive research on bananas takes place there.
   D. We should be concerned that a fungus has invaded the Americas because the government is ill-equipped to manage the situation.

2. The Cavendish is a type of banana purchased by inhabitants of Australia.
   A. True
   B. False
   C. Can't Tell

3. CRISPR will prove futile in preventing bananas from the fungus.
   A. True
   B. False
   C. Can't Tell

4. One variety of banana accounts for 1% of global banana shipments.
   A. True
   B. False
   C. Can't Tell

Question 11 - Climate Change: Should You Fly, Drive or Take the Train?

Flights produce greenhouse gases - mainly carbon dioxide (CO_2) - from burning fuel. These contribute to global warming when released into the atmosphere.

An economy-class return flight from London to New York emits an estimated 0.67 tonnes of CO_2per passenger, according to the calculator from the UN's civil aviation body, the International Civil Aviation Organization (ICAO). That's equivalent to 11% of the average annual emissions for someone in the UK, or about the same as those caused by someone living in Ghana over a year.

Aviation contributes about 2% of the world's global carbon emissions, according to the International Air Transport Association (IATA). It predicts passenger numbers will double to 8.2 billion in 2037.

And, as other sectors of the economy become greener - with more wind turbines, for example - aviation's proportion of total emissions is set to rise. It depends where passengers sit and whether they are taking a long-haul flight or a shorter one. This is because there is more space per seat, so each person accounts for a larger amount of the whole plane's pollution.

Source: Adapted from The BBC (https://www.bbc.co.uk/news/science-environment-49349566).
The text used here is for educational purposes. The contents and the copyright belong to the aforementioned source.

1. If you were to fly from London to New York, you would:
   A. add approximately 0.67 tonnes to your carbon footprint.
   B. emit the same as your colleague, who lives in the UK and does not fly, emits in an entire year.
   C. emit 5.5% of what your colleague, who lives in the UK and does not fly, emits in an entire year.
   D. increase your carbon footprint to match that of an individual in Ghana.

2. Which amongst the following assertions can be best supported by the information in the passage?
   A. Airplane travel's contribution to global carbon emissions will be 4% in 2037.
   B. Each year, 4.1 billion people travel by plane.
   C. The size of a seat on an airplane does not shape the amount of pollution emitted by that vehicle.
   D. The total proportion of the world's carbon emissions that comes from airplane travel is low.

3. People who travel from the UK to America have one of the biggest carbon footprints in the world.
   A. True
   B. False
   C. Can't Tell

4. According to the author of this passage, airplane travel:
   A. will observe a difference in travellers' habits.
   B. is a minor contributor to global warming.
   C. will become more sustainable.
   D. is monitored by IATA.

Question 12 - D-Day Landings

Troops from the UK, the US, Canada and France attacked German forces on the coast of northern France on 6 June 1944. It was the largest military, naval, air and land operation ever attempted and marked the start of the campaign to liberate Nazi-occupied north-west Europe.

D-Day involved the simultaneous landing of tens of thousands of troops on five separate beaches in Normandy. More than a year in the planning, it was originally set to start on 5 June, judged to be the most likely date to combine calm seas, a full moon and low water at first light. However, storms meant it was delayed by 24 hours to 6 June.

Airborne troops were dropped behind enemy lines in the early hours, while thousands of ships gathered off the Normandy coast for the main attack. Though they were expecting an invasion, German military leaders believed the initial attacks were only a diversionary tactic. A deception plan in the weeks ahead of the attack had led them to expect the main invasion further along the coast. The surprise element helped British troops establish a foothold on a beach codenamed Gold. In addition, Canadian forces established themselves on another beach - Juno - and the British got on to Sword beach. American soldiers also managed to land on the westernmost beach - Utah - without major casualties.

But, at nearby Omaha beach, the US force suffered serious losses. The naval barrage and bombing raids on the German defences were ineffective, and the Americans encountered a crack division of German troops.

Source: Adapted from The BBC (https://www.bbc.co.uk/news/world-48513108).
The text used here is for educational purposes. The contents and the copyright belong to the aforementioned source.

1. It was hoped that D-Day would:
   A. be the biggest operation that had ever been undertaken.
   B. lead to the removal of German forces from Europe.
   C. encourage troops already in France to assemble on certain beaches in the country.
   D. protect French citizens and lead to German surrender.

2. Which of the following statements is not supported by the passage?
   A. British troops arrived on the beach in the same area as the Canadians.
   B. Canadian troops stormed Juno beach.
   C. American troops landed on Utah and Omaha beaches.
   D. British troops secured a position on Gold beach.

3. Only American troops were killed in the D-Day Landings.
   A. True
   B. False
   C. Can't Tell

4. Which amongst the following assertions is corroborated by the information in the passage?
   A. Some troops were waiting on the beaches since they were already located in France.
   B. Only veterans are allowed on the beaches today.
   C. The D-Day Landings proved a huge success for the British.
   D. The Germans were not fully prepared for the scale of D-Day Landings.

Question 13 - Huge Knowledge Gap Over Health of Soil

A vital knowledge gap about England's environment has been uncovered by soil campaigners. They have discovered that just 0.41% of the cash invested in environmental monitoring goes on examining the soil. That is despite the fact that soils round the world, including in the UK, are said to be facing a crisis.

The figures are startling: £60.5m goes to monitoring water quality, £7.65m to checking on air, and just £284,000 to auditing soil. The mismatch was revealed in a Freedom of Information (FoI) request by the Sustainable Soils Alliance (SSA).

The Department for Environment, Food and Rural Affairs (Defra) told BBC News it was planning to design an indicator for healthy soils and to establish a new national soil monitoring scheme. It says powers in the Agriculture Bill could be used to support the monitoring. But the SSA says it has seen no evidence that Defra will commit to funding soil monitoring.

It comes as concern about the state of soil has been running high.

Source: Adapted from The BBC (https://www.bbc.co.uk/news/science-environment-51861539).
The text used here is for educational purposes. The contents and the copyright belong to the aforementioned source.

1. Soil should be examined because:
   A. a large amount of money is set aside for this exact purpose.
   B. its health is declining.
   C. too much money is spent on other areas of the environment.
   D. tougher measures have been called for by environmental campaigners.

2. According to the author of the passage,:
   A. there is no discrepancy between the amount of money spent on soil monitoring and the amount of money spent on other aspects.
   B. more money will be devoted to soil monitoring.
   C. the way in which money is spent proves surprising.
   D. the Agriculture Bill could provide the funds to support soil monitoring.

3. Based on the information in the passage, which amongst the following assertions is true?
   A. The way in which funds are spent is hidden from the public.
   B. The quality of soil is currently poor.
   C. The quality of water is more important than the quality of soil.
   D. Funding is needed to support soil monitoring.

4. Defra plays a role in the quality of soil.
   A. True
   B. False
   C. Can't Tell

Question 14 - Edward VII

Edward was king of Great Britain from 1901 to 1910, having been heir to Victoria for nearly 60 years. He was born on 9th November 1841 in London, the eldest son of Victoria and her prince consort, Albert. He was subjected to a strict regime from an early age, as his parents were keen to ensure he was prepared to rule. He attended both Oxford and Cambridge and briefly joined the army. A liaison with an actress caused considerable scandal, and Prince Albert visited his son to reprimand him. Albert died two weeks later, and Victoria held her son partly responsible for the death of his father.

Victoria withdrew almost completely from public life, and Edward was allowed to represent her at state occasions but given almost no chance to participate in affairs of state.

In January 1901, Victoria died, and Edward succeeded to the throne as Edward VII. He was crowned in August 1902. He threw himself into his new role with energy, and his reign restored sparkle to a monarchy that been rather gloomy since his father's death 40 years earlier. Related to most European royalty (he was known as the 'Uncle of Europe'), he was able to assist in foreign policy negotiations, and his well-received addresses during a state visit to Paris helped pave the way for the Anglo-French Entente Cordiale of 1904. Edward was also the first British monarch to visit Russia. In 1902, he founded the Order of Merit to reward those who distinguished themselves in science, art or literature.

In the last year of his life, Edward was involved in a constitutional crisis brought about by the refusal of the Conservative majority in the Lords to pass the Liberal budget of 1909. He died on 6th May 1910, before the situation could be resolved, and was succeeded by his son, who became George V.

Source: Adapted from The BBC (http://www.bbc.co.uk/history/historic_figures/edward_vii_king.shtml/).
The text used here is for educational purposes. The contents and the copyright belong to the aforementioned source.

1. Edward was second in line to the throne of Queen Victoria for sixty years.
    A. True
    B. False
    C. Can't Tell

2. It can be deduced from the passage that Edward VII:
    A. was the favoured child of Victoria but not of Albert.
    B. was directed by Queen Victoria to not partake in all activities as her designated ambassador.
    C. was generally considered as a contributor to the death of his father.
    D. attained degrees from both Oxford and Cambridge.

3. It is impossible to not conclude that Edward did not:
    A. have a happy childhood.
    B. rebel when he was away from direct parental control.
    C. find happiness in being allowed to marry the woman he loved.
    D. act sufficiently to resolve the constitutional crisis at the end of his reign.

4. Based on the information in the passage, which amongst the following statements is not false?
    A. Edward was responsible for initiating the Entente Cordiale.
    B. Edward's reign was marred by his indiscretions.
    C. Edward was keen to undertake a proactive role before his coronation.
    D. Edward was an enigmatic and flamboyant character.

Question 15 - Rutland Osprey Project Grows Online Audience in Lockdown

The Rutland Osprey Project said it had led to greater engagement and connection with people online. Visitors can usually observe the fish-eating birds throughout the summer from hides at Manton Bay, across from where the pair Maya and 33(11) have been nesting since 2015. They both arrived in Rutland on 16 March from Africa, with 23 other ospreys also returning, but days later the reserve was forced to close due to coronavirus. Last year saw the 150th wild chick fledge, while this spring Maya and 33(11) have had four chicks, which have been observed feeding on roach, trout and bream.

About 45,000 people logged on the project website between 14 and 20 May – more than 10 times the total number of visitors who came to see the birds last year, with 87% of those visitors being new users. Between 1 and 21 May, the project's Facebook page also had 2,000 new followers and about 900,000 minutes of its videos were viewed. Most online visitors were from the UK, but the birds were also watched in Canada, Finland, Spain and the US.

Abi Mustard, from the project, said: "With more people being engaged, hopefully we could be helping to raise the awareness of how important it is to stay connected to nature."

Source: Adapted from The BBC (https://www.bbc.co.uk/news/uk-england-leicestershire-52847850).
The text used here is for educational purposes. The contents and the copyright belong to the aforementioned source.

1. Last year saw less than 4,500 visitors.
   A. True
   B. False
   C. Can't Tell

2. Which of the following cannot be considered fictitious from the information provided in the passage?
   A. Visitors to the site were residents of the UK, Scotland, Canada, Finland and Spain.
   B. In the first three weeks of May, 900,000 minutes of videos were watched by 2,000 people.
   C. The coronavirus has led to a reduction in the number of birds migrating to the reserve.
   D. The coronavirus has been responsible for an increase in human interest in the project.

3. Based on the information in the passage, which amongst the following statements is not false?
   A. This year has seen 23 birds return to the reserve.
   B. The birds have migrated directly from Africa.
   C. The increase in online subscriptions will enable the project to recoup its losses.
   D. It has been noted that 13 percent of visitors used the site previously.

4. It is impossible to conclude that the passage does not consider which of the following to be possible?
   A. That each of the birds will continue to return each year.
   B. That awareness of the importance of nature will be enhanced.
   C. That the fledglings will have a better chance of survival now that the reserve is closed.
   D. That the number of online visitors will continue to increase at the current rate.

Question 16 - Excerpt from *The Story of A Puppet*

There was once upon a time a piece of wood. This wood was not valuable: it was only a common log like those that are burnt in winter in the stoves and fireplaces to make a cheerful blaze and warm the rooms. I cannot say how it came about, but the fact is that, one fine day, this piece of wood was lying in the shop of an old carpenter of the name of Master Antonio. He was, however, called by everybody Master Cherry on account of the end of his nose, which was always as red and polished as a ripe cherry.

No sooner had Master Cherry set eyes on the piece of wood than his face beamed with delight; and, rubbing his hands together with satisfaction, he said softly to himself:

'This wood has come at the right moment; it will just do to make the leg of a little table.'

Having said this, he immediately took a sharp axe to remove the bark and the rough surface. Just, however, as he was going to give the first stroke, he remained with his arm suspended in the air for he heard a very small voice saying imploringly:

'Do not strike me so hard!'

1. Which amongst the following statements can be best supported by the information in the passage?
   A. Furniture can be made from wood that is used to heat rooms.
   B. Master Cherry owned a shop.
   C. Master Cherry sold wood for stoves and fireplaces.
   D. Master Cherry knew he had a red nose.

2. Master Cherry's pseudonym was Master Antonio.
   A. True
   B. False
   C. Can't Tell

3. This is a fairy tale.
   A. True
   B. False
   C. Can't Tell

4. Which amongst the following statements can be verified by the information in the passage?
   A. The piece of wood asked Master Cherry not to hit it with the axe.
   B. Master Cherry's assistant asked him not to hit the piece of wood with the axe.
   C. Master Cherry was rather disinterested in the piece of wood.
   D. Master Cherry ignored the voice.

Question 17 - Job Opportunities in the Civil Service

Crown Prosecution Service: We work in partnership with other government departments and agencies throughout the criminal justice system. As criminal law continues to evolve, we work on some of the most complex and challenging cases, from fraud and firearms, to public order and corporate manslaughter. Our service employs almost 6,000 people who think objectively, act professionally, show the utmost respect for others, and continually strive for excellence.

Department for Environment, Food and Rural Affairs: People who work for the Department for Environment, Food and Rural Affairs all play their part in creating a healthier environment, developing a world-leading food and farming industry, expanding a thriving rural economy, and securing robust defences against natural threats and hazards such as flooding and animal and plant diseases. This is a particularly exciting time to join the Department for Environment, Food and Rural Affairs. We are one of the lead government departments delivering a successful exit from the European Union. This will fundamentally transform the work we do and how we deliver it. We are embracing this opportunity to become even more efficient, focused, and innovative.

HM Land Registry: Our ambition is to become the world's leading land registry for speed, simplicity, and an open approach to data. We have over 5,000 talented people working for us in 14 offices across England and Wales, each playing a vital role in building a modern, digital organisation. From updating a register to supporting registration overseas, answering parliamentary questions to maintaining infrastructure, there's a role to suit you. We are proud of our diverse and inclusive working environment, and recent awards show that our commitment to staff is a way of life.

Source: Adapted from Civil Service Careers (https://www.civil-service-careers.gov.uk/departments/).
The text used here is for educational purposes. The contents and the copyright belong to the aforementioned source.

1. Which amongst the following strengths can be corroborated by the information in the passage?
   A. Britain's relationship with the European Union gives a role to the Department for Environment, Food and Rural Affairs.
   B. Approximately 357 people work in each of HM Land Registry's offices.
   C. The Civil Service provides secure jobs that have numerous perks.
   D. The Crown Prosecution Service employs more people than the Department for Environment, Food and Rural Affairs and HM Land Registry.

2. The Crown Prosecution Service interacts with local government departments throughout the country.
   A. True
   B. False
   C. Can't Tell

3. The Department for Environment, Food and Rural Affairs plays a significant role in Britain's exit from the European Union.
   A. True
   B. False
   C. Can't Tell

4. Which amongst the following flaws, if true, can be identified from the information contained in the passage?
   A. The productivity of the Department for Environment, Food and Rural Affairs is set to increase.
   B. HM Land Registry aims to deliver a fast, world-class service.
   C. In order to join the Crown Prosecution Service, one absolutely must be determined and driven.
   D. There are a wide variety of roles available within the Civil Service.

Question 18 - The Criminal Justice System

The CPS works in partnership with the police, courts, the Attorney General's Office, the Home Office, the Ministry of Justice and other agencies throughout the criminal justice system (CJS).

There are 43 police forces across England and Wales responsible for the investigation of crime, collection of evidence, and the arrest or detention of suspected offenders. Once a suspect is held, in minor cases the police decide whether to caution him or her, take no further action, issue a fixed penalty notice, or refer to the CPS. In more serious cases, the police will send the files to the CPS to decide whether to prosecute.

The Attorney General fulfils the role of chief legal adviser to the government and superintends the Crown Prosecution Service and the Serious Fraud Office. The Attorney General also has overall responsibility for the Government Legal Department and Her Majesty's Crown Prosecution Service Inspectorate and fulfils a number of independent public interest functions.

The Solicitor General supports the Attorney across the range of his or her responsibilities.

The Ministry of Justice (MOJ) has responsibility for different parts of the justice system – the courts, prisons, probation services and attendance centres. Its work spans criminal, civil and family justice, democracy, rights and the constitution.

Source: Adapted from CPS (https://www.cps.gov.uk/criminal-justice-system). The text used here is for educational purposes. The contents and the copyright belong to the aforementioned source.

1. The relationship between the CJS and the CPS is fraught.
   A. True
   B. False
   C. Can't Tell

2. Which amongst the following does the information in the passage corroborate?
   A. Police forces superintend the way in which crime is investigated.
   B. Police officers are answerable to the CPS.
   C. The CPS possesses far more power than police forces.
   D. The CPS must monitor the activities of the police forces, especially in relation to crime.

3. According to the writer, the Attorney General assumes an important role in the criminal justice system because:
   A. he or she is directly answerable to Parliament.
   B. he or she is called on to advise a number of agencies.
   C. he or she must inform the Queen of any major changes to it.
   D. he or she can overrule the Solicitor General.

4. Based on the information in the passage, which amongst the following statements cannot be true?
   A. The Attorney General is a government minister.
   B. The MOJ plays a limited role in the CJS.
   C. The Solicitor General advises the Attorney General.
   D. The CPS is the principal agency for conducting criminal prosecutions in England and Wales.

Question 19 - The Duke of Edinburgh's Award

The Duke of Edinburgh's Award (DofE) was founded by its patron, HRH The Duke of Edinburgh, in 1956. The award is a nationally and internationally recognised, voluntary, non-competitive programme of activities for anyone aged between 14 and 24.

Doing the DofE gives young people the opportunity to experience new activities or develop existing skills. It is highly regarded by employers and higher education establishments. There are three progressive levels which, when successfully completed, lead to a Bronze, Silver or Gold Award.

The DofE aims to give young people the experience of a lifetime and raise aspirations by helping others, getting fitter, learning or developing practical skills, and taking part in an unforgettable journey.

Young people create their own DofE programme outside of study or work, and an award can be achieved by anyone who has the motivation and commitment to succeed, regardless of who you are or where you're from!

Source: Adapted from TCBC (https://www.torfaen.gov.uk/en/EducationLearning/Extra-curricularActivities/DukeofEdinburghsAward/Duke-of-Edinburghs-Award.aspx).
The text used here is for educational purposes. The contents and the copyright belong to the aforementioned source.

1. Information about which of the following can be found in the passage?
   A. The cut-off point for individuals to achieve the award.
   B. The countries in which the award is recognised.
   C. Reimbursement for undertaking activities as part of the award.
   D. The value of the award.

2. Which amongst the following statements cannot be corroborated by the information in the passage?
   A. The DofE is only for youths.
   B. The DofE encourages relationships between individuals to be established.
   C. The name of the award was chosen by The Duke of Edinburgh.
   D. The DofE is recognised by universities.

3. Which amongst the following assertions is always true?
   A. An individual should progress from Bronze level to Silver level to Gold level.
   B. Every university holds an individual who has achieved the DofE in high esteem.
   C. Those who complete the DofE acquire physical fitness.
   D. The award is not discriminative against an individual's economic background.

4. The first DofE was presented more than half a century ago.
   A. True
   B. False
   C. Can't Tell

Question 20 - Fitting A Bath

- If you are replacing an existing bath and the pipework only needs minor adjustments, then installing your new bath will be a reasonably straightforward task.
- If the bath is a new addition, or if the position of the bath is being moved and plumbing needs to be rerouted, then it's best to call in a qualified plumber.
- Ensure you have all the necessary parts, fittings, and tools before starting the project.
- Be sure to choose taps that are compatible with the pre-drilled holes in your bath.
- If you are planning to install an over bath shower, then choose a bath with a flat rim so a shower screen can create a watertight seal.
- We are fitting a 'closed in' bath so you don't need to worry about the flooring as it won't be visible. However, if you are fitting a freestanding design, then you will need to lay your chosen flooring prior to fitting.
- Whilst not essential, it's a good idea to cover the bathroom floor with a protective sheet whilst removing an old bath.
- Carefully measure and mark out all fixing points before drilling.

Source: Adapted from Wickes (https://www.wickes.co.uk/how-to-guides/bathrooms).
The text used here is for educational purposes. The contents and the copyright belong to the aforementioned source.

1. One can refer to these instructions in order to fit other bathroom appliances; they share similarities.
   A. True
   B. False
   C. Can't Tell

2. The writer believes that:
   A. fitting a bath is relatively easy.
   B. one shouldn't be worried about the way in which the flooring has been laid.
   C. fitting a bath should not raise any difficulties.
   D. it is not imperative to ask a plumber for assistance.

3. Which amongst the following statements is not supported by information contained within this passage?
   A. The type of bath will determine the complexity of the installation process.
   B. It is important to act with caution when delimiting the area in which the bath will be placed.
   C. One must, on occasions, change the structure of the plumbing in order to install a new bath.
   D. The taps should match the style of the bath.

4. Given the information in the passage, which amongst the following is true?
   A. Baths are designed with a place in which to insert taps.
   B. The individual fitting the bath should have a reasonable understanding of what to do.
   C. If a shower is to be placed over the bath, a screen is required.
   D. You shouldn't purchase any parts after you have started to install the bath.

Question 21 - A Selection of Products for Sale

Home Charcoal Oil Drum BBQ
With a cooking surface of 35 x 71cm, this oil drum charcoal BBQ is a great size for garden gatherings of around 10 people. It has an adjustable height for the grill so you can control the distance between the charcoal and cooking grill and cook your food to perfection. It's also equipped with a chrome-plated warming rack to keep food warm while you cook the next round, and its removeable ash tray makes cleaning easy.

Wooden Bench to Bistro Set
Enjoy your morning coffee and croissant in style on this solid wooden bistro set. The bench of this functional set folds flush against the wall when it's not being used. It can be transformed into a bistro set in a few simple moves. It's ideal if you only have a small space to work with but still want to eat al fresco.

Aqua Magic Mat
Great for creative play, you can help children stretch their imagination and draw anything that comes to their minds. With the amazing Aqua Magic Mat, you can fill the pen with water and watch them scribble on the mat - nothing else around your home will get marked.

Car and Home Pressure Washer
The car kit includes a foam lance to allow the application of a thick layer of foam to a surface, a soft bristle brush to allow cleaning of delicate areas like vehicle paintwork, and 500ml of car shampoo to leave an excellent shine on all vehicles.

Source: Adapted from Argos UK (https://www.argos.co.uk/).
The text used here is for educational purposes. The contents and the copyright belong to the aforementioned source.

1. The adjustable grill height intends to allow the BBQ to suit the height of the user.
   A. True
   B. False
   C. Can't Tell

2. The Wooden Bench to Bistro Set is appropriate only for breakfast.
   A. True
   B. False
   C. Can't Tell

3. The Aqua Magic Mat should not be used on a fabric surface.
   A. True
   B. False
   C. Can't Tell

4. It is recommended that you use 500ml of shampoo to leave a shine on your vehicle.
   A. True
   B. False
   C. Can't Tell

Question 22 - Red Hugh: Spanish Dig for Bones of 'Fighting Prince of Donegal'

Archaeologists have dug up a street in the city of Valladolid in a bid to find the remains of a 16th century Irish chieftain known as Red Hugh. Red Hugh O'Donnell died in Spain in 1602 while on a mission to ask the Spanish king for military assistance to drive the English army out of Ireland.

He was buried in Valladolid's Chapel of Wonders, the same church where Christopher Columbus was interred almost a century earlier. The remains of Columbus were later moved to Seville, and the ruined building eventually disappeared from view. However, archaeologists believe they have unearthed the walls of the chapel and are "close" to discovering the remains of Red Hugh. The dig in Calle Constitución (Constitution Street) began earlier this month, outside a branch of the Spanish bank Santander. Two coffins and 15 sets of unidentified human remains have been found so far.

The cause of O'Donnell's death is still disputed, so finding his remains may help either confirm or dismiss claims that he was killed by poison. His skeleton should also be missing a big toe from each foot – injuries a young Red Hugh suffered while escaping from his English captors. The team does not yet know which, if any, of the skeletons recovered so far is that of Red Hugh, but at least two can be ruled out because they were women. The others could be the remains of monks, Mr Burgos suggested, as the chapel once formed part of a large Franciscan monastery.

Red Hugh is more likely to have been buried in another part of the chapel – acrypt which may be located underneath the bank, according to the dig's spokesman.

Source: Adapted from The BBC (https://www.bbc.co.uk/news/world-europe-52832801).
The text used here is for educational purposes. The contents and the copyright belong to the aforementioned source.

1. From the information provided in the passage, which amongst the following statements cannot be corroborated?
   A. Due to his importance, the remains of the chieftain will be housed in one of the coffins.
   B. The aim of the chieftain's mission was to seek support for Independence.
   C. The burial site eventually fell into disrepair.
   D. There is a possibility that the chieftain was slain whilst on this mission.

2. If the information in the passage is presumed to be true, which of the following statements cannot be assumed not to be untrue?
   A. The chieftain secured military assistance from the Spanish.
   B. It is conceivable that the bones are situated in the catacomb of the chapel.
   C. The chieftain's loss of part of his foot might have occurred during his escape to Spain.
   D. It is possible that relics moved with those of Columbus belonged to the chieftain.

3. Which of the following is not supported by the information in the passage?
   A. Other prominent figures would not have been buried in this location.
   B. The chieftain was a rather romanticised figure.
   C. As the site was a monastery, the female bones found would have been those of nuns.
   D. The remains might not provide unequivocal information about the death.

4. If the remains are confirmed as those of Red Hugh O'Donnell, they will potentially be repatriated to Ireland.
   A. True
   B. False
   C. Can't Tell

Question 23 - Napping Keeps High Blood Pressure at Bay

The study included 212 people with a mean blood pressure of 129.9 mm Hg. They were 62 years old on average; just over half were female. About 1 out of 4 participants were smokers and/or had Type 2 diabetes. The groups were similar in terms of risk factors for heart disease except there were more smokers in the napping group. Researchers assessed and recorded blood pressure for 24 hours consecutively, midday sleep time (the average duration was 49 minutes), lifestyle habits (for example, alcohol, coffee and salt consumption, physical activity levels), and pulse wave velocity, a measure of stiffness in the arteries. Participants wore an ambulatory blood pressure monitor to measure and track blood pressure at regular intervals during routine daily living, rather than just one time in the clinic. At study recruitment, participants also underwent an echocardiogram, an ultrasound of the heart that shows its structure and function.

In their analyses, researchers adjusted for factors known to influence blood pressure levels, including age, gender, lifestyle and medications. There were no differences in terms of the number of antihypertensive medications taken between the two groups, and pulse wave velocity tests and echocardiograms were also similar.

Source: Adapted from Science Daily (https://www.sciencedaily.com/releases/2019/03/190307081029.htm).
The text used here is for educational purposes. The contents and the copyright belong to the aforementioned source.

1. The participants in the study:
   A. were more or less 62 years of age.
   B. were perhaps selected because they had a predisposition to heart disease.
   C. slept for less than one hour during the day.
   D. each had heart disease.

2. According to the information within the passage, which of the following is always true?
   A. Women are at greater risk of developing heart disease.
   B. An ABPM measures blood pressure as an individual goes about his or her daily routine.
   C. Those with Type 2 diabetes have a significant risk of developing heart disease.
   D. Echocardiograms and pulse wave velocity tests can be performed simultaneously.

3. Which amongst the following assertions is not true?
   A. The results of the study had to be tampered with as some participants had a higher blood pressure than others.
   B. Some participants were already taking medication for high blood pressure.
   C. The participants were encouraged to sleep during the day.
   D. The participants were invited to the clinic before the study started.

4. The participants were monitored for 24 hours only.
   A. True
   B. False
   C. Can't Tell

Question 24 - The Battle of Britain

The Battle of Britain, during World War II, was the successful defence of Great Britain against unremitting and destructive air raids conducted by the German air force (Luftwaffe) from July through September 1940, after the fall of France. Victory for the Luftwaffe in the air battle would have exposed Great Britain to invasion by the German army, which was then in control of the ports of France only a few miles away across the English Channel. The battle was won by the Royal Air Force (RAF) Fighter Command, whose victory not only blocked the possibility of invasion but also created the conditions for Great Britain's survival and for the eventual defeat of Nazi Germany.

Shortly after the withdrawal of British forces from the European continent in the Dunkirk evacuation (late May to early June 1940), Germany's armoured forces completed their invasion of France. The French government collapsed on June 16 and was replaced by a regime that immediately sued for peace. This left the British suddenly alone in their "island home" as the last bastion against "the menace of tyranny," in the words of their prime minister, Winston Churchill.

Source: Adapted from Britannica (https://www.britannica.com/event/Battle-of-Britain-European-history-1940). The text used here is for educational purposes. The contents and the copyright belong to the aforementioned source.

1. The Battle of Britain is considered an important event in British history because:
   A. it contributed towards the end of the Second World War.
   B. it came after British troops were forced to leave France.
   C. it helped to restore France's fallen government.
   D. it showed the world that Britain could not be defeated.

2. The RAF assumed a critical role in the Battle of Britain because:
   A. it prompted France's ports to be reopened.
   B. it returned British troops to France to help the country fight Germany.
   C. it protected Britain against the foe.
   D. it resulted in the instant collapse of the Nazi regime.

3. The Luftwaffe carried out air raids on Britain for three entire months.
   A. True
   B. False
   C. Can't Tell

4. The collapse of France's government triggered:
   A. a series of attacks on the country by Germany.
   B. a feeling of isolation in Britain.
   C. the removal of British troops from the country.
   D. the end of the Second World War.

Question 25 - India's Moon Mission

India successfully launched an unmanned spacecraft to the far side of the moon Monday, a week after aborting the mission because of a technical problem. Scientists at the mission control centre burst into applause as the rocket lifted off in clear weather as scheduled at 2:43 p.m. from Sriharikota in southern India. K. Sivan, head of India's space agency, said the rocket successfully injected the spacecraft into orbit.

The spacecraft — named Chandrayaan, the Sanskrit word for "moon craft" — is scheduled to land on the lunar south pole in September and send a rover to explore water deposits confirmed by a previous mission that orbited the moon. If India did manage the soft landing, it would be only the fourth to do so, following the U.S., Russia and China.

India's first moon mission orbited the moon in 2008 and helped confirm the presence of water. The country plans to send its first manned spaceflight by 2022.

India's launch coincided with the 50th anniversary of the Apollo 11 mission this month. It came at a time when the world's biggest space agencies are returning their gaze to the moon, seen as an ideal testing ground for technologies required for deep space exploration, and with the confirmed discovery of water, as a possible pit stop along the way. The U.S. is working to send a manned spacecraft to the moon's south pole by 2024.

Source: Adapted from The Washington Post (https://www.washingtonpost.com/world/asia_pacific/india-moon-mission-set-to-launch-a-week-after-it-was-aborted/2019/07/22/d599087e-ac45-11e9-9411-a608f9d0c2d3_story.html?utm_term=.58ee00d64008).
The text used here is for educational purposes. The contents and the copyright belong to the aforementioned source.

1. Which amongst the following statements cannot be determined by the information in the passage?
   A. India plans to continue to explore space.
   B. India is destined to be one of the few countries that has explored the moon.
   C. Explorations must be designed and scheduled in advance.
   D. India is in talks with America to launch another spacecraft.

2. The passage corroborates which of the following statements?
   A. The United Kingdom has sent a rocket to space.
   B. India has previously been successful in launching a spacecraft.
   C. India received financial support from other counties for this mission.
   D. If this mission is successful, India will become recognised for its work in this field.

3. According to the writer, which amongst the following is always true?
   A. The technologies that are required for space exploration are expensive.
   B. Water can be found on the moon.
   C. The Apollo 11 mission was launched within the last decade.
   D. The name of India's latest spacecraft derives from an unofficial language of the country.

4. India is hopeful about this mission because:
   A. it now has the tools needed to develop comprehensive data in the field.
   B. it wants to be recognised for its scientific research.
   C. it will provide new knowledge about the moon.
   D. no technical issues were encountered on this occasion.

Question 26 - The Consumption of Sugary Beverages

The average American child drinks more than 30 gallons of sugary beverages each year, including sports drinks, sodas and fruit-flavoured refreshments. This excessive sugar consumption — which is tied to a greater risk of heart disease, high cholesterol and Type 2 diabetes — has prompted the American Academy of Pediatrics and American Heart Association to endorse a set of ambitious governmental policies to help curb children's thirst for sweet drinks. But, of course, parents don't need to wait around for the government to act.

In a position paper released in March, the AAP and AHA came up with five recommendations to help children drink fewer sweetened beverages, such as taxing sugary drinks; limiting the advertising of sugary beverages directed at children and teens; making water the default beverage on children's menus; and improving the quality of nutrition labels — perhaps by adding front-of-pack labels about the health consequences of consuming sugary drinks.

Source: Adapted from The Washington Post (https://www.washingtonpost.com/lifestyle/wellness/while-companies-push-sugary-beverages-parents-should-promote-water-heres-how/2019/06/14/b40faae4-87a8-11e9-a491-25df61c78dc4_story.html?utm_term=.84f26d5539be).
The text used here is for educational purposes. The contents and the copyright belong to the aforementioned source.

1. In America, sugary drinks are only consumed by children.
   A. True
   B. False
   C. Can't Tell

2. The American Academy of Pediatrics has become involved in this issue by:
   A. single-handedly developing strategies to discourage children from consuming sugary beverages.
   B. gaining the support of the American Heart Association.
   C. warning children of the detrimental effects of sugary drinks.
   D. aiming more adverts at adults.

3. Based on the information contained within the passage, which amongst the following is false?
   A. Every child in America consumes in excess of 30 gallons of sugary drinks annually.
   B. The AAP and AHA are working collectively to reduce the over-consumption of sugary drinks.
   C. Children are encouraged to select healthier alternatives at food outlets.
   D. As part of this initiative, the price of sugary drinks will be increased.

4. According to the writer, which amongst the following assertions is true?
   A. Parents will need the support of the government to stop their children consuming sugary beverages.
   B. Children throughout America are addicted to sugary drinks.
   C. Children should choose water over soda.
   D. Fruit-flavoured water also contains a significant amount of sugar.

Question 27 - The Assassination of John F. Kennedy

As the motorcade turned southwest on Elm Street and began travelling through Dealey Plaza on the edge of downtown Dallas, the president's convertible passed the multi-story Texas School Book Depository building. Moments later, at about 1230 hours, shots rang out. A bullet pierced the base of the neck of the president, exited through his throat, and then likely (according to the Warren Report) passed through Governor Connally's shoulder and wrist, ultimately hitting his thigh. Another bullet struck Kennedy in the back of the head.

The motorcade rushed to nearby Parkland Memorial Hospital, reaching it quickly. However, doctors' efforts were futile. Kennedy was officially declared dead at 1300 hours. Connally survived his wounds.

The protocols for the funeral of another assassinated president, Abraham Lincoln, were followed for Kennedy's funeral. Kennedy's body, in a flag-draped casket, lay in repose in the East Room of the White House on November 23rd and then was transferred to the Rotunda of the U.S. Capitol to lie in state, where it was visited by some 250,000 people.

Source: Adapted from Britannica (https://www.britannica.com/event/assassination-of-John-F-Kennedy).
The text used here is for educational purposes. The contents and the copyright belong to the aforementioned source.

1. Which of the following assertions can be corroborated by the information in the passage?
   A. The same bullet that hit President Kennedy hit a woman who was travelling in the same car.
   B. Parkland Memorial Hospital was located a few metres from the place in which the bullet was fired.
   C. The same bullet that hit President Kennedy hit a man who was travelling in the same car.
   D. Connally was left with life-changing injuries.

2. Based on the information contained within the passage, which amongst the following statements is true?
   A. President Kennedy was officially pronounced dead at the scene.
   B. President Kennedy was not proclaimed dead by doctors at the hospital.
   C. At 1300 hours, it was officially announced that President Kennedy had died.
   D. President Kennedy was not pronounced dead until 1300 hours.

3. The protocols for President Kennedy's funeral:
   A. were similar to those of another president who had been murdered.
   B. were the same as those of another president who had been murdered.
   C. were distinctly comparable to those of another president who had been murdered.
   D. were the same as those of another president who had not been murdered.

4. The body of President Kennedy was placed in the Rotunda of the U.S. Capitol and:
   A. visited by thousands of mourners.
   B. seen by thousands of people.
   C. observed by thousands of Americans.
   D. visited by thousands of Europeans.

Question 28 - Abraham Lincoln

Abraham Lincoln was a self-taught lawyer, legislator and vocal opponent of slavery. He was elected 16th president of the United States in November 1860, shortly before the outbreak of the Civil War. Lincoln proved to be a shrewd military strategist and a savvy leader: His Emancipation Proclamation paved the way for slavery's abolition, while his Gettysburg Address stands as one of the most famous pieces of oratory in American history. In April 1865, with the Union on the brink of victory, Abraham Lincoln was assassinated by Confederate sympathizer John Wilkes Booth. Lincoln's assassination made him a martyr to the cause of liberty, and he is widely regarded as one of the greatest presidents in U.S. history.

Though Lincoln once maintained that his "paramount object in this struggle is to save the Union, and is not either to save or destroy slavery," he nonetheless came to regard emancipation as one of his greatest achievements, and would argue for the passage of a constitutional amendment outlawing slavery (eventually passed as the 13th Amendment after his death in 1865).

On the night of April 14, 1865, the actor and Confederate sympathizer John Wilkes Booth slipped into the president's box at Ford's Theatre in Washington, D.C. and shot him point-blank in the back of the head. Lincoln was carried to a boarding-house across the street from the theatre, but he never regained consciousness, and died in the early morning hours of April 15, 1865.

Lincoln's assassination made him a national martyr. On April 21, 1865, a train carrying his coffin left Washington, D.C. on its way to Springfield, Illinois, where he would be buried on May 4. Abraham Lincoln's funeral train travelled through 180 cities and seven states so mourners could pay homage to the fallen president.

Today, Lincoln's birthday – alongside the birthday of George Washington – is honoured on President's Day, which falls on the third Monday of February.

Source: Adapted from HISTORY.COM (https://www.history.com/topics/us-presidents/abraham-lincoln).
The text used here is for educational purposes. The contents and the copyright belong to the aforementioned source.

1. Which of the following can be measured not to be supported by the information provided?
    A. Lincoln had initially been trained to enter a career in the legal profession.
    B. Lincoln is generally recognised as the primary individual responsible for emancipation of enslavement.
    C. The country appeared to lament the events incurred at the end of Lincoln's presidency.
    D. The credence that Lincoln would endure the challenge on his life initially appeared credible.

2. Abraham Lincoln was assassinated by an opponent to emancipation.
    A. True
    B. False
    C. Can't Tell

3. What conclusion can be drawn from the passage?
    A. The assassination attempt resulted in Lincoln being regarded as a martyr.
    B. Lincoln served for only one term as president.
    C. Lincoln is widely recognised and acknowledged for his contribution to worldwide freedom.
    D. Lincoln is still considered a distinguished and noteworthy individual in the American constitution.

4. On reading the passage, it can be confirmed that there is nothing to suggest that which of the following statements is not truthful?
    A. Lincoln is considered to be a president of utmost significance.
    B. Lincoln modified his policy on slavery for reasons of political advantage.
    C. The legislation to eradicate slavery was passed as a result of the assassination.
    D. Lincoln was born on the same day as George Washington.

Question 29 - Leonardo Da Vinci

Da Vinci was one of the great creative minds of the Italian Renaissance, hugely influential as an artist and sculptor but also immensely talented as an engineer, scientist and inventor.

Leonardo da Vinci was born on 15th April 1452 near the Tuscan town of Vinci. The illegitimate son of a local lawyer, he was apprenticed to the sculptor and painter Andrea del Verrocchio in Florence and, in 1478, became an independent master. In 1483, he moved to Milan to work for the ruling Sforza family as an engineer, sculptor, painter, and architect. From 1495 to 1497 he produced a mural of 'The Last Supper' in the refectory of the Monastery of Santa Maria delle Grazie in Milan.

The fame of Da Vinci's surviving paintings has meant that he has been primarily regarded as an artist, but the thousands of surviving pages of his notebooks reveal the most eclectic and brilliant of minds. He wrote and drew on subjects including geology, anatomy (which he studied in order to paint the human form more accurately), flight, gravity, and optics, often flitting from subject to subject on a single page and writing in left-handed mirror script. He 'invented' the bicycle, airplane, helicopter, and parachute some 500 years ahead of their time.

If all this work had been published in an intelligible form, da Vinci's place as a pioneering scientist would have been beyond dispute. Yet his true genius was not as a scientist or an artist, but as a combination of the two: an 'artist-engineer'. His painting was scientific, based on a deep understanding of the workings of the human body and the physics of light and shade. His science was expressed through art, and his drawings and diagrams show what he meant, and how he understood the world to work.

Source: Adapted from The BBC (http://www.bbc.co.uk/history/historic_figures/da_vinci_leonardo.shtml).
The text used here is for educational purposes. The contents and the copyright belong to the aforementioned source.

1. According to the writer, which amongst the following assertions is false?
   A. Vinci is a town in Italy.
   B. A number of Da Vinci's works are still in existence.
   C. Da Vinci was an anatomist.
   D. One of Da Vinci's works is housed in the chapel of a monastery.

2. Da Vinci did not know who his father was.
   A. True
   B. False
   C. Can't Tell

3. Which amongst the following statements cannot be corroborated by the information in the passage?
   A. Da Vinci lived in Florence.
   B. Da Vinci was an intellectual.
   C. Da Vinci created at least one mural.
   D. Da Vinci was born in Italy.

4. Da Vinci relocated to Milan:
   A. to create 'The Last Supper'.
   B. to work for an impoverished family.
   C. and created 'The Last Supper'.
   D. because his work in Florence had come to an end.

Question 30 - World's Deepest Octopus Captured on Camera

The deepest ever sighting of an octopus has been made by cameras on the Indian Ocean floor. The animal was spotted 7,000m down in the Java Trench - almost 2km deeper than the previous reliable recording.

Researchers, who report the discovery in the journal *Marine Biology*, say it's a species of "Dumbo" octopus. The name is a nod to the prominent ear-like fins just above these animals' eyes that make them look like the 1940s Disney cartoon character.

The scientist behind the identification is Dr Alan Jamieson. He's pioneered the exploration of the deep using what are called "landers". These are instrumented frames dropped overboard from research ships. They settle on the seabed and record what passes by.

Dr Jamieson's equipment filmed two octopuses - one on a drop to 5,760m and a second to 6,957m. The individual animals were 43cm and 35cm in length. They've been placed in the Grimpoteuthis family - the group commonly known as Dumbo. Octopus fragments and eggs have been found at very great depths, but until this discovery, the previous deepest reliable sighting was at 5,145m down.

The significance of the Indian Ocean observations is that we now know that octopuses can find potentially suitable habitat across at least 99% of the global seafloor. But those animals that do live at depth will clearly need some special adaptations, says Dr Jamieson.

"They'd have to do something clever inside their cells. If you imagine a cell is like a balloon - it's going to want to collapse under pressure. So, it will need some smart biochemistry to make sure it retains that sphere," the scientist explained. "All the adaptations you need to live at pressure are at the cellular level."

Source: Adapted from The BBC (https://www.bbc.co.uk/news/science-environment-52839678).

1. Which of the following can possibly be deduced from the passage?
   A. The creatures inhabit all of the world's seafloor.
   B. The creature is named after a Disney character.
   C. The creatures may find suitable habitat in most of the seafloor.
   D. The creatures will become extinct if they are not protected.

2. According to the information presented in the passage, which amongst the following assertions cannot be untrue?
   A. The giant fins assist in helping the creature to hide.
   B. The octopus were found almost 1,000m apart.
   C. Previous discoveries placed the species at over 500m higher.
   D. Previous discoveries were found on various ocean floors.

3. Which of the following cannot not be false?
   A. The previous discoveries have located traces of the octopus in other locations.
   B. Similar equipment has not been used for previous research.
   C. The recent discovery has proved insightful for researchers in this field.
   D. The recent discovery was not reported in an outlet that deals with this specific field.

4. The passage suggests that the creatures have specifically adapted themselves to live at such depths.
   A. True
   B. False
   C. Can't Tell

Question 31 - How Many Trees Can Be Planted?

The political parties have been promising huge increases in tree planting in their election manifestos. The most eye-catching is Labour's plan to plant two billion trees by 2040. Impossible, some say - that's more than a quarter of a million trees every day. But it's not necessarily unrealistic. It's just that it will require a change in the way things are done today.

Meanwhile, the Conservatives have pledged to plant at least 30 million more trees every year, the Lib Dems and the SNP each say they will plant 60 million trees a year, while the Green Party would aim to plant 700 million trees by 2030.

How many trees are there in a hectare? It's difficult to say precisely because trees can be planted at a density of anything between 1,000 and 2,500 per hectare. But, if you take a mid-range, then planting 30,000 hectares means you are planting roughly (and we should stress this is an estimate) 50 million trees a year.

That's still a long way short of the rate of planting Labour would need to achieve in order to meet its target. But it suggests that it could be done. Experts can plant trees incredibly quickly.

Source: Adapted from The BBC (https://www.bbc.co.uk/news/50591261).
The text used here is for educational purposes. The contents and the copyright belong to the aforementioned source.

1. It is not impossible to plant 250,000 trees daily.
   A. True
   B. False
   C. Can't Tell

2. The number of trees in a hectare:
   A. can fluctuate to a potential maximum of 2,500.
   B. can be predicted precisely with minimum error.
   C. can be considered with some precision.
   D. can surge to suit the pledges of certain constitutional factions.

3. Which of the following statements is not contradicted by the information contained within the passage?
   A. Only experts can plant trees.
   B. By 2040, the Green Party would have planted half as many trees as the Labour Party.
   C. If the Liberal Democrats and the SNP combined their efforts, they would agree to plant four times as many trees as the Conservatives.
   D. Labour's plan to plant trees is preposterous.

4. Which amongst the following is always true?
   A. There are more than 1,000 trees per hectare.
   B. An area of 30,000 hectares will accommodate a maximum of 50 million trees.
   C. There are less than 2,500 trees per hectare.
   D. A total of 50 million trees could be planted in an area of 30,000 hectares.

Question 32 - Harold Wilson

Harold Wilson was a Labour politician who entered Parliament in 1945 as MP for Ormskirk. In 1947, then Prime Minister Clement Attlee made Wilson President of the Board of Trade. Aged 31, he had become the youngest member of the Cabinet in the 20th century.

Under Hugh Gaitskell's leadership of the Labour Party, Wilson served as Shadow Chancellor from 1955 to 1961, then as Shadow Foreign Secretary from 1961 to 1963. After Gaitskell passed away suddenly, Wilson fought and won a leadership contest against George Brown and James Callaghan. As Labour leader, he won four of the five General Elections he contested.

His first election victory on 15th October 1964 saw him win with a small majority of four, which increased significantly to 98 after a second General Election on 31st March 1966. As Prime Minister from 1964 to 1970, his main plan was to modernise. He believed that he would be aided by the "white heat of the technological revolution". His government supported backbench MPs in liberalising laws on censorship, divorce, abortion and homosexuality, and he abolished capital punishment.

Source: Adapted from GOV.UK (https://www.gov.uk/government/history/past-prime-ministers/harold-wilson).
The text used here is for educational purposes. The contents and the copyright belong to the aforementioned source.

1. Hugh Gaitskell, the leader of the Labour Party, was:
   A. the predecessor of Harold Wilson.
   B. the leader of the Labour Party in 1964.
   C. to become Britain's most popular prime minister.
   D. the youngest member of the government in the twentieth century.

2. According to the writer, which of the following assertions is incorrect?
   A. Harold Wilson was no longer a teenager when he entered parliament.
   B. Clement Attlee enabled Harold Wilson to enter politics.
   C. Harold Wilson's popularity soared in 70 weeks.
   D. Hugh Gaitskell's death was unexpected.

3. Harold Wilson decontrolled laws on various social issues.
   A. True
   B. False
   C. Can't Tell

4. James Callaghan later became Prime Minister of Britain.
   A. True
   B. False
   C. Can't Tell

Question 33 - Wearable Device to Detect Alzheimer's Being Developed

An ambitious project to develop a wearable device to detect early signs of Alzheimer's disease has been launched. The Early Detection of Neurodegenerative Diseases (EDoN) is being spearheaded by charity Alzheimer's Research UK. It will initially analyse data from continuing studies into the disease, using artificial intelligence. And this data will be used to design a prototype device within three years.

Wearables collect a variety of data including gait, heart rate and sleep patterns and the hope is, by analysing this data, researchers can begin to map signs of the disease years before symptoms develop. Initially, EDoN will work with the UK's national institute for data science and artificial intelligence, The Alan Turing Institute, to trawl through data from continuing studies into Alzheimer's disease.

There are currently 850,000 people living with dementia in the UK, according to Alzheimer's Research UK. And globally, the number is expected to increase from 50 million in 2018 to 152 million in 2050.

Source: Adapted from The BBC (https://www.bbc.co.uk/news/technology-51474115).
The text used here is for educational purposes. The contents and the copyright belong to the aforementioned source.

1. Based on the information in the passage, which amongst the following statements is correct?
   A. Alzheimer's Research UK is not associated with the EDoN project.
   B. EDoN is led by Alzheimer's Research UK.
   C. Alzheimer's Research UK is involved in EDoN.
   D. EDoN is supported by Alzheimer's Research UK.

2. The device that is being created:
   A. will be ready for dissemination within three years.
   B. will examine the data that it stores.
   C. will allow Alzheimer's to be detected, provided that the individual has undiscoverable symptoms.
   D. will provide researchers with a greater understanding of the disease.

3. This project is being launched because:
   A. the number of people affected by dementia is rising.
   B. the Alan Turing Institute possesses data.
   C. Alzheimer's Research UK has pledged to support those who have the disease.
   D. the early detection of Alzheimer's will offer an enhanced understanding of the disease.

4. The number of people with Alzheimer's is not anticipated to decrease by 2050.
   A. True
   B. False
   C. Can't Tell

Question 34 - Excerpt from *Alice's Adventures in Wonderland*

So she was considering in her own mind, (as well as she could, for the hot day made her feel very sleepy and stupid,) whether the pleasure of making a daisy-chain would be worth the trouble of getting up and picking the daisies, when suddenly a white rabbit with pink eyes ran close by her.

There was nothing so *very* remarkable in that; nor did Alice think it so *very* much out of the way to hear the Rabbit say to itself, 'Oh dear! Oh dear! I shall be late!' (when she thought it over afterwards, it occurred to her that she ought to have wondered at this, but at the time it all seemed quite natural); but when the Rabbit actually *took a watch out of its waistcoat-pocket,* and looked at it, and then hurried on, Alice started to her feet, for it flashed across her mind that she had never before seen a rabbit with either a waistcoat-pocket, or a watch to take out of it, and burning with curiosity, she ran across the field after it, and fortunately was just in time to see it pop down a large rabbit-hole under the hedge.

In another moment down went Alice after it, never once considering how in the world she was to get out again.

The rabbit-hole went straight on like a tunnel for some way, and then dipped suddenly down, so suddenly that Alice had not a moment to think about stopping herself before she found herself falling down what seemed to be a very deep well.

Source: Copyright © 1865 by Lewis Carroll.
The text used here is for educational purposes. The contents and the copyright belong to the aforementioned source.

1. Which amongst the following statements is corroborated by the information in the passage?
   A. Alice is a young girl.
   B. Alice is the protagonist.
   C. Alice is the Rabbit's companion.
   D. Alice is the narrator.

2. Based on the information in the passage, what can be inferred about the Rabbit?
   A. The Rabbit was late.
   B. The Rabbit is male.
   C. The Rabbit was worried that it would be late.
   D. The Rabbit ambled past Alice.

3. The Rabbit was wearing a watch.
   A. True
   B. False
   C. Can't Tell

4. At first, Alice did not find it strange that:
   A. the Rabbit possessed a watch.
   B. the Rabbit checked its watch.
   C. the Rabbit spoke to itself.
   D. the Rabbit ran past her.

Question 35 - Prince Albert

Albert was the husband of Queen Victoria. He was a significant influence on his wife, and she never recovered from his premature death.

Albert Francis Charles Augustus Emmanuel of Saxe-Coburg-Gotha was born on 26th August 1819 at Schloss Rosenau in Bavaria, the younger son of the duke of Saxe-Coburg-Gotha. When he was seven, his father divorced his mother on grounds of adultery, and she was sent to live in Switzerland and forbidden from seeing her children. Albert was educated at Bonn University. In 1840, he married his cousin, Queen Victoria. The marriage was unpopular in some quarters, and parliament resisted granting Albert what his wife regarded as a suitable allowance.

Albert's role as advisor to his wife came into full force after the death of Lord Melbourne, the Prime Minister, who had exerted a strong paternal influence over Victoria. Albert began to act as the Queen's private secretary. He encouraged in his wife a greater interest in social welfare and invited Lord Shaftesbury, the driving force behind successive factory acts, to Buckingham Palace to discuss the matter of child labour. His constitutional position was a difficult one and, although he exercised his influence with tact and intelligence, he never enjoyed great public popularity during Victoria's reign. It was not until 1857 that he was formally recognised by the nation and awarded the title 'prince consort'.

Source: Adapted from The BBC (http://www.bbc.co.uk/history/historic_figures/albert_prince.shtml).
The text used here is for educational purposes. The contents and the copyright belong to the aforementioned source.

1. Queen Victoria was the consort of Prince Albert.
   A. True
   B. False
   C. Can't Tell

2. The marriage between Victoria and Albert:
   A. was frowned upon because they were related.
   B. took place within 22 years of Albert's birth.
   C. took place in England.
   D. destroyed Victoria's relationship with parliament.

3. According to the information presented in the passage, which amongst the following assertions is true?
   A. Lord Melbourne was Queen Victoria's father.
   B. Albert did not enjoy the fact that he was in the public eye.
   C. Albert officially became a prince at the age of 38.
   D. Albert could speak more than one language.

4. Albert was not insensitive to the issues that were affecting Britain during his wife's reign.
   A. True
   B. False
   C. Can't Tell

Question 36 - Excerpt from *Gulliver's Travels*

His features are strong and masculine, with an Austrian lip and arched nose, his complexion olive, his countenance erect, his body and limbs well proportioned, all his motions graceful, and his deportment majestic. He was then past his prime, being twenty-eight years and three quarters old, of which he had reigned about seven in great felicity, and generally victorious. For the better convenience of beholding him, I lay on my side, so that my face was parallel to his, and he stood but three yards off: however, I have had him since many times in my hand, and therefore cannot be deceived in the description. His dress was very plain and simple, and the fashion of it between the Asiatic and the European; but he had on his head a light helmet of gold, adorned with jewels, and a plume on the crest. He held his sword drawn in his hand to defend himself, if I should happen to break loose; it was almost three inches long; the hilt and scabbard were gold enriched with diamonds. His voice was shrill, but very clear and articulate; and I could distinctly hear it when I stood up. The ladies and courtiers were all most magnificently clad; so that the spot they stood upon seemed to resemble a petticoat spread upon the ground, embroidered with figures of gold and silver. His imperial majesty spoke often to me, and I returned answers: but neither of us could understand a syllable. There were several of his priests and lawyers present (as I conjectured by their habits), who were commanded to address themselves to me; and I spoke to them in as many languages as I had the least smattering of, which were High and Low Dutch, Latin, French, Spanish, Italian, and Lingua Franca, but all to no purpose.

1. Which amongst the following statements is best supported by the information in the passage?
   A. The man to whom the narrator refers was foreign.
   B. The narrator did not know for certain that some of the individuals present were priests.
   C. The man to whom the narrator refers was the descendant of a rich family.
   D. The narrator is a woman.

2. The man to whom reference is made had a fair complexion.
   A. True
   B. False
   C. Can't Tell

3. Based on the information in the passage, the narrator:
   A. was not fluent in several languages.
   B. was dressed in fine clothes.
   C. was humble.
   D. was besotted with the man to whom reference is made.

4. Which amongst the following statements is not true?
   A. The man to whom the narrator refers wore clothes that were rooted in two different continents.
   B. The man to whom the narrator refers became a prince after the age of twenty years.
   C. The priests and lawyers were unable to understand the narrator.
   D. The man to whom the narrator refers spoke well.

Question 37 - Does 5G Pose Health Risks?

The 5G mobile network has been switched on in some UK cities and has led to questions about whether the new technology poses health risks.

So what are the concerns, and is there any evidence to back them up?

As with previous cellular technologies, 5G networks rely on signals carried by radio waves - part of the electromagnetic spectrum - transmitted between an antenna or mast and your phone. We're surrounded by electromagnetic radiation all the time - from television and radio signals, as well as from a whole range of technologies, including mobile phones, and from natural sources such as sunlight. 5G uses higher frequency waves than earlier mobile networks, allowing more devices to have access to the internet at the same time and at faster speeds. These waves travel shorter distances through urban spaces, so 5G networks require more transmitter masts than previous technologies, positioned closer to ground level.

The electromagnetic radiation used by all mobile phone technologies has led some people to worry about increased health risks, including developing certain types of cancer. In 2014 the World Health Organization (WHO) said that "no adverse health effects have been established as being caused by mobile phone use". However, the WHO, together with the International Agency for Research on Cancer (IARC), has classified all radio frequency radiation (of which mobile signals are a part) as "possibly carcinogenic". Eating pickled vegetables and using talcum powder are classed as having the same level of risk. Alcoholic drinks and processed meat are classed as higher risk.

Source: Adapted from The BBC (https://www.bbc.co.uk/news/world-europe-48616174).
The text used here is for educational purposes. The contents and the copyright belong to the aforementioned source.

1. Which of the following statements is best supported by the information contained within the passage?
   A. Using mobile phones does not come without any risk.
   B. One is not at any lesser risk by engaging in other day-to-day activities.
   C. The 5G network has been activated in cities throughout the UK.
   D. Many people are anxious about the health effects of mobile phones.

2. Which amongst the following statements does not represent the thoughts of the writer?
   A. The 5G network might potentially have consequences on an individual's health.
   B. The use of mobile phones does not engender harmful health effects.
   C. Electromagnetic radiation is constantly present.
   D. Certain individuals are concerned about the relationship between technology and their health.

3. The 5G network is currently available in villages and in cities.
   A. True
   B. False
   C. Can't Tell

4. The WHO has implied that the 5G network should not be a cause for concern.
   A. True
   B. False
   C. Can't Tell

Question 38 - The Science of Laughter

You don't have to be a laughter scientist - or gelotologist, as they like to be known - to know that it's good to laugh. But you might be surprised to learn just how much of an impact laughter can have on health. It alleviates the symptoms of depression and reduces stress and anxiety. It's good for the heart and boosts the immune system. And for some muscles, it provides a workout that would normally require a gym membership.

It can also help the elderly with pain management and sleeplessness. And in those with type 2 diabetes, laughter can reduce blood sugar levels and protect against some of the complications of the condition.

But as good as it is to laugh until you cry at something funny, when it comes to your mental health, simulated laughter - also known as voluntary or self-induced laughter - is even better. A recent scientific review of 86 laughter studies found that, for depression and anxiety, the therapeutic effects of simulated laughter are twice that of natural laughter.

And physically, simulated laughter can raise respiration levels in a similar way to aerobic exercise and work the internal oblique muscles to the same degree as crunches.

Source: Adapted from The Irish Independent (https://www.independent.ie/life/health-wellbeing/the-science-of-laughter-and-how-to-harness-the-benefits-39081683.html).
The text used here is for educational purposes. The contents and the copyright belong to the aforementioned source.

1. Laughter is beneficial because:
   A. it is less expensive than joining a gym.
   B. it quells negative thoughts.
   C. it can be simulated.
   D. it can cure diabetes.

2. Based on the information in the passage, which amongst the following statements is always true?
   A. Laughter eradicates depression.
   B. Simulated laughter has medicinal effects.
   C. Laughter relieves the symptoms of diabetes.
   D. Simulated laughter is sometimes created by the individual.

3. In order to become a gelotologist, one must have a degree in science.
   A. True
   B. False
   C. Can't Tell

4. The writer suggests that individuals are unaware of the close relationship between laughter and health.
   A. True
   B. False
   C. Can't Tell

Question 39 - Three Lunar Landers

NASA has announced three companies that will be helping bring humans to the moon as part of the Artemis programme. These three US firms – Blue Origin, Dynetics, and SpaceX – will receive a combined $967 million to develop and test lunar landers.

Each company will be developing its own lunar lander. Blue Origin's is called the Integrated Lander Vehicle and will be designed to launch aboard either the company's own New Glenn rocket or the United Launch Alliance's Vulcan rocket. Dynetics' lander is called the Dynetics Human Landing System and is also designed to launch aboard the Vulcan rocket. Finally, SpaceX's contract will go towards the Starship, designed to launch aboard the company's Falcon Heavy rocket.

The three landers are very different. Blue Origin's lander, which is based on the earlier Blue Moon concept, has three sections – a transfer stage to move it into a lower orbit around the moon from where it is first dropped off, a descent stage to land, and an ascent stage to return into lunar orbit. The landers from Dynetics and SpaceX are planned to each be a single structure that can perform all three of those manoeuvres.

For the first mission of the Artemis programme, which aims to send astronauts back to the moon by 2024, the plan is to launch one of the landers on a separate rocket from NASA astronauts, who are planned to launch aboard the Space Launch System (SLS) that the space agency is developing. Then, the astronauts will rendezvous with their lander in orbit around the moon before lowering down to its surface. The other two landers may be used on subsequent missions.

Source: Adapted from The New Scientist (https://www.newscientist.com/article/2242413-nasa-has-selected-three-lunar-landers-to-bring-humans-to-the-moon/).
The text used here is for educational purposes. The contents and the copyright belong to the aforementioned source.

1. Which amongst the following statements can be corroborated by the information contained within the passage?
   A. The three companies will be supported to develop a lunar lander.
   B. Each of the three companies will be required to develop its own equipment.
   C. The three companies will work collectively to build a lunar lander.
   D. Each of the three companies will launch its own rocket.

2. It is hoped that the three landers will be able to:
   A. effect all of the basic requirements.
   B. avoid carrying out three actions.
   C. each execute three actions.
   D. perform various manoeuvres.

3. Based on the information in the passage, which amongst the following statements is always true?
   A. Only one of the three landers will be used.
   B. At least one of the three landers will be used.
   C. Each of the three landers will be used simultaneously.
   D. There is potential that none of the three landers will be used.

4. It is hoped that the same astronauts who have previously landed on the moon will return to the moon by 2024.
   A. True
   B. False
   C. Can't Tell

Question 40 - Britain Goes Coal Free

When Britain went into lockdown, electricity demand plummeted; the National Grid responded by taking power plants off the network. A decade ago, just 3% of the country's electricity came from wind and solar, which many people saw as a costly distraction. Now the UK has the biggest offshore wind industry in the world, as well as the largest single wind farm, completed off the coast of Yorkshire last year.

At the same time Drax, the country's biggest power plant, has been taking a different path to renewable energy. A decade ago, it was the biggest consumer of coal in the UK but has been switching to compressed wood pellets. "We here at Drax decided that coal was no longer the future," explains Will Gardiner, the chief executive of the power group." It has been a massive undertaking and then the result of all that is we've reduced our CO_2 emissions from more than 20 million tonnes a year to almost zero."

And it is not just coal that is being eclipsed by renewables. So far this year, renewables have generated more power than all fossil fuels put together. Breaking it down, renewables were responsible for 37% of electricity supplied to the network versus 35% for fossil fuels. Nuclear accounted for about 18% and imports for the remaining 10% or so, according to figures from the online environmental journal, *Carbon Brief*. "So far this year renewables have generated more electricity than fossil fuels and that's never happened before," says Dr Simon Evans of *Carbon Brief*. "With gas also in decline, there's a real chance that renewables will overtake fossil fuels in 2020 as a whole."

Before this year, there had been a total of 154 days when the combined power created from renewable sources exceeded those from fossil fuels. *Carbon Brief* says that 91 of those days occurred in 2019. The decline in the role of fossil fuels in general and coal in particular looks set to continue. The remaining three coal plants in the UK will be shut down within five years. Then the fuel that sparked the industrial revolution here in Britain almost two centuries ago will be a thing of the past.

Source: Adapted from The BBC (https://www.bbc.co.uk/news/science-environment-52973089).
The text used here is for educational purposes. The contents and the copyright belong to the aforementioned source.

1. According to the information presented in the passage, which amongst the following assertions cannot be untrue?
   A. The UK is the superior producer of offshore wind power globally.
   B. The UK potentially houses the largest offshore wind industry in the world.
   C. The major users of fossil fuels have now adapted to greener energy supplies.
   D. Renewable energy will be the primary source of fuel for the UK in the year 2020.

2. Which of the following cannot not be false?
   A. The lockdown highlighted the dispensable nature of power stations.
   B. Coal is the main industry that has been overshadowed by renewable sources.
   C. Nuclear power will potentially continue to make a contribution to energy supplies.
   D. Renewable power was occasionally judged not to be cost effective.

3. The passage suggests that the energy that triggered a transformation might soon be eliminated.
   A. True
   B. False
   C. Can't Tell

4. Which of the following can be inferred from the passage?
   A. It would seem that the major power plants will not be turned back on after the current lockdown.
   B. In one year, combined power from renewable sources exceeded power from fossil fuels by 60%.
   C. Drax ceased the use of coal one decade ago.
   D. Since the UK has the biggest offshore wind industry, the need for imports will gradually reduce.

Question 41 - Weird Weather

Meteorologists were astounded by this unprecedented weather somersault. Some place the blame on climate change, but the Met Office says, as yet, there's no strong evidence for that. Prof Palmer told BBC News: "It would be really valuable for us to have more knowledge of how climate change is affecting weather patterns like this."

He agrees that space observations have massively improved our understanding of the climate. But he complains: "It is very frustrating to see space get quite so much attention when we can't be sure what will happen to the climate on Earth."

The strong jetstream to the south-west of England through the winter locked in place the succession of Atlantic storms that drenched the UK. The Met Office successfully predicted the wet winter in its seasonal forecast but failed to predict the sudden leap to a dry spring when the jetstream was looped over the UK, holding the sunny weather in place.

Some scientists believe it's being affected by conditions in the Arctic, which is warming faster than anywhere on the planet, because of greenhouse gases. But this is disputed. Prof Palmer said the jetstream appeared to be influenced by a climate phenomenon known as the Indian dipole – an irregular oscillating current in the Indian Ocean. This was also blamed for the wildfires in Australia.

Scientists know ocean currents on the other side of the world can influence our weather. Scientists are now planning to re-run UK climate models over recent years and remove the heating element of CO_2 emissions from the mathematical puzzle. That should offer a better understanding of British weather at least.

If warmer weather leads to more low-level clouds, that will bounce out radiation and cool the Earth. If it leads to more high-level clouds, that will trap in heat."We need to understand these processes better," he says. "Normally in science you learn about the system under study by doing laboratory experiments. With Earth's climate, there is no lab experiment you can do."

Source: Adapted from The BBC (https://www.bbc.co.uk/news/science-environment-52921479).
The text used here is for educational purposes. The contents and the copyright belong to the aforementioned source.

1. Which one of the following inferences can be deduced from the passage?
   A. The wildfires in Australia were indubitably the result of fluctuations in the Indian Ocean.
   B. The current conditions within the Arctic are potentially impacting on jetstreams.
   C. The removal of heat elements in the study will provide greater understanding of weather systems.
   D. The increase in temperatures precedes the cloud levels rising.

2. Which of the following is not supported by the information provided in the passage?
   A. Climate change is deemed the foremost cause for the recent weather anomalies.
   B. The jetstream encircling the UK was the chief component in heightened temperatures.
   C. Greenhouse gases have the potential to cause a weather phenomenon.
   D. The Atlantic storms were responsible for the amount of recent rainfall.

3. More financial support has been given to climate in space than the earth's climate.
   A. True
   B. False
   C. Can't Tell

4. Which of the following can possibly be concluded from the passage?
   A. The use of space observations has assisted in the understanding of climate change.
   B. The impact of lower-level clouds will lead to cooler temperatures.
   C. The Indian dipole has impacted on other occurrences.
   D. There are some inadequacies in the current system of forecasting.

Question 42 - A Superb Alternative History of the Space Race

At mission control we are served row upon row of men in dark-rimmed spectacles chewing pencils and doing flight calculations on bits of paper. There are women, but they are holding trays of tea or, at best, working in the back-up team.

Then comes the first "what-if" twist: the Soviet Union gets boots on the moon first. Suddenly we are plunged into an alternate timeline, in which the space race heats up rather than down, and a moon base becomes a US priority.

It is the second "what-if" twist, though, that packs the punch. While the US scrambles to get its act together, the Soviets land on the moon for a second time. On 1960s TV sets we see a cosmonaut standing on the lunar surface. Then up comes their mirror visor, and it is a woman.

This is when *For All Mankind* bursts into life. The women in those background shots at NASA and the wives watching at home can't believe their eyes. The Soviet Union has put a woman on the moon, while the US doesn't have a single woman in astronaut training.

Source: Adapted from The New Scientist (https://www.newscientist.com/article/mg24532700-500-for-all-mankind-review-a-superb-alternative-history-of-the-space-race/).
The text used here is for educational purposes. The contents and the copyright belong to the aforementioned source.

1. According to the writer of the passage, which amongst the following assertions is not false?
   A. Women are underrepresented in the space industry.
   B. Women are undervalued in the space industry.
   C. Women are suppressed in the space industry.
   D. Women are underestimated in the space industry.

2. Those who watched a woman land on the moon:
   A. were disheartened at what they saw on the TV.
   B. were delighted that they had finally been recognised.
   C. were amazed at what they witnessed.
   D. did not trust what was being shown on the TV.

3. Which of the following statements can be corroborated by the information contained in the passage?
   A. The Soviet Union wanted to annoy America by sending a female astronaut to space.
   B. America was determined to put the first astronaut on the moon.
   C. The Soviet Union wanted to irritate America by sending a second astronaut to space.
   D. America was desperate to put the second astronaut on the moon.

4. Based on the information in the passage, it can be inferred that the author:
   A. believes that women are employed by NASA to make tea.
   B. relays the disbelief felt by many that a woman landed on the moon.
   C. believes that women cannot be employed in the same capacity as men.
   D. disagrees with the way in which America treats women.

Question 43 - Measles Vaccine

Catherine Montantes was a 28-year-old college student, training to become a border patrol agent, and recently diagnosed with an autoimmune disorder. Despite being vaccinated against measles, Montantes was killed less than three months later by the disease, because her immune system was suppressed by medication to control the autoimmune disorder dermatomyositis.

In an exclusive interview with the Guardian, Montantes' mother, Ralphenia Knudson, describes how the disease, often called "harmless" by anti-vaxxers, claimed her daughter's life and upended her family.

"I understand the importance of vaccination. I had all my kids vaccinated," said Montantes' mother, Knudson, a former long-haul, semi-truck driver who lives in Juneau, Alaska. Montantes had three siblings.

Vaccine hesitancy was named a top 10 global health threat by the World Health Organization this year. By this April, measles cases had risen 300%. In its decision to call vaccine hesitancy a global health threat, the WHO attributed the virus' rise, in part, to people declining or delaying vaccines despite their availability.

Most of the cases are concentrated in conservative Orthodox Jewish communities in and around New York City. Prominent anti-vaxxers, who have targeted a close-knit Somali community in Minnesota, have visited the city to spread propaganda and false claims about the dangers of vaccines. Vaccinated children and those with suppressed immune systems – like Montantes – are the most vulnerable to measles, which kills between one and two people for every 1,000 it infects.

Source: Adapted from The Guardian (https://www.theguardian.com/society/2019/jul/10/vaccines-measles-outbreak-immune-system).
The text used here is for educational purposes. The contents and the copyright belong to the aforementioned source.

1. The World Health Organisation published a study on the measles outbreak in which it reported that cases had tripled.
   A. True
   B. False
   C. Can't Tell

2. Orthodox Jewish communities have experienced several hundred deaths due to the measles outbreak.
   A. True
   B. False
   C. Can't Tell

3. In an interview, Montantes' mother revealed that she has had all three of her children vaccinated against measles since Catherine's death.
   A. True
   B. False
   C. Can't Tell

4. If 10,000 people get measles, 20 of them will be killed by the infection.
   A. True
   B. False
   C. Can't Tell

Question 44 - Globalisation in Chile

Chile today is Latin America's richest country, with per capita GDP of about $23,000 – similar to that of central European countries. This is quite an achievement for a country that depends so heavily on copper production, and it sets Chile apart from many of its neighbours.

For example, when I led a review on antimicrobial resistance, I learned that copper has powerful antibacterial properties and is an ideal material for use in healthcare facilities where bacteria often spread. This means that copper producers such as Chile, Australia, and Canada can improve global health – and boost exports – by introducing affordable copper infrastructure into hospitals and other clinical settings around the world.

Chile is also a storehouse of knowledge for managing earthquakes and tsunamis. While I was there, I visited La Serena, which in 2015 experienced the sixth strongest earthquake ever recorded. But the ensuing tsunami killed only 11 people, though it surely would have killed far more in many other places. Chilean officials' advanced preparation and rapid response seems to have made the difference. With so much institutional experience, Chile can be a valuable resource for other countries threatened by seismic events. La Serena is also near one of the world's best stargazing sites, which attracts leading astronomers from around the globe.

Source: Adapted from The Guardian (https://www.theguardian.com/business/2017/jan/18/globalisation-world-trade-asia-global-poverty).
The text used here is for educational purposes. The contents and the copyright belong to the aforementioned source.

1. The author believes that other countries threatened by seismic events should look to Chile because:
   A. the country witnessed the sixth strongest earthquake to ever be recorded.
   B. less than a dozen people were killed when the country was hit by a tsunami.
   C. the country's preparedness for such events is admirable.
   D. officials are willing to share rapid response strategies.

2. Which of the following statements about Chile cannot be corroborated by the information in the passage?
   A. It has the potential to augment healthcare globally.
   B. It is reputed amongst astronomers.
   C. It was the first country to develop intricate plans after being hit by a deadly earthquake.
   D. It is not the poorest country in Latin America.

3. The author is a keen astronomer.
   A. True
   B. False
   C. Can't Tell

4. La Serena is a fantastic place in which to stargaze.
   A. True
   B. False
   C. Can't Tell

Question 45 - What Is Life in Space Really Like?

There is no way to anticipate the emotional impact of leaving your home planet. You look down at Earth and realize: You're not on it. It is breathtaking. It is surreal. It's a "we're not in Kansas anymore, Toto" kind of feeling. But I've spent a total of 55 days in space, over the course of five missions for NASA, and I've learned that being out there isn't just a series of breathtaking moments. It's a mix of the transcendently magical and the deeply prosaic. It can be crowded, noisy, and occasionally uncomfortable. Space travel—at least the way we do it today—isn't glamorous. But you can't beat the view!

Everyone imagines that when you're sitting on the launchpad atop 7 million pounds of explosive rocket fuel, you're nervous and worried; but the truth is, there isn't much to do for those two hours after you climb into the shuttle. Many astronauts just take a nap. You're strapped in like a sack of potatoes while the system goes through thousands of prelaunch checks. Occasionally you have to wake up and say "Roger" or "Loud and clear." But the launch itself is a whole other thing—from the pad to orbit in 8.5 minutes, accelerating the entire time until you reach the orbital velocity of 17,500 mph. That is a ride.

It turns out that once you're actually in orbit, zero-g has some upsides. Without gravity, bodily fluids move toward your head. It's a great face-lift. Your stomach gets flat. You feel long because you grow an inch or two. (I thought, "Oh cool, I'll be tall," but of course everybody else was taller too.)

Source: Adapted from Wired (https://www.wired.com/2014/11/marsha-ivins/). The text used here is for educational purposes. The contents and the copyright belong to the aforementioned source.

1. The author has completed several space missions for NASA, but she has never spent more than a fortnight in space.
   A. True
   B. False
   C. Can't Tell

2. Having read the passage, we can incur that the author believes that:
   A. being in space can be profoundly mundane.
   B. travelling to space is an insightful experience.
   C. being in space is extremely productive.
   D. going to space is not something that everyone can experience.

3. The author seems to have become bored of travelling in space.
   A. True
   B. False
   C. Can't Tell

4. Based on the information in the passage, which amongst the following statements is not false?
   A. The author is not short.
   B. Travelling to space is not challenging.
   C. It is difficult to pinpoint how space travel makes one feel.
   D. There are drawbacks to travelling to space.

Question 46 - Young People and Fast Food

One in six young people eat fast food twice a day, according to a survey of the nation's eating habits. The BBC Good Food Nation Survey found that most people ate fast food on average two days per week. But, in the 16 to 20-year-old category, one in six ate fast food at least twice a day, with one in eight among 21 to 34-year-olds eating as frequently.

The study of more than five thousand people found that half of them thought "a meal isn't a meal without meat". However, the same proportion were unaware of how much meat is a recommended daily amount. The Department of Health advises an average of no more than 70g per day, which is the equivalent of two-and-a-half rashers of bacon. But nearly one in four people thought the recommended amount of meat was at least double that.

The survey found that a fifth of men (21%), and 32% of 16 to 21-year-old men and women, ate meat at least three times a day. The typical adult now eats meat at least twice a day and has only six meat-free days a month. Christine Hayes, brand editorial director of BBC Good Food, said it showed it was "easy to be confused about the amount of meat one can enjoy while still eating a healthy, balanced diet". She added: "Those who do eat meat can still cook a Sunday roast and eat the occasional steak when balanced with some meat-free dishes."

The survey found that two in five people aged 21 to 34-year-olds had posted a photo of a meal they had cooked on social networking sites such as Instagram. A third had posted a photo of a meal they had eaten in a restaurant. Social media was identified as a contributing factor in the obesity epidemic.

Source: Adapted from The BBC (https://www.bbc.co.uk/news/health-37511554). The text used here is for educational purposes. The contents and the copyright belong to the aforementioned source.

1. The BBC Good Food Nation Survey questioned the public about its eating habits. It showed that around 16.6% of 16 to 20-year-olds are considered overweight.
   A. True
   B. False
   C. Can't Tell

2. According to the information in the passage, how often does the average adult not consume meat in any given month?
   A. 15%
   B. 20%
   C. 25%
   D. 30%

3. The negative impact that social media has on the lives of individuals is seen to contribute towards the obesity epidemic.
   A. True
   B. False
   C. Can't Tell

4. Which amongst the following statements is supported by the information in the passage?
   A. The author believes that young people consume too much fast food.
   B. In the UK, the number of vegetarians outweighs the number of meat-eaters.
   C. Young people often post pictures of their food on social media.
   D. People should not necessarily cease to eat meat.

Question 47 - Met Office Supercomputer

Better forecasting means handling more data, more rapidly, and running it through simulations of the atmosphere more accurately.

Like any huge IT installation, it'll certainly need a massive supply of electricity. That's why the Met Office is inviting the potential providers to come up with low-carbon options.

Already the Met Office is pulling in more than 200 billion observations from satellites, weather stations and buoys out in the ocean every single day, and that's set to increase.

And working out if a summer downpour will flood your home or one down the road requires more and more processing power. "We'll be streets ahead of anybody else," according to Penny Endersby, chief executive of the Met Office. "Ultimately it'll make a difference to every individual, every government department, every industry as people see forecasts becoming steadily better." It'll be the biggest investment in the 170-year history of the organisation and will dwarf the £97m bill for the current supercomputer.

It could guide Environment Agency teams deploying mobile flood barriers or help the National Grid balancing fluctuations in wind and solar power. And the prospect of rising global temperatures fuelling new and more dangerous extremes of weather makes accuracy all the more important.

The effects of the rise of 1C over the past 150 years are still not fully understood, let alone those of bigger increases to come. It should mean researchers can add more detail to their projections, weaving in factors such as the way nitrogen reacts with the carbon in the air.

And as the UK moves towards its target of net zero emissions by 2050, there'll be a chance to explore different options for how the country uses the land. For example, what will the effects be of planting new forests or protecting peat bogs or growing more biofuels?

Source: Adapted from The BBC (https://www.bbc.co.uk/news/science-environment-51504002).

1. The new supercomputer will itself leave a carbon footprint.
   A. True
   B. False
   C. Can't Tell

2. According to the information presented in the passage, which amongst the following assertions can be considered untruthful?
   A. The implementation of the device will enable UK forecasters to be the most powerful analysts.
   B. The device will allow researchers to better calculate temperature boosts.
   C. The current device is presently costing £97m.
   D. The additional methods are providing substantial interpretations.

3. According to the information presented in the passage, which amongst the following assertions cannot be untrue about the device?
   A. It will eliminate flooding.
   B. The surge in heat may be mitigated through correct usage of the device.
   C. It will effectively stabilise the use of natural resources.
   D. Its implementation will have widespread effects.

4. What conclusion can be drawn from the passage?
   A. The device will potentially need financial support from private companies.
   B. The device will play a significant role in achieving the emissions target of 2050.
   C. The necessity for intense precision is critical to effectiveness.
   D. The protection of peat bogs will have a considerable impact on emissions targets and the fuelling of this device.

Question 48 - Edward Jenner

In 1796, he carried out his now famous experiment on eight-year-old James Phipps. Jenner inserted pus taken from a cowpox pustule and inserted it into an incision on the boy's arm. He was testing his theory, drawn from the folklore of the countryside, that milkmaids who suffered the mild disease of cowpox never contracted smallpox, one of the greatest killers of the period, particularly among children. Jenner subsequently proved that, having been inoculated with cowpox, Phipps was immune to smallpox. He submitted a paper to the Royal Society in 1797 describing his experiment but was told that his ideas were too revolutionary and that he needed more proof. Undaunted, Jenner experimented on several other children, including his own 11-month-old son. In 1798, the results were finally published, and Jenner coined the word 'vaccine' from the Latin 'vacca' for cow.

Jenner was widely ridiculed. Critics, especially the clergy, claimed it was repulsive and ungodly to inocculate someone with material from a diseased animal. A satirical cartoon of 1802 showed people who had been vaccinated sprouting cow's heads. But the obvious advantages of vaccination and the protection it provided won out, and vaccination soon became widespread. Jenner became famous and now spent much of his time researching and advising on developments in his vaccine.

Source: Adapted from The BBC (http://www.bbc.co.uk/history/historic_figures/jenner_edward.shtml).
The text used here is for educational purposes. The contents and the copyright belong to the aforementioned source.

1. Which amongst the following can be corroborated by the information in the passage?
   A. The word 'vaccine' existed before the end of the eighteenth century.
   B. Jenner allowed his critics to deter his enthusiasm.
   C. No children under the age of one year were tested on.
   D. Jenner enlisted the help of adults to test his hypothesis.

2. Jenner was told that his theory:
   A. was unlikely to be viable.
   B. was supported by sufficient evidence.
   C. was far too radical.
   D. was ideally positioned to establish a cure for the smallpox.

3. Jenner found that he was:
   A. viciously attacked for his research.
   B. mocked for his research
   C. accepted for his research practices.
   D. not appreciated for his research.

4. The passage confirms that which amongst the following assertions cannot be false?
   A. Many children continued to die as a result of Jenner's experiments.
   B. Many children were saved despite Jenner's experiments.
   C. Many children continued to die despite Jenner's experiments.
   D. Many children were saved by dint of Jenner's experiments.

Question 49 - Why the Fashion Industry Faces an 'Existential Crisis'

Normally, at this time of year, many of us would be curating our perfect summer wardrobe as we prepare for sunny weather and foreign holidays. Instead, clothing sales plummeted by 34% in March as much of the world's population is currently unable to travel abroad or even socialise amid lockdown restrictions.

"It has led to a real existential crisis for the fashion industry," says Imran Amed, the founder and CEO of The Business of Fashion, a leading industry website which has produced a report about the impact of the coronavirus outbreak.

"This is an industry which is still almost entirely dependent on physical retail. More than 80% of transactions in the fashion industry still happen in physical stores."

With sales currently low, many brands have suspended advertising - although some continue to use social media influencers to promote products. Emily Canham, who has more than 700,000 Instagram followers, regularly promotes services and products including health foods, make-up, streaming services, holidays and clothes.

"For me right now it's really about listening to my followers about what feels appropriate," Canham tells BBC News. Some of her recent posts have been reflective of her current lifestyle under lockdown - not always necessarily promoting something.

She adds: "My followers generally wear what makes them feel great and powerful rather than adhering to traditional seasonal trends. It's about how you wear it, not what season it's worn in."

Source: Adapted from The BBC (https://www.bbc.co.uk/news/entertainment-arts-52394504).
The text used here is for educational purposes. The contents and the copyright belong to the aforementioned source.

1. Emily Canham is currently sharing posts that indicate her situation at present:
   A. rather than posts that promote her products.
   B. rather than posts that endorse a particular item.
   C. rather than posts that discuss topical issues.
   D. rather than posts that encourage purchases.

2. Based on the information contained in the passage, which amongst the following statements cannot be negated?
   A. The way in which the British public shops will change as a result of coronavirus.
   B. Those who work in the fashion industry are facing job losses.
   C. Many retailers have stopped advertising because they do not have the money to fund it.
   D. Emily Canham's business has survived because she has more than 700,000 followers on Instagram.

3. It is anticipated that only the summer fashion season will be affected by coronavirus.
   A. True
   B. False
   C. Can't Tell

4. The fashion industry has never encountered a crisis that compares to this one.
   A. True
   B. False
   C. Can't Tell

Question 50 - The Titanic

As it prepared to embark on its maiden voyage, the *Titanic* was one of the largest and most opulent ships in the world. The voyage nearly began with a collision, however, when suction from the *Titanic* caused the docked *New York* to swing into the giant liner's path. After an hour of manoeuvrings to prevent the accident, the *Titanic* was under way. On the evening of April 10 the ship stopped at Cherbourg, France. The city's dock was too small to accommodate the *Titanic*, so passengers had to be ferried to and from the ship in tenders. After some two hours the *Titanic* resumed its journey. On the morning of April 11 the liner made its last scheduled stop in Europe, at Queenstown (Cobh), Ireland. At approximately 1330 hours, the ship set sail for New York City. Onboard were some 2,200 people, approximately 1,300 of whom were passengers.

Throughout much of the voyage, the wireless radio operators on the *Titanic*, Jack Phillips and Harold Bride, had been receiving iceberg warnings, most of which were passed along to the bridge. The two men worked for the Marconi Company, and much of their job was relaying passengers' messages. On the evening of April 14, the *Titanic* began to approach an area known to have icebergs. Smith slightly altered the ship's course to head farther south; he maintained the ship's speed of some 22 knots. At approximately 2140 hours, the *Mesaba* sent a warning of an ice field. The message was never relayed to the *Titanic*'s bridge. At 2255 hours, the nearby Leyland liner *Californian* sent word that it had stopped after becoming surrounded by ice. Phillips, who was handling passenger messages, scolded the *Californian* for interrupting him.

Source: Adapted from Britannica (https://www.britannica.com/topic/Titanic). The text used here is for educational purposes. The contents and the copyright belong to the aforementioned source.

1. Based on the information contained in the passage, which amongst the following statements is true?
   A. The *Titanic* was considered the largest ship of its time.
   B. Some of those on board the *Titanic* were from France.
   C. Fewer than half of those on board the *Titanic* were passengers.
   D. The *Titanic* was quite close to reaching its final destination.

2. The *Titanic's* first journey took place on 10th April.
   A. True
   B. False
   C. Can't Tell

3. As the *Titanic* first departed, an accident almost occurred because:
   A. the *New Yorker* nearly strayed into its path.
   B. it strayed into the path of the *New Yorker*.
   C. the *New Yorker* strayed into its path.
   D. it almost strayed into the path of the *New Yorker*.

4. Which amongst the following statements can be corroborated by the passage?
   A. The *Titanic* should not have been steered towards an area that had icebergs.
   B. The passengers' messages took precedence over their safety.
   C. Altering the ship's speed would have changed what happened next.
   D. Human error led to the sinking of the *Titanic*.

Question 51 - Baby Boomers

In the grim, grey aftermath of war, children were born on an unprecedented scale in a population explosion: the baby boomers – born between 1946 and the mid-60s – had arrived. It was time for a new life. It was time for the young to grow up with faith in a better tomorrow.

When we baby boomers reached adolescence, creating the teenager in the process, it was as if the floodlights had been switched on, revealing a colourful, contrary, anti-authoritarian Britain. In our teens, with rock'n'roll if not much cash, we were the lucky, cocky generation.

Anthropologist Helen Fisher inelegantly described the maturing of this huge post-war bulge in the population as "like a pig moving through a python", changing society as we grew older on a scale never known before. We challenged the Victorian puritanism, censorship, class snobbery and inhibitions of the establishment. Full employment put money in the pockets of managers and factory workers alike. In spanking new houses with inside lavatories and proper bathrooms, hire purchase allowed him (and less so, her) to spend, spend, spend as if, overnight, everyone had become a toff. It could only get better.

Yet today, "baby boomer" is a toxic phrase, shorthand for greed and selfishness, for denying the benefits we took for granted to subsequent generations, notably beleaguered millennials, who reached adulthood in the early years of this century. So, where did it all go so very wrong? It may have been due partly to our irritating habit of hogging the cultural limelight, with constant references to the swinging 60s serenaded by endless revivals of Lazarus-like pop groups who refuse to die. But there are a much more serious set of charges, too. We were – and are – accused of sabotaging our children's future, hoarding power and money while expecting those with the least to foot the potentially hefty bills as we march towards our 90s.

Source: Adapted from The Guardian (https://www.theguardian.com/society/2018/apr/29/millennials-struggling-is-it-fault-of-baby-boomers-intergenerational-fairness).

The text used here is for educational purposes. The contents and the copyright belong to the aforementioned source.

1. Many millennials argue that baby boomers sabotaged their future. The author agrees with this statement.
   A. True
   B. False
   C. Can't Tell

2. Which of the following, if true, can be corroborated by the information in the passage?
   A. Several women who had a baby after the War ended brought hope to the people of Britain.
   B. Numerous babies who were born in Britain after the War ended had the opportunity to grow up in a better world.
   C. The analogy of turning on a light in a dark room is often used to describe this period.
   D. Many people wanted their children to grow up in a more hopeful world.

3. Which of the following traits does the passage not associate with baby boomers?
   A. They have very outdated morals and traditions.
   B. They took several opportunities for granted.
   C. They created problems with which the future generations had to deal, and this has ultimately damaged their future.
   D. They are hungry for power and tend to hoard it.

4. Baby boomers were born in a population explosion after World War II. The author was born in the mid-60s.
   A. True
   B. False
   C. Can't Tell

Question 52 - What Is Personality?

Personality refers to a distinctive assemblage of traits—characteristic patterns of thinking, feeling, and behaving. It derives from a mix of inborn dispositions and inclinations along with environmental factors and experiences. Although personality can change over the course of time, one's core characteristics tend to remain steady over a lifetime.

While there are countless characteristics that combine in an almost infinite number of ways, people have been trying to find a way to classify personality into types ever since Hippocrates and the ancient Greeks defined four basic temperaments. Today, psychologists generally define personality in terms of five basic traits. The so-called Big Five are openness to experience, conscientiousness, extraversion, agreeableness, and neuroticism.

For the last hundred years, employers have often sought to apply systematic approaches to employee selection, and they have utilized various assessments of personality characteristics. Currently, the Myers-Briggs Type Indicator and the DISC personality test are used widely. Critics contend that their ways of sorting people into discrete type categories are not valid psychologically and, further, that there is no evidence that the typologies predict anything meaningful about job or life performance.

Psychologists who study personality believe such typologies generally are too simplistic to account for the many ways people differ in personality. Instead, there is broad scientific consensus around the Big Five. Each of these key traits contributes to one's personality and is independent of the others.

Source: Adapted from Psychology Today (https://www.psychologytoday.com/us/basics/personality).
The text used here is for educational purposes. The contents and the copyright belong to the aforementioned source.

1. Why do critics condemn using personality tests to employ an individual?
   A. Personality tests are often inaccurate and do not reflect the person's true self.
   B. Personality tests can be expensive, and several employees cannot afford to purchase them.
   C. Personality tests do not reflect the person's true ability to carry out a particular job.
   D. Personality tests often do not accurately predict an individual's life performance.

2. What does personality not include?
   A. An individual's willingness to experience new things.
   B. An individual's disposition to care for and look after others.
   C. An individual's likeliness to experience anxiety and fear.
   D. An individual's ability to manage physical and emotional pain.

3. Certain aspects of an individual's personality can be changed. However, the majority of our personality comes from our genetics and is instinctive.
   A. True
   B. False
   C. Can't Tell

4. The Big Five were based on the five basic aspects of an individual's personality which were defined by Hippocrates in ancient Greece.
   A. True
   B. False
   C. Can't Tell

Question 53 - Secrets of the Teenage Brain

Several years ago, Frances Jensen's 16-year-old son wrote off a car. A few years earlier, her other son had returned from a friend's house with his hair dyed jet black. The University of Pennsylvania neurologist was finding her teenagers' erratic behaviour increasingly taxing, so she decided to study teenage thought processes and gathered her research in the book *The Teenage Brain*. She found that, while much had been written about teen psychology and parenting, no one had explained the neurons and cerebral connections that make those years such a unique – and terrifying – part of growing up. The teenage brain has only recently become a subject for serious research, which shows how little was known about it.

But does knowing what is going on in a teenager's brain make them any easier to live with? Without a doubt, says Jensen, who thinks that her research allowed her to be more patient with her sons. "We expect a little bit more out of adolescents than we should, given where their brains are," she says.

Tidiness needs a sophisticated level of cognitive control, and the way the teenage brain is connected means that their planning is not very good. Parts of the brain connect to each other through synapses, which are insulated, just like electric wires. That insulation is a fatty substance called myelin, which is created over time. The process takes years, and it starts at the back of the brain and slowly moves forward. The last bits of the brain to connect are the frontal and prefrontal cortices, where insight, empathy and risk taking are controlled. This means that very smart adolescents will do very stupid things in a very impulsive way. I don't think organisation is a high priority for most teenagers. They have other things to worry about – they are messy because they don't give themselves enough time to tidy up before they run off to do something else.

Source: Adapted from The Guardian (https://www.theguardian.com/lifeandstyle/2015/jan/25/secrets-of-the-teenage-brain).
The text used here is for educational purposes. The contents and the copyright belong to the aforementioned source.

1. The author of the passage strongly believes that understanding how teenagers' brains function is key to making living with them more manageable.
   A. True
   B. False
   C. Can't Tell

2. Based on the anatomy of the brain, why is it harder for teens to maintain a high level of tidiness?
   A. Tidiness requires a higher level of cognitive control which several teens do not develop until they become adults.
   B. The way in which their brain is connected means that they are unable to plan effectively.
   C. The brain is coated in myelin, which is formed over a prolonged period of time.
   D. Cleaning is not considered as a priority for teens as they deem other tasks more important.

3. Once she had completed her research on the teenage brain, Jensen realised that parents should not place so many expectations on teenagers.
   A. True
   B. False
   C. Can't Tell

4. Frances Jensen, a neurologist from the state of Pennsylvania, published a book entitled *The Teenage Brain*.
   A. True
   B. False
   C. Can't Tell

Question 54 - Ash Dieback

Ash trees are one of the UK's most abundant tree species. And it's estimated that ash dieback could cost the UK economy billions of pounds.

The fungus that causes ash dieback causes the loss of leaves and leads to parts of the tree dying.

The researchers looked at the disease's progress in an area of north-eastern France, monitoring the initial stages of its spread during 2012, which was about two years after the fungus was first recorded in the area. They then assessed the same area again between 2016 and 2018 once the disease had a chance to establish itself in the countryside.

Ash is a highly important species within the UK's hedgerows and accounts for about 10% of the nation's estimated 123 million "non-woodland" trees.

Ash dieback first arrived on UK shores back in March 2012, when it was found on some ash trees in a nursery. In October of that year, tree lovers' worst fears were realised when it was found in the wild, within a woodland in Norfolk.

Since then, the disease has spread to all parts of the UK. A recent estimate suggested that ash dieback would cost the UK economy £15bn. This estimate arises from the cost of clearing up dead and dying trees and includes lost benefits provided by the trees through water and air purification and locking in carbon from the atmosphere.

Source: Adapted from The BBC (https://www.bbc.co.uk/news/science-environment-52582304).
The text used here is for educational purposes. The contents and the copyright belong to the aforementioned source.

1. The loss of trees has the potential to lead to a major economic recession in the UK.
   A. True
   B. False
   C. Can't Tell

2. Having assessed when the disease was initially verified as being present,:
   A. it was impossible to scrutinise the early spread.
   B. it was prudent to investigate its growth.
   C. it became apparent that its spread was due to the lack of documentation in the area.
   D. it transpired that the fungus had been predominant for some time beforehand.

3. Which of the following statements can be substantiated from the information held in the passage?
   A. The disease was apparent outside of the UK prior to its discovery within the country.
   B. The initial occurrence of the disease in Britain was not identified in a garden centre.
   C. The spread of the disease was maintained within a British nursery for several months.
   D. All trees in a British nursery were affected by the disease.

4. According to the information that can be deciphered from the passage, which amongst the following assertions is not false?
   A. The spread of the disease had been expected by tree enthusiasts.
   B. The financial impact of the disease will extend beyond anything tangible.
   C. There will not be a substantial impact on the amount of carbon in the air.
   D. The clearing up operation will need to consider alternative means of water purification.

Question 55 - Murdering Hornets

The 2-inch (5cm) long Asian giant hornets, Vespa mandarinia, have been found in Washington state. Multiple stings are deadly to humans and, in their "slaughter phase", the hornets destroy honeybees, whose bodies they feed to their young. Although they typically avoid people, in Asia, "murder hornet" stings are thought to cause as many as 50 human fatalities a year, according to the *New York Times*.

The hornets are "shockingly large", said Todd Murray, a WSU scientist and invasive species specialist. "It's a health hazard, and more importantly, a significant predator of honeybees."

The insects, roughly the size of a matchbox, have large yellow-orange heads, prominent black eyes, and a black and yellow striped abdomen. The Asian giant hornet's life cycle begins in April, when queens come out of hibernation, and begin to feed and seek out subterranean dens to build their nests. Once their habitats are built in the summer and autumn months, worker hornets are sent to find food. With their sharp, spiked mandibles, the hornets decapitate honeybees, using the bodies to feed their young. The hornets can destroy a honeybee hive in a matter of hours.

The WSU scientists will begin trapping queen murder hornets this spring, aiming to detect and eradicate the species. Populations of honeybees and other pollinators in the US were already under pressure. Between 1947 and 2017, the number of honeybee colonies in the US plummeted from 6 million to 2.5 million. And last year, researchers from the University of Maryland reported that 40% of the country's honeybee colonies died in a single winter, between October 2018 and April 2019 - the largest loss of its kind.

Source: Adapted from The BBC (https://www.bbc.co.uk/news/52533585).
The text used here is for educational purposes. The contents and the copyright belong to the aforementioned source.

1. The singular resource of sustenance for the hornets is the body of the honeybee.
   A. True
   B. False
   C. Can't Tell

2. Which amongst the following assertions cannot be validated by the evidence in the passage?
   A. The hornets have had the most detrimental impact on honeybees.
   B. The hornets possess the capability of destroying human life.
   C. The hornets are substantial in mass in comparison to similar species.
   D. The hornets develop territories over two seasons.

3. According to the author of the passage, which amongst the following assertions is false?
   A. The Asian giant hornets have maintained their presence in Asia.
   B. Murder hornets may potentially decimate a hive in a comparatively short period of time.
   C. The worker hornets do not initiate habitat creation prior to the arrival of the queens.
   D. Murder hornets have evolved into a species that no longer circumvents humans.

4. The scientists have made a judgment to:
   A. undertake a method to ultimately eliminate this species.
   B. pursue action to trap the hornets who kill honeybees.
   C. take whatever methods are required to reduce the species.
   D. undertake research to trap and eliminate the hornets.

Question 56 - India's Carbon Emissions Fall

India's CO_2 emissions have fallen for the first time in four decades - and not just as a result of the country's coronavirus lockdown.

Falling electricity use and competition from renewables had weakened the demand for fossil fuels even before the coronavirus hit, according to analysis by the environmental website, *Carbon Brief*. However, it was the sudden nationwide lockdown in March that finally tipped the country's 37-year emissions growth trend into reverse.

The study finds that Indian carbon dioxide emissions fell 15% in March and are likely to have fallen by 30% in April. Virtually all of the drop-off in power demand has been borne by coal-fired generators, which explains why the emissions reductions have been so dramatic.

Coal-fired power generation was down 15% in March and 31% in the first three weeks of April, according to daily data from the Indian national grid. But even before India's sudden coronavirus lockdown, the demand for coal was weakening.

The study finds that, in the fiscal year ending March 2020, coal deliveries were down by around 2%, a small but significant reduction when set against the trend - an increase in thermal power generation of 7.5% a year set over the previous decade.

Source: Adapted from The BBC (https://www.bbc.co.uk/news/world-asia-india-52614770).

1. From the information detailed within the passage, which amongst the following inferences cannot be deduced?
   A. Analysis detects a substantial emission reduction with the passage of time.
   B. The exigence for fossil energies appears to have stimulated a decrease in emissions.
   C. The mining industry has observed a steady decline in demand.
   D. The pressure for more resourceful supplies has progressively intensified.

2. According to the passage, the author most likely agrees that the decline in the necessity for coal has:
   A. transpired following an upsurge in demand for sustainable sources.
   B. fashioned a minor, but noteworthy, bearing on emissions.
   C. occurred following the unparalleled and abrupt limitations.
   D. been the least influential factor in the recent revision of emissions.

3. Which of the following inferences can be deduced from the passage?
   A. When the current restrictions are revoked, it is plausible that emissions will return.
   B. The unparalleled constraints imposed upon the country recently have sent its emission tendencies backwards.
   C. There has not been any significant increase in demand for substitutes of non-renewable energy.
   D. The previous forty years have witnessed a consistent decline in demand for non-renewable sources of energy.

4. Based on the information in the passage, what can be inferred about the improved use of renewable supplies?
   A. Their growing popularity had been evident for some time.
   B. The present methods will decline at a rapid pace.
   C. The generators will be affected and become superfluous.
   D. It has taken over forty years for the effects of emissions to be recognised.

Question 57 - 1,000-Year-Old Bones Represent Oldest Tsunami Victims

Mjema returned to the site in 2012, 2016, and 2017, and his further excavations found bodies that were randomly oriented in the dirt – including one with intact iron bracelets around its ankles. War and disease didn't seem to account for the village's sudden demise. No cut marks or signs of illness were on any of the bones. By the looks of it, the village's men, women, and children had drowned and were buried in the shattered remains of their homes.

The sand that buried the village contained the remains of fish, rodents, birds, amphibians, and even the shells of small marine mollusc, a sign that water had washed in from the Indian Ocean, several miles downriver. And wherever the researchers dug, they kept finding more human bones. "Sometimes, it was kind of emotional, we needed to think about the science, but in the meantime, we were working with the people who died there," Maselli says.

Radiocarbon dating of charcoal and bone in the deposits confirmed that the flooding event happened about a thousand years ago. Tsunami deposits from around the Indian Ocean also date to that time, suggesting that an event similar in scale and intensity to the 2004 tsunami occurred a millennium ago.

Source: Adapted from National Geographic (https://www.nationalgeographic.com/science/2020/05/1000-year-old-bones-oldest-known-east-africa-tsunami-victims/).
The text used here is for educational purposes. The contents and the copyright belong to the aforementioned source.

1. Which of the following is supported by the information in the passage?
   A. There was a small window of opportunity that would have allowed many of the inhabitants to escape.
   B. There is sufficient evidence to establish a conclusive timeline of events.
   C. The tsunami followed an almost identical pattern to a contemporary episode.
   D. The inhabitants were self-sufficient prior to the point of the tsunami.

2. Which one of the following inferences can be presumed from the passage?
   A. The numbers found suggest the impact was somewhat mitigated.
   B. The village was a thriving dwelling close to the shoreline.
   C. The magnitude of the disaster would never be comparable with future incidents.
   D. The village had lain undiscovered for many thousands of years.

3. Which of these statements is best supported using the information contained in the passage?
   A. The inhabitants do not appear to have been killed within their own homes.
   B. There was sufficient time for evacuation, which allowed some residents to escape.
   C. It would appear plausible that the inhabitants succumbed by the influx of water.
   D. The discoveries initially intimated victims of genocide.

4. Based on the information in the passage, what can be inferred about the nature of the tsunami?
   A. It appears to have established a pattern of transpiring at distinctive interludes.
   B. The ferocity caused the inhabitants to be eradicated gradually.
   C. The intensity was of an analogous ilk to a later manifestation.
   D. The impact might have been mitigated by lower water levels and changes in the climate.

Question 58 - Longer Overlap for Modern Humans and Neanderthals

Modern humans began to edge out the Neanderthals in Europe earlier than previously thought, a new study shows. Tests on remains from a cave in northern Bulgaria suggest Homo sapiens was there as early as 46,000 years ago. This is up to 2,000 years older than evidence from Italy and the UK.

Around this time, Europe was populated by sparse groups of Neanderthals - a distinct type of human that vanished shortly after modern humans appeared on the scene.

There's considerable debate about the length of time that modern humans overlapped with Neanderthals in Europe and other parts of Eurasia. This has implications for the nature of contact between the two groups - and perhaps clues to why Neanderthals went extinct.

A tooth and four bone fragments were identified as broadly human based on their anatomical features. The bones found were associated with stone tools and artefacts, such as pendants made from cave bear teeth. These resemble examples found at later sites believed to have been occupied by Neanderthals. This could suggest the two groups interacted sufficiently for modern humans to influence Neanderthal behaviour.

Source: Adapted from The BBC (https://www.bbc.co.uk/news/science-environment-52614870).
The text used here is for educational purposes. The contents and the copyright belong to the aforementioned source.

1. One conclusion that can be drawn from the passage is that the discoveries:
   A. were all entirely human in origin and directly linked.
   B. were entirely indistinguishable from previous excavations.
   C. were comparable to specimens in other Neanderthal territories.
   D. exposed a strong likelihood that feral animals co-existed in that era.

2. The author would appear to disagree with all of the following statements with the exception of:
   A. Neanderthals are direct ancestors of the modern-day human race.
   B. Modern-day humans indubitably cohabited with alternative species.
   C. The advance of modern humans boosted the extermination of their cohorts.
   D. Modern humans directly descended from another species due to cohabitation.

3. Which of the following statements is best supported by the information contained within the passage?
   A. The modern human potentially influenced the conduct of the other group.
   B. The two groups undoubtedly mingled for an extensive period before any superiority emerged.
   C. The interaction between species led to a catastrophic impact on both of them.
   D. The potential for earlier habitations is conclusive.

4. Which factor does the author emphasise as being most likely to prove the co-existence of both races?
   A. There is clear proof that interaction indubitably led to the extinction of the weaker species.
   B. The artefacts detected were identical to those associated with modern humans.
   C. Anatomical discoveries broadly interlinked both species.
   D. There is conclusive evidence of the intermingling of numerous life types.

Question 59 - Green Energy Firms

The windfarm cluster is expected to create 600 jobs at its peak, and 280 long-term jobs, to help the UK emerge from the worst economic downturn in 300 years while taking steps to meet its climate goals.

Separately SSE and Equinor have revealed plans to use the Port of Tyne to host the operations base for the world's largest offshore wind development, which will create 200 permanent jobs and support a local supply chain industry based on clean energy.

Alok Sharma, the secretary of state for business, said projects like the Dogger Bank offshore windfarm will be "a key part of ensuring a green and resilient economic recovery, as well as reaching our target of net-zero emissions by 2050."

Keith Anderson, the boss of Scottish Power, told the Guardian that work to upgrade Scotland's first commercial windfarm, Hagshaw Hill, will come alongside two separate agreements to buy two nearby development projects to create a clean energy cluster in South Lanarkshire totalling 220MW.

"Not only do these projects help funnel money back through the supply chain and into jobs but they also make sure that the economic recovery is based on sustainable investments," he said.

Equinor and SSE Renewables picked the Port of Tyne to host the operations hub through a competitive tendering process, following its £10m overhaul to prepare for a surge in demand from windfarm developers.

Source: Adapted from The Guardian (https://www.theguardian.com/environment/2020/may/13/green-energy-firms-on-track-to-deliver-multi-billion-pound-wind-farms).

1. Based on the information in the passage, what can be inferred about the intentions of the companies?
   A. They have bowed to ecological mandates.
   B. They have forecast an opportunity to expand their local workforce.
   C. They have an intense aim to enhance the economy at the earliest opportunity.
   D. They will provide a systematic approach to promoting renewable energy.

2. Which one of these statements presents the main goal(s) of the companies?
   A. They are keen to use environmental and funding opportunities to promote their businesses.
   B. They are seizing the prospect of capturing a global market in a cost-effective location.
   C. They are keen to invest in deprived areas with high unemployment.
   D. They are looking to capitalise in an area of longevity and suitability.

3. What conclusion can be drawn from the passage?
   A. The companies are dedicated to paying urgent attention to ecological requirements.
   B. The locations are those in which the workforce will be obtained at a reduced cost.
   C. The triumph of renewable power is now leading to increased competition.
   D. There is an inference that the project is subject to lift in the economy.

4. If the information in the passage is presumed to be true, which of the following statements must also be true?
   A. The employment opportunities will be offered to those who can easily commute.
   B. The project is in receipt of support from government sources.
   C. The proposal is subject to the successful implementation in additional locations.
   D. The potential of suitable personnel was the determining factor in selecting the location.

Question 60 - America's Longest River Drier than During the Dust Bowl

For the first decade of the century, the Upper Missouri River Basin was the driest it's been in 1,200 years, even more parched than during the disastrous Dust Bowl of the 1930s, a new study says.

The drop in water level at the mouth of the Missouri, the country's longest river, was due to rising temperatures linked to climate change that reduced the amount of snowfall in the Rocky Mountains in Montana and North Dakota, scientists found. The basin has continued to experience droughts this decade — in 2012, 2013 and 2017 — but their severity in comparison with historic drought is unknown.

Researchers familiar with drought of this magnitude in the dry Southwest were surprised to find it in the Midwest. The Missouri River winds 2,300 miles from western Montana to St. Louis, where it joins the Mississippi River. It runs through the Dakotas and past Nebraska, Iowa, Kansas and Missouri, where it supports farming in several states and provides fresh water for dozens of municipalities.

Scientists at NASA and Columbia University had predicted such a drought would start sometime around 2030, but last month's study showed that the phenomenon is already here. Prolonged drought can disrupt agriculture and hurt economies, the researchers said. It affects dams that manage water resources and slows commercial traffic in rivers. On top of that, it harms marine life that must cope with lower water levels and animals such as waterfowl that rely on fish to survive. Runoff from the mountains to the Upper Missouri started decreasing in the 1950s, then dramatically declined between 1980 and 2000, the study said.

Source: Adapted from The Washington Post (https://www.washingtonpost.com/climate-environment/2020/05/11/missouri-river-drought-climate-change/).

1. It can be deduced from the passage that:
   A. the lack of comparative data has negated the trustworthiness of the research.
   B. contributing personnel did not have the essential wealth of expertise.
   C. earlier timeframes appear to have been superseded.
   D. the impact on resources may be paused with expediate action.

2. One conclusion that may be drawn from this passage is that:
   A. snowfall diminution would not appear to corroborate climate effects.
   B. the researchers are only proficient in the scale of drought in one location.
   C. the analysis has detailed the impact on climate change progression.
   D. the details in the report display contrasting worldwide impacts.

3. Based on the information in the passage, what can be inferred about a protracted absence of precipitation?
   A. It will have a bearing on aquatic species and, subsequently, their food successions.
   B. It will increase the amount of commercial travel within the area.
   C. It will instigate a replication of the Dust Bowl.
   D. It will dramatically reduce water directed for specific uses.

4. Which of the following is supported by the information in the passage?
   A. Experts had forecast the effect and ensured solutions were initiated.
   B. The severity of the drought would appear to be unparalleled.
   C. Water from elevations had potentially begun to diminish fifty years ago.
   D. It is improbable that species will endure reduced water levels.

Question 61 - Duchess Anastasia

After Nicholas II abdicated the throne on March 15, 1917, he and his family – his wife, Alexandra; son, Alexis; and four daughters, Olga, Tatiana, Maria, and Anastasia – were taken captive and eventually moved to a house in the Ural Mountains. In the cellar, they and four of their servants were executed by a Bolshevik firing squad on July 17, 1918. However, no bodies were immediately found. Moreover, reports from Russia were so unclear that the dowager empress, who had found refuge in Crimea, doubted the news of her family's death. Even the executioners' later accounts were so muddled as to invite speculation.

With such sensational accounts of the murders and the chaotic aftermath of the Revolution, anything seemed possible. Romanov imposters sprang up all over the world in the ensuing decades, offering fantastic tales of escape. The most famous claimant was Anna Anderson, whose case remained in the German courts for more than 30 years until a 1970 ruling declared no conclusive evidence proving Anderson was or was not Anastasia.

The mystery took an intriguing turn in the late 1990s when scientists using DNA evidence identified bodies found in the 1970s as the Tsar, his wife, and three of their daughters. The bodies of Alexis and of one of his sisters, however, were not among those found. Because the discovered remains had been burned, it was hard to say which Romanov daughter was absent, and the news revived speculation that Anastasia had survived. In 2007 the two missing bodies were found, and soon afterward they were identified as Alexis and probably Maria. Anastasia's remains were likely one of the bodies that had been found earlier.

Source: Adapted from Britannica (https://www.britannica.com/story/did-duchess-anastasia-survive-her-familys-execution).
The text used here is for educational purposes. The contents and the copyright belong to the aforementioned source.

1. Which one of the following inferences can be deduced from the passage?
    A. There are no specifics to accurately establish when the offspring were slaughtered.
    B. Numerous affiliates of the household absconded safely.
    C. The slayings instigated the initiation of the collapse of the realm.
    D. The precise setting of their initial incarceration has been uncovered.

2. What conclusion can be drawn from the passage?
    A. Despite the subsequent pandemonium, specific timings can be speculated.
    B. The extent of the charred relics permanently eradicated identification.
    C. The incident afforded a platform for fabricated identity claims.
    D. The Tsar elected to abdicate in the anticipation of curtailing the insurgency.

3. It can be concluded from the passage that the author:
    A. persists in the conviction that the princess escaped the massacre.
    B. deems that further investigations are still required.
    C. intimates that there was a politically motivated concealment of evidence.
    D. considers there is still no conclusive evidence of the fate of Anastasia.

4. Which of the following is not supported by the information in the passage?
    A. Anastasia's body was unquestionably one of the previous cadavers discovered.
    B. It is probable that the widow of the preceding Tsar evaded the annihilation.
    C. The assassins themselves provided capricious reports.
    D. Some pretenders have neither been established nor refuted.

Question 62 - Easter Rising

Shortly after noon on Easter Monday, Pearse, accompanied by an armed guard, stood on the steps of the GPO and read the proclamation, signalling the beginning of the Easter Rising.

Ireland's 'national right to freedom and sovereignty' was asserted. The conflict that followed was largely confined to Dublin. The British military onslaught, which the rebels had anticipated, did not at first materialise. When the rising began, the authorities had just 400 troops to confront roughly 1,000 insurgents.

The next day, Pearse surrendered unconditionally on behalf of the volunteers and issued orders to this effect. A total of 450 people were killed during the rebellion, among them 64 rebels. A total of 2,614 were injured, and nine others were reported missing, almost all in Dublin.

The British capture of a shipment of German arms three days before the rebellion was partly responsible for the failure of the nationwide mobilisation. In addition, confusion was caused by conflicting orders sent out to the Irish Volunteers by their leader Eoin MacNeill.

Dr Fearghal McGarry, from Queen's University Belfast, said "they did not expect it to win power, what they planned was a spectacle, a gesture to transform public opinion. In political terms, the rising achieved everything that the organisers thought it would. It destroyed the Irish Parliamentary Party's credibility and it derailed Home Rule. It exposed the oppressive nature of British rule and it transformed public opinion by winning public support for republicanism."

Source: Adapted from The BBC
(https://www.bbc.co.uk/news/uk-northern-ireland-35873316).

1. One conclusion that can be drawn from the passage is that:
    A. the overall sacrifice overshadowed the advances made.
    B. the rising was efficacious in terms of what was sought to be accomplished.
    C. the organisers had been assured of victory through the means used.
    D. it had been a strategic incident intended to provide a symbol of contempt.

2. Which of the following statements is not supported by the information contained in the passage?
    A. The insurgents had devised a response for the counteroffensive.
    B. The directives disseminated resulted in orders being misconstrued.
    C. The Irish population acquired an understanding of the aim of the incident.
    D. The British troops had not been fully prepared.

3. Which one of the following inferences can be deduced from the passage?
    A. The insurgence would have succeeded had there been a greater number of volunteers.
    B. The military did not deem there was any tangible threat from the rebels.
    C. The rebels were wholly conscious that the rising would not be efficacious.
    D. The rebels had not predicted the antagonism of the general public.

4. According to the passage, the author most likely agrees that:
    A. the insurgence had an adverse impact on public attitudes.
    B. the event heralded the commencement of Irish independence.
    C. the surrender was viewed as a treachery of the aims of the rebels.
    D. the mayhem between the superiors was the decisive cause for failure.

Question 63 - Mouse Embryos

Biologists have created mouse-human chimeras whose bodies were composed of up to 4 percent human cells when the early embryos were destroyed after 17 days. The highest proportion previously achieved is around 0.1 percent.

Feng's team injected around 10 human stem cells into 3.5-day-old mouse blastocysts, bundles of many cells. The human cells contributed to all kinds of tissues in the developing mouse embryo, including forming eye, liver and red blood cells.

Previous studies have shown that the reason why attempts to create mouse-human chimeras haven't been very successful is that human stem cells are in a more developmentally advanced "primed" state, whereas the mouse stem cells are in a "naïve" state. If mouse stem cells in a primed state are added to a mouse blastocyst, many of the embryos end up dying, just as when human stem cells are added.

Feng thinks that growing human organs in animals could be an essential step towards finding ways to grow organs outside bodies, in some kind of incubator. Societies need to discuss the ethical issues and potential benefits and decide on what can and cannot be done in this area, he says.

Another reason for their success, says Feng, is that the ethics committee allowed the team to let the embryos grow for 17 days, a week longer than most previous studies.

Source: Adapted from The New Scientist (https://www.newscientist.com/article/2243348-algae-transplant-could-protect-coral-reefs-threatened-by-warming-seas/).

1. Which one of the following inferences can be deduced from the passage?
   A. The experiments will generate organs for those necessitating urgent transplants.
   B. Subsequent research will necessitate investigation into the brain cells.
   C. The introduction of animal or human cells can produce a similar consequence.
   D. The cells utilised were attained from those needing transplants.

2. What conclusion can be drawn from the passage?
   A. The studies will enrich transplant development research.
   B. The studies are of minimal use to furthering human transplants.
   C. The results, to date, will be sufficient to make the process feasible.
   D. The use of small animals will not provide sufficient analysis.

3. Based on the information in the passage, what can be inferred about the development of human organs?
   A. The results will provide an indisputable solution to their production.
   B. This type of research requires a team that is significant in size.
   C. This research will serve to enhance their development in animals.
   D. They will need to be suitably matched to the cells used.

4. Which of the following is not supported by the information in the passage?
   A. The team has considered several ethical ramifications.
   B. The importance of the results for future research is immeasurable.
   C. The human cells interacted with numerous tissues in the embryo.
   D. Organs have the potential to be dominated by animal characteristics.

Question 64 - EU to Halve Pesticides

The European Commission is seeking to halve the use of chemical pesticides by 2030 to halt the decline of pollinators, in a plan likely to draw criticism both from those urging a phase-out of the substances and from farmers who say crop yields will suffer.

The Commission, the EU executive, wants to commit the European Union to a halving of the use of chemical and "high-risk" pesticides by 2030, a draft document seen by Reuters and set to be published on May 20 showed.

It did not explain what it meant by high-risk or how it would enforce the reduction. The Commission declines to comment on unpublished drafts, which are working documents and are subject to change until they are adopted.

Beekeepers in western Europe have reported a fall in the number of bees and colony losses over the last 15 years. EU lawmakers say this trend endangers the 76% of food production in Europe that depends on pollination.

Already EU regulators banned outdoor use of neonicotinoid insecticides in 2018, meaning they can only be used in closed greenhouses. Some farming groups have said a wide ban on pesticides could cause crop yields to fall and urged the Commission to assess the impact of the measures before fixing binding targets.

Bayer, among the top makers of crop chemicals, said in an emailed statement it aimed to cut the environmental impact of crop protection by 30 percent by 2030 as part of its own sustainability goals. A spokeswoman for BASF, another major crop chemical maker, said the company would not comment until the document was published.

The draft also includes a goal to plant three billion trees in the EU by 2030, to help absorb carbon dioxide from the atmosphere and make cities greener.

Source: Adapted from The Irish Independent (https://www.independent.ie/business/farming/tillage/eu-to-halve-pesticides-by-2030-to-protect-bees-biodiversity-draft-39208608.html).

1. Using the information in the passage, it can be inferred that:
   A. a reduction in the use of chemical pesticides will stop the decline of pollinators.
   B. the potential for adverse consequences is immense.
   C. the legislature will be approved with negligible obstruction.
   D. the document will encompass a constructive conservational component.

2. Which one of the following inferences cannot be deduced from the passage?
   A. The outlined article is not restricted to debating insecticides.
   B. Reduction of selected pesticides has previously been initiated.
   C. The influence of previous sanctions has been established as effective.
   D. There is a visible inclination that the annihilation of insects is increasing.

3. Which of these statements can best be supported using the information contained in the passage?
   A. There has been a proactive initiative amongst the major stakeholders to tackle the issue.
   B. Effective regulations have already been initiated to challenge the impacts of pesticides.
   C. The specifics of enforcing the reduction in usage have not been distributed.
   D. The Commission has measured the bearing on crop production.

4. One conclusion that can be drawn from the passage is that:
   A. the exclusion of insecticide will intensify the bee population.
   B. decreases are putative, but attainment targets must be pragmatic.
   C. decreasing pesticide usage will deliver a negligible impact.
   D. a widespread prohibition will have a bearing on other industries.

Question 65 - Gordon Brown

As Prime Minister, Gordon Brown oversaw the devolution of powers in Northern Ireland, the withdrawal of troops from Iraq, and the world's first ever Climate Change Act.

It was at university that he began to have problems with his sight and doctors diagnosed him with a detached retina, which was caused by an injury he received in his final game for his school rugby team.

He was Chancellor of the Exchequer during the longest ever period of economic growth. He also made the Bank of England independent and announced, at the Gleneagles Summit in 2005, an agreement to support the world's poorest countries and deal with climate change. His passion for global justice was shown in his negotiation to cancel the debts of the world's poorest nations and the tripling of the development budget.

Gordon Brown became Prime Minister on 27 June 2007, after Tony Blair left office. During his time as Prime Minister, he oversaw changes such as the introduction of neighbourhood policing in every area, a legally-enforceable right to early cancer screening and treatment, and the world's first ever Climate Change Act, which was implemented in autumn 2008.

The greatest challenge he faced in office was the worldwide financial crisis and the following recession. He also pledged to improve financial supervision and regulation.

UK combat operations in Iraq, which had begun during his predecessor's time in office, came to an end under Gordon Brown. British forces withdrew from the country at the end of April 2009.

During his time in office, he worked with his Irish counterpart Brian Cowen to negotiate the devolution of policing and justice powers in Northern Ireland. An agreement was finally reached in February 2010 and the powers were passed to Northern Ireland's government in the following April.

Source: Adapted from GOV.UK (https://www.gov.uk/government/history/past-prime-ministers/gordon-brown).
The text used here is for educational purposes. The contents and the copyright belong to the aforementioned source.

1. Which one of the following inferences can be deduced from the passage?
   A. Brown was accountable for the protracting recession within the UK.
   B. Brown initiated a proactive attack on international climate change.
   C. Brown instigated an initiative for the legal challenges in the health sector.
   D. Brown became the longest serving Chancellor of the Exchequer.

2. Which of the following is not supported by the information in the passage?
   A. Brown was instrumental in bringing the war in Iraq to a conclusion.
   B. Brown was keen to support the sharing of power in Ireland.
   C. Brown was impeded by damage to his eye which deteriorated during his ministry.
   D. Brown endeavoured to implement improved financial regulations.

3. What conclusion can be drawn from the passage?
   A. Brown was practical in addressing inequality in class structure.
   B. Brown was extremely driven in addressing global debts.
   C. Brown took charge of eradicating the influences of the fiscal institutes.
   D. Brown augmented financial pressure with his overseas aid strategy.

4. The passage suggests that all of the following statements are true except:
   A. Brown prevented further financial indiscretions through regulation.
   B. Brown enhanced local policing and security throughout the country.
   C. Brown was a powerful influence in initiating the war with Iraq.
   D. Brown exhibited an exceptional moral compass in relation to poorer states.

Question 66 - The Dunkirk Evacuation

For Britons, Dunkirk is one of the proudest moments of World War II. The evacuation of 338,226 troops and other personnel from the beaches of northern France, which took place between May 26th and June 4th 1940, was an act of stubborn defiance by a plucky island nation against Hitler's *blitzkrieg*. It was a victory snatched from the jaws of defeat. While 861 pleasure craft and fishing boats were essential to the operation's success in the shallow waters around Dunkirk, they were less significant in evacuations elsewhere.

The British retreat to Dunkirk was controversial. But poor planning, intelligence, leadership, and communications had left the Allies in a desperate situation.

The spirit of Dunkirk – the pride that the British people felt after the successful rescue of the country's men – had its own casualties, too. The crucial role of the French army has subsequently been forgotten. The RAF, criticised for failing to cover the troops on the beach adequately, actually sustained huge losses of its own, as did both the British and French navies. German errors, particularly the halt order, that allowed the escape to happen are understated.

Dunkirk has become the focal point for this moment in history, but other rescue missions took place that are not as well remembered. In total, over 558,000 British, French, Polish and Czech personnel were rescued from the beaches of northern France between May and June 1940, an additional 220,000 to those who were evacuated from Dunkirk.

Source: Adapted from The Conversation (https://theconversation.com/dunkirk-was-a-victory-for-morale-but-ultimately-a-humiliating-military-defeat-81195). The text used here is for educational purposes. The contents and the copyright belong to the aforementioned source.

1. Which of the following statements is not corroborated by the information in the passage?
   A. There had been a contentious turnaround.
   B. The incident was not a vibrant validation of British defiance.
   C. The utilisation of small vessels was not instigated from experience.
   D. The directives of the German army contributed to the accomplishment.

2. Based on the information in the passage, what can be inferred about the consequence of the expedition?
   A. A significant percentage of British troops were repatriated to safety.
   B. The event was the result of a tremendous mistake of planning.
   C. The mission was successful solely due to the smaller ships.
   D. There were negligible casualties in all of the military services.

3. Which of these statements can best be supported using the information contained in the passage?
   A. The incident succeeded against a backdrop of imminent disaster.
   B. The RAF was ultimately accountable for the defeat.
   C. The salvage operation encompassed army personnel and nationals.
   D. There were enormous casualties within the German army.

4. One conclusion that can be drawn from the passage is that:
   A. the mission was, in essence, an accomplishment due to its impact on British moral.
   B. the mission was exceptionally well orchestrated.
   C. the use of the shorelines was needed due to the obliteration of the quayside.
   D. the project has overshadowed more positive exercises.

Question 67 - Eamon De Valera

Controversially in June 1919, during the Anglo-Irish war, de Valera went to the United States; he sought unsuccessfully to gain its recognition of the Irish Republic but did raise $5 million there in funds. Returning in December 1920, he at once gave new impetus and cohesion to the Sinn Féin government. He favoured a truce with Britain but unexpectedly decided not to lead the Irish delegation which negotiated the Treaty. Critics claim he did this to evade responsibility for the inevitable compromises it entailed. His defence was that, in Dublin, he could better preserve national unity and gain acceptance of any agreement reached. In any event, he rejected the Treaty and resigned as President following its ratification by the Dail. Though he sought some basis for continuing co-operation with its supporters, both his sometimes inflammatory speeches and his attempts to mobilise opposition to it made a civil war more likely.

De Valera was somewhat marginalised during the conflict but was imprisoned afterwards for a year, which enhanced his credibility with republicans. He subsequently formed a new party, Fianna Fail, and, in 1927, it entered the Free State Dail. The next five years were spent in building up its organisation, and he established a newspaper, the 'Irish Press', in 1931. Fianna Fail's election victory in 1932 marked the beginning of 16 unbroken years in power, during which de Valera was both Prime Minister and responsible for foreign affairs. His was the most formative influence on the development of the new state. His policy initiatives included high tariffs to induce economic self-sufficiency, the gradual weakening of ties with Britain, a new and deeply conservative constitution, and neutrality in World War II. His party lost power for six years between 1948-57 but was then returned with a large majority. In 1959 de Valera resigned as Taoiseach; soon afterwards he was elected President of Ireland and, again, in 1966. He retired in 1973 and died on 29th August 1975 at the age of 92.

Source: Adapted from The BBC (https://www.bbc.co.uk/history/british/easterrising/profiles/po06.shtml).
The text used here is for educational purposes. The contents and the copyright belong to the aforementioned source.

1. If the information in the passage is presumed to be true, which of the following statements must also be true?
   A. De Valera may be considered one of the major influences in Irish politics during his time as leader.
   B. De Valera's attempt to collaborate with America had little impact on the success of independence.
   C. De Valera appeared to face a moral dilemma with the terms of the Treaty.
   D. De Valera resolved to instigate civil war in the country.

2. Which one of the following inferences can be deduced from the passage?
   A. De Valera's incarceration assisted his profile.
   B. De Valera had exercised sound judgement in abstaining from discussions in London.
   C. De Valera founded a new party following his altercation with his former faction.
   D. De Valera's personal qualities were the foundations of his success.

3. Which one of the following assertions is not supported by the information contained in the passage?
   A. De Valera's decision to maintain neutrality during the conflict was the reason for the party losing power.
   B. De Valera was active in the movement for Irish independence.
   C. De Valera was disposed to provocative outpourings.
   D. De Valera played a pivotal role in founding the autonomous country and its first government.

4. The passage infers that, if we analyse de Valera's career, he:
   A. retired from politics through age not choice.
   B. was a symbol of diplomacy and negotiation.
   C. operated primarily for his own significance.
   D. was solely responsible for the economic development of the country.

Question 68 - Ancient Tap O'Noth Hillfort

A hillfort in Aberdeenshire is one of the largest ancient settlements ever discovered in Scotland, researchers have said. University of Aberdeen archaeologists say 4,000 people may have lived in more than 800 huts perched high on the Tap O' Noth near Rhynie. Many had thought it dated from the Bronze or Iron Age. The team said carbon dating suggested it was likely to be Pictish, dating back as far as the third century AD.

They believe at its height it may have rivalled the largest known post-Roman settlements in Europe. Archaeologists from the university have conducted extensive fieldwork in the surrounding area since 2011.

Prof Gordon Noble, who led the research, described the discovery that activity at the site extended into the Pictish period as the most surprising of his career. "We took samples from the site really just to begin placing the important discoveries we have made at Rhynie over the last few years in a broader geographical context. The results of the dating were simply incredible. The Tap O' Noth discovery shakes the narrative of this whole time period. If each of the huts we identified had four or five people living in them then that means there was a population of upwards of 4,000 people living on the hill. It is truly mind-blowing and demonstrates just how much we still have to learn about settlement around the time that the early kingdoms of Pictland were being consolidated."

Aberdeenshire Council leader Jim Gifford said: "This find of historic importance will be of huge significance. I am hopeful that, once restrictions start to be lifted, and of course when it is safe to do so, visitors from far and wide will flock to Aberdeenshire to explore this find." Restrictions were imposed on the UK in March 2020 as a result of the coronavirus pandemic.

Source: Adapted from The BBC (https://www.bbc.co.uk/news/uk-scotland-north-east-orkney-shetland-52660032)
The text used here is for educational purposes. The contents and the copyright belong to the aforementioned source.

1. If the information in the passage is presumed to be true, which of the following statements must also be true?
   A. The preceding explorations had not been conducted effectively.
   B. These discoveries enhance those already documented.
   C. The utilisation of carbon dating has transformed archaeological investigations.
   D. Present constraints have impeded the promotion of all excavations.

2. From the information provided in the passage, which amongst the following statements cannot be corroborated?
   A. The site has the potential to become recognised as a world heritage site.
   B. The excavation has indicated that this was a major and central point.
   C. The periods established formerly now appear to be somewhat inappropriate.
   D. This area has been the subject of analysis for a significant period of time.

3. The author most likely agrees with all of the following statements except:
   A. the precursor to this dig proved erroneous.
   B. there will be a need to regulate visitors to ensure that the site is not endangered.
   C. it will necessitate considerable investigation to collaborate findings.
   D. there has been some discord as previous data appears incorrect.

4. The site is indubitably the most densely inhabited finding worldwide.
   A. True
   B. False
   C. Can't Tell

Question 69 - How Moral Education Could Help

There is a significant link between moral emotions and offending behaviour in young people. Moral emotions are learnt, and more attention needs to be given to the teaching of morals in childhood to address this link between morality and crime.

Moral development programmes should be developed and taught to children to reduce the likelihood of them growing up to believe that criminal behaviour could be morally acceptable. Moral education should be considered to be as crucial as nutrition, health, and formal education for our future generations to thrive.

Young people tend to spend most of their time with parents or primary caregivers, teachers and their peer groups. If a child's peers or parents don't think it's wrong to commit a crime or lack empathy or guilty feelings towards the people affected by that crime, then this a likely to affect how the young person feels as well. Research shows that lack of guilt for rule-breaking behaviour can be displayed from as young as three.

It is very likely that the primary and critical time windows for morality development begin in early childhood and extend to later childhood and adolescence. It appears that major life events - such as having stable relationships with family members or a partner, or a job, or having a child - can reinforce one's moral code and reduce the likelihood of offending behaviour.

Students absorb positive moral behaviours when surrounded with just and fair role models, rules, and interactions. Schools that foster a sense of community and hold discussions about morality can provide this environment. But if environments that foster moral development are not prolonged and sustained across several years, the effect on moral behaviour may be short lived.

Source: Adapted from The Conversation (https://theconversation.com/why-young-people-commit-crime-and-how-moral-education-could-help-new-research-131855).

1. Which of the following statements is best supported by the information contained within the passage?
   A. The stimulus of the household at a future period cannot overturn mindsets.
   B. The greatest period for felonious actions is in adolescence.
   C. Antisocial behaviours will always diminish significantly in the latter years of an individual's life.
   D. The link between childhood influences and subsequent behaviour is not deliberated sufficiently.

2. According to the writer, which amongst the following assertions cannot be considered accurate?
   A. The absence of strong guidance during childhood is not rescindable.
   B. A strong moral compass instilled from birth is impractical.
   C. The effects of influences may dissipate when not consistent.
   D. The effect of peer pressure has been shown to be significant.

3. Which of the following assertions would strengthen the case for establishing compulsory teaching of morals?
   A. The promotion of the association between morality and misconduct.
   B. The accentuation of the limitations of parental abilities.
   C. The indication that educational establishments are the solitary source of influence.
   D. The indication that life supporting subjects are more beneficial than academic focuses.

4. It can be concluded from the passage that the writer:
   A. considers that a moral compass determines cognitive behaviours.
   B. deems that class structure has an influence on moral attitudes.
   C. is convinced that instilling an understanding of behaviours at an impressionable age is vital to combatting issues.
   D. intimates that behaviours are proven to be repetitive through subsequent generations.

Question 70 - Coral Reefs

It may be possible to protect coral reefs from the warming oceans by colonising them with heat-resistant algae.

Coral reefs around the world are under threat from climate change, which is driving up ocean temperatures. Australia's Great Barrier Reef, for example, has just suffered its third mass bleaching event in five years after experiencing the hottest February sea temperatures on record.

When seas become too warm, corals lose the colourful *Symbiodiniaceae* microalgae that live in their tissues and make food for them. This causes the corals to lose their colour, giving them a bleached appearance, and to gradually starve to death.

Researchers heated *Symbiodiniaceae* algae to 31°C in a laboratory for four years to train it to tolerate more heat than it is used to. The algae eventually evolved genetic changes that hinted at greater heat resistance.

The researchers then took coral larvae from the Great Barrier Reef, mixed it with either regular algae or the heat-resistant algae and then heated it to 31°C for one week, a temperature known to cause bleaching. The coral with the regular algae quickly bleached, but the coral with the heat-resistant algae remained healthy.

The results are promising, but more research is needed to test whether the heat-resistant algae can also be used to prevent bleaching in adult coral, not just larvae, and to see whether it works for different coral species, says Buerger.

Source: Adapted from The New Scientist (https://www.newscientist.com/article/2243348-algae-transplant-could-protect-coral-reefs-threatened-by-warming-seas/).

1. What conclusion can be drawn from the passage?
   A. The investigations have conclusively proved that corals endure in heated seawater.
   B. Supplementary studies will be vital to authenticate the impact on alternative species.
   C. Algae are the solitary resource of defence for the coral reefs.
   D. At this time, research is not sufficient to corroborate the discoveries.

2. It can be deduced from the passage that:
   A. the absence of colour signifies the imminent demise of the coral.
   B. global warming will ultimately result in the extinction of corals.
   C. there appears to be a systematic cycle of the occurrence of bleaching.
   D. the emergence of shorter, cooler seasons has impacted on the coral reefs.

3. Based on the information in the passage, what can be inferred about the effects of warmer waters?
   A. The effects of the warmer waters may potentially be overturned.
   B. The effects may be counteracted through the cultivation of algae that can withstand extreme warmth.
   C. The true impact of warmer waters has emerged in the preceding five years.
   D. It will be comparatively straight forward to increase tolerance points.

4. Which of the following assertions is not supported by the information in the passage?
   A. If emissions are not reduced, artificial fortification should be considered.
   B. The solution will be equally appropriate for developed and undeveloped coral.
   C. The research has substantiated indications that the corals may be conserved.
   D. Further research will be vital for sufficient progress to be made.

Question 71 - George Best

George Best was an Irish-born football player who was one of the premier forwards in the game's history and a fashionable playboy off the field. The stylish Best became one of the iconic figures of "Swinging London" during the 1960s.

While still a schoolboy, Best was recommended to Manchester United by a local Belfast football scout, who called the youngster a "genius." Best joined the club at age 15, and he made his first-division debut two years later, in 1963. He was an immediate sensation, scoring acrobatic goals and helping United to a league title in his second season. He led the club to another league championship during the 1966–67 season. In 1968 he was named European Footballer of the Year and helped United become the first English club to win the European Cup. Best scored a total of 178 goals in his 466 career games with United.

Best was the first of many footballers to become a regular subject of the British tabloids, but it also helped foster a drinking problem that would prove to be his undoing. After a bitter departure from United in 1974, he played for numerous lesser teams in Britain, Spain, Australia, and the United States until 1983. His drinking continued to affect his play, however, and he became as well known for his squandered talent as for his undeniable brilliance. Best underwent a liver transplant in 2002 but ultimately was unable to overcome his alcoholism, and he died from a series of transplant-related infections that his compromised immune system could not combat.

Source: Adapted from Britannica (https://www.britannica.com/biography/George-Best).
The text used here is for educational purposes. The contents and the copyright belong to the aforementioned source.

1. If the information in the passage is presumed to be true, which of the following statements must also be true?
    A. Best was the most renowned signing that Manchester United has taken.
    B. Best's reputation transcended the football domain.
    C. Best did not fall prey to the burden of the media interest.
    D. Best was construed as priority for transplant.

2. Which one of the following inferences can be deduced from the passage?
    A. Best exposed an innate aptitude that was enhanced through tuition.
    B. The impact of prominence led Best to reliance on outside stimuli.
    C. Best's departure from football was in limited glaring contrast to his initial days.
    D. Best contradicted every skill he emanated through his dependences.

3. Which one of the following inferences cannot be corroborated by the information contained in the passage?
    A. Best was the stimulus for press attention amongst football players.
    B. Best failed to invigorate his career within substitute clubs.
    C. Best was the initial footballer to attract the attention of the newspapers.
    D. Best wasted his abilities due to his lack of self-discipline.

4. The passage infers that:
    A. Best was a victim of his own success.
    B. Best was refused adequate support to address his demons.
    C. Best was too immature to handle the experiences he encountered.
    D. Best continually entertained unwelcome attention from the tabloids.

Question 72 - Water Contamination within Ireland

The European Commission has put Ireland on a four-month deadline to solve a chemical contamination problem affecting the drinking water supply of 180,000 people.

It said Ireland had been in breach of the directive since 2003 and progress to address the problem was not sufficient. If the situation was not remedied within four months, the case could be referred to the European Court of Justice. "High THM levels have been linked to liver, kidneys and central nervous system diseases, bladder and colon cancer risks, as well as to effects on foetal growth, foetal viability and risks of foetal malformations," the Commission's notice stated. "Although some progress has been made, Ireland has not been complying with the rules since December 2003."

THMs form when organic matter in raw water, such as rotting vegetation or sediment from peat, reacts with chlorine, which is widely used to disinfect drinking water supplies. They are mainly ingested by drinking but can also be inhaled in the bath or shower, or from steam when washing clothes and dishes. Friends of the Irish Environment (FIE) lodged a complaint about THMs with the Commission nine years ago. The group has called for customers to be informed of any exceedances in their water supply so that they can act to protect themselves. "Consumers with supplies over the World Health Organisation levels can use simple charcoal filters to ensure that THMs are removed. They will not do this, however, unless they are made aware of the danger," it said.

"The action plans outline any measures or treatment process upgrades that Irish Water are putting in place to achieve compliance with the THMs standard, without compromising disinfection. Irish Water have indicated that all THM action plans will be completed in all supplies by 2021."

Source: Adapted from The Irish Independent (https://www.independent.ie/business/farming/forestry-enviro/environment/european-commission-give-ireland-four-months-to-solve-water-contamination-issue-affecting-180000-people-39208578.html).
The text used here is for educational purposes. The contents and the copyright belong to the aforementioned source.

1. Based on the information in the passage, it can be inferred that:
   A. the measures previously undertaken have been satisfactory.
   B. the consequences of the contamination have been unheeded.
   C. there has been a nonchalant attitude to the issues.
   D. there has been a palpable lack of perception of the impact.

2. Which of these statements can best be supported using information contained in the passage?
   A. Whilst advances have been made, the country has long been non-compliant.
   B. The foremost source of the contamination is the removal of farming waste.
   C. Subsequent research provides undeniable evidence of the impact on the unborn.
   D. The issue has been exacerbated by homeowners not adhering to directives.

3. According to the writer, which amongst the following assertions cannot be considered accurate?
   A. The issues are being supervised by suitable consultants.
   B. Compliant decontamination levels will not be compromised.
   C. Individual households might have been proactive if they had been directed accordingly.
   D. The foremost contamination is occurring in water consumption.

4. Which factor does the writer emphasise as being most likely to lead to measures being introduced?
   A. An enhanced awareness and ensuing demand for action.
   B. The effect on wellbeing if preparations are not initiated.
   C. The introduction of legislation which must be adhered to.
   D. The adverse bearing on water companies' revenues.

Question 73 - Driverless Cars

By leveraging smarter technologies we have seen extraordinary advances both in technological development and the openness of drivers to using automated vehicles. The AA believes driverless vehicles may be a common sight on UK roads in a matter of years, not decades. Driverless cars will share the road with the cars we already use for many years to come.

We're getting used to seeing the signs for "smart motorways" – major highways augmented with roadside sensors, 5G wireless communication, fibre-optic cables and CCTV systems.

It's on these roads that driverless vehicles are most likely to appear first, where motion is relatively predictable – high-speed, perhaps, but along straight lines and without traffic lights – and all those other obstacles we encounter in towns and villages.

A mini roundabout is not a big deal, but it has to be fully comprehended by the driverless tech, as do school runs and zebra crossings, bumps in the road and narrow country lanes.

For the immediate future, smart motorways will speak to drivers, advising on speed limits, lane changes, hard-shoulder availability, potential jams and roadworks. But ultimately this data will be transferred directly to vehicles, which will then respond appropriately.

They will be instructed to slow down, change lanes, brake. The driver may get a text to help plan a next move. In the future, driverless vehicles will also be able to communicate with one another, establishing safe distances and making optimum use of the road.

Source: Adapted from The Telegraph (https://www.telegraph.co.uk/cars/driving-smart/driverless-cars/?utm_campaign=tmgspk_plrbin_2847_AtpKbd7xhV0g&plr=1&utm_content=2847&utm_source=tmgspk&WT.mc_id=tmgspk_plrbin_2847_AtpKbd7xhV0g&utm_medium=plrbin&mvt=i&mvn=a41559bb0cca47feade807d0ba0878bd&mvp=NA-TELEDESK-11238861&mvl=Key-bin-advert_tmg_bin_1%20%5BWeb%20-%20Index%20-%20Sparkbrain1%5D).

1. Which of these statements can best be supported by the information contained in the passage?
   A. The programmes will safeguard the vehicle in unknown situations.
   B. Despite the steps that have already been taken in this field, further work is required.
   C. The trials have scrutinised both data and basic concepts.
   D. A blended approach that uses all technologies has been essential for the implementation of the technology.

2. Based on the information in the passage, what can be inferred about the potential dangers?
   A. There is the potential for major impediments if the technology fails.
   B. Driverless vehicles should be able to negotiate narrow lanes and roundabouts.
   C. The automobile will be meticulously regulated to safeguard safety.
   D. The vehicle will be equipped with an opportunity for passenger intervention.

3. Which one of the following inferences cannot be deduced from the passage?
   A. It is essential for the car to perform complex manoeuvres.
   B. The driverless car will interrelate effectively with human behaviours.
   C. The smart motorway network will be the principal and most suitable location for such vehicles.
   D. The initiation of this category of vehicle is now preordained.

4. One conclusion that can be drawn from the passage is that:
   A. there are still numerous deliberations required before implementation.
   B. the perception of the driver is that this will be immensely advantageous.
   C. the person within the vehicle will continue to maintain control.
   D. there will be a colossal environmental impact of a constructive quality.

Question 74 - Baroness Thatcher

Margaret Thatcher's father, a shopkeeper and Mayor of Grantham, was a major influence in her childhood. She was educated at the local grammar school and studied Chemistry at Oxford University, where she became president of the university Conservative association.

Thatcher read for the Bar before being elected as the Conservative MP for Finchley in 1959. She held junior posts before becoming Shadow Spokesperson for Education, and she entered the Cabinet as Education Secretary in 1970.

Her first two years in office were not easy – unemployment was very high, but the economy gradually showed improvement. She brought more of her supporters into the Cabinet and added to her reputation by leading the country to war against Argentina in the Falkland Islands.

The Conservatives went on to win the 1983 election by an overwhelming majority, helped by a divided opposition. Her government followed a radical programme of privatisation and deregulation, reform of the trade unions, tax cuts, and the introduction of market mechanisms into health and education. The aim was to reduce the role of government and increase individual self-reliance.

She also became a familiar figure internationally, creating a famous friendship with US President Reagan and gaining the praise of Soviet leader Gorbachev.

One great difficulty during her time in office was the issue of Europe. Her long-serving Foreign Secretary, Sir Geoffrey Howe, resigned in November 1990 in protest at her attitude to Europe. His resignation speech brought about events which were to lead to her exit from 10 Downing Street later that month.

Michael Heseltine challenged her for the leadership and, while he failed to win, he gained 152 votes, enough to make it evident that a crucial minority favoured a change. Thatcher was eventually persuaded not to go forward to the second ballot, which was won by her Chancellor of the Exchequer, John Major.

Source: Adapted from GOV.UK (https://www.gov.uk/government/history/past-prime-ministers/margaret-thatcher).
The text used here is for educational purposes. The contents and the copyright belong to the aforementioned source.

1. What conclusion can be drawn from the passage?
   A. Thatcher was one of the most unpopular of all prime ministers.
   B. Thatcher followed a strategy of eliminating much of the provisions of the welfare state.
   C. Thatcher faced issues with almost all government policies.
   D. Thatcher had immense experience prior to becoming leader.

2. It can be deduced from the passage that:
   A. Thatcher rapidly lessened the proportion of unemployment.
   B. Thatcher achieved the backing of those primarily opposing her.
   C. Thatcher had considered entering the legal profession.
   D. Thatcher found immense support from all areas after having declared a war.

3. Which of the following statements can be verified by the information in the passage?
   A. A causative reason for Thatcher's success in the election was the lack of a credible opponent.
   B. Thatcher delivered her policies through promoting her supporters to leading positions.
   C. Thatcher's altercation with a minister ultimately dictated her demise.
   D. Thatcher's decision to resign was imposed on her.

4. Geoffrey Howe was the catalyst for the promotion of another party member.
   A. True
   B. False
   C. Can't Tell

Question 75 - Biometrics and Global 'Regimes of Truth'

If you look at countries where governments have legislated and promoted new technologies both in public and private spheres of life, whether it's in renewable energy, artificial intelligence, 5G telecoms or fintech, those sectors have flourished. Authentication technology is no different.

"With biometrics, there's a lot of focus on the data privacy legal issues, but intellectual property law is also key, and we could find the two are related," says Quinn. "If developers in countries with weak regulatory oversight can innovate biometric authentication technology faster than those in countries with stricter rules, such as Europe with its General Data Protection Regulation, they could get patent protection and use it to prevent or control use of that cutting-edge technology around the world."

Some argue that the politics of a given country doesn't necessarily change whether biometrics are developed, but it does affect how it's developed and by whom. This leads to a bigger question of who you trust within society – the government, businesses, both, or neither – to spearhead its advancement.

"An authoritarian state might be more closely involved in its development. But a more democratic state is likely to promote private companies to develop technologies, often with less oversight. The increasing polarisation of politics in many countries adds tension to this debate and the perception of a widening gap between security and rights," says Dr Garfield Benjamin, a researcher at Solent University.

This is where strong regulation is playing a part. Adoption rates for authentication technology can be greater where there's more recourse with the authorities if systems go wrong. Protecting people's rights doesn't have to hamper technology development. They can go hand in hand.

Source: Adapted from The Times (https://www.thetimes.co.uk/static/future-authentication-biometrics-covid-facial-recognition-surveillance-raconteur/?utm_source=nativo).
The text used here is for educational purposes. The contents and the copyright belong to the aforementioned source.

1. Which of the following is not supported by the information in the passage?
   A. Internal frictions within administrations may ultimately hamper success.
   B. The determining factor is often the safety of the citizen.
   C. Governments will be the determining factor on who advances biometrics.
   D. The patronage of the authorities will be critical to ensure attainment of new technologies.

2. Which of these statements can best be corroborated using the information contained in the passage?
   A. Dictatorial countries will have decisive regulation over the advances.
   B. The appointment of a patent will result in enormous costs.
   C. The safeguarding of human rights will have an adverse effect.
   D. Data protection legislation will play a pivotal role.

3. It can be concluded from the passage that the author:
   A. judges that success will be seen earlier where there are limited regulatory systems.
   B. believes that regulation and advisory standards do not have to negate advances.
   C. deems it vital that all necessary data privacy measures are in place.
   D. estimates that it is important to address the standards of the outcomes.

4. There has been a global impetus for the expansion of these technologies.
   A. True
   B. False
   C. Can't Tell

Decision Making

FORMAT

In the exam, you have:
- 29 questions
- six types of questions
- 31 minutes
- +1 minute to read the instructions

In this section, there are:
- Type 1 (Logical Puzzles) – 13 exercises
- Type 2 (Syllogisms) – 9 exercises
- Type 3 (Data Interpretation) – 16 exercises
- Type 4 (Assumption Recognition) – 7 exercises
- Type 5 (Diagrams) – 16 exercises
- Type 6 (Probabilities) – 5 exercises

Objectives:
- To be able to make decisions despite uncertainty.
- To cultivate logical reasoning and confidence in judgement.
- To apply logic to reach a decision or conclusion.
- To be able to evaluate arguments and analyse statistical information.

TYPES OF QUESTIONS

Type 1 | Logical Puzzles
- A set of statements is given, from which you need to deduce information presented to arrive at a conclusion.
- Often requires the drawing of a diagram or table to make sense of the information given.

Type 2 | Syllogisms
- Arguments that take several parts, typically with two statements that are assumed to be true (or premises) that lead to a conclusion.
- Conditional syllogism: If X is true, then Y is true.
- Categorical syllogism: If X is in Z, then Y is in Z.
- Disjunctive syllogism: If X is true, then Y is false.
- Some premises may have multiple correct options.

TYPES OF QUESTIONS (Continued)

Type 3 | Data Interpretation

- Information presented in various formats (charts, graphs, tables, written passages, etc.).
- Some questions are similar to quantitative reasoning questions.

Type 4 | Assumption Recognition

- You need to choose the strongest argument that best represents the issue given.
- The issue usually represents a suggestion to implement a particular solution or debate on recent hot topics.

Type 5 | Diagrams

- Diagrams usually used in UCAT are Venn or Euler diagrams, which require you to deduce information.
- Alternatively, a list of facts is given, and you need to choose the correct Venn or Euler diagram that represents the information.

Type 6 | Probabilities

- The likelihood that an event will occur in a random experiment.
- Using simple statistics to solve questions.
- Similar to quantitative reasoning questions.

TIPS AND TRICKS TO SCORE

Revision Tips

- Practice mental math calculations. This will save a lot of time.
- Familiarise yourself with Venn diagrams, Euler diagrams, and probability.
- Get used to logical puzzles and learn decision making strategies to improve your accuracy and speed.
- We recommend starting untimed practice 12 weeks before your test date to familiarise yourself with the way questions are asked. Start doing timed practice in the next four weeks. It is all about speed and accuracy.
- Do not be afraid to draw diagrams or tables during revision or in the exam. You will be given either a whiteboard or a laminated A4 piece of paper.

TIPS AND TRICKS TO SCORE (Continued)

Answering Techniques

- It helps to shade associated shapes in Venn diagrams to reveal the answer.
- Some questions may use strange non-logical/non-scientific relationships for logical reasoning questions (e.g., all small frogs are red). It is thus crucial that you read the information that is given and answer accordingly.
- Words "several", "many", "some" and "not all" are used to try and catch you out. Pay attention to them in syllogisms.
- For assumption recognition questions, choose the argument that best addresses the point made and that is most relevant to the issue.

Question 1

Sloan, Finn, Reign and Chord each enjoy a different genre of music: rock, pop, jazz, and the blues.

- Sloan and Finn enjoy accompanying their friend to pop concerts.
- The fan of rock music and Reign have dinner together where their friend hosts jazz nights.
- Reign never attends any of the pop concerts as he lives out of town.
- Finn does not like rock music, but he will attend when his friend drives.

Who enjoys jazz?

A. Chord
B. Reign
C. Finn
D. Sloan

Question 2

A new doughnut shop has decided to hand out free doughnuts to 1000 shoppers. The shop offers half a dozen free doughnuts to anyone equal to or taller than 150cm and a dozen doughnuts to anyone shorter than 150cm.

If all those equal to or taller than 150cm and half of those shorter than 150cm accept the free samples, how many will the shop have given in total?

A. 1,000
B. 1,500
C. 3,000
D. 6,000

Question 3

In one particular year group, there are only five out of 30 international students who originate from Malaysia. All are within case group C1, which has a total of 12 students, and all identify as having only one nationality.

Answer YES if the following conclusions are correct and NO if they are not.

Q3.1	Xin is Malaysian and therefore she is in C1.	YES	NO
Q3.2	Sheryl is in C1 and is therefore Malaysian.	YES	NO
Q3.3	Yi Jie is part of the year group in question and is Singaporean, so he cannot be in C1.	YES	NO
Q3.4	Wei Teen is in C2, so she must be from Hong Kong.	YES	NO
Q3.5	Eshen is part of the year group in question. She is Malaysian and is therefore in C1.	YES	NO

Question 4

Should children bring money to school to buy lunch at recess to encourage a sense of responsibility and to learn how to count change?

Select the strongest argument from the statements below.

A. YES. Teachers find children to be better at addition and subtraction during Mathematics classes when they bring money to school.
B. YES. Children carry fewer bags to school when they do not bring lunch.
C. NO. Parents think that children are not disciplined enough to look after money.
D. NO. School hawkers would rather not accept coins and/or cash.

Question 5

Yun and Tim are organising the seating arrangements for their wedding dinner. Each table is labelled with a letter, with each letter representing the following guests: Tim's family, Yun's family, mutual friends, work colleagues, and friends from school.

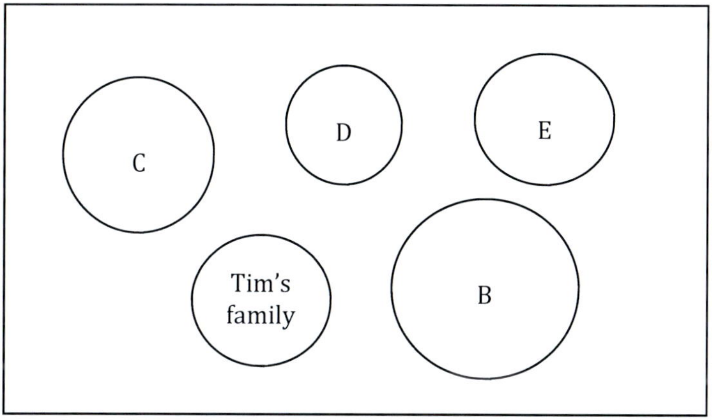

Yun's family and Tim's family are placed as far away from each other as possible to avoid any possible conflicts.

Table B was not allocated to their friends from school.

The seating area for mutual friends is equidistant from the seating area of their work colleagues as it is from the seating area of their friends from school.

Which group of people has been placed at table B?

A. Yun's family
B. Work colleagues
C. Tim's family
D. Friends from school

Question 6

Antoni placed a large order of pizzas for an upcoming event. He ordered 20 large pizzas with the following toppings: pepperoni, olives and mushrooms. Of the pizzas ordered, 17 were topped with pepperoni, five were topped with all three toppings, and eight were topped with two toppings.

Which diagram best represents the information provided above?

A. B. C. D.

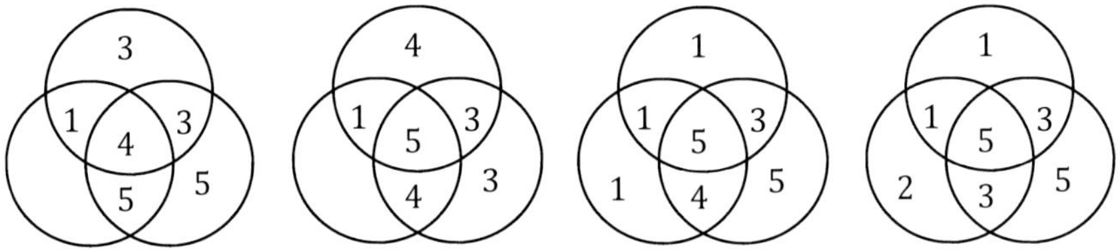

Question 7

There are 60 mice in an underground station in London. They are all scurrying for food waste: cherry tomatoes, bread and crisps. They all wish to snatch at least one of these items.

- Five mice snatch the bread only.
- 28 mice snatch the crisps only.
- 15 mice snatch the crisps and the cherry tomatoes.
- Six mice snatch the crisps and the bread.
- Three mice snatch the cherry tomatoes and the bread.

How many mice snatched the cherry tomatoes?

A. 7
B. 21
C. 3
D. 18

Question 8

Girls Anlene, Hayley, Ella, and Venice and boys Matthias, Maddox, and Marvel are siblings. They were born in seven successive years, albeit in a different order.

- Anlene and Maddox were born five years apart.
- Matthias is two years older than Marvel.
- Ella is one year older than Marvel.
- Venice is the youngest in the family.
- Each brother has a sister who is one year older than them.

Which of the following statements is true?

A. Hayley is the fifth child of the family.
B. Anlene is younger than Matthias.
C. Ella is older than Anlene.
D. Maddox is older than Marvel.

Question 9

Snow has been invited to Echo's Christmas party. Snow has prepared six slices of cheesecake, three slices of durian cake, and seven slices of carrot cake. On the way to the party, Snow drops three slices and throws them away.

Answer YES if the following conclusions are correct and NO if they are not.

Q9.1	There are more slices of cheesecake than there are slices of durian cake.	YES	NO
Q9.2	There could be the same number of cheesecake slices and carrot cake slices remaining.	YES	NO
Q9.3	There are equal slices of each type of cake.	YES	NO
Q9.4	There are fewer durian cake slices than there are carrot cake slices.	YES	NO
Q9.5	There is at least one slice of durian cake remaining.	YES	NO

Question 10

Should the NHS charge patients a fee for medications to decrease excessive prescriptions?

Select the strongest argument from the statements below.

A. YES. The NHS can use the extra income to fund budget cuts.
B. YES. It will encourage doctors to put patients on fewer medications and will encourage healthier living.
C. NO. Non-working and needy elderly patients will be most affected.
D. NO. Requiring patients to pay for their medications may trigger strikes against the NHS.

Question 11

Which diagram correctly represents the relationship between milk, cheese, ice cream, squid, calamari and octopus?

A.

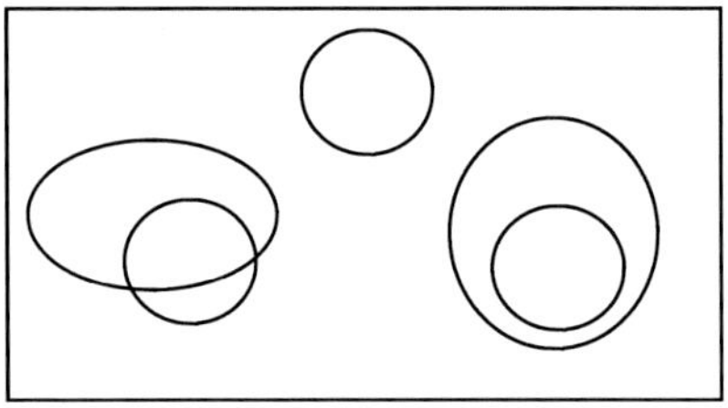

C.

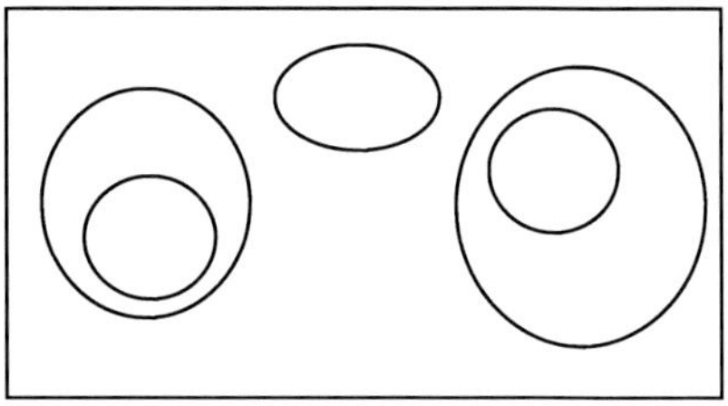

B.

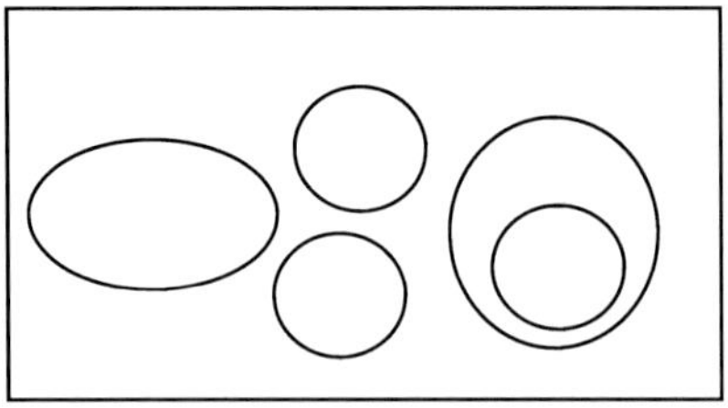

D.

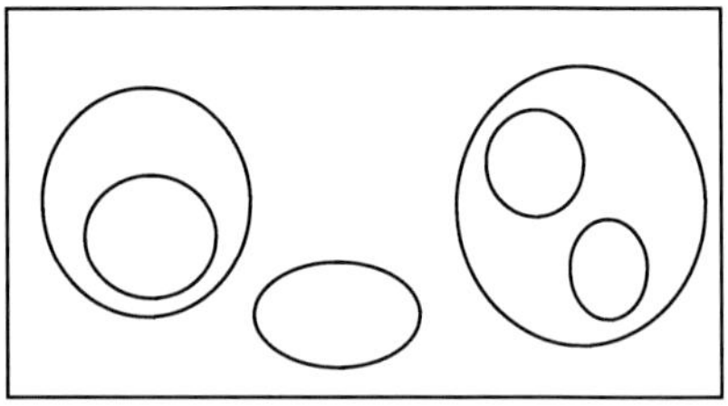

Question 12

A group of friends - Scott, Henry, Lupita, Amarit and Huang - visit their local fish and chips shop. They all buy a regular fish and chips, with a side of either gravy, curry, cheese, peas or baked beans.

- Huang does not like eating any food that is green in colour.
- Scott loves cheese.
- All of them order a different side to each other.
- Henry and Lupita prefer to have a sauce as a side to take away the dryness of the deep-fried fish and chips.

Who chose peas?

A. Lupita
B. Huang
C. Amarit
D. Henry

Question 13

Lilah plans to bake 100 gingerbread cookies for an upcoming Christmas dinner. Of the 100 gingerbread cookies baked, 10 contain raisins, 29 contain icing, and 52 contain chocolate chips. Of those containing chocolate chips, 17 also have icing, while four of those containing raisins also have icing.

Which of the following diagrams best represents the above data?

A.
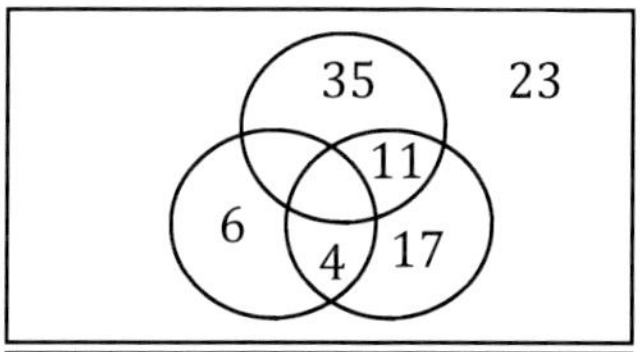

C.
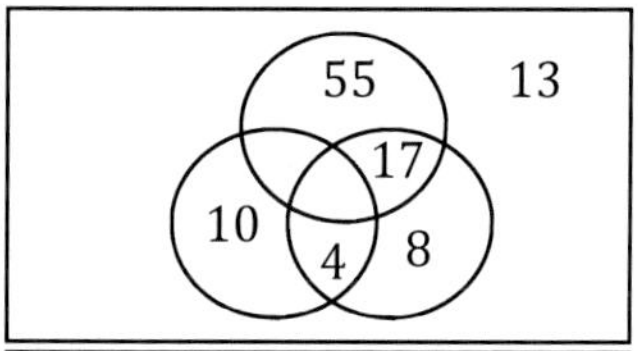

B.
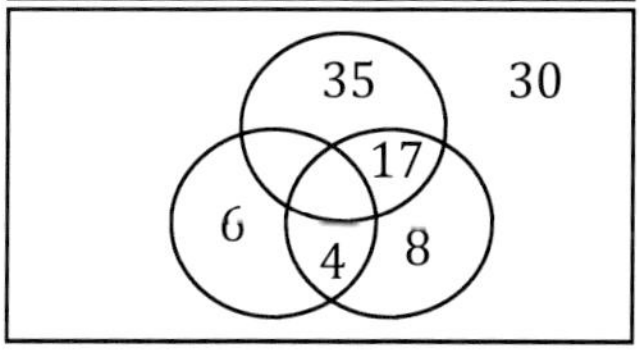

D.
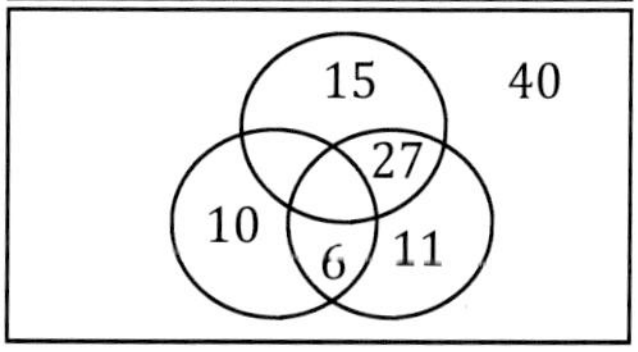

Question 14

Three teachers, Mrs Ball, Miss Holiday and Mr Phillips, teach at St George's. They each teach two of the following subjects: English, Mathematics and Drama. Each subject is taught by two teachers.

Mr Phillips and Miss Holiday have a passion for the arts.
Mrs Ball and Miss Holiday teach English.

Which of the following statements is true?

A. Mrs Ball teaches Mathematics and Drama.
B. Mr Phillips teaches Mathematics too.
C. Miss Holiday does not teach English.
D. Mathematics is taught by two female teachers.

Question 15

Vanessa is expecting a baby in one month. She would like to start setting up a nursery. She attends a sale at her nearest shopping mall selling items relating to motherhood.

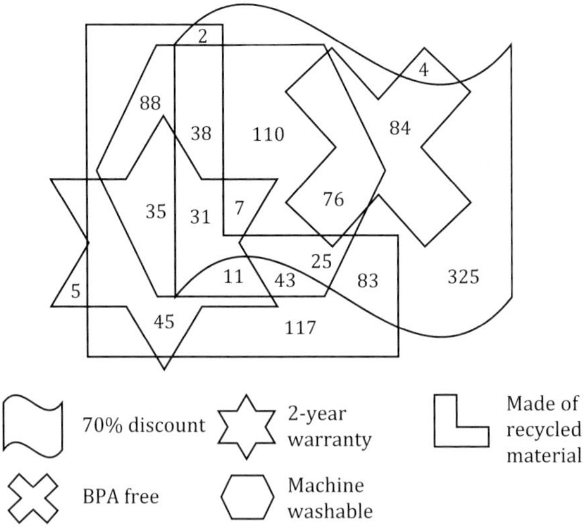

From how many items can Vanessa choose if she only wants to shop in the 70% discounted aisle with a 2-year warranty?

A. 44
B. 2
C. 38
D. 43

Question 16

An on-call shift consists of three junior doctors, two registrars, and one consultant.

There are three crash call bleeps between the members of the team.

Only one registrar carries a crash call bleep.
Consultants do not carry a crash call bleep.
Doctors who call in sick do not carry a crash call bleep.

Answer YES if the following conclusions are correct and NO if they are not.

Q16.1	One of the junior doctors does not carry a crash call bleep.	YES	NO
Q16.2	The consultant called in sick.	YES	NO
Q16.3	The other registrar has called in sick.	YES	NO
Q16.4	No doctors have called in sick.	YES	NO
Q16.5	Doctors do not carry the crash call bleep if they are not working on an on-call shift.	YES	NO

Question 17

Brandon's family has a family history of cystic fibrosis, an autosomal recessive disorder. Both parents must be carriers of the gene for a child to have cystic fibrosis.

- Brandon's uncle has cystic fibrosis.
- His father does not have cystic fibrosis.
- No one in Brandon's maternal side of the family has cystic fibrosis, and his mother has been identified as a non-carrier of the gene.

What are the chances that Brandon has cystic fibrosis?

A. 0%
B. 25%
C. 50%
D. 100%

Question 18

A newly-opened bubble milk tea shop is giving away one free drink in the months of February, May, June and August, coinciding with the public holidays. The lucky winner will be able to choose from different bubble milk tea flavours (Assam, oolong, winter melon and taro). The winners were Ashley, Pathma, Arun, and Baskie.

- None of the flavours were chosen twice.
- Arun won the lucky draw three months after Pathma (who chose winter melon).
- Ashley was the last winner, and she chose taro.
- Baskie loves oolong milk tea with tapioca pearls.

Who won the lucky draw in May?

A. Pathma
B. Arun
C. Ashley
D. Baskie

Question 19

Should the government impose a healthcare surcharge on migrants working and studying in the UK in anticipation of them using the NHS?

Select the strongest argument from the statements below.

A. YES. This will reduce the number of migrants seeking opportunities in the UK. This will ensure that there are more jobs and university spaces for UK nationals.
B. YES. Not all migrants pay tax, especially students.
C. NO. This will mean that migrants will be unable to use the NHS. They might then present with complications and in emergency situations at a later date.
D. NO. This will affect lower-income families and their future in the UK.

Question 20

The following diagram represents the number of pieces of jewelry owned by 100 households in Pembrokeshire. Each home has at least one piece of jewelry.

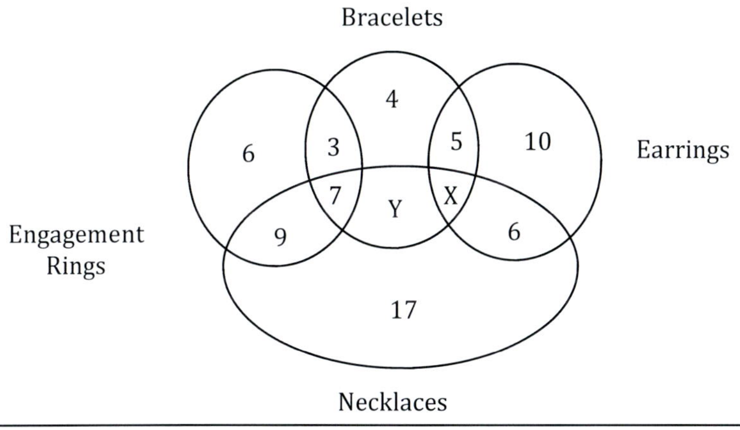

Which of the following statements is true?

A. There are more households with necklaces than earrings.
B. The number of households with all four types of jewelry cannot be determined.
C. There are more households with bracelets than necklaces.
D. There are exactly 35 households with only one type of jewelry.

Question 21

- Green frogs like the rain.
- Frogs with red eyes are rare.
- Frogs who do not have red eyes are green.
- Small frogs are not rare.
- In one particular pond, none of the frogs like rain.
- Harold is a frog from this particular pond.

Answer YES if the following conclusions are correct and NO if they are not.

Q21.1	Harold is a green frog.	YES	NO
Q21.2	Frogs with red eyes are not small frogs.	YES	NO
Q21.3	Harold is not a small frog.	YES	NO
Q21.4	Frogs that like the rain are not from the pond.	YES	NO
Q21.5	Common frogs are not green.	YES	NO

Question 22

Chiharu, Matsuri, Sasuke, Enoki, and Shizumi are travelling together. They each have one suitcase. The suitcases are either black, white, or grey.

- Three suitcases are medium-sized, and the rest are cabin-sized.
- All cabin-sized suitcases are grey.
- All medium-sized suitcases are either black or white.
- Chiharu and Shizumi do not have medium-sized suitcases.
- Only Sasuke has a white suitcase.

Which of the following is true?

A. There are three black suitcases.
B. Enoki has a cabin-sized black suitcase.
C. There are two white suitcases.
D. Matsuri has a medium-sized black suitcase.

Question 23

Should the government introduce a national exam for all students leaving primary school before entering secondary school?

Select the strongest argument from the statements below.

A. YES. It is a good way to rank students across the nation.
B. YES. Exams are a good indicator of knowledge and understanding.
C. NO. This will apply enormous pressure on young students and can be very stressful.
D. NO. Secondary schools will be ranked based on performance so that top-ranked students can get into the best schools.

Question 24

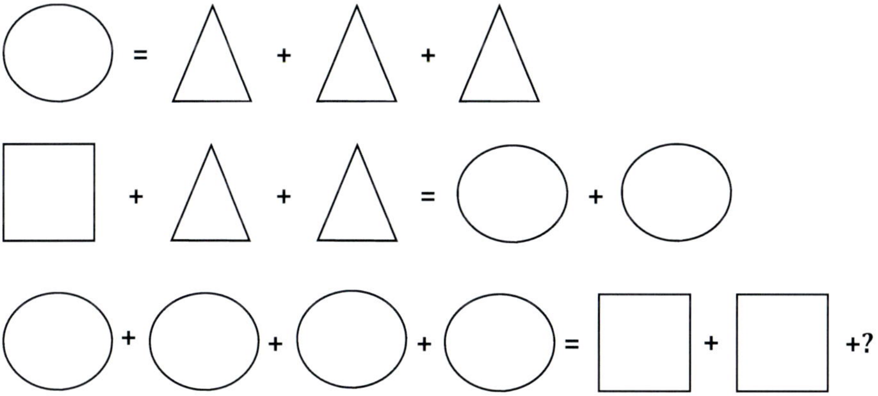

Which of the following shapes completes the equation?

A. Triangle
B. Circle
C. Square
D. Pentagon

Question 25

The NHS recommendations on alcohol intake are as follows:

- Men and women are advised not to drink more than 14 units a week on a regular basis.
- An individual should spread his/her drinking over three or more days if he/she regularly drinks as much as 14 units a week.
- If an individual wants to cut down, he/she should try to have several drink-free days each week.
- Pregnant women are not advised to drink alcohol.

Small glass of wine (125ml, ABV 12%)	1.5 units	Pint of lager/beer/ cider (473ml, ABV 5.2%)	3 units
Can of lager/beer/cider (440ml, ABV 5.5%)	2 units	Alcopop (275ml, ABV 5.5%)	1.5 units
Single small shot of vodka (25ml, ABV 40%)	1 unit	Large glass of wine (250ml, ABV 12%)	3 units

- Judith has 10 shots of vodka on a night out with her friends once a week.
- Cindy is in her second trimester of pregnancy; she drinks a small glass of wine each night with her dinner.
- Garrett regularly drinks up to 14 pints of lager each week.
- Sally uses a large glass of white wine when she cooks her famous beef stew once a week.

Which of the following statements is true?

A. Sally has the greatest alcohol intake among the group.
B. Garrett is well within his recommendations for alcohol intake.
C. Cindy has a higher alcohol intake than Judith.
D. Judith consumes a total of 15 units of alcohol in one week.

Question 26

Morgan would like to design a layout for a new building that he is constructing, The Green, which encompasses 55 levels of deluxe apartments. Each apartment will consist of a bathroom, a bedroom, a balcony, a walk-in wardrobe, a kitchen, and a living area.

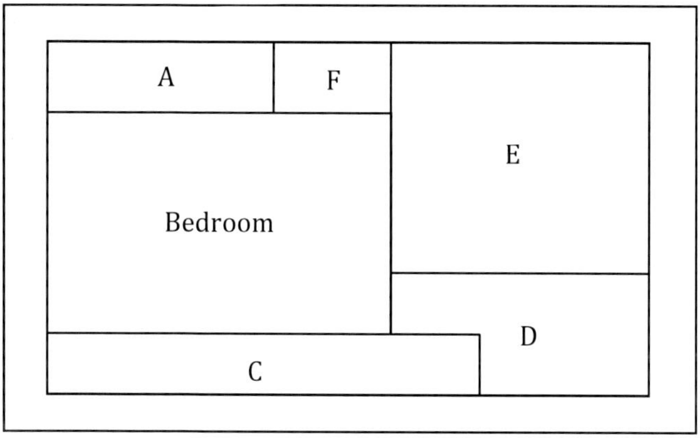

- The bathroom is located in between the living area and the walk-in wardrobe.
- The kitchen is furthest away from the walk-in wardrobe to prevent the clothes from smelling.
- The balcony is the longest and narrowest area.
- From the kitchen, you could see the view from the balcony.

What is represented by area A?

A. Walk-in wardrobe
B. Living area
C. Kitchen
D. Bathroom

Question 27

Should the government provide an incentive for food providers to put healthier carbohydrate options on menus (such as brown rice, red rice, wholewheat spaghetti, and rye bread) to encourage healthy living?

Select the strongest argument from the statements below.

A. YES. It will encourage greater production of healthier carbohydrates.
B. YES. Healthier carbohydrates contain more fibre, vitamins and minerals.
C. NO. Healthier carbohydrates are less popular and may affect local businesses.
D. NO. Healthier carbohydrates will generate more waste.

Question 28

No doctor has diabetes.
Many people who are obese become diabetics.

Answer YES if the following conclusions are correct and NO if they are not.

Q28.1	No doctor is obese.	YES	NO
Q28.2	Some people who are obese may be doctors.	YES	NO
Q28.3	No diabetic is a doctor.	YES	NO
Q28.4	All people who are obese are also diabetic.	YES	NO
Q28.5	A diabetic obese person cannot be a doctor.	YES	NO

Question 29

As part of his Geography project, David performed a survey of 100 households in his neighbourhood on the recycling of glass, paper and plastic.

- 10 households recycled paper, plastic and glass.
- 14 households recycled paper and glass.
- 15 households recycled paper and plastic.
- 21 households recycled glass and plastic.
- 32 households recycled glass.
- 52 households recycled plastic.
- 46 households recycled paper.

How many households recycled neither glass nor plastic?

A. 27
B. 37
C. 36
D. 26

Question 30

Buzz, Woolos, Gwent and Manor visited Penang this summer. Each participated in one of the following beach activities: a banana boat ride; scuba diving; jet skiing; parachuting. The costs for these activities were, in no particular order: RM40, RM48, RM95, and RM103.

Woolos spent RM8 more than Manor, and Buzz spent RM8 more than Gwent. Manor spent the least amount and opted for the banana boat ride.

Who spent RM95 on his activity?

A. Woolos
B. Buzz
C. Gwent
D. Manor

Question 31

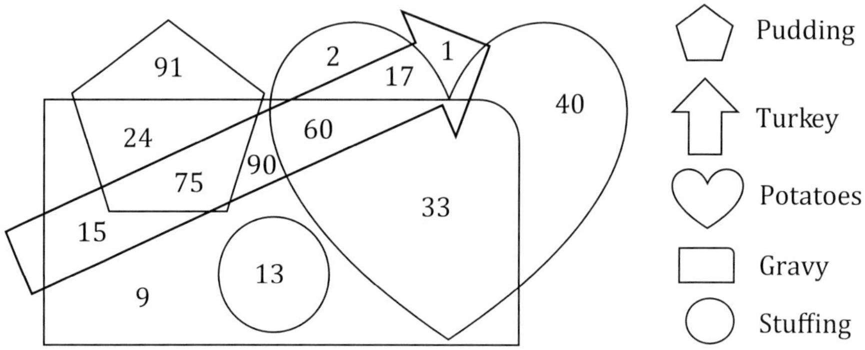

How many guests had turkey, potatoes and gravy but not pudding and stuffing at the Christmas dinner buffet?

A. 60
B. 50
C. 45
D. 75

Question 32

Lily, Petal, Rose and Bea are being weighed as part of their sports class assessment.

If Lily is lighter than Petal and Rose, and if Bea is heavier than Petal, which of the following must be true?

A. Rose is the heaviest.
B. Lily is heavier than Bea.
C. Bea is heavier than Rose.
D. None of the above.

Question 33

Thomas, the manager of a ticket-selling company, would like to know how many tickets have been sold for a particularly famous concert.

The following table shows the sales of the concert tickets on three separate days. There are two types of tickets: standing and seating. The standing tickets cost £40 each, whereas the seating tickets cost £70 each.

Tickets	Friday	Saturday	Sunday
Standing	41	60	70
Seating	24	19	22

Which of the following statements is true?

A. Sunday made more revenue through its standing tickets than its seating tickets.
B. There were more sales for seating tickets than standing tickets.
C. Seating tickets were found to be more cost effective by customers.
D. Overall, more tickets were sold for Friday than Saturday.

Question 34

Should large food companies hire staff with learning disabilities to encourage self-development?

Select the strongest argument from the statements below.

A. YES. This will encourage people with learning disabilities to work and to be independent.
B. YES. Large food companies will gain publicity for social inclusion.
C. NO. People with learning disabilities are more vulnerable to criticism in the workplace.
D. NO. Impatient customers are more likely to avoid these food companies which may subsequently affect businesses.

Question 35

Three out of 10 students eat pasta.
Six out of 10 students eat rice.
Five out of 10 students eat potatoes.

Answer YES if the following conclusions are correct and NO if they are not.

Q35.1	At most, one of the 10 students eats rice and potatoes.	YES	NO
Q35.2	At least two of the 10 students eat neither potatoes nor pasta.	YES	NO
Q35.3	Some students eat all three carbohydrates.	YES	NO
Q35.4	At most, one of the 10 students does not eat rice or pasta.	YES	NO
Q35.5	At most, three out of the 10 students eat all three carbohydrates.	YES	NO

Question 36

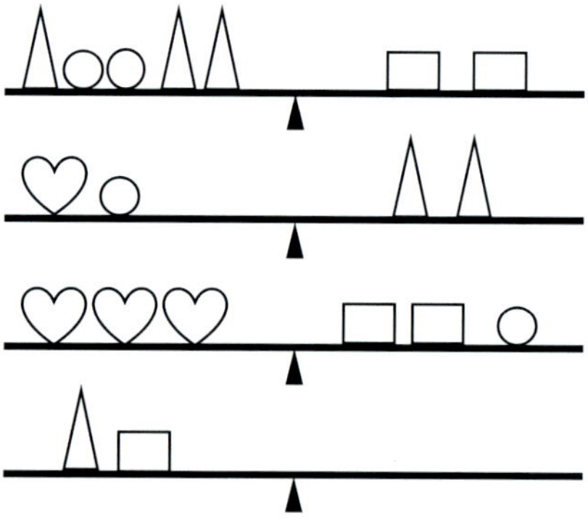

Which of the following completes the above diagram?

A 

C 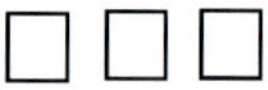

B 

D 

Question 37

Almost every child in Kuala Lumpur learns to play a musical instrument. A survey was conducted to find out the number of musical instruments played by 100 children, the results of which are represented in the following diagram. Every child in the study plays at least one musical instrument.

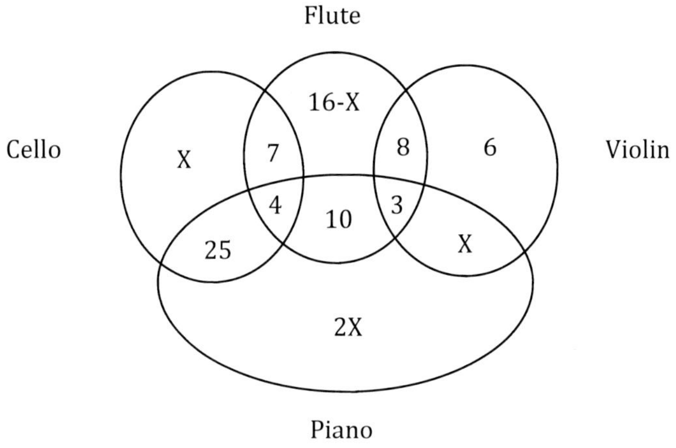

Which of the following statements is true?

A. The total number of children who play three musical instruments is six.
B. The total number of children who play the piano is less than the total number of children who play either the cello or the violin.
C. More children play only the violin than only the cello.
D. The number of children who play the flute is the same as the number of children who play both the cello and the piano.

Question 38

For the next entry into a UK Medical School, the admissions team has decided on a cut-off score based on predicted pre-university grades (A Levels; IB; Scottish Highers), interview, personal statement, and UCAT.

Applicants who scored 88 and above were given an offer, while those who scored below 75 were rejected.

The following table represents the number of students who were offered a place, put on the waiting list, and rejected. It is categorised by nationality.

Results	UK	Non-UK / EU	International
Offered	250	33	20
Waitlisted	169	7	430
Rejected	2570	100	1377

Which of the following statements is true?

A. In total, the university received 4,500 applications this year.
B. The percentage of UK students who received an offer was ten times greater than the percentage of international students who received an offer.
C. There were fewer UK applicants than international and non-UK applicants combined.
D. Overall, 12% of applicants were rejected.

Question 39

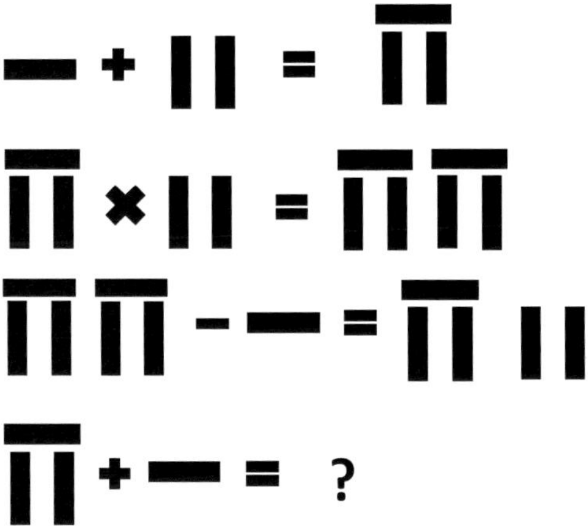

Which of the following shapes completes the above equation?

A.

C.

B.

D.

Question 40

Which diagram correctly represents the relationship between tapioca pearls, flour, bread, and roe?

A.

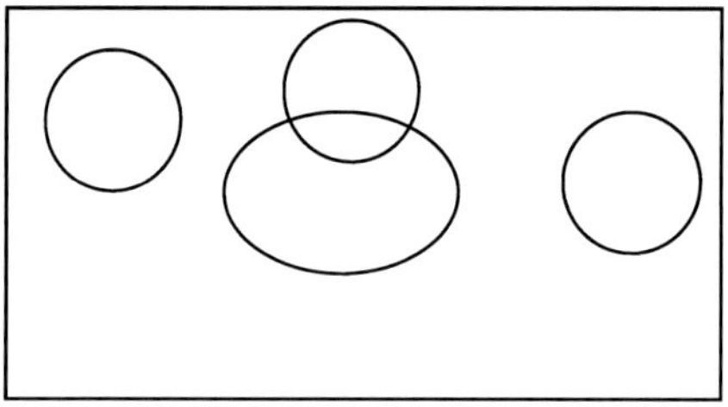

C.

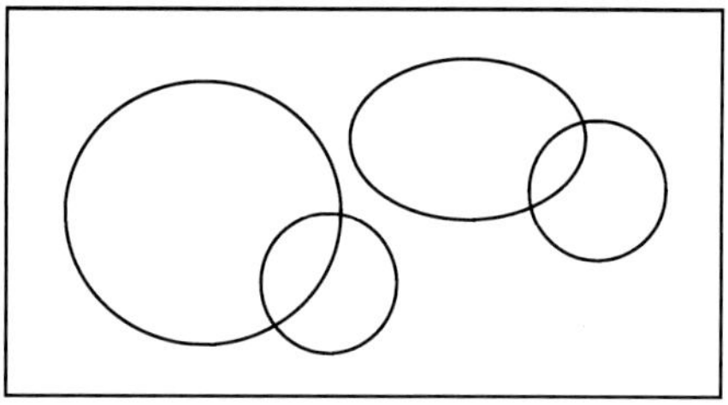

B.

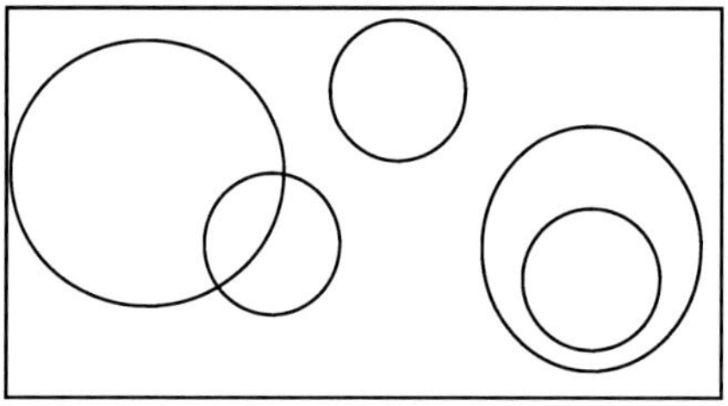

D.

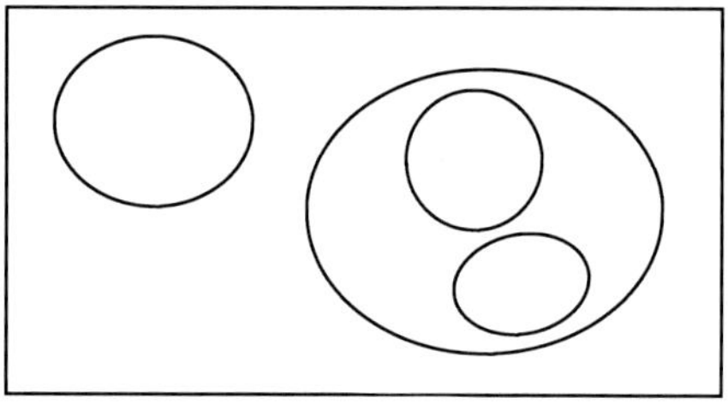

Question 41

Angelica's music playlist is set to play songs at random from thirty different songs. Any song can be played at any time, and a song might be repeated. There are five songs by Band P, seven songs by Band Q, 10 by Band R, and eight by Band S. If Angelica has just played five songs in a row by Band R, what is the probability that the next two songs will also be by Band R?

A. 1/2
B. 1/3
C. 1/4
D. 1/9

Question 42

A paper company produces six different sizes of paper: A0, A1, A2, A3, A4 and A5.

Each piece of paper has a long and short edge.

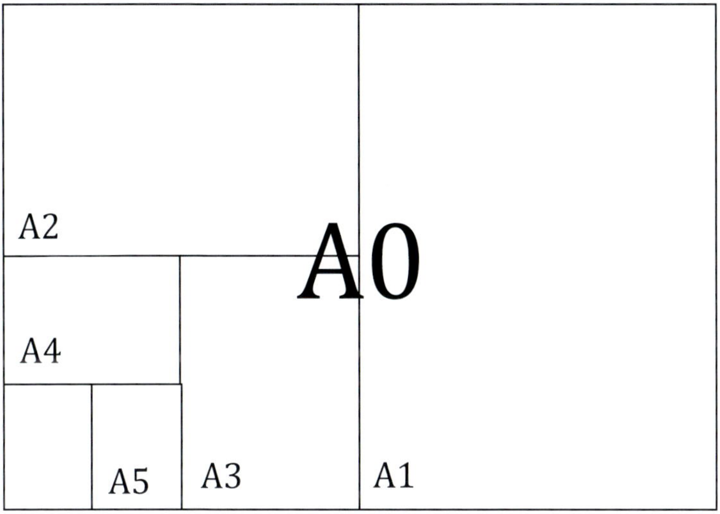

Which of the following statements is true?

A. The area of an A2 piece of paper is equivalent to ten pieces of A5 paper.
B. Thirty-two pieces of A5 can completely fit into an A0.
C. An A1 piece of paper is six times larger than an A4 piece of paper.
D. The area of an A0 piece of paper can accommodate ten pieces of A3 paper.

Question 43

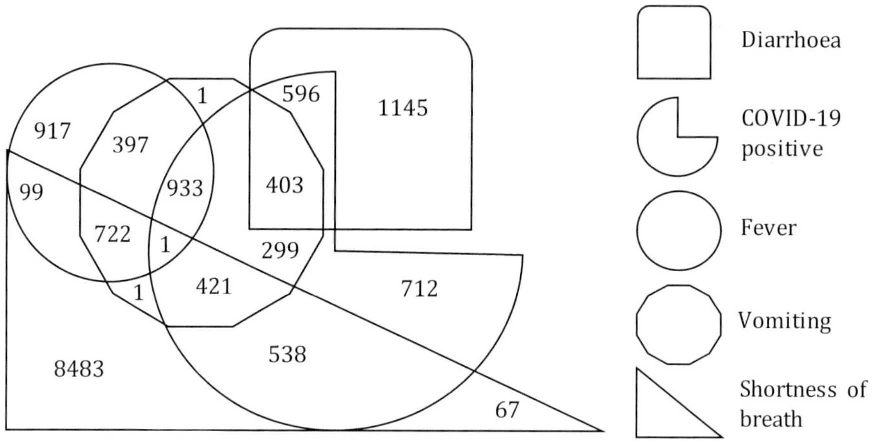

How many patients who had both diarrhoea and vomiting tested positive for COVID-19?

A. 999
B. 720
C. 596
D. 403

Question 44

An area of a rectangle can be calculated by multiplying the length of its sides.

Rectangle P has sides measuring X and 2X.
Rectangle Q has sides measuring 2X and 4X.
Rectangle R has sides measuring 3X and 6X.
Rectangle S has sides measuring 4X and 8X.

Which of the following statements is true?

A. P + P + P = Q
B. P + P + P + Q = R
C. R + R = S
D. Q + Q + Q + P + P + P + P = S

Question 45

Logan notices that everyone in his family likes Tteokbokki except him. More than one family member in his house likes Bibimbap.

Answer YES if the conclusion follows and NO if it does not.

Q45.1	If a person in the family does not like Tteokbokki , it must be Logan.	YES	NO
Q45.2	Logan likes Bibimbap.	YES	NO
Q45.3	If only two people in his family like Bibimbap, Logan must be one of them.	YES	NO
Q45.4	Someone in the family likes both Tteokbokki and Bibimbap.	YES	NO
Q44.5	If a person in the family does not like Bibimbap, he/she must like Tteokbokki.	YES	NO

Question 46

Phenotype is the term used in genetics for the composite observable characteristics or traits of an organism, such as the number of petals, the colour of the fruit, or the height.

Each organism obtains genes in pairs called alleles, consisting of maternal and paternal alleles. As long as one of the alleles is dominant, the trait will be expressed. On the other hand, the recessive trait will only be expressed if the organism receives the recessive allele from both parents.

Possible maternal alleles

Possible paternal alleles

	GH	**Gh**	**gH**	**gh**
GH	**GGHH**	**GGHh**	**GgHH**	**GgHh**
Gh	**GGHh**	**GGhh**	**GgHh**	**Gghh**
gH	**GgHH**	**GgHh**	**ggHH**	**ggHh**
gh	**GgHh**	**Gghh**	**ggHh**	**gghh**

G = Dominant allele for pink flower
g = Recessive allele for purple flower

H = Dominant allele for sweet fruit
h = Recessive allele for sour fruit

A farmer would like to harvest fruits to make compote.

Which of the following statements is true?

A. All the trees have sweet fruits and pink flowers.
B. There is a 50% chance that the tree will have pink flowers and sweet fruits.
C. There is a six out of sixteen chance that the tree has only one dominant trait (either pink flower or sweet fruit).
D. It is impossible for the tree to have purple flowers and sour fruits.

Question 47

A survey was conducted on a cohort of 88 students on the genre of films they like. Eleven enjoy crime, 50 enjoy animation, and 48 enjoy comedy. Twenty-seven of those who enjoy animation also like comedy films. Only one person enjoys crime and comedy.

Which of the following diagrams best represents the above data?

A.

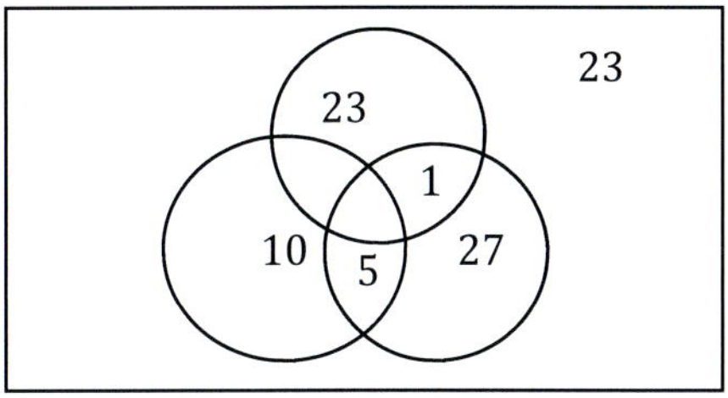

C.

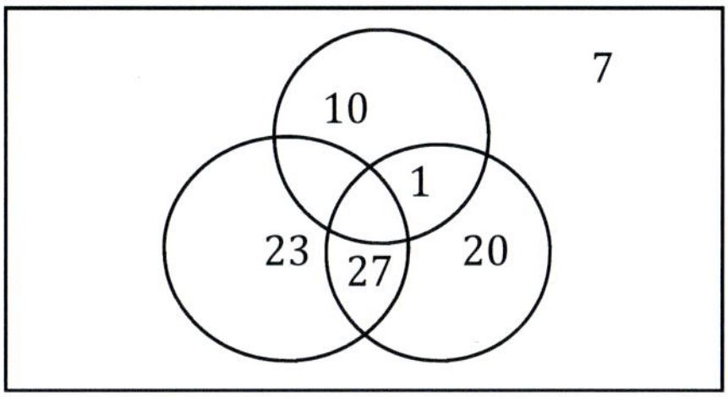

B.

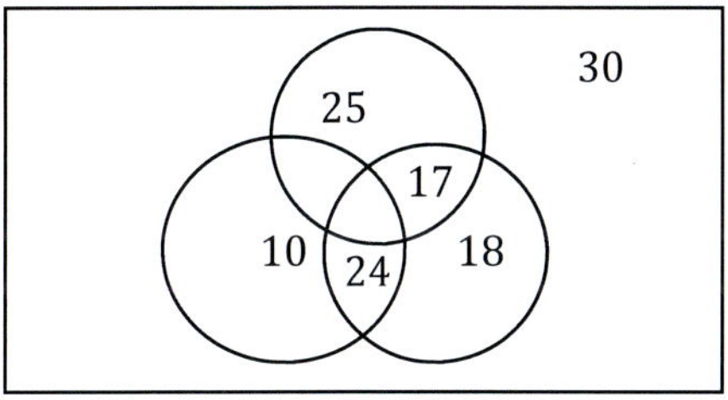

D.

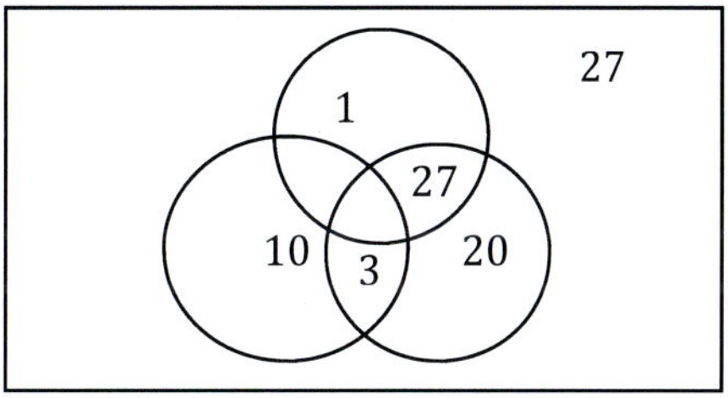

Question 48

On Ward B6, there are 35 people who are either patients or doctors.
There are five more females than males.
Fifteen of the 28 patients are male.

How many male doctors are there on Ward B6?

A. 6
B. 4
C. 3
D. 0

Question 49

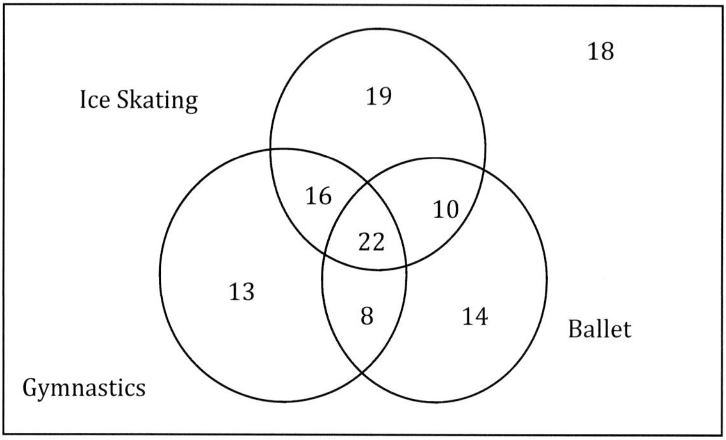

The diagram provides information about the number of students who participated in different types of sports.

Based on the diagram, which of the following statements is true?

A. More students took part in ice skating than those who did not.

B. Thirty students took part in neither gymnastics nor ice skating.

C. More students participated in ballet than ice skating.

D. There were more students who did not do either ice skating, ballet or gymnastics than those who did.

Question 50

In a lucky draw box, there are a certain number of £5 notes, 40 £10 notes, and five £20 notes. The probability of Eleanor drawing a £20 note is a 1 in 25 chance.

How many £5 notes are in the lucky draw box?

A. 110
B. 100
C. 90
D. 80

Question 51

Four pre-schools (A, B, C, and D) organised a school trip to a local zoo. Altogether there were 50 children who joined the trip. The entrance ticket was charged at $5 for children equal to or above 5 years old and $2.50 for children under 5 years old.

Pre-school B has 24 children who went to the zoo and is twice the size of A, three times the size of C, and four times the size of D. C has as many children equal to or above 5 years old as D has under 5 years old. A has equal children in both age groups, and B has as many children under 5 years old as C. There are 16 children equal to or above 5 years old from B who went to the zoo.

How many of the four pre-schools have children only in one age group (either equal to or above 5 years old or under 5 years old)?

A. 0
B. 1
C. 2
D. 3

Question 52

In the Intensive Care Unit, half of the 100 patients have shortness of breath and have tested positive for Coronavirus. Forty patients do not have shortness of breath, and 20 patients have tested negative for Coronavirus.

How many patients have neither the Coronavirus nor shortness of breath?

A. 5
B. 10
C. 15
D. 20

Question 53

The diagram shows the profile of chefs in Paris.

The triangle represents poissonniers.
The rectangle represents those equal to or taller than 170cm.
The hexagon represents patissiers.
The parallelogram represents entremetiers.
The numbers in the diagram represent the number of professionals in each category.

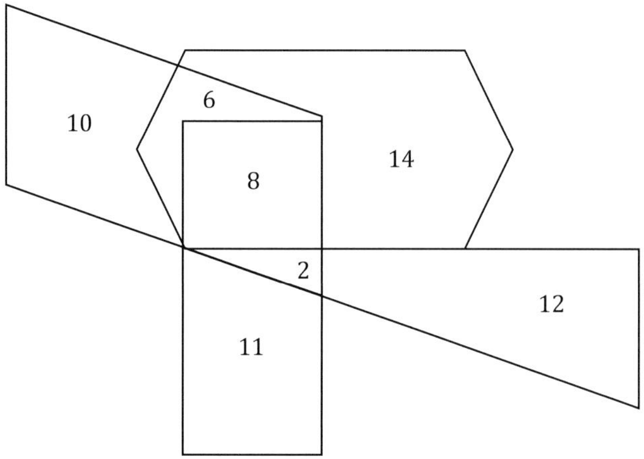

Which of the following statements is true?

A. More than 30% of all the entremetiers and patissiers who are shorter than 170cm are entremetiers only.
B. More than half of those equal to or taller than 170cm work in professions other than patissiers and entremetiers.
C. None of the poissonniers equal to or taller than 170cm are patissiers or entremetiers.
D. Amongst the chefs who work with both pastry and vegetables, four out of seven are shorter than 170cm.

Question 54

The diagram below shows the office layout of the 88th floor in the Patronus Twin Towers.

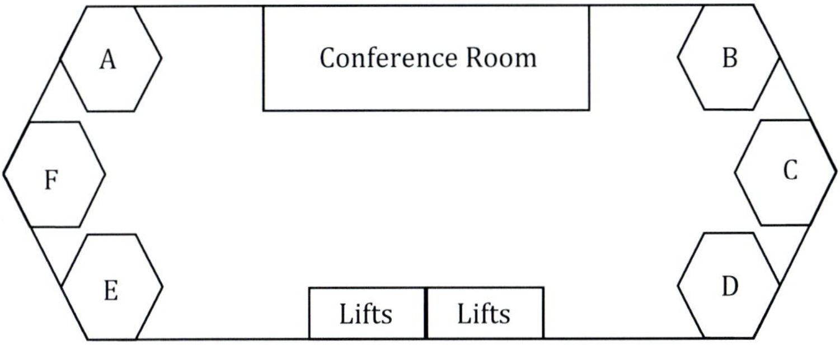

Amore's office is diagonally opposite Malachi's office.
Khalid's office is diagonally opposite Min Ju's office.
Amore's office is closer to Khalid's office than to Min Ju's office.
Malachi's office is closer to Min Ju's office than to Khalid's office.
The reception desk is between Amore's and Khalid's offices.
The coffee room is between Min Ju's and Malachi's offices.
The conference room is directly in front of the lifts.

Andrew exits one of the lifts, turns left, and heads towards the reception desk to sign in prior to the next meeting.

Which of the following statements is true?

A. The conference room is closest to Khalid's and Min Ju's offices.
B. The coffee room is diagonally opposite the reception desk.
C. If A is Amore's office, then E represents Malachi's office.
D. If Andrew exits the lift and turns right, he will see Malachi's office, the coffee room, and Min Ju's office.

Question 55

This painting is an impressionist portrait. All impressionist portraits are treasures.

Answer YES if the conclusion follows and NO if it does not.

Q55.1	All the things that are not treasures are not impressionist portraits.	YES	NO
Q55.2	Some treasurable impressionist portraits are paintings.	YES	NO
Q55.3	All paintings are treasures.	YES	NO
Q55.4	Some paintings are treasures.	YES	NO
Q55.5	All paintings are impressionist portraits.	YES	NO

Question 56

Michiko would like to buy a bowl of poke, but she only has ¥4000.

Step 1	White rice ¥150	Brown rice ¥304	Quinoa ¥456	Salad ¥305	Egg noodles ¥102
Step 2	Ahi tuna ¥3285	Salmon ¥3543	Tofu ¥3060	Albacore ¥3330	Grilled eel ¥3690
Step 3	Tamago ¥300	Seaweed ¥202	Jicama ¥265	Takuan ¥188	Avocado ¥333

Which one of the following is a possible combination?

A. White rice, grilled eel, jicama
B. Quinoa, ahi tuna, avocado
C. Salad, salmon, takuan
D. Brown rice, albacore, tamago

Question 57

Miskin would like to create a brine to tenderise meat. She prepares three beakers (T, U, V). Each beaker contains 500ml of water and different amounts of salt. She inserts identical pieces of chilli into each beaker and leaves them for 24 hours. The chilli was weighed at the beginning and after 24 hours.

Chilli	Beaker T	Beaker U	Beaker V
Weight before (mg)	500mg	488mg	495mg
Weight after (mg)	400mg	488mg	510mg

Which of the following statements is true?

A. If T had 50g of salt added, then V had 100g of salt added.
B. The chilli shrunk in V.
C. The solution in V is hypotonic.
D. If T had 30g of salt added and V had 20g of salt added, then no salt was added to U.

Question 58

The table below shows how much nicotine each smoking product contains.

Smoking products	Average nicotine content
Cigarette	12mg (one cigarette)
Cigar	15.4mg (large cigar)
Chewing tobacco	144mg (whole can)
E-cigarette	15.4mg (15 puffs)
Hookah	16.6mg (15 puffs)
Pipe (tobacco)	50.89mg (one pipe)

Annalise smokes one pack of cigarettes a day.
Oliver smokes 60 puffs of Hookah a day and uses an e-cigarette (150 puffs).
Aafaaq's grandfather smokes four pipes daily.
Gigi enjoys chewing tobacco with her best friend Schmitz. They both finish two whole cans each in a day.

Which of the following statements is true?

A. Aafaaq's grandfather smokes the least amount of nicotine in a day.
B. Gigi smokes the same amount of nicotine as Oliver.
C. Oliver smokes the most amount of nicotine out of the group.
D. Annalise smokes twice the amount of nicotine in comparison to Schmitz.

Question 59

The diagram below shows how students in Singapore attend tuition classes using different forms of transport.

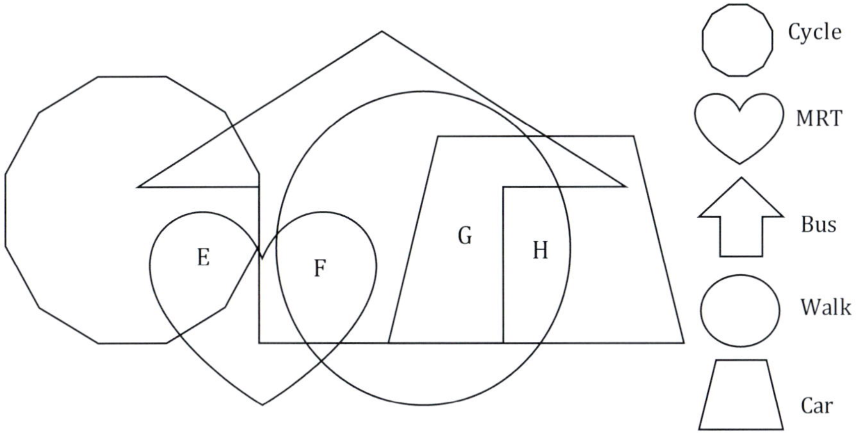

Which of the following letters represents students who travel via a combination of MRT, walking and bus?

A. E
B. F
C. G
D. H

Question 60

Should the government fine those who do not follow lockdown measures (e.g., social distancing; one form of exercise per day) to prevent the further spread of Coronavirus?

Select the strongest argument from the statements below.

A. YES. This will reduce the number of people violating lockdown measures and hopefully reduce the number of affected cases.
B. YES. This will help reduce the number of admissions to hospital.
C. NO. Due to non-essential workers lacking income, this will affect the poorer population largely.
D. NO. Administering fines will not prevent others from violating the rules.

Question 61

On Valentines Day, the average of 20 students in Class 6 at St. Thomas' School who received a gift from a secret admirer is 3.3. Eight students received four each, and seven students received three each. Julin received three times as many gifts as Shu Min, Nia and Jee Nee. Assuming Shu Min, Nia and Jee Nee received the same number of gifts each, they each have twice as many as Melessa.

How many gifts did Julin receive?

A. 5
B. 6
C. 7
D. 8

Question 62

A bag contains 24 yellow, 16 purple, 12 blue, and 8 pink seashells. Twenty-five seashells are removed from the bag randomly. The chance of drawing a purple seashell from the bag is now 2 out of 5.

How many of the removed seashells were purple?

A. 1
B. 2
C. 3
D. 4

Question 63

A regular deck of cards has 52 cards. Assume that you do not replace the card you had drawn before the next draw.

What is the probability of drawing three queens in row?

A. 1 in 1275
B. 1 in 2025
C. 1 in 5525
D. 1 in 10125

Question 64

Famous hotels are painted gold.
All receptionists speak Hangugeo.
Only receptionists work in famous hotels.
All those who speak Hangugeo love watching Korean dramas.

Answer YES if the conclusion follows and NO if it does not.

Q64.1	A receptionist who works in a famous hotel does not necessarily love watching Korean dramas.	YES	NO
Q64.2	People who love watching Korean dramas work in famous hotels.	YES	NO
Q64.3	A receptionist can't have worked in an unknown hotel.	YES	NO
Q64.4	All gold hotels have workers who speak Hangugeo.	YES	NO
Q64.5	All those who love watching Korean dramas are receptionists.	YES	NO

Question 65

Mr Ri would like to send a secret message to his fellow soldiers who are at sea. He is aware that the message can be intercepted by external spies.

On Monday, he sent this message:
BANANA-TENTACLES-APPLE-ORANGE-RASPBERRY-EGG-GUAVA-MELON

His fellow soldiers met him in Prague at 10:00 am.

On Friday, he sent this message:
CORN-NETWORK-LENTILS-SPINACH-SILVERBEET-CHERRY

Where will Mr Ri's fellow soldiers meet him?

A. Ankara at 17:00 pm
B. Nile at 02:00 am
C. Saigon at 06:00 am
D. Lisbon at 12:00 pm

Question 66

A safe box containing five million dollars has been shipped across to the island Aitutaki. Whoever cracks the passcode will get to keep the five million dollars.

A clue is attached to the safe box:

Men want treasure without much haste,
Calm, obedient and work at a fast pace,
Whoever breaks the code, wins the race,
Use it with honour and grace.

This safe box is a treasure,
Crack the code and your life will be filled with pleasure,
Take your time and work under leisure,
For whoever sees the clue will not need to measure.

To crack this code, you must go back in time,
Follow the treasure and you will find,
If you are obedient, you don't have to look far,
For the code only has four numbers,
Each found next to the other,
In the word, what you see is what you seek,
Listen carefully,
What is below men,
Higher than honour,
Next to life,
And above measure.

What is the code?

A. 8-4-6-4
B. 4-6-9-2
C. 9-2-6-4
D. 2-8-4-9

Quantitative Reasoning

FORMAT

In the exam, you have:

- 36 questions
- 9 different scenarios
- 24 minutes
- +1 minute to read the instructions

In this section, there are:

- 60 scenarios (256 questions)

Objectives:

- To solve numerical problems under pressure.
- To review and research data.
- To extract and manipulate information.
- To substitute numbers into formula.

TYPES OF QUESTIONS

Type | GCSE-Level Mathematics

- Basic arithmetic
- Proportionality
- Ratios
- Percentage, fractions and changes
- Speed, distance and time
- Geometry
- Money, tax and exchanges
- Population densities
- Rates
- Time
- Averages and ranges

TIPS AND TRICKS TO SCORE

Revision Tips

- Brush up on your GCSE mathematics and mental arithmetic.
- Have a list of basic formulas commonly used:
  - ⇒ Area of a square = a^2
  - ⇒ Area of of a circle = πr^2
  - ⇒ Circumference of a circle = $2\pi r$
  - ⇒ Pythagoras theorem à $a^2 + b^2 = c^2$
  - ⇒ Area of triangle = ½ x base x height
  - ⇒ Volume of cuboid = length x width x height
  - ⇒ Area of parallelogram = base x height
  - ⇒ Change in percentage = (new number – original number) /original number x 100
  - ⇒ Convert currency (eg. £ to $)
  - ⇒ Distances (eg. miles to kilometer)
  - ⇒ Weight (eg. kg to pounds)
  - ⇒ Speed – time – distance formula
    - ♦ Speed = distance / time
    - ♦ Time = distance / speed
    - ♦ Distance = speed x time
- Try and use mental calculation, if possible, to build up your confidence in using quick mental arithmetic.
- Learn to estimate and eliminate.
- Get used to using the online screen calculator by using the keyboard. You could practice this for both untimed and timed practice. Make sure **NUM LOCK is ON**. Avoid clicking the numbers using the mouse or trackpad.
- Practice using a classic calculator instead of a scientific calculator, as it best represents the on-screen calculator.
- We recommend starting untimed practice 12 weeks before your test date. After the first four weeks, we recommend starting timed practice. Make sure that your practice in the last few weeks is done on an online platform as this will best simulate the real test.
- Reflect and review how answers are obtained.
- In the 'answer' section of this book, you will find tips on how you can save time. It would be useful to make notes on these tips as you go along.

Answering Techniques

- Try and answer as many questions correctly rather than answering all questions hastily.
- The test is not negatively marked, so don't leave a question unanswered if you have not been able to arrive at a sensible answer.
- There are multiple strategies on how to approach QR questions. Find one that suits you and stick to it.
- Do not waste your time trying to decide whether a question is easy or not.
- We recommend doing the questions as they appear, and if the question turns out to be difficult, flag it then return to it later.
- Skim the text / graph to look at where you can find information. Then approach the questions individually and answer accordingly.
- You can sometimes find important information outside the graph or table itself (e.g., within the text).
- Make full use of the whiteboard given during practice and the official test.

Question 1

The table below shows the ticket prices* for the "All Wales Tennis Open Championship 2019".

	Centre Court	No. 1 Court	No. 2 Court	Ground Admission
Saturday 1 / Sunday 2 June	£75	£53	£43	£15
Monday 3 / Tuesday 4 June	£95	£68	£50	£15
Wednesday 5 June	£117	£100	£86	£10
Thursday 6 June	£123	£115	£92	£10
Friday 7 June	£166	£140	-	£10
Saturday 8 June	£189	-	-	£7
Sunday 9 June	£214	-	-	£7

** The ticket prices shown are for regular adult seats only. Children under the age of 12 receive a £15 discount which is deducted after seat selection. Tickets for VIP seats are 30% more expensive than the regular tickets, and there are no VIP seats at ground admissions. The child's discount does not apply for ground admissions.*

Q1.1 A father and his two sons, aged 11 and 13, want to buy VIP seats for the men's quarter-final match that will take place on the Wednesday at Centre Court. How much will he have to pay for the tickets altogether?

A. £443.10
B. £439.50
C. £336.00
D. £441.30
E. £456.30

Q1.2 A tennis fan and his wife bought regular tickets online to the Friday game at No. 1 Court and chose to have the tickets delivered to them for an extra fee of £2.50. However, they forgot to bring their tickets with them on the day of the event and decided to watch from the grounds. How much did they lose due to their mistake?

A. £280.00
B. £282.50
C. £285.20
D. £300.00
E. £302.50

Q1.3 A businessman and his family are in town for the week. He is deciding between watching the show with his six-year-old daughter on regular seats at Centre Court for Thursday or a VIP seat to himself at No. 2 Court on the same day. How much, in ratio, would he need to spend if he brings his daughter along with him compared to going alone?

A. 0.52:1
B. 1.54:1
C. 1.93:1
D. 2.01:1
E. 2.14:1

Q1.4 A group of four teenagers buys VIP tickets to the match on the 9th from an authorised reseller. Two of them had a one-time-use promo code that gets them a 15% discount each. Given that the boys decided to split the final cost of the tickets equally, how much, in percentage, did each of them save compared to the original ticket price? Round your answer to one decimal place.

A. 7.5%
B. 8.1%
C. 9.8%
D. 11.6%
E. 20.3%

Question 2

The table below shows the annual income tax bracket rates and thresholds in pounds (£).

Brackets	Taxable Income (£)	Tax Rate
1	Up to 10,000	5%
2	10,000 - 25,000	15%
3	25,000 - 45,000	25%
4	Over 45,000	40%

An example of how to calculate your income tax: If you earn £15,000, you will have to pay (0.05 x 10,000 + 0.15 x 5,000) £1,250.

Q2.1 Parker earns £5,500 every three months. How much annual income tax does she have to pay?

A. £192
B. £275
C. £575
D. £1,150
E. £2,300

Q2.2 Jake has a monthly income tax of £500. How much is his annual income?

A. £10,000
B. £24,000
C. £38,000
D. £41,000
E. £45,000

Q2.3 If the government introduces a 50% tax on income over £50,000, how much more will Jennifer have to pay each month if she has an annual income of £60,000? Round your answer to the nearest pound.

A. £1,229
B. £2,459
C. £13,459
D. £14,750
E. £17,750

Q2.4 The following year, the government revised the tax rates and increased brackets 2 and 3 to 17% and 30%, respectively. If Kelly earns £36,000 in both years, how much is the percentage increase of her payable tax? Round your answer to the nearest percent.

A. 13%
B. 15%
C. 16%
D. 17%
E. 19%

Question 3

A science student buys himself a cylindrical container that is 50cm tall and 28cm wide.

He writes the following down before he begins his experiments:

- $\pi = 3.14$
- 1 litre = $1dm^3$, where 1dm = 10cm
- density of water = $1.00gcm^{-3}$ and density of ice = $0.92gcm^{-3}$, where $1gcm^{-3} = 1kgdm^{-3}$

Q3.1 The student fills up 70% of the container with $0.12moldm^{-3}$ of salt. How much salt, in grams, has he added? (Molar mass of salt = 58g/mol)

A. 219.7g
B. 150.7g
C. 313.9g
D. 150.4g
E. 149.9g

Q3.2 The student fills half of the container with water and leaves it in the freezer. What is the volume of ice after all the water freezes, assuming that no water was lost or gained during the freezing process?

A. $14{,}155cm^3$
B. $16{,}724cm^3$
C. $28{,}310cm^3$
D. $30{,}772cm^3$
E. $33{,}448cm^3$

Q3.3 The student found the container to be leaky after filling it with water to the brim. Before patching up the hole, he measures the rate of leakage and found it to be 5ml/s. What is the percentage decrease of water if the leakage is only stopped after an hour, assuming the rate of leakage is constant?

A. 1.0%
B. 41.5%
C. 58.5%
D. 61.3%
E. 71.0%

Q3.4 The student pours 23dm^3 of water into the container before leaving it in the rain for three hours. The level of water rose at 0.2cm/min. What is the percentage increase of the volume of water after 1.5 hours?

A. 36.0%
B. 48.2%
C. 63.3%
D. 72.0%
E. 96.4%

Question 4

A medical school's Glee Club decided to raise funds for cancer support organisations by singing solos at an open concert. They agreed to divide the funds between two charities - We Are Warriors and Cancer Survivors - in the ratio of 3:2.

The table below summarises the total number of songs each student performed and how much money they managed to raise.

Student	Number of Songs	Amount of Funds Raised (£)
Rachel	5	45.60
Blaine	7	61.10
Kurt	3	24.00
Quinn	4	56.80
Jesse	4	39.50

Q4.1 How much did Cancer Survivors receive from the concert?

A. £90.80
B. £95.00
C. £101.60
D. £113.50
E. £136.20

Q4.2 What is the difference in the total amount of money raised between the student with the most money per song and least money per song?

A. £5.08
B. £5.47
C. £6.20
D. £6.50
E. £8.50

Q4.3 We Are Warriors was generous enough to give some money to Cancer Survivors such that they both received the same amount. What is the percentage increase in the amount of money Cancer Survivors received?

A. 20%
B. 20.5%
C. 23%
D. 24.6%
E. 25%

Q4.4 Another student, Sam, joined in to perform at the last minute. The average of the amount of funds raised per student became £52.00. How much did Sam raise from his performance?

A. £53.20
B. £44.40
C. £31.20
D. £72.90
E. £85.00

Question 5

Q5.1 Rhys loves playing basketball. He practices shooting hoops in the playground outside his house for 30 minutes every day. In April, there were seven days when he shot eight hoops, nine days when he shot 12 hoops, six days when he shot 15 hoops, and he shot an average of 10 hoops for the rest of the days. The mean number of hoops scored in April was:

A. 9
B. 10
C. 11
D. 12
E. 30

Q5.2 Rettz, who is the head of a village, wants to set up a night market for people to sell their goods. He and a few villagers build a shelter for the market; the size of the shelter is 50m by 30m. Each stall is given a space of 5m by 4m. He estimates that the walking area for customers will take about 30% of the market area. What is the maximum number of stalls that can fit under the shelter?

A. 22
B. 52
C. 60
D. 75
E. 93

Q5.3 Raine carried out a survey on a random sample of medical students to determine whether the Annual Welsh Surgical Conference should be held on the first or second week of March. A total of 238 students responded, and the results showed that 34.5% would prefer to have it on the second week of March. What is the approximate number of students in the entire medical school of 755 students that Raine could expect to prefer having it on the first week of March?

A. 260
B. 156
C. 339
D. 400
E. 495

Q5.4 Roo just returned from her two-week skiing trip. She wants to upload the pictures she has taken with her camera to her Facebook. A typical photo taken is about 32 megabytes. Her mother only allows her to use the laptop for a maximum of 12 hours each day. If the internet speed in her house is 25 megabit per second, what is the maximum number of images that the tracking station could receive from the camera each day? (1 megabyte = 8 megabit)

A. 101,322
B. 5,913
C. 270,000
D. 4,218
E. 12,098

Question 6

The table below shows a few types of spices and their respective compositions.

Spice	% of turmeric	% of cumin	% of coriander
A	49	30	21
B	15	10	75
C	55	42	3
D	70	-	30
E	30	45	25

Q6.1 How much more cumin is there in 250g of Spice A compared to 100g of Spice E?

A. 0.03g
B. 30kg
C. 3.0g
D. 300mg
E. 0.03kg

Q6.2 If all the five spices are mixed together in equal amounts, what percentage of turmeric, in the final mixture, is from Spice D?

A. 14%
B. 19%
C. 20%
D. 32%
E. 70%

Q6.3 Two parts of Spice C was mixed with three parts of Spice D. What is the percentage increase of turmeric compared to the original of Spice C?

A. 16%
B. 9%
C. 116%
D. 482%
E. 454%

Q6.4 A customer claimed that it is possible to make one spice out of another by adding one of the three main ingredients. Which ingredient would that be?

A. Turmeric
B. Cumin
C. Coriander
D. The claim is false

Question 7

Firdaus is a university student who is enthusiastic about going to the gym for an hour every day during the week. The graph below shows the number of times he visited the gym in each week against his n^{th} week in university.

Total hours spent in the gym each week vs n^{th} week in university

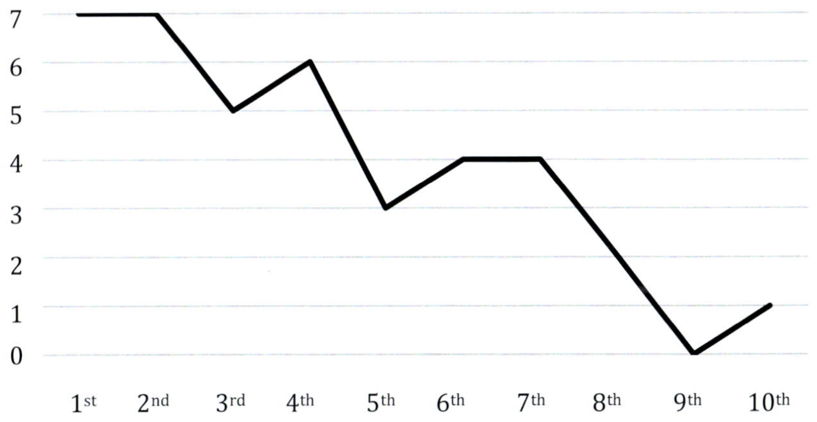

Q7.1 What is his mean time spent in the gym each week across the 10 weeks?

A. 3.7 hours
B. 3.9 hours
C. 4.0 hours
D. 4.3 hours
E. 4.5 hours

Q7.2 At which periods below did Firdaus have the greatest decline in gym time?

A. 7th - 8th week
B. 2th - 3rd week
C. 8th - 9th week
D. 4th - 5th week
E. 6th - 7th week

Q7.3 What is the percentage decrease in the mean gym time of the first five weeks compared to the mean gym time of the last five weeks?

A. 16%
B. 116%
C. 61%
D. 255%
E. 216%

Q7.4 Firdaus' friend, Neary, frequents the gym every alternative week. The sum of both their mean time spent per week is 4.8 hours. How much time does Neary spend in the gym each visit if she has a consistent regime throughout the term?

A. 1.2 hours
B. 1.8 hours
C. 2.25 hours
D. 9 hours
E. 11.4 hours

Question 8

Jian Yang receives a cruiser motorcycle from his father as a gift on his 21st birthday. The next morning, he takes his brand new bike out for a ride to town to meet his friends.

Q8.1 The time taken to travel is 45 minutes. Assuming that Jian Yang travelled at an average speed of 25mph, how long was the journey, in km? (1 mile = 1.609km)

A. 8.9km
B. 18.8km
C. 25.1km
D. 30.2km
E. 34.2km

Q8.2 His friend, Chris, wanted to test his bike on a circuit. His ride can be described as below:

- Steadily accelerated from 0 to 40mph in 4 minutes
- Maintained constant speed for 10 minutes
- Steadily decelerated to a stop in 9 minutes

What was his average speed, in m/s, throughout the journey?

A. 4.4
B. 7.8
C. 11.8
D. 12.3
E. 15.6

Q8.3 If each circuit lap is a 850m loop, how many laps can be completed in a minute if one rides the bike at 80mph?

A. 2.36
B. 2.52
C. 2.84
D. 2.99
E. 3.70

Q8.4 After the group dismissed, Jian Yang decided to take a different route on his way back. He knows that two thirds of the route has a speed limit of 60mph and the rest of it has a speed limit of 20mph. If the total distance ahead of him was 15 miles, how long will he take to reach home if he were to ride his bike at the maximum legal speed?

A. 10mins
B. 15mins
C. 20mins
D. 25mins
E. 35mins

Question 9

In a classroom, there are 13 boys and 27 girls. The average height of the girls is 163.9cm whereas the average height of the boys is 172.2cm.

Treat Q9.2 and Q9.3 as individual scenarios.

Q9.1 What is the average height of the whole classroom?

A. 126.4cm
B. 169.5cm
C. 168.1cm
D. 165.9cm
E. 166.6cm

Q9.2 A pair of male twins were enrolled in the class. If the new average is 167.3cm and if the twins are of the same height, what is the height of each twin?

A. 181.4cm
B. 140.5cm
C. 170.7cm
D. 105.8cm
E. 178.7cm

Q9.3 The tallest boy in the class was transferred to another school because his family had to move. His height was 190.9cm. What is the percentage reduction in the average height of the boys?

A. 0.94%
B. 0.90%
C. 1.4%
D. 0.86%
E. 0%

Q9.4 During their recess break, everyone stayed in class except for five girls who left for the canteen. The average height of the girls in the class increased by 1.2%. What is the average height of the five girls?

A. 163.1cm
B. 155.2cm
C. 196.7cm
D. 161.3cm
E. 153.4cm

Question 10

Research has discovered that it is possible to calculate the approximate age, in years, of a tree. The way to do it is to multiply the diameter of the tree, in inches, with a constant, which is the growth factor for that particular species. The table below gives the growth factor for eight species of trees.

Species of Tree	Growth Factor
Sugar Maple	5.0
Green Ash	4.0
Black Cherry	5.0
River Birch	3.5
Dogwood	7.0
Aspen	2.0
Shagbark Hickory	7.5
Black Walnut	4.5

Additional information:
1 inch = 2.5 centimetres
1 foot = 12 inches
$\pi = 3.14$

Q10.1 What is the approximate age of the Dogwood tree when its circumference is 113cm?

A. 252yrs
B. 101yrs
C. 791yrs
D. 42yrs
E. 63yrs

Q10.2 If the mean, mode and median of the information in the table were to be arranged in descending order, which order would it be?

A. Mode, median, mean
B. Median, mean, mode
C. Mode, mean, median
D. Mean, mode, median
E. Median, mode, mean

Q10.3 If an Aspen tree and a Sugar Maple tree have a radius of one foot, which of the following will be the closest to the difference, in inches, of their diameters 10 years from now?

A. 18 inches
B. 24 inches
C. 36 inches
D. 40 inches
E. Can't tell

Q10.4

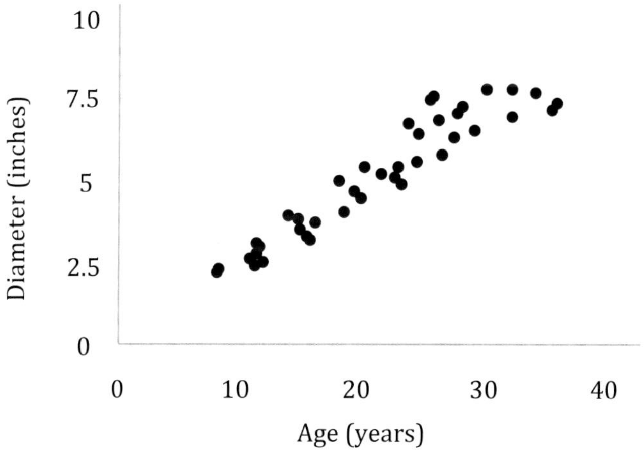

The scatterplot above gives a tree diameter plotted against age for 26 trees in a single species. The growth factor of this species is closest to that of which species?

A. Aspen
B. Black Cherry
C. Dogwood
D. Green Ash
E. Shagbark Hickory

Question 11

The pie chart below shows the different shoe brands sold by a sports shop during a year. A total of 267,500 pairs of shoes were sold that year.

Shoe Sales

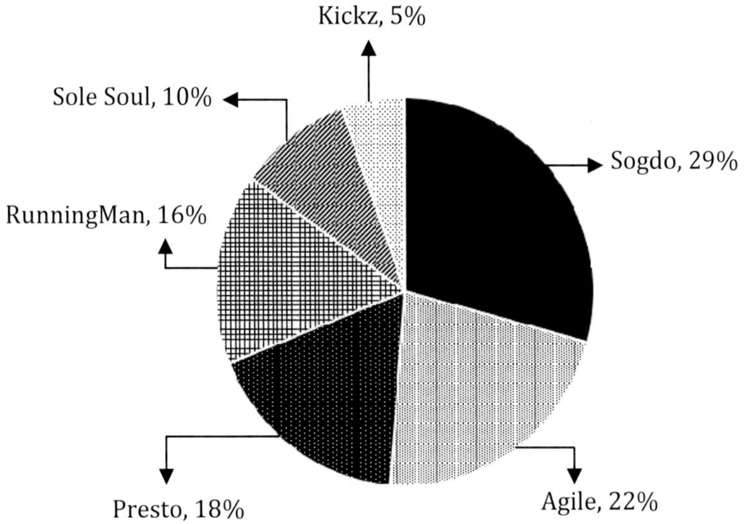

Q11.1 How many of the total shoes sold that year were RunningMan and Kickz shoes?

A. 58,065
B. 56,175
C. 74,655
D. 72,225
E. 101,650

Q11.2 If a mean profit of £40 was made from each pair of Presto shoes sold and £55 was made from each pair of Agile shoes, how much more profit did Agile sales generate compared to Presto, in pounds?

A. £294,250
B. £294,520
C. £675,300
D. £1,310,570
E. £1,310,750

Q11.3 During a year end audit, they found that 12,550 pairs of Sole Soul shoes were sold but were unrecorded. How much will the angle size of Sogdo's sector decrease once a new pie chart is made?

A. 0°
B. 1.3°
C. 2.3°
D. 4.7°
E. 5.1°

Q11.4 The total profit made from RunningMan shoes alone was £8M. What is the estimated mean profit made from each pair of its shoes?

A. £187
B. £181
C. £176
D. £125
E. £136

Question 12

The specific heat capacity of an object is defined by the formula c = ΔQ / (m x Δθ), where ΔQ is the change in thermal energy (in J), m is the mass (in kg), and Δθ is the change in temperature (in °C) of the object.

$$c = \frac{\Delta Q}{m \times \Delta\theta}$$

$$\Delta Q = m \times c \times \Delta\theta$$

The specific heat capacity, c changes depending on the material of the substance. A few materials with their respective c are given below:

Material	Specific Heat Capacity, c
Water	4,181
Methanol	2,530
Ethanol	2,440
Propanol	2,390
Sodium	1,214
Potassium	754
Gold	122

Assume that no heat is lost to the surroundings nor used for a change in the state of the materials in the questions below.

Q12.1 What is the temperature change observed if 3,000J of heat were supplied to 500g of water?

A. 1×10^{-3}°C
B. 1.4°C
C. 0.7°C
D. 12°C
E. 5.1°C

Q12.2 For the same mass of liquid, what is the ratio in the rise in temperature of methanol to propanol if the same amount of energy was supplied to both the alcohols?

A. 0.94:1
B. 1.05:1
C. 1.12:1
D. 1:2.12
E. 1:1.22

Q12.3 The amount of energy supplied to give a rise of 15°C in 0.750kg of solid sodium is supplied in equal amounts to an unknown mass of solid potassium. Assuming that the temperature change in potassium is the same as that of sodium, what is the difference in mass between the two solids?

A. 0.485kg
B. 2.11kg
C. 1.21kg
D. 1.12kg
E. 0.458kg

Q12.4 An experiment was carried out to determine the specific heat capacity of an unknown solid material. It was found that, for 35% the equivalent mass of solid gold, it gives a temperature rise that is four times greater than the mass of gold when both solids are supplied with the same amount of energy. What is the estimated specific heat capacity of the material?

A. 10.7
B. 170.8
C. 87.1
D. 1,394.2
E. 99.2

Question 13

The bar graph below shows the number of students scoring straight As in their GCSEs between two rival schools across different years.

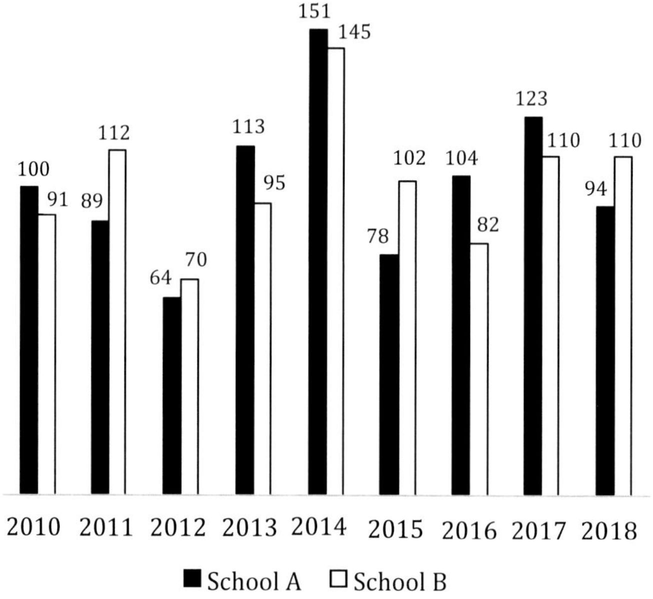

Q13.1 Of the total number of students scoring straight As in School B across all the years shown in the graph, what percentage of the total is the year with the least straight As?

A. 6.2%
B. 7.0%
C. 7.6%
D. 8.9%
E. 9.1%

Q13.2 What was the greatest percentage increase in the number of students scoring straight As in their GCSEs in School A compared to the previous year's performance?

A. 33.3%
B. 33.6%
C. 43.4%
D. 76.6%
E. 83.2%

Q13.3 In the year in which there was the smallest percentage change in the number of students scoring straight As compared to the year before in School A, what is the percentage change between those two years in School B?

A. +34.1%
B. -19.6%
C. +74.5%
D. +35.7%
E. -45.4%

Q13.4 Which of the following statements is true?

A. For six times within the nine years, School A has had more straight A students in a year compared to School B.
B. The smallest change in the number of straight A students in School B between two consecutive years is a decrease of 16.
C. The greatest difference between the number of straight A students in both schools is 23.
D. School B has a higher average of straight A students across the nine years compared to School A.
E. The biggest change in the number of straight A students in School A between two consecutive years is an increase of 73.

Question 14

The graph below shows the amount of profit made in different sectors by a multinational conglomerate corporation based in Southeast Asia, named iSEAN.

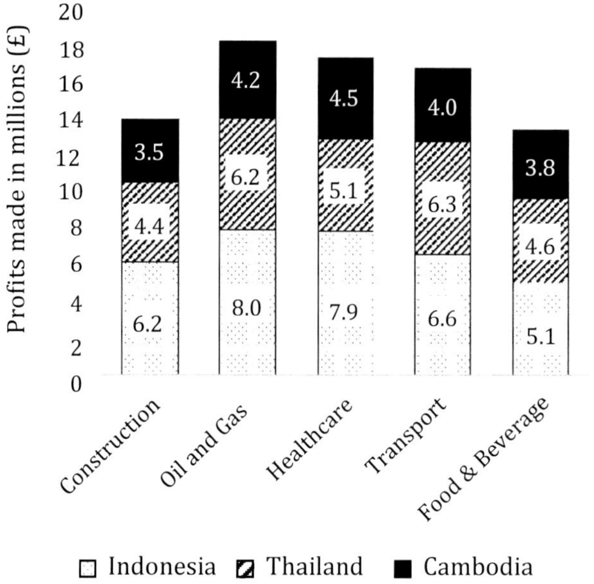

Q14.1 Which of the five sectors represents approximately 21% of the profits made?

A. Construction
B. Oil & Gas
C. Healthcare
D. Food & Beverage
E. Transport

Q14.2 If the ratio of profit to turnover of contracts in Thailand was reported to be 3:17, what was the Oil & Gas turnover in Thailand?

A. £1.1M
B. £35.1M
C. £1.4M
D. £45.3M
E. £14.7M

Q14.3 iSEAN had a target for Food & Beverage profits to be a quarter of the total profits. Assuming profits in the other areas remain the same, by how much did the Food & Beverage profits miss this target?

A. £8.8M
B. £6.6M
C. £6.1M
D. £5.3M
E. £9.7M

Q14.4 A competitor wants to buy iSEAN and offers a price of nine times the current profits. iSEAN shareholders reject this offer and suggest a price that is at least 27% more than the competitor's initial offer. What is this suggested price?

A. £930M
B. £1,245M
C. £897M
D. £919M
E. £1,012M

Question 15

The following information is for questions Q15.1 and Q15.2.

Benkk is an international bank which issues its credit cards for travellers worldwide. When a customer makes a purchase using a Benkk traveller card in a currency different from the customer's home currency, the bank converts the purchase price at the daily foreign exchange rate and then charges a 4% fee on the converted cost.

Sara lives in London, but she is on vacation in China. She used her Benkk card for a purchase that cost 185 Yuan (Chinese currency). The bank posted a charge of £19.76 to her account that included the 4% fee.

Q15.1 What foreign exchange rate, in Chinese Yuan per one British pound, did the bank use for Sara's purchase?

A. 9.74 Yuan
B. 9.37 Yuan
C. 9.00 Yuan
D. 8.85 Yuan
E. 8.28 Yuan

Q15.2 A bank in China sells prepaid credit cards worth 800 Yuan. Sara can buy the prepaid card using dollars at the daily exchange rate with no fee, but she will lose any money left unspent on the prepaid card. What is the least amount of the 800 Yuan on the prepaid card Sara must spend for the prepaid card to be cheaper than charging all her purchases on the Benkk card?

A. 768
B. 769
C. 770
D. 771
E. 772

The following information is for questions Q15.3 and Q15.4.

The Lavender Property Group invested in the five properties listed in the table below. The table shows the amount, in pounds, the company paid for each of the property and the corresponding monthly rental price, in pounds, the company charges for the property for each of the five respective locations.

Property Location	Purchase Price (£)	Monthly Rental Price (£)
Kek Lok Si Lane	192,000	1,425
Georgetown Street	264,000	1,965
Butterworth Drive	105,200	774
Convent Green Lane	210,000	1,560
Gurney Drive	675,200	5,049

Q15.3 Lavender Property Group purchased a Convent Green Lane property and received a 30% discount off the original price, along with an additional 15% off the discounted price for purchasing the property in cash. Which of the following best estimates the original price, in pounds, of the Convent Green Lane property?

A. £4.67M
B. £823,529
C. £2M
D. £352,941
E. £31.5M

Q15.4 The relationship between the monthly rental price *m*, in pounds, and the property's purchase price *p*, in thousands of pounds, can be represented by a linear function. Which of the following functions below represents the relationship?

A. $m(p) = 7.5p - 15$
B. $m(p) = 3.5p + 650$
C. $m(p) = 5p + 75$
D. $m(p) = 2.5p - 160$
E. $m(p) = 8p - 90$

Question 16

Camdyn and Elspeth agreed to a friendly race to see who is the faster cyclist. The graph below shows the relationship of velocity against time of their cycle.

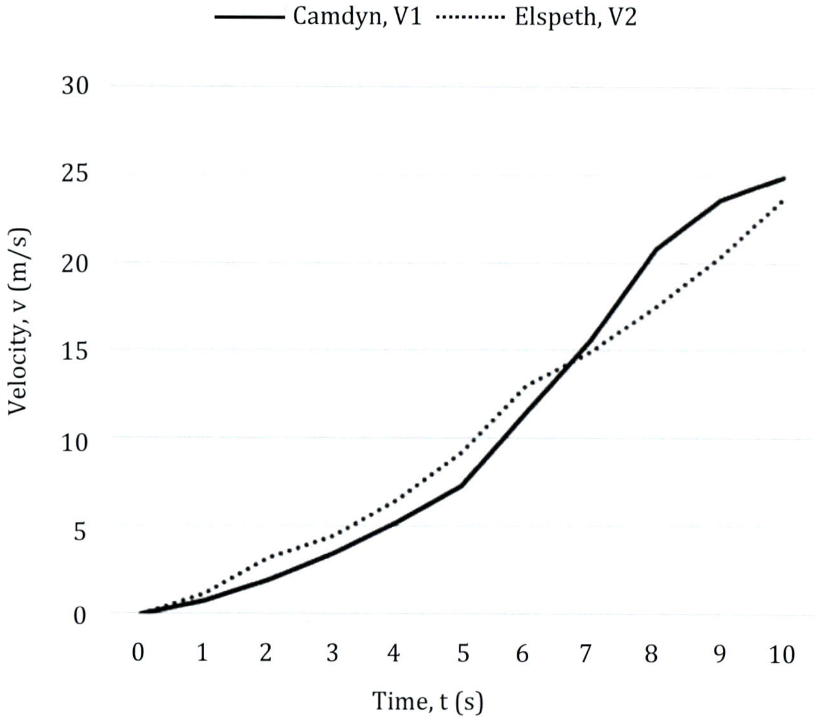

t, s	**0**	**1**	**2**	**3**	**4**	**5**	**6**	**7**	**8**	**9**	**10**
V1, m/s	0	0.8	2.0	3.5	5.3	7.3	11.5	15.6	20.8	23.6	24.9
V2, m/s	0	1.2	3.2	4.5	6.5	9.2	13.0	14.9	17.5	20.3	13.6

The formula for acceleration, a is given by:

$$a = \frac{v_f - v_i}{\Delta t}$$

where v_i is the initial velocity, v_f is the final velocity and Δt is the change in time.

Q16.1 What is the ratio of the greatest acceleration of Camdyn's to Elspeth's?
- A. 1.34:1
- B. 1.29:1
- C. 1.37:1
- D. 1.14:1
- E. Can't tell

Q16.2 What is the difference in the distance travelled between Camdyn and Elspeth in the first five seconds?
- A. 5.7m
- B. 4.3m
- C. 5.25m
- D. 4.75m
- E. Can't tell

Q16.3 At the nth second, Elspeth's acceleration decreased such that her velocity at the $(n+1)^{th}$ second was less than Camdyn's. If she had maintained her acceleration for another three seconds and kept at a constant velocity after, what would be her percentage increase in distance travelled from the nth second onwards?
- A. 13.4%
- B. 39.7%
- C. 23.4%
- D. 17.3%
- E. Can't tell

Q16.4 There is 1,609 metres in a mile. What is the difference in their average velocities in miles per hour (mph)?
- A. 0.21
- B. 1.65
- C. 3.41
- D. 2.63
- E. 0.17

Question 17

A mathematics teacher is quizzing his students about the relationship between time, distance and speed. He delivers his teaching using models of planets and stars. He explains the below to his students:

"Class, I want you to imagine a moon that revolves around Planet X, which is located 195.3 thousand miles from it. The moon reflects light from the Sun and onto Planet X. The diameter of Planet X is 65,370 miles, and the diameter of the moon is 5,463 kilometres."

1 mile = 1,609 metres

Volume of sphere = $\frac{4}{3}\pi r^3$, $\pi = 3.14$

Q17.1 The speed of light is given as $3 \times 10^8 ms^{-1}$. How long does it take for the light reflected by the moon to reach Planet X?

A. 1,074s
B. 1.75 mins
C. 1.05s
D. 7.98 mins
E. 967s

Q17.2 Assuming the moon and Planet X are perfectly spherical, how many times larger is the volume of the planet compared to the moon?

A. 8,135
B. 6,786
C. 7,137
D. 10,905
E. 7,255

Q17.3 The speed of the orbit of Planet X around the Sun is 680 meters per second, and the orbit has a diameter of 944 million miles. How long does it take for the planet to complete one orbit, in years?

A. 14
B. 112
C. 222
D. 567
E. 813

Q17.4 If the orbit of the moon around Planet X is circular and one complete orbit occurs in four fifths of a year, what is the orbital speed in miles per hour?

A. 33
B. 207
C. 4,968
D. 10,796
E. 3.34×10^5

Question 18

Seven adults were selected to be part of a TV series weight loss programme "Weight No More". The programme runs over the summer for three months, and the participants are expected to reach a specific weight target by the end of the programme. Additional points are given to those who exceed their target appropriately.

The table below shows the height and weight measurements of the participants taken at the start of the programme.

Name of Participant	Height (m)	Starting Weight	Target Loss (%)
Draco	1.71	50st 1lb	24
Rubeus	1.91	234lb	30
Neville	1.77	317kg	20
Fleur	1.65	45st	22
Myrtle	1.60	202kg	8
Quirinus	1.80	60st	25
Dolores	1.78	52st 2lb	23

1 stone (st) = 6.35kg
1 pound (lb) = 2.20kg

Q18.1 Which participant has the median starting weight in the group?

A. Rubeus
B. Fleur
C. Dolores
D. Draco
E. Quirinus

Q18.2 At the end of the programme, Neville reaches his targeted weight. If Dolores has the same final weight as Neville, how many percent of additional weight did Dolores lose compared to her initial weight?

A. 1.2%
B. 3.4%
C. 4.5%
D. 24.2%
E. 31.9%

Q18.3 The Body Mass Index (BMI) of an individual is given as:

$$BMI = \frac{\text{Mass (kg)}}{\text{Height}^2\ (\text{m}^2)}$$

What is Rubeus' BMI at the end of the programme assuming that he only reaches two sevenths of his target?

A. 101
B. 45.8
C. 131
D. 246
E. 129

Q18.4 Which participant has the lowest starting BMI?

A. Dolores
B. Draco
C. Myrtle
D. Quirinus
E. Rubeus

Question 19

Shinji and his wife had opened a new bubble milk tea shop, Thirst-Tea, in Manchester a year ago. The shop opens from 0900 – 2200 hours on weekdays and 1000 – 1700 hours on weekends.

Q19.1 At any time during opening hours, two members of staff are required, except during peak times (1100 – 1300 hours and 1800 – 2100 hours) when four members of staff are required. What is the minimum total number of staff hours required to cover the shop for the week?

A. 4
B. 158
C. 180
D. 216
E. 243

Q19.2 Shinji replaces his bubble tea machine with a newer model to keep up with the speed of his business. The old machine measured the milk tea in millilitres, but the new machine measures the milk tea in ounces. There are 28.4 millilitres in an ounce. A standard sized cup contained 500ml of bubble tea. How much is this in ounces (oz)?

A. 17.6oz
B. 20.2oz
C. 1.8oz
D. 24.8oz
E. 16.0oz

Q19.3 To optimise the use of resources, Shinji decides to calculate how many cups can be made from each 1.5kg bag of tapioca pearls from his supplier. The pearls gain approximately 12.5% of weight during roasting. Each cup requires 25g of roasted pearls. How many cups of bubble milk tea can be made from each bag of pearls?

A. 54.5
B. 720
C. 67.5
D. 150
E. 750

Q19.4 Thirst-Tea has a loyalty card scheme in place for customers. Customers receive eight loyalty points on their card for every pound spent in a single purchase. At any time, a customer can redeem a 10p discount in exchange for five points. (N.B. If a customer with 16 points makes a redemption, he/she can only redeem 30p, and one point will remain on the card.) Ji-hye usually buys a cup of milk tea for herself on the way home from work. If each cup is £3.20, how many purchases would Ji-hye need to make to be able to redeem a free cup for herself?

A. 5
B. 6
C. 7
D. 9
E. 12

Question 20

Q20.1 The area of a square field, Field X, is given by 4,900m². Its length is increased by 20m whilst its width is decreased by 20m to give Field Y. Which of the statements below is true?

A. Area X = Area Y; Perimeter X < Perimeter Y
B. Area X < Area Y; Perimeter X = Perimeter Y
C. Area X < Area Y; Perimeter X > Perimeter Y
D. Area X > Area Y; Perimeter X = Perimeter Y
E. Area X = Area Y; Perimeter X > Perimeter Y

Q20.2 A wealthy businessman wants to buy a piece of square land to build a mansion. He wants the length of each side of his plot to be 100m long. He does his research and summarises his findings below:

"Red land is £5,400 per acre. Yellow land is £50,000 per m^2. Green land is £1.2 million per hectare. Blue land is £450k per acre. Each land is adjacent to two other lands such that they are arranged in a 2 by 2 order. I want one third of my plot to be on the Blue land and the rest of it on the Green land."

1 hectare = 10,000m^2 = 2.47 acres

Which of the amounts below is closest in value to the cost of buying the land he wants?

A. £170k
B. £4.51M
C. £1.21M
D. £1.17M
E. £2.35M

Q20.3 A marathon runner normally runs six rounds around his neighbourhood. His personal best is to complete this run in 3 hours and 4.3 minutes.

Round 1	Round 2	Round 3	Round 4	Round 5
24mins 33s	34mins 5s	29mins 42s	28mins 53s	39mins 21s

How much shorter does his sixth round have to be compared to his fifth round if he wants to meet his best record?

A. 11mins 27s
B. 11.7mins
C. 0.19hrs
D. 667s
E. 697s

Q20.4 In Chelsea's photo gallery on her phone, 1,789 pictures are from her trip to Italy. This takes up approximately 12% of her photos. What is the approximate size of her photo album, in GB, if the average picture takes up 3MB?

1MB = 1,000,000B = 0.001GB

A. 47.0
B. 44,725
C. 44.7
D. 0.64
E. 64,230

Question 21

Papoutsia is a UK-based shoe factory that deals with clients both locally and internationally. It is known to make all types of shoes, such as sport shoes, walking shoes and boots. For local orders within the UK, the shipping cost is at a flat rate of £10, irrespective of the order size. Express local delivery would cost an added 25% charge. For international orders, the shipping rates vary depending on which continent the country is in and the size of the order. The shipping costs for the respective continents and the order sizes are shown in the first table below. Order sizes of above a thousand units have their shipping fee waived off. Papoutsia also offers an express service for delivery (i.e. order arrives within three working days) at a extra cost of £55, regardless of the order size.

The prices for the shoes (per unit) also vary depending on the order size. The second table below lists the prices for the different zones and order sizes. The prices of the shoes do not vary based on size, colour or model. Clients can opt to have customised embroidery on their shoes for a fee of £10 per side of shoe, regardless of the size of the print.

	Shipping Cost for International Orders (£)		
Continents	≤ 200 units	201 ≤ units ≤ 500	501 ≤ units ≤ 1000
Europe	12	10	7
Asia	16	13	9
Africa	20	17	12
America	25	18	14
Australia	30	24	16

Order Size	Price Per Unit (£)
≤ 200	15
201 - 500	12
501 - 1000	10
> 1000	8

Q21.1 An American dancing school is going to send a few of its best groups for the Annual World Dance Competition in South Korea in five days time. The school had ordered 40 pairs of each colour of red, neon yellow, grey, black and white from a local factory. However, the order was rejected at short notice and, while searching for an alternative, they came across Papoutsia online. They added two more pairs of black shoes to their previous order and opted for the express delivery service from Papoutsia. How much does the school have to pay for this?

A. £3,709
B. £3,691
C. £2,479
D. £6,115
E. £2,497

Q21.2 "Smash", one of the largest badminton academies in Europe, wants to order shoes for 60 coaches and 600 students. A total of 40 coaches and 40% of the students want to have their names embroidered on their shoes. To standardise it, first names will be embroidered on the left shoe and surnames will be embroidered on the right shoe. The academy places the order for coaches and students separately, and it opts for the standard delivery for both orders. Calculate how much Papoutsia will charge in total.

A. £9,407
B. £12,219
C. £8,970
D. £9,419
E. £10,520

Q21.3 During the Christmas season, Papoutsia offered 6% off the total price if full payment is made within two days. Excited by the offer, a performing arts academy in London quickly places an order, as follows, and opts for express delivery so that the shoes arrive in time for their Christmas Arts Festival.

Order: 184 pairs for the Opera section. 302 pairs for the Drama section. 253 pairs shoes for the Orchestra section. 271 pairs for the Spoken Words section. All shoes must be black in colour and the academy's logo must be embroidered on the right-sided shoe.

Calculate how much money, to the nearest pound, the academy has to have ready if it wants to make an immediate full payment.

A. £17,089
B. £17,101
C. £18,193
D. £17,402
E. £18,923

Q21.4 A school's alumni goes on an overseas expedition trip to the peak of Matterhorn Mountain, Switzerland to celebrate the school's bicentenary establishment. The group places two different orders, both with standard delivery, on Papoutsia. The group receives two invoices, which makes a total of £5,298. The group cannot retrieve the detailed information of the order. Fortunately, the person-in-charge who placed the order can recall some of the information as follows.

First Order: 80 sized-10 pairs of shoes with one-sided embroidery and 15 sized -11 shoes without embroidery.

Second Order: £17 delivery charge and an unknown number of shoes without embroidery.

Find out how many pairs of shoes without embroidery were ordered.

A. 253
B. 252
C. 269
D. 254
E. 268

Question 22

The table below shows the nutritional information for different flavours of Welsh cakes.

Nutritional information	**Lemon Poppy**	**Cherry Almond**	**Maple Syrup**	**Bailey's**	**RDA***
Weight per packet (g)	55	120	90	75	-
Nutritional information given per 100g					
Energy (kcal)	601	575	831	676	2,000
Protein (g)	6.2	8.5	5.9	7.3	45
Carbohydrates (g) *(of which sugars)*	53 15	46 12	78 21	44 14	235 92
Fat (g) *(of which saturates)*	40 2.6	32 1.4	56 3.0	45 4.3	75 25
Fibre (g)	3	2	1	2	27
Salt (g)	1.1	0.5	0.7	1.2	2.7
*RDA - Recommended daily allowance					

Q22.1 Approximately what percentage of the RDA of salt will an individual consume if he/she eats three packets of maple syrup cakes?

A. 35%
B. 56%
C. 70%
D. 81%
E. 83%

Q22.2 Approximately how much energy (kcal) would the consumption of three packets of lemon poppy cakes and two packets of Bailey's cakes produce?

A. 1,967
B. 2,006
C. 2,038
D. 2,650
E. 3,178

Q22.3 How much fat, in grams, to the nearest whole number, would the consumption of half a packet of cherry almond cakes provide?

A. 19.2
B. 23.4
C. 27.6
D. 38.4
E. 55.2

Q22.4 By how many percent would an individual have missed his/her RDA of fibre (g) if he/she consumes eight packets of maple syrup cakes?

A. 26.7%
B. 34.5%
C. 55.6%
D. 73.3%
E. 96.7%

Q22.5 By how many percent would an individual have exceeded his/her RDA of salt (g) if he/she consumes 14.5 packets of lemon poppy cakes?

A. 23%
B. 165%
C. 225%
D. 270%
E. 320%

Question 23

The table below shows the number of different species of animals in different zoos in the Western region.

Animal	Quintal	Tuin	Jardins	Parque	Garten
Lion	36	40	3	56	245
Rhinoceros	45	242	7	84	421
Elephant	121	234	75	78	550
Gorilla	135	52	10	44	156
Other	80	115	32	24	110

Q23.1 What percentage of all animals in the Western region is in Parque Zoo?

A. 4.3%
B. 9.5%
C. 12.5%
D. 12.9%
E. 22.8%

Q23.2 If the number of gorillas in Tuin Zoo increased by 34%, what percentage of animals in the zoo would be lions?

A. 4%
B. 6%
C. 9%
D. 10%
E. 11%

Q23.3 If the number of elephants in Garten was reduced by 68%, what would the approximate ratio of elephants in Garten to animals in Garten in the 'Other' category be?

A. 17:5
B. 4:9
C. 8:5
D. 7:3
E. 7:10

Q23.4 If Jardin Zoo increases its number of rhinoceros by 225%, by what percentage would it have to reduce its current count of elephants in order to maintain the same total number of animals in the zoo?

A. 9%
B. 12%
C. 21%
D. 31%
E. 33%

Question 24

The table below shows the numbers of medals won by eight sports houses in their annual Inter-House Games. The houses are arranged in the order of number of gold medals won.

	Gold	Silver	Bronze
Hamilton	132	91	62
Wu Lien Teh	100	50	70
Hargreaves	88	55	50
Cheeseman	34	23	44
Pinhorn	22	24	26
Sirajuddin	20	12	35
Tunku Putra	17	19	35
P. Ramlee	15	22	36

The Parent-Teacher Association (PTA) offered to donate the funds below to the houses for their achievements:

- For each gold medal won, the house will receive £20.
- For each silver medal won, the house will receive £10.
- For each bronze medal won, the house will receive £5.
- The house whose athlete won the 'Sportsman of the Year Award' will receive £200.

Q24.1 What percentage of all the gold medals in the event was won by Cheeseman?

A. 7.1%
B. 7.9%
C. 8.1%
D. 8.9%
E. 10.0%

Q24.2 Hamilton decided to donate 50% of its raised funds to the house that made the least money from the games. If the houses were to be arranged by amount of funds raised, what would be the position of the house after receiving Hamilton's donation?

A. 1st
B. 2nd
C. 3rd
D. Tied 3rd
E. 4th

Q24.3 The PTA special award went to a student who is from P. Ramlee. What is the percentage increase in the total funds raised by P. Ramlee?

A. 6.8%
B. 23.0%
C. 26.8%
D. 28.6%
E. 45.5%

Q24.4 A student claims that 60% of the gold medals won by Hamilton, Wu Lien Teh and Hargreaves combined were won by national-level athletes who just so happened to be placed in those sport houses. Wu Lien Teh's captain claimed that only 25% of its gold medals were won by those athletes, whereas Hargreave's captain claimed only 40% for the same statement. Assuming that all their claims are true, what is the estimate for the percentage of Hamilton's gold medals won by national athletes?

A. 44%
B. 71%
C. 96%
D. 100%
E. The claim cannot be true

Question 25

It is understood in clinical practice that:

- 1% means 1g in 100ml for weight/volume (w/v) calculations or 1g in 100g for weight/weight (w/w) calculations.
- 1 in 1,000 means 1g in 1,000ml.

Q25.1 A nurse is about to use a 1% Lidocaine solution to locally anaesthetise an area on the buttock for the excision of a cyst. How many mg are in 2ml of a 1% Lidocaine solution?

A. 200
B. 20
C. 2
D. 0.2
E. 0.02

Q25.2 In patients who experience nausea and vomiting acutely, it might be necessary to administer histamine H1-receptor antagonist, Drug X, by the IV route. The IV preparation contains 250 micrograms per millilitre. What is this value expressed as a percentage?

A. 250
B. 25
C. 0.25
D. 0.025
E. 0.0025

Q25.3 A patient has accidentally eaten some nuts, and this has caused an allergic reaction. He is immediately given an intramuscular injection of 0.5mg of Adrenaline 1 in 1,000 to treat his suspected anaphylaxis. What volume of the solution was given to him?

A. 0.5l
B. 0.5μl
C. 0.5ml
D. 5ml
E. 5μl

Q25.4 A patient is prescribed the antispasmodic Mebeverine to alleviate symptoms of irritable bowel syndrome. The medication is supplied as a liquid containing 50mg/5ml. Sufficient Mebeverine is dispensed to provide a 100mg dose twice daily for four weeks. What is the total volume, in litres, of Mebeverine required?

A. 560
B. 80
C. 280
D. 0.08
E. 0.56

Question 26

Two years ago, Krisada started his own durian trading business, named Kris', and he has successfully expanded his business into a franchise with stores all over the UK. He imports a variety of durians from Southeast Asian countries, such as Thailand, Indonesia and Malaysia, and sells them at the prices shown below. His business has a '20 for 20 deal' where customers get a 20% discount if an order for any particular product is over 20kg.

Customers can simply purchase the durians as a whole fruit on their own. However, customers can also opt for a service to have the durian flesh removed from the skin and packed into a container. This service costs £3 per fruit, regardless of its weight and species.

Delivery is available and costs 10% of the order. Minimum order for delivery is £20.

The table below shows the trading price per unit mass of the different durian species. These rates are for the whole fruit and not just the flesh.

Type of Durian	Buying Price per kg (£)	Selling Price per kg (£)
D2	7.00	9.99
D24	9.00	12.99
D88	6.50	8.99
D101	8.00	10.99
Musang King	12.00	15.99

Q26.1 Ellie hosts a 'fruits and scones' party in her house. On the morning, she places an order with Kris' for 30kg of D24, 45kg of D2, 50kg of D88, and 12kg of Musang King. She schedules for the fruits to be delivered, in containers, at 4:45 pm on the same day. How much does Ellie have to pay, in total, if a total of 36 durians were used to prepare her order?

A. £1,278.20
B. £1,588.63
C. £1,747.49
D. £1,330.88
E. £1,463.97

Q26.2 Hann wants to sell durian products (i.e. durian fruit, durian milkshake, and durian ice cream) at a regional cultural festival. He makes a list and plans to have 300kg of D2, 360kg of D24, 300kg of D88, 270kg of D101, and 100kg of Musang King.

He emails his list to Kris' and says that he wants to have two thirds of each durian species on the list, except the Musang King, packed in containers. These containers will be collected by himself on the day of the event. He would like the rest to be delivered to his school. If the grand total of his order costs him £14,073.95, how many durians were used for his collection order?

A. 489
B. 547
C. 454
D. 530
E. 521

Q26.3 Kris' normally gets its D2 and D24 durians from Indonesia because of their quality and reasonable price. However, due to the recent bad weather, the majority of the yield was affected. Kris' made a decision to get those species of durian from Malaysia instead, which so happens to charge a price that is 15% higher than Indonesia. As this was a temporary problem, Kris' decided to maintain its selling price. A customer orders 50kg each of all the durians in the D species. The customer did not opt for any extra services. Calculate the profit (+) or loss (-) that Kris' will make from this purchase.

A. -£35.35
B. +£394.25
C. -£17.35
D. +£193.40
E. -£27.65

Q26.4 On Monday morning, an old lady buys the D24, D88 and D101 for her grandchildren. None of the products of her purchase qualify for the '20 for 20 deal' discount, but she remembers that Kris' did give some discount as it was celebrating its anniversary that whole week. She went back the next day to enjoy the same discount. She realises that the discount does not apply to the D24 durian.

On Thursday, her neighbour asks her about the discount. The lady recalls buying 10kg of D101, 15kg of D88, and 10kg of D24 on Monday and was charged £335.25. On Tuesday, she bought 15kg of D101, 20kg of D88, and 10kg of D24 and was charged £418.50. She has misplaced both receipts and now wants to know how much she paid, per kg, for the D88 and D101. She did not opt for any extra services on either occasion. Calculate the price, per kg, in pounds, for those two durian species.

A. £6.99; £8.99
B. £7.50; £9.50
C. £7.99; £9.99
D. £7.77; £8.88
E. £6.75; £9.00

Question 27

Yinxien is baking a cake for a friend's birthday. The recipe lists ingredients in ounces (oz) but her local supermarket, where she buys the ingredients, sells products by the kilogram (kg). 1 gram is equivalent to 0.04 ounces (oz). The list of ingredients is:

- 10.4 ounces of butter
- 12.6 ounces of sugar
- 3 eggs
- 11.0 ounces of flour

The prices of the ingredients at her local supermarket are:

- Butter: £3.50 for 0.5 kg
- Sugar: £4.55 for 3 kg
- Eggs: £1.80 for a packet of 6 eggs
- Flour: £3.80 for 1 kg

Q27.1 How much is the cost of one cake?

A. £3.71
B. £4.25
C. £5.24
D. £6.75
E. £13.65

Q27.2 Yinxien is making more than one cake and buys 1.65kg of flour, which is the exact amount she needs. How much sugar does she need?

A. 1.98kg
B. 0.81kg
C. 1.67kg
D. 1.89kg
E. 2.11kg

Q27.3 Yinxien has £40.00. What is the maximum number of cakes she can make?

A. 7
B. 8
C. 9
D. 10
E. 11

Q27.4 When Yinxien visits the supermarket, she finds that the price of butter has increased by 25% and the price of sugar has decreased such that it is now seven eighths of its previous price. What is the difference between the new cost of each cake compared to its original cost?

A. -4p
B. +4p
C. +£2.22
D. +40p
E. +£1.18

Question 28

Rachel is a fresh graduate who takes the same modes of public transport to and from her legal firm. Every morning, she takes the nearest underground, which is a five-minute walk from her place, to arrive at a ferry terminal to catch a ferry, before walking seven minutes to a central station to catch a bus. The bus stops at a station that is a two-minute walk from her firm. Rachel's boss is strict on having her employees arrive by 8:30 am each day.

Underground	Ferry
7:13 - 7:25	7:17 - 7:32
7:19 - 7:31	7:30 - 7:45
7:29 - 7:41	7:45 - 8:00
7:35 - 7:47	7:51 - 8:06
7:44 - 7:56	8:00 - 8:15
7:56 - 8:08	8:07 - 8:22
8:14 - 8:26	8:12 - 8:27

- Underground costs £2.40 per journey.
- Ferry costs £1.50 per journey.
- Bus costs 60p per journey.
- The fares are the same for weekdays and weekends.
- The bus starts operating from 6:09 am and frequents every 10 minutes. Rachel's bus journey from central station to her stop is usually eight minutes.

Q28.1 What is the shortest travelling time possible for Rachel to arrive at her workplace?

A. 52mins
B. 54mins
C. 55mins
D. 59mins
E. 1hr

Q28.2 One day, Rachel was scheduled to have an important interview, and she decided to take the taxi to the ferry departure terminal instead of the underground. She knows that it will take her 13 minutes to arrive at the terminal. What is the latest time she should leave her house in order to still arrive at the office five minutes early?

A. 7:23 am
B. 7:32 am
C. 8:12 am
D. 7:45 am
E. 7:52 am

Q28.3 Rachel goes to work five days a week for 40 weeks a year. On every other week, she has to go to work on a Saturday as well. Rachel is currently deciding if she should invest in an unlimited annual travel pass (valid for all modes of transport). It is available to purchase for £1,250. What is the percentage increase (+) or decrease (-) between purchasing an annual travel pass compared to paying for each journey individually?

A. +26.3%
B. +58.4%
C. -20.8%
D. -36.9%
E. +14.5%

Q28.4 Rachel saves up enough money and decides to drive to work, which is 27km away. As she is new to driving, she often travels at an average speed of 20m/s. However, she knows that the traffic normally increases her journey time by approximately 24 minutes. If it takes her five minutes to park her car before arriving in person at the firm, approximately what is the latest time Rachel should leave her house for work?

A. 7:38 am
B. 7:23 am
C. 7:43 am
D. 6:59 am
E. 7:11 am

Question 29

Caitlin runs a strawberry farm as her part-time job. The farm produces an average of 600kg of strawberries each day. She sells her strawberries in a morning market at £2.35 per kilo. Over the years, she has been able to expand her strawberry business. She learns that every 1kg of strawberries produces 100g of strawberry extract. 1kg of strawberry ice cream has 12% of extract. She sells the ice cream at £4.00 for a 1kg tub.

Q29.1 Caitlin receives an order from a friend to provide 400kg of ice cream for a local food festival. What amount of strawberries, in kg, would be used to prepare this amount of ice cream?

A. 4,000
B. 480
C. 400
D. 48
E. 40

Q29.2 Over the course of a year, Caitlin expands the land of her farm such that her produce increases by 40%. How much more extract, in kg, is Caitlin able to produce in the month of January?

A. 744
B. 84
C. 24
D. 2,604
E. 7,440

Q29.3 On Christmas day, Caitlin decides to sell 300kg of strawberries and some ice cream made from an equal weight of strawberries. How much more does she make from the ice cream compared to the strawberries alone, as a percentage? Assume the cost of making the ice cream is negligible.

A. 141%
B. 104%
C. 70.2%
D. 29.5%
E. 14.6%

Q29.4 Caitlin decides to produce strawberry jam containing 57% of extract. She sells the jam in jars of 454g. The cost of processing each jar of jam until its final product is 65p. If each jar is sold at 140% of the cost price. How much profit does she make from every kg of strawberries?

A. £3.48
B. 87p
C. 96p
D. 91p
E. £1.00

Question 30

Q30.1 Snow Blanket is a company that supplies duvets to retailers. The manager estimated that the cost C, in pounds, of producing n hearing aids is $C = 5n + 810$. Each duvet is sold at the price of £14. The manager did some calculations and found that a profit is made when the total income from selling a quantity of duvets is greater than the production cost for that quantity of items. Which of the following inequalities gives all possible vales of n for which a profit will be made?

A. $n > 70$
B. $n > 90$
C. $n < 70$
D. $n < 90$
E. Can't tell

Q30.2 Coin A and Coin B are in non-overlapping contact. Coin A's radius is four times smaller than the radius of Coin B. Coin A rolls around Coin B once and returns to its original position. How many times will Coin A revolve till it reaches its initial position? Diameter of a circle = $2\pi r$; area of a circle = πr^2; $\pi = 3.14$.

A. 6
B. 5.5
C. 5
D. 4.5
E. 4

Q30.3 The expression $\frac{1}{(7x-1)}$ is written to be equivalent to $\frac{49x^2}{(7x-1)}$ - P. What is P expressed in terms of x?

A. $7x - 1$
B. $7x + 1$
C. $49x^2$
D. $49x^2 - 1$
E. $x^2 - 1$

Q30.4 A man buys his wife a pair of hexagonal shaped earrings with a circular hole in the centre. All the sides of the hexagon are 2cm long, and the diameter of the hole is also 2cm. If the earrings were to be fully coated with gold, what would be the total surface area covered by gold, in cm^2, to the nearest whole number? The thickness of the earrings is negligible.

A. $6\sqrt{3}$
B. $6\sqrt{3} - 2\pi$
C. $12\sqrt{3} - \pi$
D. $12\sqrt{3} - 2\pi$
E. $12\sqrt{3} - 4\pi$

Question 31

The diagram below shows the model drawing of a swimming pool. It is 20cm long, 10cm wide and 0.1cm deep. (The diagram is not drawn to scale.)

Note: Do not relate any of the sub-questions to each other.

Q31.1 The real dimensions of the pool are measured, and it is found that its length is 50m. What is the scale used on the drawing?

A. 1:200
B. 1:250
C. 1:500
D. 1:1000
E. 1:2000

Q31.2 An architect wants to modify the pool such that the base of the pool is inclined so that there will be an area that is safe for children to swim. If one side of the pool's length is made to be one fifth of the other side, what is the reduction in volume of the pool's total capacity?

A. 1,000m^3
B. 1,250m^3
C. 1,750m^3
D. 2,000m^3
E. 2,500m^3

Q31.3 If the pool was made to be in the shape of a cube but with the same surface area, how will the perimeter of the pool change?

A. Lesser
B. Greater
C. Equal
D. Can't tell

Q31.4 An architect intends to extend the length of the pool by 5% of its initial length. What is the increase in the perimeter of the pool?

A. 2.5m
B. 10m
C. 52.5m
D. 210m
E. 320m

Question 32

Zen purchased his favourite vanilla hazelnut pillows, Vanillow, from his local food store. The nutritional facts on the box state that a serving of the cereal is two thirds of a 500ml cup and provides 240 calories, 60 of which are calories from fat. Furthermore, each serving of the cereal provides 210 milligrams of potassium, which is 5% of the recommended daily intake for adults.

Q32.1 What is the recommended daily intake of potassium, in g, for an average teenager if his/her recommended value is 40% less than that of an adult?

A. 1680
B. 1.68
C. 2.52
D. 4.2
E. 6.3

Q32.3 Zen normally prepares himself a bowl of cereal as supper if he stays up late to complete his work. However, his supper cereal is a mix of Vanillow and Choconut. Choconut provides 280 calories per cup. If the total calories in one full cup of the Vanillow and Choconut mixture is 310, what proportion of the mixture is Chocout?

A. 3/7
B. 4/7
C. 3/8
D. 3/4
E. 5/8

Q32.2 If m servings of a cereal named Bananana provides n grams of potassium, which is 6% of an adult's recommended daily potassium intake, which of the following expresses n in terms of m for this cereal?

A. 6m
B. 0.06m
C. 0.252m
D. 2.52m
E. 252m

Q32.4 The fat content in Carameltz cereal contributes to half of the calories it provides in one third of a cup. Carameltz cereal box states that the recommended serving is three fourths of the same 500ml cup as Vanillow. If a serving of Carameltz were to the provide the same calories as two full cups of Vanillow, what would the fat content in Carameltz be, in calories?

A. 160
B. 320
C. 480
D. 640
E. 960

Question 33

The diagram below shows the difference in the energy usage in a private school in years 2000 and 2010.

2010

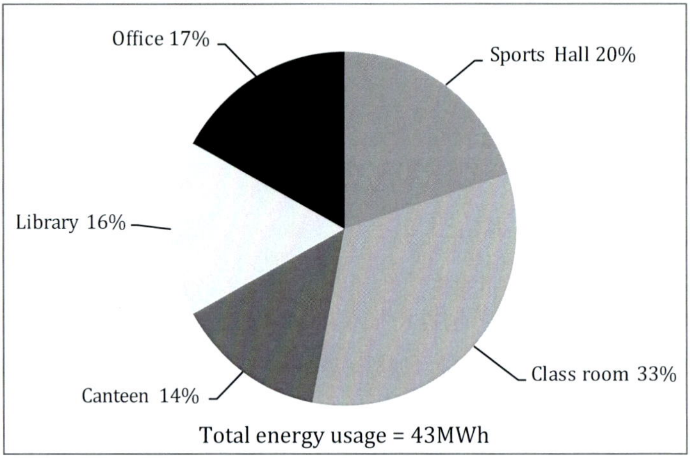

2000

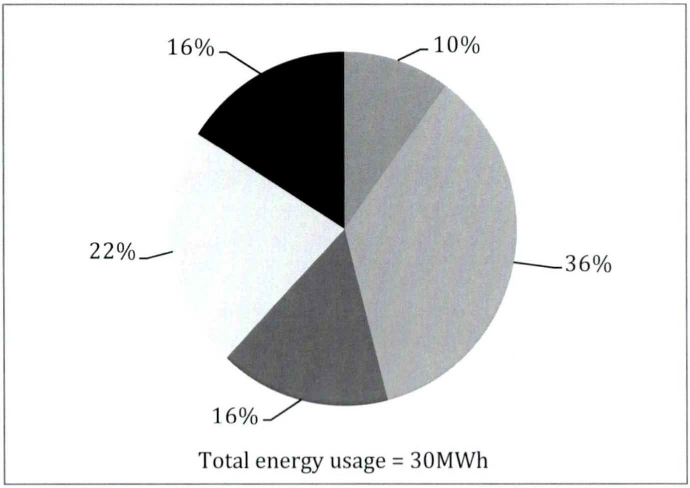

Q33.1 What is the change in the total energy used, in MWh, for the classroom, canteen and sports hall between 2000 and 2010?

A. -10.21
B. +4.18
C. +8.41
D. +10.21
E. -4.18

Q33.2 Which space had the smallest change in energy consumption between the two years?

A. Library
B. Classroom
C. Canteen
D. Office
E. Sports Hall

Q33.3 The school has expanded over the years, allowing for a greater intake of students. If the number of classrooms has increased such that the amount of energy consumed by classrooms has increased by 7.5% compared to 2010, what is the increase in the energy usage when compared to 2000?

A. 5.4MWh
B. 7.3MWh
C. 4.5MWh
D. 14.0MWh
E. 6.7MWh

Q33.4 In 2010, the school aimed to reduce the overall energy consumption by 16% in the next 10 years by encouraging students and staff to switch off the lights when a space is not in use. Assuming that this was achieved only in classrooms and all other spaces were to have the same energy consumption in 2020 as in 2010, what percentage of a pie chart would classrooms consume?

A. 13.1%
B. 41.3%
C. 27.7%
D. 35.6%
E. 29.2%

Question 34

The diagram and the table below shows the distances between 10 towns, labelled in Roman numerals. These are the only routes of which any form of travel is possible. (The diagram is not drawn to scale.)

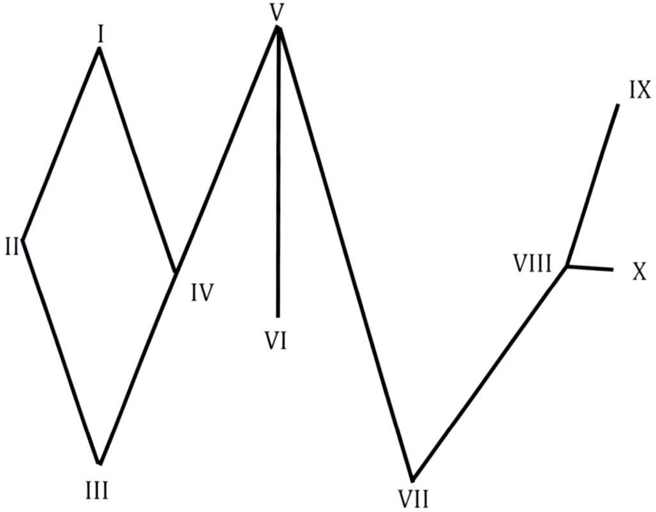

Route	Distance (km)	Route	Distance (km)
I - II	5	V - VI	9
II - III	6	V - VII	15.5
III - IV	5	VII - VIII	7
I - IV	6	VIII - IX	4.5
IV - V	7.5	VIII - X	1

Q34.1 Rhys lives in town IV. He rides his bike at approximately 20.6 miles per hour and arrives at his destination 20 minutes later. There is 1.6 kilometres in a mile. What is his most likely destination?

A. Town I
B. Town II
C. Town III
D. Town VI
E. Town VII

Q34.2 Caius takes 45 minutes to travel from his house, in town VI, to town IV to pick up his friend, Cathleen. From there, they want to watch a movie at a cinema that is in town IX. Assuming that he takes 1 hour 10 minutes to travel from Cathleen's house to the cinema, what is the ratio of his average speed in this journey compared to his previous journey (VI - IV)?

A. 1.3:1
B. 0.7:1
C. 1.4:1
D. 2.6:1
E. 1:1.3

Q34.3 Shi Hui resides in town VI but works in town III. On a Friday, she clocks out of work at 5:15 pm to drive herself straight to the airport, located in town IX, to catch a flight that departs at 7:15 pm. She suddenly realises that she has left her passport at home and she is aware that the check-in counter strictly closes an hour before take-off. If she normally takes 45 minutes to get to the airport from her workplace, what is the percentage increase in her average driving speed if she wants to arrive at the airport ten minutes before the check -in counter closes?

A. 10%
B. 31%
C. 44%
D. 9%
E. 14%

Q34.4 Every year, a marathon challenge named 'Survival of the Fittest' is organised. The participants have to visit all the 10 towns during the run and return to the starting point at the end of the marathon. The starting points rotate among the towns each year. Which town would host the marathon with the longest route?

A. Town II
B. Town V
C. Town VIII
D. Town VI
E. All are the same

Question 35

Q35.1 Octavius is a 63-year-old patient who weighs 80kg. He is given 4ml of Furosemide 50mg in 5ml solution intravenously. What dose, in milligrams, of Furosemide was he given?

A. 40
B. 32
C. 50
D. 20
E. 4

Q35.2 Jacques, who is a newborn, weighs 2.85kg and requires a daily maintenance dose of Digoxin of 0.025g intravenously. The drug is available as 500mg/2ml ampoules. What volume would give in microlitres (μl)?

A. 0.001
B. 0.1
C. 1
D. 10
E. 100

Q35.3 Perla, a 48kg 67-year-old patient, has a swollen right calf. A doctor carries out some investigations and reports the findings as below:

- D-dimer: positive
- Well's score: 7
- Serum creatinine: 64 mol/l (creatinine clearance >30ml/min)

The doctor decides a treatment plan to give the patient Enoxaparin (LMW Heparin) at a dose of 1.5mg/kg. What dose, in g, is given to her?

A. 0.1
B. 0.072
C. 96
D. 72
E. 101

Q35.4 Luke is a neurosurgical patient who is prescribed Phenytoin capsules 300mg daily. A few days after his operation, he complains of difficulty swallowing the capsules. The nurse asks the FY1 doctor if she can prescribe him the liquid form of the drug instead. The doctor knows that the liquid form contains Phenytoin base rather than the sodium salt of Phenytoin as in capsules. This means that the therapeutic effect of 100mg of the capsule form has approximately the same therapeutic effect as 92mg of the liquid form. What dose of liquid Phenytoin should the doctor prescribe?

A. 326mg
B. 362mg
C. 267mg
D. 276mg
E. 306mg

Question 36

The table below shows the cost of renting certain types of boats from a jetty. The table, however, is incomplete.

Type	Deposit (£)	Rate Per Hour (£)
Canoe	100	75
Dinghy	180	145
Sailboat	-	190
Motorboat	250	-
Catamaran	330	400
Yacht	-	-

- Every rent requires the payment of a non-refundable deposit fee.
- Customers renting the canoe, dinghy or sailboat have the option to hire a staff member to manoeuvre the boat for them. It costs £50 per hour to hire a member of staff.
- All rents for the motorboat, catamaran and yacht are inclusive of a staff member who will manoeuvre the boat.
- All figures shown in the table, including the omitted ones, will effectively increase by 15% starting the 1st of March 2020.
- However, there will be no changes to the fee to hire a member of staff for the canoe, dinghy and sailboat.

Q36.1 A couple celebrated the first day of 2020 by going on a sailboat ride for five hours. They did not opt for a member of staff. They split the cost evenly, and each had to pay £585. How much is the deposit of the sailboat?

A. £150
B. £180
C. £220
D. £420
E. £445

Q36.2 Haziq went on a solo getaway during Christmas in 2019 and decided to sit on the motorboat ride for an hour. He enjoyed the staff on-board service but felt that the trip ended too quickly. He returns two months later and decides to go for the cheapest boat option. He still wants the staff service. This time, his trip lasts for four hours, and he still pays the same price as before. How much is the rate per hour for a motorboat?

A. £150
B. £250
C. £300
D. £360
E. £420

Q36.3 Alex and Alexa rent a canoe for an hour on the 23rd of February 2020. They returned exactly a week later for a two-hour trip and decided to have a staff on board to navigate the canoe this time. By how much does their total cost increase on the second trip?

A. £162.50
B. £277.50
C. £262.50
D. £212.50
E. £220

Q36.4 Daliah and her family once rented the yacht for five hours and had to pay £2,545, whilst Adeola and her family rented the same yacht for three hours and had to pay £1,695. Both rents occurred in January 2020. How much more expensive, as a percentage, is the deposit of the yacht compared to the catamaran?

A. 6.8%
B. 16.2%
C. 21.4%
D. 27.3%
E. 150%

Question 37

Tokyo, Japan			
8,915	**Berlin, Germany**		
18,570	10,013	**Rio, Brazil**	
7,583	7,726	12,933	**Male, Maldives**

- The local time in Male is four hours behind Tokyo.
- The local time in Berlin is four hours ahead of Rio.
- The local time in Rio is 12 hours behind Tokyo.

All figures shown in the diagram above are in kilometres.

Q37.1 Ricardo flies from Tokyo to Berlin. The plane was said to have flown over Male instead of taking a direct route. What is the percentage increase in his duration of flight if the plane has travelled at its usual speed?

A. 73.2%
B. 82.8%
C. 81.1%
D. 71.7%
E. 86.8%

Q37.2 Xavier flies directly from Tokyo to Male. He notices that the airplane flies at an average speed of 550 mph (1 mile = 1.6 km). What is his time of arrival in Male if his plane departs Tokyo at 1315 hours?

A. 1815
B. 1752
C. 2034
D. 2125
E. 0152 (+1)

Q37.3 Shanice regularly flies directly between Berlin and Rio. The duration of the flight used to be 18 hours, but it has now reduced by 13%. The increase in the average speed of flight is:

A. 83km/h
B. 85km/h
C. 74km/h
D. 137km/h
E. 69km/h

Q37.4 Elsa and Anna depart from Male at 1745 hours, and they fly to Tokyo and Rio, respectively. If both airplanes were to fly at the same average speed of 400 mph, what is the earliest time possible, in Rio time, for them to contact each other? Assume that getting in contact during flights is not possible.

A. 0805 (+1)
B. 1357 (+1)
C. 0157 (+1)
D. 1805 (+2)
E. 0557 (+1)

Question 38

The table below shows the price of papers and their respective sizes and types sold in a printing company.

Size	Width x Height (mm)	Uncoated Paper (£)	Matt Coated Paper (£)	Bond Paper (£)
A4	210 x 297	0.50	2.50	4.00
A3	297 x 420	1.20	4.00	7.00
A2	420 x 594	2.00	9.00	13.50
A1	594 x 841	3.00	15.00	20.00
A0	841 x 1189	4.50	22.50	30.00

- The paper cutting and stapling services are free of charge.
- The prices shown above are for one-sided print.
- Two-sided print is only available for uncoated papers.
- The price for a two-sided print is 1.5 times the price of a one-sided print. (e.g., two-sided print on A1 is 3.00 x 1.5 = £4.50.)
- 1 inch = 25.4mm

Q38.1 Eren wants to work out the size of an A8 paper. From the table given, what would be the best estimate of the size of an A8 paper, in inches?

A. 1.5 x 2.0
B. 2.0 x 2.9
C. 25 x 37
D. 37 x 52
E. Can't tell

Q38.2 Jared prints two A2 matt coated papers and an A1 uncoated paper for a project, whilst his friend, Chris, prints an A0 bond paper and 25 A4 uncoated papers for a bake sale. How much more does Chris spend than Jared?

A. £11.50
B. £17.00
C. £18.50
D. £21.50
E. £24.20

Q38.3 Angharad wants to print a few A4 posters on matt coated paper. She's deciding between printing them individually and arranging many copies on an A0 paper and then using the cutting service to get A4-sized posters. Assuming that the number of A4-sized copies she needs perfectly fits a full A0 paper, using the second method above (i.e. print on A0) will be equivalent to getting an approximate discount off the first method by how much?

A. 44%
B. 47%
C. 58%
D. 78%
E. Can't tell

Q38.4 George wants to print booklets for a door gift for a musical he is organising. The specifications of the booklet are as follows:

- Double-sided print
- 8 pages (including front and back cover)
- Stapled at the centre as a 'backbone' to secure the pages
- Each page must be A4-sized

With a budget of £600, what is the maximum number of booklets he can print if his order only deals with a particular size of paper?

A. 41
B. 83
C. 100
D. 176
E. 200

Question 39

The table below shows the changes in carbon dioxide emissions from Factory X from 2010 to 2019.

Year	Carbon Dioxide Emissions (tonnes)
2010	577.9
2011	464.1
2012	372.7
2013	299.3
2014	240.4
2015	193.0
2016	155.0
2017	124.5
2018	100.0
2019	80.3

From 2015 onwards, the factory had installed a filter that reduces the amount of carbon dioxide emitted by 15%.

1 tonne of carbon dioxide contains 556m^3.

Q39.1 What is the average amount of carbon dioxide produced by the factory per year, in m^3?

A. 261
B. 5,675
C. $1.34x10^6$
D. $1.45x10^5$
E. $1.45x10^6$

Q39.2 The factory strictly operates on weekdays only. If the amount of carbon dioxide produced in February is 6% of 2012's total, what is the likely minimum average of carbon dioxide produced per day in the given month, in tonnes?

A. 1.02
B. 1.06
C. 1.12
D. 0.77
E. 0.89

Q39.3 How much more carbon dioxide, in m^3, would have been emitted from the factory had the filter not been installed at all?

A. 120
B. $7.7x10^3$
C. $2.6x10^4$
D. $4.3x10^5$
E. $6.4x10^4$

Q39.4 If the graph of carbon dioxide emissions against time were to be plotted using the figures given in the table, what graph shape would you expect to see?

A. Negative quadratic function downward slope
B. Decreasing linear function
C. Negative quadratic function upward slope
D. Reciprocal exponential decay
E. Negative quadratic function upward slope

Question 40

Aeiou Ristorante is a nationwide food and beverage franchise which is famous for its pizzas, cinnamon bread and milkshakes.

Q40.1 The cinnamon bread is sold in the shape of an isosceles right-angled triangle. The thickness of the bread is negligible. If Aeiou were to increase the length of the equal sides by 30%, by what percent does the area of the triangle increase?

A. 30%
B. 130%
C. 169%
D. 196%
E. 215%

Q40.2 The pizzas are round in shape. The thickness of the pizzas is negligible. The diameter of a large pizza is 60% larger than the diameter of a small pizza. What percentage of a large pizza is a small pizza?

A. 39%
B. 44%
C. 51%
D. 63%
E. 71%

Q40.3 The milkshakes are sold in cylindrical cups of different sizes. However, the diameter of the cup of any size is equal to its height. In the production of the small sized cups, the height and width of the big sized cups are decreased by 15%. To the nearest integer, by what percent does the volume decrease?

A. 9%
B. 15%
C. 39%
D. 42%
E. 61%

Q40.4 Qwerty walked from his house to Aeiou's for lunch. He brought X amount of cash with him. He spent 1/4 of this on some pizzas, bought himself a milkshake that cost £9, and then spent two thirds of the remaining by taking a cab home. When he got home, he had £7 left in his pocket. What was the value of X?

A. £32
B. £36
C. £40
D. £42
E. £44

Question 41

The diagram below shows the exchange rate between the British Pound Sterling and currencies in other countries of the world. Assume that the figures shown below represent both buying and selling rates of the British pound.

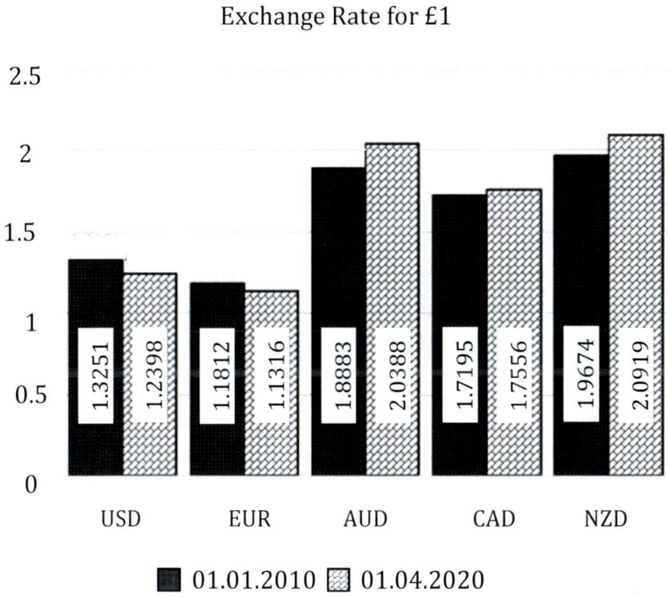

Key:
USA – US Dollar
EUR – Euros
AUD – Australian Dollar
CAD – Canadian Dollar
NZD – New Zealand Dollar

Q41.1 What was the ratio of AUD to USA on 01.04.2020?

A. 8:5
B. 16:1
C. 3:5
D. 4:5
E. 7:3

Q41.2 Tong Chuan exchanged £180,000 for NZD on 01.01.2020 and then exchanged it to EUR on 01.04.2020. How much more EUR would he hold if he had directly converted the pounds to EUR back in January?

A. 12,123
B. 21,051
C. 8,928
D. 15,325
E. 32,675

Q41.3 What is the percentage increase between the difference in the exchange rate of USD and CAD in April compared to January?

A. 13%
B. 24%
C. 29%
D. 31%
E. 136%

Q41.4 Which currency experienced the greatest percentage change between January and April in 2020?

A. USD
B. EUR
C. AUD
D. CAD
E. NZD

Q41.5 A 6% fee is applied to the final currency after every transaction. How many British Pound Sterlings did Joanna exchange to New Zealand Dollar in April if she paid the equivalent of £7,500 as an exchange fee?

A. £108,000
B. £113,000
C. £119,500
D. £122,550
E. £125,000

Question 42

Hateem is flooring his newly built single-storey home. He looks at the blueprint that his architect once drew to help plan this process. The diagram below shows the floor plan of a single story house drawn in a 1:250 scale.

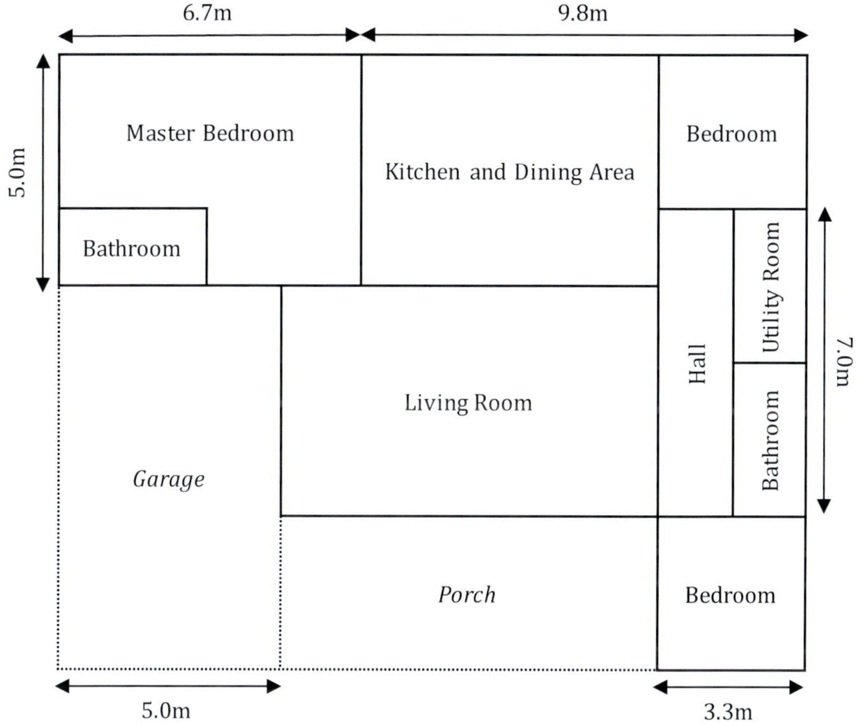

There is a door between:

- The master bedroom and the bathroom (the door is built along the wall with the narrower width).
- The master bedroom and the kitchen and dining area.
- The living room and the kitchen and dining area.
- The living room and the garage (this is the main entrance).
- The hall and both bedrooms.
- The hall and the utility room.
- The hall and the living room.
- The hall and the bathroom.

Additional Information:

- The floor of the regular bedrooms is square in shape.
- The utility room and the bathroom adjacent to it are of the same size.
- There is a total of five windows in the house.
- The main entrance door (with door frame included) is 3m in width and 2.5m in height.
- All other doors (with door frame included) are of the same height but half of the width of the entrance door.
- The doors take up two thirds the height of the entire house.
- All windows are square in shape and are sized $1m^2$.
- Spaces in italics are not within the interior of the house.
- Each metre is 3.28 foot (ft) long.
- On the blueprint, 'width' is measured horizontally and 'length' is measured vertically.
- Do not assume that the total space of the utility room and the adjacent bathroom is equal to the space of the hall.
- Do not assume that the bathrooms are of the same size.

Q42.1 What is the perimeter of the house (excluding the exteriors)?

A. 195.7ft
B. 60.2cm
C. 179.5ft
D. 62.0m
E. 197.5ft

Q42.2 What is the maximum possible width of the utility room?

A. 1.3m
B. 1.8m
C. 2.4m
D. 3.5m
E. Can't tell

Q42.3 The master bedroom has an area of $316.83ft^2$. What is the maximum (approximate) length of the longer portion of the wall separating the master bedroom and the master bathroom?

A. 5.25m
B. 4.05m
C. 2.7m
D. 2.3m
E. Can't tell

Q42.4 What is the total exterior area of the house drawn on the architect's blueprint, to the nearest hundredths place?

A. 70.06cm^2
B. 34.62cm^2
C. 20.48cm^2
D. 11.21cm^2
E. 9.81cm^2

Q42.5 Hateem wants to floor the interior of his house with marble in all areas except for the bathroom, which will have vinyl. The cost of marble and vinyl is £26.50 and £9.10 per square foot, respectively. How much will this cost him in total? You can assume that both bathrooms are of the same size and one of its sides is 1.8m in length.

A. £3,870.77
B. £17,468.84
C. £38,238.46
D. £41,643.24
E. Can't tell

Q42.6 Hateem plans to repaint all the walls of the house. He estimates that he will be able to finish painting the whole house in a fortnight. How much area would he cover on average each day? You can assume that both bathrooms are of the same size and one of its sides is 2.0m in length. You can also assume that the thickness of the wall is negligible.

A. 17.29m^2
B. 24.77m^2
C. 28.07m^2
D. 49.54m^2
E. 56.14m^2

Question 43

The table below shows the recruitment statistics for a nationwide legal firm.

Year	Number of applications received	Number of interviews offered	Number of applications accepted
2011	13,583	3,524	530
2012	14,205	3,677	555
2013	17,366	4,002	550
2014	19,239	4,451	590
2015	22,011	4,153	610

Q43.1 In which of the five years was the number of interviews offered, as a percentage of the number of applications received, the second lowest?

A. 2011
B. 2012
C. 2013
D. 2014
E. 2015

Q43.2 Expressed in terms of percentage, what was the difference between the percentage of all applicants who received an interview offer and the percentage of applicants accepted in 2012?

A. 10.8%
B. 13.6%
C. 16.2%
D. 19.7%
E. 21.98%

Q43.3 As a percentage, how much higher was the rate of accepted applications in 2011 than in 2015?

A. 0.8%
B. 1.2%
C. 1.5%
D. 2.7%
E. 3.9%

Q43.4 Which two years had the greatest percentage difference in number of interviews offered?

A. 2011 to 2012
B. 2012 to 2013
C. 2013 to 2014
D. 2014 to 2015
E. Can't tell

Question 44

A group of 13 friends travelled from Southampton to Edinburgh. Three were appointed as drivers, and they had to bring their cars along. They spent seven nights in Edinburgh before heading back to Southampton. They stayed in a student bed-n-breakfast, which charged £11.50 per person per night. Their meals for the trip cost £2,206 altogether. They set their car metres to 0 (zero) before travelling and discovered upon return that each car had travelled 896 miles. Each driver is paid £0.40 per mile for fuel. Each person had contributed £300 at the start of the journey. In order to keep track of the finances, a treasurer was elected. Assume that everyone equally shared the expenses of the trip.

Q44.1 How much should each driver be paid for fuel?

A. £347.60
B. £358.40
C. £415.70
D. £1,042.80
E. £1,075.20

Q44.2 Was the money enough to cover all the expenses?

A. Yes, and there was extra money
B. Yes, but they broke even
C. No
D. Can't tell

Q44.3 How much did each person receive or have to contribute to balance the accounts?

A. £15.75
B. £32.90
C. £54.65
D. £64.75
E. No change

Q44.4 On their way back, they had to drive through a few tolls. A total of £12 was paid for each car. This had been forgotten by the treasurer and was not accounted for. Provided no one has received or paid any extra money yet, how much more money does each person need to contribute to clear the balance?

A. £1.89
B. £2.13
C. £2.77
D. £4.34
E. £5.65

Question 45

The table below shows five individuals and their respective data deals of the service, CO_2.

Name	Deal	Years with current contract	Total GB per month
Fatt	Individual	5	8
Swann	Family	4	10
Barbossa	Business	7	15
Sparrow	Premium	3	9
Jones	Happy-Three-Friends	2	6

- An additional 1GB of data per month is added for every two years of contract.
- 1GB = 1,000MB

Q45.1 Barbossa continues with his contract for another six years. How many GBs of data will he get per year in five years time?

A. 18
B. 64
C. 144
D. 180
E. 216

Q45.2 What is the ratio of the initial number of GBs per month that Swann received at the start of her contract, to the number of monthly GBs Jones will get if he continues with his contract for another five years?

A. 1.5:1
B. 4:3
C. 8:3
D. 8:5
E. 6:5

Q45.3 What is the percentage increase from initial yearly GBs to yearly GBs after 11 years for an individual on a premium deal?

A. 24.5%
B. 32.6%
C. 43.5%
D. 55.6%
E. 62.5%

Q45.4 If an individual uses an average of 423MB daily and has just started his/her contract on a 'Happy-Three-Friends' deal, how many months will he/she have to stay with this contract before his/her monthly entitlement matches his/her mobile data usage? Assume that there are 30 days in a month.

A. 14
B. 16
C. 36
D. 48
E. 192

Question 46

The graph below shows the trend of sales in the real estate market in the UK from 2007 to 2011.

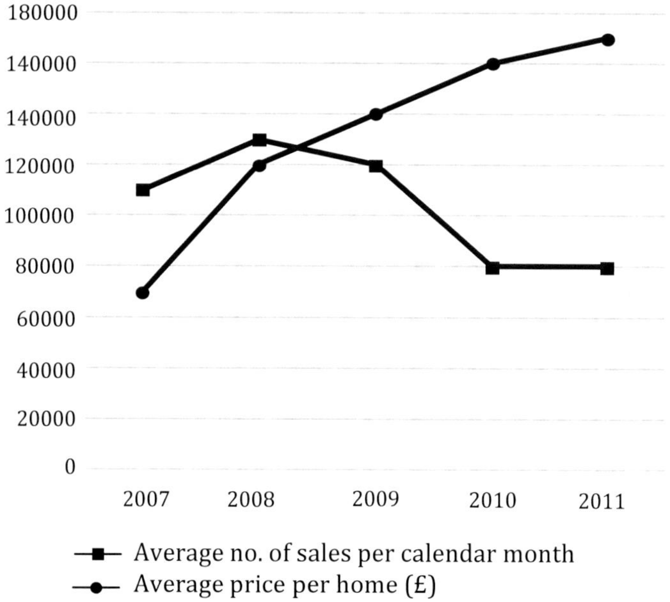

Q46.1 Which year saw the largest amount of money spent on buying houses in the UK?

A. 2007
B. 2008
C. 2009
D. 2010
E. 2011

Q46.2 What was the difference in the amount of money spent, to the nearest million, on buying houses between the years 2007 and 2011?

A. £70,800M
B. £68,500M
C. £66,500M
D. £62,700M
E. £59,250M

Q46.3 If the percentage increase in the average price per home between 2007 and 2008 had continued consistently for each of the following years until 2011, what would be the percentage increase of the apparent average price of a house compared to its actual average price? Round your answer to the nearest integer.

A. 114%
B. 195%
C. 256%
D. 435%
E. 509%

Q46.4 What was the percentage decrease in average monthly sales from 2009 to 2010?

A. 7.7%
B. 23.8%
C. 31.3%
D. 35.4%
E. 192

Q46.5 What was the ratio between the average number of sales per month and the average price per home in 2009?

A. 7:6
B. 8:3
C. 3:4
D. 5:4
E. 6:7

Q46.6 If the decline in the average number of sales per calendar month observed between 2008 and 2009 continued at this rate for the following years, in which year would the average number of sales per year be equal to 360,000?

A. 2015
B. 2016
C. 2017
D. 2018
E. 2019

Question 47

The table below shows the number of phones sold over the years by different companies.

	Dianhua	Hailo	Oppa
2006	59,039	56,193	38,262
2007	54,267	42,566	40,066
2008	56,137	58,046	36,100
2009	38,700	50,937	48,618
2010	57,466	48,874	47,662

Dianhua

- Sells phones in China only
- Average phone retail price: 3,300 Yuan

Hailo

- Sells phones in India only
- Average phone retail price: 26,300 Rupees

Oppa

- One third of phones sold in China; two thirds sold in India
- Average phone retail price: 4,110 Yuan in China; 39,500 Rupees in India

Exchange Rate

- 1 Yuan = 10.6 Rupees
- Constant for all the years

Q47.1 In 2007, what proportion of the total phones sold were sold in India?

A. 19.5%
B. 31.3%
C. 40.8%
D. 59.2%
E. 60.4%

Q47.2 What was the total value of phones sold in China in 2009, to the nearest million Yuan?

A. 191M
B. 194M
C. 205M
D. 222M
E. 239M

Q47.3 What was the average yearly income for Oppa over the five years, to the nearest million Yuan?

A. 58M
B. 74M
C. 102M
D. 162M
E. 1,167M

Q47.4 Amara calculates the total income of the three companies. She standardises the numbers by making sure that they are all expressed in Rupees. What is the least number of phones Oppa has to sell to match the income of the company with the greatest income?

A. 9,379
B. 17,277
C. 20,374
D. 15,665
E. 21,356

Question 48

The table below shows the employee distribution by department in Geongang International Network, which is a global private healthcare provider.

Department	2015	2016	2017	2018	2019	Average Annual Salary for Role (£)
GP	37%	33%	32%	29%	25%	97,761
Medicine	17%	23%	24%	25%	23%	102,438
Surgery	19%	20%	18%	20%	21%	108,873
Admin	12%	8%	11%	11%	13%	79,441
Other	15%	16%	15%	15%	18%	63,635
Total No. of Employees	-	322,092	346,993	387,686	449,708	-

Q48.1 What was the total approximate cost of monthly salaries paid to the Department of Medicine in 2018, in millions?

A. £525M
B. £773M
C. £827M
D. £1,254M
E. £9,928M

Q48.2 In which year did the company pay out the most in salaries for GPs? Assume the total number of employees in 2015 increased by 6% when progressing into 2016.

A. 2015
B. 2016
C. 2017
D. 2018
E. 2019

Q48.3 The number of employees in Surgery in 2016 was equal to the number of employees in both Admin and Other combined in 2015. What was the percentage increase in the number of employees from 2015 to 2016?

A. 17%
B. 26%
C. 35%
D. 39%
E. 41%

Q48.4 What is the percentage increase in the average individual monthly salary if one, who had been an 'Other' employee since 2015, was promoted to take up an Admin role in 2019?

A. 19.9%
B. 22.4%
C. 24.8%
D. 25.7%
E. 26.9%

48.5 If the trend (i.e. rate of increase) for total number of employees from 2018 to 2019 had started earlier from 2016 and remained constant in the following years, approximately how many extra employees would there be in 2019?

A. 24,873
B. 36,481
C. 42,583
D. 53,044
E. 60,193

Question 49

Tambun Bites is a snack factory that specialises in making mung bean paste biscuits. The biscuit is known for its sweet taste and its hemispheric shape. Over the years, the company has expanded its business on a global scale, and it now has operating factories in the UK. In the local factory, the hourly pay for a factory worker is £8.20. The factory runs at the usual 9:00 am to 5:00 pm hours, with an hour in between for lunch. Any overtime payment is paid time and a quarter. The production of the biscuit utilises trays and trolleys to bake the biscuits. Each trolley can carry up to 16 trays, and each tray can hold a maximum of 72 biscuits. (The formula for the volume of a sphere is $\frac{88}{23}$ r^3.)

Q49.1 One bowl of biscuit mix fills eight trolleys, and the mix has a density of $6g/cm^3$. To the nearest integer, how much does one bowl weigh, in kilograms, if the radius of the mix is 1.1cm?

A. 127kg
B. 154kg
C. 254kg
D. 308kg
E. 508kg

Q49.2 A factory worker works four shifts per week plus six hours overtime. Approximately how much does he make in a year, to the nearest £?

A. £16,843
B. £16,203
C. £18,984
D. £26,346
E. £26,437

Q49.3 It takes nine seconds for a worker to fill a tray with biscuits and to place it on a trolley for baking. On an anniversary celebration, the owner wants to make an artwork of the company's logo using the biscuits. He encourages all factories to make the biscuits for a full shift. If a factory has five workers, how many trolleys will be sent for baking in total?

A. 675
B. 750
C. 875
D. 950
E. 1,000

Q49.4 There are X trays filled with biscuits. However, 5% of the biscuits in each tray were burnt and cannot be sold. If a standard box for sale has 22 biscuits and X trays managed to fill 34 boxes, what does X represent?

A. 9
B. 10
C. 11
D. 12
E. 13

Question 50

Blingg is a company which is known to sell bracelets and necklaces with star-shaped pendants. One day, a customer visits the stall and asks for a bracelet with a seven-point star rose gold pendant. Blingg has that particular shape and colour available in three different sizes, all of which are mathematically similar. The customer wants two pendants on her bracelet.

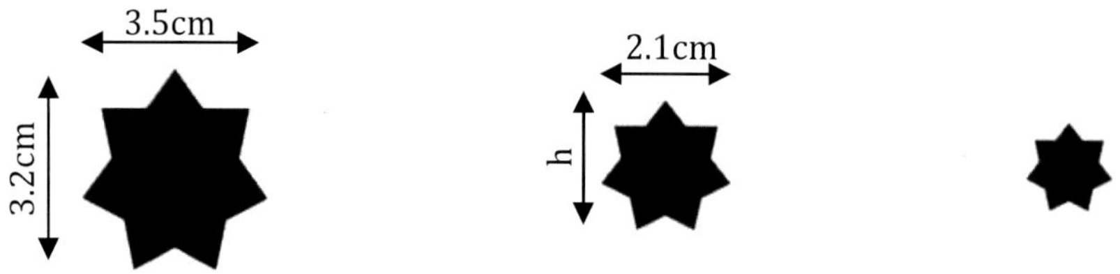

Q50.1 Calculate the height (h) of the medium-sized pendant, expressed in cm.

A. 1.68cm
B. 1.92cm
C. 3.23cm
D. 5.33cm
E. Can't tell

Q50.2 Given that the area of the medium star is 3.24cm^2, calculate the area, in cm^2, of the large star?

A. 4.56cm^2
B. 6.34cm^2
C. 7.50cm^2
D. 9.00cm^2
E. Can't tell

Q50.3 Assuming the 'area scale factor' for the large star to the small star is 12.3906, what would be the width of the small star in mm, to the nearest tenths place?

A. 2.6mm
B. 4.7mm
C. 5.4mm
D. 8.6mm
E. 9.1mm

Q50.4 Assume that the area of the small star is $1.12cm^2$. The pendants need to be coated in the rose gold. What is the total surface area of the small star in the bracelet, in mm^2? You can assume that the thickness of the pendant is negligible.

A. $2.24mm^2$
B. $4.48mm^2$
C. $162mm^2$
D. $224mm^2$
E. $448mm^2$

Question 51

The table below shows the revenue, for the month of July 2019, for different types of membership in a sports club.

Membership types	Total number of members	Members who were unable to regulate their payments	Average business cost per customer (£)	Monthly retail price per customer (£)
Student	158,743	2,004	75.26	89.99
Basic Access	202,718	1,696	122.12	199.99
Full Service	186,846	2,348	215.71	259.99
Concession	161,896	1,852	143.07	169.99
National Athlete	54,921	883	137.54	159.99

Q51.1 Which membership category contributed the second lowest profit to the sports club in July 2019?

A. Student
B. Basic Access
C. Full Service
D. Concession
E. National Athlete

Q51.2 What percentage of all members, in July 2019, were unable to regulate their payments?

A. 0.98%
B. 1.05%
C. 1.15%
D. 1.68%
E. 2.31%

Q51.3 Expressed as a percentage, to what extent do the sales of the two most profitable membership categories represent the sales of the other three categories at the sports club in July 2019? (i.e. a 100% representation means that the profit made from the top two categories is equal to the profit made from the other three categories.)

A. 247%
B. 277%
C. 289%
D. 304%
E. 412%

Q51.4 What was the sports club's total business cost due to the five membership categories offered, to the nearest thousand?

A. £98,583k
B. £101,235k
C. £107,724k
D. £108,938k
E. £112,420k

Q51.5 Adjusting for wastage cost of customers who failed on their payments, what percentage of the total actual profits of the sports club in July 2019 was accounted for by the median of the profits made by all categories?

A. 11.2%
B. 13.6%
C. 14.1%
D. 14.7%
E. 15.2%

Question 52

The graph below shows the Economic Index (value of economy) of five companies across different quarters over two years.

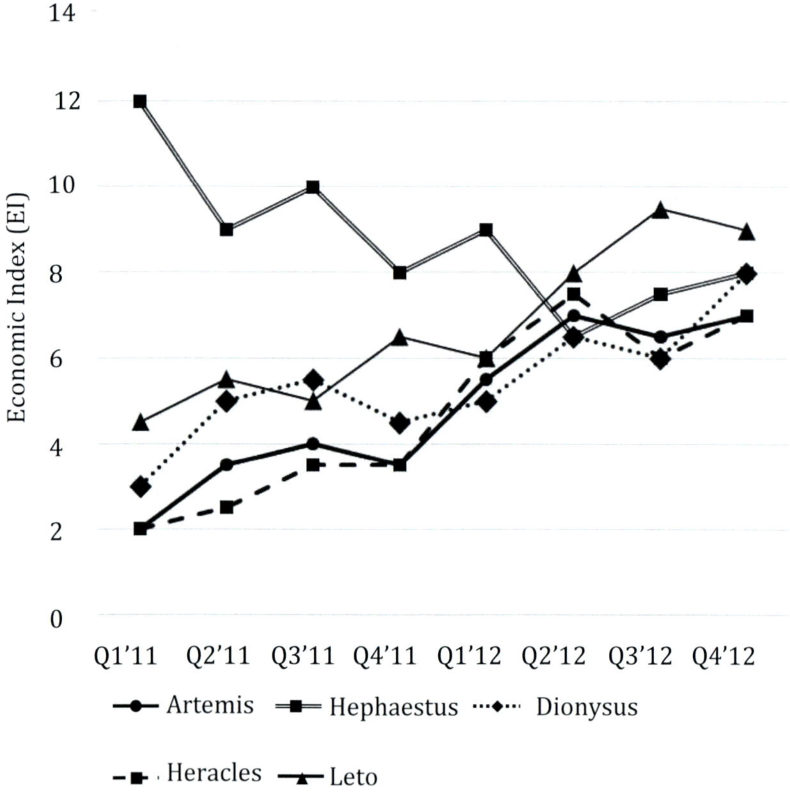

Q52.1 What was the difference in the combined Economic Index for the five companies between Q2'11 and Q3'12?

A. 9
B. 9.5
C. 10
D. 10.5
E. 11

Q52.2 What was the combined Economic Index, for all five companies, mid-way between Q4'11 and Q1'12?

A. 26.5
B. 29.5
C. 24
D. 25.25
E. 28.75

Q52.3 Which company experienced the least decline in its Economic Index over 2011 and 2012?

A. Artemis
B. Hephaestus
C. Dionysus
D. Heracles
E. Leto

Q52.4 In which quarter did the combined Economic Index for all five companies remain constant with the quarter preceding it?

A. Q2'11
B. Q4'11
C. Q1'12
D. Q3'12
E. Q4'12

Q52.5 Which company experienced the greatest increase in its Economic Index between Q2 of 2011 and Q3 of 2012?

A. Artemis
B. Hephaestus
C. Dionysus
D. Heracles
E. Leto

Q52.6 Which one of the companies experienced the least change in its economy over the two years?

A. Artemis
B. Hephaestus
C. Dionysus
D. Heracles
E. Leto

Q52.7 What was the average Economic Index for each company in Q1 of 2012?

A. 5.1
B. 5.6
C. 6.3
D. 6.5
E. 6.8

Q52.8 What is the difference in Economic Index for the two companies that experienced the greatest percentage change in economic growth over the two years?

A. 0
B. 0.25
C. 0.5
D. 0.75
E. 1

Question 53

The table below shows the cost of supplies required in a typical hospital.

Cost (£) per unit					
Order Quantity	**1-10**	**11-100**	**101-1,000**	**1,001-10,000**	**10,001+**
Vacutainer bottle set	35.41	27.44	22.34	16.31	13.36
Winged infusion set	6.99	5.13	4.05	3.23	2.54
Box of tourniquets	14.56	12.54	10.27	8.82	7.98
Box of syringes	11.23	10.66	8.77	7.03	6.90
Otoscope specula pack	19.35	17.48	15.86	13.28	11.14
*Price excludes VAT - VAT charged at 21%					

Q53.1 What would be the total cost (VAT included), in pounds, for the order of 786 vacutainer bottle sets, 54 boxes of tourniquets, and 1,961 otoscope specula packs?

A. £44,176.96
B. £53,625.36
C. £43,876.36
D. £53,454.12
E. £53,090.40

Q53.2 What is the percentage decrease in unit price, including VAT, for winged infusion sets when purchased in quantities of more than 10,001 compared to quantities under 10?

A. 36.3%
B. 175.1%
C. 62.3%
D. 54.8%
E. 63.7%

Q53.3 How much more would a buyer have to pay on his/her order, including VAT, for the purchase of 1,384 boxes of syringes, 836 boxes of tourniquets, and 11,053 vacutainer bottle sets if the VAT rate increased to 25%?

A. £6,693.39
B. £6,235.43
C. £6,688.27
D. £6,639.33
E. £6,710.35

Q53.4 With VAT excluded, what is the maximum number of winged infusion sets that could be bought with one third of the money saved from reducing an order of 7,368 otoscope specula packs to 459?

A. 8,914
B. 9,347
C. 6,253
D. 7,009
E. 11,887

Q53.5 With VAT included, what is the ratio of the price a buyer has to pay for 559 boxes of syringes to the price he/she has to pay for 89 boxes of tourniquets?

A. 3.9:1
B. 4.0:1
C. 4.2:1
D. 4.4:1
E. 4.5:1

Q53.6 An order of winged infusion sets and vacutainer bottle sets costs a total of £52,024.68, including VAT. The cost for the winged infusion sets comes to £27,871.42, excluding VAT. How many vacutainer bottle sets were ordered?

A. 1,224
B. 1,122
C. 908
D. 845
E. 677

Question 54

The diagram below shows the share prices in the electronics industry.

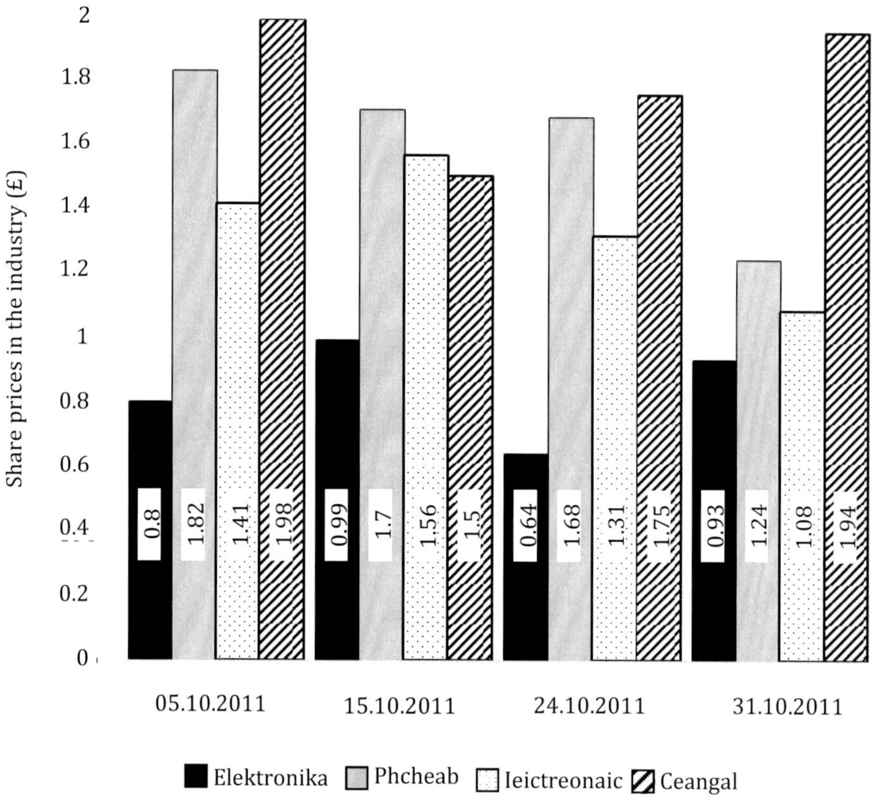

Q54.1 How many more shares of Elektronika could one buy for £22,440 on 05.10.2011 compared to the number of Ieictreonaic shares one could buy for the same amount on 31.10.2011?

A. 5,234
B. 6,954
C. 7,273
D. 9,864
E. 12,135

Q54.2 If an investor bought 16,500 shares of Caengal on 05.10.2011 and sold 7,200 of these on 15.10.2011, how much loss would he/she have made from the shares sold?

A. 1,656
B. £3,456
C. £5,370
D. 6,783
E. 7,349

Q54.3 An investor sold 20,000 Phcheab shares on 15.10.2011 and used this money to buy some share units from one of the companies on 24.10.2011, which he happily sold at the end of the month as he made a profit. What is the greatest possible profit he could have made on this trading? Round your answer to the nearest pound (if necessary).

A. £9,860
B. £10,352
C. £13,246
D. £15,406
E. £16,359

Q54.4 An investor purchased £27,000 worth of Ieictreonaic shares on 05.10.2011 and then sold two thirds of these ten days later. Following this, she used all of the money from the sale to later purchase Elektronika shares on 31.10.2011. What is the approximate total number of shares held by the investor, assuming that she did not have any shares before this trading?

A. 18,237
B. 19,347
C. 21,412
D. 23,472
E. 27,795

Question 55

The table below shows the number of schools in five different provinces and the number of students in the respective provinces who qualified for the final round of a national Science, Technology, Engineering and Mathematics (STEM) competition held in China.

	Yunnan	**Jiangsu**	**Xian**	**Hubei**	**Suzhou**	***China Avg.**
No. of participating schools	125	25	50	150	100	-
Number of students qualified for finals per 100 schools						
Biology	6	43	11	28	99	31
Physics	36	30	18	72	80	65
Chemistry	72	7	36	82	20	45
Mathematics	82	99	78	57	84	24
Further Mathematics	51	82	9	34	64	95
General Knowledge in STEM	35	101	54	7	23	29
*China Average - the average across 31 participating provinces						

Q55.1 What is the ratio of students who qualified for finals in Physics from Hubei to the number of students who qualified for finals in Further Mathematics from Yunnan?

A. 27:16
B. 24:17
C. 48:19
D. 144:85
E. 34:25

Q55.2 Approximately how many more schools from Xian would have to participate to meet the national average for Chemistry?

A. 27
B. 50
C. 65
D. 75
E. 125

Q55.3 Given the total number of students for each of the five individual provinces taking part in the finals, which province is the median?

A. Yunnan
B. Jiangsu
C. Xian
D. Hubei
E. Suzhou

Q55.4 Which province has the second highest number of students qualified for the finals in Mathematics and General Knowledge combined?

A. Yunnan
B. Jiangsu
C. Xian
D. Hubei
E. Suzhou

Q55.5 Approximately how many schools in Hubei would have to participate to have the number of finalists in Biology equate to the national average?

A. 46
B. 90
C. 111
D. 134
E. 162

Question 56

Kaiya is a student residing in Philadelphia. This coming weekend, she plans to visit her friend in New York to watch a musical together. She calculates that it is 95 miles to travel by car to New York and that petrol costs 82p per mile. There are two routes via train to Victoria. The direct bus takes 1 hour 38 mins and costs £35. The indirect bus stops at Princeton and costs £42. This journey takes 2 hours 30 mins. She has a coach card that allows her 30% off bus journeys that are longer than two hours.

Q56.1 If Kaiya goes by the cheapest possible route, how much would it cost her to get to New York?

A. £10.50
B. £12.60
C. £24.50
D. £29.40
E. £34.50

Q56.2 She decides to take the car, and it turns out that her friend would like to tag along for a visit to Philadelphia. The friend says she will evenly split the cost of the journey back. How much would the entire journey cost Kaiya?

A. £38.95
B. £58.43
C. £77.90
D. £116.85
E. £155.80

Q56.3 Travelling on the bus at off peak times is cheaper by 15%. This cannot be applied to the journey to New York, but it can be applied to the return. How much would a round trip cost if Kaiya were to take the direct bus?

A. £29.75
B. £32.55
C. £54.65
D. £64.75
E. £70.00

Q56.4 Kaiya takes the car and needs to pay a parking fee. She arrives at 10:30 am and leaves at a certain time. Visitors can opt to pay a parking rate of £1.50 an hour or a flat rate of £10 for the day. If she had opted for the hourly rate ticket, what time must she leave the place if she doesn't want to regret not taking the flat rate? How much would the total journey cost?

A. 3:30 pm; £163.80
B. 4:30 pm; £165.30
C. 5:10 pm; £165.80
D. 5:20 pm; £166.20
E. 5:30 pm; £166.40

Question 57

The table below summarises the results of a survey that considers the key qualities needed to be successful in the acting industry.

	Necessary	Important	Irrelevant
Education	44	30	78
Network	63	51	38
Determination	69	74	9
Risk-Taking	80	54	18
Multitalented (e.g. able to sing and dance)	39	29	84

Q57.1 What percentage of actors said that 'Network' is 'Necessary'?
A. 28.3%
B. 34.2%
C. 41.4%
D. 50.4%
E. 52.6%

Q57.2 What is the ratio of the number of actors who deem 'Risk-Taking' 'Important' to the number of actors who deem 'Education' irrelevant?
A. 9:13
B. 3:10
C. 9:5
D. 3:5
E. 3:13

Q57.3 What is the difference, as a percentage, of the total responses across all qualities in the 'Irrelevant' category compared to the 'Necessary' category?

A. 1.4%
B. 1.6%
C. 7.5%
D. 8.9%
E. 10.1%

Q57.4 Assuming all of the 'Important' responses were regarded as 'Necessary' by all respondents, which one of the characteristics would correspond to the median 'Necessary' responses?

A. Education
B. Network
C. Determination
D. Risk-Taking
E. Multitalented

Question 58

The table below shows the profit statement of a Michelin-star Russian restaurant, Khleb & Co., in 2015 and 2016 in pounds.

Year	Quarter	SR (000s)	FC (000s)	VC (000s)	MS (000s)	NoC
'15	Q1	31.5	9.8	5.4	1.24	121
	Q2	33.8	10.7	6.6	2.67	125
	Q3	33.6	10.5	6.1	3.56	147
	Q4	34.5	11.0	6.8	3.78	150
'16	Q1	36.5	10.9	7.0	3.91	163
	Q2	39.7	12.5	8.1	3.83	158
	Q3	42.1	12.2	9.5	4.01	176
	Q4	51.8	12.1	9.6	4.22	167

Key:

SR - Sales Revenue
FC - Fixed Costs
VC - Variable Costs
MS - Marketing Spend
NoC - Number of Customers

Q1 - January to March
Q2 - April to June
Q3 - July to September
Q4 - October to December

Profit = Sales Revenue (SR) - Total Costs (TC)
Total Costs (TC) = Fixed Costs (FC) + Variable Costs (VC)
Average Transaction = Sales Revenue (SR) / No. of Customers (NoC)

Q58.1 In which quarter of 2015 and 2016 was the profit per Khelb & Co.'s customer the highest?

A. Q1 2015
B. Q2 2016
C. Q3 2015
D. Q1 2016
E. Q2 2015

Q58.2 What is the ratio of the profit to the marketing spend for Q4 2015?

A. 4.21:1
B. 3.85:1
C. 5.16:1
D. 4.03:1
E. 4.42:1

Q58.3 What was the percentage change in the fixed cost per customer between the last quarter of 2015 and the following quarter?

A. -8.8%
B. +10.2%
C. -9.7%
D. +21.3%
E. -35.1%

Q58.4 Which quarter between Q3 2015 and Q3 2016 experienced the greatest percentage change in sales revenue compared to the previous quarter?

A. Q3 2015
B. Q4 2015
C. Q1 2016
D. Q2 2016
E. Q3 2016

Q58.5 Assume that the average transaction value continued to increase with the trend seen between Q1 2015 and Q2 2015. How much higher would it be than the actual average transaction value in Q4 2016?

A. £13.54
B. £29.37
C. £31.40
D. £42.55
E. £50.49

Question 59

The table below shows the data collected by *Worldometer* for the recorded number of cases of the COVID-19 viral outbreak in 2020. For the sake of this question, you can assume that, as of 1st of January, there were 89 cases of people infected with the virus and all these cases occurred in December. There are no reported mortalities before January. The table below shows the cumulative data for the months January to April.

Incidence is defined as the number of new cases. Prevalence is defined as the total number of cases at a specific point in time (i.e. deaths and recovered cases not included).

Month	Cumulative Cases	*Active Cases	Mortality
January	11,950	11,448	259
February	86,604	41,297	2,718
March	863,184	640,973	41,066
April	3,301,083	2,028,231	189,781

*The numbers shown are the number of ongoing active cases recorded on the last day of each respective month.

Q59.1 A medical student is given this data for his examinations and asked to calculate the average number of deaths that occurred across the four months. Calculate the answer, assuming that the student does it correctly, rounding up to the next integer.

A. 58,456
B. 28,546
C. 70,267
D. 70,725
E. 70,276

Q59.2 A health statistician has been asked to calculate which month had the second highest percentage increase in incidence of a given month compared to the previous month. Which month would it be?

A. January
B. February
C. March
D. April
E. Can't tell

Q59.3 A professor in infectious diseases is planning to deliver a specific intervention to address this infection in an international webinar and wants to know the prevalence of the disease at the end of April. Based on the information provided in the table, calculate the total number of recovered cases that had been reported by the 30th of April 2020.

A. 1,231,786
B. 1,124,137
C. 1,039,028
D. 1,083,071
E. 931,543

Q59.4 The government of Country X declared a strict nationwide lockdown at the beginning of May. The cumulative number of cases, active cases and deaths in Country X is 6% of the global number at any time. The data was retrospectively studied by a student at the end of the month. It was found that the number of new cases was 34% less than *expected and the number of deaths was reported as 24% of the *expected number of deaths.

The student makes the below assumptions:

- *Expected means the percentage increase of March - April is equal to that of April - May.
- None of the new cases in May had led to recovery by the end of the month.
- Any calculations products that directly represent the number of people should be rounded off immediately.

Calculate the prevalence at the end of May.

A. 1,282,234
B. 309,173
C. 948,539
D. 412,131
E. 2,318,668

Question 60

The table below shows the shares of the market for handbags in 2018.

Company	Revenue (£M)	Number of transactions (in 1000s)	Number of shops	Number of employees
Handtasche	17,720	457,920	610	25,087
Bag Llaw	13,015	684,302	573	23,344
Handobaggu	20,959	1,539,924	489	15,314
Queens' Bags	16,900	986,403	945	20,906
Hendabega	15,187	740,249	721	17,690

Q60.1 Which of the companies had the greatest revenue per transaction that year?

A. Handtasche
B. Bag Llaw
C. Handobaggu
D. Queens'
E. Hendabega

Q60.2 Which of the following is the closest to the approximate ratio of the revenue, per shop, for Bag Llaw to Hendabega?

A. 6:5
B. 27:25
C. 61:50
D. 51:50
E. 1:1

Q60.3 On average, across all the companies, what is the number of employees per shop to the nearest integer?

A. 28
B. 29
C. 30
D. 31
E. 32

Q60.4 What percentage of the total revenue in the handbag market in 2018 is Handobaggu and Handtasche?

A. 41.3%
B. 43.1%
C. 45.2%
D. 47.6%
E. 51.2%

Abstract Reasoning

FORMAT

In the exam, you have:

- 55 items associated with shapes
- 13 minutes
- +1 minute to read instructions
- Four types of questions
- 50 items of Types 1 and 4 (total of 10 exercises, each with 5 test shapes to allocate)
- 5 items of Types 2 and 3 (each a separate exercise)

In this section, there are:

- Type 1 – 25 exercises
- Type 2 – 30 exercises
- Type 3 – 25 exercises
- Type 4 – 21 exercises

Objective:

- To be able to recognise a pattern in a mass of data / information.

TYPES OF QUESTIONS

Type 1 | Which set does it belong to? Or neither?

- Set A and B are always different from each other.
- Is there a numerical order to the pattern? (e.g., lock hands, number of coloured sectors, number of objects, number of edges, planes of symmetry).
- Number of edges – Is there a repetition (do they all have the same number of edges)?
- Correlation of colours – Does the colour of an object have any meaning / pattern?
- Is there a constant in all the boxes in a set?
- Size – Is there a reason why one object is bigger than the others? Can all the other objects fit into one? Does the biggest object represent a constant?
- Scattering of objects - Helpful when a group of similar objects are gathered in one set and the others are scattered.

TYPES OF QUESTIONS (Continued)

- Number and type of angles – Are the angles more or less than 90 degrees or 180 degrees?
- Intersections – Do the shapes all line up? Do they cross each other?
- Direction and position of arrows – Do they all point in the same direction? If opposite, what changes?

Type 2 | Which figure completes the series?

- Patterns following a logical series – Is it a progressive pattern (e.g. 2, 4, 6, 8 or 4, 3, 2, 1) or alternating pattern (e.g. +1, -2, +1, -2)? If it is progressive, be sure to check for linear or non-linear patterns.
- Number of edges, sectors and angles.
- Rotations - Are there any rotating patterns within the shapes (e.g., 90, 180, 270 degrees)? Do they rotate clockwise or anti-clockwise? Or perhaps could they be mirror images instead of rotations?
- Horizontal or vertical flipping.

Type 3 | A is to B as C is to X. Which is X?

- Each feature has a purpose.
- Does the colour of an object mean anything to the next?
- Do they move in a direction?
- Do the colours correlate to other things such as the number of edges or angles?
- Do the arrows move in a particular direction when proceeding to the next box?
- Do the arrows signify a change in direction or size?
- Do the shapes move in a particular manner (e.g., rotation, flipping)?

Type 4 | Which subsets belong to: A? B?

- Similar to Type 1
- Which of these subsets belongs to: Set A? Set B?

TIPS AND TRICKS TO SCORE

Revision Tips

- When revising, write down all of the pattern conditions that can appear for each type of question.

TIPS AND TRICKS TO SCORE (Continued)

- It is useful to have common patterns noted on a flashcard or poster to help you recognise them as you go along. These include:
  - ⇒ Number of sides
  - ⇒ Relationship between colours
  - ⇒ Adding and subtracting number of sides
  - ⇒ Assigning a value to a particular shape
  - ⇒ Significance of shapes within shapes
  - ⇒ Symmetry
  - ⇒ Angles / right angles
  - ⇒ Arrangement
  - ⇒ Numbers
  - ⇒ Size
  - ⇒ Position
  - ⇒ Orientation
  - ⇒ Simple logical series or arithmetic progression (prime numbers, division, multiplication)
- Learn to spot patterns or 'triggers' during practice.
- Common triggers are:
  - ⇒ Arrows: Usually hints a question on direction or may be pointing to a certain shape.
  - ⇒ Clocks: Think about the long and short hands. Do they represent an angle, or minutes and hours, or are they pointing to a number for multiplication?
  - ⇒ Colours: Usually the same shapes have the same colour or represent a series.
  - ⇒ Letters and numbers: They represent shapes. Usually related to the number of right angles or symmetry.
- Common patterns examiners use to design questions in the exam:
  - ⇒ Alternate patterns: A pattern that is common in Type 2 questions where a certain shape only changes its character (appear, move, etc.) in some boxes.
  - ⇒ Conditional patterns: A pattern where the characteristics of one object in a box dictates the characteristics of another item in the same box.
- Watch out for distractors (shapes that have no relationships to the pattern).

TIPS AND TRICKS TO SCORE (Continued)

- Give yourself plenty of time to prepare (recommended 10 – 12 weeks). The more questions you practice, the more familiar you will become with question types and patterns.
- Start by practicing questions untimed for the first four weeks to ease yourself into the UCAT format. The next four weeks should include timed practice.
- After each exercise, check and review the answers.

Answering Techniques

- Have a mnemonic that works for you as it will come in handy to cover as many possible patterns in a short amount of time. There are multiple mnemonics; choose one and improvise as you go along. There is no one right method.
- If you find yourself stuck on a question for more than 30 seconds, flag the question and return to it later. It may give you a new perspective on the question.
- Find a pattern before answering. Trying to match each answer to the given set is time consuming and confusing.
- Start with the simplest subset; it has the least distractors.
- Don't get too entangled on minute details. Sometimes looking at the bigger picture makes sense.
- Sit back, relax and take a deep breath.

TYPE I - Question 1

Match the following subsets to the sets above.

Set A	Set B
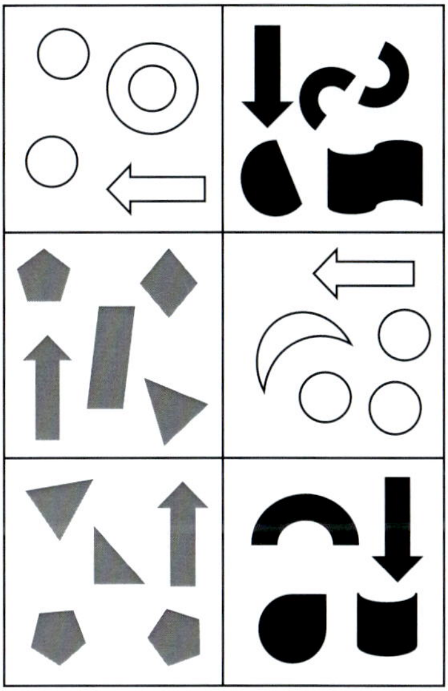	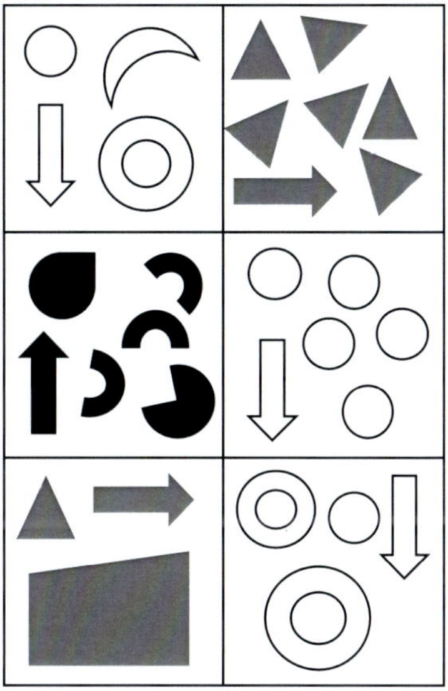

Subset 1.1	Subset 1.2	Subset 1.3	Subset 1.4	Subset 1.5
				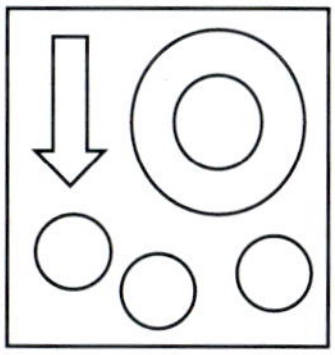
☐ Set A	☐ Set A	☐ Set A	☐ Set A	☐ Set A
☐ Set B	☐ Set B	☐ Set B	☐ Set B	☐ Set B
☐ Neither	☐ Neither	☐ Neither	☐ Neither	☐ Neither

TYPE I - Question 2

Match the following subsets to the sets above.

Set A

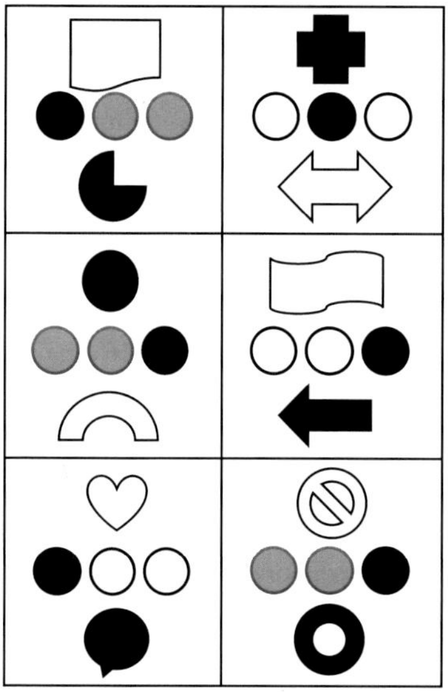

Set B

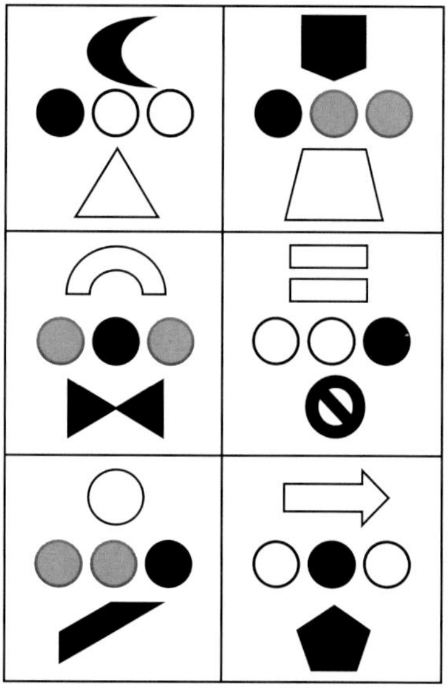

Subset 2.1

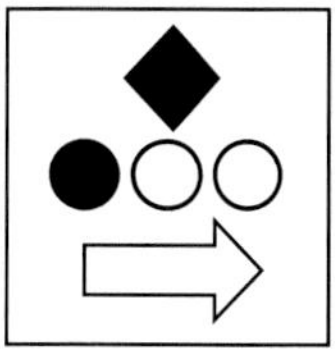

☐ Set A
☐ Set B
☐ Neither

Subset 2.2

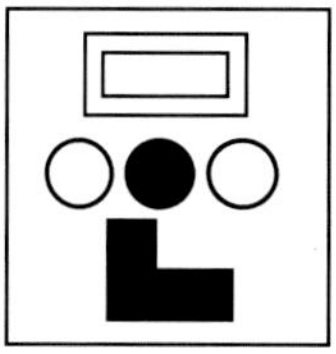

☐ Set A
☐ Set B
☐ Neither

Subset 2.3

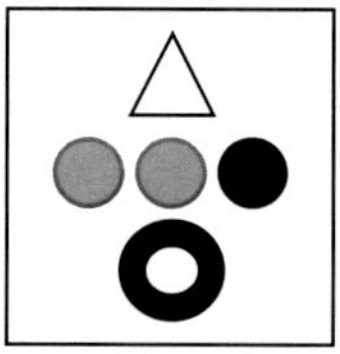

☐ Set A
☐ Set B
☐ Neither

Subset 2.4

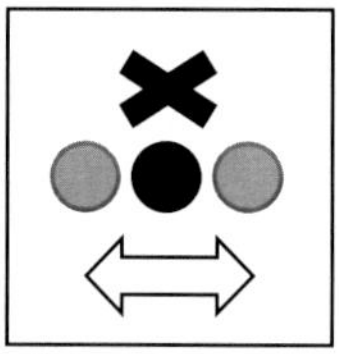

☐ Set A
☐ Set B
☐ Neither

Subset 2.5

☐ Set A
☐ Set B
☐ Neither

TYPE I - Question 3

Match the following subsets to the sets above.

Set A

Set B

Subset 3.1

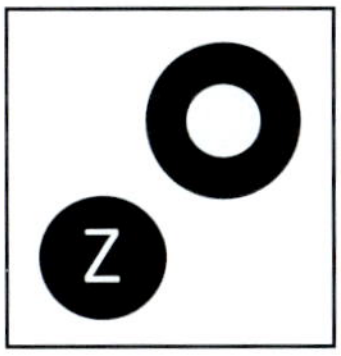

Subset 3.2

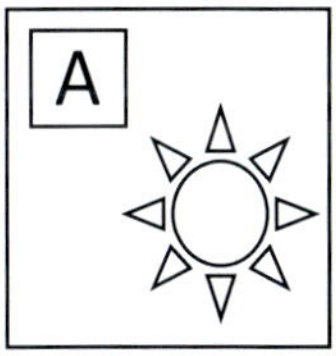

Subset 3.3

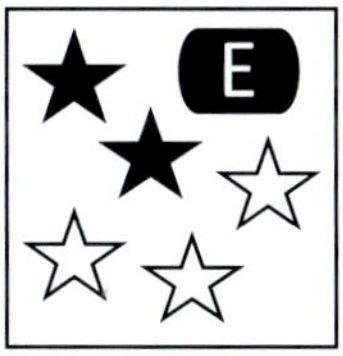

Subset 3.4

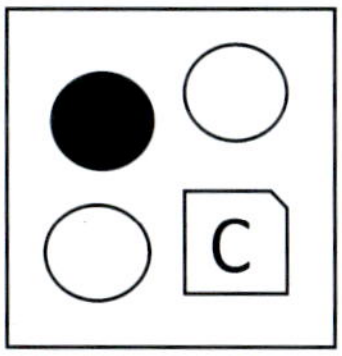

Subset 3.5

☐ Set A	☐ Set A	☐ Set A	☐ Set A	☐ Set A
☐ Set B	☐ Set B	☐ Set B	☐ Set B	☐ Set B
☐ Neither	☐ Neither	☐ Neither	☐ Neither	☐ Neither

TYPE I - Question 4

Match the following subsets to the sets above.

Set A

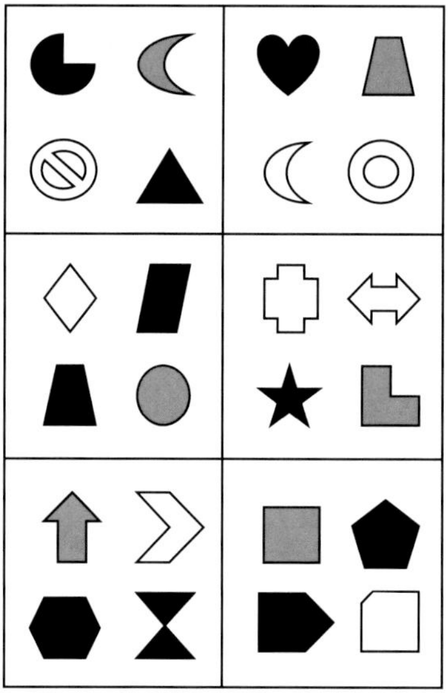

Set B

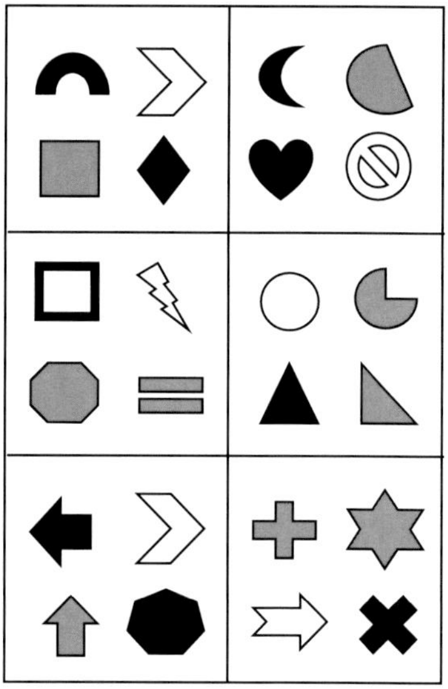

Subset 4.1

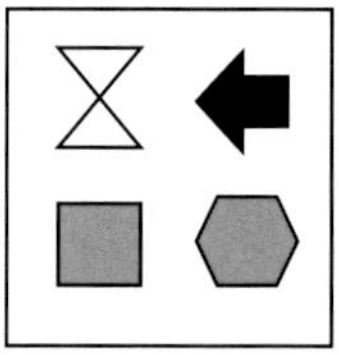

☐ Set A

☐ Set B

☐ Neither

Subset 4.2

☐ Set A

☐ Set B

☐ Neither

Subset 4.3

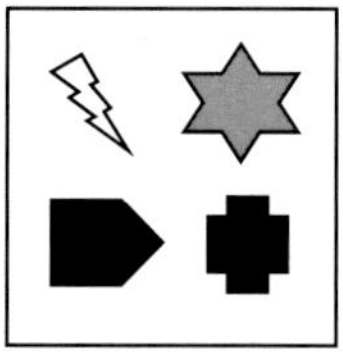

☐ Set A

☐ Set B

☐ Neither

Subset 4.4

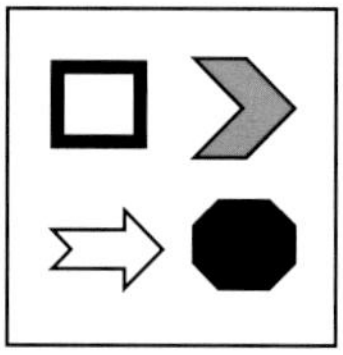

☐ Set A

☐ Set B

☐ Neither

Subset 4.5

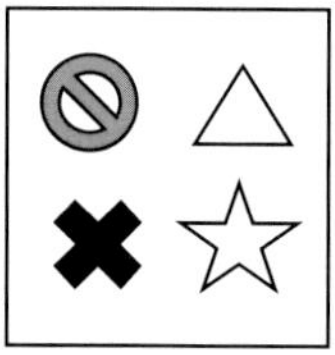

☐ Set A

☐ Set B

☐ Neither

TYPE I - Question 5

Match the following subsets to the sets above.

Set A

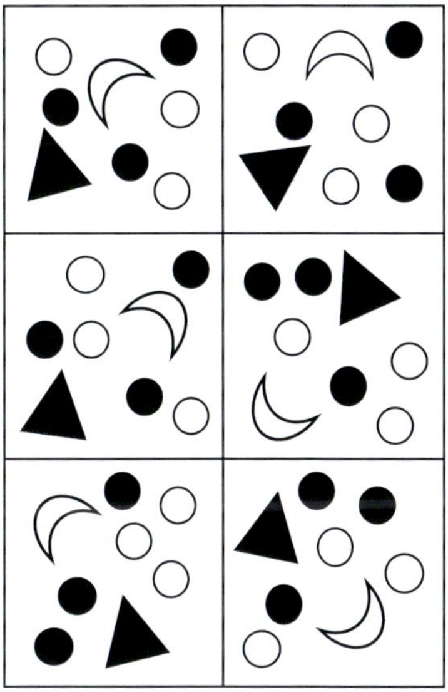

Set B

Subset 5.1

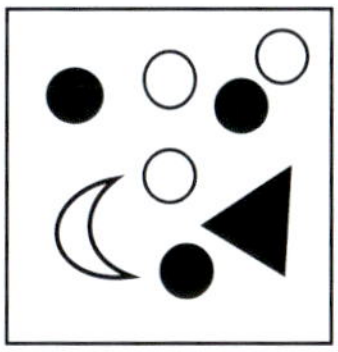

☐ Set A
☐ Set B
☐ Neither

Subset 5.2

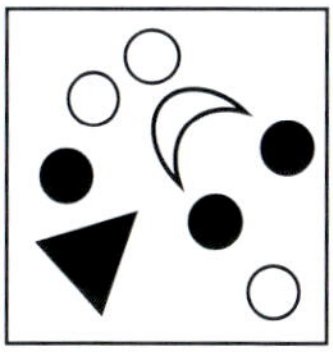

☐ Set A
☐ Set B
☐ Neither

Subset 5.3

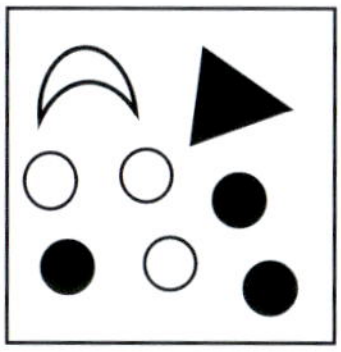

☐ Set A
☐ Set B
☐ Neither

Subset 5.4

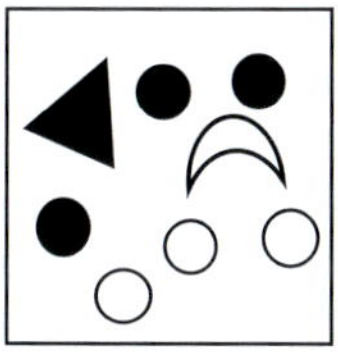

☐ Set A
☐ Set B
☐ Neither

Subset 5.5

☐ Set A
☐ Set B
☐ Neither

TYPE I - Question 6

Match the following subsets to the sets above.

Set A

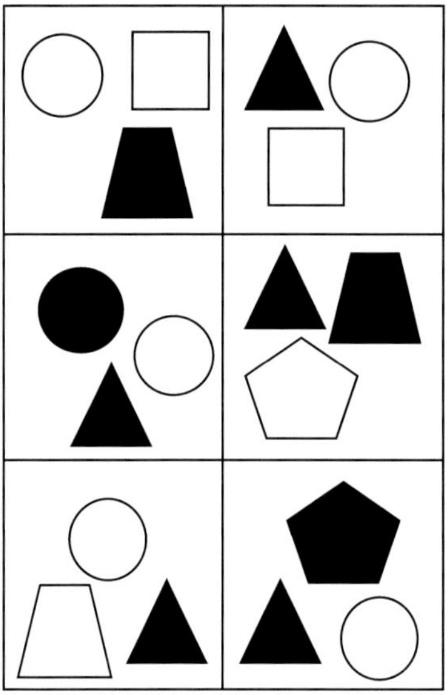

Set B

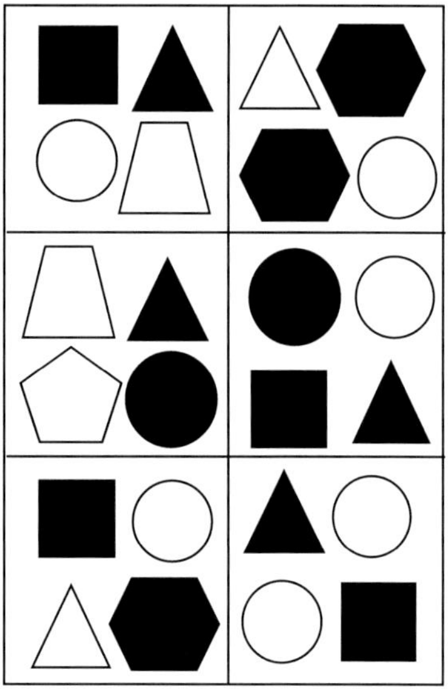

Subset 6.1

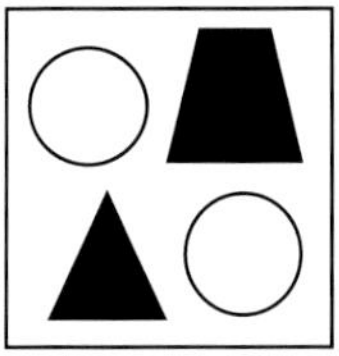

- ☐ Set A
- ☐ Set B
- ☐ Neither

Subset 6.2

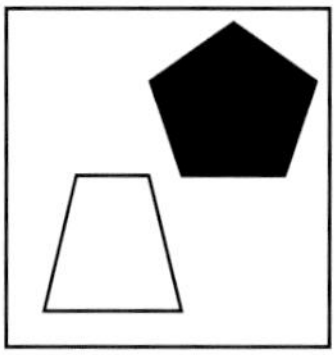

- ☐ Set A
- ☐ Set B
- ☐ Neither

Subset 6.3

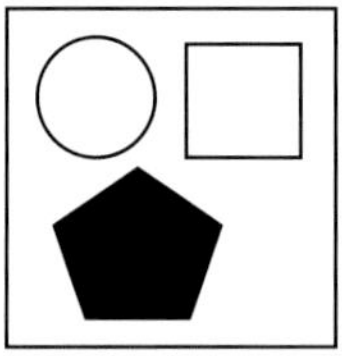

- ☐ Set A
- ☐ Set B
- ☐ Neither

Subset 6.4

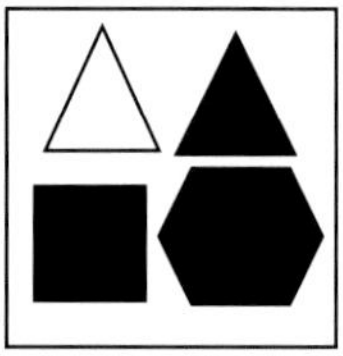

- ☐ Set A
- ☐ Set B
- ☐ Neither

Subset 6.5

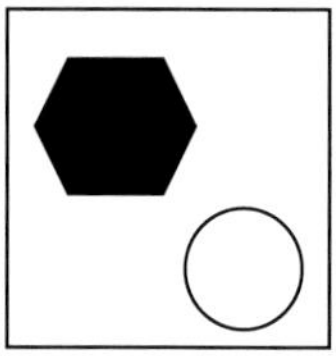

- ☐ Set A
- ☐ Set B
- ☐ Neither

TYPE I - Question 7

Match the following subsets to the sets above.

Set A

Set B

Subset 7.1

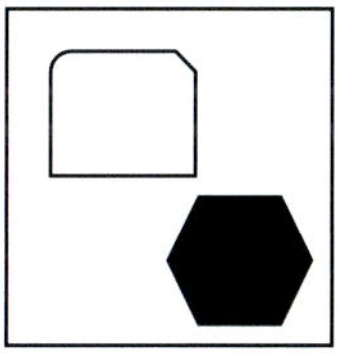

- ☐ Set A
- ☐ Set B
- ☐ Neither

Subset 7.2

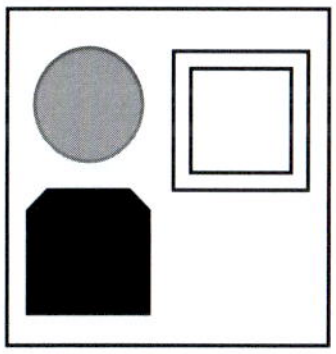

- ☐ Set A
- ☐ Set B
- ☐ Neither

Subset 7.3

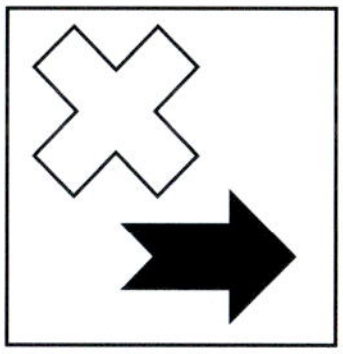

- ☐ Set A
- ☐ Set B
- ☐ Neither

Subset 7.4

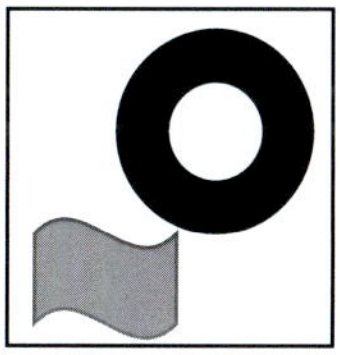

- ☐ Set A
- ☐ Set B
- ☐ Neither

Subset 7.5

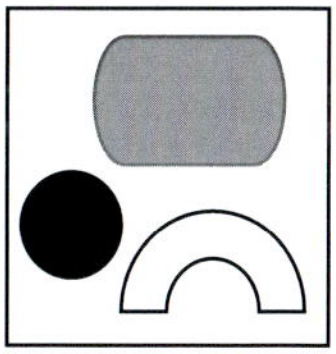

- ☐ Set A
- ☐ Set B
- ☐ Neither

TYPE I - Question 8

Match the following subsets to the sets above.

Set A

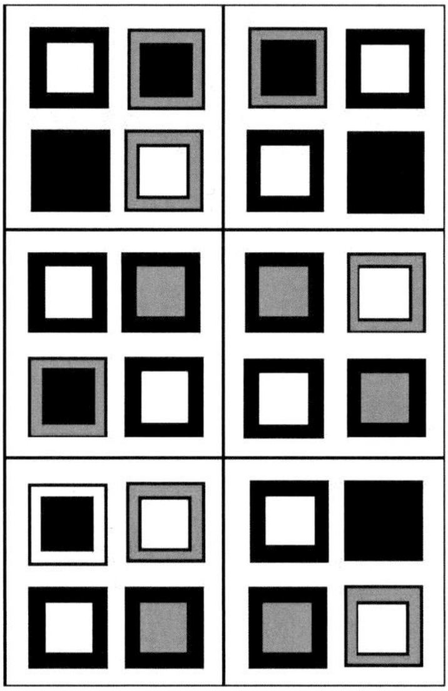

Set B

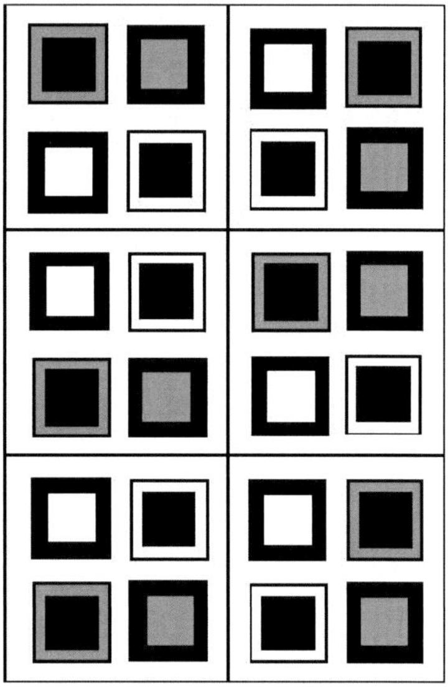

Subset 8.1

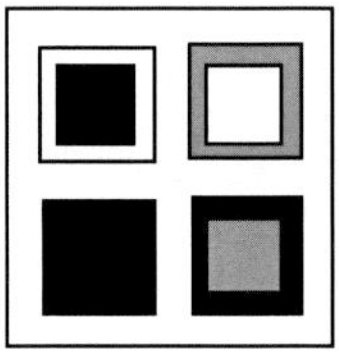

Subset 8.2

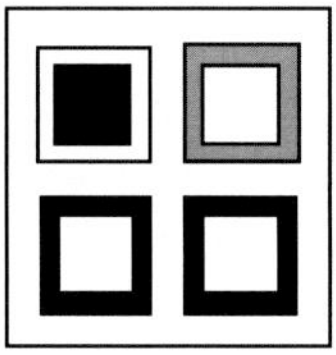

Subset 8.3

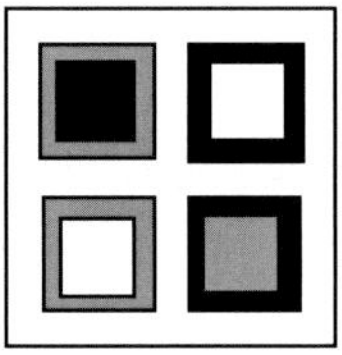

Subset 8.4

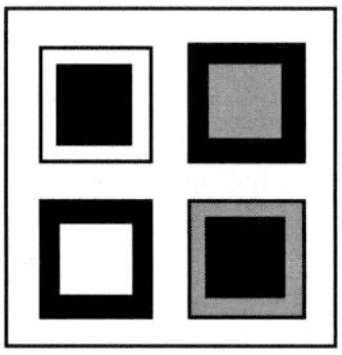

Subset 8.5

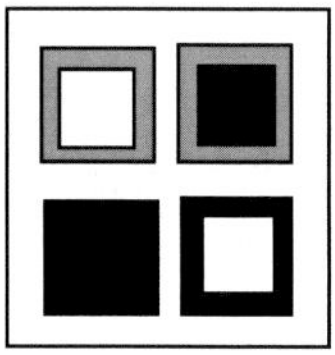

Subset 8.1	Subset 8.2	Subset 8.3	Subset 8.4	Subset 8.5
☐ Set A	☐ Set A	☐ Set A	☐ Set A	☐ Set A
☐ Set B	☐ Set B	☐ Set B	☐ Set B	☐ Set B
☐ Neither	☐ Neither	☐ Neither	☐ Neither	☐ Neither

TYPE I - Question 9

Match the following subsets to the sets above.

Set A

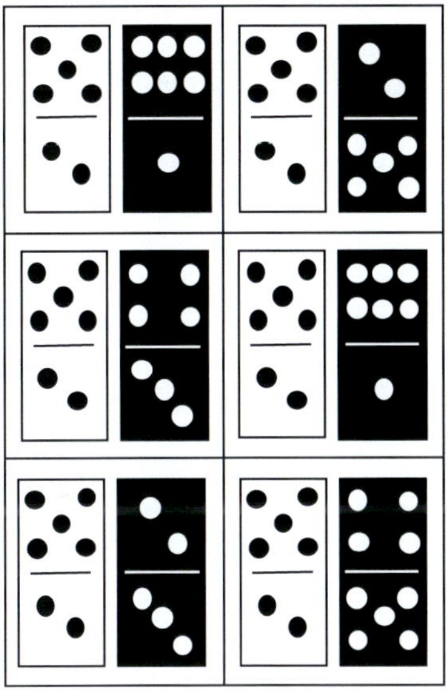

Set B

Subset 9.1	Subset 9.2	Subset 9.3	Subset 9.4	Subset 9.5
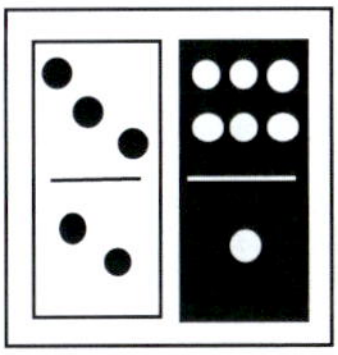	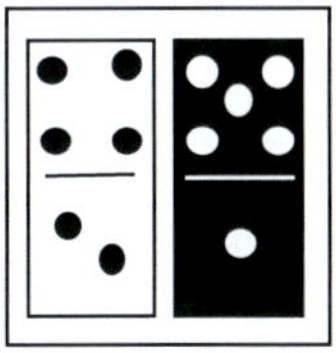		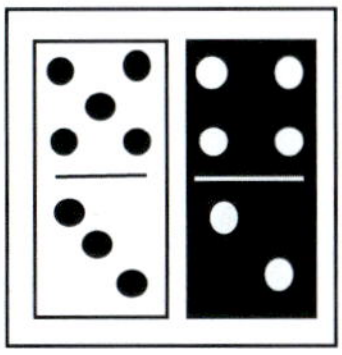	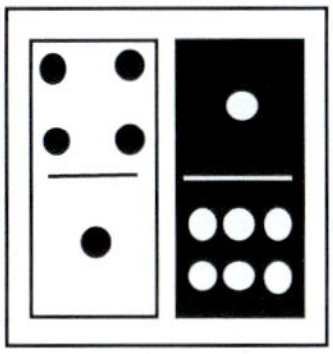
☐ Set A	☐ Set A	☐ Set A	☐ Set A	☐ Set A
☐ Set B	☐ Set B	☐ Set B	☐ Set B	☐ Set B
☐ Neither	☐ Neither	☐ Neither	☐ Neither	☐ Neither

TYPE I - Question 10

Match the following subsets to the sets above.

Set A

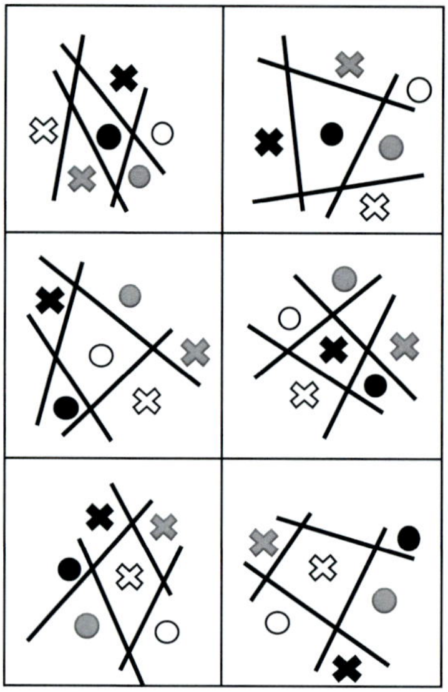

Set B

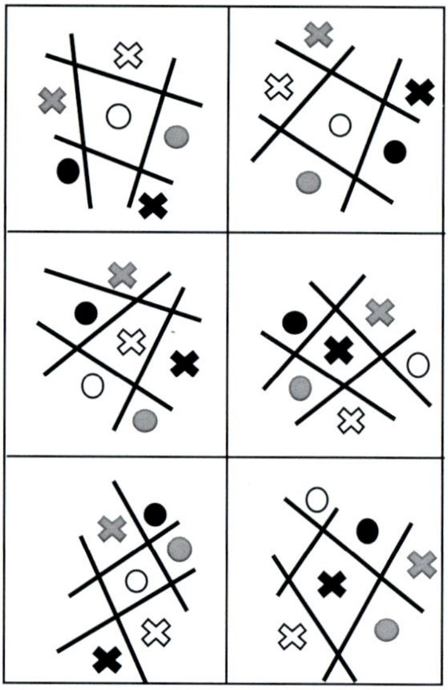

Subset 10.1

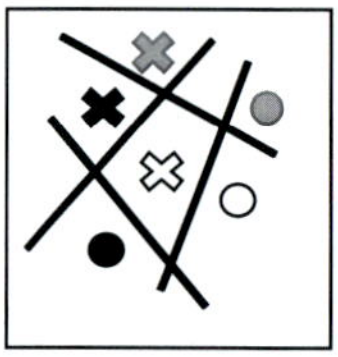

☐ Set A

☐ Set B

☐ Neither

Subset 10.2

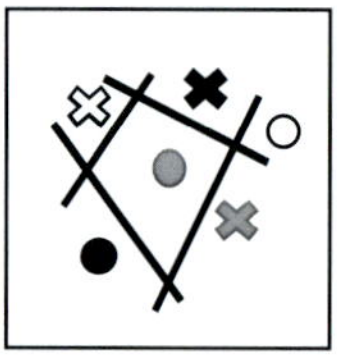

☐ Set A

☐ Set B

☐ Neither

Subset 10.3

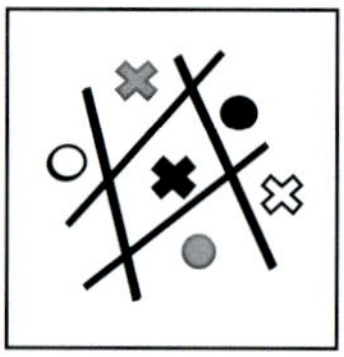

☐ Set A

☐ Set B

☐ Neither

Subset 10.4

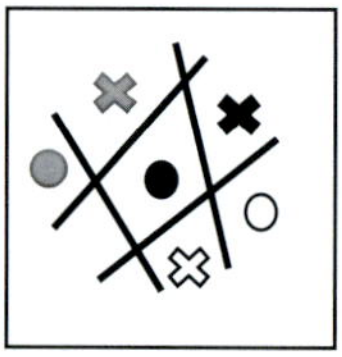

☐ Set A

☐ Set B

☐ Neither

Subset 10.5

☐ Set A

☐ Set B

☐ Neither

TYPE I - Question 11

Match the following subsets to the sets above.

Set A

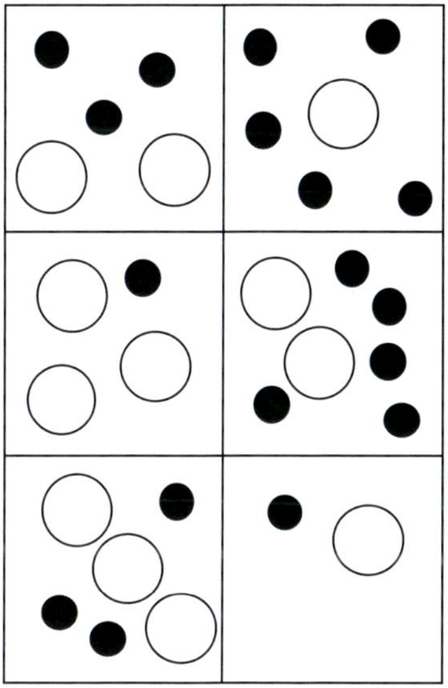

Set B

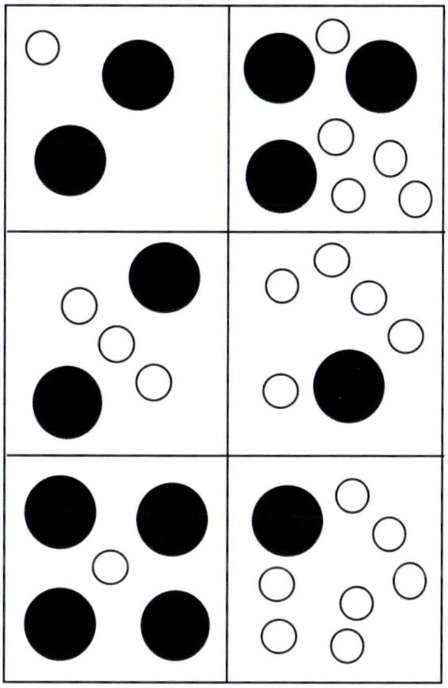

Subset 11.1	Subset 11.2	Subset 11.3	Subset 11.4	Subset 11.5
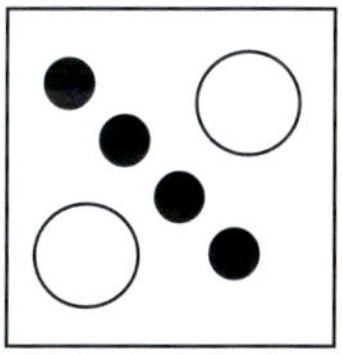	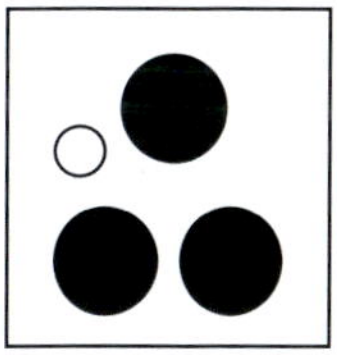	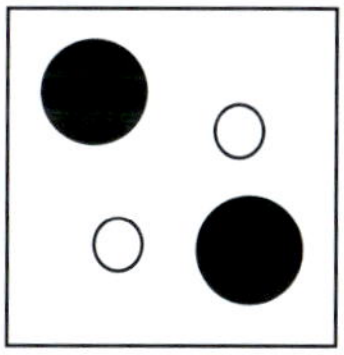	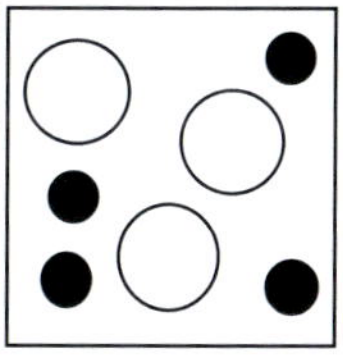	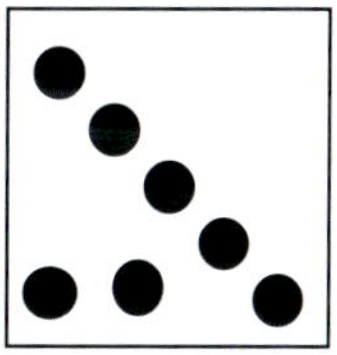
☐ Set A	☐ Set A	☐ Set A	☐ Set A	☐ Set A
☐ Set B	☐ Set B	☐ Set B	☐ Set B	☐ Set B
☐ Neither	☐ Neither	☐ Neither	☐ Neither	☐ Neither

TYPE I - Question 12

Match the following subsets to the sets above.

Set A

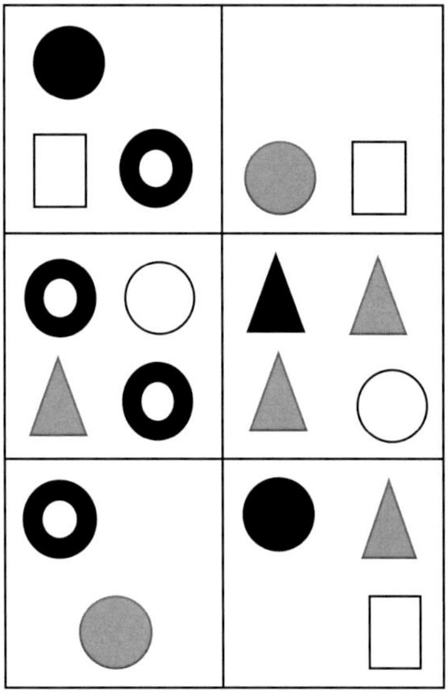

Set B

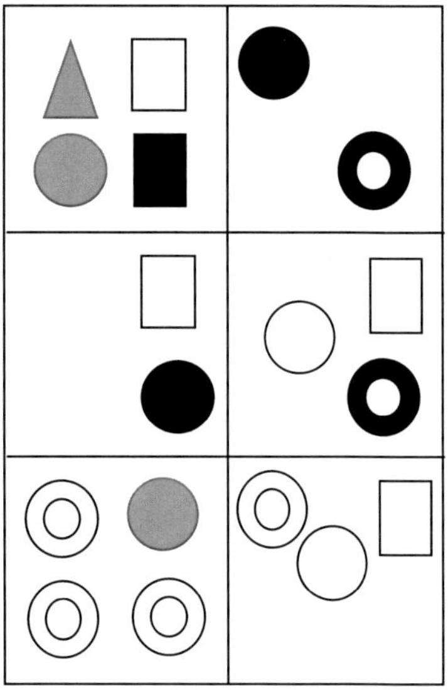

Subset 12.1

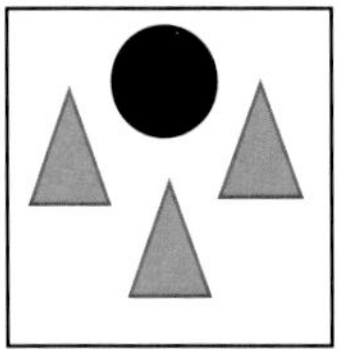

☐ Set A
☐ Set B
☐ Neither

Subset 12.2

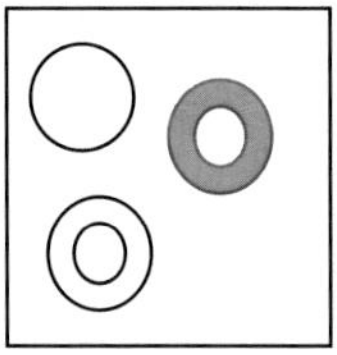

☐ Set A
☐ Set B
☐ Neither

Subset 12.3

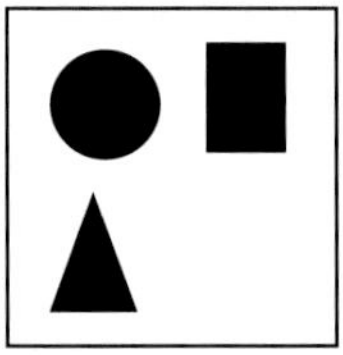

☐ Set A
☐ Set B
☐ Neither

Subset 12.4

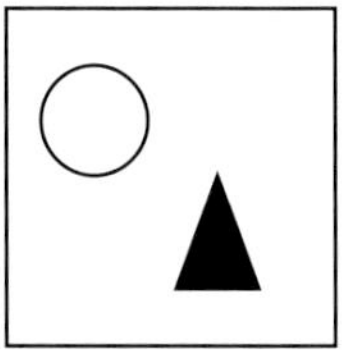

☐ Set A
☐ Set B
☐ Neither

Subset 12.5

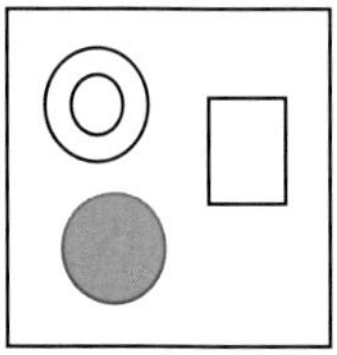

☐ Set A
☐ Set B
☐ Neither

TYPE I - Question 13

Match the following subsets to the sets above.

Set A

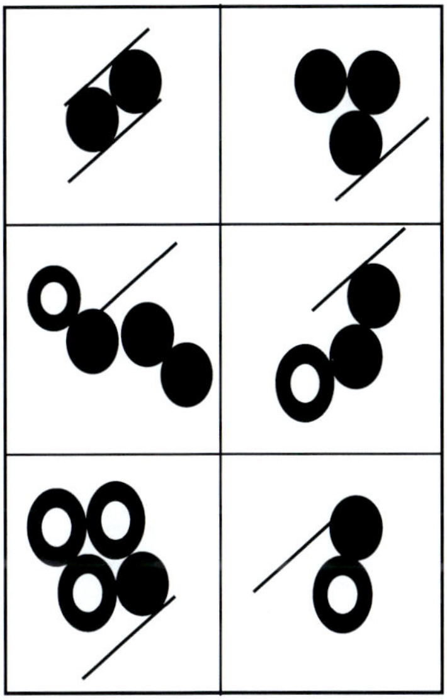

Set B

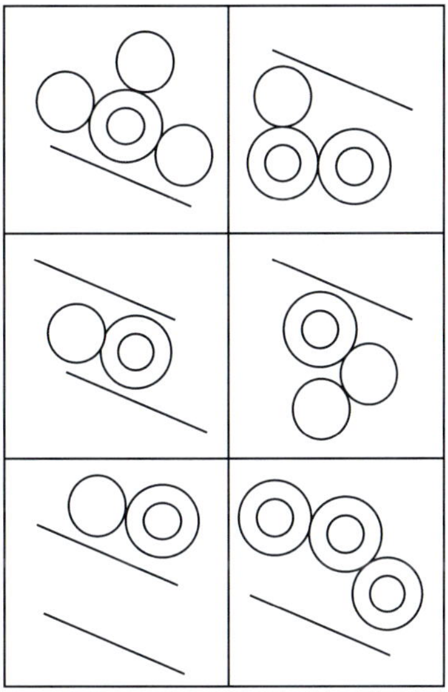

Subset 13.1	Subset 13.2	Subset 13.3	Subset 13.4	Subset 13.5
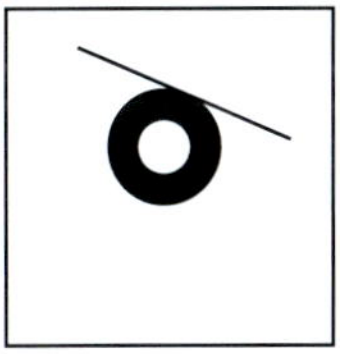	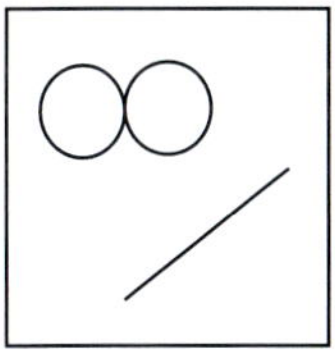		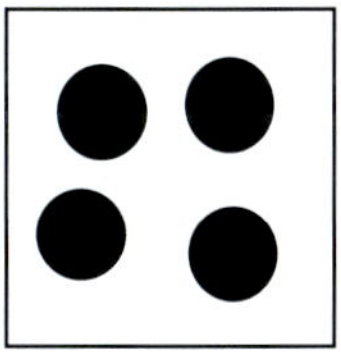	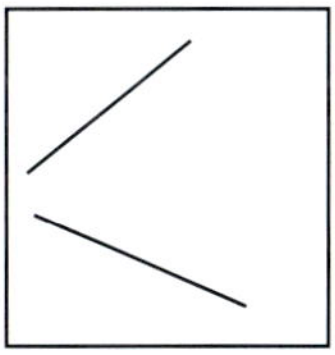
☐ Set A	☐ Set A	☐ Set A	☐ Set A	☐ Set A
☐ Set B	☐ Set B	☐ Set B	☐ Set B	☐ Set B
☐ Neither	☐ Neither	☐ Neither	☐ Neither	☐ Neither

TYPE I - Question 14

Match the following subsets to the sets above.

Set A

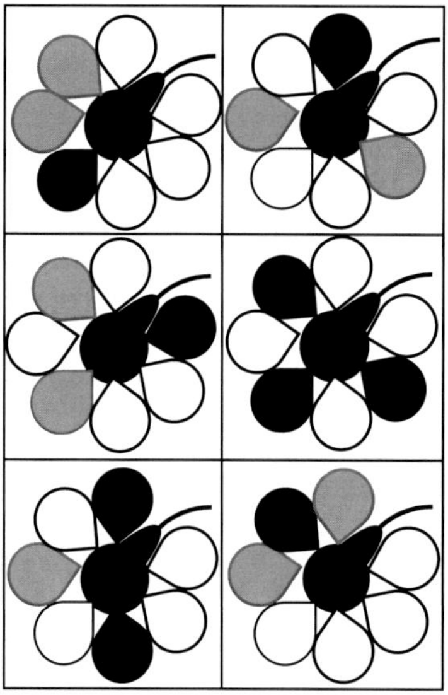

Set B

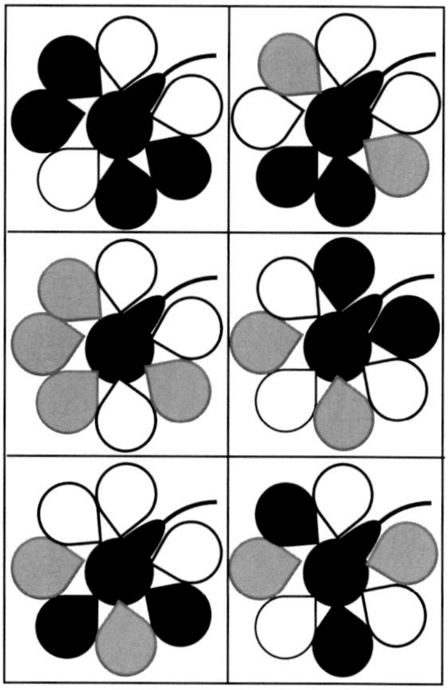

Subset 14.1

Subset 14.2

Subset 14.3

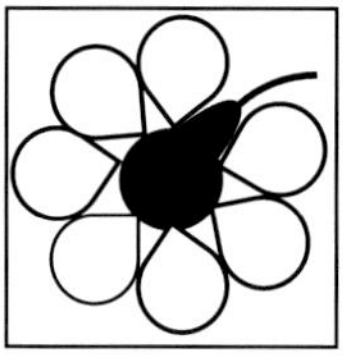

Subset 14.4

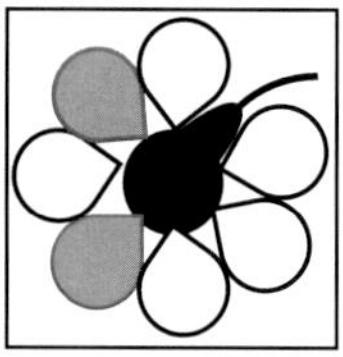

Subset 14.5

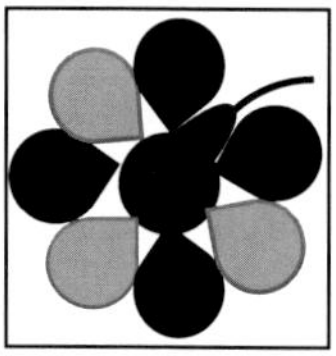

Subset 14.1	Subset 14.2	Subset 14.3	Subset 14.4	Subset 14.5
☐ Set A	☐ Set A	☐ Set A	☐ Set A	☐ Set A
☐ Set B	☐ Set B	☐ Set B	☐ Set B	☐ Set B
☐ Neither	☐ Neither	☐ Neither	☐ Neither	☐ Neither

TYPE I - Question 15

Match the following subsets to the sets above.

Set A

Set B

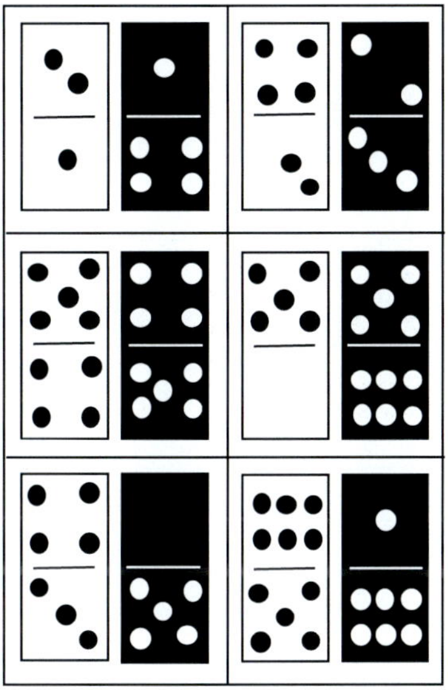

Subset 15.1	Subset 15.2	Subset 15.3	Subset 15.4	Subset 15.5
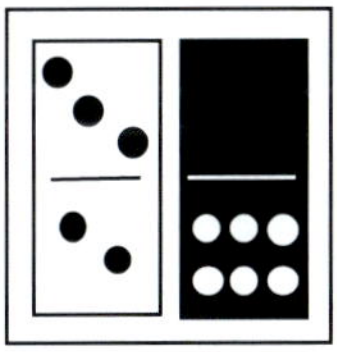		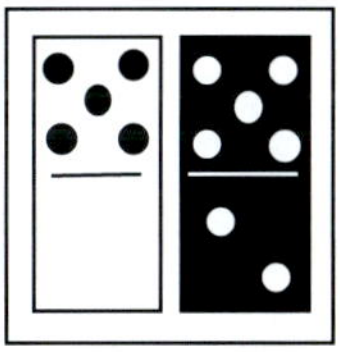	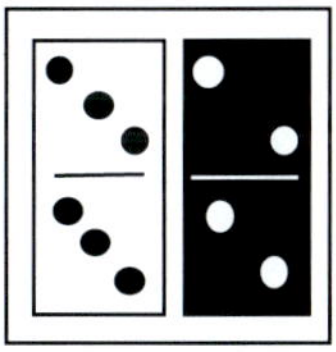	
☐ Set A	☐ Set A	☐ Set A	☐ Set A	☐ Set A
☐ Set B	☐ Set B	☐ Set B	☐ Set B	☐ Set B
☐ Neither	☐ Neither	☐ Neither	☐ Neither	☐ Neither

TYPE I - Question 16

Match the following subsets to the sets above.

Set A	Set B
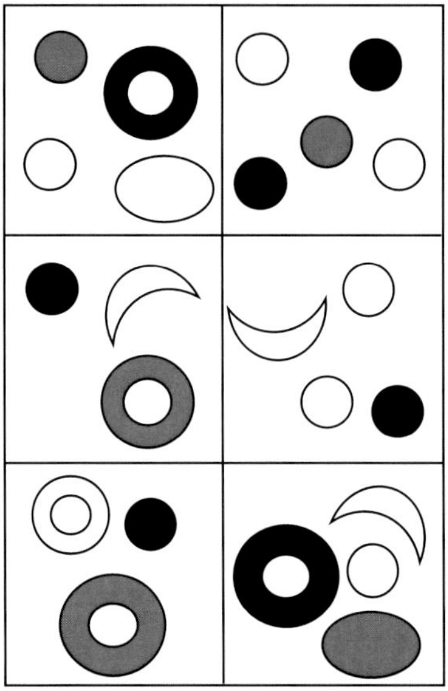	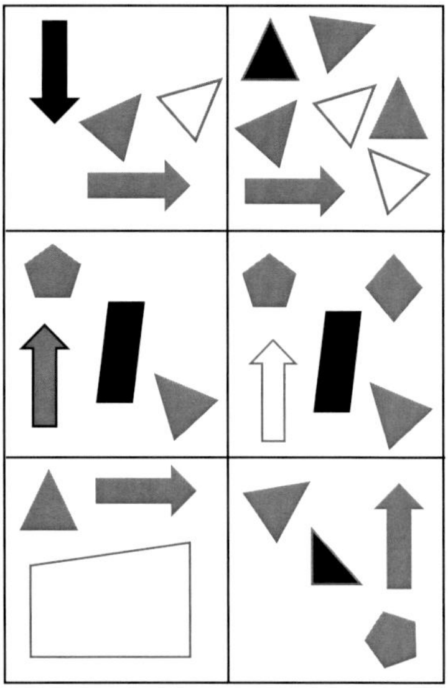

Subset 16.1	Subset 16.2	Subset 16.3	Subset 16.4	Subset 16.5
				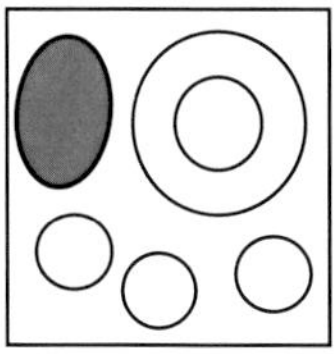
☐ Set A	☐ Set A	☐ Set A	☐ Set A	☐ Set A
☐ Set B	☐ Set B	☐ Set B	☐ Set B	☐ Set B
☐ Neither	☐ Neither	☐ Neither	☐ Neither	☐ Neither

TYPE I - Question 17

Match the following subsets to the sets above.

Set A

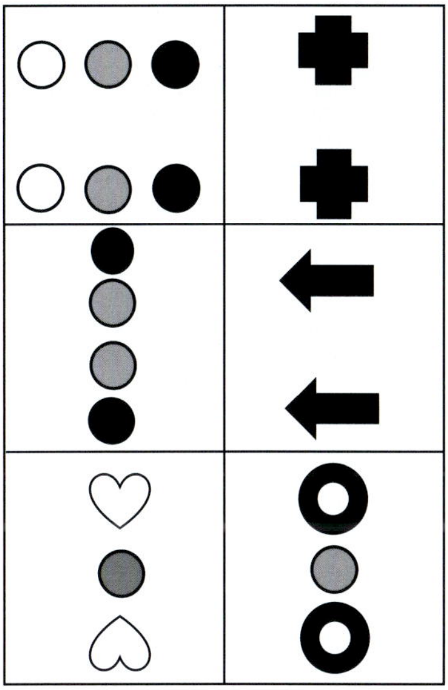

Set B

Subset 17.1 | Subset 17.2 | Subset 17.3 | Subset 17.4 | Subset 17.5

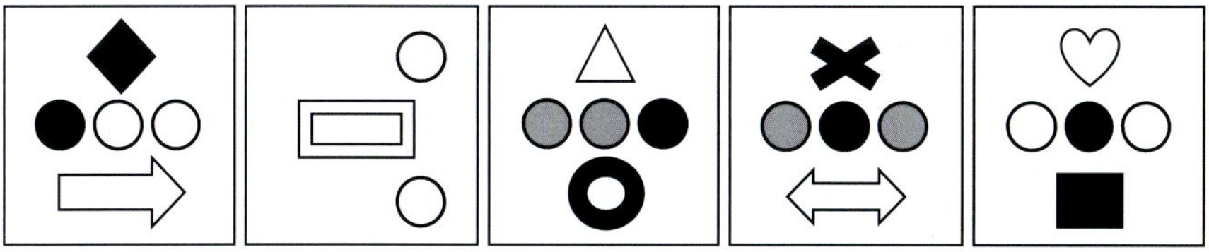

Subset 17.1	Subset 17.2	Subset 17.3	Subset 17.4	Subset 17.5
☐ Set A	☐ Set A	☐ Set A	☐ Set A	☐ Set A
☐ Set B	☐ Set B	☐ Set B	☐ Set B	☐ Set B
☐ Neither	☐ Neither	☐ Neither	☐ Neither	☐ Neither

TYPE I - Question 18

Match the following subsets to the sets above.

Set A

Set B

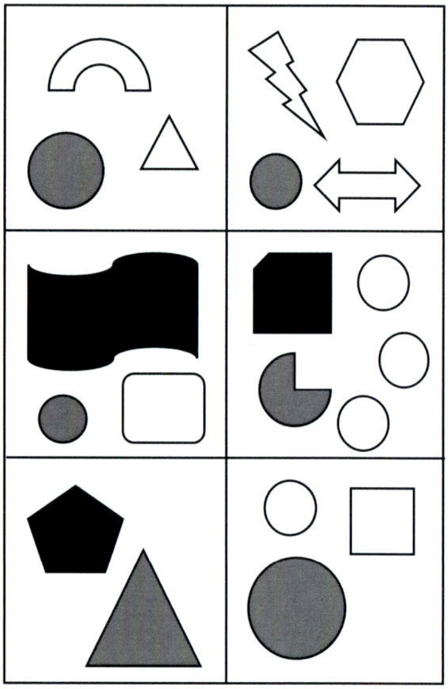

Subset 18.1

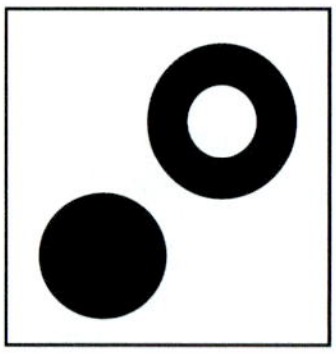

Subset 18.2

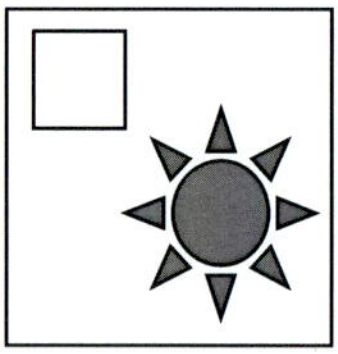

Subset 18.3

Subset 18.4

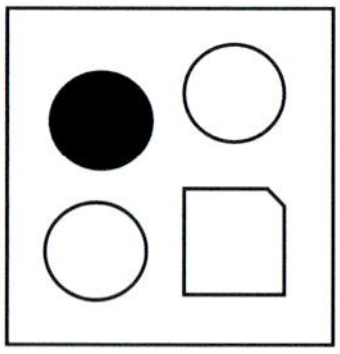

Subset 18.5

Subset 18.1	Subset 18.2	Subset 18.3	Subset 18.4	Subset 18.5
☐ Set A	☐ Set A	☐ Set A	☐ Set A	☐ Set A
☐ Set B	☐ Set B	☐ Set B	☐ Set B	☐ Set B
☐ Neither	☐ Neither	☐ Neither	☐ Neither	☐ Neither

TYPE I - Question 19

Match the following subsets to the sets above.

Set A

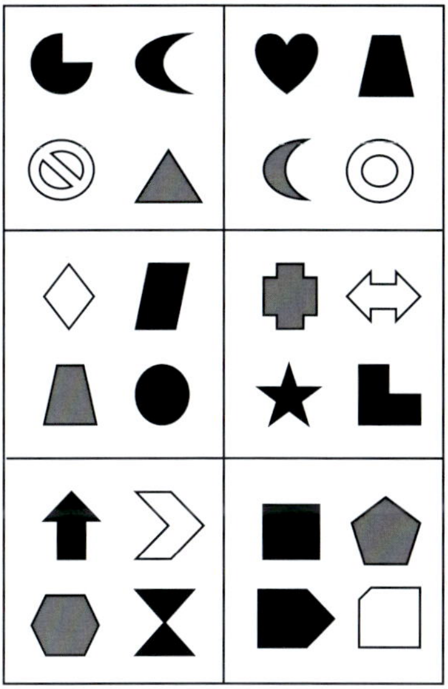

Set B

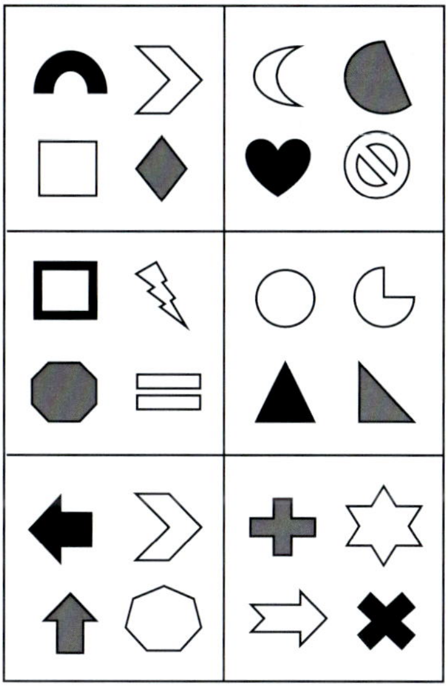

Subset 19.1

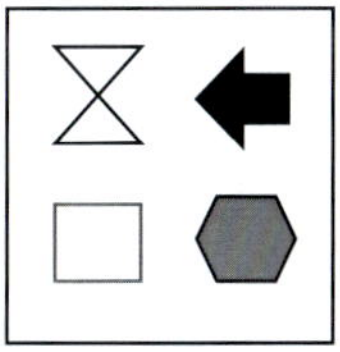

- ☐ Set A
- ☐ Set B
- ☐ Neither

Subset 19.2

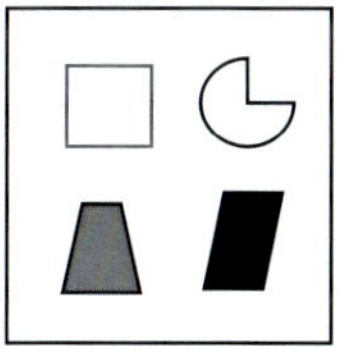

- ☐ Set A
- ☐ Set B
- ☐ Neither

Subset 19.3

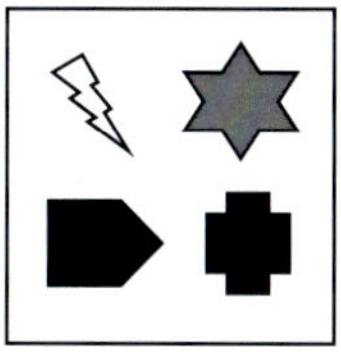

- ☐ Set A
- ☐ Set B
- ☐ Neither

Subset 19.4

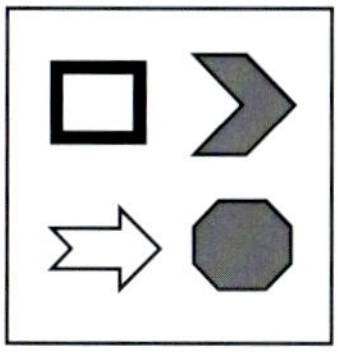

- ☐ Set A
- ☐ Set B
- ☐ Neither

Subset 19.5

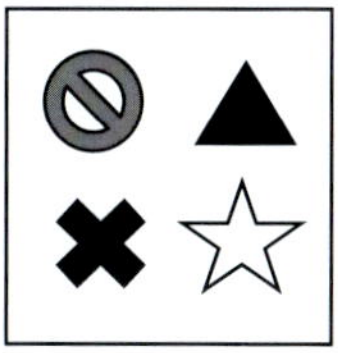

- ☐ Set A
- ☐ Set B
- ☐ Neither

TYPE I - Question 20

Match the following subsets to the sets above.

Set A

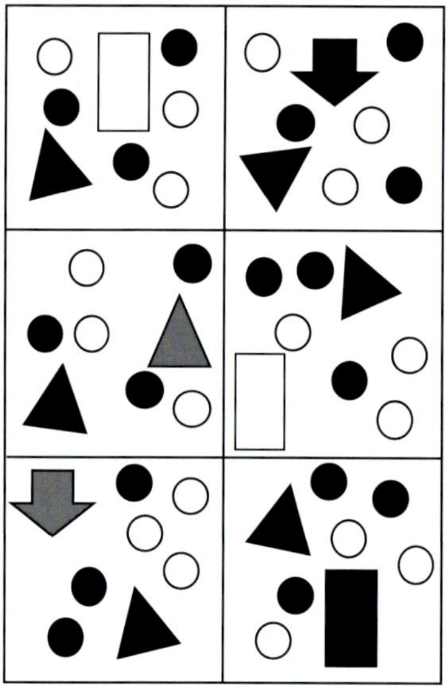

Set B

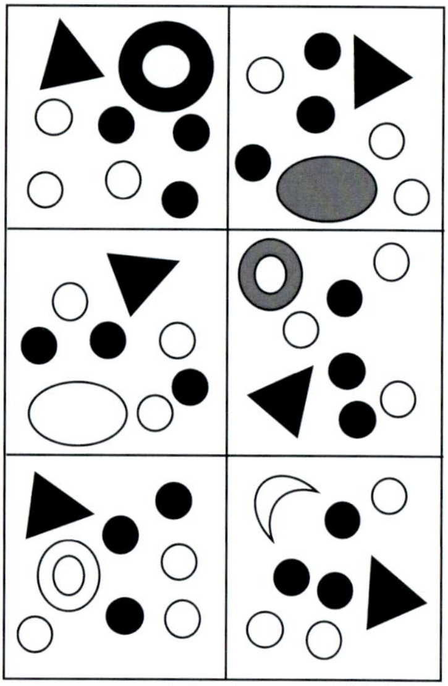

Subset 20.1

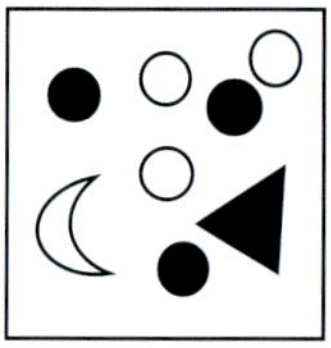

Subset 20.2

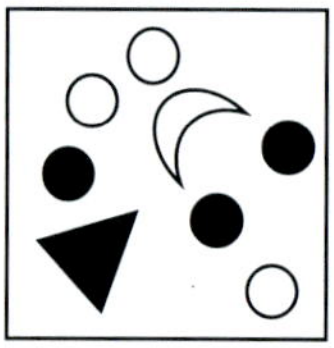

Subset 20.3

Subset 20.4

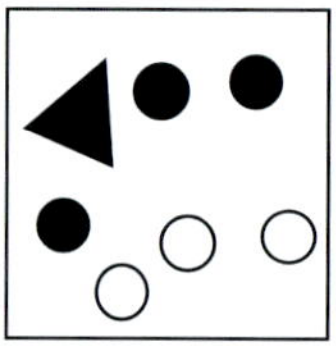

Subset 20.5

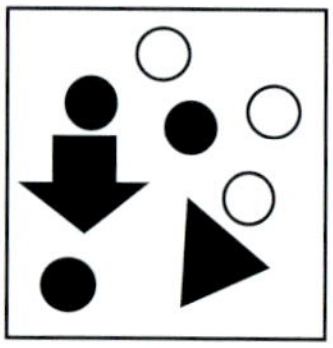

Subset 20.1	Subset 20.2	Subset 20.3	Subset 20.4	Subset 20.5
☐ Set A	☐ Set A	☐ Set A	☐ Set A	☐ Set A
☐ Set B	☐ Set B	☐ Set B	☐ Set B	☐ Set B
☐ Neither	☐ Neither	☐ Neither	☐ Neither	☐ Neither

TYPE I - Question 21

Match the following subsets to the sets above.

Set A

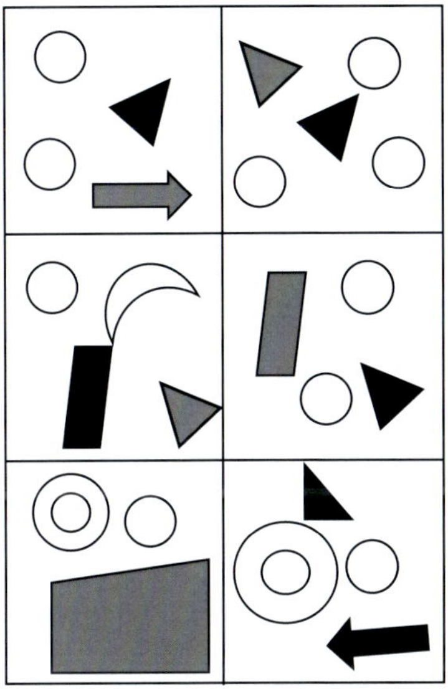

Set B

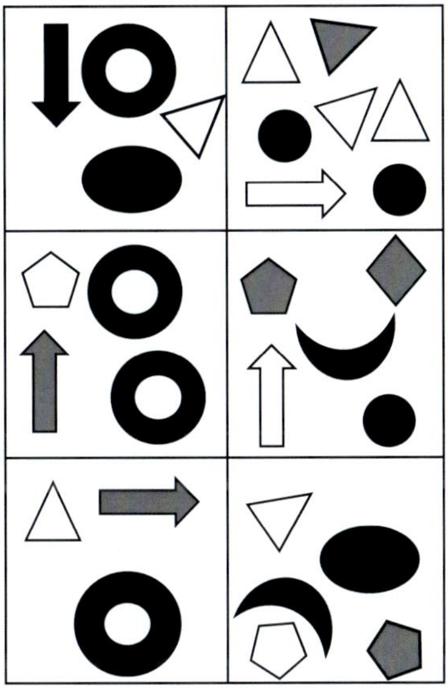

Subset 21.1

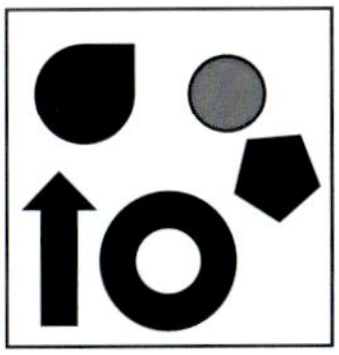

Subset 21.2

Subset 21.3

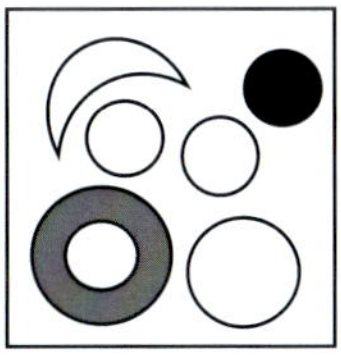

Subset 21.4

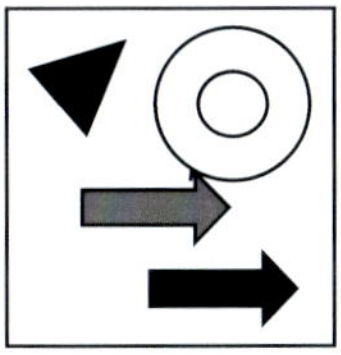

Subset 21.5

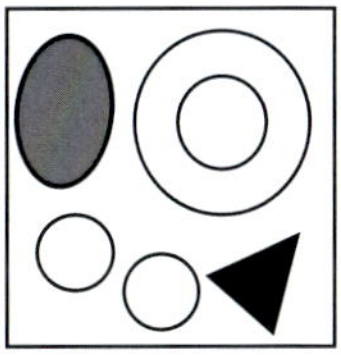

Subset 21.1	Subset 21.2	Subset 21.3	Subset 21.4	Subset 21.5
☐ Set A	☐ Set A	☐ Set A	☐ Set A	☐ Set A
☐ Set B	☐ Set B	☐ Set B	☐ Set B	☐ Set B
☐ Neither	☐ Neither	☐ Neither	☐ Neither	☐ Neither

TYPE I - Question 22

Match the following subsets to the sets above.

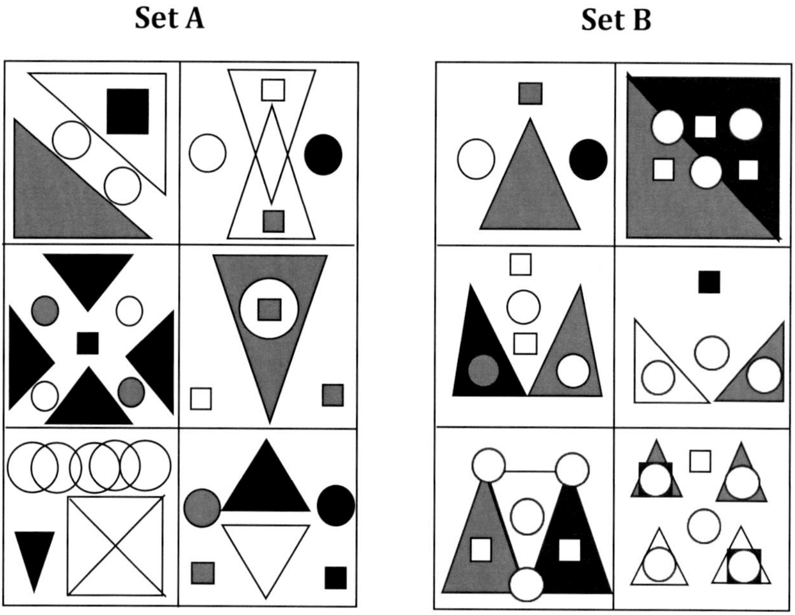

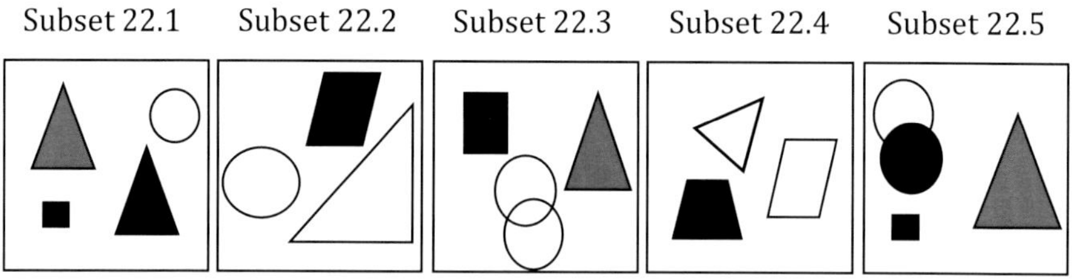

Subset 22.1	Subset 22.2	Subset 22.3	Subset 22.4	Subset 22.5
☐ Set A	☐ Set A	☐ Set A	☐ Set A	☐ Set A
☐ Set B	☐ Set B	☐ Set B	☐ Set B	☐ Set B
☐ Neither	☐ Neither	☐ Neither	☐ Neither	☐ Neither

TYPE I - Question 23

Match the following subsets to the sets above.

Set A **Set B**

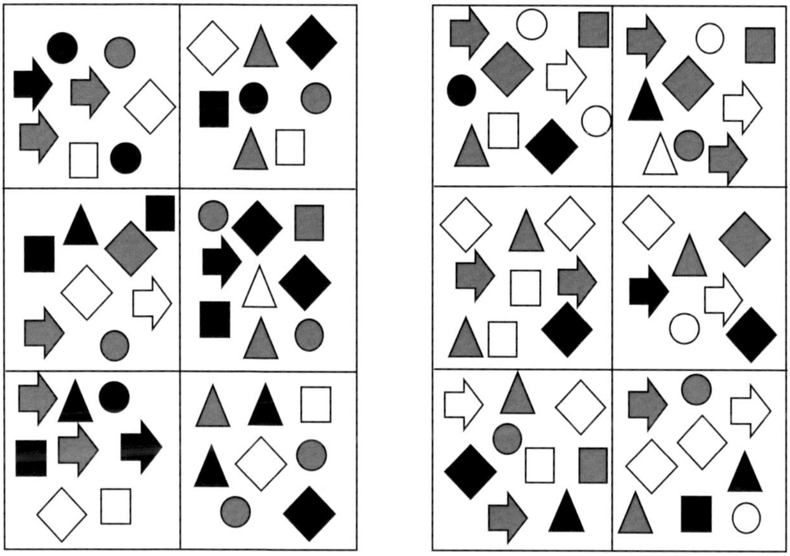

Subset 23.1 Subset 23.2 Subset 23.3 Subset 23.4 Subset 23.5

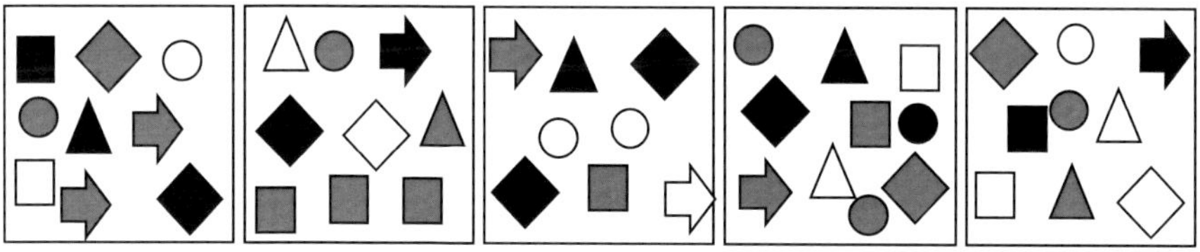

Subset 23.1	Subset 23.2	Subset 23.3	Subset 23.4	Subset 23.5
☐ Set A	☐ Set A	☐ Set A	☐ Set A	☐ Set A
☐ Set B	☐ Set B	☐ Set B	☐ Set B	☐ Set B
☐ Neither	☐ Neither	☐ Neither	☐ Neither	☐ Neither

TYPE I - Question 24

Match the following subsets to the sets above.

Set A

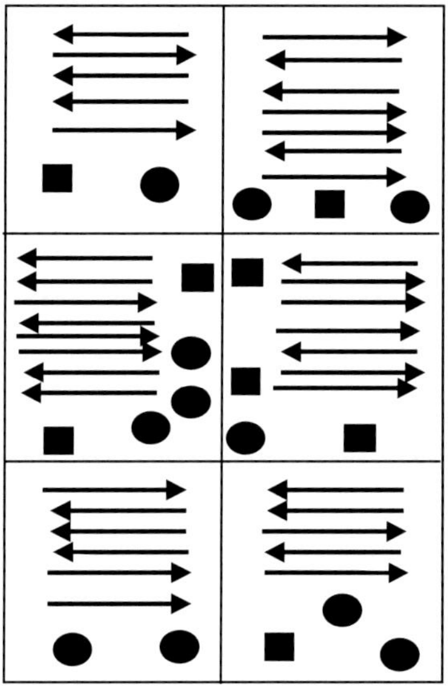

Set B

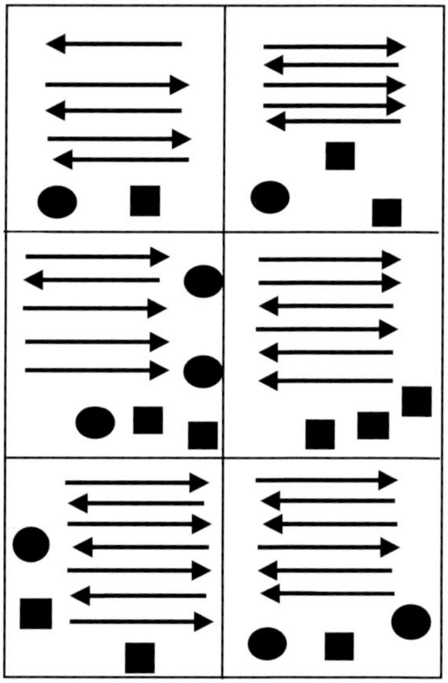

Subset 24.1

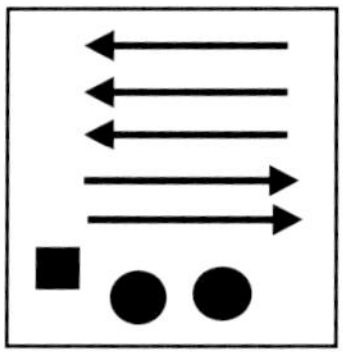

- ☐ Set A
- ☐ Set B
- ☐ Neither

Subset 24.2

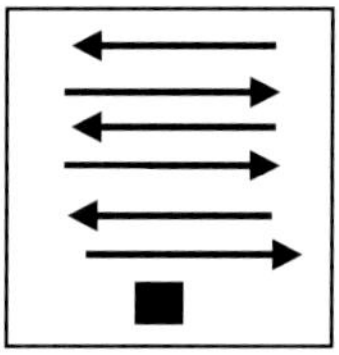

- ☐ Set A
- ☐ Set B
- ☐ Neither

Subset 24.3

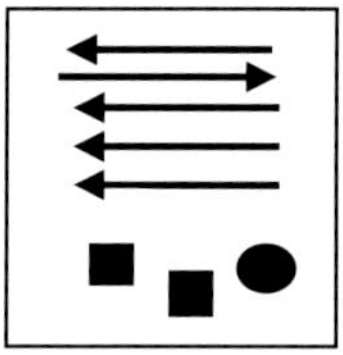

- ☐ Set A
- ☐ Set B
- ☐ Neither

Subset 24.4

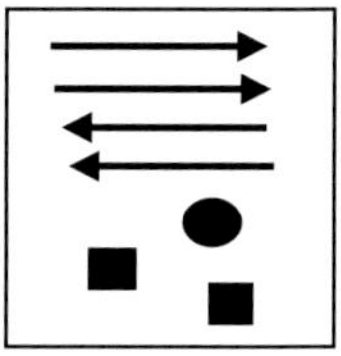

- ☐ Set A
- ☐ Set B
- ☐ Neither

Subset 24.5

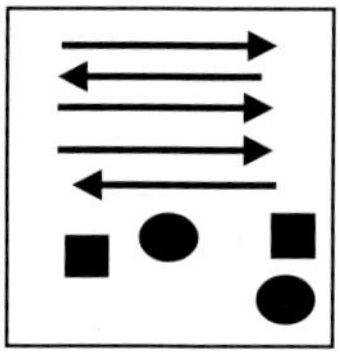

- ☐ Set A
- ☐ Set B
- ☐ Neither

TYPE I - Question 25

Match the following subsets to the sets above.

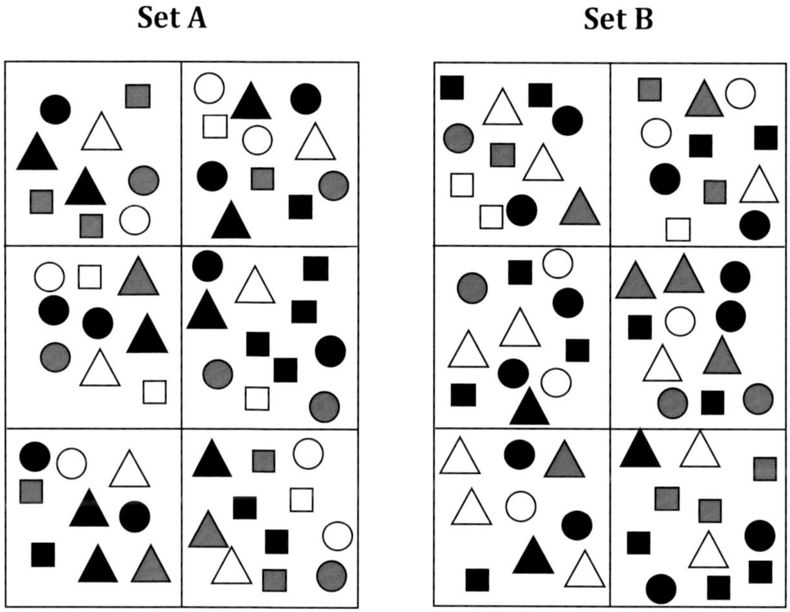

Subset 25.1 | Subset 25.2 | Subset 25.3 | Subset 25.4 | Subset 25.5

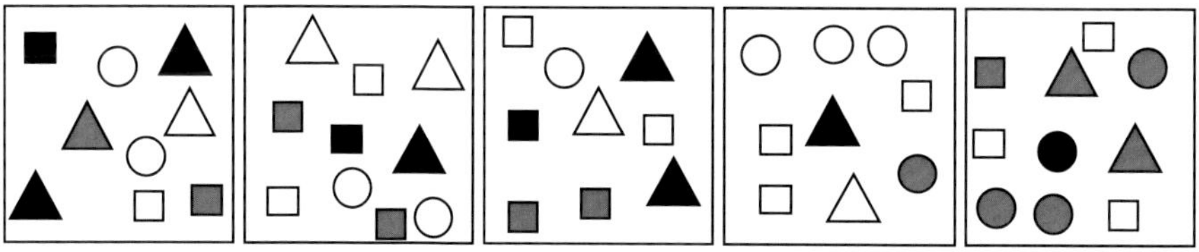

Subset 25.1	Subset 25.2	Subset 25.3	Subset 25.4	Subset 25.5
☐ Set A	☐ Set A	☐ Set A	☐ Set A	☐ Set A
☐ Set B	☐ Set B	☐ Set B	☐ Set B	☐ Set B
☐ Neither	☐ Neither	☐ Neither	☐ Neither	☐ Neither

TYPE II - Question 1

Which figure completes the series?

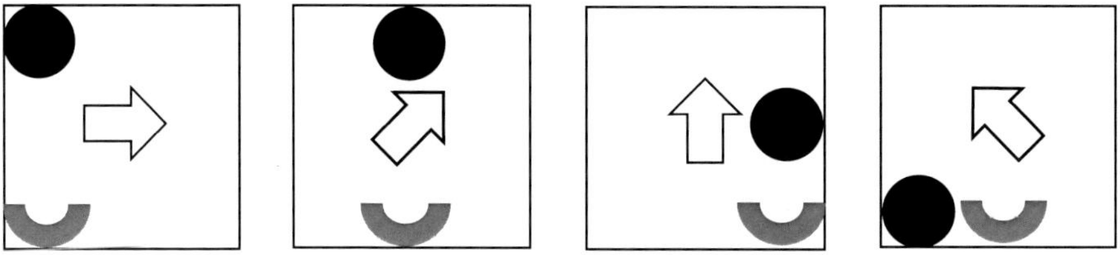

A B C D

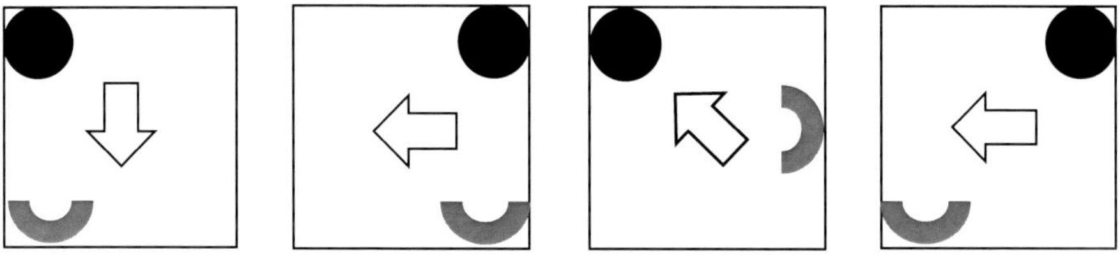

TYPE II - Question 2

Which figure completes the series?

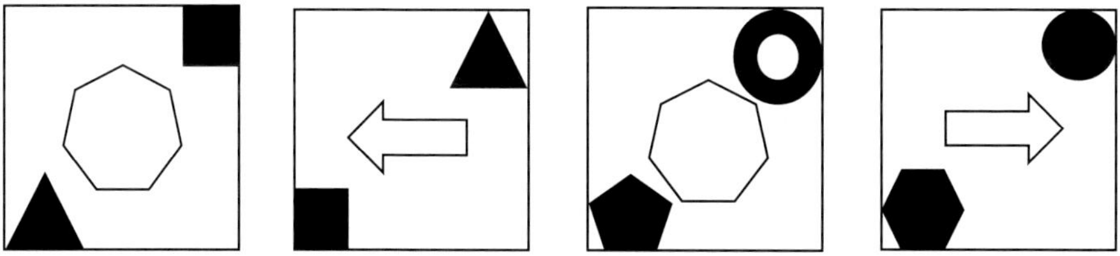

A B C D

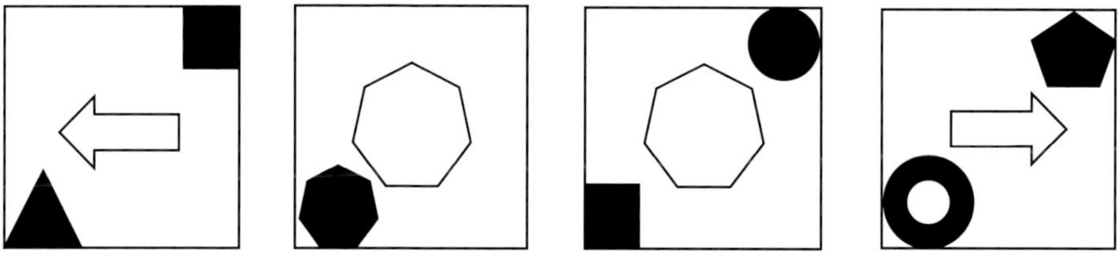

TYPE II - Question 3

Which figure completes the series?

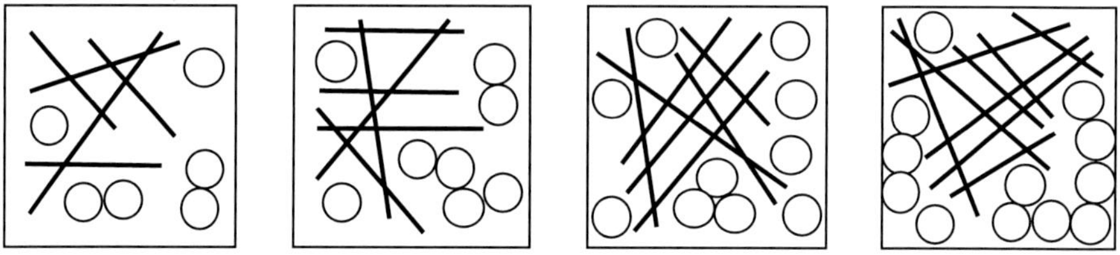

A B C D

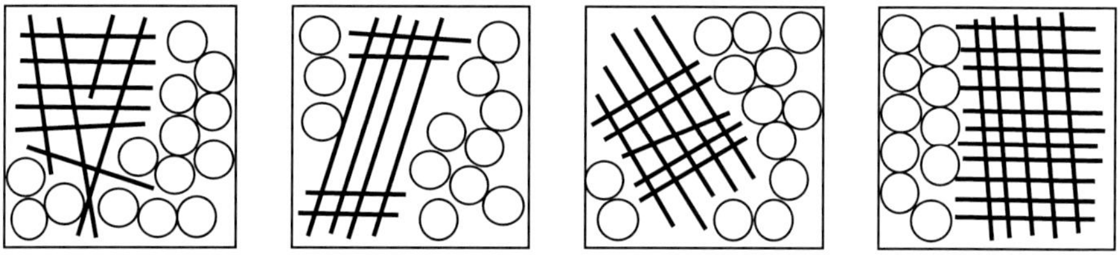

TYPE II - Question 4

Which figure completes the series?

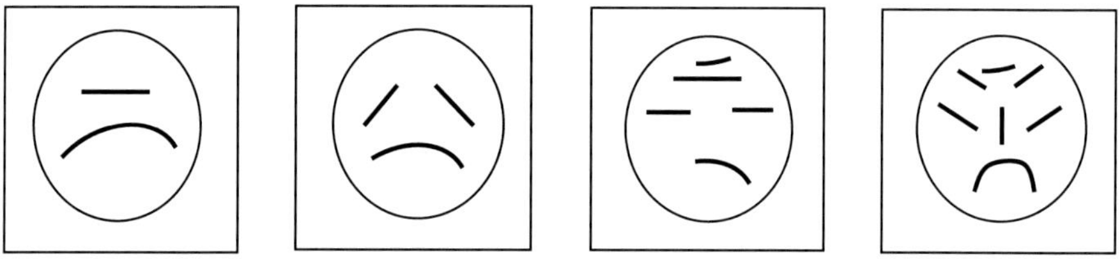

A B C D

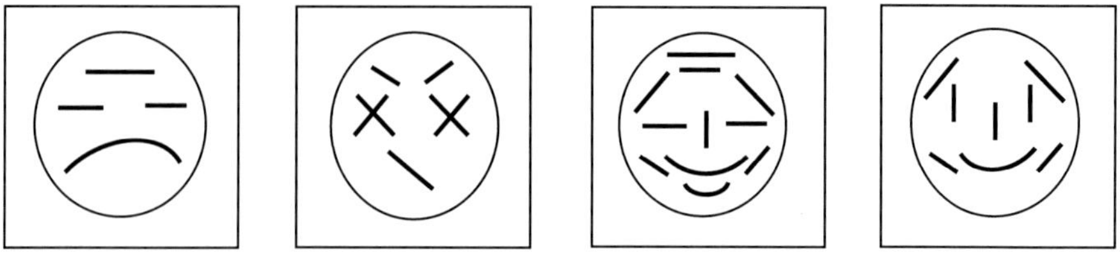

TYPE II - Question 5

Which figure completes the series?

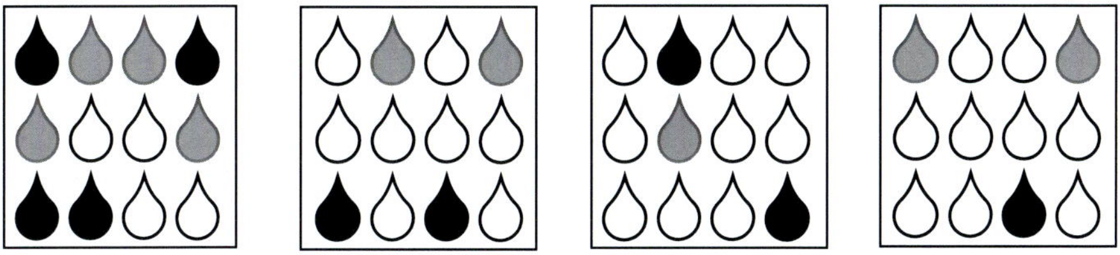

A B C D

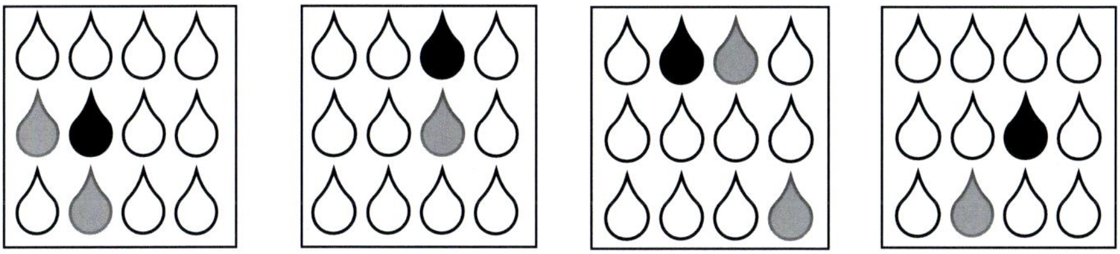

TYPE II - Question 6

Which figure completes the series?

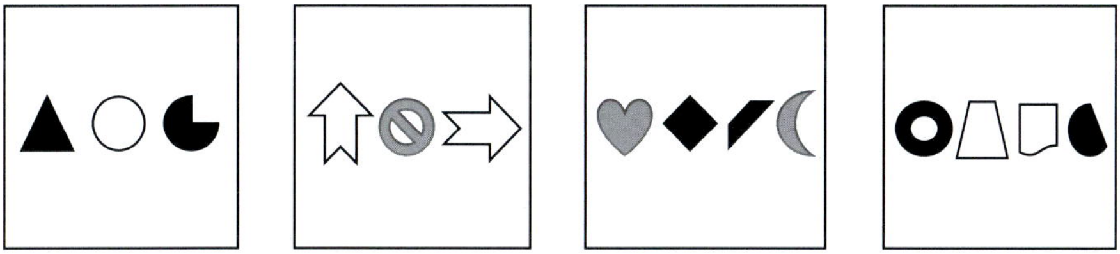

A B C D

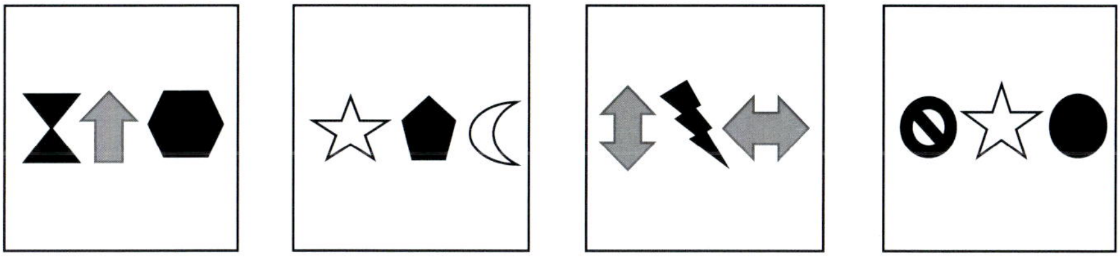

TYPE II - Question 7

Which figure completes the series?

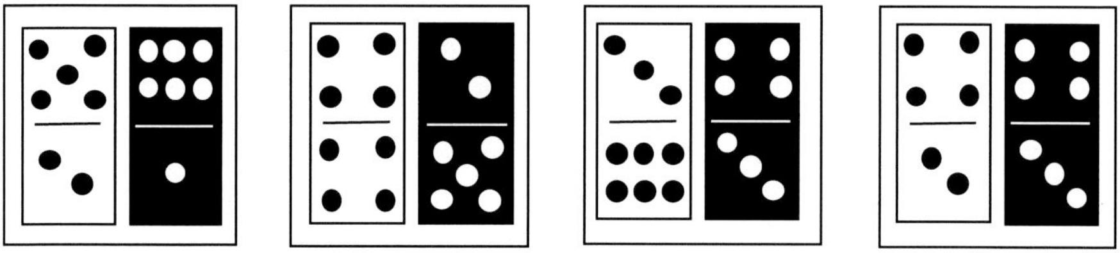

A

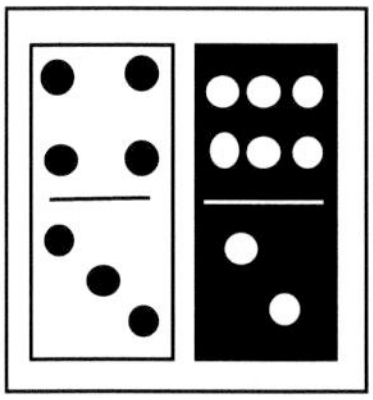

B

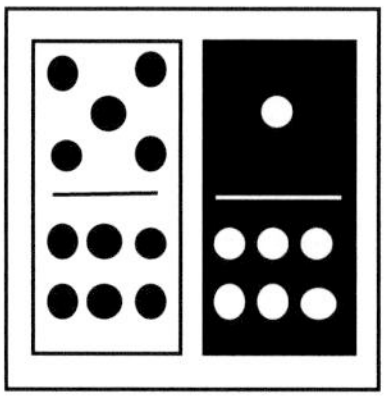

C

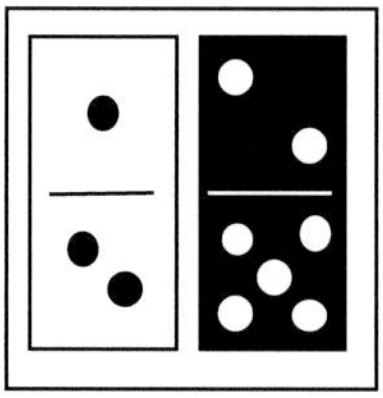

D

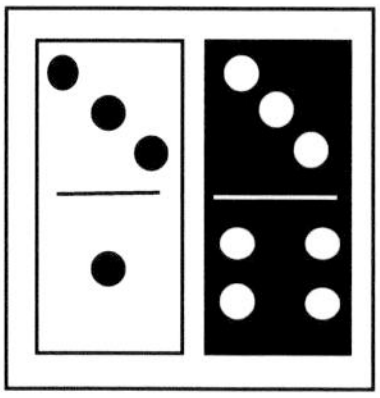

TYPE II - Question 8

Which figure completes the series?

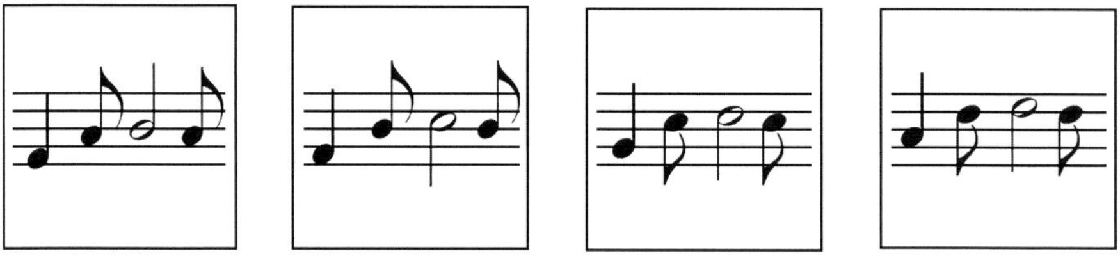

A

B

C

D

TYPE II - Question 9

Which figure completes the series?

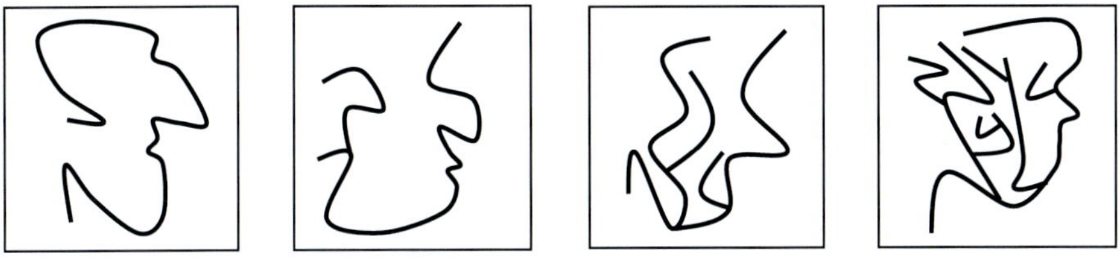

A B C D

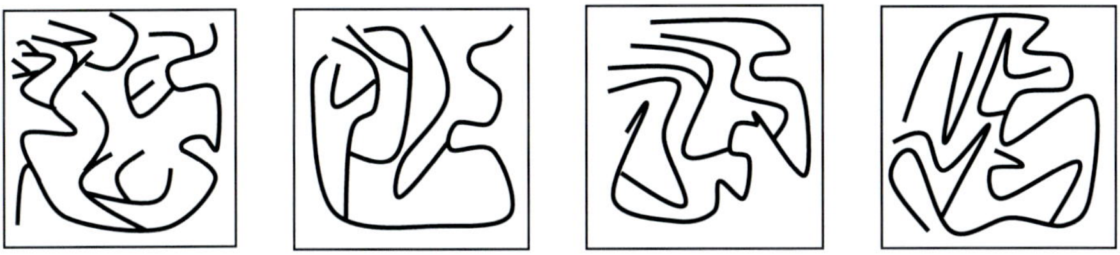

TYPE II - Question 10

Which figure completes the series?

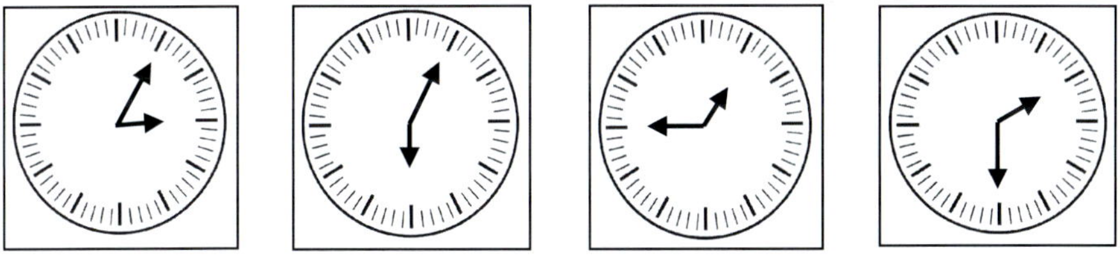

A B C D

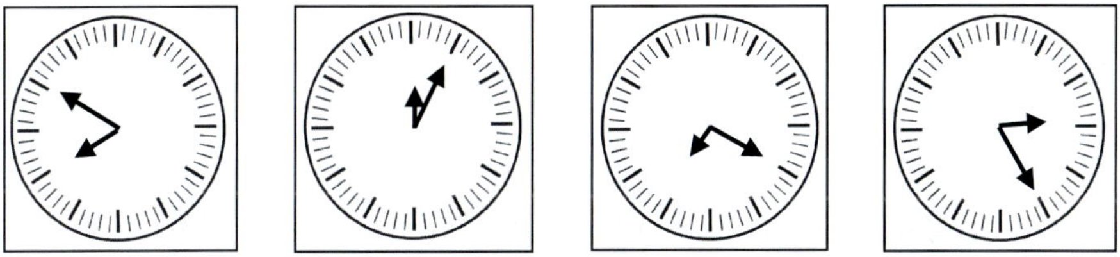

TYPE II - Question 11

Which figure completes the series?

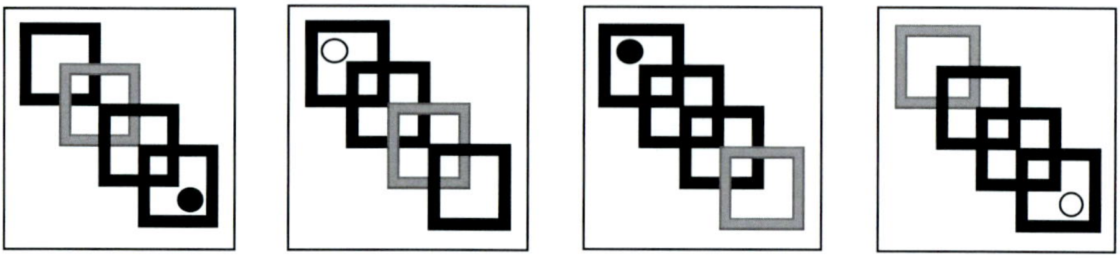

A B C D

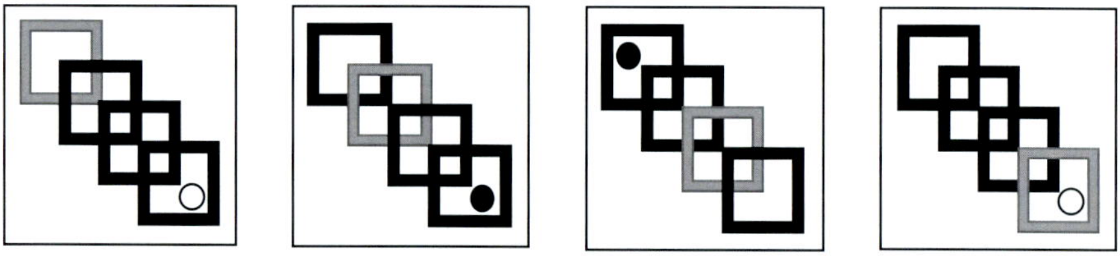

TYPE II - Question 12

Which figure completes the series?

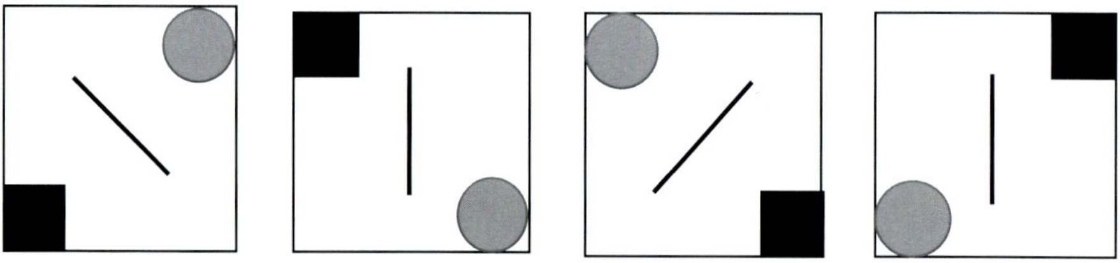

A B C D

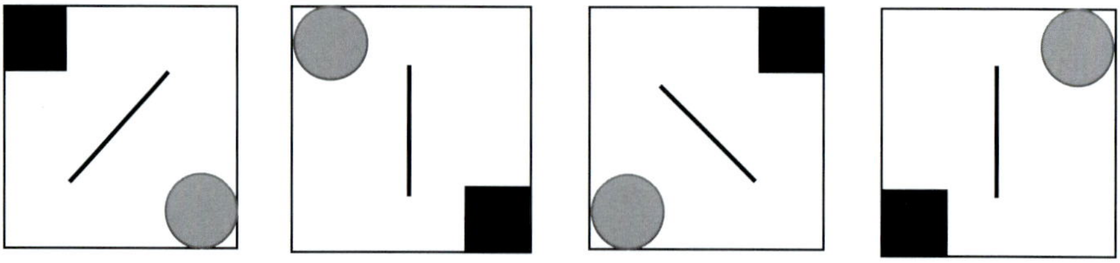

TYPE II - Question 13

Which figure completes the series?

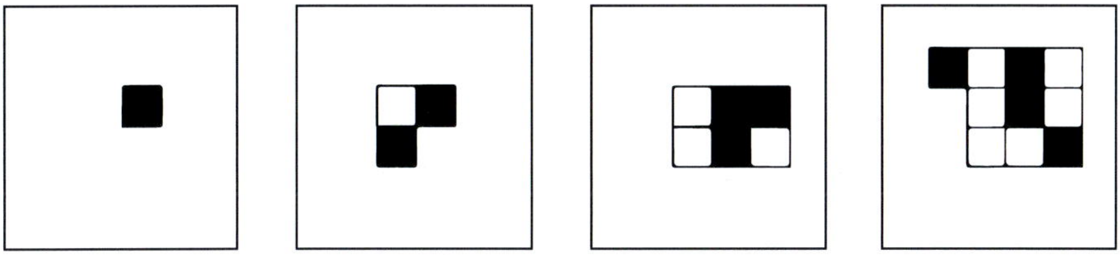

A B C D

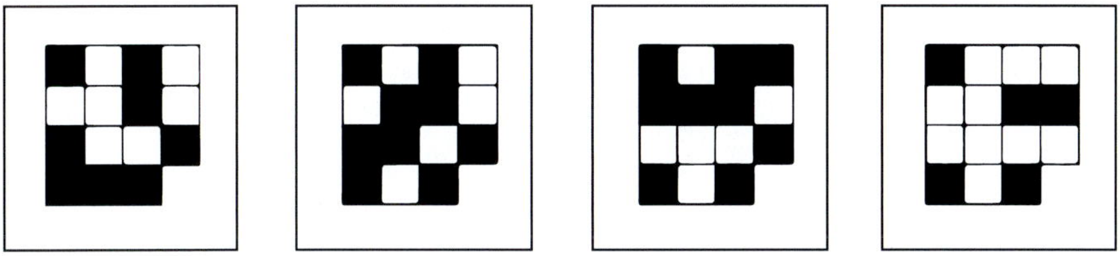

TYPE II - Question 14

Which figure completes the series?

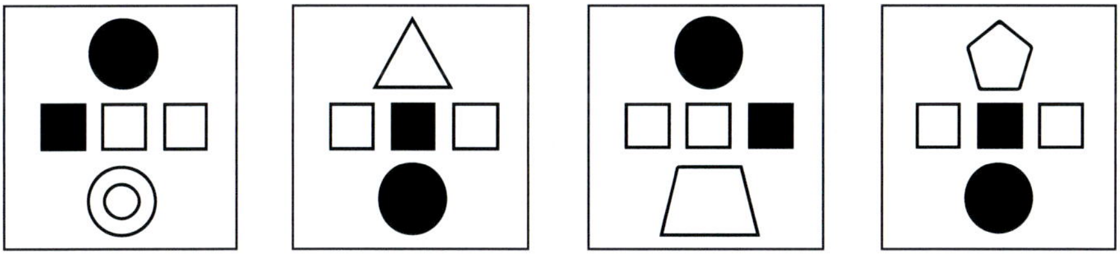

A B C D

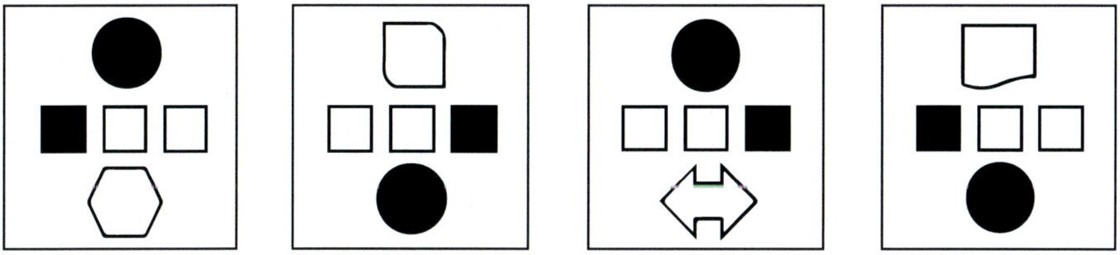

TYPE II - Question 15

Which figure completes the series?

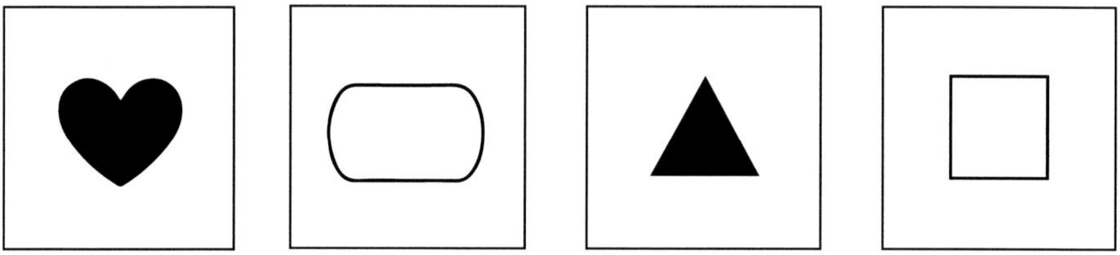

A B C D

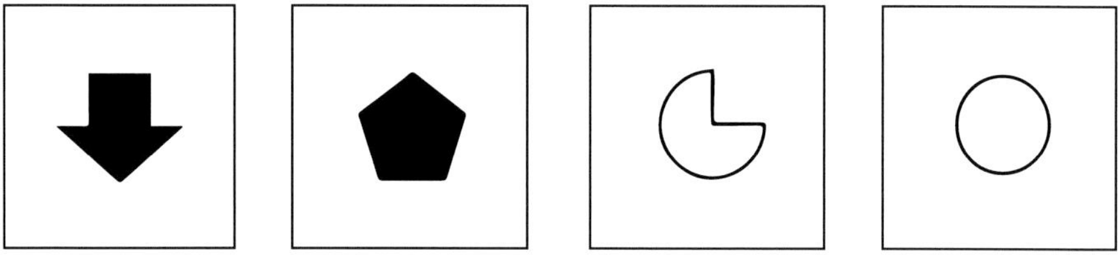

TYPE II - Question 16

Which figure completes the series?

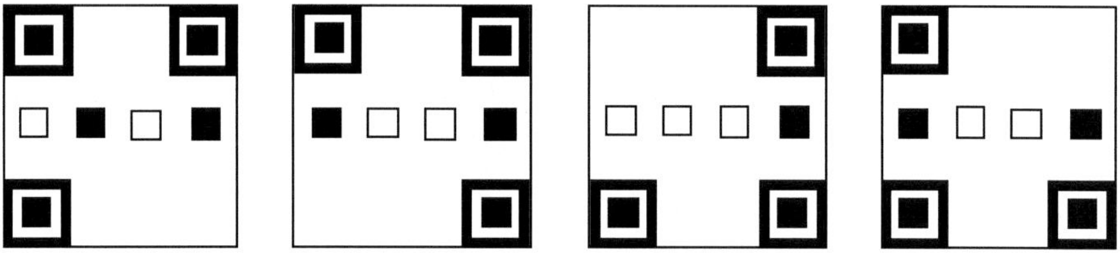

A B C D

TYPE II - Question 17

Which figure completes the series?

A

B

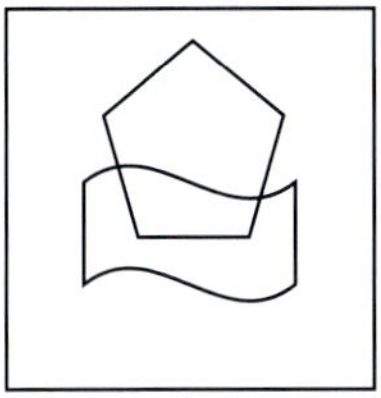

C

D

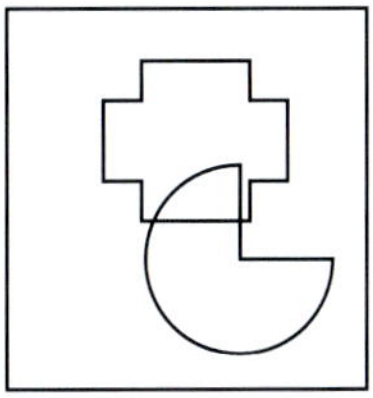

TYPE II - Question 18

Which figure completes the series?

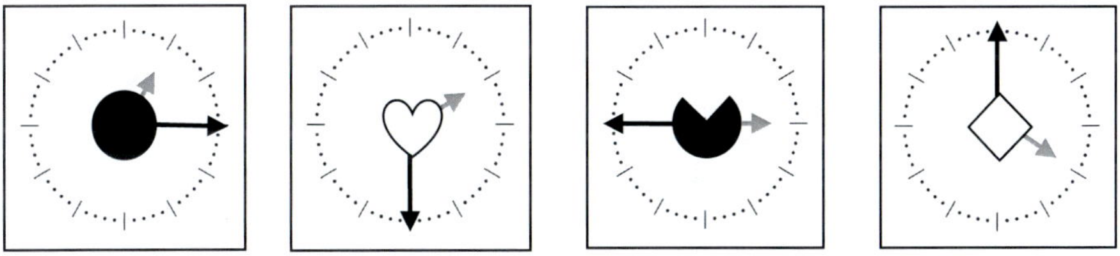

A

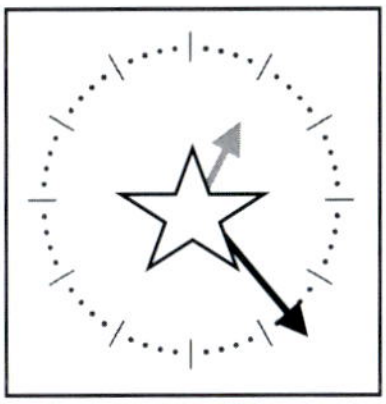

B

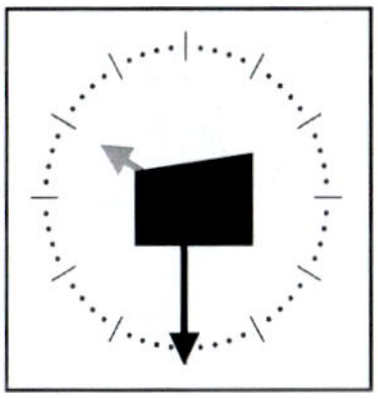

C

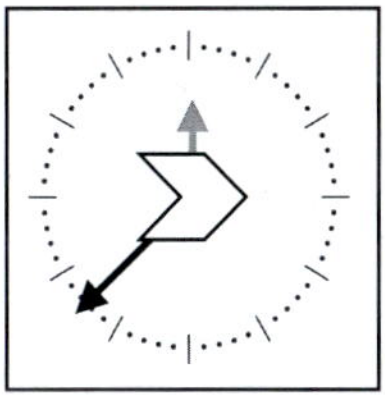

D

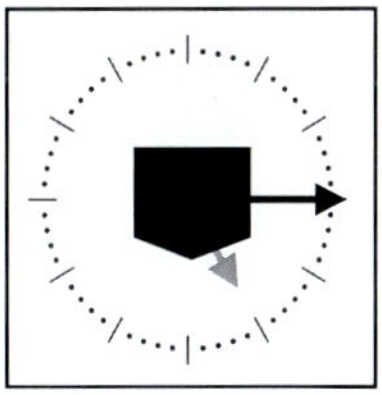

TYPE II - Question 19

Which figure completes the series?

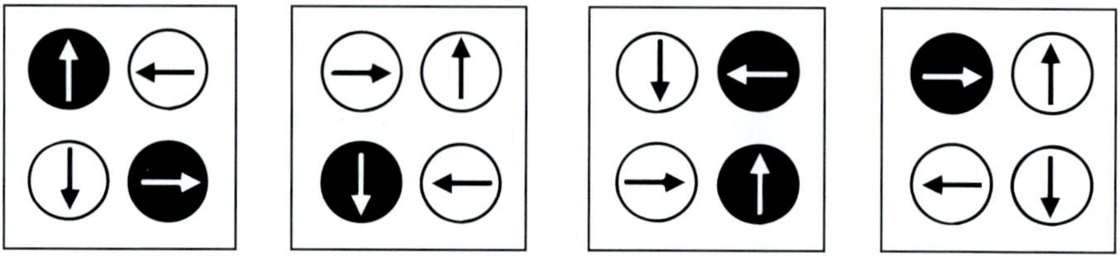

A B C D

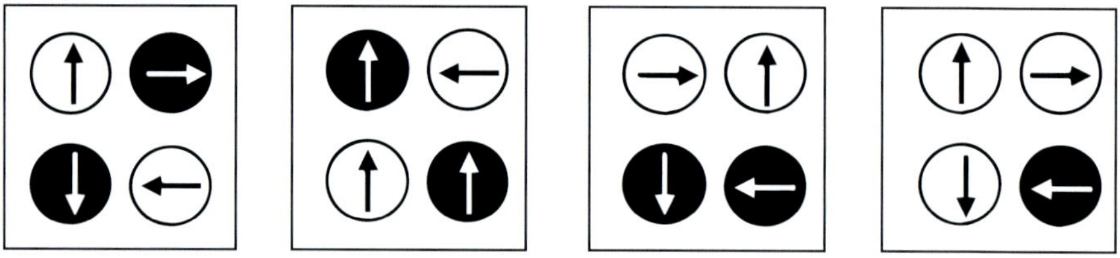

TYPE II - Question 20

Which figure completes the series?

A B C D

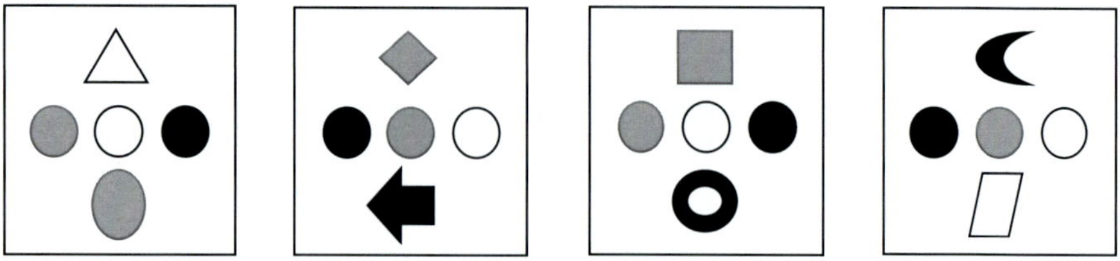

TYPE II - Question 21

Which figure completes the series?

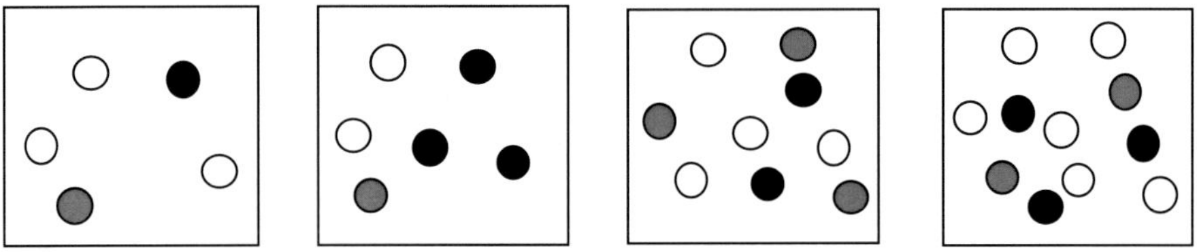

A B C D

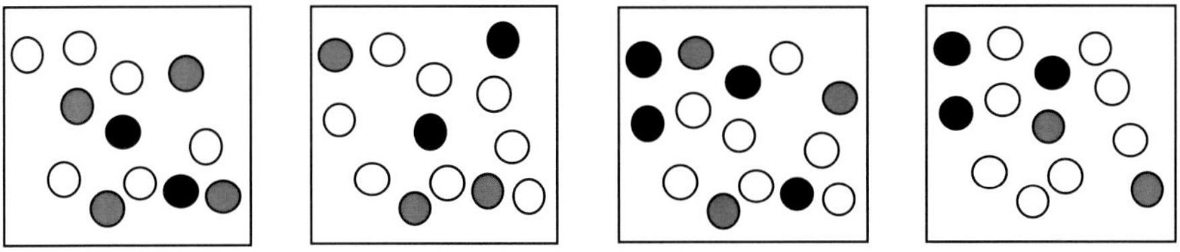

TYPE II - Question 22

Which figure completes the series?

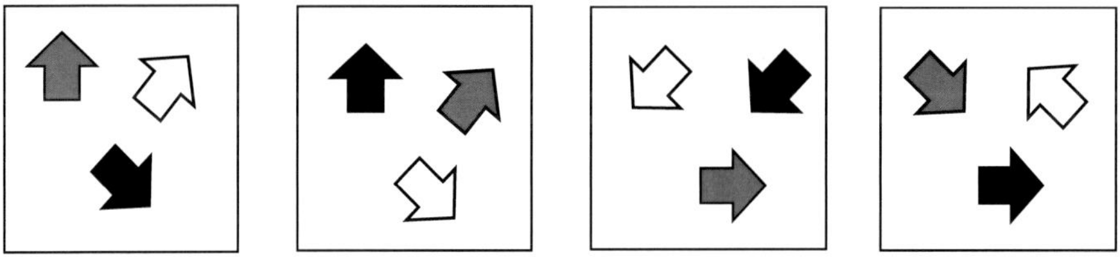

A B C D

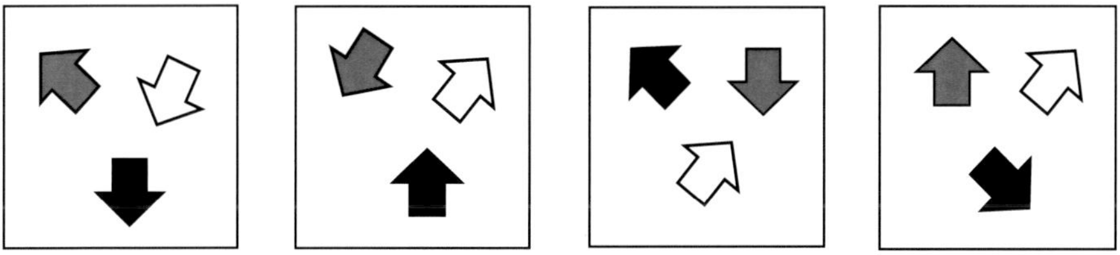

TYPE II - Question 23

Which figure completes the series?

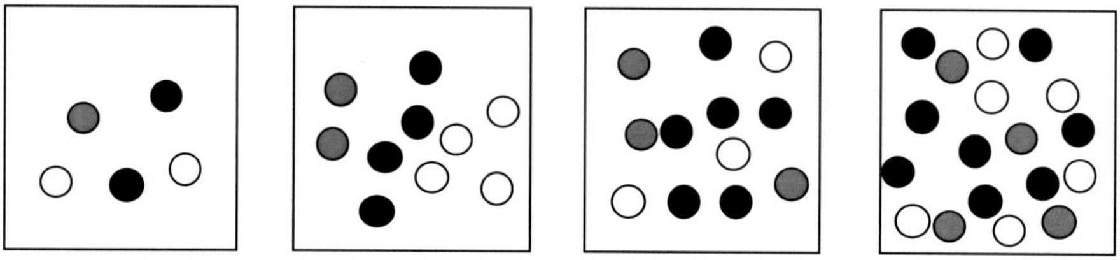

A B C D

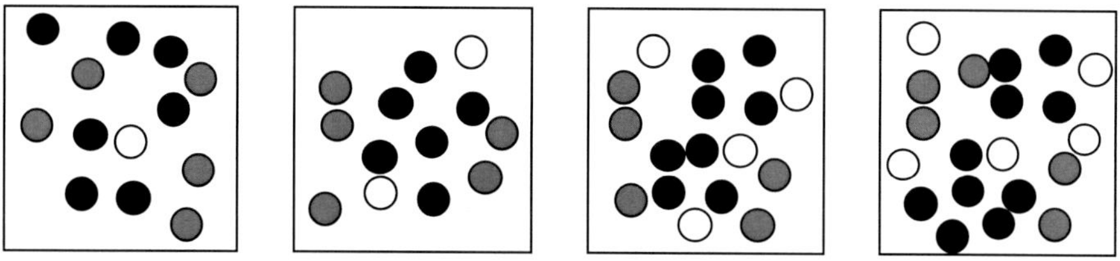

TYPE II - Question 24

Which figure completes the series?

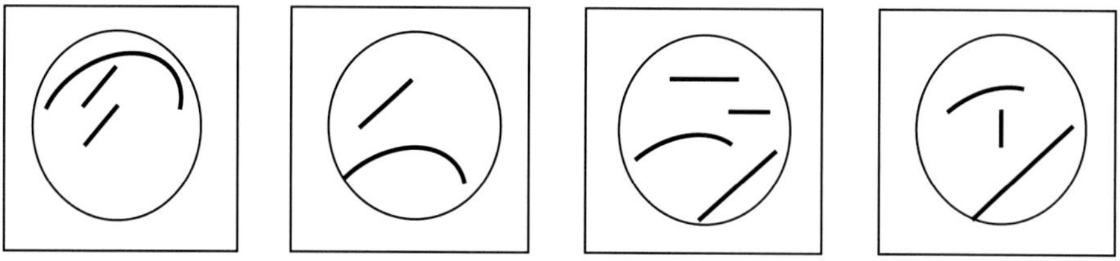

A B C D

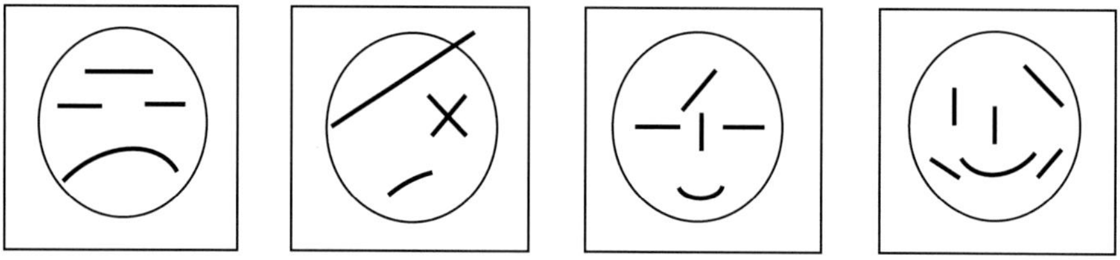

TYPE II - Question 25

Which figure completes the series?

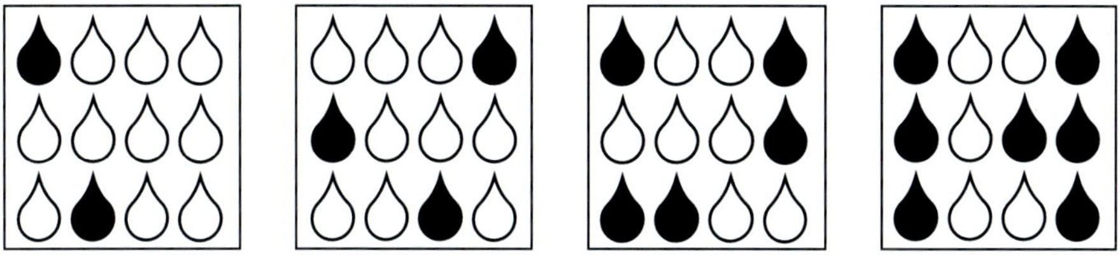

A

B

C

D

TYPE II - Question 26

Which figure completes the series?

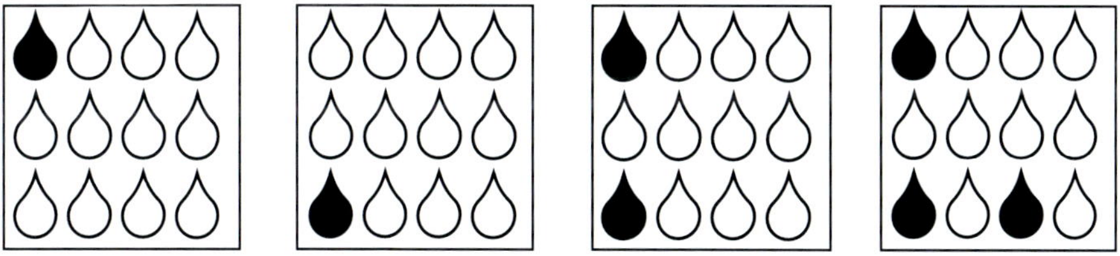

A

B

C

D

TYPE II - Question 27

Which figure completes the series?

A B C D

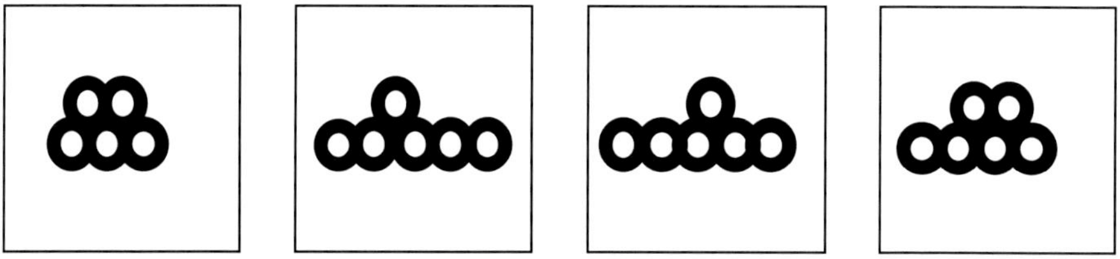

TYPE II - Question 28

Which figure completes the series?

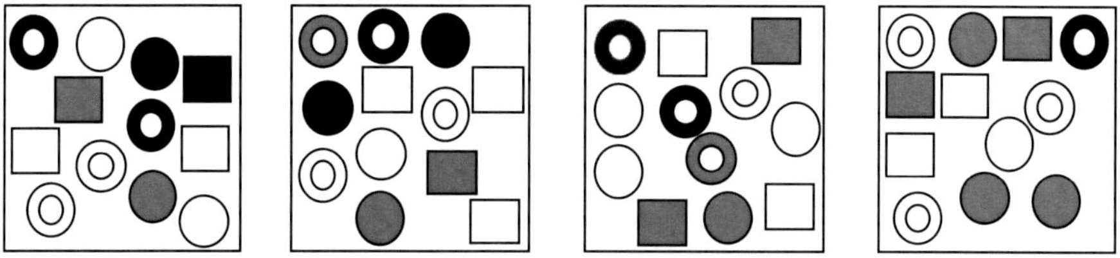

A B C D

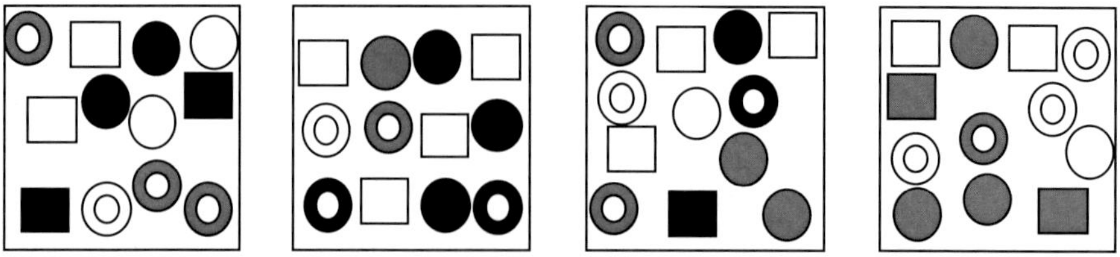

TYPE II - Question 29

Which figure completes the series?

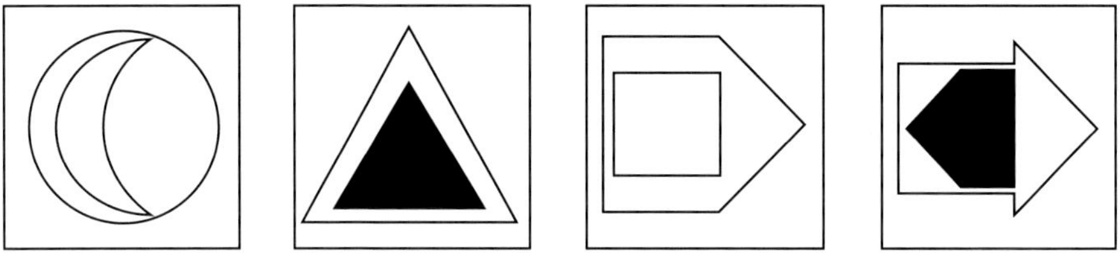

A B C D

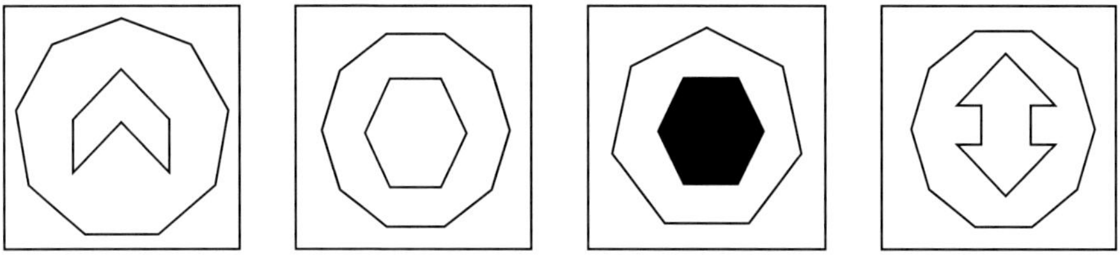

TYPE II - Question 30

Which figure completes the series?

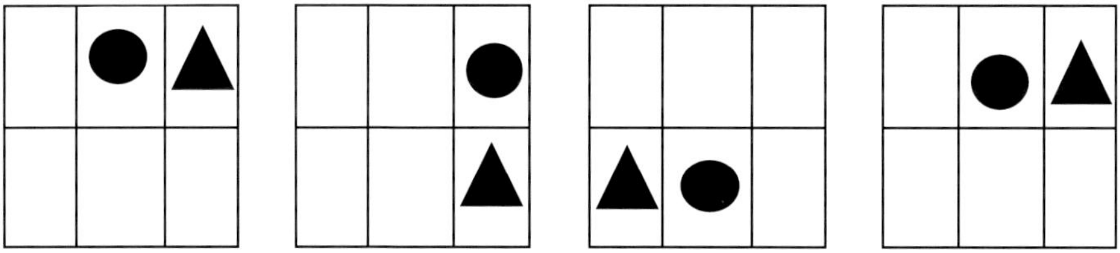

A B C D

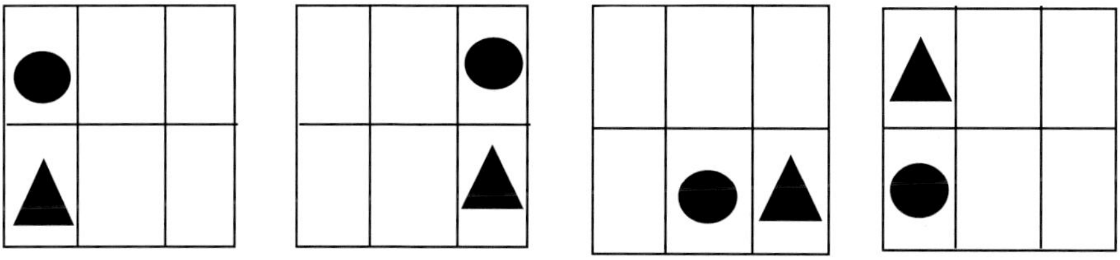

TYPE III - Question 1

Which of the following completes the statement?

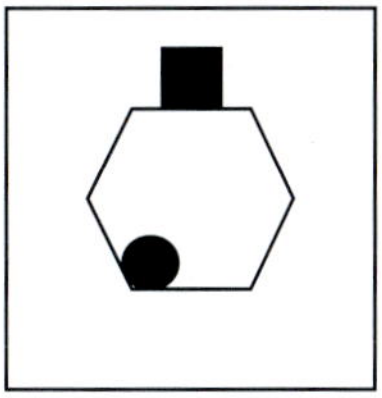

is to

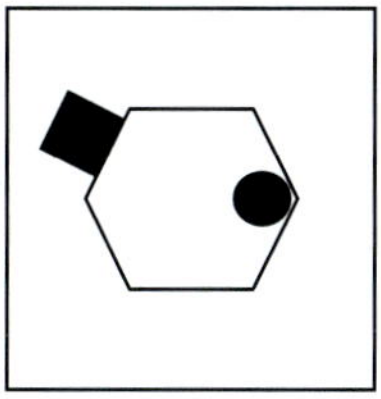

as

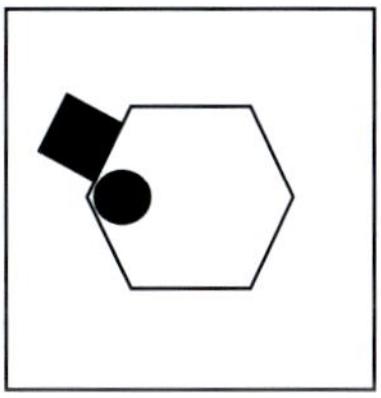

is to

A

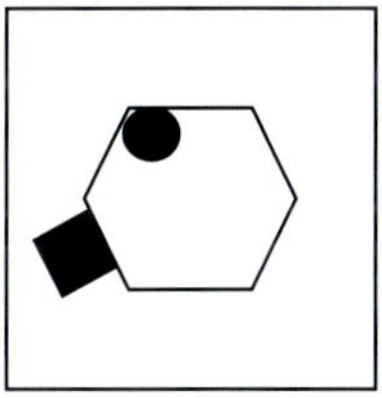

B

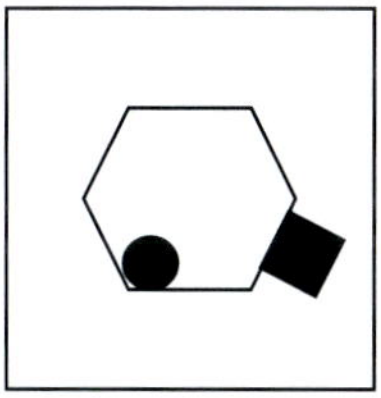

C

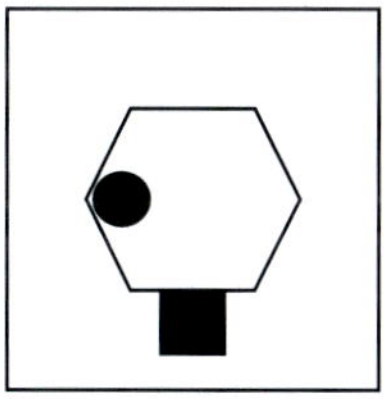

D

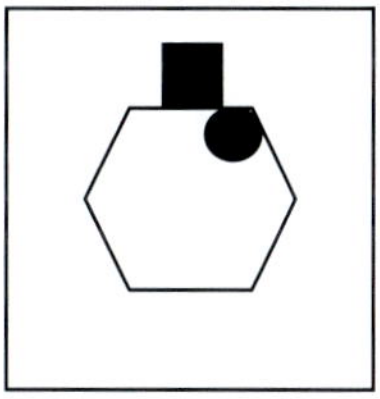

TYPE III - Question 2

Which of the following completes the statement?

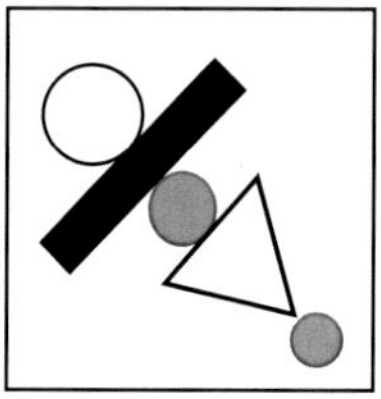

is to

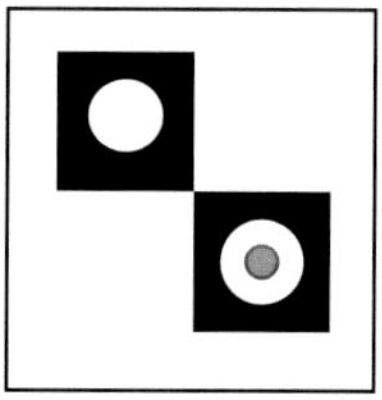

as

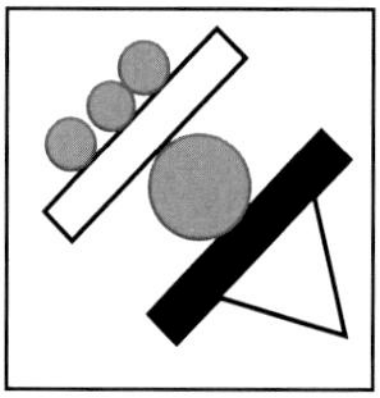

is to

A

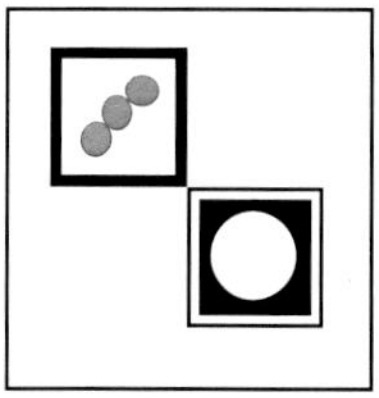

B

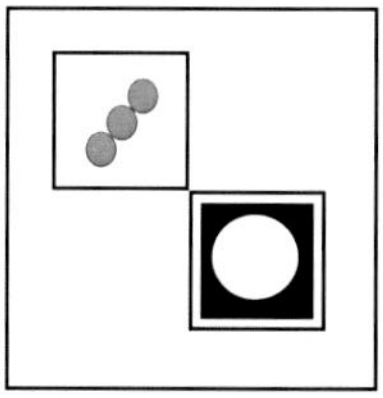

C

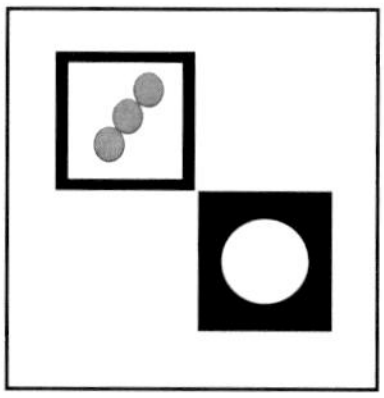

D

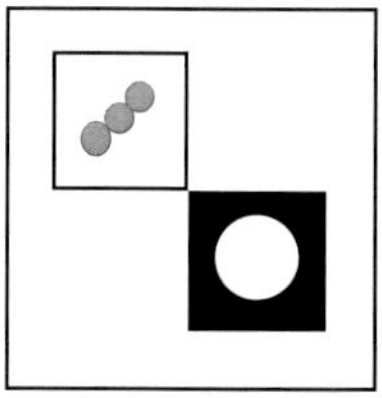

TYPE III - Question 3

Which of the following completes the statement?

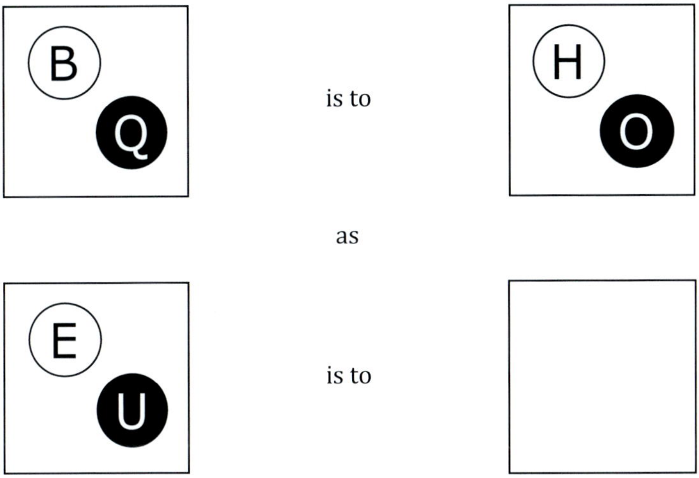

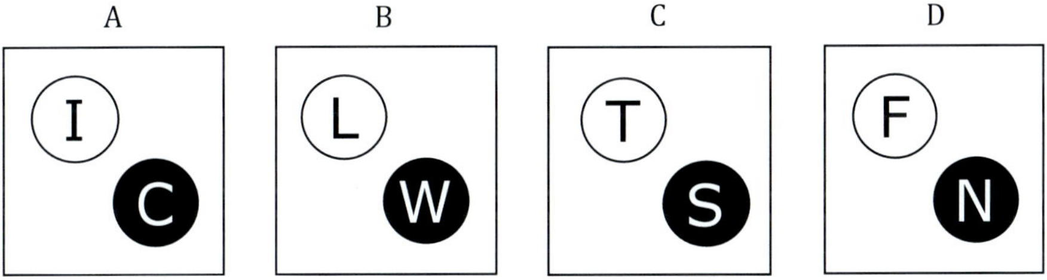

TYPE III - Question 4

Which of the following completes the statement?

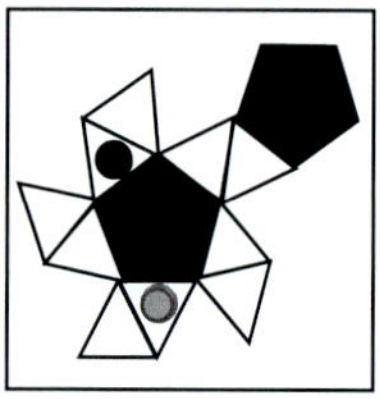

is to

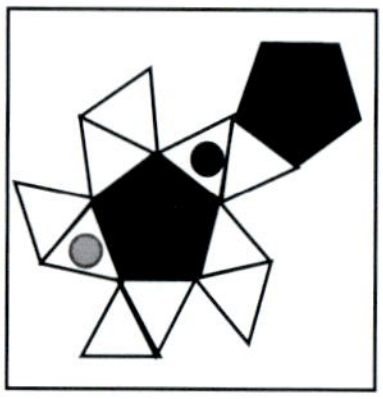

as

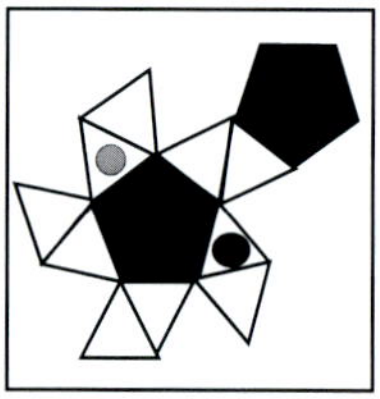

is to

A

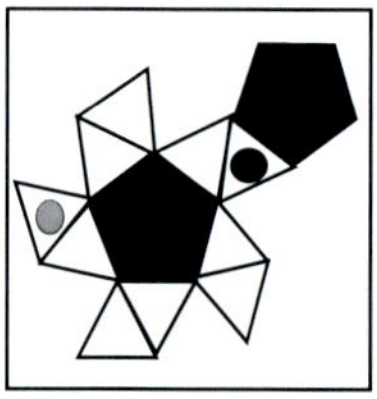

B

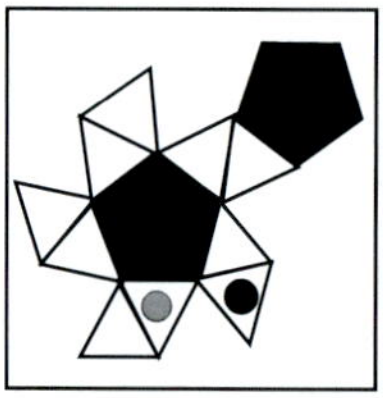

C

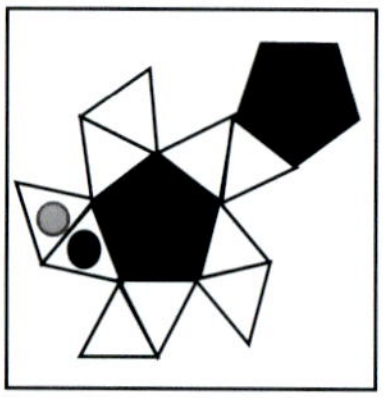

D

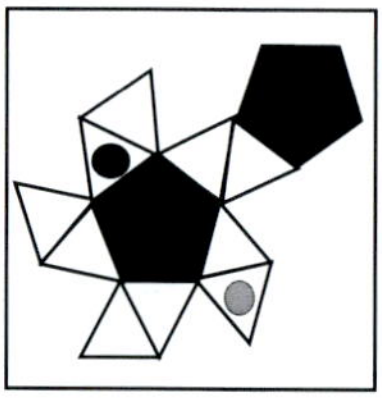

Abstract Reasoning

TYPE III - Question 5

Which of the following completes the statement?

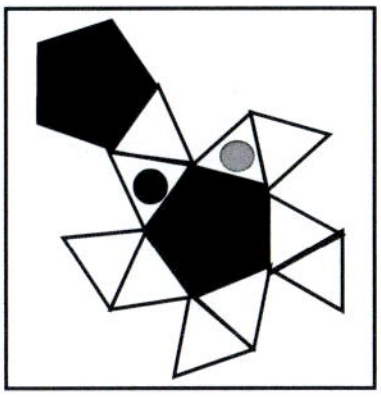

is to

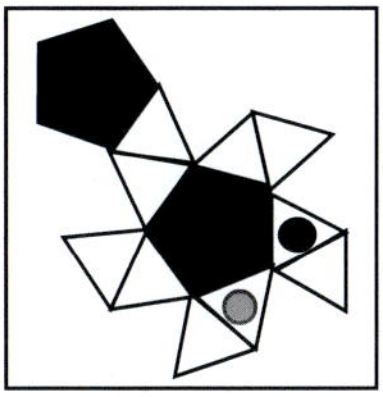

as

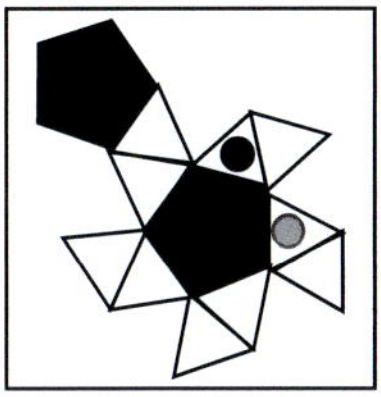

is to

A

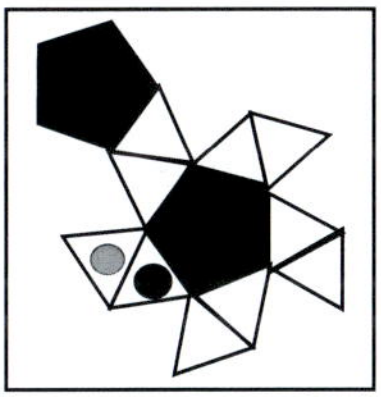

B

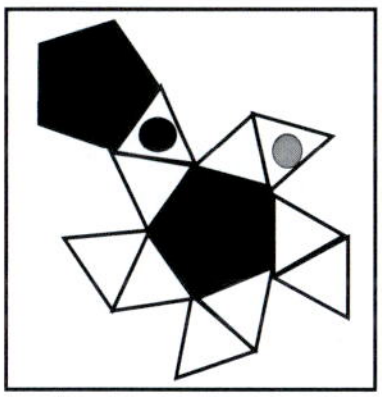

C

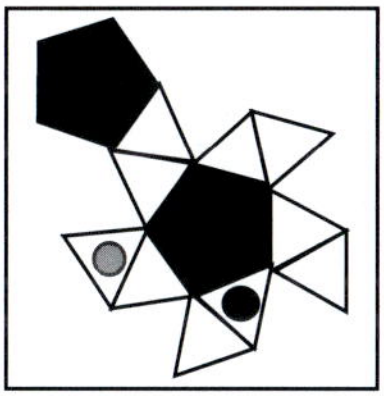

D

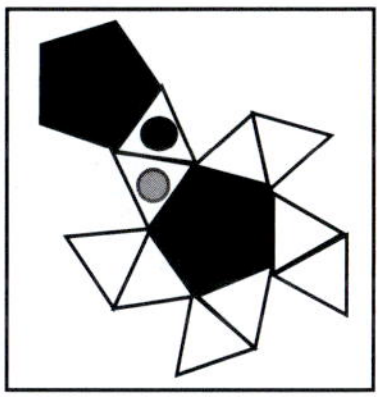

TYPE III - Question 6

Which of the following completes the statement?

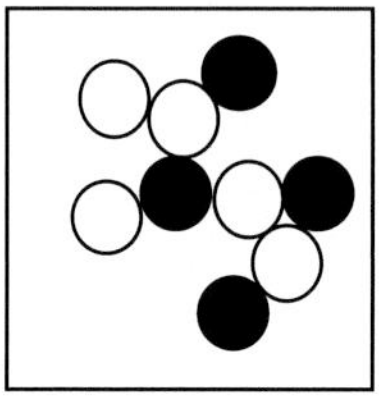

is to

as

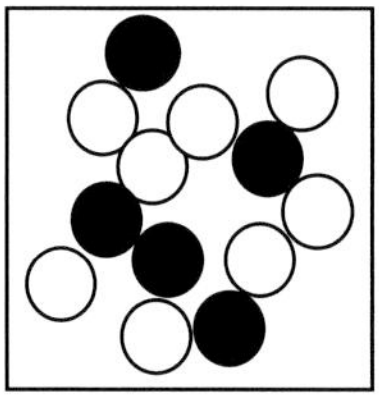

is to

A

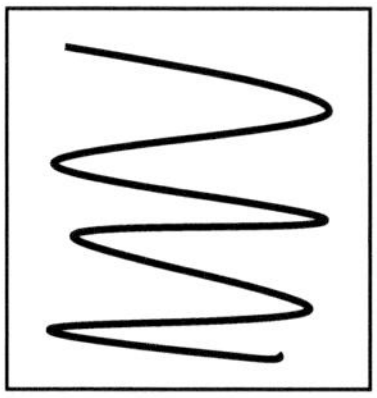

B

C

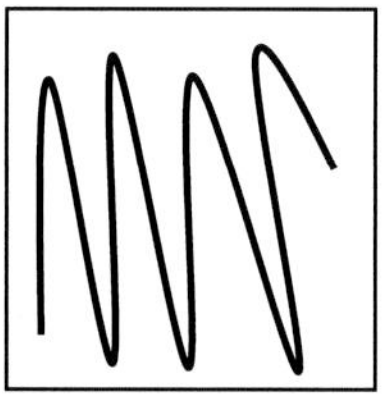

D

TYPE III - Question 7

Which of the following completes the statement?

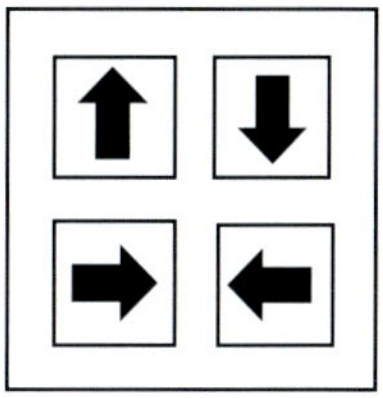

is to

as

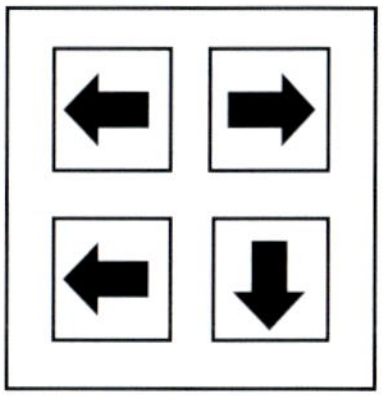

is to

A

B

C

D

TYPE III - Question 8

Which of the following completes the statement?

is to

as

is to

A

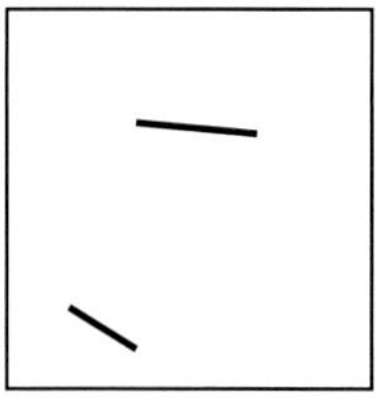

B

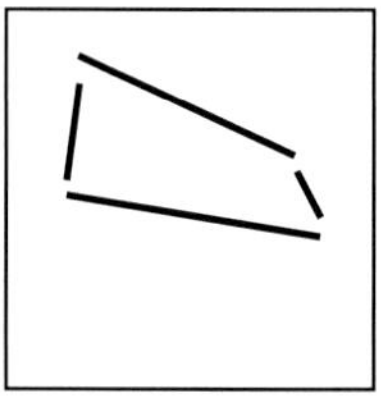

C

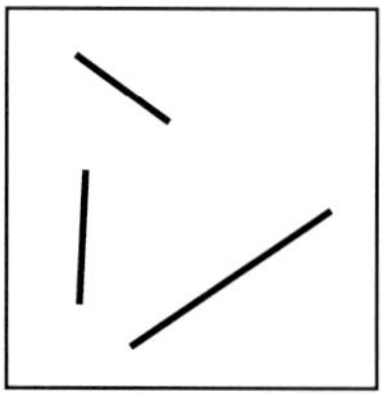

D

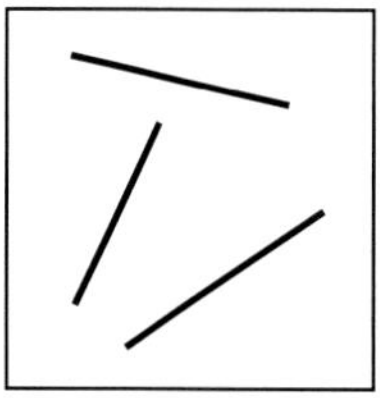

TYPE III - Question 9

Which of the following completes the statement?

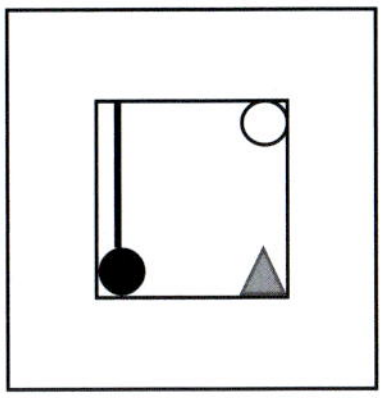

is to

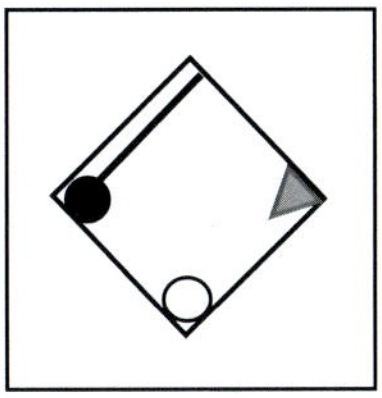

as

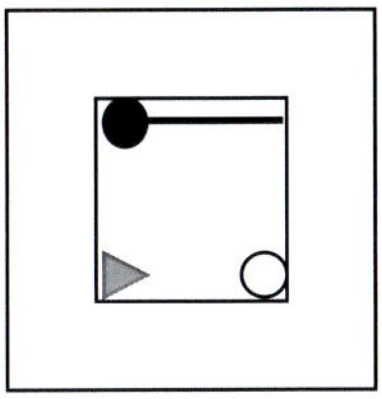

is to

A

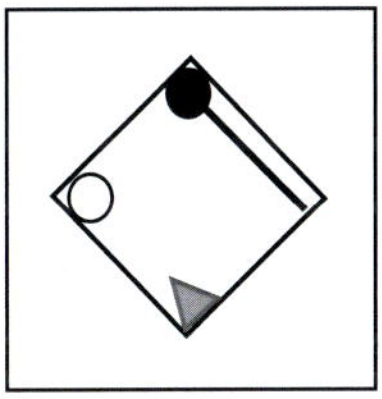

B

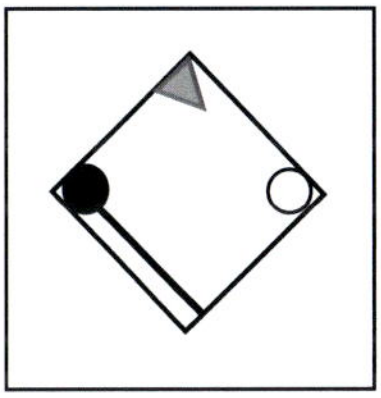

C

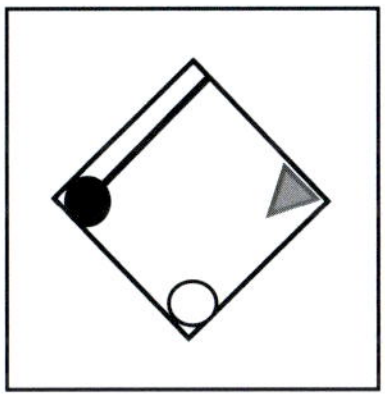

D

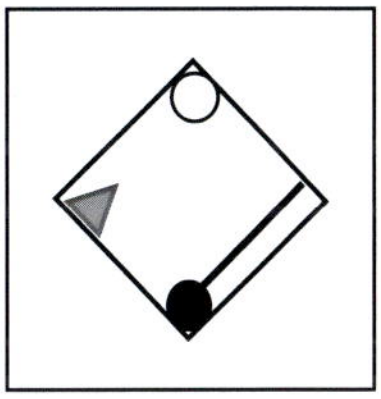

TYPE III - Question 10

Which of the following completes the statement?

is to

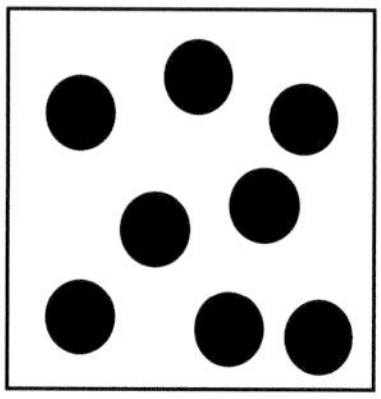

as

is to

A

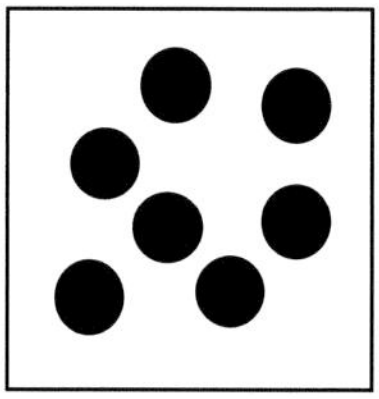

B

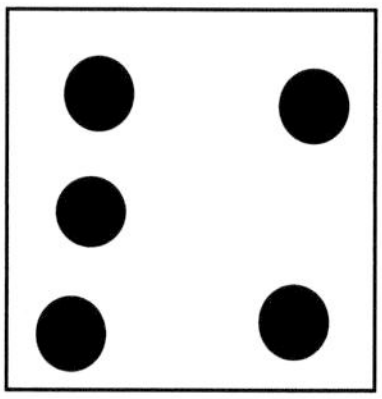

C

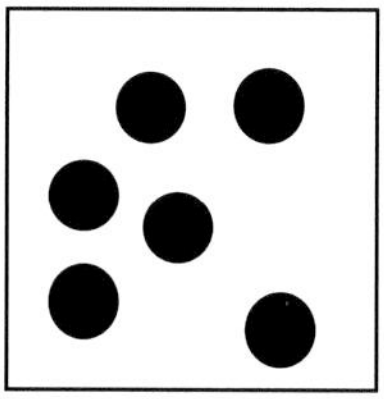

D

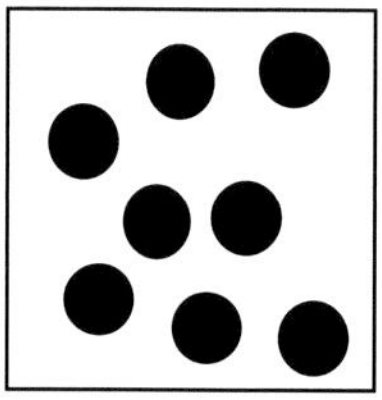

TYPE III - Question 11

Which of the following completes the statement?

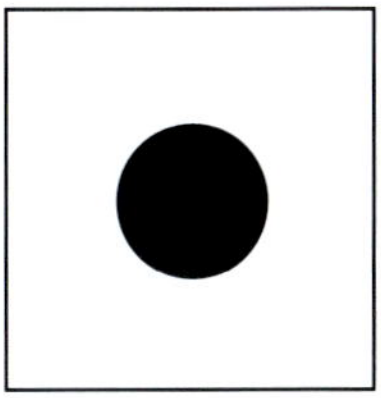

is to

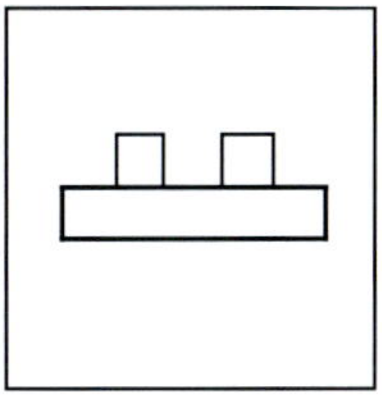

as

is to

A

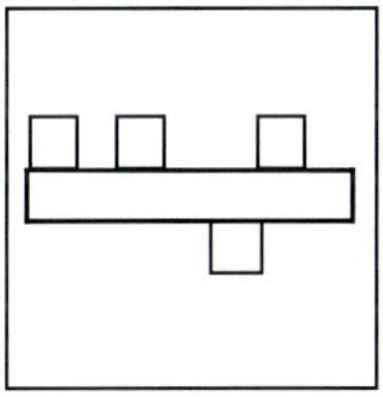

B

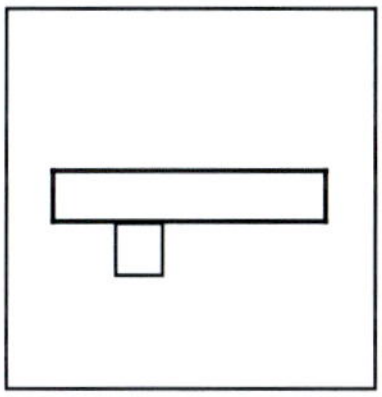

C

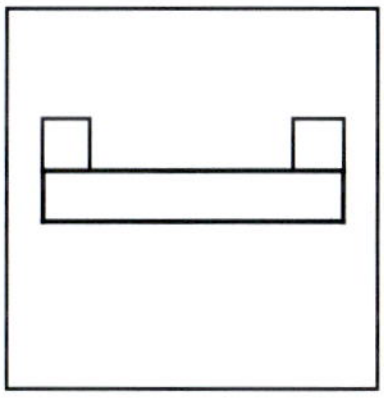

D

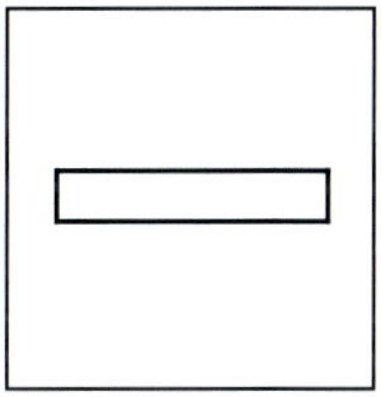

TYPE III - Question 12

Which of the following completes the statement?

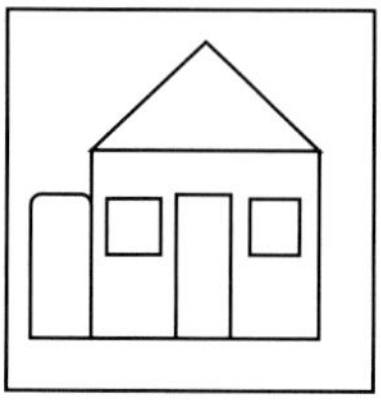

is to

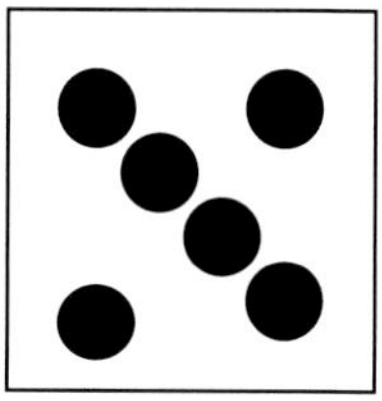

as

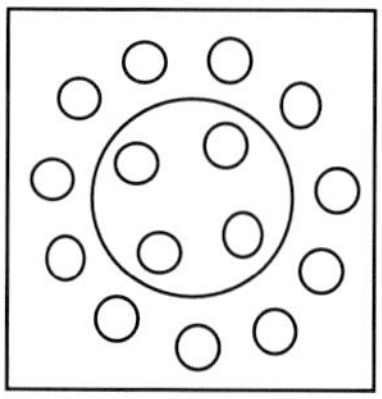

is to

A

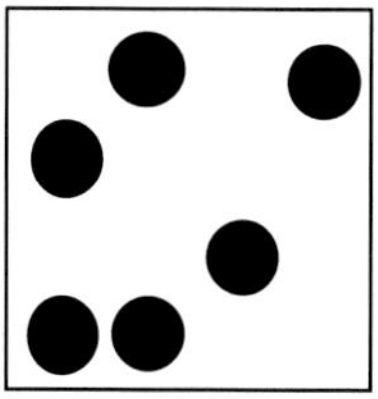

B

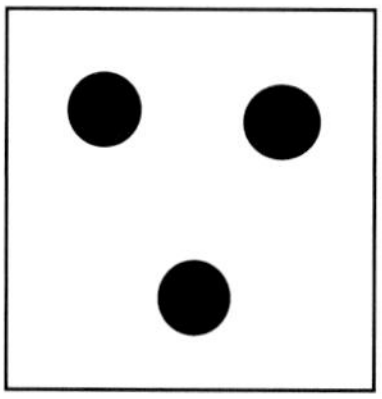

C

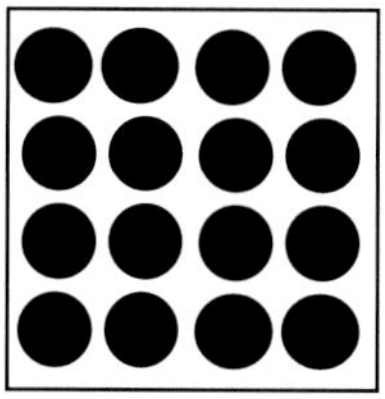

D

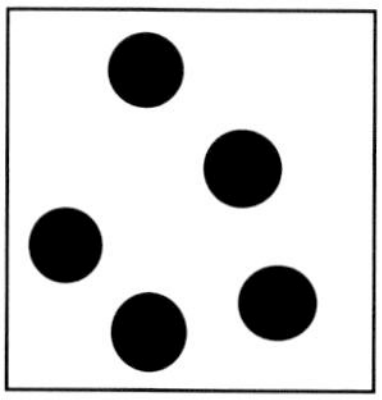

TYPE III - Question 13

Which of the following completes the statement?

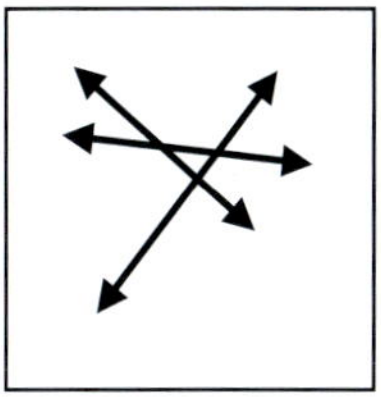

is to

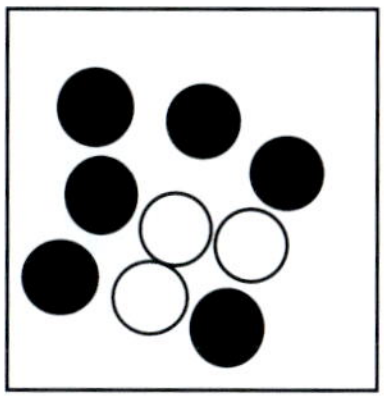

as

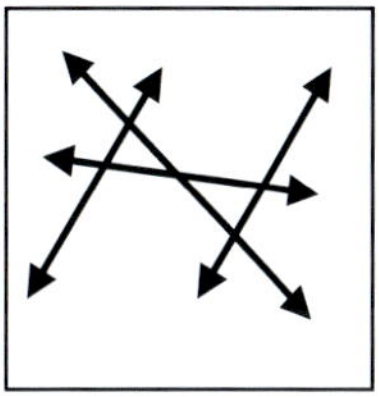

is to

A

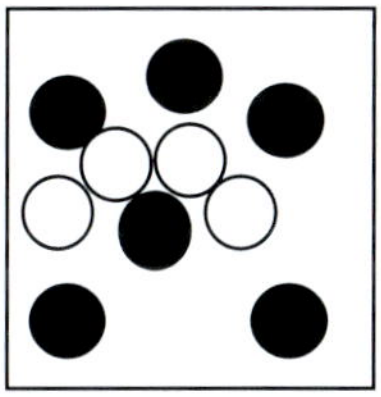

B

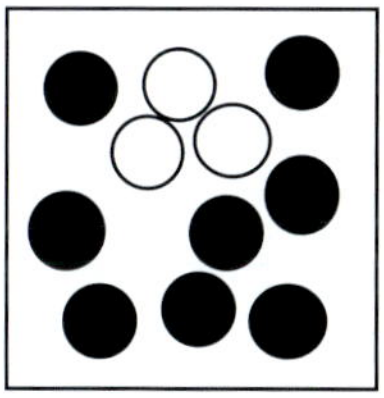

C

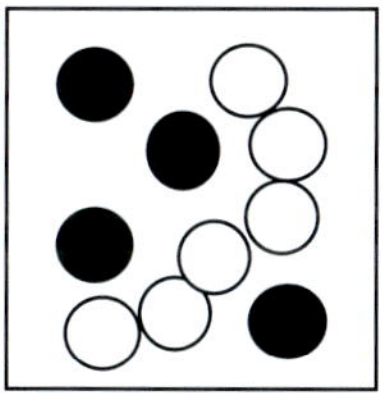

D

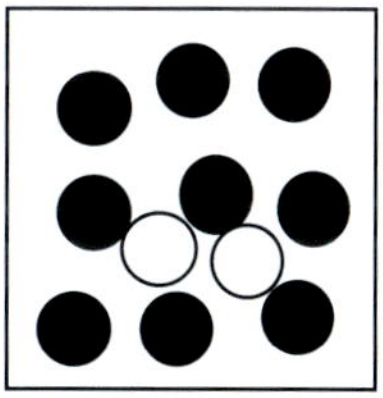

TYPE III - Question 14

Which of the following completes the statement?

is to

as

is to

A

B

C

D

Abstract Reasoning

TYPE III - Question 15

Which of the following completes the statement?

is to

as

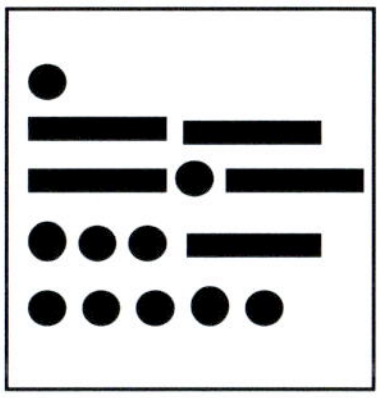

is to

A

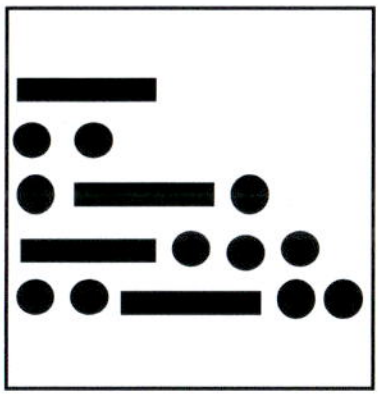

B

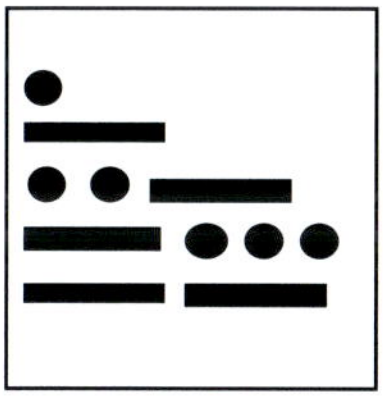

C

D

TYPE III - Question 16

Which of the following completes the statement?

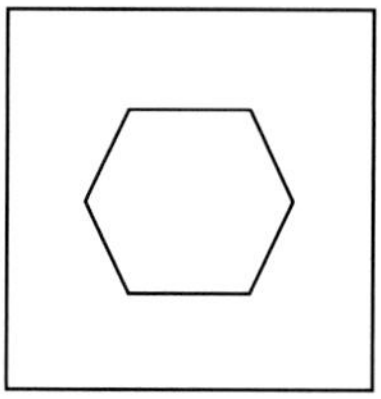

is to

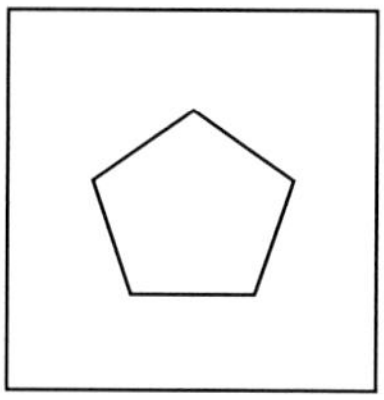

as

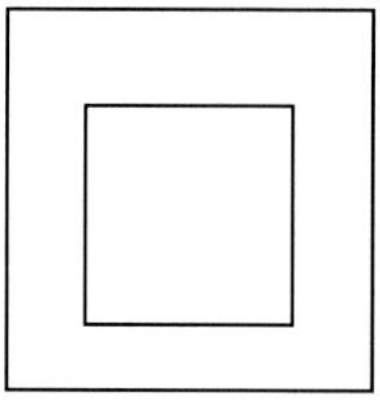

is to

A

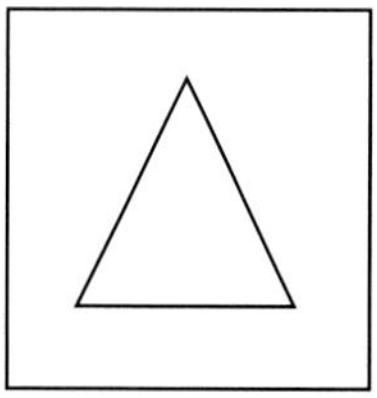

B

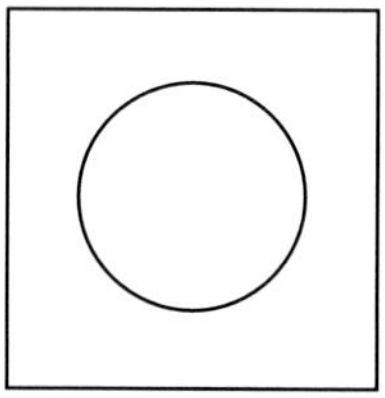

C

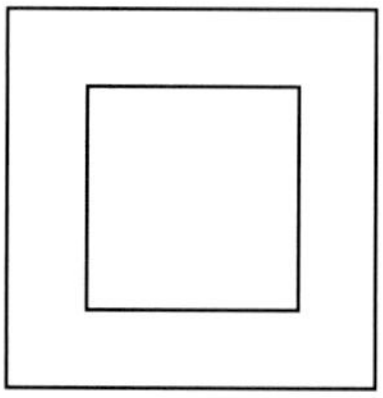

D

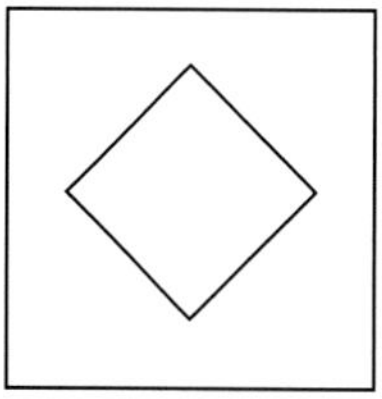

TYPE III - Question 17

Which of the following completes the statement?

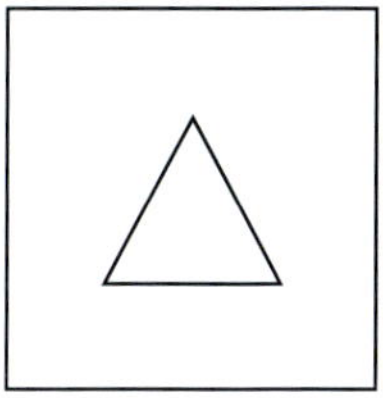

is to

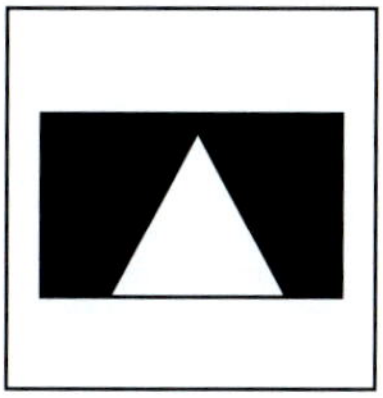

as

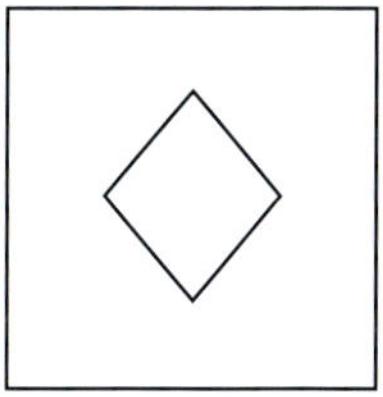

is to

A

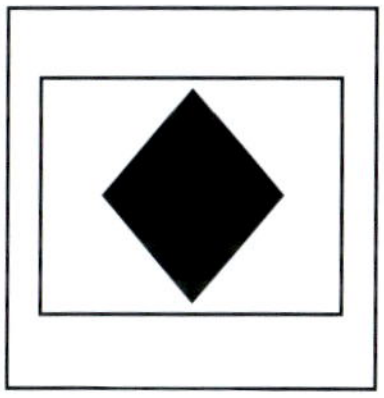

B

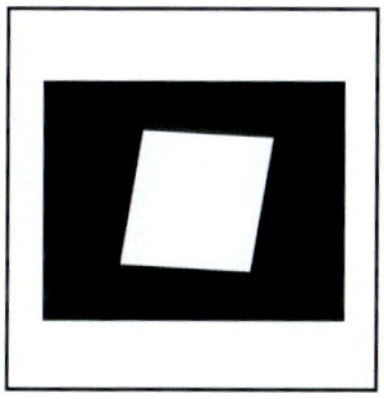

C

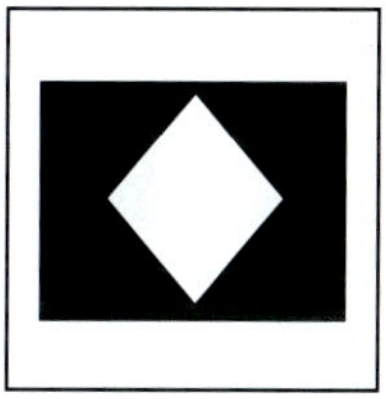

D

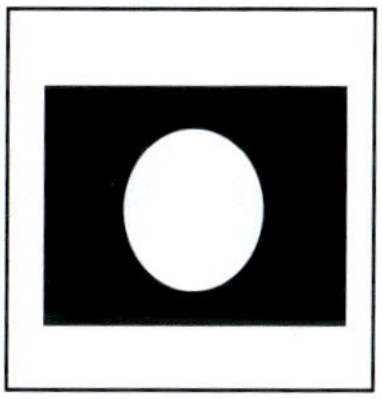

TYPE III - Question 18

Which of the following completes the statement?

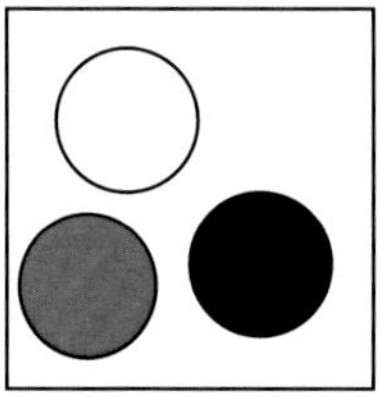

is to

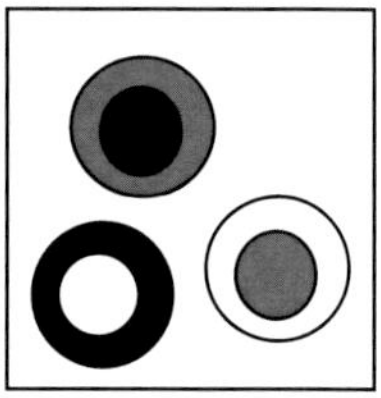

as

is to

A

B

C

D

TYPE III - Question 19

Which of the following completes the statement?

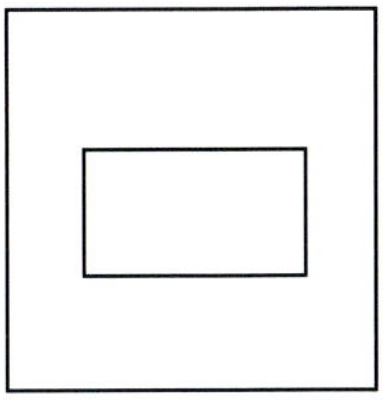

is to

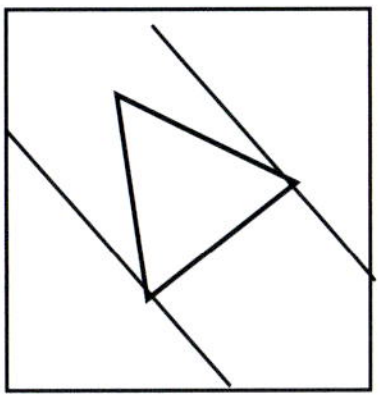

as

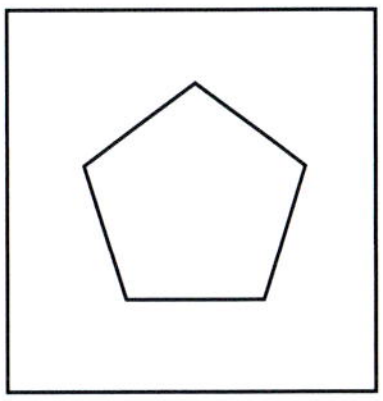

is to

A

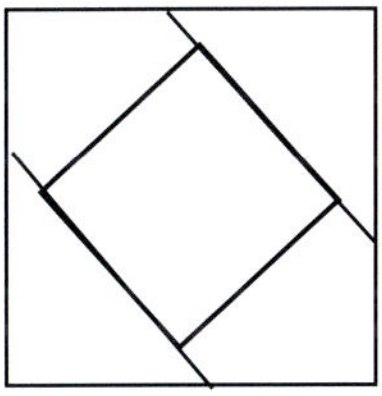

B

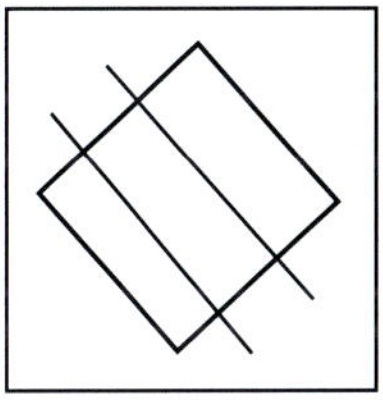

C

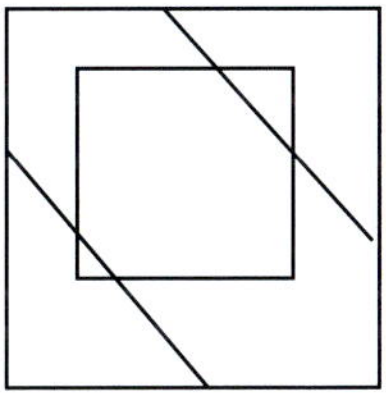

D

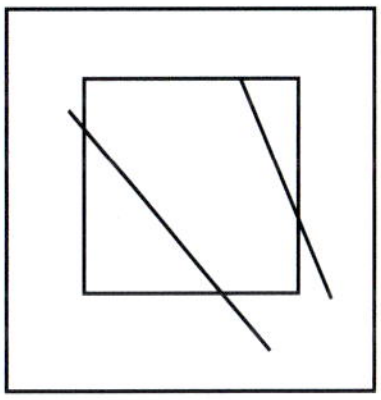

TYPE III - Question 20

Which of the following completes the statement?

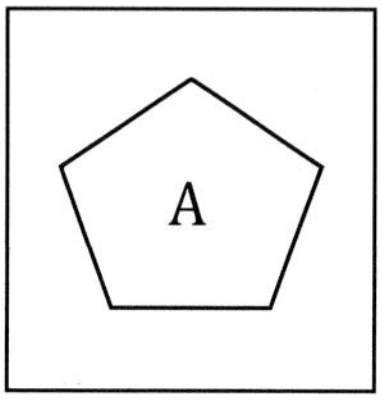

is to

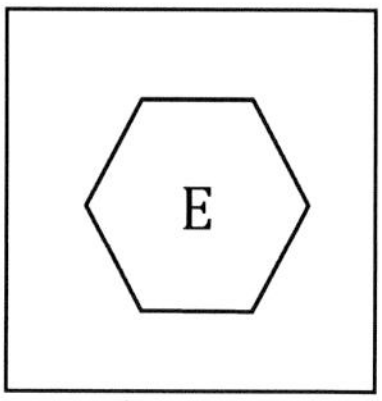

as

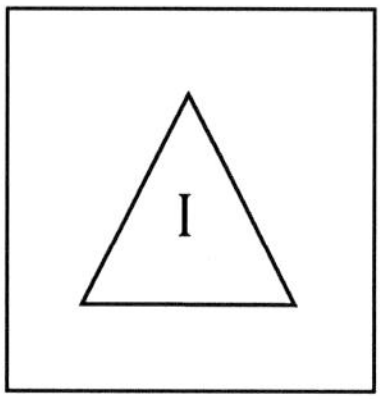

is to

A

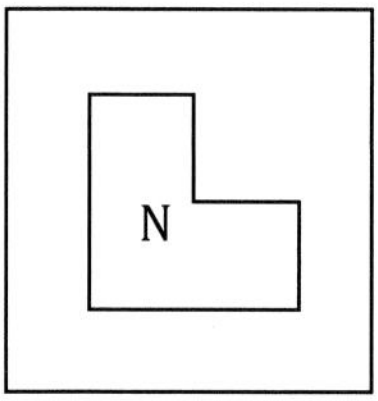

B

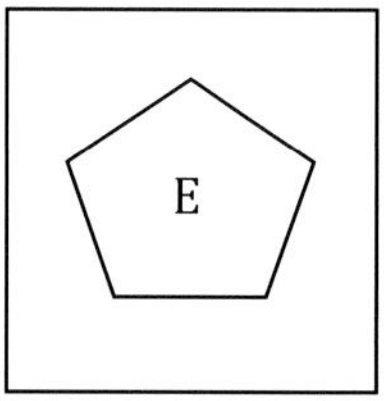

C

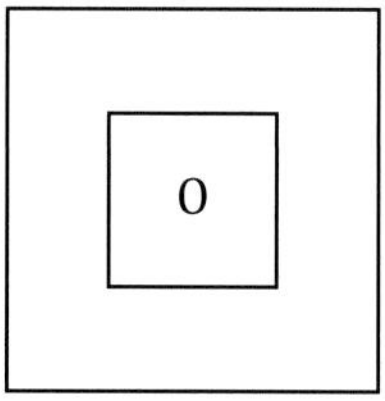

D

TYPE III - Question 21

Which of the following completes the statement?

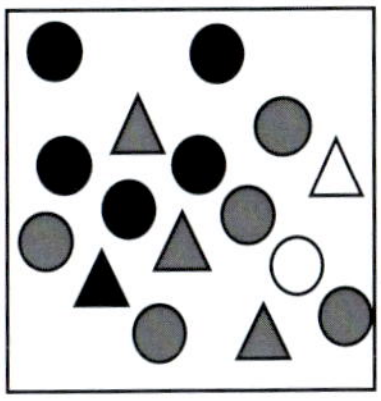

is to

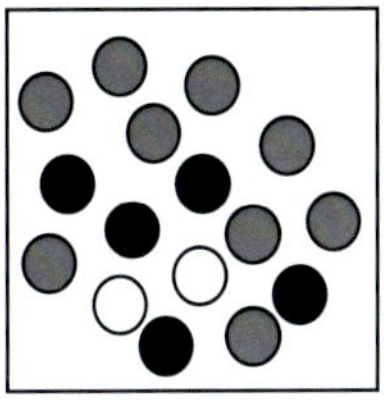

as

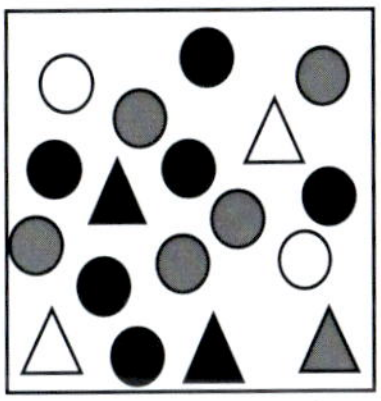

is to

A

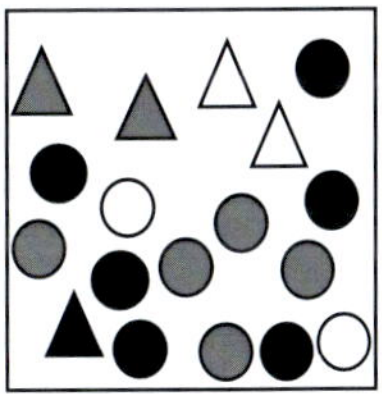

B

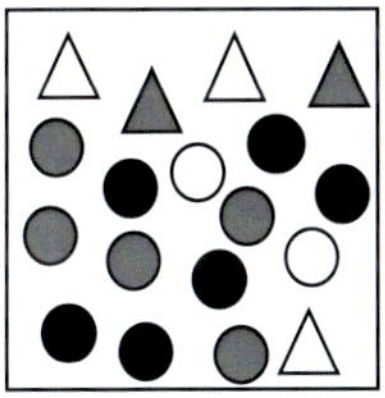

C

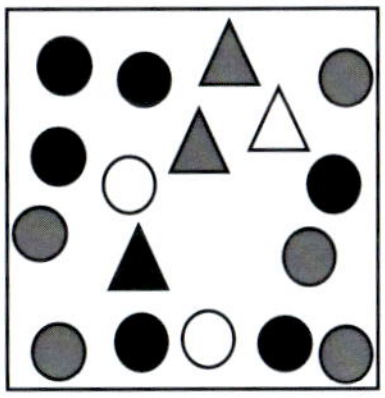

D

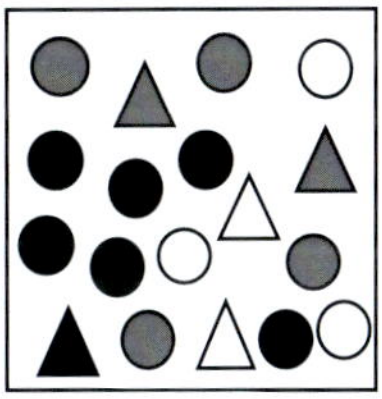

TYPE III - Question 22

Which of the following completes the statement?

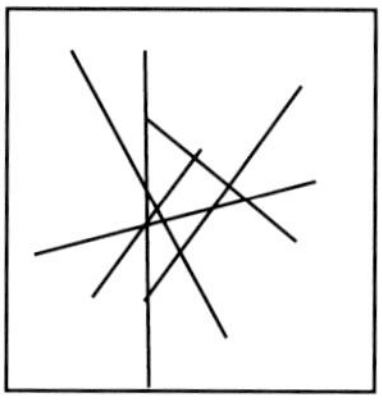

is to

as

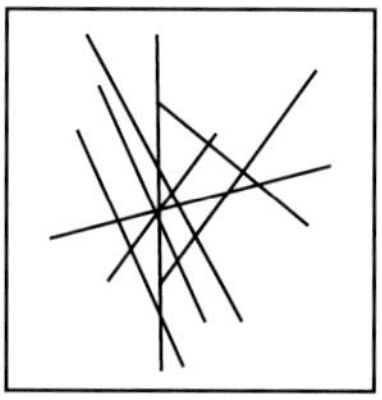

is to

A

B

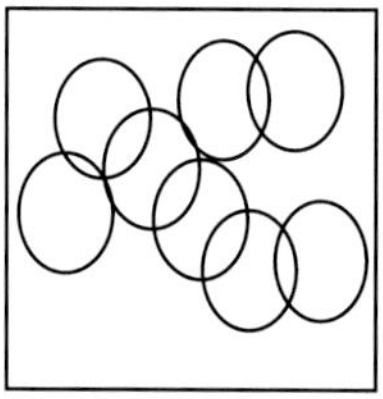

C

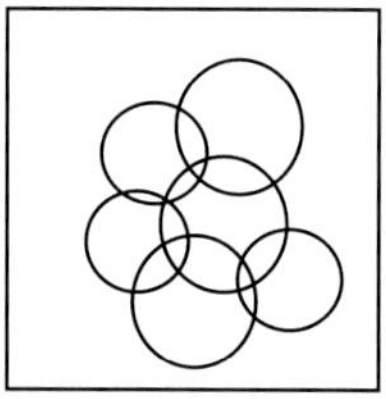

D

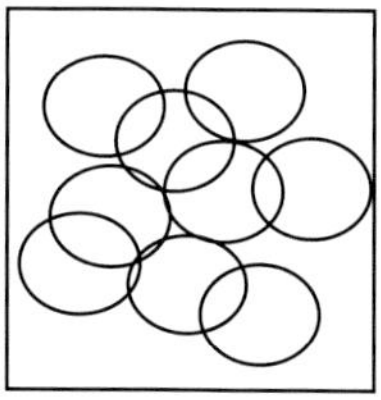

TYPE III - Question 23

Which of the following completes the statement?

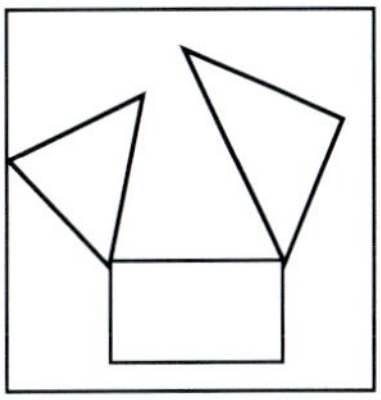

is to

as

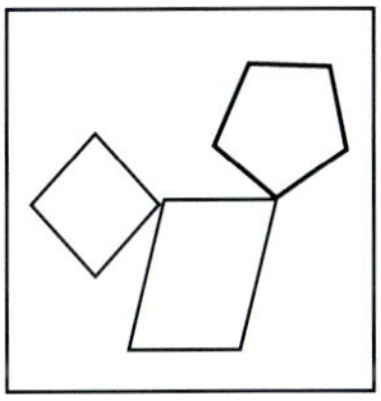

is to

A

B

C

D

TYPE III - Question 24

Which of the following completes the statement?

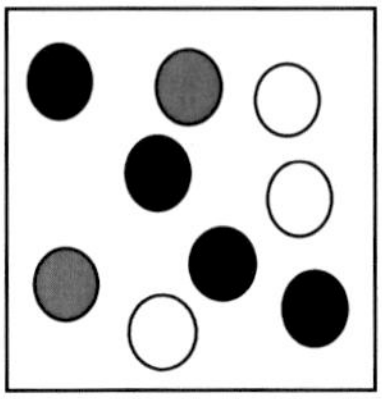

is to

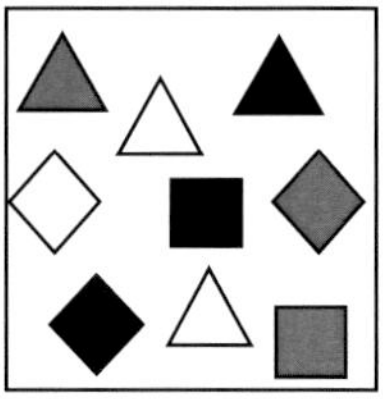

as

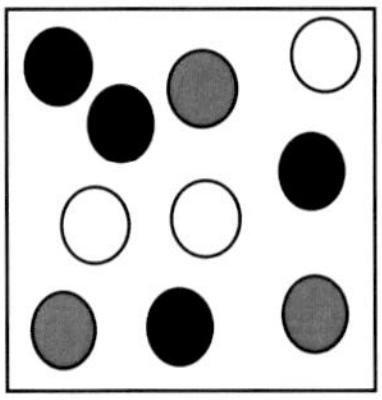

is to

A

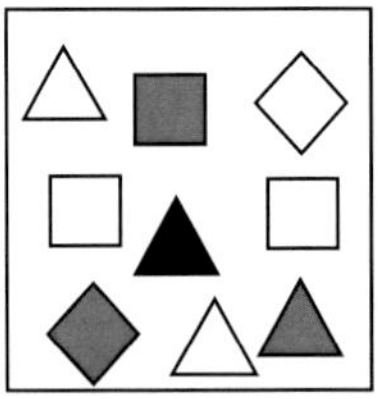

B

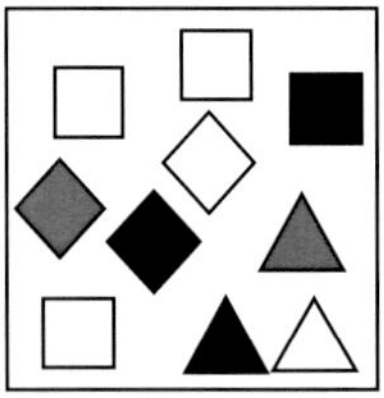

C

D

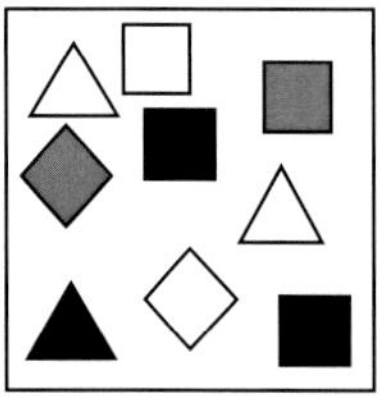

TYPE III - Question 25

Which of the following completes the statement?

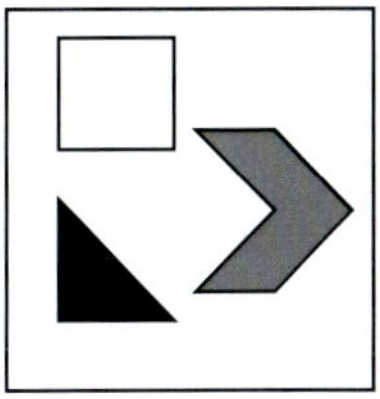

is to

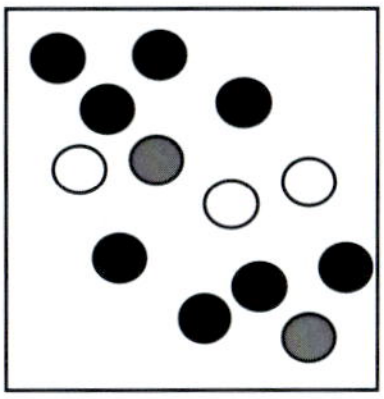

as

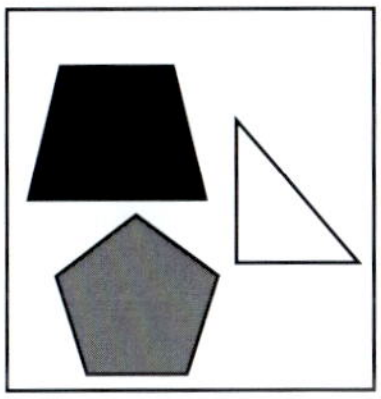

is to

A

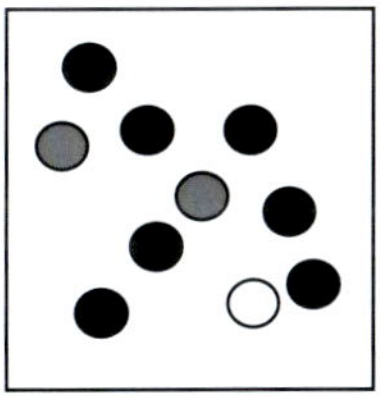

B

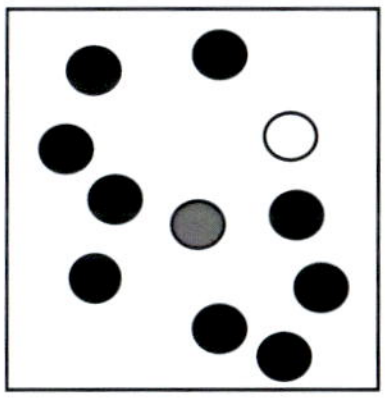

C

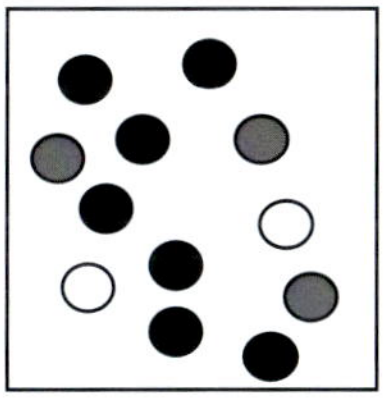

D

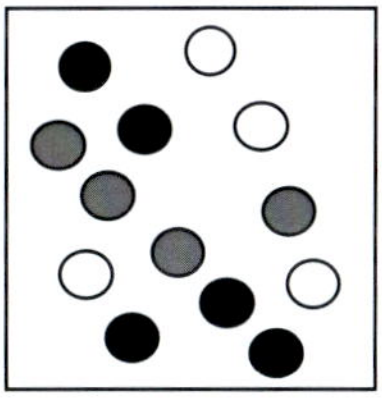

TYPE IV - Question 1

Set A | **Set B**

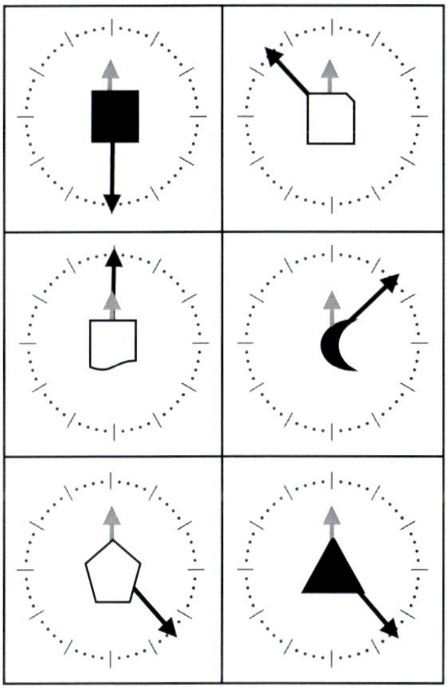

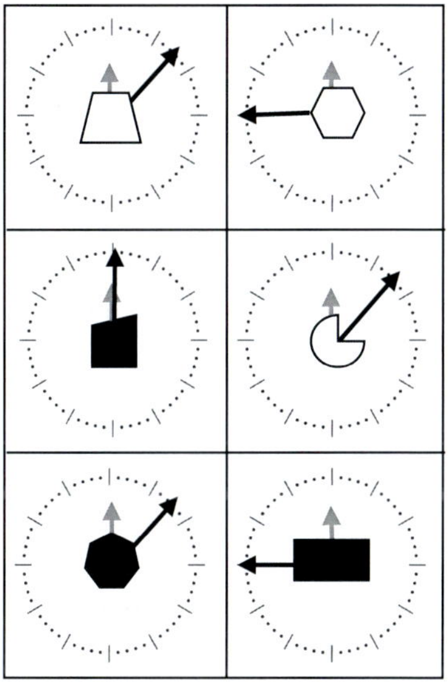

Which of the following test shapes belongs to Set A?

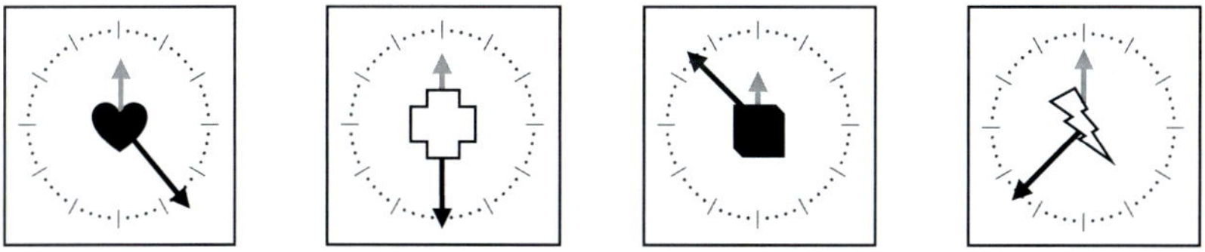

A B C D

Which of the following test shapes belongs to Set B?

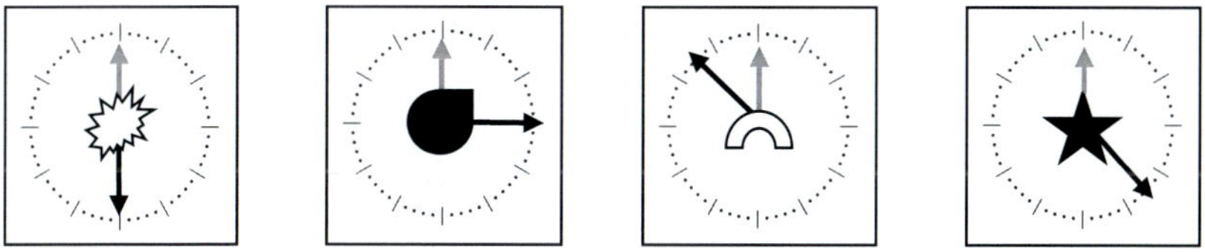

A B C D

TYPE IV - Question 2

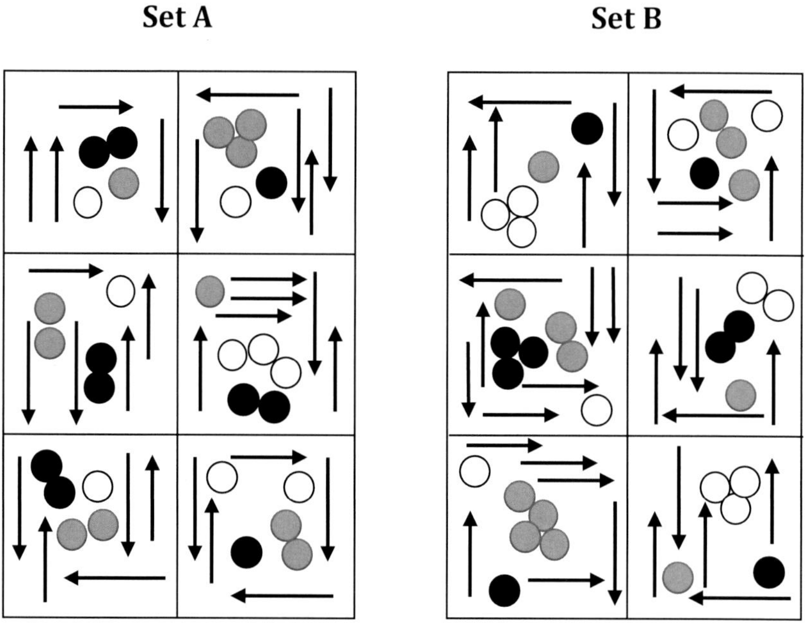

Which of the following test shapes belongs to Set A?

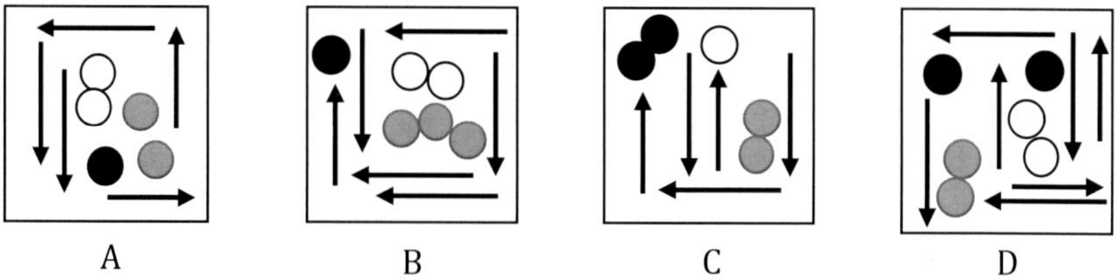

Which of the following test shapes belongs to Set B?

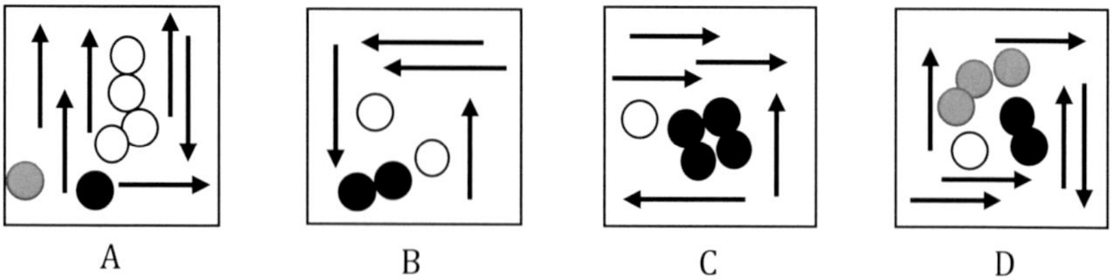

TYPE IV - Question 3

Set A

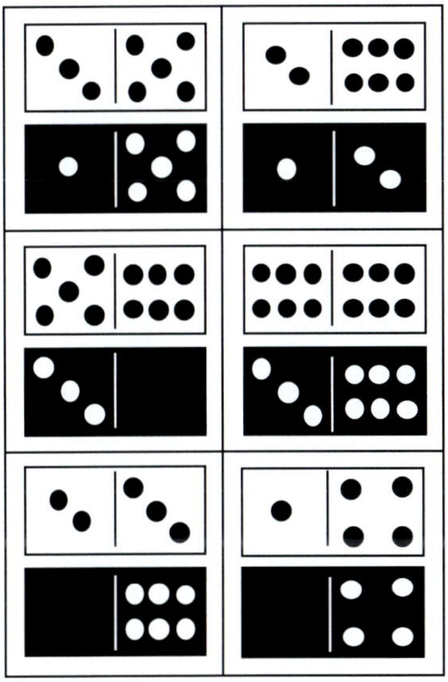

Set B

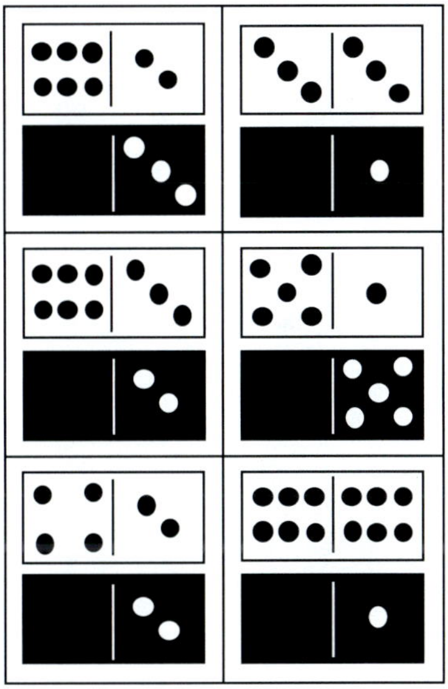

Which of the following test shapes belongs to Set A?

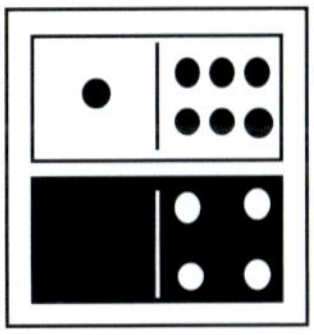

A

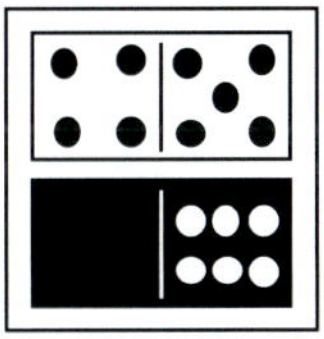

B

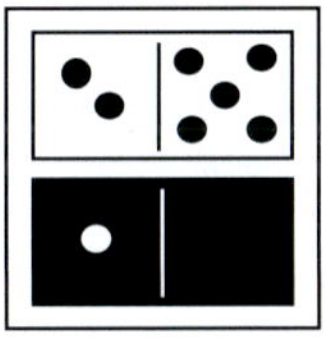

C

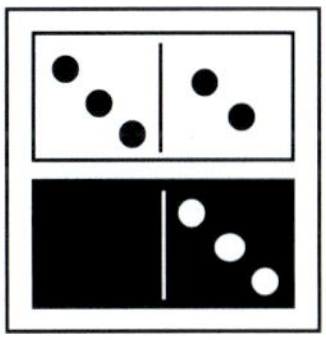

D

Which of the following test shapes belongs to Set B?

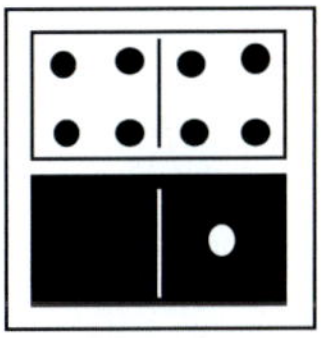

A

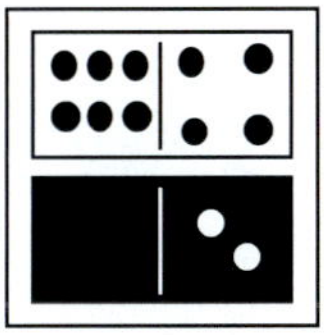

B

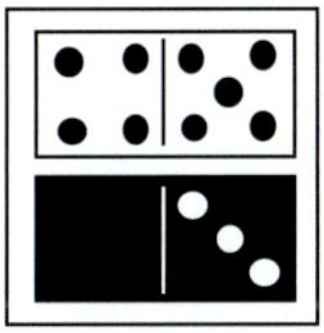

C

D

TYPE IV - Question 4

Set A

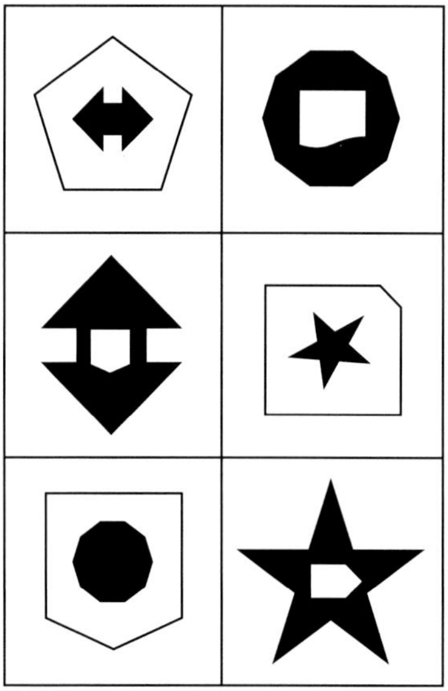

Set B

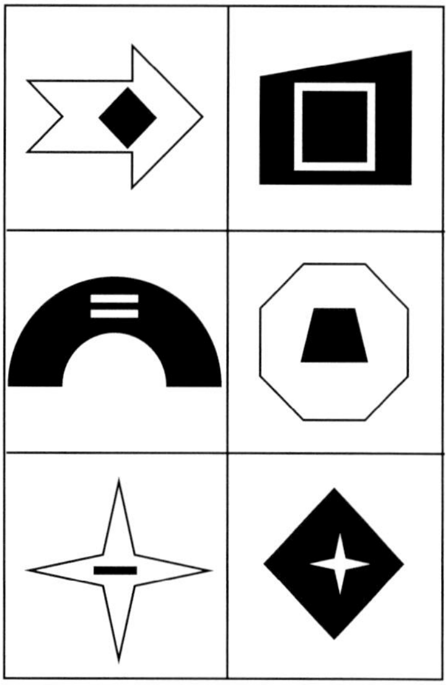

Which of the following test shapes belongs to Set A?

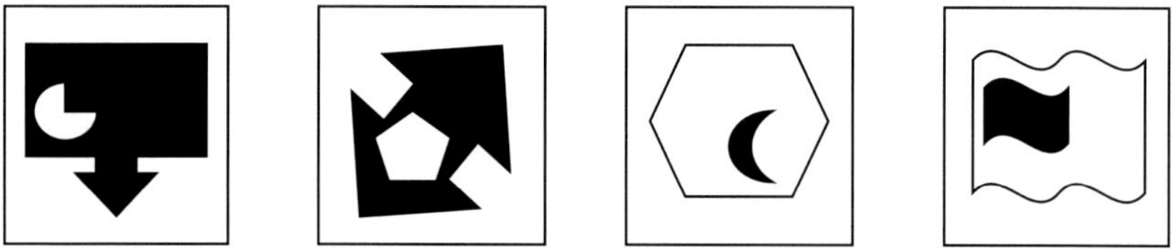

A B C D

Which of the following test shapes belongs to Set B?

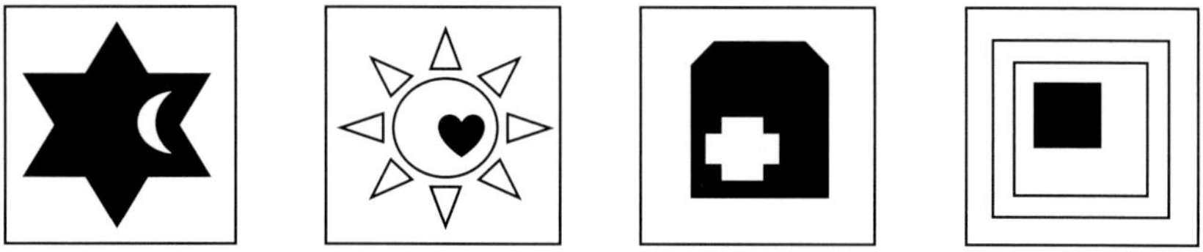

A B C D

TYPE IV - Question 5

Set A

Set B

Which of the following test shapes belongs to Set A?

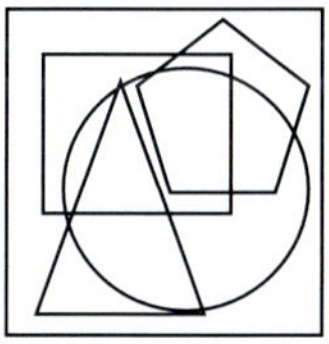

A

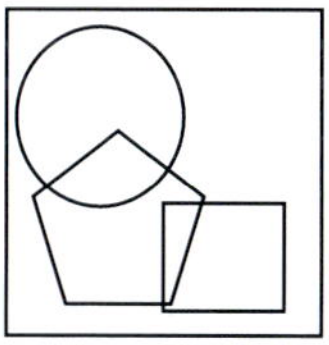

B

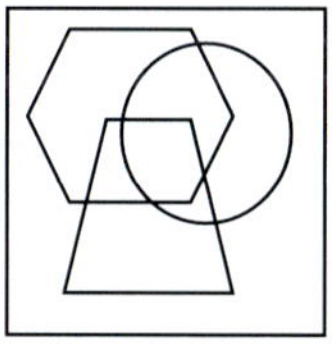

C

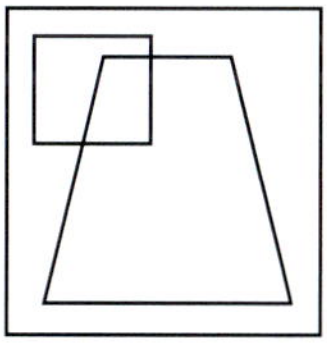

D

Which of the following test shapes belongs to Set B?

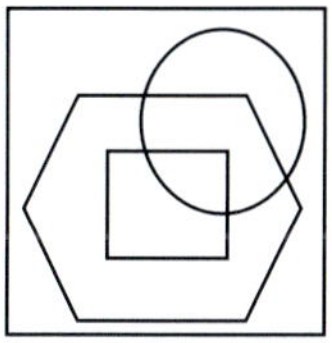

A

B

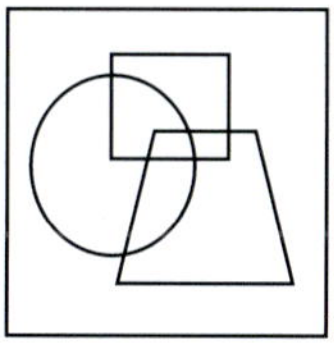

C

D

TYPE IV - Question 6

Set A

Set B

Which of the following test shapes belongs to Set A?

A

B

C

D

Which of the following test shapes belongs to Set B?

A

B

C

D

TYPE IV - Question 7

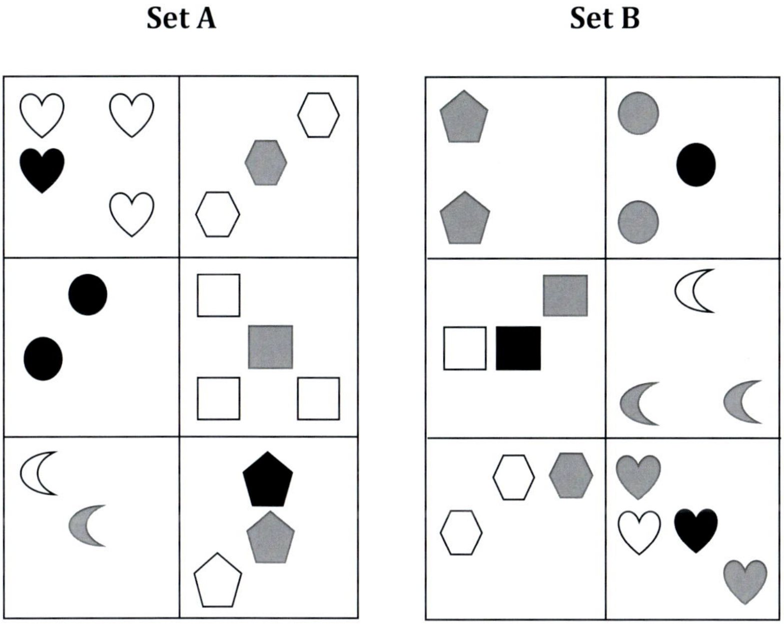

Which of the following test shapes belongs to Set A?

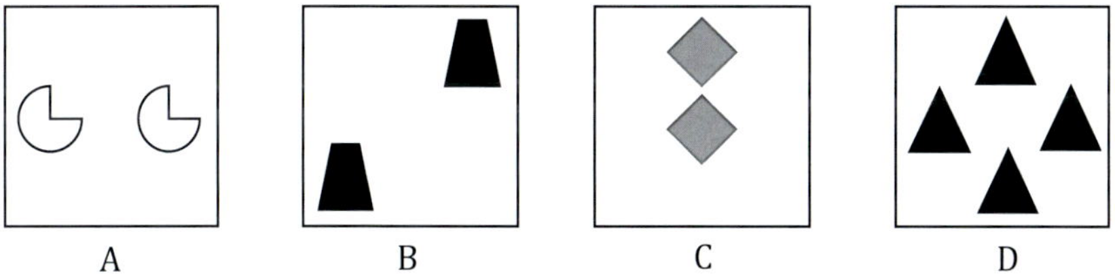

Which of the following test shapes belongs to Set B?

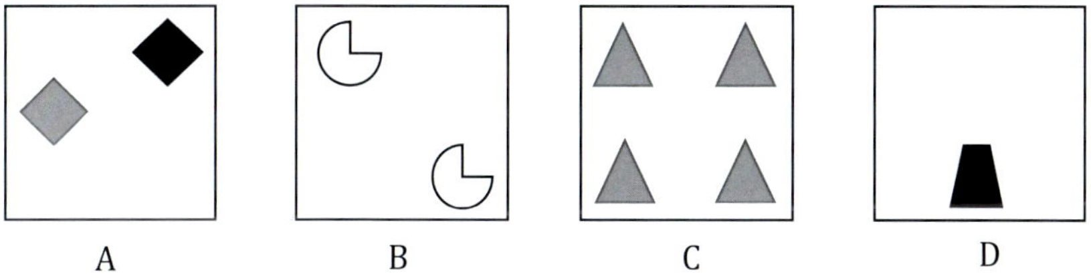

TYPE IV - Question 8

Set A

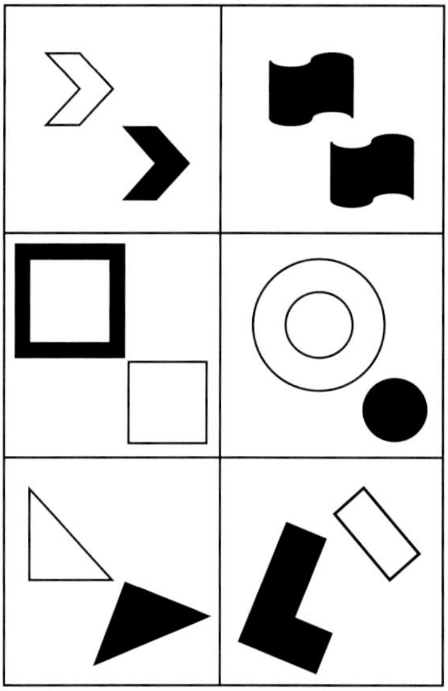

Set B

Which of the following test shapes belongs to Set A?

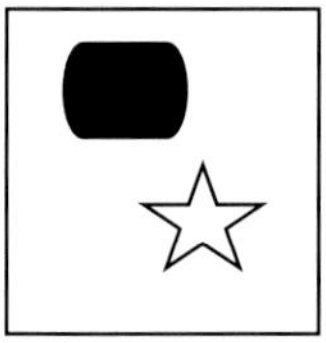
A

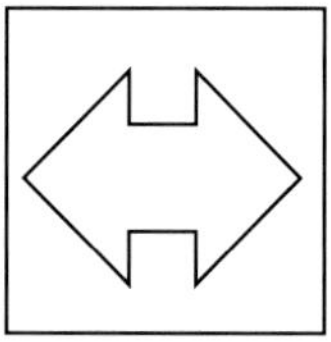
B

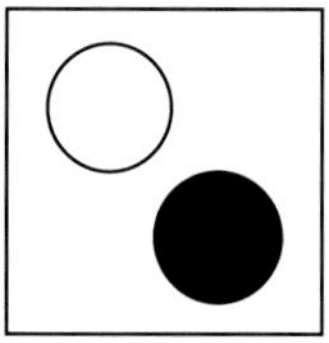
C

D

Which of the following test shapes belongs to Set B?

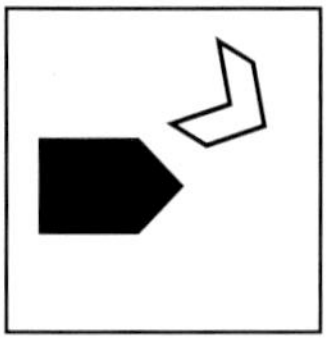
A

B

C

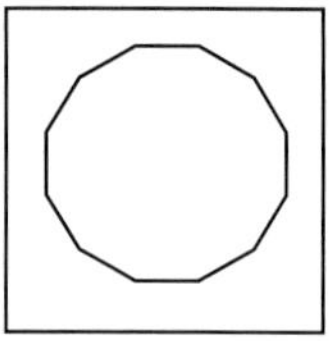
D

TYPE IV - Question 9

Set A **Set B**

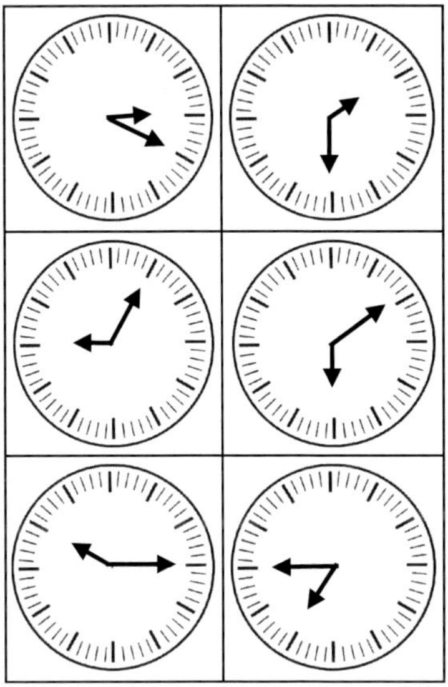

Which of the following test shapes belongs to Set A?

A

B

C

D

Which of the following test shapes belongs to Set B?

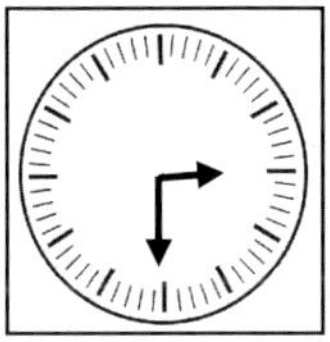
A

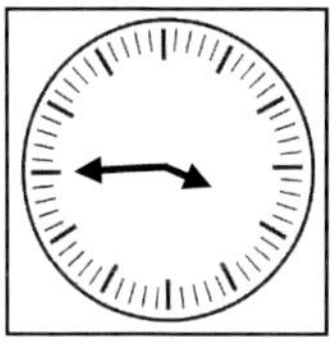
B

C

D

TYPE IV - Question 10

Set A **Set B**

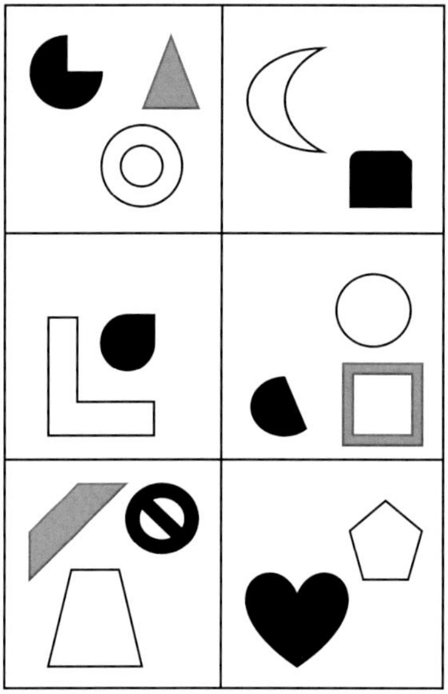

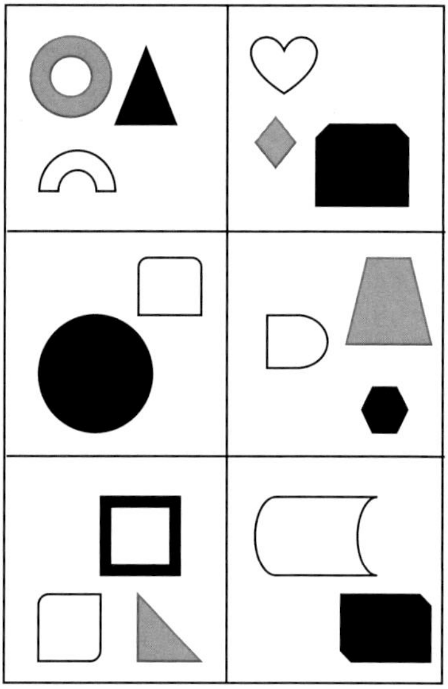

Which of the following test shapes belongs to Set A?

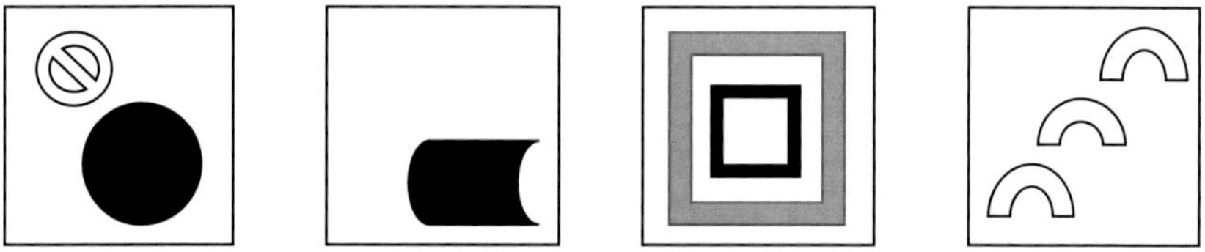

A B C D

Which of the following test shapes belongs to Set B?

A B C D

TYPE IV - Question 11

Set A **Set B**

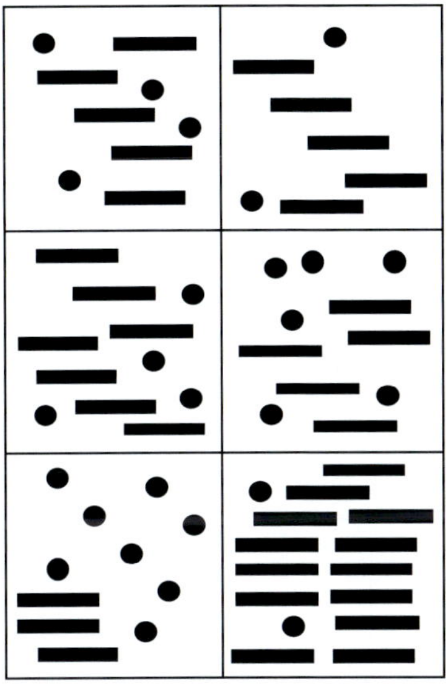

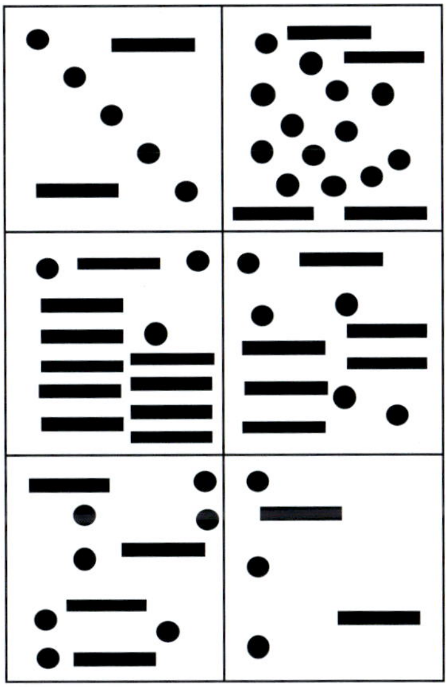

Which of the following test shapes belongs to Set A?

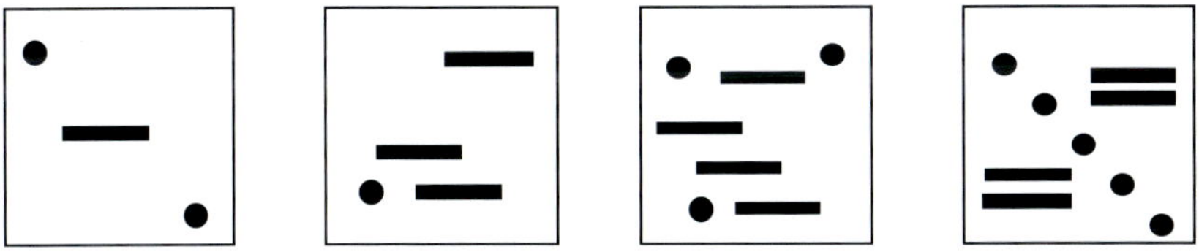

A B C D

Which of the following test shapes belongs to Set B?

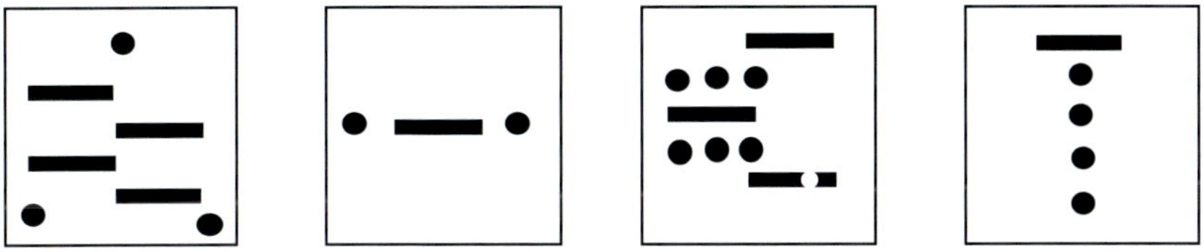

A B C D

TYPE IV - Question 12

Set A

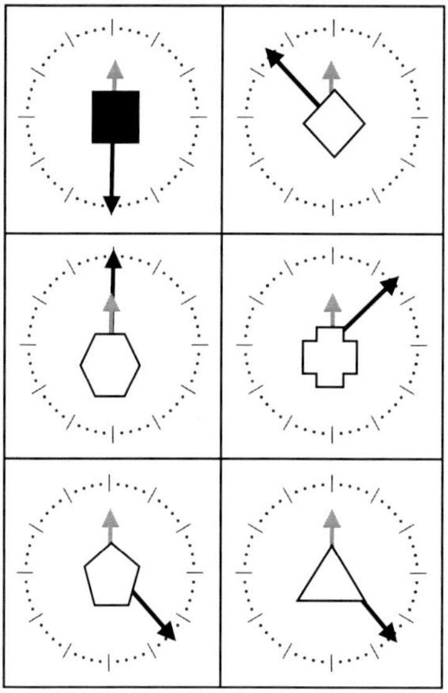

Set B

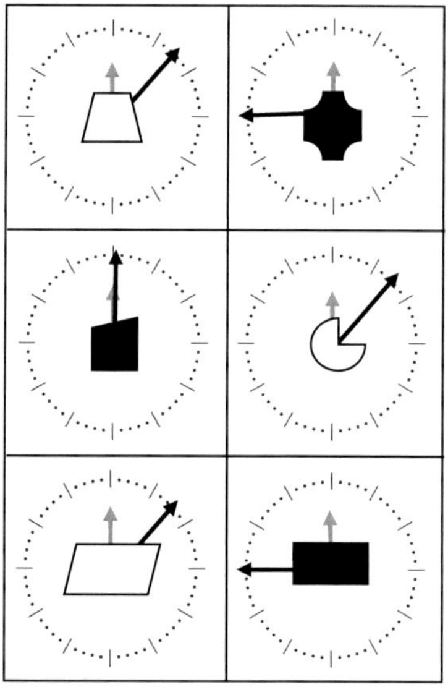

Which of the following test shapes belongs to Set A?

A

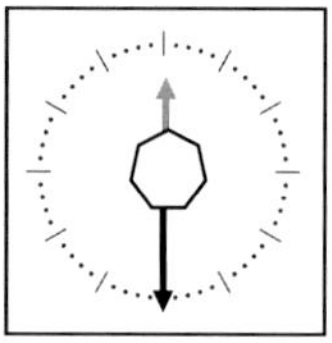

B

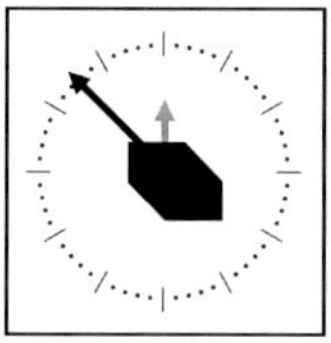

C

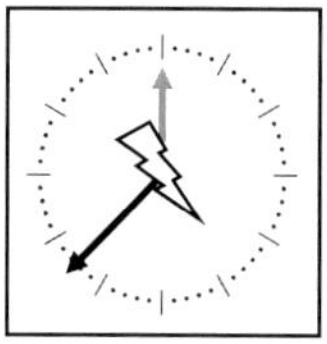

D

Which of the following test shapes belongs to Set B?

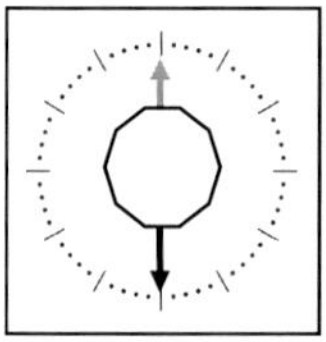

A

B

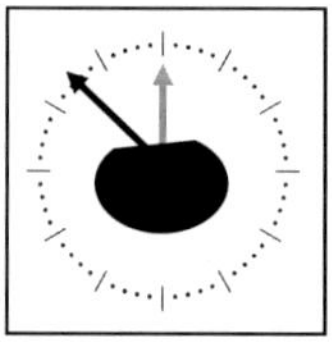

C

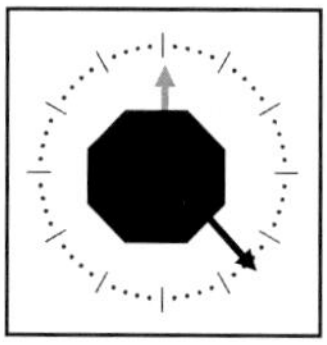

D

TYPE IV - Question 13

Set A **Set B**

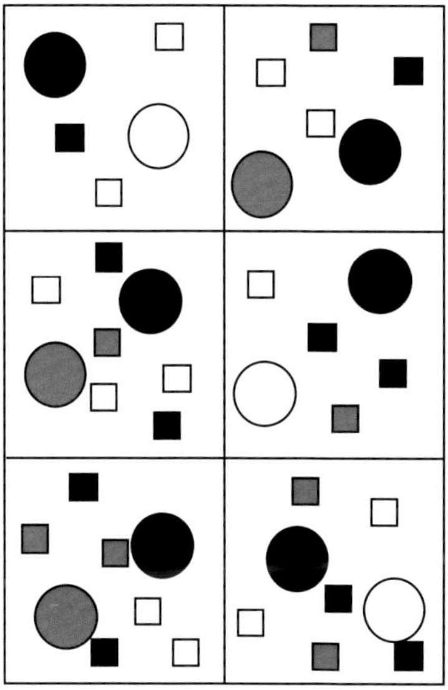

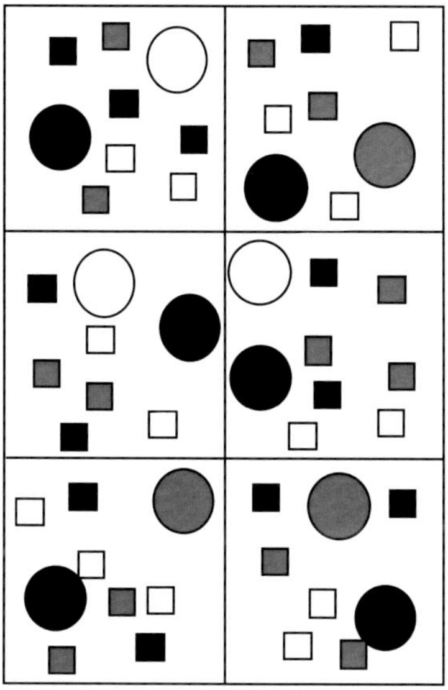

Which of the following test shapes belongs to Set A?

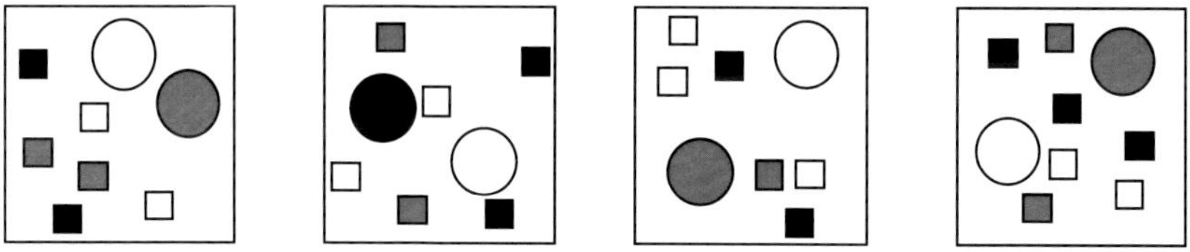

A B C D

Which of the following test shapes belongs to Set B?

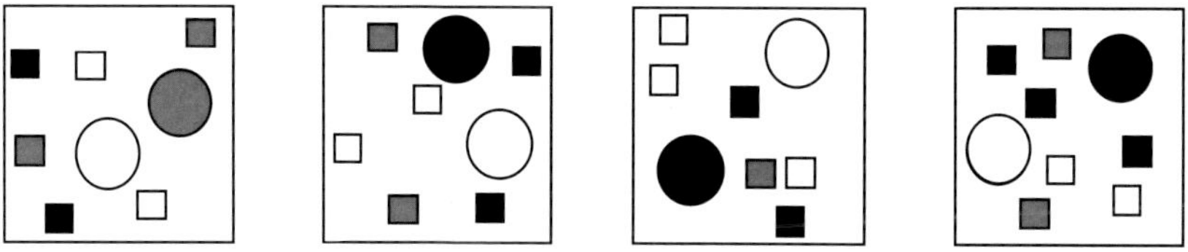

A B C D

TYPE IV - Question 14

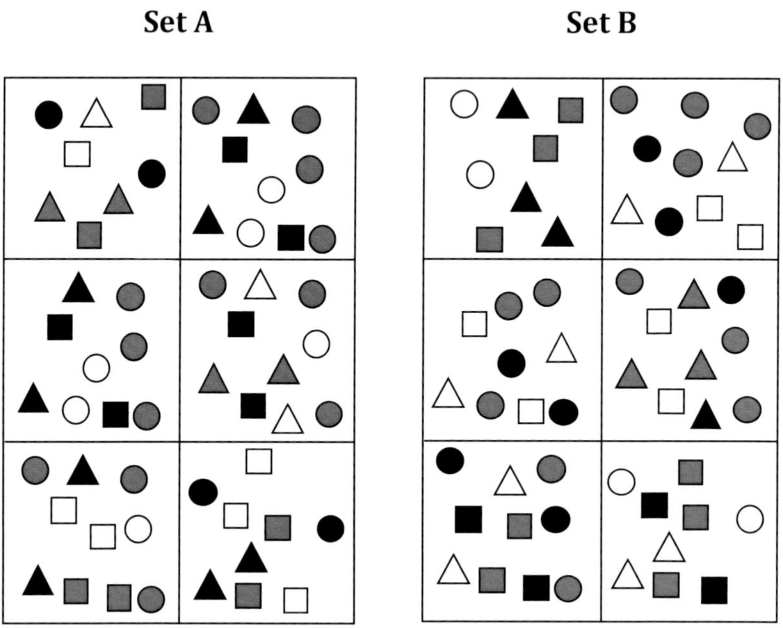

Which of the following test shapes belongs to Set A?

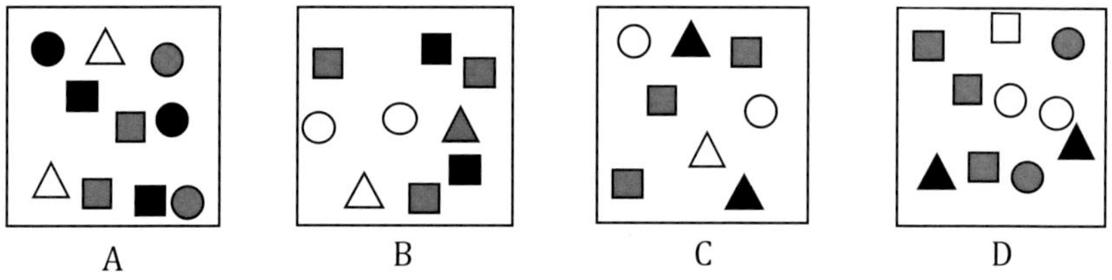

Which of the following test shapes belongs to Set B?

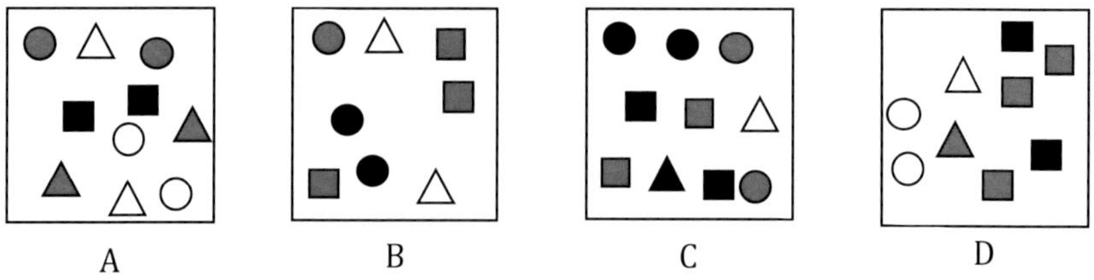

TYPE IV - Question 15

Set A **Set B**

Which of the following test shapes belongs to Set A?

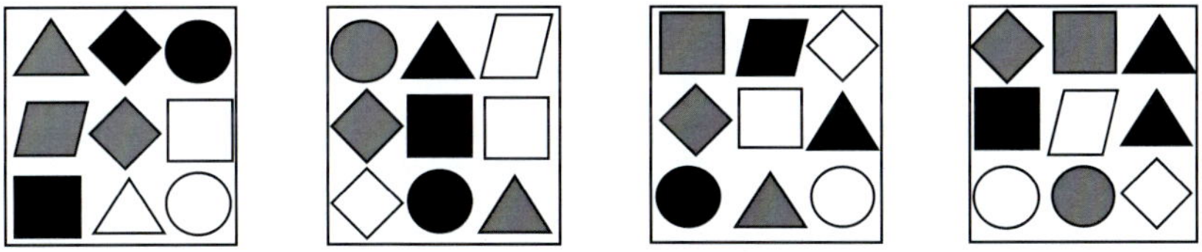

A B C D

Which of the following test shapes belongs to Set B?

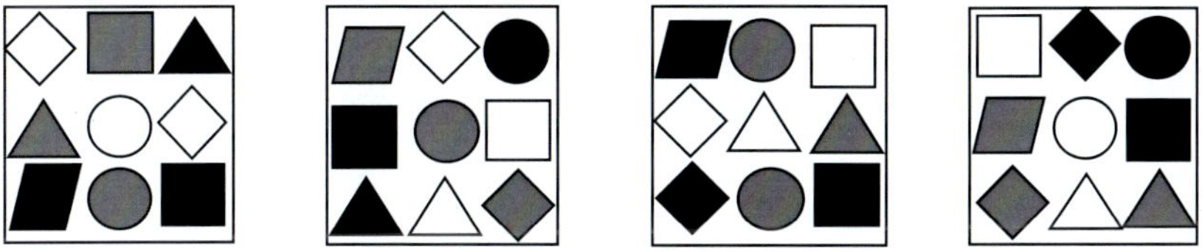

A B C D

TYPE IV - Question 16

Set A | **Set B**

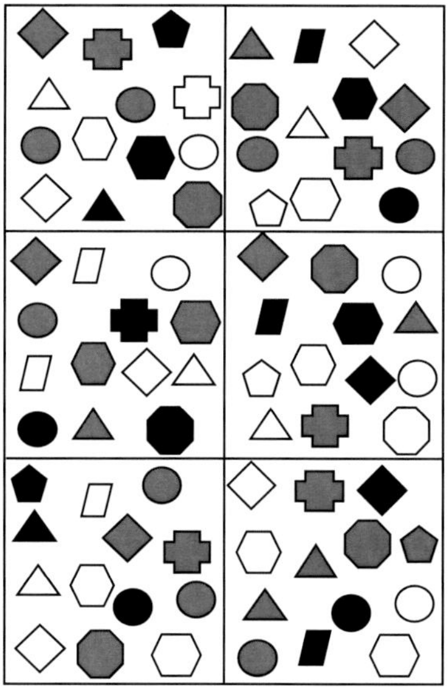

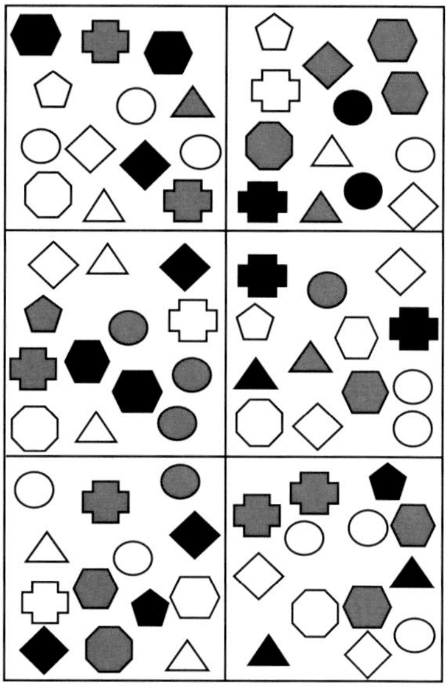

Which of the following test shapes belongs to Set A?

A

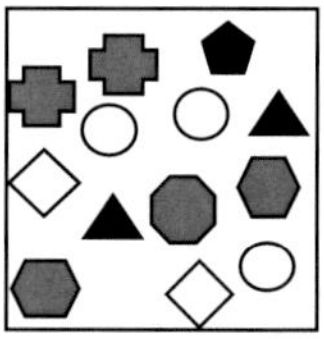

B

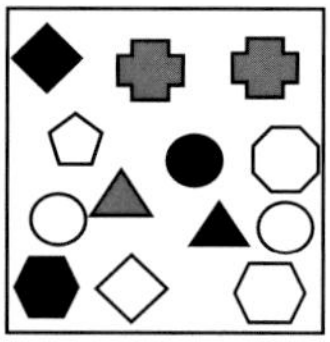

C

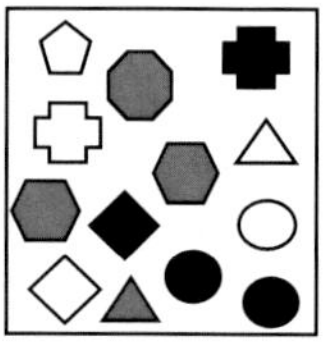

D

Which of the following test shapes belongs to Set B?

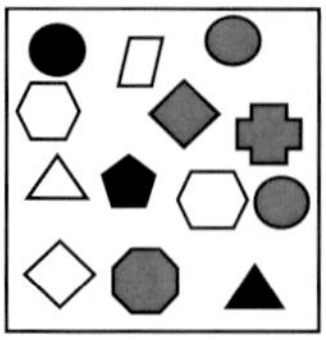

A

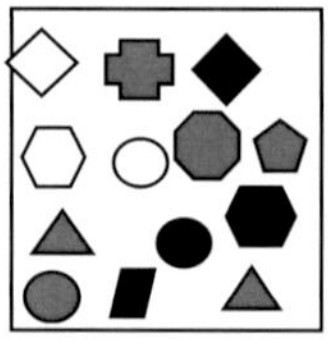

B

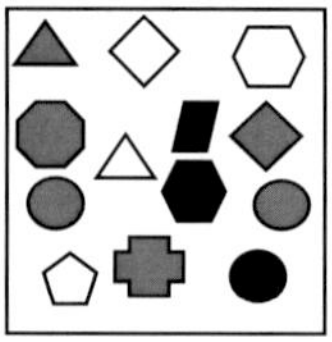

C

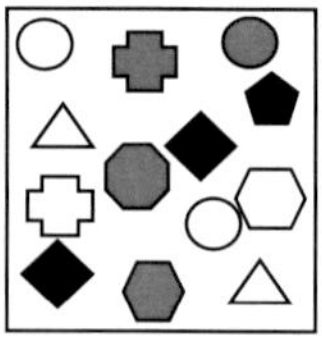

D

TYPE IV - Question 17

Set A

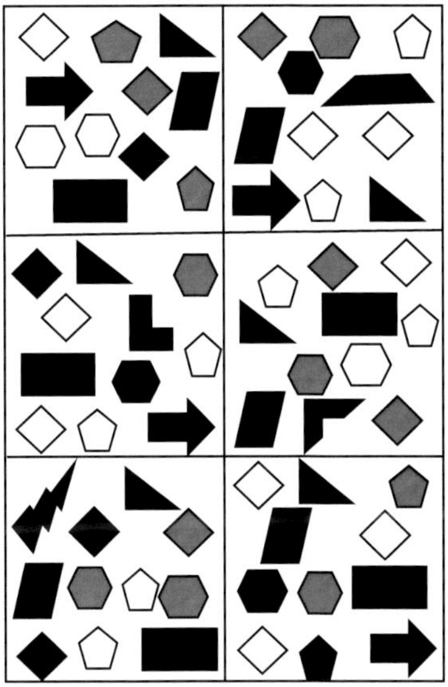

Set B

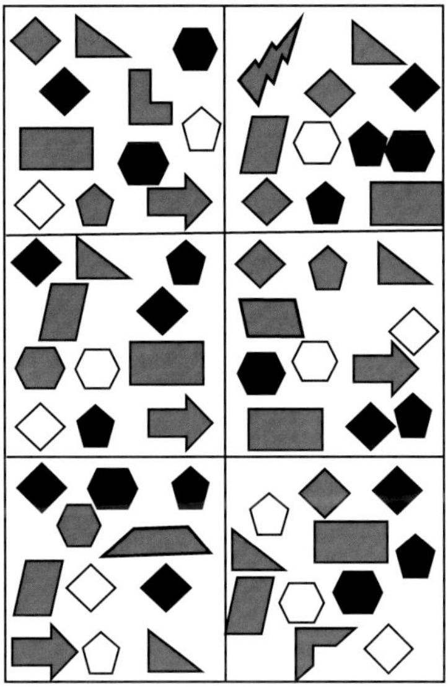

Which of the following test shapes belongs to Set A?

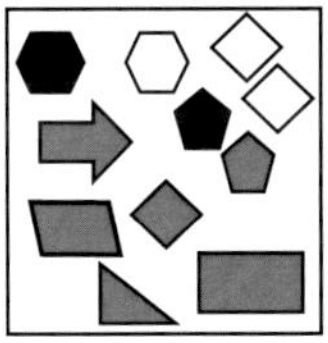
A

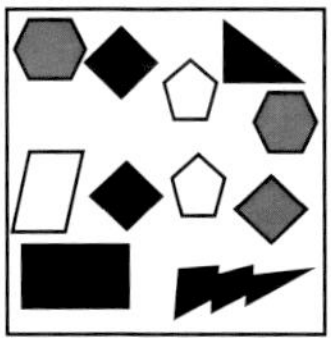
B

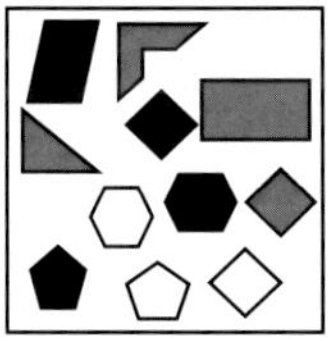
C

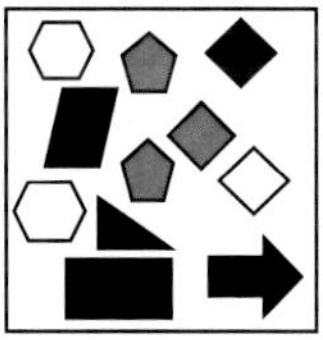
D

Which of the following test shapes belongs to Set B?

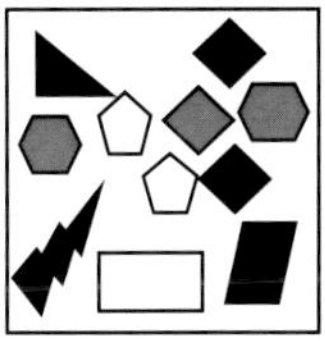
A

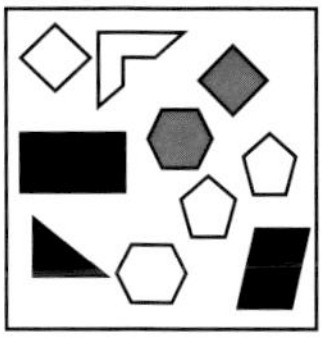
B

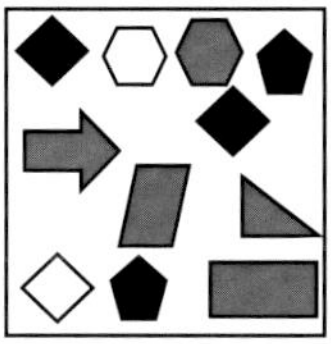
C

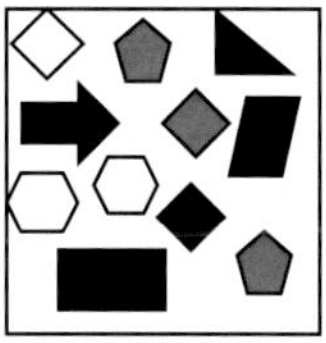
D

TYPE IV - Question 18

Set A

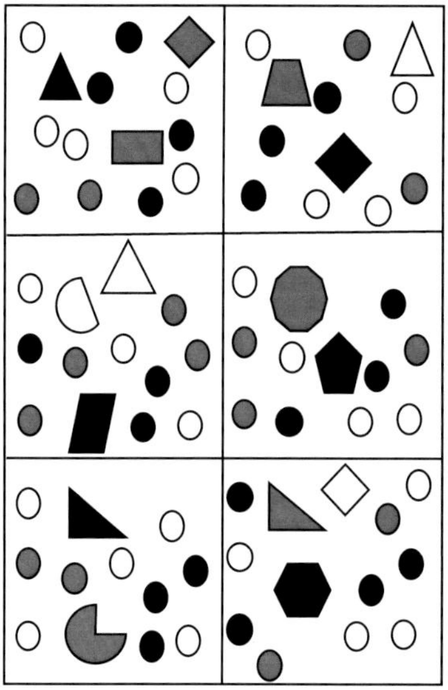

Set B

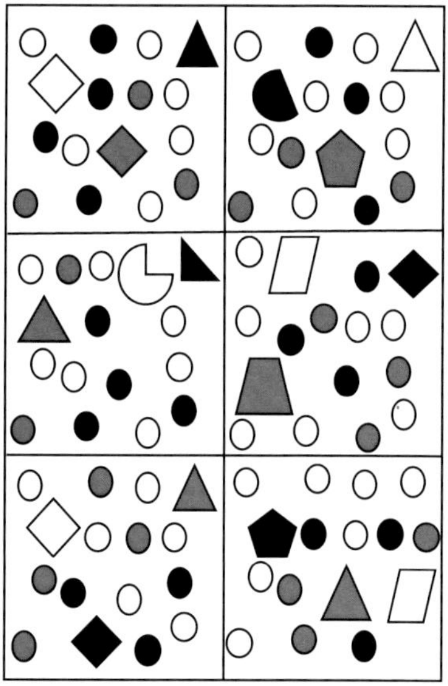

Which of the following test shapes belongs to Set A?

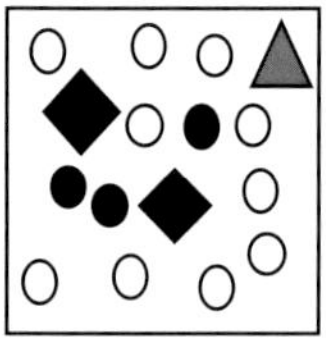

A

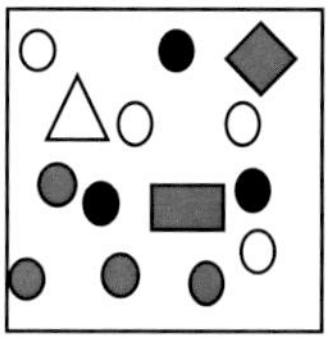

B

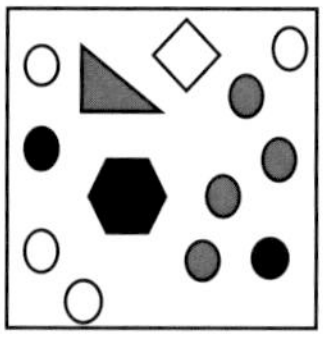

C

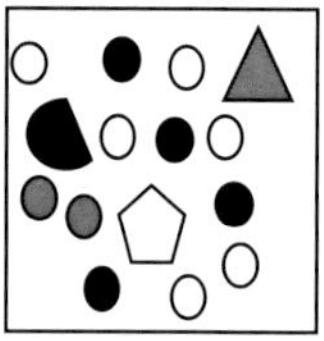

D

Which of the following test shapes belongs to Set B?

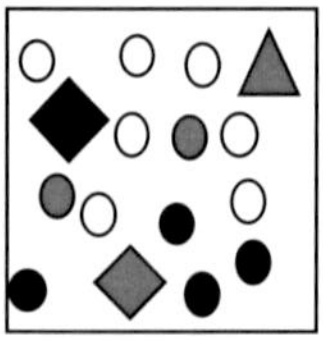

A

B

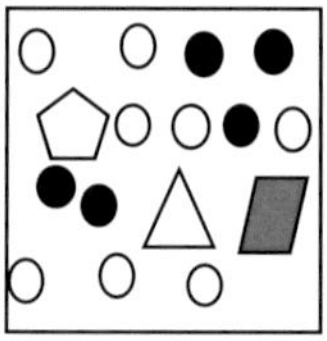

C

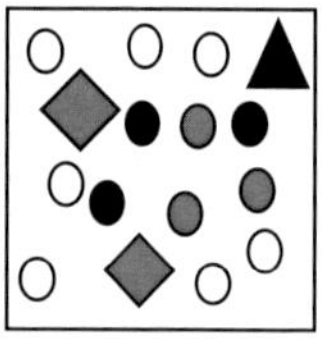

D

TYPE IV - Question 19

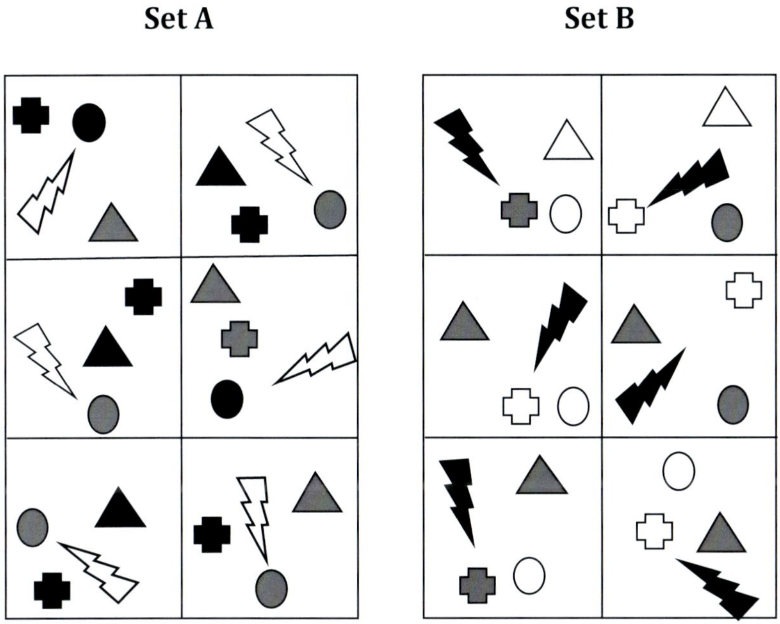

Which of the following test shapes belongs to Set A?

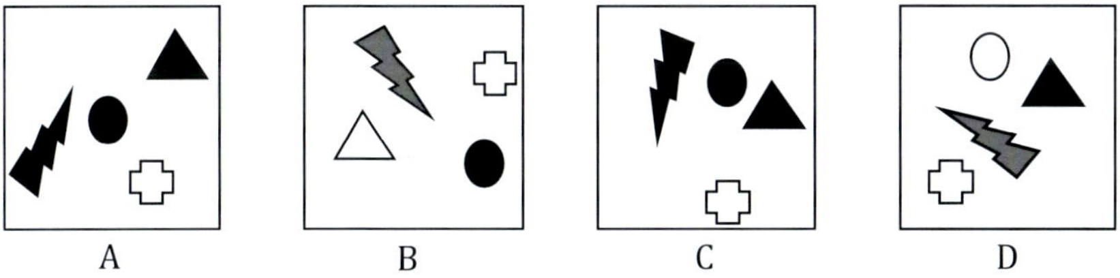

Which of the following test shapes belongs to Set B?

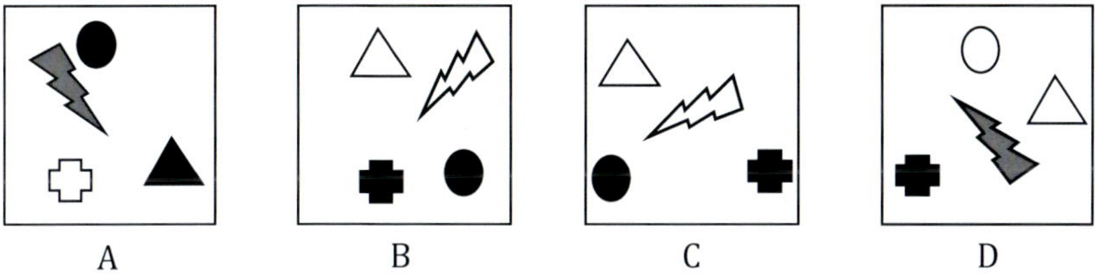

TYPE IV - Question 20

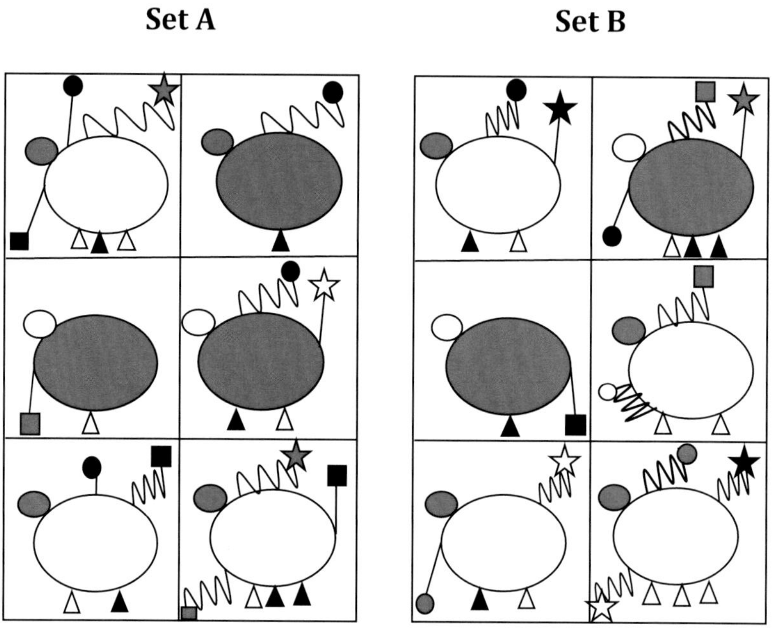

Which of the following test shapes belongs to Set A?

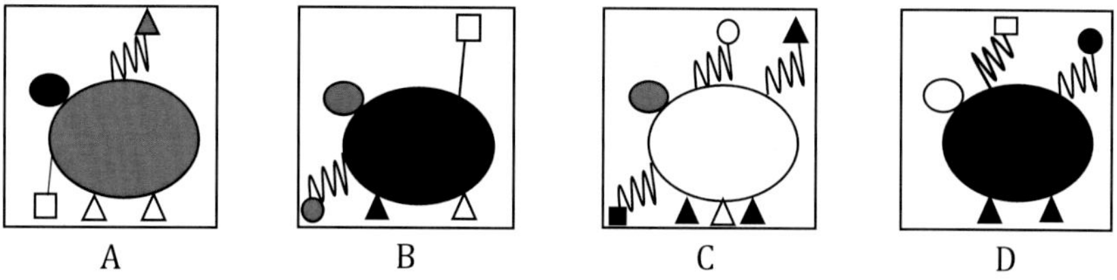

Which of the following test shapes belongs to Set B?

TYPE IV - Question 21

Set A **Set B**

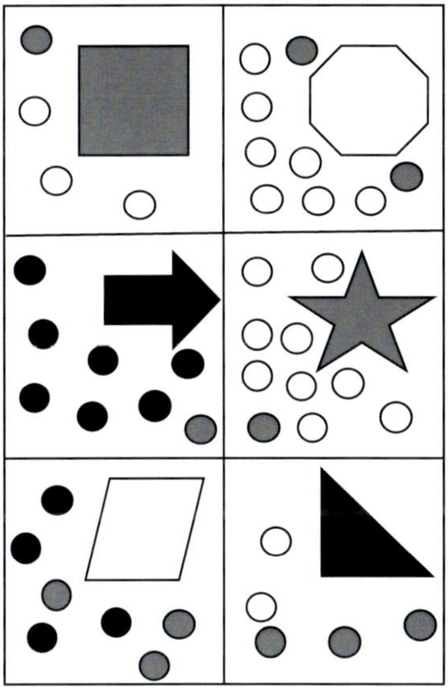

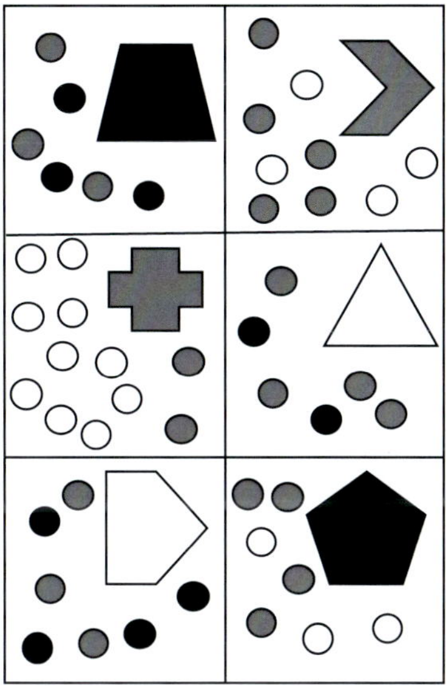

Which of the following test shapes belongs to Set A?

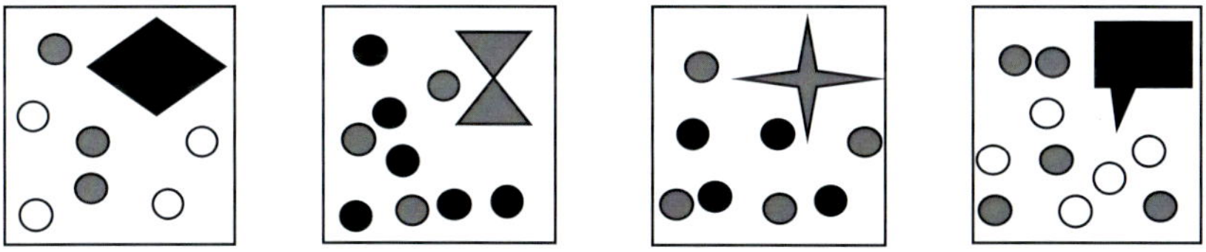

A B C D

Which of the following test shapes belongs to Set B?

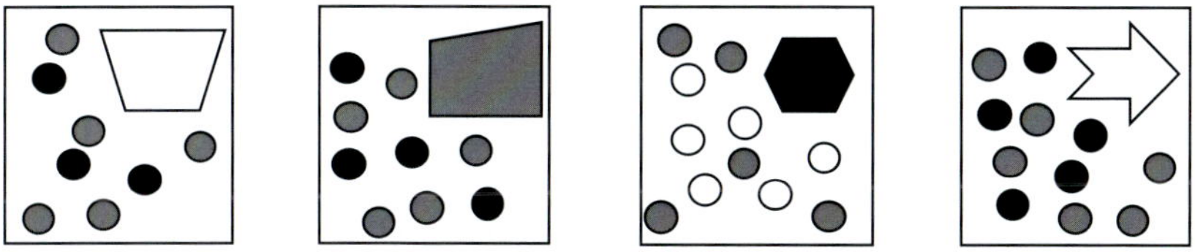

A B C D

Situational Judgement

FORMAT

In the exam, you have:

- 69 questions
- 20 different scenarios
- Each scenario has 2 to 5 questions
- 26 minutes
- +1 minute to read the instructions
- You do not receive a score out of 900. Rather, you are assessed from Band 1 to Band 4.

In this section, there are:

- Type 1 – 40 scenarios
- Type 2 – 35 scenarios

Objectives:

- To understand real world situations.
- To identify critical factors.
- To assess understanding of medical ethics.

TYPES OF QUESTIONS

Type 1 | Rank the appropriateness of courses of action

- **A very appropriate thing to do** – An action that solves the issue (either part or all) in a competent way.
- **Appropriate, but not ideal** – Something that can be done but is not the most preferred response.
- **Inappropriate but not awful** – Should be avoided but not the worst thing that can happen.
- **Very inappropriate thing to do** – Should be avoided as it will make the situation worse.

Type 2 | Consider the importance of certain factors that will inform your course of action

- **Very important** – Cannot be ignored.
- **Important** – Not vital but may have a positive impact.
- **Of minor importance** – Wouldn't make much of a difference if forgotten.
- **Not important at all** – This is something that should definitely not be taken into account.

FOUR 'Cs' OF MEDICAL ETHICS

Capacity

- Consent can only be taken from patients who have the capacity to make a decision.
- Bad decisions do not indicate lack of capacity.
- In the UK, everyone above the age of 16 is assumed to have capacity, unless proven otherwise.
- All healthcare professionals assess capacity.
- Only regard a patient as lacking capacity if he/she is unable to retain, understand, use, weigh up, or communicate information needed to make a decision.
- You should maximise a patient's ability to make decisions.
  - ⇒ Provide a translator.
  - ⇒ Speak using non-medical terms.
- Capacity is time and decision specific.
  - ⇒ Having the capacity to decide on taking paracetamol is different from having the capacity to decide on whether to have an amputation.
  - ⇒ Decision on whether to undergo major surgery can change throughout time depending on the patient's current fitness and age.
- If you doubt a patient's capacity to make a decision, you should seek advice from:
  - ⇒ Nursing staff or others involved in patient's care.
  - ⇒ Those close to the patient who will be able to communicate the patient's needs.
  - ⇒ Specialist doctors such as psychiatrists, neurologists, and speech and language therapists.
- Making decisions when a patient lacks capacity:
  - ⇒ Make the care of your patient your first concern.
  - ⇒ Treat patients as individuals and respect their dignity.
  - ⇒ Support and encourage patients to be involved in their treatment and care.
  - ⇒ Treat patients with respect and do not discriminate.
- *Key things to remember for common scenarios:*
  - ⇒ Bad decisions do not indicate a lack of capacity.
  - ⇒ Capacity is time and decision specific.

FOUR 'Cs' OF MEDICAL ETHICS (Continued)

⇒ Patients lack capacity when they are unable to **retain -> understand -> weigh -> communicate** information needed to make a decision.
⇒ Maximise patient's ability to make a decision.
⇒ **Provide a translator and use non-medical terms.**

Competence

- Everyone **aged 16 and over is presumed** to be competent to give his/her consent to medical treatment.
- If the patient demonstrates competence and is under 16 years of age, we describe the patient as being *Gillick* competent (if he/she meets the criteria of Fraser guidelines).
  ⇒ Able to **understand** that there is a choice and that choices have consequences.
  ⇒ Able to **weigh** the information and arrive at a decision
  ⇒ A willingness to make a choice.
  ⇒ Understand the nature and purpose of the proposed intervention.
  ⇒ Understand the proposed intervention's risks and side effects.
  ⇒ Understand the alternatives to the proposed intervention and the risks associated to them.
  ⇒ Freedom from undue pressure.

Consent

- Process of obtaining permission from a patient.
- Work in partnership with your patients to ensure good care.
- In emergency situations where consent cannot be obtained, check for an advanced directive (legal document with patient's wishes).
- If not, act in the patient's best interest.
- Listen to patients and respect their views about their health.
- Discuss with patients what their diagnosis, prognosis, treatment and, care involve.
- Respect patients' decisions.
- Give patients all the information they want or need (Montgomery law).
- *Key things to remember for common scenarios:*
  ⇒ Answer patients' questions honestly.
  ⇒ **Do not coerce patients** into consenting for a procedure.
  ⇒ Person who obtains patient's consent has to:

FOUR 'Cs' OF MEDICAL ETHICS (Continued)

- Be suitably **trained and qualified.**
- Have sufficient knowledge of the proposed investigation or treatment and understand the risks involved.

⇒ Does the patient have the **capacity to consent**?

⇒ Tailoring your approach to discussions with patients according to:
- their needs, wishes and priorities.
- complexity of the treatment.
- level of knowledge about and understanding of their condition, prognosis and treatment options.

⇒ **Do not make assumptions** about patients' wants or needs.

Confidentiality

- Use the minimum necessary personal information.
- Manage and protect information.
- Maintain patients' trust.
- *Key things to remember for common scenarios:*
  - ⇒ Do not discuss patients **outside of work** especially patient identifiable information (DOB, name, address).
  - ⇒ Do not share patient details **over social media** (personal email, WhatsApp, Instagram, Facebook, Tik Tok, etc.).
  - ⇒ Do not bring **home** patient identifiable information (ward lists, patient files).
  - ⇒ Do not share details of diagnosis, treatment or plan without the patient's explicit consent.
  - ⇒ Do not share patient information **over the phone.**
    - If a relative, friend or neighbour calls, do not confirm patient's presence on the ward without prior consent from the patient.
    - Signpost them to speak directly with the patient if they would like any updates.
    - In certain instances, patients give you the permission to discuss their medical care in advance of an anticipated phone call.
    - Pictures, photographs, videos, audiotape or other images of patients should not be shared.
  - ⇒ **Anonymise patients if able.**
- *When can you disclose personal information?*
  - ⇒ Patient has given **consent** -> for the sake of his/her own care or for local clinical audit.

FOUR 'Cs' OF MEDICAL ETHICS (Continued)

⇒ Patient has given explicit consent for specific purposes.
⇒ Disclosure is of overall benefit to a patient who lacks capacity to consent (does the patient have capacity to make a particular decision?).
⇒ Disclosure **required by law** (ordered by a judge or presiding officer of court).
⇒ Disclosure can be justified in the **public interest** (e.g., communicable diseases or serious crime).

TIPS AND TRICKS TO SCORE

Revision Tips

- Have a basic knowledge of the four pillars of medical ethics (consent, capacity, confidentiality and competence) and key principles of medical professionalism.
- Familiarise yourself with the roles of a doctor and medical student.
- The General Medical Council's Good Medical Practice and Outcomes for Graduates online resources provide detailed advice on how a doctor should behave, the knowledge, skills and performance required, maintaining trust, safety and quality, communication partnership, and teamwork.
- Reflect and review on the questions as you practice.
- Remember your hospital attachments.
- Practice speed reading (recommended four weeks before your test date) to improve your reading comprehension skills and save precious time.

Answering Techniques

- Answer the questions according to what you **SHOULD** do, not what you **WOULD** do.
- Each question is independent of the question before. It is possible to have several courses of actions that are very appropriate.
- Read the questions properly and answer accordingly. If the question is asking specifically in relation to patient safety, then choose the answer that best reflects whether the safety of the patient has been put first.

TYPE I - Question 1 - A Little Too Late

A junior doctor, Priya, is working her normal day shift which is meant to finish at 5:00 pm. However, she has a list of patients to discharge and she must write up their medications before the pharmacy closes at 4:30 pm. It is now 3:30 pm, and she still has to chase blood results of eight patients and prepare four discharge letters which will take about 20 minutes each. She is the only junior doctor covering the ward today, and there is no one on-site to help. She is eager to leave work at 5:00 pm as she has to get ready for a date tonight. She decides to rush through the discharge letters and leave the blood results for the on-call doctor, Maura, to chase. Maura will be covering all 16 wards in the hospital from 5:30 pm onwards.

How **appropriate** are each of the following responses by the junior doctor **Priya** in this situation?

1.1 Leave at 5:00 pm as planned, rush through the discharge letters, and leave the blood results for the on-call doctor to chase.

A. A very appropriate thing to do
B. Appropriate, but not ideal
C. Inappropriate, but not awful
D. A very inappropriate thing to do

1.2 Leave at 5:00 pm as planned and check the blood results in the morning if Maura has not done them.

A. A very appropriate thing to do
B. Appropriate, but not ideal
C. Inappropriate, but not awful
D. A very inappropriate thing to do

1.3 Stay and finish the discharge letters and chase the blood results, even though that means that she might be late for her date.

A. A very appropriate thing to do
B. Appropriate, but not ideal
C. Inappropriate, but not awful
D. A very inappropriate thing to do

TYPE I - Question 1 (Continued) - A Little Too Late

1.4 Contact Maura's supervisor, Dr O'Shea, to make sure that he is aware of the blood results that Maura needs to chase.

A. A very appropriate thing to do
B. Appropriate, but not ideal
C. Inappropriate, but not awful
D. A very inappropriate thing to do

TYPE I - Question 2 - A Professional Relationship

A new junior doctor, Santana, started working on the Trauma and Orthopaedics Ward about a month ago. One of the long-stay patients, Jonathan, has taken a liking to Santana and looked her up on Facebook. Jonathan sends a request to Santana and starts sending her flirty messages. Santana recognises him as one of her patients and responds.

How **appropriate** are each of the following responses by **Santana** in this situation?

2.1 Santana accepts his friend request and flirts back as she is feeling lonely.

A. A very appropriate thing to do
B. Appropriate, but not ideal
C. Inappropriate, but not awful
D. A very inappropriate thing to do

2.2 Santana accepts his friend request and politely rejects him.

A. A very appropriate thing to do
B. Appropriate, but not ideal
C. Inappropriate, but not awful
D. A very inappropriate thing to do

2.3 Santana does not accept his friend request, ignores him on the ward, and asks the other junior doctor on the team to treat him as she feels uncomfortable.

A. A very appropriate thing to do
B. Appropriate, but not ideal
C. Inappropriate, but not awful
D. A very inappropriate thing to do

2.4 Santana ignores his messages and decides to share a screenshot of the messages on Twitter, but she anonymises him and doesn't identify him as a patient.

A. A very appropriate thing to do
B. Appropriate, but not ideal
C. Inappropriate, but not awful
D. A very inappropriate thing to do

TYPE I - Question 2 (Continued) - A Professional Relationship

2.5 Santana politely refuses him, but she jokes about his advances to her colleagues during lunch in the Junior Doctor Mess.

A. A very appropriate thing to do
B. Appropriate, but not ideal
C. Inappropriate, but not awful
D. A very inappropriate thing to do

TYPE I - Question 3 - A HIV Positive Patient

A junior doctor, Eoin, just found out that one of the new patients on the ward, Will, has been diagnosed as HIV positive, and his social history shows that he has had multiple sexual partners. After the 9:00 am ward round, Eoin's consultant puts him in charge of taking some urgent blood samples from Will to be sent to the lab immediately for his ongoing acute infection. Eoin has a personal stigma against people with HIV and frequently shares his opinion on Twitter publicly.

How **appropriate** are each of the following responses by **Eoin** in this situation?

3.1 Eoin gives the task to his fellow colleague and explains that he is uncomfortable treating patients who are HIV positive.

A. A very appropriate thing to do
B. Appropriate, but not ideal
C. Inappropriate, but not awful
D. A very inappropriate thing to do

3.2 Eoin puts his opinions aside and completes the task. However, he expresses his reluctance to the patient.

A. A very appropriate thing to do
B. Appropriate, but not ideal
C. Inappropriate, but not awful
D. A very inappropriate thing to do

3.3 Eoin ignores the task and hopes the on-call doctor picks it up at 5.30 pm.

A. A very appropriate thing to do
B. Appropriate, but not ideal
C. Inappropriate, but not awful
D. A very inappropriate thing to do

3.4 Eoin completes the task efficiently but takes precaution in double gloving himself.

A. A very appropriate thing to do
B. Appropriate, but not ideal
C. Inappropriate, but not awful
D. A very inappropriate thing to do

TYPE I - Question 3 (Continued) - A HIV Positive Patient

3.5 Eoin politely asks his fellow colleague, who is also on the team and is free at the moment, to carry out the task and says that it is urgent.

A. A very appropriate thing to do
B. Appropriate, but not ideal
C. Inappropriate, but not awful
D. A very inappropriate thing to do

TYPE I - Question 4 - An Angry Partner

A medical student, Jozsef, has been asked to help clerk some patients in the waiting area of the Emergency Unit. He reads a patient's notes briefly, which say 'abdominal pain'. His patient is a young Caucasian 15-year-old girl, Leia, who is accompanied by a much older looking man, Mr Buggati. Jozsef noticed that, during the history taking, the man answered on behalf of her and took charge of the conversation, not allowing her to speak. Mr Buggati seems to believe the tummy ache is caused by a bad dinner that she ate and that it is probably nothing to worry about. He hurries the conversation and is asking to leave now.

How **appropriate** are each of the following responses by **Jozsef** in this situation?

4.1 Leia is probably shy and prefers Mr Buggati to tell her story. Jozsef discusses her care and further treatment options with Mr Buggati.

A. A very appropriate thing to do
B. Appropriate, but not ideal
C. Inappropriate, but not awful
D. A very inappropriate thing to do

4.2 Leia probably doesn't speak English so Mr Buggati is being helpful towards Leia. Jozsef listens to Mr Buggati, agrees, and lets them leave.

A. A very appropriate thing to do
B. Appropriate, but not ideal
C. Inappropriate, but not awful
D. A very inappropriate thing to do

4.3 Jozsef stops Mr Buggati and asks if he could speak to Leia alone.

A. A very appropriate thing to do
B. Appropriate, but not ideal
C. Inappropriate, but not awful
D. A very inappropriate thing to do

4.4 As per hospital policy, he asks if he could examine Leia in a different room with a chaperone.

A. A very appropriate thing to do
B. Appropriate, but not ideal
C. Inappropriate, but not awful
D. A very inappropriate thing to do

TYPE I - Question 5 - An Unconscious Bias

Two medical students, Kevin and Andrea, are on the same surgical team for placement. Kevin has noticed recently that the surgical registrar, Mr White, has taken a liking to him as he only asks him to help out in theatre, engages in conversations only with him despite Andrea being next to him, and offers to teach him some surgical techniques whilst waiting for patients to arrive. Kevin notices that Andrea, although bothered, doesn't say or do anything.

How **appropriate** are each of the following responses by **Kevin** in this situation?

5.1 Kevin involves Andrea in conversations with Mr White and takes turns with Andrea in helping out in theatre, despite Mr White's offer.

A. A very appropriate thing to do
B. Appropriate, but not ideal
C. Inappropriate, but not awful
D. A very inappropriate thing to do

5.2 Kevin discusses his concerns with Mr White that Andrea hasn't been receiving the same treatment as him, and he finds this uncomfortable.

A. A very appropriate thing to do
B. Appropriate, but not ideal
C. Inappropriate, but not awful
D. A very inappropriate thing to do

5.3 Kevin ignores the situation since Andrea hasn't said anything; perhaps she isn't interested in surgery.

A. A very appropriate thing to do
B. Appropriate, but not ideal
C. Inappropriate, but not awful
D. A very inappropriate thing to do

5.4 Kevin speaks to the surgical team consultant regarding Mr White's actions. Hopefully the consultant will have a word with Mr White.

A. A very appropriate thing to do
B. Appropriate, but not ideal
C. Inappropriate, but not awful
D. A very inappropriate thing to do

TYPE I - Question 6 - A Message Bearer

Sakura is a medical student on placement in the delivery unit. Mrs Johansson has just given birth to a baby girl. On delivery, the midwife notices the baby has some distinct features of Down's Syndrome. The midwife, Jessica, asks if Sakura could break the news to Mrs Johansson that the child may have Down's Syndrome as she is quickly called to another delivery suite to help with a complex case.

How **appropriate** are each of the following responses by **Sakura** in this situation?

6.1 Sakura breaks the news to Mrs Johansson following the order from Jessica.

A. A very appropriate thing to do
B. Appropriate, but not ideal
C. Inappropriate, but not awful
D. A very inappropriate thing to do

6.2 Sakura agrees with Jessica but asks her to break the news to Mrs Johansson very quickly before she goes to the other delivery suite.

A. A very appropriate thing to do
B. Appropriate, but not ideal
C. Inappropriate, but not awful
D. A very inappropriate thing to do

6.3 Sakura involves the medical obstetric team and asks for advice regarding breaking bad news.

A. A very appropriate thing to do
B. Appropriate, but not ideal
C. Inappropriate, but not awful
D. A very inappropriate thing to do

6.4 Sakura ignores Jessica's request and leaves to go for lunch.

A. A very appropriate thing to do
B. Appropriate, but not ideal
C. Inappropriate, but not awful
D. A very inappropriate thing to do

TYPE I - Question 7 - A Ward List

Jonah, a medical student, is on placement in the Endocrine Ward. On the ward round this morning, he was introduced to multiple interesting cases that he would like to write up for self-directed learning. He notices that all the doctors on the team have a ward list which includes details of each patient, including their presenting symptoms, tests required, and management plans. He politely asks the ward clerk to print out a copy of the ward list for his own reference. He has made some notes on the ward list and is considering whether he should take the ward list home.

How **appropriate** are each of the following responses by **Jonah** in this situation?

7.1 Jonah takes the ward list home as he feels that it will definitely benefit his learning.

A. A very appropriate thing to do
B. Appropriate, but not ideal
C. Inappropriate, but not awful
D. A very inappropriate thing to do

7.2 Jonah asks the ward clerk to print out another copy of the list without including patient demographics.

A. A very appropriate thing to do
B. Appropriate, but not ideal
C. Inappropriate, but not awful
D. A very inappropriate thing to do

7.3 Jonah takes the ward list home and returns it the next day, pretending he accidentally brought it home.

A. A very appropriate thing to do
B. Appropriate, but not ideal
C. Inappropriate, but not awful
D. A very inappropriate thing to do

7.4 Since no one else knows of Jonah's intentions, he takes the list home.

A. A very appropriate thing to do
B. Appropriate, but not ideal
C. Inappropriate, but not awful
D. A very inappropriate thing to do

TYPE I - Question 8 - A Medical Emergency

James, a medical student, is on a placement in the Emergency Department. He notices that one of the patients admitted on the ward today is one of his classmates, Donna. He recalls Donna being a very shy and private person who doesn't converse much. James starts to express curiosity in Donna's admission.

How **appropriate** are each of the following responses by **James** in this situation?

8.1 James looks up Donna's case notes and test results without the knowledge of the junior doctor looking after Donna and Donna herself.

A. A very appropriate thing to do
B. Appropriate, but not ideal
C. Inappropriate, but not awful
D. A very inappropriate thing to do

8.2 James copies Donna's hospital number and searches for her GP record.

A. A very appropriate thing to do
B. Appropriate, but not ideal
C. Inappropriate, but not awful
D. A very inappropriate thing to do

8.3 James asks the junior doctor who is looking after Donna if Donna is happy to speak to him about her admission.

A. A very appropriate thing to do
B. Appropriate, but not ideal
C. Inappropriate, but not awful
D. A very inappropriate thing to do

8.4 James shares on social media with his other classmates that Donna is in hospital for a suspected miscarriage.

A. A very appropriate thing to do
B. Appropriate, but not ideal
C. Inappropriate, but not awful
D. A very inappropriate thing to do

TYPE I - Question 8 (Continued) - A Medical Emergency

8.5 James looks up Donna's GP record and finds that her next of kin is her mother. James phones Donna's mother and tells her she is in the Emergency Unit for a suspected miscarriage.

A. A very appropriate thing to do
B. Appropriate, but not ideal
C. Inappropriate, but not awful
D. A very inappropriate thing to do

TYPE I - Question 9 - A Telephone Call

Nikki, a medical student, is on placement in the Psychiatry Ward. The telephone on the ward rings. Nikki, being the closest to the telephone, answers the call. Fred is on the line and would like to ask about his friend and neighbour, Parry. Nikki finds that there is no one else available to speak to Fred as all the doctors and nurses are currently seeing other patients. Fred is being very polite but persistent. He insists that he is Parry's only friend and that they are neighbours.

How **appropriate** are each of the following responses by **Nikki** in this situation?

9.1 Nikki refers to the online case notes on Parry and updates Fred on Parry's progress in the hospital.

A. A very appropriate thing to do
B. Appropriate, but not ideal
C. Inappropriate, but not awful
D. A very inappropriate thing to do

9.2 Nikki recommends Fred to call Parry himself and ask about his progress in the hospital.

A. A very appropriate thing to do
B. Appropriate, but not ideal
C. Inappropriate, but not awful
D. A very inappropriate thing to do

9.3 Nikki recommends Fred to come to the ward during visiting times to see Parry if he would like to know more about Parry's care.

A. A very appropriate thing to do
B. Appropriate, but not ideal
C. Inappropriate, but not awful
D. A very inappropriate thing to do

9.4 Nikki denies Fred's questions and hangs up the phone.

A. A very appropriate thing to do
B. Appropriate, but not ideal
C. Inappropriate, but not awful
D. A very inappropriate thing to do

TYPE I - Question 9 (Continued) - A Telephone Call

9.5 Nikki interrupts the doctor who is taking care of Parry and asks for advice regarding Fred's request.

A. A very appropriate thing to do
B. Appropriate, but not ideal
C. Inappropriate, but not awful
D. A very inappropriate thing to do

TYPE I - Question 10 - A Lazy Student

Chidi, a medical student is on placement at his GP surgery along with five of his colleagues. Chidi and his colleagues have been assigned to do house visits in pairs. Chidi is paired with Eleanor, who seems to enjoy house visits and has always managed to carry a conversation well with the patients, unlike him; he feels a little awkward about the idea of house visits. In the past few weeks, Chidi has managed to create an excuse to back out of doing house visits with Eleanor at least once a week. Eleanor starts to feel suspicious about Chidi's frequent absences.

How **appropriate** are each of the following responses by **Eleanor** in this situation?

10.1 Eleanor confronts Chidi about his behaviour and threatens to report him.

A. A very appropriate thing to do
B. Appropriate, but not ideal
C. Inappropriate, but not awful
D. A very inappropriate thing to do

10.2 Eleanor speaks to Chidi and explores why he doesn't enjoy house visits. She tries to make him feel more comfortable.

A. A very appropriate thing to do
B. Appropriate, but not ideal
C. Inappropriate, but not awful
D. A very inappropriate thing to do

10.3 Eleanor writes a complaint to the medical school regarding Chidi's lack of professionalism and frequent absences.

A. A very appropriate thing to do
B. Appropriate, but not ideal
C. Inappropriate, but not awful
D. A very inappropriate thing to do

10.4 Eleanor ignores Chidi's actions and allows Chidi to be absent from house visits.

A. A very appropriate thing to do
B. Appropriate, but not ideal
C. Inappropriate, but not awful
D. A very inappropriate thing to do

TYPE I - Question 10 (Continued) - A Lazy Student

10.5 Eleanor gossips on social media to her colleagues about Chidi's absences and humiliates him.

A. A very appropriate thing to do
B. Appropriate, but not ideal
C. Inappropriate, but not awful
D. A very inappropriate thing to do

TYPE I - Question 11 - A Data Collector

Flora, a medical student, is helping Tim, a foundation doctor, to collect data for an audit. He creates an Excel sheet, which includes a column of patient demographics (name, address and hospital number). At the end of the day, Flora has managed to collect data for a hundred patients. Tim sends a text message to Flora to check on her progress and tells her to save the data on to a pen drive which he will collect from her at the end of the week. Close to finishing, she is considering whether to save the Excel sheet on to her personal pen drive.

How **appropriate** are each of the following responses by **Flora** in this situation?

11.1 Flora saves it on her personal pen drive and brings it home as she will meet Tim only at the end of the week.

A. A very appropriate thing to do
B. Appropriate, but not ideal
C. Inappropriate, but not awful
D. A very inappropriate thing to do

11.2 Flora asks whether she could meet Tim today to email the data to his NHS email address using her NHS email address.

A. A very appropriate thing to do
B. Appropriate, but not ideal
C. Inappropriate, but not awful
D. A very inappropriate thing to do

11.3 Flora ignores Tim's advice and saves the Excel sheet onto the NHS computer desktop.

A. A very appropriate thing to do
B. Appropriate, but not ideal
C. Inappropriate, but not awful
D. A very inappropriate thing to do

11.4 Flora ignores Tim's advice and emails the Excel sheet to her personal email account.

A. A very appropriate thing to do
B. Appropriate, but not ideal
C. Inappropriate, but not awful
D. A very inappropriate thing to do

TYPE I - Question 12 - A Close Observation

Garrett, a junior doctor, has been late to work 10 times this month. To his surprise, no one in his team has noticed this. However, one of the ward nurses, Angela, has kept a record of Garrett's poor punctuality. She confronts Garrett and gives him a warning that, if he is ever late again, she will report him to his supervisor.

How **appropriate** are each of the following responses by **Garrett** in this situation?

12.1 Garrett shouts at Angela and reminds her that, as a ward nurse, she has no business meddling with his punctuality.

A. A very appropriate thing to do
B. Appropriate, but not ideal
C. Inappropriate, but not awful
D. A very inappropriate thing to do

12.2 Garrett admits that he is in the wrong, but he asks Angela not to tell anyone on the team.

A. A very appropriate thing to do
B. Appropriate, but not ideal
C. Inappropriate, but not awful
D. A very inappropriate thing to do

12.3 Garrett feels threatened and treats Angela coldly on the ward; he starts to ignore her.

A. A very appropriate thing to do
B. Appropriate, but not ideal
C. Inappropriate, but not awful
D. A very inappropriate thing to do

12.4 Garrett apologises to Angela and tries his best to arrive at work earlier from now on.

A. A very appropriate thing to do
B. Appropriate, but not ideal
C. Inappropriate, but not awful
D. A very inappropriate thing to do

TYPE I - Question 12 (Continued) - A Close Observation

12.5 Garrett admits his mistakes to the team and makes an effort to change.

A. A very appropriate thing to do
B. Appropriate, but not ideal
C. Inappropriate, but not awful
D. A very inappropriate thing to do

TYPE I - Question 13 - A Clashed Event

Diana, a junior doctor, has been booked to do an on-call shift tomorrow. She has known for a while that one of the conferences she has booked and paid for in advance clashes with the on-call shift. She, unfortunately, hasn't been able to swap her on-call shift with anyone.

How **appropriate** are each of the following responses by **Diana** in this situation?

13.1 Diana calls in sick the morning of the shift and attends the conference.

A. A very appropriate thing to do
B. Appropriate, but not ideal
C. Inappropriate, but not awful
D. A very inappropriate thing to do

13.2 Diana attends her on-call shift and misses the conference.

A. A very appropriate thing to do
B. Appropriate, but not ideal
C. Inappropriate, but not awful
D. A very inappropriate thing to do

13.3 Diana does not turn up for the on-call shift and attends the conference.

A. A very appropriate thing to do
B. Appropriate, but not ideal
C. Inappropriate, but not awful
D. A very inappropriate thing to do

13.4 Diana begs one of her colleagues, Emma, a junior doctor, to replace her and do an additional on-call shift. Emma reluctantly agrees, and Diana attends the conference.

A. A very appropriate thing to do
B. Appropriate, but not ideal
C. Inappropriate, but not awful
D. A very inappropriate thing to do

TYPE I - Question 14 - A Racist Comment

Ratata, a junior doctor, is currently taking history from Mr Touille who has been admitted to the Emergency Unit with central chest pain. Hana, another junior doctor, overhears rude and racist comments from Mr Touille. Ratata seems to have ignored his comments and continues to take Mr Touille's history.

How **appropriate** are each of the following responses by **Hana** in this situation?

14.1 Hana interrupts Ratata and Mr Touille's conversation and confronts Mr Touille about his rude and racist comments.

A. A very appropriate thing to do
B. Appropriate, but not ideal
C. Inappropriate, but not awful
D. A very inappropriate thing to do

14.2 Hana speaks to Mr Touille privately regarding his comments after Ratata finishes clerking him.

A. A very appropriate thing to do
B. Appropriate, but not ideal
C. Inappropriate, but not awful
D. A very inappropriate thing to do

14.3 Hana interrupts Ratata and Mr Touille's conversation and asks Mr Touille to apologise to Ratata immediately.

A. A very appropriate thing to do
B. Appropriate, but not ideal
C. Inappropriate, but not awful
D. A very inappropriate thing to do

14.4 Hana uses her mobile phone to film Mr Touille and Ratata's conversation and shares it on social media, humiliating Mr Touille.

A. A very appropriate thing to do
B. Appropriate, but not ideal
C. Inappropriate, but not awful
D. A very inappropriate thing to do

TYPE I - Question 14 (Continued) - A Racist Comment

14.5 Hana speaks to Ratata privately after his clerking to check on how he is doing.

A. A very appropriate thing to do
B. Appropriate, but not ideal
C. Inappropriate, but not awful
D. A very inappropriate thing to do

TYPE I - Question 15 - A Missed Teaching

Caius, a junior doctor on the ward, is due to give a departmental teaching that afternoon. He is expecting his fellow colleague, Tom, to attend to give him some feedback on his teaching. The feedback is important evidence for his annual review with his supervisor. The registrar, Dr Roberts, recommended both Caius and Tom to do as many ward jobs as they can in the next 30 minutes before Caius' teaching. Tom has been given the challenging job of discussing and requesting radiology scans with the radiologist for two patients on the ward. Unfortunately, Tom hasn't been able to make it to Caius' teaching, despite Caius leaving five missed calls on Tom's phone. Caius is bothered and upset. He thinks that Tom missed his teaching on purpose.

How **appropriate** are each of the following responses by **Caius** in this situation?

15.1 Caius confronts Tom for not answering any of his calls and leaves a bad review of Tom for their annual team review.

A. A very appropriate thing to do
B. Appropriate, but not ideal
C. Inappropriate, but not awful
D. A very inappropriate thing to do

15.2 Caius reports Tom to the consultant for purposely missing his teaching.

A. A very appropriate thing to do
B. Appropriate, but not ideal
C. Inappropriate, but not awful
D. A very inappropriate thing to do

15.3 Caius asks Tom politely whether the scans have been requested and offers to repeat his teaching at a later date.

A. A very appropriate thing to do
B. Appropriate, but not ideal
C. Inappropriate, but not awful
D. A very inappropriate thing to do

TYPE I - Question 15 (Continued) - A Missed Teaching

15.4 Caius misses Tom's teaching next week on purpose.

A. A very appropriate thing to do
B. Appropriate, but not ideal
C. Inappropriate, but not awful
D. A very inappropriate thing to do

TYPE I - Question 16 - A Wrong Prescription

Bolton, a junior doctor, notices that one of the prescriptions made by his fellow junior doctor colleague, Henry, was three times the normal dose. Bolton approaches Henry and tells him about his mistake. Henry performs a quick assessment of the patient and finds that he is asymptomatic. Henry asks Bolton not to make a report against him as this is the third prescription error he has made in the past two months.

How **appropriate** are each of the following responses by **Bolton** in this situation?

16.1 Bolton makes an incident report against Henry.

A. A very appropriate thing to do
B. Appropriate, but not ideal
C. Inappropriate, but not awful
D. A very inappropriate thing to do

16.2 Bolton asks for a favour in exchange for not reporting Henry.

A. A very appropriate thing to do
B. Appropriate, but not ideal
C. Inappropriate, but not awful
D. A very inappropriate thing to do

16.3 Bolton ignores Henry's request and reports Henry's recurrent prescription errors to Henry's supervisor.

A. A very appropriate thing to do
B. Appropriate, but not ideal
C. Inappropriate, but not awful
D. A very inappropriate thing to do

16.4 Bolton asks Henry to apologise to the patient, even though the patient is asymptomatic.

A. A very appropriate thing to do
B. Appropriate, but not ideal
C. Inappropriate, but not awful
D. A very inappropriate thing to do

TYPE I - Question 17 - A Needlestick Inury

Joloff, a medical student on placement in the Emergency Unit, has offered to help perform an arterial blood gas (ABG) on one of the acute patients in Majors. As Joloff has recently received competency in performing ABGs, he performs the skill unsupervised. He successfully managed to get blood from the patient's radial artery and is attempting to cover the needle with a rubber bung. As he tries to poke the needle into the rubber bung, he pierces through it and into his middle finger. He quickly removes the needle and runs his finger under cold water.

How **appropriate** are each of the following responses by **Joloff** in this situation?

17.1 Joloff reports his needlestick injury to Occupational Health and books an appointment for follow up.

A. A very appropriate thing to do
B. Appropriate, but not ideal
C. Inappropriate, but not awful
D. A very inappropriate thing to do

17.2 Joloff files a clinical incident form against himself on the system.

A. A very appropriate thing to do
B. Appropriate, but not ideal
C. Inappropriate, but not awful
D. A very inappropriate thing to do

17.3 Joloff looks up the patient's case notes to look for any previous blood test results which would suggest that he has a blood-borne virus, especially HIV.

A. A very appropriate thing to do
B. Appropriate, but not ideal
C. Inappropriate, but not awful
D. A very inappropriate thing to do

17.4 Joloff wraps his finger with a plaster and carries on clerking other patients in the Emergency Unit.

A. A very appropriate thing to do
B. Appropriate, but not ideal
C. Inappropriate, but not awful
D. A very inappropriate thing to do

TYPE I - Question 18 - Another Doctor, Please

Tom Jones, a junior doctor, is called by one of the nurses to see a patient who is demanding to speak to any other doctor except his colleague, Morris. Before seeing the patient, Tom reads the case notes. His colleague, Morris, has recently spoken to Prakash about his upcoming colonoscopy, which Morris will be performing. Prakash reveals to Tom that he found "something weird about Morris" and would prefer Tom to do the procedure instead.

How **appropriate** are each of the following responses by **Tom** in this situation?

18.1 Tom swaps Prakash with one of his own patients on his colonoscopy list without telling Morris.

A. A very appropriate thing to do
B. Appropriate, but not ideal
C. Inappropriate, but not awful
D. A very inappropriate thing to do

18.2 Tom reassures Prakash that Morris is good at his job and he does not need to worry.

A. A very appropriate thing to do
B. Appropriate, but not ideal
C. Inappropriate, but not awful
D. A very inappropriate thing to do

18.3 Tom explores Prakash's concerns about Morris further.

A. A very appropriate thing to do
B. Appropriate, but not ideal
C. Inappropriate, but not awful
D. A very inappropriate thing to do

18.4 Tom discusses with Morris and agrees to remove Prakash from Morris' list and place him on the waiting list for another doctor to perform the colonoscopy.

A. A very appropriate thing to do
B. Appropriate, but not ideal
C. Inappropriate, but not awful
D. A very inappropriate thing to do

TYPE I - Question 19 - An Intimate Examination

Noah is a junior doctor on the Endocrine Ward. During the ward round this morning, one of the patients, Mr Higgins, mentions to Noah in passing that one of the medical students was a bit stroppy yesterday when he examined his testicles. Noah is a bit puzzled because there is no indication that would explain a need for Mr Higgins to have a testicular examination. Upon checking Mr Higgins' notes, there is no documentation of a testicular examination being performed yesterday. Noah is aware of two medical students, Cyan and Monet, who have been on the ward recently.

How **appropriate** are each of the following responses by **Noah** in this situation?

19.1 Noah confronts both Cyan and Monet and forces both of them to apologise to Mr Higgins.

A. A very appropriate thing to do
B. Appropriate, but not ideal
C. Inappropriate, but not awful
D. A very inappropriate thing to do

19.2 Noah asks both Cyan and Monet about the need for having performed the testicular examination and the reasons for the lack of documentation in the notes.

A. A very appropriate thing to do
B. Appropriate, but not ideal
C. Inappropriate, but not awful
D. A very inappropriate thing to do

19.3 Noah discusses Mr Higgins' concerns with the ward consultant.

A. A very appropriate thing to do
B. Appropriate, but not ideal
C. Inappropriate, but not awful
D. A very inappropriate thing to do

19.4 Noah apologises to Mr Higgins and explains the complaint procedure.

A. A very appropriate thing to do
B. Appropriate, but not ideal
C. Inappropriate, but not awful
D. A very inappropriate thing to do

TYPE I - Question 19 (Continued) - An Intimate Examination

19.5 Noah reports both the students to the Dean of Medical Education.

A. A very appropriate thing to do
B. Appropriate, but not ideal
C. Inappropriate, but not awful
D. A very inappropriate thing to do

TYPE I - Question 20 - A Bad Practice

Snow, a medical student, overhears one of the nurses, Genevieve, telling her fellow colleagues that one of the patients, Mr Hamish, is extremely smelly and reeks of alcohol and that she will be grateful when the patient leaves the ward. Genevieve then carries on about how lazy the junior doctors on the ward have been and she can't wait for the next rotation.

How **appropriate** are each of the following responses by **Snow** in this situation?

20.1 Snow interrupts Genevieve and confronts her in front of her colleagues, stating that her comments are inappropriate.

A. A very appropriate thing to do
B. Appropriate, but not ideal
C. Inappropriate, but not awful
D. A very inappropriate thing to do

20.2 Snow records Genevieve's conversation using his mobile phone and plays it to the current junior doctors.

A. A very appropriate thing to do
B. Appropriate, but not ideal
C. Inappropriate, but not awful
D. A very inappropriate thing to do

20.3 Snow waits until the conversation ends, approaches Genevieve, and asks her to reflect on her comments.

A. A very appropriate thing to do
B. Appropriate, but not ideal
C. Inappropriate, but not awful
D. A very inappropriate thing to do

20.4 Snow ignores Genevieve's comments and dismisses it as "locker room talk".

A. A very appropriate thing to do
B. Appropriate, but not ideal
C. Inappropriate, but not awful
D. A very inappropriate thing to do

TYPE I - Question 20 (Continued) - A Bad Practice

20.5 Snow joins in the conversation and agrees with Genevieve that Mr Hamish is abusing the NHS.

A. A very appropriate thing to do
B. Appropriate, but not ideal
C. Inappropriate, but not awful
D. A very inappropriate thing to do

TYPE I - Question 21 - A Cancelled Operation

Schofield, a junior doctor, has been part of the colorectal team for three months. He recognises one of the patients on the operating list, Mr Burrows, who has returned to have an operation to remove a tumour. Towards the end of his shift, Schofield's consultant, Prof Rasheed, tells Schofield that Mr Burrows' operation will have to be cancelled and rescheduled to a later date due to the lack of theatre staff and operating time. Schofield is aware that this will be the second time Mr Burrows' operation has been cancelled at such short notice. Mr Burrows did not take the news well during the first cancellation.

How **appropriate** are each of the following responses by **Schofield** in this situation?

21.1 Schofield approaches Mr Burrows in a calm manner and takes him to a side room to break the news.

A. A very appropriate thing to do
B. Appropriate, but not ideal
C. Inappropriate, but not awful
D. A very inappropriate thing to do

21.2 Schofield asks the ward nurse to break the news to Mr Burrows instead as he is aware Mr Burrows will not take the news well.

A. A very appropriate thing to do
B. Appropriate, but not ideal
C. Inappropriate, but not awful
D. A very inappropriate thing to do

21.3 Schofield talks to Mr Burrows privately and explains why his operation is cancelled.

A. A very appropriate thing to do
B. Appropriate, but not ideal
C. Inappropriate, but not awful
D. A very inappropriate thing to do

TYPE I - Question 21 (Continued)- A Cancelled Operation

21.4 Schofield documents Prof Rasheed's instructions into Mr Burrows' hospital notes and discharge letter. Schofield then tells the ward clerk that Mr Burrows will not be needing a bed tonight.

A. A very appropriate thing to do
B. Appropriate, but not ideal
C. Inappropriate, but not awful
D. A very inappropriate thing to do

TYPE I - Question 22 - A Leaking Bathroom Tap

Kellen, a medical student, is rushing to his allocated ward to attend the medical ward round at 9:00 am sharp. On his way down the extremely long corridor of Llandough Hospital, he notices water seeping from under one of the bathroom doors, forming a pool of water in the corridor. A quick glance of his watch shows that it is 8:57 am.

How **appropriate** are each of the following responses by **Kellen** in this situation?

22.1 Kellen checks the tap out and attempts to turn it off.

A. A very appropriate thing to do
B. Appropriate, but not ideal
C. Inappropriate, but not awful
D. A very inappropriate thing to do

22.2 Kellen ignores the pool of water and continues towards the ward. He makes it in time for the ward round.

A. A very appropriate thing to do
B. Appropriate, but not ideal
C. Inappropriate, but not awful
D. A very inappropriate thing to do

22.3 Kellen goes to the nearest sluice, grabs the "Wet Floor" sign, and places it above the pool of water.

A. A very appropriate thing to do
B. Appropriate, but not ideal
C. Inappropriate, but not awful
D. A very inappropriate thing to do

22.4 Kellen attempts to turn the tap off. He then calls Maintenance and reports the matter. He is late to the ward round.

A. A very appropriate thing to do
B. Appropriate, but not ideal
C. Inappropriate, but not awful
D. A very inappropriate thing to do

TYPE I - Question 23 - A Xenophobic Attack

Sao Feng, a junior doctor, is on his way to his local hospital in Seattle for a night shift. About two metres from the entrance, he is stopped by a group of men who then precede to punch him in the stomach and shout racial slurs at him.

How **appropriate** are each of the following responses by **Sao Feng** in this situation?

23.1 Sao Feng immediately leaves the hospital for home and calls in sick.

A. A very appropriate thing to do
B. Appropriate, but not ideal
C. Inappropriate, but not awful
D. A very inappropriate thing to do

23.2 Sao Feng attends A&E and lies about his injuries.

A. A very appropriate thing to do
B. Appropriate, but not ideal
C. Inappropriate, but not awful
D. A very inappropriate thing to do

23.3 Sao Feng consoles himself in the toilet, takes pictures of his injuries, and tweets about them with the hashtag "Hate is a virus".

A. A very appropriate thing to do
B. Appropriate, but not ideal
C. Inappropriate, but not awful
D. A very inappropriate thing to do

23.4 Sao Feng goes to the toilet and cries. He ignores incoming calls from his colleagues. He is one hour late for his shift.

A. A very appropriate thing to do
B. Appropriate, but not ideal
C. Inappropriate, but not awful
D. A very inappropriate thing to do

23.5 Sao Feng tries to fight off the group of men by retaliating with racial slurs against their race.

A. A very appropriate thing to do
B. Appropriate, but not ideal
C. Inappropriate, but not awful
D. A very inappropriate thing to do

TYPE I - Question 24 - A Sick Colleague

Jamaluddin, one of the junior doctors, has been self-isolating due to the Coronavirus for the past seven days. He has tested positive for the Coronavirus. He is aware that he is due to be on-call for the next four days. However, he still has fever and a dry cough. His colleagues have been asking him when he will be returning to work.

How **appropriate** are each of the following responses by **Jamaluddin** in this situation?

24.1 Jamaluddin attends his four-day on-call shift, despite having ongoing symptoms.

A. A very appropriate thing to do
B. Appropriate, but not ideal
C. Inappropriate, but not awful
D. A very inappropriate thing to do

24.2 Jamaluddin lies to his colleagues about his Coronavirus status and hugs them after a long hiatus of not seeing them.

A. A very appropriate thing to do
B. Appropriate, but not ideal
C. Inappropriate, but not awful
D. A very inappropriate thing to do

24.3 Jamaluddin calls NHS111 and reports his current symptoms. They advise him to self-isolate for another seven days. He calls his line manager to let her know that he will be absent for his upcoming on-call shifts.

A. A very appropriate thing to do
B. Appropriate, but not ideal
C. Inappropriate, but not awful
D. A very inappropriate thing to do

24.4 Jamaluddin self-medicates with antibiotics in an attempt to resolve his symptoms prior to his on-call shift.

A. A very appropriate thing to do
B. Appropriate, but not ideal
C. Inappropriate, but not awful
D. A very inappropriate thing to do

TYPE I - Question 25 - An Online Video

A group of junior doctors decided to record a video of them dancing after a long night shift on one of the Coronavirus wards. They then proceed to upload the video on a popular social media platform website using the hashtags #NHS and #Coronavirus. Badrul Baltasar, a fellow colleague, comes across the video and recognises his colleagues and the ward they were on.

How **appropriate** are each of the following responses by **Badrul Baltasar** in this situation?

25.1 Badrul reports the video as inappropriate content and asks for it to be removed.

A. A very appropriate thing to do
B. Appropriate, but not ideal
C. Inappropriate, but not awful
D. A very inappropriate thing to do

25.2 Badrul confronts the group of junior doctors and shouts at them for being unprofessional.

A. A very appropriate thing to do
B. Appropriate, but not ideal
C. Inappropriate, but not awful
D. A very inappropriate thing to do

25.3 Badrul downloads the video and publicly shames the junior doctors online by naming each of them.

A. A very appropriate thing to do
B. Appropriate, but not ideal
C. Inappropriate, but not awful
D. A very inappropriate thing to do

25.4 Badrul approaches the group and discusses the implications of their video in a private setting.

A. A very appropriate thing to do
B. Appropriate, but not ideal
C. Inappropriate, but not awful
D. A very inappropriate thing to do

TYPE I - Question 26 - A Precious Stone

Two medical students, Joanna and Badawee, find a diamond ring in one of the cadavers during dissection. No one else in their dissection group is aware of this discovery.

How **appropriate** are each of the following responses by **Joanna and Badawee** in this situation?

26.1 Joanna and Badawee wash the diamond ring with antiseptic and keep it.

A. A very appropriate thing to do
B. Appropriate, but not ideal
C. Inappropriate, but not awful
D. A very inappropriate thing to do

26.2 Joanna and Badawee report the diamond ring to their supervisor.

A. A very appropriate thing to do
B. Appropriate, but not ideal
C. Inappropriate, but not awful
D. A very inappropriate thing to do

26.3 Joanna and Badawee clean the diamond ring and attempt to sell it on an online website.

A. A very appropriate thing to do
B. Appropriate, but not ideal
C. Inappropriate, but not awful
D. A very inappropriate thing to do

TYPE I - Question 27 - A Waiting Patient

Dove, a junior doctor working in the Emergency Department, recognises one of the patients in the waiting room as her colleague, Ashton. Looking at the number of patients on the waiting list, it would be at least four hours until Ashton sees a doctor. She is aware that Ashton is currently on annual leave.

How **appropriate** are each of the following responses by **Dove** in this situation?

27.1 Dove calls Ashton's name next, so that he skips the long queue.

A. A very appropriate thing to do
B. Appropriate, but not ideal
C. Inappropriate, but not awful
D. A very inappropriate thing to do

27.2 Dove continues seeing patients according to the waiting list.

A. A very appropriate thing to do
B. Appropriate, but not ideal
C. Inappropriate, but not awful
D. A very inappropriate thing to do

27.3 Dove asks her fellow colleague to see Ashton next. Ashton shouldn't be wasting his annual leave waiting in the Emergency Department.

A. A very appropriate thing to do
B. Appropriate, but not ideal
C. Inappropriate, but not awful
D. A very inappropriate thing to do

27.4 Dove looks up Ashton's case notes privately to see what brought him into hospital.

A. A very appropriate thing to do
B. Appropriate, but not ideal
C. Inappropriate, but not awful
D. A very inappropriate thing to do

TYPE I - Question 28 - A Negative Feedback

Rory, one of the junior doctors, just completed her 'End of Placement' meeting with her clinical supervisor. During the meeting, it was highlighted that one of her colleagues, Prabath, had made a negative comment about her confidence, management skills, and lack of ability to manage acutely unwell patients alone on a night shift. Rory feels upset by this.

How **appropriate** are each of the following responses by **Rory** in this situation?

28.1 Rory approaches Prabath in a private setting and asks for advice on how to improve her management skills and confidence.

A. A very appropriate thing to do
B. Appropriate, but not ideal
C. Inappropriate, but not awful
D. A very inappropriate thing to do

28.2 Rory gossips about Prabath's negative comment to the other junior doctors to get sympathy in return.

A. A very appropriate thing to do
B. Appropriate, but not ideal
C. Inappropriate, but not awful
D. A very inappropriate thing to do

28.3 Rory, in return, writes a negative comment about Prabath's lack of approachability as a colleague out of anger.

A. A very appropriate thing to do
B. Appropriate, but not ideal
C. Inappropriate, but not awful
D. A very inappropriate thing to do

28.4 Rory reflects on her performance as a Foundation Year 1 doctor and strives to be more confident in her next job rotation.

A. A very appropriate thing to do
B. Appropriate, but not ideal
C. Inappropriate, but not awful
D. A very inappropriate thing to do

TYPE I - Question 29 - A Crying Child

Seto, a junior doctor, has been asked to urgently cannulate and take blood from an acutely unwell 12-month old baby. This is Seto's first paediatric patient since he started working eight months ago. The baby is crying and screaming in his mother's arms. The baby's mother is increasingly anxious.

How **appropriate** are each of the following responses by **Seto** in this situation?

29.1 Seto tries to calm and distract the baby by playing some songs on his iPhone whilst he quickly completes the task.

A. A very appropriate thing to do
B. Appropriate, but not ideal
C. Inappropriate, but not awful
D. A very inappropriate thing to do

29.2 Seto checks his watch and sees that it is almost the end of his shift. He passes the task on to his fellow colleague instead.

A. A very appropriate thing to do
B. Appropriate, but not ideal
C. Inappropriate, but not awful
D. A very inappropriate thing to do

29.3 Seto brings both the mother and baby to a quiet room, gives instructions to the mother on how to distract the baby, and completes the task.

A. A very appropriate thing to do
B. Appropriate, but not ideal
C. Inappropriate, but not awful
D. A very inappropriate thing to do

29.4 Seto completes the task with much difficulty whilst the baby continues to cry and scream in pain.

A. A very appropriate thing to do
B. Appropriate, but not ideal
C. Inappropriate, but not awful
D. A very inappropriate thing to do

TYPE I - Question 30 - A Prison Break

Leia is a female doctor working in an all-male prison. One of her regular patients, Immanuel, has been needing more insulin injections, resulting in more visits to the infirmary. From reading Immanuel's case notes, Leia is convinced that he is innocent and that he was framed for a crime he didn't commit. Over time, they have started to develop mutual feelings for each other. One day, Immanuel asks for Leia's help to escape via the infirmary.

How **appropriate** are each of the following responses by **Leia** in this situation?

30.1 Leia leaves the infirmary unlocked at the end of her shift so that Immanuel can escape.

A. A very appropriate thing to do
B. Appropriate, but not ideal
C. Inappropriate, but not awful
D. A very inappropriate thing to do

30.2 Leia reports Immanuel's intentions, risking any potential relationship with Immanuel.

A. A very appropriate thing to do
B. Appropriate, but not ideal
C. Inappropriate, but not awful
D. A very inappropriate thing to do

30.3 Leia frames her colleague to help Immanuel escape from prison.

A. A very appropriate thing to do
B. Appropriate, but not ideal
C. Inappropriate, but not awful
D. A very inappropriate thing to do

30.4 Leia prescribes an overdose of insulin on the day of the escape, causing Immanuel to seek medical attention and stopping him from escaping.

A. A very appropriate thing to do
B. Appropriate, but not ideal
C. Inappropriate, but not awful
D. A very inappropriate thing to do

TYPE I - Question 31 - A Family Affair

Dr Tancrady works in the Palliative Unit. She is a widow. Her husband and her children were involved in a staged accident by an illegal company. One day, Dr Tancrady comes across a patient on her ward who was involved in the murder of her husband and children.

How **appropriate** are each of the following responses by **Dr Tancrady** in this situation?

31.1 Dr Tancrady asks her colleague to take over the patient's care.

A. A very appropriate thing to do
B. Appropriate, but not ideal
C. Inappropriate, but not awful
D. A very inappropriate thing to do

31.2 Dr Tancrady 'accidentally' prescribes the wrong medications, resulting in a cardiac arrest.

A. A very appropriate thing to do
B. Appropriate, but not ideal
C. Inappropriate, but not awful
D. A very inappropriate thing to do

31.3 Dr Tancrady investigates the patient's family background and uses it as leverage to get the patient to confess about the company's illegal wrongdoings.

A. A very appropriate thing to do
B. Appropriate, but not ideal
C. Inappropriate, but not awful
D. A very inappropriate thing to do

31.4 Dr Tancrady continues to treat the patient unconditionally. She learns to forgive him, despite not receiving an apology.

A. A very appropriate thing to do
B. Appropriate, but not ideal
C. Inappropriate, but not awful
D. A very inappropriate thing to do

TYPE I - Question 32 - A Calming Effect

A surgical trainee, Sook Han, is performing her very first unassisted open appendicectomy on an old man today. Prior to the operation, she feels anxious. One of her colleagues, Lynn, suggests that she should take an anxiolytic tablet to calm her nerves. Lynn reassures Sook Han that the tablet works, and she has found it very useful.

How **appropriate** are each of the following responses by **Sook Han** in this situation? Assume that each of the following responses would be said politely.

32.1 "No, thank you, Lynn. However, I will have to report you for self-medicating."

A. A very appropriate thing to do
B. Appropriate, but not ideal
C. Inappropriate, but not awful
D. A very inappropriate thing to do

32.2 "Yes, please. I'll have two tablets."

A. A very appropriate thing to do
B. Appropriate, but not ideal
C. Inappropriate, but not awful
D. A very inappropriate thing to do

32.3 "Lynn, I think you are addicted to the tablets. I'm going to report you."

A. A very appropriate thing to do
B. Appropriate, but not ideal
C. Inappropriate, but not awful
D. A very inappropriate thing to do

32.4 "Where can I get the tablets from? Please don't tell anyone else."

A. A very appropriate thing to do
B. Appropriate, but not ideal
C. Inappropriate, but not awful
D. A very inappropriate thing to do

TYPE I - Question 33 - An Angry Boss

Dr Winston, a consultant, is due to start the medical ward round at 8:00 am this morning. At 8:30 am, he is still absent from work. He finally turns up at 9:00 am. Without further explanation, he shouts at the senior registrar, David, for not taking charge of the ward round at 8:00 am. Now Dr Winston has to see patients in a rush as he has a meeting at 12:00 pm.

How **appropriate** are each of the following responses by **David** in this situation?

33.1 David shouts back at Dr Winston and storms off the ward.

A. A very appropriate thing to do
B. Appropriate, but not ideal
C. Inappropriate, but not awful
D. A very inappropriate thing to do

33.2 David files a complaint against Dr Winston for verbal abuse without his knowledge.

A. A very appropriate thing to do
B. Appropriate, but not ideal
C. Inappropriate, but not awful
D. A very inappropriate thing to do

33.3 David tries to calm Dr Winston down by speaking in a polite manner.

A. A very appropriate thing to do
B. Appropriate, but not ideal
C. Inappropriate, but not awful
D. A very inappropriate thing to do

33.4 David holds a grudge against Dr Winston and writes about how he has been mistreated in a public newspaper article.

A. A very appropriate thing to do
B. Appropriate, but not ideal
C. Inappropriate, but not awful
D. A very inappropriate thing to do

TYPE I - Question 34 - A Simple Favour

Jeevaraja, a specialty trainee, is due to have his annual review soon. He is aware that one of the consultants in his hospital, Mr Babatunde, will be performing the review. He knows that some of his colleagues have managed to form good connections with Mr Babatunde and that this has had a positive influence on their reviews.

How **appropriate** are each of the following responses by **Jeevaraja** in this situation? Assume that each of the following responses would be said politely.

34.1 "Mr Babatunde, would you like to join my family for dinner tonight? We could perhaps discuss my annual review over dinner too."

A. A very appropriate thing to do
B. Appropriate, but not ideal
C. Inappropriate, but not awful
D. A very inappropriate thing to do

34.2 "Here is a box of chocolates for you, Mr Babatunde. You've been an excellent consultant."

A. A very appropriate thing to do
B. Appropriate, but not ideal
C. Inappropriate, but not awful
D. A very inappropriate thing to do

34.3 "I have heard that you'll be performing my annual review, Mr Babatunde. I look forward to it."

A. A very appropriate thing to do
B. Appropriate, but not ideal
C. Inappropriate, but not awful
D. A very inappropriate thing to do

34.4 "I have spoken to your secretary, Mr Babatunde, and she tells me that you are busy over the next few days. If you give me your log in details, I could write my own review."

A. A very appropriate thing to do
B. Appropriate, but not ideal
C. Inappropriate, but not awful
D. A very inappropriate thing to do

TYPE I - Question 35 - A Small Secret

Jalaludeen and Stimson are two medical students on their GP placement. They have been assigned a patient, Mr Haemaraj, to follow through his journey as a newly-diagnosed brain cancer patient. They were tasked to write a reflective piece on their experiences. From their visits to Mr Haemaraj's house, they have started to form a close bond with him. One day, whilst they are chatting with Mr Haemaraj in his living room, he has an odd request. He wants to see Jalaludeen give Stimson a kiss. It would remind him of fun times in his youth. If they disobey him, Mr Haemaraj would report them to the medical school for misconduct, although this never happened.

How **appropriate** are each of the following responses by **Jalaludeen and Stimson** in this situation?

35.1 Jalaludeen and Stimson ignore Mr Haemaraj's request and immediately leave his house.

A. A very appropriate thing to do
B. Appropriate, but not ideal
C. Inappropriate, but not awful
D. A very inappropriate thing to do

35.2 Jalaludeen gives Stimson a kiss reluctantly. Mr Haemaraj forces them to promise each other that this will be their little secret.

A. A very appropriate thing to do
B. Appropriate, but not ideal
C. Inappropriate, but not awful
D. A very inappropriate thing to do

35.3 Jalaludeen calls the police whilst Stimson distracts Mr Haemaraj.

A. A very appropriate thing to do
B. Appropriate, but not ideal
C. Inappropriate, but not awful
D. A very inappropriate thing to do

TYPE I - Question 36 - A Sexual Act

A medical student, Quason, is on his placement in Psychiatry. Jean-Pierre, a psychiatric ward nurse, is one of the longest staff members on the ward. One day, Quason witnesses a sexual act between Jean-Pierre and one of the psychiatric patients, Akira. The sexual act involved Jean-Pierre groping Akira in the buttock region.

How **appropriate** are each of the following responses by **Quason** in this situation?

36.1 Quason ignores Jean-Pierre's actions and carries on with his work.

A. A very appropriate thing to do
B. Appropriate, but not ideal
C. Inappropriate, but not awful
D. A very inappropriate thing to do

36.2 Quason confronts Jean-Pierre and threatens to report him.

A. A very appropriate thing to do
B. Appropriate, but not ideal
C. Inappropriate, but not awful
D. A very inappropriate thing to do

36.3 Quason shares the story with two of his close friends in a house party that evening and asks them to keep it strictly confidential.

A. A very appropriate thing to do
B. Appropriate, but not ideal
C. Inappropriate, but not awful
D. A very inappropriate thing to do

36.4 Quason confronts Jean-Pierre, reports him to the staff manager, and files a police report.

A. A very appropriate thing to do
B. Appropriate, but not ideal
C. Inappropriate, but not awful
D. A very inappropriate thing to do

TYPE I - Question 37 - A Change in Behaviour

Slavik and Nadiah are the only married couple among the junior doctors working in Royal Sloan Hospital. One day, Charles, a junior doctor, notices dark bruises on Nadiah's forearms. He also starts to realise that Nadiah has become more timid than usual and has been wearing long-sleeved t-shirts to work. Slavik has also appeared to become more protective over Nadiah in the past few days, never leaving her alone at work.

How **appropriate** are each of the following responses by **Charles** in this situation?

37.1 Charles passes a secret note to Nadiah saying "I'm here if you need me."

A. A very appropriate thing to do
B. Appropriate, but not ideal
C. Inappropriate, but not awful
D. A very inappropriate thing to do

37.2 Charles immediately makes a report against Slavik for domestic abuse.

A. A very appropriate thing to do
B. Appropriate, but not ideal
C. Inappropriate, but not awful
D. A very inappropriate thing to do

37.3 Charles asks Nadiah about her bruises privately and encourages her to make a report.

A. A very appropriate thing to do
B. Appropriate, but not ideal
C. Inappropriate, but not awful
D. A very inappropriate thing to do

37.4 Charles confronts Slavic about Nadiah's bruises and threatens to report him.

A. A very appropriate thing to do
B. Appropriate, but not ideal
C. Inappropriate, but not awful
D. A very inappropriate thing to do

TYPE I - Question 38 - A Blood Stain

A medical student, Asha, is helping the medical team on Ward West One. One day, Sarah, the junior doctor on the ward, notices a blood stain on the back of Asha's trousers. Sarah thinks Asha may be on her period.

How **appropriate** are each of the following responses by **Sarah** in this situation? Assume that each of the following responses would be said politely.

38.1 "Asha, I think you might be having your period. I have a sanitary pad if you need one."

A. A very appropriate thing to do
B. Appropriate, but not ideal
C. Inappropriate, but not awful
D. A very inappropriate thing to do

38.2 Speaking loudly, Sarah says "Asha, did you sit on something? There is blood on your trousers."

A. A very appropriate thing to do
B. Appropriate, but not ideal
C. Inappropriate, but not awful
D. A very inappropriate thing to do

38.3 "Asha, I have taken a picture of your trousers from the back. Here, let me show you. I think you might be on your period."

A. A very appropriate thing to do
B. Appropriate, but not ideal
C. Inappropriate, but not awful
D. A very inappropriate thing to do

38.4 "Asha, please go to the toilet and change your trousers. This is very unprofessional of you."

A. A very appropriate thing to do
B. Appropriate, but not ideal
C. Inappropriate, but not awful
D. A very inappropriate thing to do

TYPE I - Question 39 - A Team Effort

Timothy, has recently been elected as the representative of the Junior Doctor Mess. He has been tasked to lead the organisation of the Winter Ball for the end of term. Timothy feels that his co-workers (Henry, Ruru and Mia) are not putting as much effort as he is into the event organisation.

How **appropriate** are each of the following responses by **Timothy** in this situation? Assume that each of the following responses would be said politely.

39.1 Timothy meets with Henry privately and says "Henry, please let Ruru and Mia know that they are slacking in their work."

A. A very appropriate thing to do
B. Appropriate, but not ideal
C. Inappropriate, but not awful
D. A very inappropriate thing to do

39.2 Timothy calls for a group meeting and announces "I will be stepping down as the lead organiser of the Winter Ball as, although I appreciate all of your talents, I do not see us working as a team."

A. A very appropriate thing to do
B. Appropriate, but not ideal
C. Inappropriate, but not awful
D. A very inappropriate thing to do

39.3 Timothy meets with Mia privately and says "Mia, it has come to my attention that Henry and Ruru feel that you have not been completing your tasks. I am very disappointed in you."

A. A very appropriate thing to do
B. Appropriate, but not ideal
C. Inappropriate, but not awful
D. A very inappropriate thing to do

39.4 Timothy sends a text message in the group chat saying "Team, how is everyone doing? Let's catch up on our recent progress regarding the Winter Ball."

A. A very appropriate thing to do
B. Appropriate, but not ideal
C. Inappropriate, but not awful
D. A very inappropriate thing to do

TYPE I - Question 40 - A Rule Breaker

Harikrishna is a specialty registrar currently working in the NHS on a Tier 2 visa. He is married and has four children. He earns about £30,000 per year. For a family of six, Harikrishna feels pressured to make more money.

How **appropriate** are each of the following responses by **Harikrishna** in this situation?

40.1 Harikrishna signs up for multiple locum shifts on top of his current job. This exceeds the number of working hours allowed by his visa.

A. A very appropriate thing to do
B. Appropriate, but not ideal
C. Inappropriate, but not awful
D. A very inappropriate thing to do

40.2 Harikrishna steals some Morphine from the stock cupboard and sells it illegally online.

A. A very appropriate thing to do
B. Appropriate, but not ideal
C. Inappropriate, but not awful
D. A very inappropriate thing to do

40.3 Harikrishna signs up for locum shifts on the weekend in keeping with his visa allowance. However, this means he gets to spend less time with his family.

A. A very appropriate thing to do
B. Appropriate, but not ideal
C. Inappropriate, but not awful
D. A very inappropriate thing to do

40.4 Harikrishna uses NHS premises and conducts private practice without the knowledge of the hospital's management team.

A. A very appropriate thing to do
B. Appropriate, but not ideal
C. Inappropriate, but not awful
D. A very inappropriate thing to do

TYPE II - Question 1 - A Confused Patient

A junior doctor, Chiamaka, is covering his ward alone today. All of his team members are either on-call or in clinic. One of the patients on the ward, Thanos, who doesn't speak English, suddenly has an unwitnessed fall and, when the nurses attend to him, he starts shouting at them in Greek. Chiamaka goes to Thanos' bedside immediately to try and calm him down, but he becomes more agitated.

How **important** is it for Chiamaka to take into account the following considerations when deciding how to respond to the situation?

1.1 That Thanos just had an unwitnessed fall and could have potentially hit his head.

A. Very important
B. Important
C. Of minor importance
D. Not important at all

1.2 That Thanos is being violent towards the nurses verbally.

A. Very important
B. Important
C. Of minor importance
D. Not important at all

1.3 That Chiamaka calls for a translator as Thanos doesn't speak English and is becoming more confused.

A. Very important
B. Important
C. Of minor importance
D. Not important at all

1.4 That Chiamaka is the only doctor on the ward and perhaps there is a need to call for senior help.

A. Very important
B. Important
C. Of minor importance
D. Not important at all

TYPE II - Question 1 (Continued) - A Confused Patient

1.5 That the cause of Thanos' fall is still unknown and other patients are at risk.

A. Very important
B. Important
C. Of minor importance
D. Not important at all

TYPE II - Question 2 - A Drunk Colleague

A junior doctor, Lyndon, who just finished his on-call shift, is on his way home at 12:00 am. He finds his colleague and friend, Gaël, in a semi-conscious state and reeking of alcohol in the living room of their residency hall. Gaël is due to start work tomorrow at 7:00 am and normally leaves to drive to work at 6:00 am when it's still dark outside. Lyndon is considering raising the issue with Gaël's supervisor.

How **important** is it for **Lyndon** to take into account the following considerations when deciding how to respond to the situation?

2.1 That Gaël is known to be good at his job as a junior doctor.

A. Very important
B. Important
C. Of minor importance
D. Not important at all

2.2 That Gaël's patients are at risk if he goes into work tomorrow in a hungover state.

A. Very important
B. Important
C. Of minor importance
D. Not important at all

2.3 That Gaël recently went through a break-up, and Lyndon should be understanding of his situation.

A. Very important
B. Important
C. Of minor importance
D. Not important at all

2.4 That it is a common occurrence to see Gaël in a drunken state.

A. Very important
B. Important
C. Of minor importance
D. Not important at all

TYPE II - Question 2 (Continued) - A Drunk Colleague

2.5 That Gaël has a supportive team of doctors who will ensure that his job is done well.

A. Very important
B. Important
C. Of minor importance
D. Not important at all

2.6 That Lyndon has just ended a 13-hour shift and is extremely tired. He is due to start work tomorrow at 7:00 am too.

A. Very important
B. Important
C. Of minor importance
D. Not important at all

TYPE II - Question 3 - A Bruised Child

George is a medical student doing a GP rotation which involves him sitting in clinic to observe. One of the patients is a mother who has brought her child in. She is worried about a cough that the child has developed; it hasn't resolved after one week. The GP uses a stethoscope to examine the child with his shirt off. George notices a distinct bruise on the child's neck and shoulder. The GP seems to have missed this and informs the mother that the cough is self-limiting and likely to be a viral infection. The mother and child leave the GP clinic.

How important is it for **George** to take into account the following considerations when deciding how to respond to the situation?

3.1 That George is only a medical student; the GP will probably ignore his accusation.

A. Very important
B. Important
C. Of minor importance
D. Not important at all

3.2 That George thinks this could be a sign of abuse.

A. Very important
B. Important
C. Of minor importance
D. Not important at all

3.3 That the mother looks attentive to her child's health and would probably bring the child back if she noticed the bruise.

A. Very important
B. Important
C. Of minor importance
D. Not important at all

3.4 That the child is active, able to walk, and able to climb. The bruise is most likely from an accident.

A. Very important
B. Important
C. Of minor importance
D. Not important at all

TYPE II - Question 3 (Continued) - A Bruised Child

3.5 That the GP might have seen it and probably dismissed it based on his clinical judgement.

A. Very important
B. Important
C. Of minor importance
D. Not important at all

TYPE II - Question 4 - A Prescribing Error

Ben Stew is a medical student on placement. On a very busy ward round, the consultant asks Mustafa, the junior doctor, to start a patient on antibiotics. Mustafa immediately prescribes the patient a penicillin-based antibiotic and hands the drug chart to Ben Stew, giving him the task to ask the nurse in charge to dispense the antibiotic immediately. As Mustafa hands Ben Stew the drug chart, Ben Stew's eyes briefly catch the allergies section on the front which says that the patient, Mr Hakeem, is allergic to penicillin. Mustafa reminds Ben Stew that the antibiotic is required immediately and signals him to hurry as he keeps up with the ward round.

How **important** is it for **Ben Stew** to take into account the following considerations when deciding how to respond to the situation?

4.1 That there is a possibility that the consultant was aware of the patient's penicillin allergy but asked Mustafa to prescribe it anyway. He is the consultant so he knows what he is doing.

A. Very important
B. Important
C. Of minor importance
D. Not important at all

4.2 That Mustafa has been working on the ward for months and knows the patient better than Ben Stew.

A. Very important
B. Important
C. Of minor importance
D. Not important at all

4.3 That the patient needs the antibiotic immediately.

A. Very important
B. Important
C. Of minor importance
D. Not important at all

4.4 That interrupting Mustafa on the busy ward round regarding the patient's allergy will upset both Mustafa and the consultant.

A. Very important
B. Important
C. Of minor importance
D. Not important at all

TYPE II - Question 4 (Continued) - A Prescribing Error

4.5 That Ben Stew is only a medical student and he should do as he is told.

A. Very important
B. Important
C. Of minor importance
D. Not important at all

TYPE II - Question 5 - A Dyslexic Colleague

Caru and Killian are both working on the same team as junior doctors. Killian notices that Caru takes a long time to write up drug charts and doesn't include much information in discharge letters. When Killian approaches Caru regarding the matter, she gets upset and stops talking to him for the next few hours. Killian suspects Caru is dyslexic and is considering whether to speak to Caru's educational supervisor himself.

How **important** is it for **Killian** to take into account the following considerations when deciding how to respond to the situation?

5.1 That it may upset Caru that Killian goes to her supervisor.

A. Very important
B. Important
C. Of minor importance
D. Not important at all

5.2 That Caru hasn't talked to anyone regarding her difficulties and probably doesn't want anyone to know.

A. Very important
B. Important
C. Of minor importance
D. Not important at all

5.3 That Caru's difficulty may put patients at risk.

A. Very important
B. Important
C. Of minor importance
D. Not important at all

5.4 That Killian has to take the additional responsibility of checking Caru's work without her knowledge and correct it if she makes mistakes.

A. Very important
B. Important
C. Of minor importance
D. Not important at all

TYPE II - Question 6 - A Gift

Laskna, a junior doctor who has been working on the ward for the past few months, receives a holiday voucher as a gift from one of her long-stay patients, Gaîlo. Gaîlo is particularly thankful to the team, especially Laskna, for all their hard work and the support he has received on the ward whilst he was ill. Laskna has a long weekend coming up during which she was planning to go on holiday. The voucher is perfect for those dates.

How **important** is it for **Laskna** to take into account the following considerations when deciding how to respond to the situation?

6.1 That no one else knows about the gift.

A. Very important
B. Important
C. Of minor importance
D. Not important at all

6.2 That Gaîlo has been a difficult patient to manage and the gift was well earned.

A. Very important
B. Important
C. Of minor importance
D. Not important at all

6.3 That refusing to accept the gift may upset the patient.

A. Very important
B. Important
C. Of minor importance
D. Not important at all

6.4 That other staff members seem to accept gifts from patients all the time.

A. Very important
B. Important
C. Of minor importance
D. Not important at all

TYPE II - Question 7 - An Odd Request

Benny is a medical student on placement in the Medical Emergency Unit, shadowing Samuel, a junior doctor. Benny has a list of clinical skills that he needs signed off whilst on placement. He feels quite confident that he can perform most of these skills unsupervised. One of the patients on the ward needs a lumbar puncture urgently. Benny recalls that lumbar puncture is not on the clinical skills list provided by the medical school. Samuel casually asks Benny whether he would like to start the procedure first as he is currently busy with another patient. He promises that he will return to supervise Benny after.

How **important** is it for **Benny** to take into account the following considerations when deciding how to respond to the situation?

7.1 That the patient needs the lumbar puncture urgently.

A. Very important
B. Important
C. Of minor importance
D. Not important at all

7.2 That all the other doctors, including Samuel, are busy at the moment with other patients.

A. Very important
B. Important
C. Of minor importance
D. Not important at all

7.3 That Benny feels confident he is able to perform a lumbar puncture as he has previously watched one being performed.

A. Very important
B. Important
C. Of minor importance
D. Not important at all

7.4 That Samuel trusts Benny to start the procedure and promises to return later.

A. Very important
B. Important
C. Of minor importance
D. Not important at all

TYPE II - Question 8 - A Late Morning

Joffrey, a medical student, is due to start placement at 8:30 am sharp. He had a late night yesterday since he was studying for his test next week and, despite setting an alarm, he wakes up late. Joffrey rushes to get ready and reaches at 10:00 am. To his surprise, no one on the team has noticed his absence this morning as they've had a very busy ward round. His fellow medical student colleague, Aisling, has, however, noticed that it is the fifth time Joffrey has turned up late to placement in the past month. Aisling is considering whether to report Joffrey to the medical school due to his lack of punctuality.

How **important** is it for **Aisling** to take into account the following considerations when deciding how to respond to the situation?

8.1 That no one else on the team has noticed Joffrey's frequent lack of punctuality.

A. Very important
B. Important
C. Of minor importance
D. Not important at all

8.2 That Aisling feels it is unprofessional for Joffrey to be late to placement.

A. Very important
B. Important
C. Of minor importance
D. Not important at all

8.3 That Joffrey will be upset with Aisling if she reports his behaviour to his educational supervisor.

A. Very important
B. Important
C. Of minor importance
D. Not important at all

TYPE II - Question 8 (Continued) - A Late Morning

8.4 That other medical students have been late to placements and still seem to do well in their monthly tests.

A. Very important
B. Important
C. Of minor importance
D. Not important at all

TYPE II - Question 9 - A Sibling Bond

Yuzu, a medical student, has been helping out with the multiple mini interviews (MMIs) for prospective medical students for the past couple of years. His younger brother, Taeyang, recently received news that he has been shortlisted and will be attending the MMIs at Yuzu's university in the next few months. Yuzu is considering whether to declare to the University Board that Taeyang is his brother.

How **important** is it for **Yuzu** to take into account the following considerations when deciding how to respond to the situation?

9.1 That no one else knows they are siblings.

A. Very important
B. Important
C. Of minor importance
D. Not important at all

9.2 That Taeyang has received rejections from two other universities.

A. Very important
B. Important
C. Of minor importance
D. Not important at all

9.3 That Yuzu's past experiences are valuable to the MMI panel.

A. Very important
B. Important
C. Of minor importance
D. Not important at all

9.4 That Yuzu feels responsible to help Taeyang do well in his interview and stays on the panel.

A. Very important
B. Important
C. Of minor importance
D. Not important at all

TYPE II - Question 10 - A Suspicious Email

Milo, a junior doctor who is working a night shift on the Psychiatry Ward, receives an email addressing one of his current patients on the ward, Habib. The sender's email address is from an external domain which he doesn't recognise as a work email. The email demands personal information of Habib and sends a death threat to Milo if he doesn't reply with the wanted information within the next 24 hours. Milo is considering whether to reply to the email.

How **important** is it for **Milo** to take into account the following considerations when deciding how to respond to the situation?

10.1 That no one else knows about the email.

A. Very important
B. Important
C. Of minor importance
D. Not important at all

10.2 That Habib used to have a past social history of dealing with drug cartels.

A. Very important
B. Important
C. Of minor importance
D. Not important at all

10.3 That Milo is the only member of staff working on the ward that night, and he feels threatened.

A. Very important
B. Important
C. Of minor importance
D. Not important at all

10.4 That the sender asked to not involve the police.

A. Very important
B. Important
C. Of minor importance
D. Not important at all

TYPE II - Question 10 (Continued) - A Suspicious Email

10.5 That the sender included Milo's personal details in the email as blackmail.

A. Very important
B. Important
C. Of minor importance
D. Not important at all

TYPE II - Question 11 - A Hurt Colleague

Kurt and Amornsri work on the same team in General Medicine. Kurt overhears a patient being rude to Amornsri on the ward round and demanding to see another doctor instead. Kurt sees Amornsri removing herself from the ward with her face buried in her hands. This isn't the first time Amornsri has been shouted at on the ward by a patient. Amornsri has also received multiple complaints from previous patients regarding her conduct as a doctor. Kurt is considering whether to talk to Amornsri's educational supervisor.

How **important** is it for **Kurt** to take into account the following considerations when deciding how to respond to the situation?

11.1 That Amornsri has received a lot of complaints regarding her conduct as a doctor.

A. Very important
B. Important
C. Of minor importance
D. Not important at all

11.2 That Amornsri will be upset if Kurt speaks to her educational supervisor.

A. Very important
B. Important
C. Of minor importance
D. Not important at all

11.3 That Amornsri is currently going through a bereavement for a close relative.

A. Very important
B. Important
C. Of minor importance
D. Not important at all

11.4 That Kurt is getting frustrated with Amornsri's general conduct with patients.

A. Very important
B. Important
C. Of minor importance
D. Not important at all

TYPE II - Question 11 (Continued) - A Hurt Colleague

11.5 That Amornsri has been working on the ward for four months.

A. Very important
B. Important
C. Of minor importance
D. Not important at all

TYPE II - Question 12 - A Tough Week

Avery, a junior doctor, has been working on the ward and is completing the last day of a 12-day shift which included a weekend of long day shifts. Avery is feeling extremely tired on the ward today. Her fellow colleague, Shelby, notices that Avery has started to make mistakes in routine tasks. Shelby is considering whether to report Avery to the consultant in-charge today.

How **important** is it for **Shelby** to take into account the following considerations when deciding how to respond to the situation?

12.1 That no one else knows about Avery's mistakes.

A. Very important
B. Important
C. Of minor importance
D. Not important at all

12.2 That no patients have been affected by Avery's mistakes.

A. Very important
B. Important
C. Of minor importance
D. Not important at all

12.3 That Avery is trying her best, given it is her last day of a 12-day shift.

A. Very important
B. Important
C. Of minor importance
D. Not important at all

12.4 That the consultant will be frustrated with Avery and probably reflect on Avery's performance in her work portfolio.

A. Very important
B. Important
C. Of minor importance
D. Not important at all

TYPE II - Question 13 - A Lost Sample

Seren, a junior doctor, has been asked to take crossmatch samples from a couple of patients this morning during the ward round prior to their respective operations. Seren tries her best to double-check her work as she goes along completing urgent tasks. Later in the afternoon, Seren receives a call from theatre asking for two units of red blood cells to be transfused for Mr Groff who has suffered a major blood loss. Seren immediately calls the blood bank to put in an urgent request for Mr Groff. To Seren's surprise, the blood bank denies having received any request for crossmatch samples for Mr Groff this morning.

How **important** is it for **Seren** to take into account the following considerations when deciding how to respond to the situation?

13.1 That Seren was confident that she took a crossmatch sample from Mr Groff this morning and the blood bank should look for it.

A. Very important
B. Important
C. Of minor importance
D. Not important at all

13.2 That Mr Groff needs blood urgently.

A. Very important
B. Important
C. Of minor importance
D. Not important at all

13.3 That Seren is known to never make a mistake on the ward.

A. Very important
B. Important
C. Of minor importance
D. Not important at all

13.4 That Mr Groff's consultant will be frustrated if he finds out.

A. Very important
B. Important
C. Of minor importance
D. Not important at all

TYPE II - Question 14 - A Medication Request

Zack, a junior doctor, has been asked to complete Mrs Dolby's medication chart and discharge letter prior to sending her home. Mrs Dolby pulls Zack aside and asks if she can have Codeine instead of her regular Paracetamol to take home as her pain is relieved only by Codeine.

How **important** is it for **Zack** to take into account the following considerations when deciding how to respond to the situation?

14.1 That Mrs Dolby does not have a history of illicit drug usage and is unlikely to overdose on Codeine.

A. Very important
B. Important
C. Of minor importance
D. Not important at all

14.2 That Mrs Dolby hasn't had Codeine in the past three days prior to her discharge and is perhaps asking for Codeine as an emergency supply if her pain returns.

A. Very important
B. Important
C. Of minor importance
D. Not important at all

14.3 That Zack is able to prescribe Codeine without needing to consult with a senior clinician.

A. Very important
B. Important
C. Of minor importance
D. Not important at all

14.4 That Mrs Dolby's real reason for asking for regular Codeine on discharge is that she thinks it will help her husband's arthritis.

A. Very important
B. Important
C. Of minor importance
D. Not important at all

TYPE II - Question 15 - A Lying Patient

Bennett, a medical student, is currently on placement in the Acute Medical Ward. One of the patients, Crystal, an elderly lady who was previously admitted with abdominal pain, tells the team that she is feeling well enough to go home. The team starts to plan Crystal's discharge. Bennett calls in to say goodbye to Crystal as she packs her bags. Crystal whispers to Bennett that she actually still has tummy aches but can't wait to go home to see her pet parrot. Bennett remembers reading in Crystal's notes that she lives alone. No family members have been in to see her whilst she has been in hospital.

How **important** is it for **Bennett** to take into account the following considerations when deciding how to respond to the situation?

15.1 That the team is currently planning Crystal's discharge and it'll be a hassle to stop now.

A. Very important
B. Important
C. Of minor importance
D. Not important at all

15.2 That Crystal might not understand the severity of her condition and is putting herself at risk of a bowel perforation.

A. Very important
B. Important
C. Of minor importance
D. Not important at all

15.3 That Crystal will leave the hospital this afternoon, regardless of what the doctors say.

A. Very important
B. Important
C. Of minor importance
D. Not important at all

15.4 That Crystal will lose confidence in Bennett for breaking her trust.

A. Very important
B. Important
C. Of minor importance
D. Not important at all

TYPE II - Question 16 - A Collapsed Passerby

Adele, a final year medical student, has left placement for the day. She is walking home when a passerby suddenly collapses on the pavement about a foot from her. The passerby's relative is shouting for help. Adele, who is yet to have her Advanced Life Support training, is considering whether to introduce herself as a doctor and begin chest compressions.

How **important** is it for **Adele** to take into account the following considerations when deciding how to respond to the situation?

16.1 That no one else knows that Adele is a medical student and has not undertaken her Advanced Life Support training.

A. Very important
B. Important
C. Of minor importance
D. Not important at all

16.2 That there is no one else more qualified at the moment to start chest compressions on the patient.

A. Very important
B. Important
C. Of minor importance
D. Not important at all

16.3 That Adele has watched chest compression videos on YouTube and roughly remembers the algorithm.

A. Very important
B. Important
C. Of minor importance
D. Not important at all

16.4 That the relative is shouting for help and asking for a doctor.

A. Very important
B. Important
C. Of minor importance
D. Not important at all

TYPE II - Question 17 - An Epileptic Colleague

Aber and Melor are both working night shifts this weekend. On Friday night, Aber found Melor in an epileptic seizure in the Junior Doctor Mess. Aber found Melor's anti-epileptic injection and delivered it into Melor's thigh, which quickly resolved her epileptic seizure. Melor manages to get some rest that night as the wards are quiet, whilst Aber completes any new tasks coming through. Melor confesses to Aber that this is the second time in the past week she has had an epileptic seizure due to the odd sleeping hours required of a night shift. Melor drives to work every day and asks Aber to promise not to report any of the incidents to her supervisor or GP. Aber is aware that an individual with epilepsy isn't allowed to drive a car unless he/she has been free of seizures for at least a year.

How **important** is it for **Aber** to take into account the following considerations when deciding how to respond to the situation?

17.1 That the DVLA doesn't know about Melor's frequent epileptic history and she is still driving.

A. Very important
B. Important
C. Of minor importance
D. Not important at all

17.2 That Melor will be cross with Aber for breaking her promise.

A. Very important
B. Important
C. Of minor importance
D. Not important at all

17.3 That Melor's supervisor will be able to provide extra support during her night shifts.

A. Very important
B. Important
C. Of minor importance
D. Not important at all

TYPE II - Question 17 (Continued) - An Epileptic Colleague

17.4 That Melor is known to be a responsible doctor and is good at her job.

A. Very important
B. Important
C. Of minor importance
D. Not important at all

TYPE II - Question 18 - A Different Approach

Rebecca, a medical student, is attending placement at a GP surgery. Her GP tutor isn't in today so she decides to sit in with a more senior GP, Mr Agarwal, who is a partner of the surgery. Rebecca finds that Mr Agarwal is very fond of his patients and his patients, likewise, adore him. However, Rebecca notices that Mr Agarwal's management plans are out of date with the current guidelines.

How **important** is it for **Rebecca** to take into account the following considerations when deciding how to respond to the situation?

18.1 That Mr Agarwal is a senior GP and probably has more experience with patients, despite what current guidelines suggest.

A. Very important
B. Important
C. Of minor importance
D. Not important at all

18.2 That Rebecca is a medical student and her role is to observe and learn.

A. Very important
B. Important
C. Of minor importance
D. Not important at all

18.3 That the patients are fond of Mr Agarwal and adore him.

A. Very important
B. Important
C. Of minor importance
D. Not important at all

18.4 That there haven't been any complaints from patients regarding Mr Agarwal's medical advice.

A. Very important
B. Important
C. Of minor importance
D. Not important at all

TYPE II - Question 19 - A Private Doctor

Pamela, a medical student, is on placement in an Antenatal Clinic. She notices that Mrs Wakowski, the obstetrician, has been actively promoting her private services during clinic in the NHS hospital by offering her business card and suggesting that elective caesarean sections are safer performed in a private hospital.

How **important** is it for **Pamela** to take into account the following considerations when deciding how to respond to the situation?

19.1 That Mrs Wakowski is a consultant; she knows what is safer for patients as she has many years of experience.

A. Very important
B. Important
C. Of minor importance
D. Not important at all

19.2 That all the patients have been receptive towards Mrs Wakowski's medical advice.

A. Very important
B. Important
C. Of minor importance
D. Not important at all

19.3 That Pamela admires Mrs Wakowski's work and would like to build a good rapport with her.

A. Very important
B. Important
C. Of minor importance
D. Not important at all

19.4 That Mrs Wakowski is Pamela's educational supervisor.

A. Very important
B. Important
C. Of minor importance
D. Not important at all

TYPE II - Question 20 - A Simple Procedure

Samuel, a medical student, is on placement in the Acute Medical Unit. Samuel would like to sign off some clinical skills and has volunteered to help the junior doctors with their blood forms. Ponnuswammy, another medical student on placement, notices that Samuel doesn't wash his hands between patients and hasn't been wearing gloves.

How **important** is it for **Ponnuswammy** to take into account the following considerations when deciding how to respond to the situation?

20.1 That none of the doctors on the ward, including the consultants, have washed their hands between seeing patients.

A. Very important
B. Important
C. Of minor importance
D. Not important at all

20.2 That the majority of the patients in the Acute Medical Unit are admitted with diarrhoea and vomiting.

A. Very important
B. Important
C. Of minor importance
D. Not important at all

20.3 That Samuel is doing his best to help ease the workload of the junior doctors on the ward. Washing his hands between every patient will take up more time.

A. Very important
B. Important
C. Of minor importance
D. Not important at all

20.4 That Ponnuswammy himself tends to forget to wash his hands and wear gloves whilst taking blood from patients.

A. Very important
B. Important
C. Of minor importance
D. Not important at all

TYPE II - Question 20 (Continued) - A Simple Procedure

20.5 That none of the patients have made a complaint about Samuel's lack of hand hygiene.

A. Very important
B. Important
C. Of minor importance
D. Not important at all

TYPE II - Question 21 - A Lost Badge

Adam, a junior doctor, notices that he has misplaced his identification badge a few hours after starting work. He is unable to remember when he last saw or used it. His badge contains important information, such as his full name, licence number, and log in details.

How **important** is it for **Adam** to consider the following considerations when deciding how to respond to the situation?

21.1 That his badge enables access to all the wards in the hospital.

A. Very important
B. Important
C. Of minor importance
D. Not important at all

21.2 That his badge enables access onto the NHS computers under his log in details.

A. Very important
B. Important
C. Of minor importance
D. Not important at all

21.3 That this is the third time Adam has lost his badge only to find, on previous occasions, that he forgot to bring it to work.

A. Very important
B. Important
C. Of minor importance
D. Not important at all

21.4 That there is a security number on the back of his badge; if someone else found it, he/she could report it as "lost and found".

A. Very important
B. Important
C. Of minor importance
D. Not important at all

21.5 That today is Adam's last week working in the hospital.

A. Very important
B. Important
C. Of minor importance
D. Not important at all

TYPE II - Question 22 - An Unexpected Report

Mr Proctor is a patient on the ward who is awaiting the results of his CT scan. The medical team who looks after Mr Proctor has seen the report of his CT scan and has proceeded to discuss it with an oncologist and radiologist. They have arrived at a decision that Mr Proctor is not suitable for further active treatment and should receive palliative care. The medical consultant asks Conway, the junior doctor looking after Mr Proctor, to break the news to Mr Proctor as soon as possible.

How **important** is it for **Conway** to consider the following considerations when deciding how to respond to the situation?

22.1 That the medical consultant has asked Conway to break the news as soon as possible.

A. Very important
B. Important
C. Of minor importance
D. Not important at all

22.2 That Conway was not involved in the multidisciplinary team discussion about Mr Proctor's scan and is unsure of the reason why Mr Proctor is not suitable for active treatment.

A. Very important
B. Important
C. Of minor importance
D. Not important at all

22.3 That Conway has not seen the CT scan report himself.

A. Very important
B. Important
C. Of minor importance
D. Not important at all

22.4 That Conway is aware that Mr Proctor is increasingly agitated since he has not received any news about his CT scan.

A. Very important
B. Important
C. Of minor importance
D. Not important at all

TYPE II - Question 23 - A Stubborn Patient

Dr Katya is the attending doctor in the lung clinic today. One of her patients, Mr Pring, is a long-term smoker and has no intention of stopping. Mr Pring has had a lung removed due to a previous lung tumour. Today, he has returned to clinic for a post-operative follow-up. Mr Pring admits that he has resumed smoking since he left hospital, going against Dr Katya's advice. Dr Katya is increasingly frustrated by Mr Pring's stubbornness.

How **important** is it for **Dr Katya** to consider the following considerations when deciding how to respond to the situation?

23.1 That Katya is aware of Mr Pring's stressful lifestyle; smoking is a coping mechanism for him.

A. Very important
B. Important
C. Of minor importance
D. Not important at all

23.2 That Mr Pring has just recovered from a major operation and has resumed smoking.

A. Very important
B. Important
C. Of minor importance
D. Not important at all

23.3 That Dr Katya has exhausted all options of smoking cessation techniques offered to Mr Pring in the past.

A. Very important
B. Important
C. Of minor importance
D. Not important at all

23.4 That Mr Pring is easy to anger and has raised his voice at Dr Katya in the past.

A. Very important
B. Important
C. Of minor importance
D. Not important at all

TYPE II - Question 24 - A Selfish Act

Victoria is a junior doctor working on the frontline during the Coronavirus pandemic. She is aware of the difficulties in purchasing surgical masks online and in pharmacies. Victoria's elderly parents live with her and are completely dependent on her. She discovers a large stock of surgical masks on the ward on which she is working. She is contemplating whether to take a box of 100 surgical masks home.

How **important** is it for **Victoria** to consider the following considerations when deciding how to respond to the situation?

24.1 That no one else is around on the ward.

A. Very important
B. Important
C. Of minor importance
D. Not important at all

24.2 That there is no tally of stock usage by the ward.

A. Very important
B. Important
C. Of minor importance
D. Not important at all

24.3 That her colleague, Susan, has stolen a box previously and there were no repercussions.

A. Very important
B. Important
C. Of minor importance
D. Not important at all

24.4 That she is the sole carer of her dependent parents and it is in their best interests.

A. Very important
B. Important
C. Of minor importance
D. Not important at all

TYPE II - Question 25 - A Missing Child

Ara is a junior doctor working in the Emergency Department. She receives a bleep and a handover from the nurses that there is a patient, who is suffering from severe chest pain, to be seen. Ara suspects the patient is having a heart attack. She quickly makes her way towards the patient's cubicle. On her way, she finds a child crying in the corridor alone. He looks lost and afraid.

How **important** is it for **Ara** to consider the following considerations when deciding how to respond to the situation?

25.1 That the crying child is lost and afraid.

A. Very important
B. Important
C. Of minor importance
D. Not important at all

25.2 That the patient has severe chest pain and time is crucial.

A. Very important
B. Important
C. Of minor importance
D. Not important at all

25.3 That there have been increasing reports of missing children in the area.

A. Very important
B. Important
C. Of minor importance
D. Not important at all

25.4 That the child is too young to speak and answer questions.

A. Very important
B. Important
C. Of minor importance
D. Not important at all

25.5 That the child could be related to the patient.

A. Very important
B. Important
C. Of minor importance
D. Not important at all

TYPE II - Question 26 - A Crash Call

Somashekar is the junior doctor on-call tonight. He has been in-charge of carrying the crash bleep. It has been five months since he completed his Advanced Life Support training. At 4:00 am, he receives a crash call and is awoken from his sleep. Still half asleep, he rushes to the patient's bed. The ward nurses ask Somashekar what they need to do. He is unable to recall his training and is unsure of what to do.

How **important** is it for **Somashekar** to consider the following considerations when deciding how to respond to the situation?

26.1 That calling for senior help would mean a short delay in treating the patient.

A. Very important
B. Important
C. Of minor importance
D. Not important at all

26.2 That the nurses will file a complaint against him and he may potentially lose his GMC licence.

A. Very important
B. Important
C. Of minor importance
D. Not important at all

26.3 That the patient is unresponsive and the nurses are increasingly worried.

A. Very important
B. Important
C. Of minor importance
D. Not important at all

26.4 That it has been five months since he had his Advanced Life Support training and is unable to recall anything.

A. Very important
B. Important
C. Of minor importance
D. Not important at all

TYPE II - Question 27 - A High Risk Patient

Emmett, one of the junior doctors on-call, has been bleeped to see a patient who is highly suspected of having Coronavirus. The patient is on a 'Red Zone' ward. On arrival, Emmett notices that there is insufficient 'personal protective equipment' such as the N95 respirator mask. He feels uncomfortable to assess the patient.

How **important** is it for **Emmett** to consider the following considerations when deciding how to respond to the situation?

27.1 That there is insufficient 'personal protective equipment' on a 'Red Zone' ward (a.k.a. suspected COVID ward).

A. Very important
B. Important
C. Of minor importance
D. Not important at all

27.2 That the patient is increasingly unwell and requires urgent medical attention.

A. Very important
B. Important
C. Of minor importance
D. Not important at all

27.3 That Emmett has a past medical history of asthma and is at high risk of developing severe Coronavirus symptoms.

A. Very important
B. Important
C. Of minor importance
D. Not important at all

27.4 That Emmett has recently recovered from Coronavirus himself.

A. Very important
B. Important
C. Of minor importance
D. Not important at all

27.5 That Emmett has recently lost a family member to Coronavirus.

A. Very important
B. Important
C. Of minor importance
D. Not important at all

TYPE II - Question 28 - A Phone Call

Marc is a junior doctor working on one of the infectious disease wards. One of his patients, Selah, is on end-of-life care and may not survive another day. The patient's family has been calling the ward daily for regular updates. They have not been able to speak to Selah directly on the phone as she does not have a mobile phone and the ward phone is attached to the work station. They would really like to visit and speak to Selah directly but, due to the nature of the ward, no visitors are allowed. Marc is contemplating lending his mobile phone to Selah.

How **important** is it for **Marc** to take into account the following considerations when deciding how to respond to the situation?

28.1 That Selah is in her last few hours of life.

A. Very important
B. Important
C. Of minor importance
D. Not important at all

28.2 That lending Selah his mobile phone is against recommended infection control guidelines.

A. Very important
B. Important
C. Of minor importance
D. Not important at all

28.3 That Selah's family is really upset and would desperately like to speak to her.

A. Very important
B. Important
C. Of minor importance
D. Not important at all

28.4 That Selah's family has not been able to visit her due to the ward restrictions in place.

A. Very important
B. Important
C. Of minor importance
D. Not important at all

TYPE II - Question 29 - A Special Delivery

Llewellyn, a senior surgical registrar on-call, is anxiously awaiting the delivery of his firstborn son. His wife went into labour early this morning. At about 3:00 pm, in the midst of an operation, he receives a bleep from the Labour Ward that his wife is ready to push and the baby's head is crowning. He is halfway through a high-risk operation, and his surgical assistant is unfamiliar with finishing the operation alone.

How **important** is it for **Llewellyn** to consider the following considerations when deciding how to respond to the situation?

29.1 That his wife is about to deliver his firstborn son.

A. Very important
B. Important
C. Of minor importance
D. Not important at all

29.2 That he is in the middle of a high-risk operation.

A. Very important
B. Important
C. Of minor importance
D. Not important at all

29.3 That the other surgeon is unable to complete the operation alone.

A. Very important
B. Important
C. Of minor importance
D. Not important at all

29.4 That he will not forgive himself if he misses the birth of his son.

A. Very important
B. Important
C. Of minor importance
D. Not important at all

TYPE II - Question 30 - A Sly Fox

Kofi is a junior doctor applying for a surgical training post. During his interview for the post, he exaggerated and forged some sections of his portfolio so that he attains the maximum points in each section. Badr, his colleague who is attending the same interview, notices that some of Kofi's claims are false.

How **important** is it for **Badr** to consider the following considerations when deciding how to respond to the situation?

30.1 That Badr is competing with Kofi for the same surgical training post.

A. Very important
B. Important
C. Of minor importance
D. Not important at all

30.2 That Kofi will be publicly embarrassed if he reports it.

A. Very important
B. Important
C. Of minor importance
D. Not important at all

30.3 That Kofi and Badr have been friends since high school.

A. Very important
B. Important
C. Of minor importance
D. Not important at all

30.4 That Kofi saved his daughter's life in a drowning incident a month ago.

A. Very important
B. Important
C. Of minor importance
D. Not important at all

30.5 That reporting Kofi could mean that he loses his licence to practice as a medical doctor.

A. Very important
B. Important
C. Of minor importance
D. Not important at all

TYPE II - Question 31 - A Leap of Faith

Steve is the on-call junior surgical registrar today. He is known to be extremely good at his work. A patient who has just suffered a stab wound has been brought into the Emergency Unit. The patient has lost a large amount of blood and requires immediate surgical attention. The on-call consultant is arriving in 40 minutes. Steve feels that the patient will have a better outcome if he performs the surgery immediately. Steve is confident that he will be able to perform the surgery, despite him being a junior surgical registrar.

How **important** is it for **Steve** to consider the following considerations when deciding how to respond to the situation?

31.1 That Steve feels confident that he can perform the surgery immediately as he has observed the procedure many times before.

A. Very important
B. Important
C. Of minor importance
D. Not important at all

31.2 That the on-call consultant will only arrive in 40 minutes.

A. Very important
B. Important
C. Of minor importance
D. Not important at all

31.3 That Steve feels the patient will have a better outcome if he performs the surgery immediately.

A. Very important
B. Important
C. Of minor importance
D. Not important at all

31.4 That Steve is a junior surgical registrar and he has never performed this operation before.

A. Very important
B. Important
C. Of minor importance
D. Not important at all

TYPE II - Question 32 - A Paralysed Man

Beatrice is a junior doctor on her GP rotation. One of her patients, Juan Manuel, is a 27-year-old man who is paralysed from the waist down. Before his car accident three years ago, Juan Manuel was a very active man who did extreme sports. Since his accident, he has been riddled with depression due to the sudden change in lifestyle. He plans to fly to Switzerland for euthanasia.

How **important** is it for **Beatrice** to consider the following considerations when deciding how to respond to the situation?

32.1 That Juan Manuel is depressed and struggling to cope with his current lifestyle.

A. Very important
B. Important
C. Of minor importance
D. Not important at all

32.2 That none of Juan Manuel's family members are supportive of his decision for euthanasia.

A. Very important
B. Important
C. Of minor importance
D. Not important at all

32.3 That Beatrice has exhausted all possible options to help him cope with his current disability.

A. Very important
B. Important
C. Of minor importance
D. Not important at all

32.4 That Juan Manuel is a 27-year-old man. There are a lot of opportunities that he could still explore in his life.

A. Very important
B. Important
C. Of minor importance
D. Not important at all

TYPE II - Question 33 - A Contraceptive Pill

Nakupenda is a junior doctor working in a Sexual Health Clinic. Makiko, a 15-year-old patient, attends the clinic for a prescription of the combined oral contraceptive pill (COCP). She admits that she is currently sexually active with her 16-year-old boyfriend, Eros, and he doesn't like to wear condoms. She understands the side effects and risks of taking the oral contraceptive pill and seems mature for her age.

How **important** is it for **Nakupenda** to consider the following considerations when deciding how to respond to the situation?

33.1 That Makiko understands the risks and side effects of the COCP.

A. Very important
B. Important
C. Of minor importance
D. Not important at all

33.2 That Makiko is 15 years old and is currently sexually active with her boyfriend, Eros, who is 16 years old.

A. Very important
B. Important
C. Of minor importance
D. Not important at all

33.3 That Makiko's parents are unaware of her relationship with Eros.

A. Very important
B. Important
C. Of minor importance
D. Not important at all

33.4 That Makiko is at risk of an unwanted pregnancy if Nakupenda does not prescribe the COCP.

A. Very important
B. Important
C. Of minor importance
D. Not important at all

TYPE II - Question 34 - A Blood Transfusion

Imogen is on her night shift when a child is suddenly rushed into the Emergency Department with massive blood loss following a bus collision. His parents are on their way to the hospital and will take roughly an hour to arrive. Imogen discovers that the child is a Jehovah's Witness from his identity card. The child is unconscious and is unable to answer questions. Imogen orders two units of red blood cells to begin blood transfusion.

How **important** is it for **Imogen** to consider the following considerations when deciding how to respond to the situation?

34.1 That the child is a Jehovah's Witness.

A. Very important
B. Important
C. Of minor importance
D. Not important at all

34.2 That the child may not survive if he does not receive a blood transfusion immediately.

A. Very important
B. Important
C. Of minor importance
D. Not important at all

34.3 That neither the child nor the child's parents are able to consent for a blood transfusion.

A. Very important
B. Important
C. Of minor importance
D. Not important at all

34.4 That the child is unconscious and unable to answer questions.

A. Very important
B. Important
C. Of minor importance
D. Not important at all

TYPE II - Question 35 - Ability to Decide

Catrina is a junior surgical registrar. Mr Mason, a 55-year-old gentleman, has recently been diagnosed with bowel perforation. Despite Catrina's efforts in explaining to Mr Mason the risks and benefits of surgery, Mr Mason is not keen to consent. Upon further questioning, Mr Mason expresses that he would like to be left alone. "If I am meant to die, no surgery is going to cure me." Catrina is certain that the surgery will save Mr Mason's life.

How **important** is it for **Catrina** to consider the following considerations when deciding how to respond to the situation?

35.1 That Mr Mason has the capacity to make a decision.

A. Very important
B. Important
C. Of minor importance
D. Not important at all

35.2 That Catrina does not have Mr Mason's consent to perform the surgery.

A. Very important
B. Important
C. Of minor importance
D. Not important at all

35.3 That Mr Mason does not understand the benefits of having surgery.

A. Very important
B. Important
C. Of minor importance
D. Not important at all

35.4 That Catrina does not agree with Mr Mason's decision to not have surgery.

A. Very important
B. Important
C. Of minor importance
D. Not important at all

Verbal Reasoning

Answer 1

Q1.1: C - the public is completely reliant on the knowledge that restaurant staff possess.

Explanation: The first paragraph of the passage maintains that people with food allergies in Europe depend on restaurant staff to provide suitable food when they eat out. Members of the public thus depend on the knowledge that those working in a restaurant possess in order to ensure that they eat food to which they are not allergic.

- **A: the number of Europeans with one has increased.** While the passage states that more than 10% of people in Europe have food allergies, it does not infer that the number of people in Europe with a food allergy has increased.
- **B: limited studies have been conducted on attitudes towards them.** The first paragraph does claim that most studies have addressed neither the attitudes of staff towards food allergies nor which factors might determine attitudes towards food allergies. However, the passage does not suggest that this is the reason for which food allergies should be taken seriously.
- **D: less than 50% of those interviewed have sufficient knowledge of food allergies.** The passage confirms that '30 percent of the interviewees could correctly name three common food allergens, and 41 percent correctly answered five true-or-false statements about food allergies'. Hence, the passage corroborates the fact that less than 50% of those interviewed have limited knowledge of food allergies. However, we cannot be certain what the author of the question considers as 'sufficient' knowledge. It could be that being able to correctly name one food allergy is deemed 'sufficient'.

Q1.2: B - Those who were interviewed are supportive of customers with food allergies.

Explanation: The third paragraph informs us that many of the staff 'held positive attitudes regarding their and their colleagues' responsibility to help meet the needs of customers with food allergies'. It can thus be inferred that those interviewed tended to be supportive of customers with food allergies.

- **A: Those who were interviewed understand their responsibility towards customers with food allergies.** The passage states that 'most of the staff held positive attitudes regarding their and their colleagues'

Answer 1 (Continued)

responsibility to help meet the needs of customers with food allergies'. This phrase does not necessarily indicate that those interviewed understand their responsibility to help customers who have food allergies. They might be supportive of those with food allergies, but this does not definitely mean that they comprehend the responsibility that is bestowed upon them as restaurant workers.

- **C: Those working in restaurants in the UK are positive about supporting customers with food allergies.** The study was conducted in Germany. The passage does not mention restaurant staff in the UK.
- **D: Those who were interviewed are entirely dependent on what the customer tells them about his or her food allergy.** The information in the passage does not tell us if this is true or false. The third paragraph states that those interviewed 'had negative attitudes regarding the accuracy of customers' reports of their own food allergies'. However, it does not indicate the occurrence or absence of dependency.

Q1.3: A - True

Explanation: The first paragraph argues that 'most studies have not adequately addressed staff attitudes toward food allergies, nor which factors might determine food allergy knowledge and food allergy attitudes'. We can thus deduce that existing studies on food allergies are limited.

Q1.4: D - those with a sound educative background are more alert to concerns surrounding food allergies.

Explanation: The final paragraph of the passage states that restaurant workers with the highest school degree possessed a greater degree of knowledge of food allergies. It is assumed that those with the highest school degree will have a solid educative background.

- **A: only one in three restaurant workers in Germany is able to name three common food allergies.** While the study did find that only 30% (or approximately one in three) of the interviewees could correctly name three common food allergens, the study was conducted in a specific area of Germany (15 districts of Düsseldorf). It therefore did not provide the opportunity for restaurant workers throughout the country to be interviewed. We cannot assume that the results in these districts are reflected throughout Germany.

Answer 1 (Continued)

- **B: more than 181 interviewees had adequate knowledge of food allergies.** We know that a total of 295 individuals were interviewed, of which 41 percent could correctly answer five true-or-false statements about food allergies. Therefore, 120.95 individuals could correctly answer five true-or-false statements about food allergies. It should also be noted that we cannot be certain what the author of the question considers as 'adequate' knowledge. It could be that being able to correctly answer three statements is deemed 'adequate'.
- **C: every corner of society exhibits gendered distinctions.** The final paragraph of the passage does distinguish between male and female staff. However, the passage does not speak about other aspects of society.

Answer 2

Q2.1: A - True

Explanation: The course entitled 'Diploma Units Law and Practice (Legal Studies)' will provide the attendee with the **platform** to become a member of the Chartered Institute of Legal Executives. The passage declares that the attendee will need to complete the qualification in order to gain membership to the professional body; membership is not automatic upon enrolment in the course.

Q2.2: A - True

Explanation: The passage states that the course entitled 'Professional Diploma in Accounting' will assist those who wish to enhance the amount of money they are able to earn.

Q2.3: B - False

Explanation: The passage informs us that the course entitled 'IOSH Certificate in Managing' is suitable for managers 'from any organisation or sector'. This suggests that it will be appropriate for those who work in an office, and the statement is therefore false.

Answer 2 (Continued)

Q2.4: B - False

Explanation: The course entitled 'City and Guilds Award in Employability' provides attendees with numerous basic skills required for career development. These skills will presumably enhance the attendee's CV, and the course will therefore prove beneficial for those who wish to enhance their CV.

Answer 3

Q3.1: A - The number of nightingales in parts of the UK has decreased over the last fifty years.

Explanation: The final paragraph states that 'numbers here have declined markedly over the last half century'. This phrase indicates that the last 50 years have seen a decrease in the number of nightingales. We know that the word 'here' refers to the UK since the final sentence of the previous paragraph speaks of England.

- **B: Nightingales can be found in Spain.** While the passage asserts that the researchers who conducted this study are based in Spain, it does not necessarily inform us that the birds can be found in that country.
- **C: Skylarks are found in Europe.** The penultimate paragraph compares the nightingale's ability to sing with that of the skylark. Since the nightingale is the subject of this paragraph, the phrase 'although common in many parts of Europe and Asia, the bird is mainly seen and heard in southern England' refers to this creature.
- **D: Nightingales can be found throughout the world.** The passage states that the nightingale is common in parts of Europe and Asia, but it does not mention the other continents of the world.

Q3.2: C - Can't Tell

Explanation: We know that the researchers reside in Spain, but we do not know where they studied the nightingale and if this was its natural habitat.

Answer 3 (Continued)

Q3.3: D - Skylarks are less popular than nightingales.

Explanation: We are told that nightingales can produce more sounds than skylarks, but the passage does not confirm that nightingales are more popular than skylarks. This statement is, therefore, not corroborated by the information in the passage.

- **A: Nightingales are bred due to their ability to sing.** The penultimate paragraph states that nightingales are farmed due to their ability to sing. This statement is, therefore, corroborated by the information in the passage.
- **B: The consequences of climate change are affecting the livelihood of the nightingale.** The final paragraph associates the decline in the number of nightingales with the fact that the climate is changing. This statement is, therefore, corroborated by the information in the passage.
- **C: The researchers mentioned in this passage have studied data from less than twenty years ago.** The first paragraph informs us that these researchers have discovered that nightingales' wingspans have become smaller over a 20-year period. It is, therefore, assumed that some of this data has come from a time that is less than twenty years ago. This statement is thus corroborated by the information in the passage.

Q3.4: B - False

Explanation: The passage asserts that the skylark can produce 340 different sounds whilst the nightingale can produce over 1,000 different sounds. Since the nightingale can produce more sounds than the skylark, the statement 'skylarks produce three times as many sounds as nightingales' must be false.

Answer 4

Q4.1: C - Can't Tell

Explanation: While the passage confirms that the narrator had been outdoors that morning, it does not indicate whether the narrator enjoyed it. The passage states that the narrator 'never liked long walks', but we are told that a long walk was 'out of the question' that day due to the rain. It therefore cannot be deduced whether the narrator enjoyed being outdoors that particular morning, and the answer is 'can't tell'.

Q4.2: C - The narrator is often scolded.

Explanation: The narrator talks about what usually happens on a walk. We are told that the narrator becomes saddened by the fact that Bessie chides him/her. It can therefore be assumed that he/she is often reprimanded.

- **A: Eliza is Georgiana's only sister.** We cannot be certain that Eliza is Georgiana's only sister. We know that Eliza is Georgiana's sister since we are told that they sit around 'their' mother. This implies that they have the same mother and are, therefore, sisters (although it is also possible that the two girls are stepsisters). However, the passage does not tell us if the narrator is related to Eliza and Georgiana or if he/she is female. If the narrator is female, she might also be Georgiana's sister. In addition, the passage does not inform us if Georgiana has another sister who is not present in this scene. We therefore cannot be certain that Georgiana has only one sister.
- **B: The narrator is related to John.** We are not told who the narrator is nor if he/she is related to the other children.
- **D: The narrator is younger than the other children.** While we are informed that the narrator is physically inferior to Eliza, John, and Georgiana, we cannot be certain if he/she is younger in age.

Q4.3: B - False

Explanation: While the mother of Eliza, John and Georgiana mentions that she must learn from Bessie if the narrator has behaved as is expected of a child, she declares that she also needs to see this for herself: we are told that she would need to 'discover by her own observation'. Bessie will determine if the narrator had behaved appropriately, but she is not the person to do so since the mother will also play a role in this. The statement is, therefore, false.

Answer 4 (Continued)

Q4.4: A - resemble other children.

Explanation: The mother suggests that the narrator should attempt to adopt a more 'childlike disposition', which indicates that the narrator has been advised to mirror the behaviour of a good child. This statement is thus the correct option; the narrator is told to behave in a similar manner to other children.

- **B: adopt different characteristics to other children.** As we have seen above, the mother suggests that the narrator should behave like a good child. He/She is not advised to adopt different characteristics to a child but, rather, to embody and echo them. This assertion is, therefore, false.
- **C: sit with the other children.** We are told that the narrator has been 'dispensed from joining the group' until he/she adopts more appropriate behaviour. Hence, the narrator cannot sit with the other children.
- **D: stop arguing with the other children.** While we learn that the narrator does not behave in the same manner as the other three children, we are not informed that he/she argues with them. In addition, the second paragraph of the passage suggests that Eliza, John, and Georgiana often quarrel, but it does not make reference to the narrator here.

Answer 5

Q5.1: C - Can't Tell

Explanation: The passage does not inform us if the abbot did or did not take care of his physical appearance. The sentence 'he found satisfaction in attaining the greatest possible perfection outwardly as well as inwardly' might encourage us to believe that the statement is true. However, this sentence implies that the abbot aimed to exhibit decent behaviour through his actions, such as singing in the choir. Therefore, the answer is 'can't tell'.

Answer 5 (Continued)

Q5.2. B - dismissed any antipathetic sentiments.

Explanation: We can clearly tell that Abbot Kasatsky was devoted to his vocation. This devotion prompted him to be meek and obedient and to undertake his duties with content and joy; his faithfulness prevented him from having any hostile thoughts or feelings.

- **A: was able to compare himself to the other abbots in the monastery.** Abbot Kasatsky draws attention to 'the bad qualities of the other monks'. However, he does not explicitly compare himself to them. In addition, a dutiful temperament would not permit such judgmental and hypercritical sentiments. This answer thus cannot be correct.
- **C: pleased those in charge of the monastery.** While we are told that the abbot performed all of the tasks assigned to him in a compliant and joyful manner, we do not learn what those in charge of the monastery thought.
- **D: encouraged many visitors to speak to him.** We discover that the monastery was 'much frequented' and that there was a 'bustle of the many visitors'. Yet, we are not told if Abbot Kasatsky interacted with the visitors or if they approached him. As such, we cannot be certain if his pleasant characteristics encouraged visitors to speak to him.

Q5.3: C - Abbot Kasatsky's faith prompted him to put up with things that he thought were tedious.

Explanation: We learn that the abbot's obedience to the elders of the monastery (starets), which was presumably triggered by his faith, prevented him from becoming disheartened by the monotonous church services. This statement can, therefore, be verified by the information in the passage.

- **A: Abbot Kasatsky felt superior to the other monks in the monastery.** While it is suggested that the other monks had undesirable characteristics, we do not know if the monks to which reference is made resided in the same monastery as Abbot Katasky. This statement thus cannot be corroborated by the information in the passage.
- **B: Abbot Kasatsky served in the army.** We learn that he had been involved in a regiment, but the passage does not provide us with details of what he did. Answer option C is, therefore, better supported by the information in the passage than answer option B.

Answer 5 (Continued)

- **D: Abbot Kasatsky was required to speak to many people who came to the monastery.** We discover that the monastery was 'much frequented' and that there was a 'bustle of the many visitors'. Yet, we are not told if Abbot Kasatsky was required to interact with them. This statement thus cannot be corroborated by the information in the passage.

Q5.4: C - Can't Tell

Explanation: The passage informs us that, as a monk, Abbot Katasky **tried** to be perfect. It is important to note that we are not told if he managed to achieve perfection. In addition, we do not know how he led his life before this moment, and we therefore cannot tell if he achieved perfection throughout his life.

Answer 6

Q6.1: C - Can't Tell

Explanation: The passage confirms that inulin causes gas, bloating and abdominal pain, but it does not discuss the side effects of **insulin**. We therefore cannot tell from the information that we are given if insulin causes gas, bloating and abdominal pain.

Q6.2: B - Certain foods contain more fibre than others.

Explanation: It can be inferred from the passage that some foods contain more fibre than others since we are told that manufacturers are adding fibre to certain foods (cereals; energy bars; protein supplements; cookies; diet ice cream). Hence, it is evident that some foods will contain more fibre than others. This is the correct answer option.

- **A: Americans are trying to increase the amount of fibre they ingest.** A keyword in this question is 'always'. If you overlook this important word, you might select the wrong answer. The first paragraph informs us that **most** Americans are trying to add more fibre to their diet, but it does not confirm that **all** Americans are attempting to increase their intake of fibre. This statement therefore cannot be **always** true.

Answer 6 (Continued)

- **C: "Healthier" cookies are made up of more fibre than regular cookies.** We are told that fibre is added to some "healthier" cookies, but the passage does not compare them with regular cookies. We therefore cannot be certain of the extent to which the amount of fibre in each type of cookie differs.
- **D: Inulin causes side-effects.** The word 'always' in this question implies that, while it is possible that more than one statement might be true, you must select the statement that is **always** true. The second paragraph declares that inulin **can** cause gas, bloating and abdominal pain. The keyword here is 'can', which does not confirm that inulin **always** provokes side-effects.

Q6.3: A - cannot be digested by the human body.

Explanation: The passage states that inulin is a type of prebiotic. Prebiotics cannot be digested by humans, but the bacteria inside one's gut can digest them. This answer option is, therefore, the most appropriate.

- **B: is not worth taking since the consequences outweigh the benefits.** The writer does not argue that this is true. It is suggested that the consumption of inulin has side-effects and health benefits.
- **C: can replace fibre.** The passage states that inulin is a type of fibre. It thus cannot replace fibre since it is a fibre. This answer option thus cannot be true.
- **D: should not be consumed in large quantities, and one should eat products that contain it slowly.** The passage does claim that inulin can cause side-effects if it is consumed too quickly or in large quantities. A keyword in this answer option is 'should'. The passage does not declare that inulin **should** or **must** be consumed slowly and in small quantities. It simply implies that this could prevent side-effects. This answer option is, therefore, not true.

Q6.4: B - False

Explanation: The first paragraph argues that the **average** American consumes half the recommended amount of fibre each day.

Answer 7

Q7.1: A - Florence rejected the trainees as she had not initiated their enrolment.

Explanation: The final paragraph implies that Florence refused to accept the sisters who were sent to Scutari because she had not agreed for them to come to train at the hospital. We can, therefore, conclude that this is true.

- **B: Florence was dedicated to welcoming any recruits enlisted.** The final paragraph informs us that Florence initially refused to accept 15 sisters who had been sent from Ireland to train at the hospital. We learn that she eventually accepted five, but she sent the others to a different hospital. Hence, we cannot conclude that she welcomed **any** recruit.
- **C: Florence initiated some antagonism within the staff under her supervision.** The passage does not mention this. The penultimate paragraph states that Florence did not **tolerate** opposition, but the passage neither claims that she instigated it nor confirms that her staff were involved.
- **D: Florence was deficient in the level of education to follow a more appropriate career.** While the first paragraph states that nursing was 'a disreputable occupation' which assumed a low position on the social scale, we are not told why Florence became a nurse or what qualifications she possessed.

Q7.2: C - Florence was committed to developing and educating laywomen.

Explanation: Based on the information provided in the passage, we cannot be certain that this is true. We are informed that she supervised laywomen, but we are not told that she developed and educated them. It can be assumed that she would have helped the laywomen who worked under her to develop their ability to care for patients. However, this is an assumption that is not verified by the information in the passage. In addition, we do not learn if she educated the laywomen. We simply cannot tell how Florence treated laywomen, and this assertion cannot be supported by the information within the passage.

Answer 7 (Continued)

- **A: Florence was efficacious in plummeting death levels.** The passage states that Florence was (mostly) successful in introducing hygiene into the hospital, as well as other basic necessities. We learn that 'mortality from cholera and typhoid had halved' under Florence's watch, which means that this statement can be corroborated by the information in the passage.
- **B: Florence was instrumental in the enhancement of sanitation.** The passage states that Florence was (mostly) successful in introducing hygiene into the hospital. This assertion can, therefore, be supported by the information within the passage.
- **D: Florence was committed to an occupation that was belittled.** The passage confirms Florence's commitment to her profession: she cared enough to reform the hospital in which she worked, and she fought to improve conditions. With regards to the fact that her occupation was 'belittled', the first paragraph highlights that nursing was considered as unglamorous as scullery work. This implies that her occupation was undervalued. This assertion can, therefore, be verified by the information within the passage.

Q7.3: C - believes that Florence was somewhat supercilious and formidable.

Explanation: The final paragraph portrays Florence as rather pretentious since she did not allow sisters from Ireland to train at the hospital simply because she was not informed that they were arriving. This supports the assertion that the author considers her to be quite supercilious. The fact that she sent the sisters away and held her ground (she only allowed five into the hospital) shows why the author might see her as formidable. The author does not seem to agree with the depiction of her as a 'kindly' lady since this is quickly brushed over in order to discuss her negative actions.

- **A: deems that Florence had a negligible impact on the nursing vocation.** While the third paragraph highlights how Florence improved the hospital and helped to reduce deaths, the passage does not confirm that she did or did not change the profession. The word 'negligible' will not necessarily determine whether you see this assertion as true or false. What is important here is that, based on the information in the passage, we do not know if Florence's impact was insignificant or crucial. You might be aware that she is considered as the

Answer 7 (Continued)

founder of modern nursing. However, the passage discusses her work in one hospital; it does not reveal the influence she had on the nursing profession. Here, it is important that you use only the information in the passage.

- **B: considers the reputation of Florence to be wholly vindicated.** In the penultimate paragraph, the author juxtaposes the fact that Florence is still considered as an affectionate lady with a more negative characteristic that she possessed. The author acknowledges that Florence is seen as a kindly lady, but he/she does not necessarily corroborate it. Therefore, this statement cannot be true.
- **D: implies that Florence has not obtained the acknowledgement she warrants.** This cannot be confirmed. The author does not suggest that Florence has or has not gained the recognition she deserves.

Q7.4: B - Florence begrudged any usurping of her authority.

Explanation: The penultimate paragraph asserts that Florence did not tolerate any opposition, and the following paragraph highlights how she refused to accept nurses whom since she had not invited. The first paragraph states that she had the authority to select and dismiss staff. Hence, the fact that she reacted adversely when nurses were sent to her hospital without her approval shows that she did not allow anyone to overrule her authority.

- **A: Florence instantly exhibited empathy to all who encountered her.** The passage does not mention this, and we cannot confirm that it is true. We might assume that, as a nurse, she was empathetic. However, we cannot be certain if she was empathetic at all or if she was empathetic towards everyone.
- **C: Florence's parents did not encourage her to enrol in the nursing profession.** The passage does not mention Florence's parents. We cannot confirm that it is true.
- **D: Florence had a profound trepidation of rodents.** While Florence wrote that the hospital was filled with vermin, we are not told if she was afraid of them. We cannot confirm that it is true.

Answer 8

Q8.1: D - it would prove advantageous for patients.

Explanation: The first paragraph of the passage indicates that a test that uses saliva has been developed as an alternative to the current practice of monitoring glucose. This same paragraph also suggests that the current method is invasive and painful. Hence, it can be inferred that a test that uses saliva will not embody these negative aspects and will, therefore, prove favourable for patients.

- **A: it is more reliable than blood.** While the passage argues that lab tests of the saliva process have a fairly high accuracy rate and that this 'shows promising results for monitoring diabetes', it does not confirm that a test that uses saliva is more reliable than one that uses blood. The accuracy rate for a test that uses blood is not provided, and we cannot compare this with the accuracy rate for a test that uses saliva.
- **B: fifty percent of people with diabetes are unaware that they have the condition.** The passage states that around half of the global cases of diabetes are 'undiagnosed'. The keyword in this phrase is 'around'. The word 'around' suggests 'approximately'; it could be that slightly more than half of the global cases of diabetes are undiagnosed, or it could be that slightly less than half of the global cases of diabetes are undiagnosed. We thus cannot be certain that exactly 50% of people with diabetes are unaware that they have the disease. In addition, the words 'undiagnosed' and 'unaware' are not directly synonymous. The individual might be fully aware that he or she has the disease because he or she is manifesting the common symptoms, but it might be undiagnosed due to a wealth of reasons (such as a fear of visiting the GP that prevents the individual from obtaining a diagnosis).
- **C: it is easier to obtain than blood.** We are told that the current method of monitoring blood glucose can be invasive and painful. The passage implies that a test that uses saliva would alleviate these consequences. However, the passage does not state if obtaining saliva for the purpose of such a test is **easier** than obtaining blood.

Q8.2: A - People with severe diabetes will benefit from this type of test.

Explanation: The passage does not tell us about the type of diabetes for which this test will be beneficial. We cannot assume that the test is only for certain types of diabetes or that it will be appropriate for all types and at all stages of the

Answer 8 (Continued)

disease. This assertion cannot be supported by the information in the passage and is, therefore, the correct answer.

- **B: This research involved scholars in Brazil.** The final paragraph confirms that this is true.
- **C: Researchers in the UK were involved in this study.** The first paragraph states that the University of Strathclyde (Scotland) was involved in this research.
- **D: The test that relies on saliva is accurate.** The passage claims that the test has an accuracy rate of 95.2% and thus argues that the test is accurate.

Q8.3: B - False

Explanation: The passage states that diabetes 'affects an estimated 425 million people worldwide'. The population of the world (in May 2020) is 7.8 billion. A quarter of the world's population would therefore be 1.95 billion (in May 2020). Hence, the assertion that a quarter of the world's population has diabetes is incorrect since only 425 million people worldwide have the disease.

Q8.4: C - There are two universities in Brazil.

Explanation: The keyword in this question is 'always'. The final paragraph of the passage confirms that there are two universities in Brazil. While it does not suggest that these are the **only** universities in the country, we know that there are **always** two universities in Brazil. This answer option is, therefore, correct.

- **A: Tests that use saliva will replace those that use blood.** The passage does not corroborate this. It does not confirm if saliva will replace blood, if saliva will be used only in certain cases, or if saliva will end up being used at all. Hence, this answer option cannot be **always** true.
- **B: Such research is published in reliable journals.** There are two important keywords here: 'always' in the question and 'reliable' in the answer option. The final paragraph states that this particular research has been published in the journal *PLOS ONE*. However, we do not know if this journal is **reliable**. Even if we assume that this journal is reliable, we are not told that such research is **always** published in **reliable** journals. Hence, this answer option cannot be corroborated by the information in the passage.

Answer 8 (Continued)

- **D: Blood enables diabetes to be monitored effectively.** The passage informs us that blood is the current prevalent method for monitoring diabetes. We might assume that it enables diabetes to be monitored effectively, but the passage does not confirm this. Moreover, we are not told if blood **always** allows diabetes to be monitored effectively; the passage does not provide the accuracy rate. We also do not know if there is also another method of monitoring diabetes. After all, it is possible that blood is not **always** used and that there is another method about which the passage does not speak.

Answer 9

Q9.1: C - Portier and Richet were awarded the Nobel Prize in Physiology or Medicine.

Explanation: The final sentence of the passage's first paragraph infers that Richet was awarded the Nobel Prize in Physiology or Medicine for his discoveries into how the immune system can be prompted to behave in a self-destructive manner. While the passage largely focuses on Richet and mentions Portier only once, it does state that the two worked together on this research. This assertion can, therefore, be supported by the information contained in the passage.

- **A: The immune system did not start to be studied recently.** Since we do not know when this passage was written or when Richet conducted his research, the information in the passage does not confirm that the immune system started to be studied recently. You might know that anaphylaxis was discovered in the early twentieth century, and you might be able to deduce that researchers did not start to study the immune system only recently. You might, therefore, be tempted to select this answer option. However, it is important that you use only the knowledge that is given in the passage as a basis for answering a question.
- **B: The Nobel Prize in Physiology or Medicine is awarded every year.** The passage does not state how often the Nobel Prize in Physiology or Medicine is awarded. Based on the information in the passage, we cannot say if this is true or false. Once again, it is vital to use

Answer 9 (Continued)

only the information in the passage to answer the question. You might know that the Nobel Prize in Physiology or Medicine is not awarded every year, but this information is not given in the passage.

- **D: Richet used only animals as experimental subjects.** The second paragraph of the passage describes how Richet tested his theories on dogs. However, the passage does not confirm if he did or did not turn to another experimental subject. Hence, we cannot be certain that this assertion is true.

Q9.2: A - True

Explanation: The second paragraph of the passage states quite explicitly that dogs died during Richet's experiments.

Q9.3: C - Richet's findings led him to confute what other scientists had proposed.

Explanation: The passage states that Richet demonstrated that anaphylaxis was neither an accident nor an aberration. Yet, 'many scientists in the field had thought' that this response was either an accident or an aberration. We can, therefore, conclude that Richet's discovery enabled him to contradict what other scientists had previously suggested.

- **A: Dogs are the only animal on which this research was conducted.** While the passage does not mention that Richet tested his theories on any other type of animal, the passage similarly does not mention that Richet **did not** test his theories on any other type of animal. We therefore cannot be certain that this assertion is true.
- **B: Richet had to apply for ethical approval.** While ethical approval would certainly need to be sought for such research today, the passage does not inform us when this research took place and if Richet needed to apply for ethical approval.
- **D: Richet administered poison into dogs only.** The passage does not mention that Richet injected poison into any other type of animal, but it also does not mention that Richet **did not** inject poison into any other type of animal. We therefore cannot be certain that this assertion is true.

Answer 9 (Continued)

Q9.4: B - poses a risk to his or her life.

Explanation: The first paragraph describes this reaction as 'fatal', which suggests that anaphylactic shock poses a risk to an individual's life.

- **A: had been suspected for many years.** While scientists knew that the body was undergoing an adverse response, it was thought that this response was an accident or an aberration. It was not known that this was a type of shock.
- **C: often occurs after he or she has been poisoned.** The keyword here is 'often'. Anaphylaxis does occur after an individual has been poisoned. This is not **often** the case but, rather, it is almost always the case.
- **D: can be alleviated with medicine.** You might know that this is true, but it is not mentioned in the passage. Hence, this answer option cannot be selected here. Remember that all answers should be based on the information that is contained within the passage only.

Answer 10

Q10.1: B - We should be concerned that a fungus has invaded the Americas because a significant number of bananas are grown there.

Explanation: The first paragraph in the passage states that the Americas represent the source of much of the world's banana supply. The entire passage is underpinned by the concern that a fungus might wipe out bananas. This assertion can, therefore, be verified by the information in the passage.

- **A: We should be concerned that a fungus has invaded the Americas because a significant number of bananas are sold there.** The passage does not infer that any bananas are sold in the Americas, and it certainly does not state that a significant number of bananas are sold there. This statement thus cannot be verified by the information in the passage.
- **C: We should be concerned that a fungus has invaded the Americas because extensive research on bananas takes place there.** The passage does not confirm that research is undertaken in the Americas. While it states that scientists are attempting to save the banana, we do not

Answer 10 (Continued)

know where they are based. This statement thus cannot be verified by the information in the passage.

- **D: We should be concerned that a fungus has invaded the Americas because the government is ill-equipped to manage the situation.** The passage does not inform us how the government will deal with the situation. This statement thus cannot be verified by the information in the passage.

Q10.2: A - True

Explanation: The second paragraph asserts that researchers in Australia have inserted a gene into Cavendish bananas, which is the top commercial variety of the fruit. While the passage does not explicitly state that people in Australia buy this type of banana, it can be assumed from the way in which this information is presented.

Q10.3: C - Can't Tell

Explanation: The title states that CRISPR **might** be the banana's only hope against fungus. While we cannot be certain that the tool will not prove futile in protecting bananas from the fungus, we cannot be certain that it will prove futile. Hence, the answer must be 'can't tell'.

Q10.4: C - Can't Tell

Explanation: The final paragraph of the passage maintains that the Cavendish banana accounts for 99% of global banana shipments. The passage does not state if one type of banana accounts for the remaining 1% of global banana shipments or if more than one type of banana accounts for the remaining 1% of global banana shipments. Therefore, the answer must be 'can't tell'.

Answer 11

Q11.1: C - emit 5.5% of what your colleague, who lives in the UK and does not fly, emits in an entire year.

Explanation: The second paragraph of the passage states that, by flying from London to New York and back to London (return flight), a person emits an amount that is equivalent to 11% of what the average person in the UK emits in one year. Therefore, if you were to fly from London to New York (but you do not fly back to London, as the question infers), you would presumably emit half of 11%, which is 5.5.%.

- **A: add approximately 0.67 tonnes to your carbon footprint.** This would be correct if you were to fly from London to New York and back to London. The second paragraph of the passage states that 'an economy-class **return** flight from London to New York emits an estimated 0.67 tonnes of CO_2 per passenger'.
- **B: emit the same as your colleague, who lives in the UK and does not fly, emits in an entire year.** This cannot be true since we are told that a return flight from London to New York emits, per passenger, what is equivalent to 11% (and not 100%) of the average annual emissions for an individual in the UK. We also must remember that the question discusses flying from London to New York, but it does not mention flying back to London. This figure of 11% will presumably decrease if the person does not return.
- **D: increase your carbon footprint to match that of an individual in Ghana.** We are told that a passenger on a return flight from London to New York will emit the same amount of CO_2 as an individual in Ghana emits over one year. Hence, if you were to take a **return** flight from London to New York, you would emit the same amount of CO_2as an individual in Ghana emits over one year, and the flight would thus cause your carbon footprint to match that of an individual in Ghana. However, we must remember that the question does not speak of a **return** flight. Flying to New York from London but not flying back **might** cause your carbon footprint to match that of an individual in Ghana since, as the passage infers, you would also be emitting CO_2 in other ways. However, we cannot presume that this is true from the information in the passage. This answer option is, therefore, incorrect.

Answer 11 (Continued)

Q11.2: D - The total proportion of the world's carbon emissions that comes from airplane travel is low.

Explanation: The third paragraph of the passage asserts that 'aviation contributes about 2% of the world's global carbon emissions'. We can suggest that 2% is relatively low. In addition, we know that the other three answer options cannot be true (see below). Hence, this answer option is the one that is **best supported** by the information in the passage.

- **A: Airplane travel's contribution to global carbon emissions will be 4% in 2037.** The passage states that 'aviation contributes about 2% of the world's global carbon emissions'. The same paragraph also maintains that the number of passengers is expected to double by 2037. However, it does not affirm that, because passenger numbers will double, the global carbon emissions from airplane travel will also double.
- **B: Each year, 4.1 billion people travel by plane.** While the passage does state that passenger numbers are expected to double to 8.2 billion in 2037, we are not given sufficient additional information to corroborate this answer option. We are not told how many passengers travel by plane each year. It is also unlikely that the passage infers that 4.1 billion people travel by plane each year and this figure will suddenly double in 2037 to 8.2 billion.
- **C: The size of a seat on an airplane does not shape the amount of pollution emitted by that vehicle.** The final paragraph of the passage relates an increase in aviation's total emissions with the fact that emissions are influenced by where a passenger sits (business class or economy class) since 'there is more space per seat'. The passage infers that there is a difference in the amount of space in the two classes and that this contributes to the plane's emissions.

Q11.3: C - Can't Tell

Explanation: While the passage asserts that an individual who flies from London to New York and back to London emits an estimated 0.67 tonnes of CO_2, we are not told how his or her carbon footprint compares to that of an individual who flies between other countries or engages in other activities. In addition, this statement considers individuals who travel from the UK to America; it does not explicitly imply return journeys. Based on the information in the passage, we cannot be certain if this statement is true or false.

Answer 11 (Continued)

Q11.4: A - will observe a difference in travellers' habits.

Explanation: The passage states that IATA predicts the number of airplane passengers will double. This implies that people will travel by plane more, which means that their current habits will change. This statement is thus true.

- **B: is a minor contributor to global warming.** The author relays information provided by IATA and states that air travel contributes about 2% of the world's global carbon emissions. Yet, the author does not position this within the context of global warming. We are not told how this 2% translates to the phenomenon of global warming.
- **C: will become more sustainable.** In the final paragraph, the author states that, while other sectors of the economy will become "greener", the total emissions produced by aviation is likely to rise. This statement thus cannot be true.
- **D: is monitored by IATA.** The passage does not confirm this. We know that IATA has provided statistics on air travel, but we are not given any detailed information about its role. Therefore, we cannot be certain if this statement is true.

Answer 12

Q12.1: B - lead to the removal of German forces from Europe.

Explanation: The first paragraph of the passage explains that the D-Day Landings were the beginning of the campaign to free north-west Europe from Nazi occupation. This would then lead to the liberation of the rest of Europe from German forces. As such, this statement is corroborated by the information within the passage.

- **A: be the biggest operation that had ever been undertaken.** Although we are told that this was a large-scale operation, the passage does not suggest that it was the largest in history.
- **C: encourage troops already in France to assemble on certain beaches in the country.** Although there were many troops on the beaches, the passage does not imply that resident troops were relocated to the beaches.

Answer 12 (Continued)

- **D: protect French citizens and lead to German surrender.** While this might seem a logical conclusion, it is not confirmed by the information in the passage.

Q12.2: B - Canadian troops stormed Juno beach.

Explanation: We are told that, while Canadian troops did land on Juno beach, they 'established themselves'. The passage does not support the supposition that they **stormed** the beach, and this statement cannot be verified by the information that we are given.

- **A: British troops arrived on the beach in the same area as the Canadians.** The passage describes how troops landed on the coast of northern France. It also notes that there was a 'simultaneous landing of tens of thousands of troops on five separate beaches in Normandy'. Taking into account both explanations, this statement can be supported.
- **C: American troops landed on Utah and Omaha beaches.** The third paragraph of the passage states that American troops were successful in landing on Utah beach. In addition, the final paragraph of the passage claims that a further delegation of American troops 'suffered serious losses' at Omaha beach, which infers that they did land there.
- **D: British troops secured a position on Gold beach.** The third paragraph of the passage advises that British troops established a foothold on the beach which had been given the codename 'Gold'. This statement can, therefore, be supported by the information within the passage.

Q12.3: C - Can't Tell

Explanation: Although it would be reasonable to assume that all areas suffered losses, the passage does not provide us with this information. As such, we cannot tell if only American troops were killed in the D-Day Landings.

Q12.4: D: The Germans were not fully prepared for the scale of D-Day Landings.

Explanation: Despite the information regarding the counterattack, there is clear support for the fact that the Germans were not prepared. The passage

Answer 12 (Continued)

affirms that the Germans had believed that the attack would take place at a different location and, as such, had not planned sufficiently. This statement is thus corroborated by the information within the passage.

- **A: Some troops were waiting on the beaches since they were already located in France.** Although this might be possible, the passage does not offer any information to support this.
- **B: Only veterans are allowed on the beaches today.** You might be aware that this is false. Yet, it is vital to answer the question using only the information provided. The passage neither discusses this nor provides any information to suggest that access is restricted today. This statement cannot be supported by the information within the passage.
- **C: The D-Day Landings proved a huge success for the British.** Whilst the D-Day Landings are overwhelmingly recognised as a success and a turning point in the Second World War, the passage does not provide this information.

Answer 13

Q13.1: B - its health is declining.

Explanation: The passage infers that soil should be examined because its health is declining. The first paragraph states plainly that worldwide crops are 'facing a crisis', whilst the final paragraph details measures that are needed to incubate healthy soils. This statement is, therefore, supported by the information within the passage.

- **A: a large amount of money is set aside for this exact purpose.** This statement suggests that soil should be examined purely because the money is available. However, the passage does not claim that money is unreservedly available to monitor the soil. As such, this statement cannot be considered as true.
- **C: too much money is spent on other areas of the environment.** The author does highlight that money is unequally distributed and that a greater amount of money is spent on other areas. However, he/she does not claim that **too much** money is spent on other areas. This statement thus cannot be corroborated by the information in the passage.

Answer 13 (Continued)

- **D: tougher measures have been called for by environmental campaigners.** Again, this cannot be inferred from the information in the passage.

Q13.2: C - the way in which money is spent proves surprising.

Explanation: This can be confirmed as a view of the author as the second paragraph indicates that the figures are 'startling'. The author then goes on to detail the allocation of the funds and emphasising the 'mismatch' in allocation.

- **A: there is no discrepancy between the amount of money spent on soil monitoring and the amount of money spent on other aspects.** This is not the view of the author: the inequalities in distribution are highlighted in the second paragraph.
- **B: more money will be devoted to soil monitoring.** The author states that 'there is no evidence that Defra will commit to funding soil monitoring'. Hence, this statement cannot be corroborated by the information within the passage.
- **D: the Agriculture Bill could provide the funds to support soil monitoring.** The author does not suggest this. He/She does state that the powers contained in the Bill will hopefully support soil monitoring. However, the passage does not confirm that the Bill will include the necessary legislation to provide appropriate funding.

Q13.3: D - Funding is needed to support soil monitoring.

Explanation: This is a clear observation throughout the passage. The author notes the 'mismatch' of funding and explains that, unless this is addressed, the health of the soil will face a continued crisis. The author also claims that concern 'has been running high' already. This statement can thus be supported by the information within the passage.

- **A: The way in which funds are spent is hidden from the public.** This cannot be true as the second paragraph explains that the distribution of funding was detailed following a Freedom of Information (FoI) request. This may be requested by anyone and, as such, information cannot be considered as hidden.
- **B: The quality of soil is currently poor.** We cannot be certain if this is true. The passage only highlights that there is a concern about the condition of the soil; it does not specifically state that the soil is in a poor condition.

Answer 13 (Continued)

- **C: The quality of water is more important than the quality of soil.** While the passage notes that water monitoring receives more funding than soil monitoring, it does not, at any time, suggest that water quality is considered more important.

Q13.4: A - True

Explanation: This can be confirmed as true by noting the information in paragraph three. The passage indicates that Defra has discussed a plan to establish a monitoring scheme.

Answer 14

Q14.1: B - False

Explanation: The first paragraph of the passage states that Edward was 'heir to Victoria for nearly 60 years'. This statement is, therefore, false. Firstly, Edward was first in line to the throne (and not second in line to the throne). Secondly, the passage states that he was heir to the throne for **nearly** 60 years (and not **exactly** 60 years).

Q14.2: B - was directed by Queen Victoria to not partake in all activities as her designated ambassador.

Explanation: The second paragraph of the passage notes that Edward was 'given almost no chance to participate in affairs of state'. It is therefore evident that Victoria would only allow him to represent her in certain circumstances and would not permit him to participate in all activities. This statement can thus be corroborated by the information within the passage.

- **A: was the favoured child of Victoria but not of Albert.** It is not possible to presume this from the details in the passage. The author does not provide information to confirm that this is true. **C: was generally considered as a contributor to the death of his father.** This cannot be confirmed from the information provided. While the passage indicates that Queen Victoria blamed Edward for his father's death, it does not indicate that this was the **general** opinion.

Answer 14 (Continued)

- **D: attained degrees from both Oxford and Cambridge.** The author details that Edward attended both Oxford and Cambridge. It does not, however, detail the qualifications obtained. As such, this statement cannot be confirmed by the information within this passage.

Q14.3: B - rebel when he was away from direct parental control.

Explanation: Based on the information within the passage, it is possible to conclude that Edward rebelled when he was not in close proximity to his parents. The passage describes how 'a liaison with an actress caused considerable scandal' and notes that 'Prince Albert visited his son to reprimand him'. It is, therefore, impossible to disprove that this statement is true.

- **A: have a happy childhood.** It is not possible to confirm that Edward had a happy childhood since the passage provides minimal information of this. It does indicate that he underwent a 'strict regime', but this is not a sufficient indicator to prove that he did not have a happy childhood. Indeed, we are not told how he reacted to this 'regime'.
- **C: find happiness in being allowed to marry the woman he loved.** This cannot be determined from the information in the passage as there is only a brief reference to Edward's romantic involvement with one actress. The author does not suggest that Edward had any interest in marrying the actress (or, indeed, anyone else).
- **D: act sufficiently to resolve the constitutional crisis at the end of his reign.** There is not enough detail within the passage to confirm this. The reason for which he did not resolve the crisis could have been his death, but the author does not provide sufficient information to support this statement. Therefore, it is impossible to conclude (but not impossible not to conclude) that this statement is true.

Q14.4: C - Edward was keen to undertake a proactive role before his coronation.

Explanation: The passage infers that Edward acted as the representative of the Queen. The author states that Edward was 'given almost no chance to participate in affairs of state', which implies that he was not allowed to be as active as he might have wished. In addition, we are told that, when he became King, he 'threw himself into his new role' and rejuvenated the monarchy. This statement can, therefore, be considered as true.

Answer 14 (Continued)

- **A: Edward was responsible for initiating the Entente Cordiale.** The passage does not suggest that Edward was responsible for this. Although he 'helped pave the way', he was not responsible for the agreement.
- **B: Edward's reign was marred by his indiscretions.** The only indiscretion mentioned within the passage was his liaison with an actress, and this occurred before he became king. Hence, based on the information within the passage, we cannot confirm that this statement to be true.
- **D: Edward was an enigmatic and flamboyant character.** Although the passage advises that he 'restored sparkle' to the monarchy and was well respected internationally, there is nothing within the passage to indicate that this statement is true.

Answer 15

Q15.1: B - False

Explanation: The passage notes that there were 45,000 visitors to the online site in one week (between 14th and 20th May). The passage states that this was over ten times the number of people who physically went to see the birds the previous year. We can therefore calculate that 4,500 people visited the birds last year, and this statement is thus false.

Q15.2: D - The coronavirus has been responsible for an increase in human interest in the project.

Explanation: This can be confirmed as true since the passage details the huge increase in visitors to the website after the reserve was forced to close. The number of people who are watching the birds online far exceeds the number of people who were visiting the reserve, and the pandemic has increased awareness of the availability of the online resource.

- **A: Visitors to the site were residents of the UK, Scotland, Canada, Finland and Spain.** This statement is not true as the passage does not confirm that any of the visitors were based in Scotland.

Answer 15 (Continued)

- **B: In the first three weeks of May, 900,000 minutes of videos were watched by 2,000 people.** While the passage does state that the project's Facebook page received 2,000 new visitors between 1st and 21st May, it does not assert that all 2,000 individuals watched all 900,000 minutes of video. This statement is, therefore, false.
- **C: The coronavirus has led to a reduction in the number of birds migrating to the reserve.** There is nothing in the passage to suggest that less birds have migrated to the reserve since the pandemic began. Hence, this statement cannot be corroborated by the information within the passage.

Q15.3: D - It has been noted that 13 percent of visitors used the site previously.

Explanation: The passage states that 87% of visitors to the website were new users. As such, it can be confirmed that 13% used the site previously. This statement is, therefore, not false.

- **A: This year has seen 23 birds return to the reserve.** The passage tells us that Maya and 33(11) returned 'with 23 other ospreys'. The total number of ospreys to return thus totals 25, and this statement is false.
- **B: The birds have migrated directly from Africa**. The keyword in this statement is 'directly'. Although the passage does assert that the birds arrived from Africa, it does not categorically state that they came **directly** from Africa. It is not known if they stopped elsewhere before arriving at the reserve and, as such, this statement cannot be considered as not false.
- **C: The increase in online subscriptions will enable to project to recoup its losses.** Since the passage does not provide information to indicate any losses that the project has suffered or that online subscriptions will assist in this regard, this statement cannot be considered as true. In addition, we are not told if viewers must pay to watch the birds online.

Q15.4: B - That awareness of the importance of nature will be enhanced.

Explanation: The passage concludes with the comment 'With more people being engaged, hopefully we could be helping to raise the awareness of how important it is to stay connected to nature.' It is therefore possible to conclude that the passage considers this to be possible.

Answer 15 (Continued)

- **A: That each of the birds will continue to return each year.** The passage does not suggest whether this is true or false. As such, we cannot conclude that the passage does or does not consider this to be possible.
- **C: That the fledglings will have a better chance of survival now that the reserve is closed.** The fledglings are kept from human interference even when the reserve is open to visitors: visitors make use of the hides at Manton Bay. In addition, fledglings have prospered in previous years at the reserve. It is therefore possible (and not impossible) to conclude that the passage does not consider this to be true.
- **D: That the number of online visitors will continue to increase at the current rate.** The passage does not suggest whether this is true or false. As such, we cannot conclude that the passage does or does not consider this to be possible.

Answer 16

Q16.1: A - Furniture can be made from wood that is used to heat rooms.

Explanation: The first paragraph compares the piece of wood that Master Cherry envisaged as the leg of a table with a log that is burnt in stoves and fireplaces to warm a room. The passage therefore confirms that one can use the same wood to heat a room as to make furniture, and this statement is thus correct.

- **B: Master Cherry owned a shop.** We cannot assume that Master Cherry owned the shop. It could be that he rented it or that he owned only part of it. From the information that the passage provides, we cannot confirm that this is true.
- **C: Master Cherry sold wood for stoves and fireplaces.** The passage does not confirm this. It does compare the piece of wood to logs that are burnt in the winter in stoves and fireplaces, but we are not told if Master Cherry sold such logs.
- **D: Master Cherry knew he had a red nose.** The passage does not affirm this. It states that the end of Master Cherry's nose was red, and we might assume that he was aware of this. However, we cannot be certain if he knew.

Answer 16 (Continued)

Q16.2: B - False

Explanation: The carpenter's name was Master Antonio. His penname was Master Cherry.

Q16.3: C - Can't Tell

Explanation: While the passage possesses characteristics that belong to the fairy tale (such as the opening phrase 'once upon a time'), we cannot be certain that this is a fairy tale. Texts often exhibit characteristics of a number of literary genres and cannot be positioned within the boundaries of one.

Q16.4: A - The piece of wood asked Master Cherry not to hit it with the axe.

Explanation: The final paragraph asserts that, as Master Cherry was about to strike the piece of wood with an axe, he heard a small voice that said: 'Do not strike me so hard!' Since the voice said 'me' and Master Cherry was about to hit the wood, we can assume that it was the wood that spoke.

- **B: Master Cherry's assistant asked him not to hit the piece of wood with the axe.** We are not told that Master Cherry has an assistant. Therefore, this statement cannot be corroborated by the information in the passage.
- **C: Master Cherry was rather disinterested in the piece of wood.** The passage claims that Master Cherry 'beamed with delight' and 'rubbed his hands together with satisfaction' upon seeing the wood. He decided to use it to make the leg of a table. Hence, we know that he was not disinterested in the piece of wood.
- **D: Master Cherry ignored the voice.** We are told that Master Cherry 'remained with his arm suspended in the air' when he heard the voice. We can therefore assume that he did not ignore it.

Answer 17

Q17.1: A - Britain's relationship with the European Union gives a role to the Department for Environment, Food and Rural Affairs.

Explanation: The passage asserts that the Department for Environment, Food and Rural Affairs is 'one of the lead government departments delivering a successful exit from the European Union'. We can thus deduce that the Department has tasks to complete due to the fact that Britain is leaving the European Union. This statement is, therefore, true.

- **B: Approximately 357 people work in each of HM Land Registry's offices.** The passage states that approximately 5,000 people work in HM Land Registry's 14 offices across England and Wales. Since 5,000 divided by 14 is 357.1, this statement could be construed as true. However, there are a few aspects to address here. Firstly, we do not know if HM Land Registry owns more than 14 offices. The passage affirms that 5,000 people work 'in 14 offices', which does not negate the fact that it might possess more offices in which people do not work. If this is the case, this answer option cannot be true since it says 'each'. Secondly, we cannot assume that these 5,000 people are equally divided between 14 offices. This statement is, therefore, not supported by the information in the passage.
- **C: The Civil Service provides secure jobs that have numerous perks.** While the passage highlights the benefits of each role, it does not confirm that any of the jobs are **secure**.
- **D: The Crown Prosecution Service employs less people than the Department for Environment, Food and Rural Affairs and HM Land Registry.** The passage states that the Crown Prosecution Service employs 'almost 6,000 people'. It asserts that HM Land Registry employs 'over 5,000 people', but it does not confirm the number of people employed by the Department for Environment, Food and Rural Affairs. It is **possible** that, cumulatively, the Department for Environment, Food and Rural Affairs and HM Land Registry employ a greater number of people than the Crown Prosecution Service (we know that HM Land Registry alone employs more than 5,000 people). However, we must remember that we are not told how many people are employed by the Department for Environment, Food and Rural Affairs. In addition, the statement does not necessarily suggest that the Crown Prosecution Service employs less people than the Department for Environment, Food and Rural Affairs and HM Land Registry **cumulatively**.

Answer 17 (Continued)

Hence, this statement cannot be supported by the information in the passage.

Q17.2: C - Can't Tell

Explanation: The passage states that the Crown Prosecution Service 'works in partnership with other government departments and agencies throughout the criminal justice system'. However, we cannot tell if it works with **local** government departments or if it interacts with government departments **throughout the country**.

Q17.3: C - Can't Tell

Explanation: We are told that the Department for Environment, Food and Rural Affairs is 'one of the lead government departments delivering a successful exit from the European Union'. Yet, we do not learn what role the Department assumes and whether it is crucial or insignificant.

Q17.4: C - In order to join the Crown Prosecution Service, one absolutely must be determined and driven.

Explanation: The passage asserts that the Crown Prosecution Service employs people who 'continually strive for excellence'. This infers that one must be determined and driven to work here. It is important to note that the question asks us to identify a **flaw**. The fact that one must be determined and driven can be considered a flaw within the context of a job advert since it will prevent individuals who are not determined and driven from being able to apply for and successfully fulfil that role.

- **A: The productivity of the Department for Environment, Food and Rural Affairs is set to increase.** This information can be found in the passage: the passage states that the Department for Environment, Food and Rural Affairs is set to become 'even more efficient'. However, an increase in productivity cannot be considered as **flaw**. As such, this statement is not correct.
  B: HM Land Registry aims to deliver a fast, world-class service. This information can be identified in the passage: the passage asserts that HM Land Registry aims to become 'the world's leading land registry for speed', which implies that it will deliver a fast service that is world-class. Yet, a service of this calibre cannot be considered as **flaw.** As such, this statement is not correct.

Answer 17 (Continued)

- **D: There are a wide variety of roles available within the Civil Service.** Once again, this information can be identified in the passage: we are told of the various roles that are available within the Civil Service, and the passage infers that there are jobs to suit people of different personalities and with different interests. However, the fact that a plethora of roles exists and that there are roles to accommodate different people cannot be considered as **flaw**. As such, this statement is not correct.

Answer 18

Q18.1: C - Can't Tell

Explanation: We are not given any details on the relationship between the CJS and the CPS. Based on the information in the passage, we cannot tell if this statement is true or false.

Q18.2: A - Police forces superintend the way in which crime is investigated.

Explanation: The second paragraph asserts that the 43 police forces across England and Wales are responsible for the investigation of crime. Hence, this statement is corroborated by the information in the passage.

- **B: Police officers are answerable to the CPS.** While the passage states that police forces can ask the CPS to decide whether an offender should be prosecuted, it does not explicate if police officers must answer to the CPS.
- **C: The CPS possesses far more power than police forces.** Once again, while the passage maintains that police officers can ask the CPS to decide whether an offender should be prosecuted, it does not confirm that the CPS has **far more** power than police forces. We might assume that the CPS holds more power than police forces, but we cannot be certain of the minute details from the information that we are given. In addition, this statement is vague: it does not specify the area(s) of power to which it refers. We cannot confidently state that this assertion is true.

Answer 18 (Continued)

- **D: The CPS must monitor the activities of the police forces, especially in relation to crime.** The passage does not offer a detailed explanation of the relationship between the CPS and police forces. We know that police officers can ask the CPS to decide whether an offender should be prosecuted, but we are not told if or how the CPS regulates police forces.

Q18.3: B - he or she is called on to advise a number of agencies.

Explanation: The third paragraph delineates the bodies that the Attorney General advises and oversees. It lists a number of bodies, suggesting that the Attorney General advises a number of agencies.

- **A: he or she is directly answerable to Parliament.** While you might be aware, from your own knowledge, that this is true, the passage neither supports nor negates it. It cannot be selected as the correct option here since it is not mentioned within the passage.
- **C: he or she must inform the Queen of any major changes to it.** This information is not delineated within the passage.
- **D: he or she can overrule the Solicitor General.** Once again, you might be aware, from your own knowledge, that this is true. Yet, we must consider the information that the passage provides. The passage states that the Solicitor General supports the Attorney General, which does suggest that the Attorney General can overrule the Solicitor General. However, we can only make this assumption; the passage does not explicate that this is true. In addition, the question seeks the reason for which the Attorney General assumes an **important** role in the criminal justice system. We are not told whether the fact that the Attorney General is supported by the Solicitor General gives him or her importance. This answer option, therefore, cannot be selected here.

Q18.4: B - The MOJ plays a limited role in the CJS.

Explanation: The final paragraph of the passage describes the parts of the CJS for which the MOJ is responsible. It lists a number of areas, suggesting that the MOJ does not assume a limited role in the CJS. This statement thus cannot be true.

- **A: The Attorney General is a government minister.** The passage states that the Attorney General is the chief legal adviser to the government. He/She must therefore be a minister.

Answer 18 (Continued)

- **C: The Solicitor General advises the Attorney General.** The penultimate paragraph of the passage confirms that the Solicitor General supports the Attorney. It is therefore assumed that he or she will advise the Attorney General.
- **D: The CPS is the principal agency for conducting criminal prosecutions in England and Wales.** The passage affirms that the police requests the CPS to decide whether to prosecute an offender in serious cases. Therefore, this statement can be supported by the information in the passage.

Answer 19

Q19.1: D - The value of the award.

Explanation: The penultimate paragraph asserts that the DofE provides 'the experience of a lifetime and raises aspirations by helping others, getting fitter, learning or developing practical skills, and taking part in an unforgettable journey'. The second paragraph also states that it is 'highly regarded by employers and higher education establishments'. These aspects make the award valuable, and this statement is thus supported by the information within the passage.

- **A: The cut-off point for individuals to achieve the award.** While the passage asserts that anyone aged between 14 and 24 years can participate in the award, it does not clarify whether an individual must start or complete the award by the age of 24 years. The passage does not tell by when an individual must complete the award.
- **B: The countries in which the award is recognised.** The first paragraph states that the award is recognised both nationally and internationally, but it does not specify the exact countries in which it is recognised.
- **C: Reimbursement for undertaking activities as part of the award.** While the first paragraph of the passage claims that the award is voluntary, the passage does not state whether the activities undertaken as part of the award are or are not remunerated.

Answer 19 (Continued)

Q19.2: C - The name of the award was chosen by The Duke of Edinburgh.

Explanation: We are informed that the award is named after its founder and patron, The Duke of Edinburgh. However, we are not told how the name was conceived or who selected it. This statement therefore cannot be corroborated by the information in the passage.

- **A: The DofE is only for youths.** The first paragraph states that it is for anyone aged between 14 and 24 years, whilst the final two paragraphs relate the undertaking of the award to 'young people'. This statement can, therefore, be supported by the information in the passage.
- **B: The DofE encourages relationships between individuals to be established.** The passage states that the DofE allows young people to help others. We can thus assume that this aspect of the award encourages relationships to be built between individuals, and this statement can be supported by the information in the passage.
- **D: The DofE is recognised by universities.** The second paragraph maintains that the award is highly regarded by higher education establishments. This statement is, therefore, true.

Q19.3: D - The award is not discriminative against an individual's economic background.

Explanation: The final paragraph confirms that the award can be achieved by anyone, regardless of who he or she is or where he or she is from. This suggests that an individual's economic background will never determine if he or she can achieve the award.

- **A: An individual should progress from Bronze level to Silver level to Gold level.** The keyword in this question is 'always'. While the passage maintains that an individual **can** progress from Bronze level to Silver level to Gold level, it does not state that an individual **must** or **should**. Hence, this assertion is not **always** true.
- **B: Every university holds an individual who has achieved the DofE in high esteem.** While the passage states that the award is recognised by higher education establishments, it does not state that **every** university recognises it. In addition, while we are told that universities recognise the award, we are not informed how they consider those who are awarded it. In other words, the passage does not necessarily confirm that universities hold those with the award in 'high esteem'.

Answer 19 (Continued)

- **C: Those who complete the DofE acquire physical fitness.** While the penultimate paragraph states that the DofE helps individuals to become fitter, this might not **always** be the case. An individual who is completing the award might already be very fit and not need to acquire physical fitness. Hence, this statement is not **always** true.

Q19.4: C - Can't Tell

Explanation: The first paragraph claims that the award was founded in 1956. Hence, it was **founded** more than half a century ago. Yet, we do not know when the first award was **presented**; the passage does not provide this information. You might know that the award was first presented more than fifty years ago, but the information in the passage does not confirm if this is true or false. The correct answer is, therefore, 'can't tell'.

Answer 20

Q20.1: C - Can't Tell

Explanation: We might assume that this statement is false since it seems unlikely that instructions to fit a bath can be used to fit a different type of appliance. However, the passage does not confirm if this is true or false. Therefore, based on the information that the passage provides, we cannot tell if this statement is true or false.

Q20.2: D - it is not imperative to ask a plumber for assistance.

Explanation: The second bullet point states that, in some instances, 'it's best to call in a qualified plumber'. The passage infers that, on some occasions, it might be advisable to ask a qualified plumber for assistance. However, it does not assert that one **must** seek a plumber's assistance. This statement is, therefore, corroborated by the information within the passage.

- **A: fitting a bath is relatively easy.** The first bullet point suggests that replacing an old bath with a new bath should be reasonably uncomplicated. However, the second bullet point implies that, if the bath is a new addition or if the position of the bath is being changed, one

Answer 20 (Continued)

might need to ask a plumber for help since this is a little more difficult. The writer thus does not confirm that fitting any bath will be an easy task.

- **B: one shouldn't be worried about the way in which the flooring has been laid.** The passage states that the flooring is not visible with a 'closed in' bath and, as such, one does not need to be concerned with the way in which it has been laid. Yet, the same bullet point affirms that the flooring will be visible if a freestanding bath is being fitted and, in this instance, one will need to consider the flooring prior to fitting the bath. This statement is, therefore, false.
- **C: fitting a bath should not raise any difficulties.** While the passage does not explicitly say that fitting a bath will be difficult, its use of the words 'be sure', 'ensure that' and 'carefully' implies that problems could occur. It also suggests that one might need the help of a plumber, indicating that this part could prove challenging. This statement thus cannot be supported by the information within the passage.

Q20.3: D - The taps should match the style of the bath.

Explanation: The passage advises the user to 'choose taps that are compatible with the pre-drilled holes in the bath', suggesting that the taps should fit into the holes that were made in the bath before it was purchased. The passage does not advocate that the style of the taps should match that of the bath, and this statement is thus incorrect.

- **A: The type of bath will determine the complexity of the installation process.** The first two bullet points confirm that this statement is true. We learn that, if an existing bath is being replaced, the installation of the new bath should be 'a reasonably straightforward task'. However, the passage suggests that the process might prove more difficult if the bath is a new addition or if the position of the bath is being changed. Hence, this statement is true.
- **B: It is important to act with caution when delimiting the area in which the bath will be placed.** The final bullet point demonstrates that this statement is true: the user is told to '**carefully** measure and mark out all fixing points'.
- **C: One must, on occasions, change the structure of the plumbing in order to install a new bath.** The second bullet point affirms that the plumbing might need to be rerouted in order to install the new bath. This statement is, therefore, true.

Answer 20 (Continued)

Q20.4: A - Baths are designed with a place in which to insert taps.

Explanation: The passage advises the user to 'choose taps that are compatible with the pre-drilled holes in the bath', suggesting that holes in which the taps will sit are made in the bath before it is purchased. This statement is, therefore, true.

- **B: The individual fitting the bath should have a reasonable understanding of what to do.** We are not told at whom this guide is aimed; the passage does not distinguish between complete novices and those with experience of fitting bathroom appliances. From the information that we are given, we cannot be certain if an understanding of how to fit a bath is required in order to follow these instructions.
- **C: If a shower is to be placed over the bath, a screen is required.** The passage states that, if the user plans to install an over bath shower, he or she should select a bath with a flat rim to allow a shower screen to create a watertight seal. However, the passage does not confirm that one **must** have a shower screen; it seems to be a suggestion. Therefore, we cannot deem this statement to be true.
- **D: You shouldn't purchase any parts after you have started to install the bath.** While the third bullet point advises the user to acquire all the necessary parts, fittings, and tools before starting to fit the bath, it does not state that one **must** do this. Again, it is only a suggestion. This statement thus cannot be supported by the information in the passage.

Answer 21

Q21.1: B - False

Explanation: The reason for which the grill can be adjusted is to move the food closer to or further from the charcoal. Its primary intention is not to match the height of the user, and this statement is thus false.

Answer 21 (Continued)

Q21.2: C - Can't Tell

Explanation: Although the description explicitly mentions breakfast items, it does not state that the Wooden Bench to Bistro Set is explicitly for breakfast. We therefore cannot tell if this statement is true or false.

Q21.3: B - False

Explanation: The description of the Aqua Magic Mat states that no items 'will get marked'. We can thus presume that a fabric surface would not be affected, and this statement is thus false.

Q21.4: C - Can't Tell

Explanation: While the item includes 500ml of car shampoo, it is not possible for the reader to ascertain if this amount of shampoo is required each time. The description does not mention how many washes can be completed with 500ml of car shampoo.

Answer 22

Q22.1: A - Due to his importance, the remains of the chieftain will be housed in one of the coffins.

Explanation: This cannot be corroborated using the information provided. The passage states that it has not yet been confirmed if the chieftain's remains are at this site. As such, we cannot be certain if his remains will be in one of the coffins.

- **B: The aim of the chieftain's mission was to seek support for Independence.** This can be validated from the information within the passage since the author notes that O'Donnell sought military support to remove the English from Ireland.
- **C: The burial site eventually fell into disrepair**. Red Hugh was buried in Valladolid's Chapel of Wonders. The second paragraph states that, after Columbus' remains were moved to Seville, the Chapel of Wonders, which was a 'ruined building', disappeared from view. Hence, this statement can be corroborated by the information within the passage.

Answer 22 (Continued)

- **D: There is a possibility that the chieftain was slain whilst on this mission.** The final paragraph asserts that there are 'claims that he was killed by poison'. We are thus told that it is **possible** that Red Hugh was murdered whilst he was conducting this mission. This statement can, therefore, be supported by the information in the passage.

Q22.2: B - It is conceivable that the bones are situated in the catacomb of the chapel.

Explanation: The final paragraph of the passage indicates that Red Hugh is 'more likely to have been buried in another part of the chapel', possibly the crypt. As such, this statement can be corroborated by the information within the passage.

- **A: The chieftain secured military assistance from the Spanish.** This cannot be verified by the information within the passage. The passage notes that his intention was to secure military assistance from the Spanish, but it does not confirm that he obtained it.
- **C: The chieftain's loss of part of his foot might have occurred during his escape to Spain.** The passage notes that the chieftain sustained these injuries 'while escaping from his English captors'. It does not suggest that they were sustained as he attempted to travel to Spain for this mission. As such, this statement cannot be corroborated by the information within the passage.
- **D: It is possible that relics moved with those of Columbus belonged to the chieftain.** The passage does not give any indication that the remains of any other person were transferred to Seville with those of Columbus. We therefore cannot consider this statement to be true.

Q22.3: C - As the site was a monastery, the female bones found would have been those of nuns.

Explanation: This is not supported by the information in the passage. While the passage asserts that two of the skeletons recovered 'were women', it does not suggest that these women were nuns. Indeed, we are not provided with any details of who these individuals were, and we cannot assume that they would have been nuns simply because the site was a monastery.

- **A: Other prominent figures would not have been buried in this location.** The passage states that Christopher Columbus, a famous explorer,

Answer 22 (Continued)

was buried at the site. As such, this statement can be corroborated by the information within the passage.

- **B: The chieftain was a rather romanticised figure.** This statement can be considered as true since the passage infers that Red Hugh was a somewhat idealised figure. For example, the fact that his injuries were sustained whilst fleeing captivity suggests that he was a fighting hero.
- **D: The remains might not provide unequivocal information about the death.** This is verified in the third paragraph of the passage, which states that finding the remains 'may help' to confirm the precise cause of Red Hugh's death. The author indicates that, even if the remains are those of Red Hugh, they will not necessarily deliver a firm conclusion of the cause of death.

Q22.4: C - Can't Tell

Explanation: Although the chieftain was Irish, there is nothing within the passage to suggest that he will (or will not) be returned to his native land. As such, we cannot be certain if this is true or false.

Answer 23

Q23.1: B - were perhaps selected because they had a predisposition to heart disease.

Explanation: The passage infers that some participants had risk factors for heart disease, but it does not state that all of them had risk factors for heart disease or if any actually had heart disease. Since the study monitored blood pressure, it can be assumed that some (or even all) participants **might** have been selected because they had a predisposition to heart disease. We cannot be certain, and the fact that the word 'perhaps' appears in this answer option allows us to select it as the correct answer.

- **A: were more or less 62 years of age.** The passage states that the participants were 62 years old 'on average'. The terms 'more or less' and 'on average' have different meanings. Through the use of the term 'more or less', the answer option implies that some participants were a little younger than 62 years, other participants were a little older than 62 years, and some participants were 62 years old. Yet, through the use

Answer 23 (Continued)

of the term 'on average', the passage suggests that the age of each participant was added up and divided by the total number of participants, which totalled 62. This statement is, therefore, incorrect.

- **C: slept for less than one hour during the day.** The passage does mention that the average duration of the participants' midday sleep was 49 minutes, which is less than one hour. However, we cannot be certain if **all** of the participants slept during the day (which is what this question asks). The passage also alludes to a "napping group", which suggests that some of the participants were asked to sleep and others were not. We are not provided sufficient information to assert that this statement is correct.
- **D: each had heart disease.** The passage infers that some participants had risk factors for heart disease, but it does not confirm if any had heart disease. It certainly does not state that **each** participant had heart disease, and we thus cannot be certain that this statement is correct.

Q23.2: B - An ABPM measures blood pressure as an individual goes about his or her daily routine.

Explanation: The passage states that participants wore an ambulatory blood pressure monitor (ABPM) to measure blood pressure at regular intervals during routine daily living. It therefore suggests that the role of an ABPM is to measure blood pressure as an individual goes about his or her daily routine. Based on the information contained within the passage, this statement can be considered as always true; an ABPM will **always** be able to measure blood pressure as an individual goes about his or her daily routine.

- **A: Women are at greater risk of developing heart disease.** The passage does not contain any information to suggest that this is true (or false). It cannot be deduced from the information within the passage.
- **C: Those with Type 2 diabetes have a significant risk of developing heart disease.** Once again, the passage does not contain any information to suggest that this is true (or false). It cannot be deduced from the information within the passage.
- **D: Echocardiograms and pulse wave velocity tests can be performed simultaneously.** We know that both an echocardiogram and a pulse wave velocity test were performed on the participants, but the information

Answer 23 (Continued)

in the passage does not suggest that they should **always** be performed together. Based on the information in the passage, we cannot deduce if this statement is **always** true.

Q23.3: A - The results of the study had to be tampered with as some participants had a higher blood pressure than others.

Explanation: The passage affirms that the researchers 'adjusted for factors known to influence blood pressure levels, including age, gender, lifestyle and medications'. This does not, however, suggest that the results were altered to take into account an individual's blood pressure. This statement is, therefore, false.

- **B: Some participants were already taking medication for high blood pressure.** The passage states that 'there were no differences in terms of the number of antihypertensive medications taken between the two groups', which implies that some participants were taking medication to control high blood pressure. This statement can, therefore, be considered as true.
- **C: The participants were encouraged to sleep during the day.** The first paragraph of the passage makes reference to 'the napping group', which implies that at least one group was encouraged to take naps. However, we do not know how many groups were asked to nap (we do not even know how many groups there were), and we cannot be certain of the exact time they took a nap. Since we do not know if all of the participants were asked to nap and when they napped, we cannot confirm if this is untrue.
- **D: The participants were invited to the clinic before the study started.** We are informed that the participants wore an ABPM at regular intervals and not only once 'in the clinic'. It is thus assumed that the participants visited the clinic before the study in order to undergo certain tests. This statement is thus true.

Q23.4: B - False

Explanation: While 'researchers assessed and recorded blood pressure for 24 hours consecutively', we are told that they also conducted preliminary tests and study recruitment with the participants. This means that the participants would have been monitored for more than 24 hours, and this statement is thus false.

Answer 24

Q24.1: A - it contributed towards the end of the Second World War.

Explanation: The passage states that the victory of the Royal Air Force Fighter Command created the conditions for the eventual defeat of Nazi Germany. The defeat of Nazi Germany signalled the end of the Second World War, and this statement is thus correct.

- **B: it came after British troops were forced to leave France.** While the Battle of Britain took place shortly after the withdrawal of British forces from Europe, the passage does not infer that this is the reason for which the event is considered as an important part of British history. We cannot be certain that this statement is correct.
- **C: it helped to restore France's fallen government.** The passage claims that the French government collapsed on 16th June and that the Battle of Britain took place from July to September. However, we do not know what role the Battle of Britain played in France's fallen government.
- **D: it showed the world that Britain could not be defeated.** While this might be considered as true, the passage does not explicitly state it. Based on the information within the passage, we cannot be certain that this statement is correct.

Q24.2: C - it protected Britain against the foe.

Explanation: We are told that the victory of the Royal Air Force Fighter Command blocked the possibility of an invasion of Britain. This statement is, therefore, correct.

- **A: it prompted France's ports to be reopened.** The passage does not confirm if or when France's ports reopened and, more importantly, if the RAF enabled this to happen. We cannot be certain that this statement is correct.
- **B: it returned British troops to France to help the country fight Germany.** The passage does not inform us if British troops returned to France or that the RAF enabled this to happen. We cannot be certain that this statement is correct.
- **D: it resulted in the instant collapse of the Nazi regime.** The passage states that the victory of the Royal Air Force Fighter Command created the conditions for the **eventual** (and not the instant) defeat of Nazi **Germany**. The passage does not assert that the entire Nazi regime throughout Europe was defeated; it makes reference to Germany alone.

Answer 24 (Continued)

This statement thus cannot be corroborated by the information in the passage.

Q24.3: C - Can't Tell

Explanation: We are told that the Luftwaffe carried out unremitting air raids on Britain 'from July through September 1940'. However, we are not informed of the exact date in July on which these air raids started or the exact date in September on which they finished. We cannot be certain that the air raids lasted for three **entire** months.

Q24.4: B - a feeling of isolation in Britain.

Explanation: The passage asserts that the collapse of the French government left the British 'alone'. It quotes Winston Churchill, whose words emphasise the fact that Britain was left alone to face the enemy after the collapse of France's government. This statement is, therefore, correct.

- **A: a series of attacks on the country by Germany.** While we are told that the French government collapsed on 16th June 1940, we are not informed whether Germany attacked the country following this. In fact, we are told that the collapse of France's government led to the empowerment of a new regime that sought peace, which implies that there was no further fighting. We thus cannot be certain that this statement is true.
- **C: the removal of British troops from the country.** We are told that British forces were withdrawn from Europe between late May and early June 1940 and that the French government collapsed on 16th June 1940. Hence, British troops had already been removed from France when its government collapsed. This statement is, therefore, incorrect.
- **D: the end of the Second World War.** The passage infers that the Battle of Britain led to the end of the Second World War. It does not state that the collapse of France's government triggered it. This statement is, therefore, incorrect.

Answer 25

Q25.1: D - India is in talks with America to launch another spacecraft.

Explanation: While the passage states that India 'plans to send its first manned spaceflight by 2022' and that 'the U.S. is working to send a manned spacecraft to the moon's south pole by 2024', it does not confirm that the two countries are discussing a collaboration. This statement cannot be corroborated by the information within the passage.

- **A: India plans to continue to explore space.** The passage affirms that India intends to send a manned spaceflight by 2022. This suggests that it plans to continue to explore space.
- **B: India is destined to be one of the few countries that has explored the moon.** The passage claims that, if Chandrayaan is successful in landing on the lunar south pole in September, India would be the fourth country to achieve the soft landing on the moon (after the U.S., Russia and China). This statement is thus supported by the information in the passage.
- **C: Explorations must be designed and scheduled in advance.** The passage infers that India is now planning to send a spaceflight by 2022 and that the U.S. is working to send a spacecraft by 2024, which suggests that explorations need to be planned in advance. This statement is, therefore, true.

Q25.2: B - India has previously been successful in launching a spacecraft.

Explanation: The passage states that 'India's first moon mission orbited the moon in 2008'. This confirms that India has successfully launched a spacecraft in the past.

- **A: The United Kingdom has sent a rocket to space.** While the passage mentions the U.S., Russia, China and, of course, India, it does not inform us that the UK has sent a rocket to space. This statement cannot be corroborated by the information in the passage.
- **C: India received financial support from other counties for this mission.** The passage does not confirm if this is true or false. We cannot be certain that this is true.
- **D: If this mission is successful, India will become recognised for its work in this field.** The passage does not corroborate this. It could be that India is already recognised for its work in this field. Since the passage does not provide sufficient information to suggest that this statement is true, we cannot select it as the correct answer.

Answer 25 (Continued)

Q25.3: B - Water can be found on the moon.

Explanation: The passage claims that, after it lands on the moon, Chandrayaan will send a rover to explore water deposits 'confirmed by a previous mission that orbited the moon'. The passage also asserts that India's first moon mission in 2008 'helped confirm the presence of water'. The information within the passage therefore confirms that water can be found on the moon; this statement is **always** true.

- **A: The technologies that are required for space exploration are expensive.** While you might know that this is true, the passage does not mention the cost of such technologies. It is important that you answer the questions with the information you are given alone. This sentence cannot be corroborated by the information provided within the passage.
- **C: The Apollo 11 mission was launched within the last decade.** The passage states that India's recent launch 'coincided with the 50th anniversary of the Apollo 11 mission'. This confirms that the Apollo 11 mission was not launched within the last decade, and this statement is thus false.
- **D: The name of India's latest spacecraft derives from an unofficial language of the country.** We are informed that the spacecraft is named Chandrayaan, which is the Sanskrit word for "moon craft". Since Sanskrit is an official language of India, this statement is false.

Q25.4: C - it will provide new knowledge about the moon.

Explanation: We are told that Chandrayaan will 'send a rover to explore water deposits'. This infers that the mission will hopefully provide new knowledge about the moon, and this statement is thus correct.

- **A: it now has the tools needed to develop comprehensive data in the field.** The passage does not confirm if this is true or false. Since the passage does not provide sufficient information to suggest that this statement is true, we cannot select it as the correct answer.
- **B: it wants to be recognised for its scientific research.** The passage does not corroborate this. It could be that India is already recognised for its scientific research. It is also important to note that this statement does not refer to a specific scientific field in which India might want to be recognised. Since the passage does not provide sufficient information to suggest that this statement is true, we cannot select it as the correct answer.

Answer 25 (Continued)

- **D: no technical issues were encountered on this occasion.** The first sentence of the passage states that India successfully launched an unmanned spacecraft on Monday, 'a week after aborting the mission because of a technical problem'. The fact that it says '**the** mission' suggests that the initial unsuccessful launch and the subsequent successful launch are both considered part of the same mission. Since the question refers to '**this** mission', this statement is thus false; this mission did encounter technical issues at first.

Answer 26

Q26.1: C - Can't Tell

Explanation: While the passage discusses the fact that children in America consume sugary beverages, it does not specify if other individuals also consume sugary drinks. We can, of course, assume that children are not the only consumers of sugary drinks. However, we must remember that the question should be answered **only** with the information we are given in the passage. Since the passage makes reference to children alone, we cannot tell if this statement is true or false.

Q26.2: C - warning children of the detrimental effects of sugary drinks.

Explanation: The second paragraph notes that the American Academy of Pediatrics and the American Heart Association intend to highlight the consequences of sugary drinks on a child's health by potentially adding labels to packaging. Such labels will detail the 'health consequences of consuming sugary drinks'. This confirms that this statement is correct.

- **A: single-handedly developing strategies to discourage children from consuming sugary beverages.** This is not supported by the information within the passage since the author notes that the American Academy of Pediatrics and the American Heart Association are working in collaboration to develop such strategies.
- **B: gaining the support of the American Heart Association.** According to the information that we are provided, the American Academy of Pediatrics has not gained the support of the American Heart Association. Rather, they are working in collaboration. This statement cannot be confirmed by the information within the passage.

Answer 26 (Continued)

- **D: aiming more adverts at adults.** The passage does not discuss an intention to address adverts for sugary drinks towards adults. This statement is, therefore, not supported by the information in the passage.

Q26.3: A - Every child in America consumes in excess of 30 gallons of sugary drinks annually.

Explanation: This is false as the passage states that 'the **average** American child consumes more than 30 gallons of sugary beverages each year'. It does not state that **every** child in America consumes 30 gallons of sugary beverages each year, and this statement is thus not true.

- **B: The AAP and AHA are working collectively to reduce the over-consumption of sugary drinks.** The passage highlights this very early on by stating how the effects of sugary drinks have prompted this collaboration. This statement is, therefore, true.
- **C: Children are encouraged to select healthier alternatives at food outlets.** The second paragraph asserts that one of the initiatives developed by the American Academy of Pediatrics and the American Heart Association is to offer water as a 'default beverage on children's menus'. This statement can thus be considered as true.
- **D: As part of this initiative, the price of sugary drinks will be increased.** The second paragraph of the passage notes that one of the recommendations proposed by the American Academy of Pediatrics and the American Heart Association is to tax sugary drinks. This would increase their cost, and this statement is thus true.

Q26.4: B - Children throughout America are addicted to sugary drinks.

Explanation: The author discusses the 'average American child', which implies that reference is made to children throughout the country and not in specific areas. In addition, the passage notes the need to 'curb children's thirst for sweet drinks'. The use of the generic term 'children' infers that the passage is not speaking of certain areas within the country.

- **A: Parents will need the support of the government to stop their children consuming sugary beverages.** This cannot be ascertained from the information within the passage. In fact, the author states that 'parents don't need to wait around for the government to act'. The passage therefore urges parents to act independently, and this statement is untrue.

Answer 26 (Continued)

- **C: Children should choose water over soda.** While one of the initiatives developed by the American Academy of Pediatrics and the American Heart Association is to offer water as a 'default beverage on children's menus', the passage does not state that water **should** be selected.
- **D: Fruit-flavoured water also contains a significant amount of sugar.** In the first sentence of the passage, the author names 'fruit-flavoured refreshments' amongst sugary drinks. However, he/she does not specifically speak of fruit-flavoured **water**. In addition, the author does not provide detailed information on the amount of sugar contained in different types of drinks. Therefore, we cannot be certain if this assertion is true.

Answer 27

Q27.1: C - The same bullet that hit President Kennedy hit a man who was travelling in the same car.

Explanation: The initial paragraph details the journey of the bullet. It states that, having passed through the neck and throat of the President, the bullet went on to hit Governor Connally in three places. We know that Governor Connally is a man; if this person were a woman, the salutation would be 'Governess'. This statement can thus be confirmed using the information specified in the passage.

- **A: The same bullet that hit President Kennedy hit a woman who was travelling in the same car.** The first paragraph tells us that the bullet passed through the neck and throat of the President and went on to hit Governor Connally in three places. We know that Governor Connally is a man; if this person were a woman, the salutation would be 'Governess'. In addition, we are not informed that the same bullet hit a third individual. This statement therefore cannot be corroborated by the information within the passage.
- **B: Parkland Memorial Hospital was located a few metres from the place in which the bullet was fired.** Whilst the passage advises that the motorcade reached the **nearby** Parkland Memorial Hospital quickly, it does not explicitly state that the hospital was only a few metres away.

Answer 27 (Continued)

- **D: Connally was left with life-changing injuries.** The passage only states that Connally survived; it does not detail the injuries that he suffered. As such, this statement cannot be corroborated by the information within the passage.

Q27.2: D - President Kennedy was not pronounced dead until 1300 hours.

Explanation: The second paragraph states that Kennedy was shot at around 1230 hours and was rushed to Parkland Memorial Hospital. It claims that the efforts of the doctors were futile, and he was 'officially declared dead' at 1300 hours. This statement is, therefore, true.

- **A: President Kennedy was officially pronounced dead at the scene.** This is not true. The passage states that Kennedy was shot at around 1230 hours and was rushed to Parkland Memorial Hospital. It claims that the efforts of the doctors were futile, and he was 'officially declared dead' at 1300 hours. Hence, he was not pronounced dead at the scene.
- **B: President Kennedy was not proclaimed dead by doctors at the hospital.** The second paragraph confirms that Kennedy was pronounced dead at the hospital. We can therefore assume that the doctors at the hospital were the ones who formally confirmed his death, and this statement is not true.
- **C: At 1300 hours, it was officially announced that President Kennedy had died.** Based on the information within the passage, we can assume that this is not true. We are told that the President was declared dead at 1300 hours, and we can assume that it would have been unlikely that his death was **officially announced** the moment he died.

Q27.3: B - were the same as those of another president who had been murdered.

Explanation: The final paragraph of the passage notes that the protocols for the funeral of 'another assassinated president' were followed for Kennedy's funeral. This statement is, therefore, corroborated by the information within the passage.

Answer 27 (Continued)

- **A: were similar to those of another president who had been murdered.** The final paragraph of the passage notes that the protocols for the funeral of 'another assassinated president' were **followed** for Kennedy's funeral. This statement is thus incorrect; the protocols for Kennedy's funeral were **the same** as those of another murdered president and not merely **similar**.
- **C: were distinctly comparable to those of another president who had been murdered.** The final paragraph of the passage notes that the protocols for the funeral of 'another assassinated president' were **followed** for Kennedy's funeral. This statement is thus incorrect; the protocols for Kennedy's funeral were **the same** as those of another murdered president and not merely **comparable**.
- **D: were the same as those of another president who had not been murdered.** The final paragraph of the passage notes that the protocols for the funeral of 'another **assassinated** president' were followed for Kennedy's funeral. This statement is, therefore, false.

Q27.4: B - seen by thousands of people.

Explanation: The passage notes that 250,000 people visited Kennedy's body while it lay in state at the Rotunda. This statement can, therefore, be corroborated by the information within the passage.

- **A: visited by thousands of mourners.** Although thousands of people visited Kennedy's body, we are not told that they were all mourners. Many people might have visited out of respect or curiosity; they might not have necessarily been mourning the death of the President. This statement cannot be verified by the information in the passage.
- **C: observed by thousands of Americans.** While we might assume that this is true, the passage does not confirm the number of Americans who visited Kennedy's body. As such, this statement cannot be corroborated by the information within the passage.
- **D: visited by thousands of Europeans.** Similarly to the above explanation, the passage does not confirm who visited Kennedy's body. As such, this statement cannot be verified by the information within the passage.

Answer 28

Q28.1: A - Lincoln had initially been trained to enter a career in the legal profession.

Explanation: The passage advises that Lincoln was a 'self-taught lawyer', but it does not state that he formally qualified as a lawyer. It also does not confirm that he had been trained. In addition, the passage does not indicate that he practiced as a lawyer. As such, this statement cannot be supported by the information within the passage.

- **B: Lincoln is generally recognised as the primary individual responsible for emancipation of enslavement.** The author notes that Lincoln's Emancipation Proclamation ultimately led to the abolition of slavery. This statement can, therefore, be supported by the information in the passage.
- **C: The country appeared to lament the events incurred at the end of Lincoln's presidency.** The passage supports this statement. It describes that Lincoln's body was taken through a large number of cities and states of America to enable mourners to pay homage to the fallen president.
- **D: The credence that Lincoln would endure the challenge on his life initially appeared credible.** This can be supported by the information in the passage as the author details how, having been carried from the theatre, Lincoln did not die until the next day. The fact that the passage states 'but he never regained consciousness' implies that it was initially thought he might survive.

Q28.2: C - Can't Tell

Explanation: Although the passage notes that Lincoln's death made him a 'martyr to the cause of liberty', the author does not detail the beliefs of the Confederates. We are not told if they were for or against emancipation and, as such, we cannot be certain if this statement is true or false.

Q28.3: D - Lincoln is still considered a distinguished and noteworthy individual in the American constitution.

Explanation: This can be concluded from the passage as the author notes that Lincoln is 'regarded as one of the greatest presidents in U.S. history'. As a president directly relates to political activities and the constitution or establishment, this statement can be supported by the information we are provided.

Answer 28 (Continued)

The passage also notes that Lincoln is recognised on President's Day, which emphasises the esteem in which he is held.

- **A: The assassination attempt resulted in Lincoln being regarded as a martyr.** This is not a conclusion that can be supported by the information provided. There was not an assassination attempt. Lincoln was killed and, as such, the assassination was carried out.
- **B: Lincoln served for only one term as president.** This cannot be confirmed by the information in the passage. While we are told that he was elected in 1860 and was killed in 1865, we are not informed if he was re-elected in that time or if he underwent a continuous period in office.
- **C: Lincoln is widely recognised and acknowledged for his contribution to worldwide freedom.** The passage states that he was acknowledged for his contribution to the 'cause of liberty'. However, it does not confirm if this was solely within America or throughout the world. This statement thus cannot be corroborated by the information within the passage.

Q28.4: A - Lincoln is considered to be a president of utmost significance.

Explanation: This can be concluded from the passage. The first paragraph notes that Lincoln is deemed one of the greatest presidents in the history of America. Furthermore, the passage advises that he is honoured on President's Day.

- **B: Lincoln modified his policy on slavery for reasons of political advantage.** Whilst the passage does describe his change in policy, it does not indicate that it was solely for political gain. This statement cannot be supported by the information within the passage.
- **C: The legislation to eradicate slavery was passed as a result of the assassination.** The author details how the amendment that brought in the prohibition of slavery was introduced by Lincoln. While it notes that the legislation was passed after his death, it does not suggest that his death facilitated the passing of the law.
- **D: Lincoln was born on the same day as George Washington.** The passage does not confirm that they were born on the very same day. We might infer from the final paragraph that the two individuals shared the same birthday, but we cannot be certain that they were both

Answer 28 (Continued)

born on the same day in the same year. This statement cannot be verified by the information within the passage.

Answer 29

Q29.1: D - One of Da Vinci's works is housed in the chapel of a monastery.

Explanation: The passage makes reference to one of Da Vinci's works that is housed in the refectory (or dining room) of the Monastery of Santa Maria delle Grazie in Milan. It is not housed in the monastery's chapel. This statement is, therefore, false.

- **A: Vinci is a town in Italy.** The passage mentions 'the Tuscan town of Vinci'. This statement can thus be corroborated by the information in the passage.
- **B: A number of Da Vinci's works are still in existence.** The author notes this in the third paragraph of the passage. It is stated that the fame of Da Vinci's surviving paintings has led him to be primarily considered as an artist.
- **C: Da Vinci was an anatomist.** The final paragraph of the passage details that Da Vinci's paintings were 'based on a deep understanding of the workings of the human body'. As such, it can be inferred from the information within the passage that he was also an anatomist.

Q29.2: C - Can't Tell

Explanation: The passage notes that Da Vinci was 'the illegitimate son of a local lawyer'. However, it does not state whether Da Vinci was aware of his parentage during his lifetime or, indeed, if the lawyer really was his father. Based on the information within the passage, we cannot be certain if he was aware of who his father was.

Q29.3: A - Da Vinci lived in Florence.

Explanation: Although Da Vinci was an apprentice to Andrea del Verrocchio in Florence, the author does not state that he ever lived in that city. After all, he might have lived elsewhere and travelled to Florence. As such, this statement cannot be corroborated from the details within the passage.

Answer 29 (Continued)

- **B: Da Vinci was an intellectual.** This is validated by the information within the passage since the author details a wide range of subjects that Da Vinci studied. A variety of fields are noted, including anatomy, engineering, science and geology. This statement can thus be considered as true.
- **C: Da Vinci created at least one mural.** Based on the information that we are given, we can be certain that this is true: the passage makes reference to the mural of 'The Last Supper'.
- **D: Da Vinci was born in Italy.** The second paragraph of the passage states that Da Vinci was born 'near the Tuscan town of Vinci'. This statement is thus true.

Q29.4: C - and created 'The Last Supper'.

Explanation: The second paragraph states that Da Vinci moved to Milan to work for the Sforza family. Hence, we can deduce that the reason for which he relocated to Milan was to work for them. The passage goes on to assert that Da Vinci produced a mural of 'The Last Supper' in the refectory of a Milanese monastery. The purpose of his relocation was not to create the mural. Rather, he ended up creating the mural while he was in Milan. This statement can, therefore, be considered as true.

- **A: to create the Last Supper.** The author does not suggest that Da Vinci moved to Milan specifically to create this mural. The second paragraph states that Da Vinci moved to Milan to work for the Sforza family. Hence, we can deduce that the reason for which he relocated to Milan was to work for them. As such, this statement cannot be confirmed as true.
- **B: to work for an impoverished family.** The passage notes that Da Vinci began to work for the 'ruling Sforza family'. The fact that the author calls the family 'ruling' suggests that they were not impoverished.
- **D: because his work in Florence had come to an end.** We might assume that this is true, but it cannot be confirmed by the information within the passage. The author does not explicitly state that his work in Florence had come to an end.

Answer 30

Q30.1: C - The creatures may find suitable habitat in most of the seafloor.

Explanation: The passage asserts that the creatures 'can find potentially suitable habitat across at least 99% of the global seafloor'. Hence, this statement can be corroborated by the information within the passage.

- **A: The creatures inhabit all of the world's seafloor.** The passage does not state that the creatures inhabit **all** of the world's seafloor. Rather, it affirms that the creatures **can potentially find** habitat across approximately 99% of the world's seafloor. This statement is, therefore, incorrect.
- **B: The creature is named after a Disney character.** The passage asserts that the name of the creature is associated with the fact that it has prominent ear-like fins. We are told that these ear-like fins cause the creature to resemble the Walt Disney cartoon character Dumbo, but the passage does not imply that the creature is named after this character. This statement is, therefore, false.
- **D: The creatures will become extinct if they are not protected.** The passage does not discuss this issue, and we cannot be certain if this statement is true or false. We are not provided with any information to determine if this is correct.

Q30.2: C - Previous discoveries placed the species at over 500m higher.

Explanation: The passage informs us that the previous deepest sighting was at 5,145m, whilst the recent sightings were at 5,760m and 6,957m. Hence, previous discoveries placed the species at over 500m higher than the recent discoveries. This statement can be confirmed as true.

- **A: The giant fins assist in helping the creature to hide.** This cannot be confirmed as true from the information with which we are provided. The passage does not offer any information to support the significance of the creature's fins.
- **B: The octopus were found almost 1,000m apart.** The passage notes that one creature was found at 6,957m and another was found at 5,760m. This is **more than** 1,000m apart and not **almost** 1,000m apart. This statement is thus false.
- **D: Previous discoveries were found on each ocean floor.** We are not told where the previous discoveries took place. The passage confirms that the recent research found the creatures in the Indian Ocean, and it asserts that these observations highlight that octopuses can

Answer 30 (Continued)

find suitable habitat across at least 99% of the global seafloor. However, we are not certain where the creature has previously been sighted.

Q30.3: D - The recent discovery was not reported in an outlet that deals with this specific field.

Explanation: The second paragraph asserts that the discovery has been reported in the journal *Marine Biology*. From the title of the journal, we can deduce that it deals with this field (marine biology). This statement is thus false.

- **A: The previous discoveries have located traces of the octopus in other locations.** The fourth paragraph informs us that the creature has recently been sighted at 5,760m and at 6,957m. It continues that the previous deepest reliable sighting was at 5,145m. Hence, the previous discovery located the octopus at a different depth. This statement is, therefore, true.
- **B: Similar equipment has not been used for previous research.** This statement can be considered true. We are told that Dr Alan Jamieson has 'pioneered the exploration of the deep using what are called "landers"'. This implies that Dr Jamieson developed this equipment and first used it in his recent discovery.
- **C: The recent discovery has proved insightful for researchers in this field.** The passage discusses the 'significance' of these observations since they have highlighted that octopuses can find habitat across at least 99% of the global seafloor. This statement can thus be considered true.

Q30.4: A - True

Explanation: The penultimate paragraph states that the creatures that live at depth will need special adaptations. Since it has been confirmed that this particular creature can live at depth, it is assumed that its composition would have adjusted in order to enable it to survive. This statement can thus be considered true.

Answer 31

Q31.1: A - True

Explanation: The first paragraph states that Labour plans to plant a quarter of a million trees every day. That the author advises that this is 'not necessarily unrealistic' confirms that this statement is true.

Q31.2: A - can fluctuate to a potential maximum of 2,500.

Explanation: The third paragraph explains that the density at which trees are planted will determine the number of trees that can be planted. It states that 'between 1,000 and 2,500 [trees] per hectare' can be planted. As such, this statement is correct.

- **B: can be predicted precisely with minimum error.** The passage delineates the difficulties in assessing how many trees are in a particular area. Indeed, paragraph three asserts that 'it's difficult to say precisely'. This statement is thus incorrect.
- **C: can be considered with some precision.** The third paragraph stresses that the number of trees planted can only be estimated. The passage does not confirm that the number of trees in a hectare can be measured with **any** degree of precision, and this statement is thus incorrect.
- **D: can surge to suit the pledges of certain constitutional factions.** The number of trees planted does vary according to the promises of various political parties. However, the passage maintains that trees can be planted at a density of between 1,000 and 2,500 per hectare. Therefore, regardless of the number of trees that a political party pledges to plant, the number of trees per hectare cannot exceed 2,500. This statement is, therefore, not corroborated by the information within the passage.

Q31.3: C - If the Liberal Democrats and the SNP combined their efforts, they would agree to plant four times as many trees as the Conservatives.

Explanation: The passage does not contradict this statement. The total number of trees planted by the Liberal Democrats and the SNP collectively would equate to 120 million. The Conservatives would plant 30 million trees, which is one quarter of 120 million.

- **A: Only experts can plant trees.** The passage does not imply that **only** experts can plant trees. It simply indicates that experts can plant

Answer 31 (Continued)

trees **quickly**. As such, this statement cannot be corroborated by the information within the passage.

- **B: By 2040, the Green Party would have planted half as many trees as the Labour Party.** The passage asserts that Labour plans to have planted two billion trees by 2040.It claims that the Green Party would have planted 700 million trees by 2030, but it does not detail how many trees the Green Party plans to plant between 2030 and 2040. As such, we cannot be certain if the Green Party would have planted half as many trees as the Labour Party by 2040.
- **D: Labour's plan to plant trees is preposterous.** The passage does not suggest that Labour's plan is absurd. The first paragraph states that 'it's not necessarily unrealistic', whilst the final paragraph asserts that 'it could be done'. As such, this statement is contradicted by the information within the passage.

Q31.4: D - A total of 50 million trees could be planted in an area of 30,000 hectares.

Explanation: The passage states that an estimated 50 million trees could be planted in an area of 30,000 hectares. While the author maintains that this is an estimate, he/she implies that it is possible to plant 50 million trees in 30,000 hectares. This statement can therefore be considered as always true.

- **A: There are more than 1,000 trees per hectare.** The keyword in this question is 'always'. While more than 1,000 trees can be planted in a hectare, there are not **always** more than 1,000 trees in a hectare. The passage indicates that the number of trees per hectare is dependent on the density at which they are planted. Hence, this statement is not **always** true.
- **B: An area of 30,000 hectares will accommodate a maximum of 50 million trees.** This cannot be considered as true. The passage states that 2,500 trees can be planted in one hectare. This means that up to75 million trees could be accommodated in an area of 30,000 hectares (30,000 multiplied by 2,500).
- **C: There are less than 2,500 trees per hectare.** The keyword in this question is 'always'. While less than 2,500 trees can be planted in a hectare, there are not **always** less than 2,500 trees in a hectare. Indeed, 2,500 trees can be planted in a hectare. Hence, this statement is not **always** true.

Answer 32

Q32.1: A - the predecessor of Harold Wilson.

Explanation: The second paragraph of the passage explains how, following the sudden death of Hugh Gaitskell, Harold Wilson successfully won the contest to become leader of the Labour Party. This statement is, therefore, correct.

- **B: the leader of the Labour Party in 1964.** Based on the information with which we are provided, we cannot confirm if this is true. The passage does not state when Gaitskell died, and it is not possible to deduce whether he was the leader of the Labour Party in 1964.While we are told that Wilson won his first election victory in October 1964, we do not know for how long before this he was leading the party or whether Gaitskell was also the leader of the party in the same year.
- **C: to become Britain's most popular prime minister.** There is nothing within the passage to confirm or deny this statement.
- **D: the youngest member of the government in the twentieth century.** The passage states that **Wilson** was the youngest member of the Cabinet in the 20th century. Hence, this statement cannot be corroborated by the information within the passage.

Q32.2: B - Clement Attlee enabled Harold Wilson to enter politics.

Explanation: This statement is not correct. While Attlee made Wilson President of the Board of Trade in 1947, Wilson had already entered politics when he was elected as MP for Ormskirk in 1945. Attlee enabled Wilson to enter the Cabinet, but Wilson was already involved in politics at this time.

- **A: Harold Wilson was no longer a teenager when he entered parliament.** We can infer from the first paragraph of the passage that Wilson was around 29 years of age when he became MP for Ormskirk in 1945 (the passage explicitly states that he was 31 years old in 1947).This statement is, therefore, correct. Wilson was 29 years of age when he became a member of parliament; he was no longer a teenager.
- **C: Harold Wilson's popularity soared in 70 weeks.** This can be corroborated by the final paragraph of the passage. We are told that Wilson's first election victory on 15th October 1964 saw him win with a small majority of four, but this increased significantly to 98 after a second General Election on 31st March 1966. His popularity soared between these two dates. There are 70 weeks and two days between 15th October 1964 and 31st March 1966, and this statement is thus true.

Answer 32 (Continued)

- **D: Hugh Gaitskell's death was unexpected.** This can be inferred from the second paragraph of the passage, which notes that Gaitskell 'passed away **suddenly**'.

Q32.3: A - True

Explanation: The final paragraph of the passage confirms that this is true. Here, the author details the support that Wilson's government gave to a variety of laws, which had a direct impact on common topics.

Q32.4: C - Can't Tell

Explanation: Based on the information within the passage, it is not possible to confirm whether this is true or false. The only mention of James Callaghan is that he fought Wilson for leadership of the Labour Party; the passage does not advise that he became prime minister. While you might know that James Callaghan did become the Prime Minister of the Britain, you must answer the question only with the information you are given in the passage. The correct answer, on this occasion, is 'can't tell'.

Answer 33

Q33.1: B - EDoN is led by Alzheimer's Research UK.

Explanation: The first paragraph of the passage states that EDoN is 'being spearheaded' by Alzheimer's Research UK. This statement is, therefore, corroborated by the information within the passage.

- **A: Alzheimer's Research UK is not associated with the EDoN project.** Since the first paragraph of the passage states that EDoN is 'being spearheaded' by Alzheimer's Research UK, we know that Alzheimer's Research UK is associated with the project. This statement is thus incorrect.
- **C: Alzheimer's Research UK is involved in EDoN.** This statement suggests that Alzheimer's Research UK is simply a participant in the research. However, the first paragraph of the passage states that EDoN is 'being spearheaded' by Alzheimer's Research UK. The charity assumes a leading role in the project and, as such, the word 'involved' is not correct.

Answer 33 (Continued)

- **D: EDoN is supported by Alzheimer's Research UK**. This statement infers that Alzheimer's Research UK is merely offering assistance to EDoN in some form. However, we know what Alzheimer's Research UK is 'spearheading' this project. The words 'supported by' are not correct here.

Q33.2: D - will provide researchers with a greater understanding of the disease.

Explanation: The passage states that the device will help to detect early signs of Alzheimer's and assist researchers to identify signs of the disease before symptoms start to develop. This statement can, therefore, be verified by the information within the passage.

- **A: will be ready for dissemination within three years.** The first paragraph of the passage states that a prototype should be available within three years. It does not state that the device will be ready for distribution within three years.
- **B: will examine the data that it stores.** It is true that the device will collect and store data, but this data will then be analysed by researchers. As such, the device will not examine the data that it stores, and this statement is false.
- **C: will allow Alzheimer's to be detected, provided that the individual has undiscoverable symptoms.** We cannot confirm that this statement is true. The passage indicates that the device will help researchers to 'map signs of the disease years before symptoms develop'. The device will thus assist in the detection of Alzheimer's before symptoms have **developed**. The passage does not draw an association between the device and symptoms that have not been or cannot be **discovered**.

Q33.3: D - the early detection of Alzheimer's will offer an enhanced understanding of the disease.

Explanation: The passage claims that the project aims to produce a wearable device which will detect early signs of Alzheimer's. It maintains that such a device will enable researchers to map signs of the disease before symptoms start to develop. This statement can thus be considered as true; the passage infers that the project will provide a greater understanding of the disease even before symptoms start to appear.

Answer 33 (Continued)

- **A: the number of people affected by dementia is rising.** Whilst the passage does confirm that this is true, it does not suggest that it is the reason for the launch of the project. The aim of the project is to assist those who might develop Alzheimer's.
- **B: the Alan Turing Institute possesses data.** While the second paragraph states that EDoN will work with the Alan Turing Institute to analyse data, there is no indication that the project has been launched **because** the Institute possesses data.
- **C: Alzheimer's Research UK has pledged to support those who have the disease.** The passage describes how the project aims to detect the disease, but it does not suggest that the reason for the project is to enable Alzheimer's Research UK to support those with the disease.

Q33.4: B - True

Explanation: The final paragraph details how, by 2050, the number of people diagnosed with Alzheimer's is expected to increase to 152 million. The number of people with Alzheimer's is thus not expected to decrease, and this statement is true.

Answer 34

Q34.1: B - Alice is the protagonist.

Explanation: This statement is true since the entire passage details Alice's experiences.

- **A: Alice is a young girl.** You might be familiar with Lewis Carroll's *Alice's Adventures in Wonderland*, and you might therefore be aware that Alice is a young girl. However, the passage does not state that she is young. There is no mention of her age, and this statement cannot be corroborated by the information within the passage.
- **C: Alice is the Rabbit's companion.** We cannot deem this to be true. The passage intimates that Alice had not met the Rabbit before and that she follows him out of curiosity rather than companionship.
- **D: Alice is the narrator.** The passage tells the story of Alice and describes what is happening in the third person. If Alice were the narrator,

Answer 34 (Continued)

the passage would have been written in the first person (with the use of 'I' instead of 'Alice').

Q34.2: C - The Rabbit was worried that it would be late.

Explanation: This statement can be considered true since the Rabbit rushes past Alice and states 'Oh dear! Oh dear! I shall be late!' We can thus infer that the Rabbit was concerned that it would be late.

- **A: The Rabbit was late.** The Rabbit says 'I **shall be** late'; it does not say that it was **already** late. This statement cannot be corroborated by the information within the passage.
- **B: The Rabbit is male.** Although we might assume that the Rabbit is male, particularly as he wears a waistcoat, the passage does not validate this.
- **D: The Rabbit ambled past Alice**. The first paragraph states that the Rabbit 'ran close by' Alice, whilst the second paragraph asserts that it 'hurried on'. This statement is, therefore, not true.

Q34.3: B - False

Explanation: The passage states that the Rabbit 'took a watch out of its waistcoat-pocket', which indicates that it was not wearing a watch. This statement is, therefore, false.

Q34.4: C - the Rabbit spoke to itself.

Explanation: The second paragraph explains that, when Alice thought afterwards, she realised that she should have been surprised that the Rabbit said to itself 'Oh dear! Oh dear! I shall be late!' We are told that, at the time, it seemed 'quite natural'. This statement is, therefore, true.

- **A: the Rabbit possessed a watch.** We are informed that, when the Rabbit took a watch out of its waistcoat-pocket, Alice started to her feet. This implies that the fact that the Rabbit possessed a watch made Alice curious to follow it. We can, therefore, deduce that she **did** find it strange that the Rabbit possessed a watch, and this statement is thus not true.
- **B: the Rabbit checked its watch.** We are informed that, when the Rabbit took a watch out of its waistcoat-pocket and looked at it, Alice started to her feet. This suggests that the fact that the Rabbit checked its

Answer 34 (Continued)

watch made her curious to follow it. We can thus assume that she **did** find it strange that the Rabbit checked its watch, and this statement is false.

- **D: the Rabbit ran past her.** The passage states that 'there was nothing so very remarkable' in the fact that the Rabbit ran close by her, which indicates that Alice did not find it strange that the Rabbit ran past her. However, we are not informed that she later realised this was strange. While she does find the fact that the Rabbit said to itself 'Oh dear! Oh dear! I shall be late!' strange at a later moment, we are not told that she considers the fact that the Rabbit ran past her strange at all. This statement is, therefore, not corroborated by the information in the passage.

Answer 35

Q35.1: B - False

Explanation: This statement is false as Prince Albert was the consort of Queen Victoria. As he was married to the Queen, he was termed her consort or companion.

Q35.2: B - took place within 22 years of Albert's birth.

Explanation: Although Albert's age is not made explicit, we can deduce that he had married before he reached the age of 22 years. The passage states that he was born in 1819 and married in 1840.

- **A: was frowned upon because they were related.** We are told that Albert and Victoria were related and that there was some dissent towards the marriage. However, the passage does not imply that the disapproval was due to the fact that they were related. We therefore cannot be certain that this statement is true.
- **C: took place in England.** The passage does not provide any information of the location of the ceremony, and we cannot confirm that this statement is true.
- **D: destroyed Victoria's relationship with parliament.** The passage notes that the marriage between Victoria and Albert caused some tensions with parliament members. However, it does not indicate that Victoria's relationship with parliament was completely destroyed.

Answer 35 (Continued)

Q35.3: D - Albert could speak more than one language.

Explanation: Albert was born in Bavaria and educated in Germany; his native language would have been German. He was married to the Queen of England, and it is therefore presumed that he would have spoken English. This statement can easily be true.

- **A: Lord Melbourne was Queen Victoria's father.** Although the passage suggests that Lord Melbourne held a 'strong paternal influence over Victoria', he was not her biological father. The passage does not, in any way, suggest this.
- **B: Albert did not enjoy the fact that he was in the public eye.** This is not hinted by the information within the passage. Following the death of Lord Melbourne, Albert took on a prominent role as advisor to the Queen. This would have presumably involved considerable public attention, but we are not told whether he enjoyed it or not.
- **C: Albert officially became a prince at the age of 38.** We cannot be certain of how viable this is. The passage does not detail the exact date upon which he was awarded the title of 'prince consort', and it is possible that it happened before his 38th birthday.

Q35.4: A - True

Explanation: This statement can be considered as true. The passage states that Albert encouraged his wife's interest in social welfare and was keen to discuss the matter of child labour.

Answer 36

Q36.1: B - The narrator did not know for certain that some of the individuals present were priests.

Explanation: The narrator states that 'there were several of his priests and lawyers present (as I conjectured by their habits)'. He/She was not certain that these individuals were priests since he/she 'conjectures'; he/she guessed that they were priests due to their mannerisms. This statement can, therefore, be supported by the information within the passage.

Answer 36 (Continued)

- **A: The man to whom the narrator refers was foreign.** The passage does confirm that the man had an 'Austrian lip', but it is not clearly stated that he was Austrian or of Austrian descent. Having said this, we do not know where this passage is set, and we cannot define what the term 'foreign' means in this context. The passage might be set in Austria, which would mean that this man was not 'foreign'. Hence, this statement cannot be supported by the information within the passage.
- **C: The man to whom the narrator refers was the descendant of a rich family.** The passage notes that the man wore a 'helmet of gold, adorned with jewels' and that the hilt and scabbard of his sword were made of gold and enriched with diamonds. This might suggest that he was rich, but it does not confirm that he was a **descendant** of a rich family. This statement cannot be corroborated by the information within the passage.
- **D: The narrator is a woman.** The passage does not contain any details that suggest that the narrator is a man or a woman. As such, this statement cannot be confirmed as true.

Q36.2: B - False

Explanation: The narrator describes the man's complexion as 'olive'. This indicates that the man did not have a fair complexion, and this statement is false.

Q36.3: A - was not fluent in several languages.

Explanation: This can be confirmed from the information towards the end of the passage. The narrator attempted to speak to the priests and lawyers in many languages. However, these were languages of which he/she 'had a smattering'. This affirms that the narrator was not fluent in these languages; he/she only knew a little of each.

- **B: was dressed in fine clothes.** The passage does not provide any details of the clothes worn by the narrator; it describes only those worn by the individuals he/she describes. As such, we cannot be certain of the clothing that the narrator wore.
- **C: was humble.** The passage does not give any indication of the personality of the narrator. We cannot deduce if he/she was humble or not.

Answer 36 (Continued)

- **D: was besotted with the man to whom reference is made.** The information in the passage does not suggest that the narrator was in any way besotted with the man to whom reference is made. It seems that the narrator was intrigued by the man, but we cannot be certain that he/she was obsessed with him.

Q36.4: B - The man to whom the narrator refers became a prince after the age of twenty years.

Explanation: The passage explains that the man was twenty-eight years and three quarters and that he had happily reigned for about seven years. Firstly, we do not know if the man was a prince. The fact that he had 'reigned' does not necessarily confirm that he was a prince. Secondly, the passage states that the man had reigned 'in great felicity' for about seven years. It is possible that he had reigned under different (and not happy) circumstances before that. If that were true, he might have started to reign before the age of 20 years. Based on the information with which we are provided, this statement cannot be confirmed as true.

- **A: The man to whom the narrator refers wore clothes that were rooted in two different continents.** The passage describes the man's clothes as a mix between the Asiatic and the European styles. Hence, this statement can be corroborated by the information within the passage.
- **C: The priests and lawyers were unable to understand the narrator.** This can be confirmed as true. We are told that, even though the narrator attempted to address the priests and lawyers in as many languages of which he had at least a little knowledge, it was futile.
- **D: The man to whom the narrator refers spoke well.** This can be supported by the information within the passage since the narrator tells how the man's voice was 'very clear and articulate'.

Answer 37

Q37.1: B - One is not at any lesser risk by engaging in other day-to-day activities.

Explanation: This statement can be verified by the information in the final paragraph of the passage. It implies that an individual can be subjected to the same level, or even a higher level, of risk through eating pickled vegetables, using talcum powder, drinking alcohol, and eating processed meat. The passage does not suggest that individuals are at a lesser risk by engaging in other day-to -day activities.

- **A: Using mobile phones does not come without any risk.** Based on the information with which we are provided, we cannot be certain if this is true. The passage states that, while the WHO did say that "no adverse health effects have been established as being caused by mobile phone use", the WHO and IARC have classified all radio frequency radiation as "possibly carcinogenic". However, the passage does not explicitly confirm or disprove that the use of a mobile phone can pose a risk, and we cannot be certain that this statement is true.
- **C: The 5G network has been activated in cities throughout the UK.** The first paragraph states that the network has been switched on 'in **some** UK cities'. It does not confirm that the network has been activated in cities throughout the country, and this statement is thus not true.
- **D: Many people are anxious about the health effects of mobile phones.** The final paragraph asserts that '**some** people' are worried about increased health risks posed by the electromagnetic radiation used by mobile phone technologies. Since the words 'some' and 'many' are not synonymous, this statement cannot be supported by the information within the passage.

Q37.2: B - The use of mobile phones does not engender harmful health effects.

Explanation: The final paragraph notes the impacts of radiation used in mobile phone technology and, quoting the IARC, states that all radio frequency radiation is "possibly carcinogenic". Although the writer has noted that this is a minimal risk, the fact that he/she has included this comment shows that he/she is not entirely convinced that there is **no** risk. This statement can, therefore, be selected as the correct answer.

Answer 37 (Continued)

- **A: The 5G network might potentially have consequences on an individual's health.** The writer does not explicitly state that the 5G network cannot affect an individual's health. The passage discusses this exact issue, but it does not conclude that the 5G network is not harmful. Hence, this statement can be considered as a thought of the writer.
- **C: Electromagnetic radiation is constantly present.** This can be supported by the information within the passage. The writer states that 'we're surrounded by electromagnetic radiation all the time - from television and radio signals, as well as from a whole range of technologies, including mobile phones, and from natural sources such as sunlight'.
- **D: Certain individuals are concerned about the relationship between technology and their health.** The final paragraph asserts that 'the electromagnetic radiation used by all mobile phone technologies has led some people to worry about increased health risks'. This statement can, therefore, be considered as a thought of the writer.

Q37.3: B - False

Explanation: The first paragraph of the passage advises that the 5G network is available only in a limited number of cities in the UK at present. It does not state that it is available in villages. This statement is thus false.

Q37.4: C - Can't Tell

Explanation: The passage does not include any reference to the thoughts of the WHO on the 5G network. The final paragraph does state that the WHO spoke about the relationship between adverse health effects and mobile phone use, but it does not discuss the 5G network specifically. Hence, it is not possible to ascertain the opinions of the organisation. We cannot tell if this statement is true or false.

Answer 38

Q38.1: B - it quells negative thoughts.

Explanation: The first paragraph states that laughter 'alleviates the symptoms of depression and reduces stress and anxiety'. This reinforces the idea that laughter can allay negative thoughts. This statement is further supported by paragraph three, which highlights the therapeutic effects of laughter.

- **A: it is less expensive than joining a gym.** While we might assume that laughter is less expensive than joining a gym, the passage does not position this as the reason for which laughter is beneficial. The passage does note that laughter 'provides a workout that would normally require a gym membership', but it does not discuss the economic differences. This statement is, therefore, not correct.
- **C: it can be simulated**. The passage does explain that laughter can be simulated, but it does not suggest that such simulation is the reason for which laughter is beneficial. This statement is thus false.
- **D: it can cure diabetes**. The passage notes that laughter can reduce blood sugar levels and protect against some complications of diabetes. It does not, however, suggest that laughter can cure diabetes.

Q38.2: B - Simulated laughter has medicinal effects.

Explanation: The third paragraph of the passage states that studies have found that simulated laughter has therapeutic effects for depression and anxiety. As such, this statement can be confirmed as always true; research has proven that simulated laughter has medicinal effects.

- **A: Laughter eradicates depression.** While the passage notes that laughter alleviates the symptoms of depression, it does not state that laughter can eliminate depression. We cannot confirm that this statement is true.
- **C: Laughter relieves the symptoms of diabetes.** The passage states that laughter **can** reduce blood sugar levels and **can** protect against **some** complications of type 2 diabetes. Hence, this statement cannot be confirmed as **always** true.
- **D: Simulated laughter is sometimes created by the individual.** Since simulated laughter is 'voluntary or self-induced', it will **always** be created by the individual. This statement suggests that simulated laughter is **sometimes** created by the individual, which is incorrect.

Answer 38 (Continued)

Q38.3: C - Can't Tell

Explanation: We are unable to confirm if this is true or false from the information provided in the passage. The passage opens by stating that a 'laughter scientist' is called a 'gelotologist', but it does not give any indication of whether one requires a science degree to become a gelotologist.

Q38.4: A - True

Explanation: The first paragraph of the passage asserts 'you might be surprised to learn just how much of an impact laughter can have on health'. This implies that many people are unaware of the close connection between the two aspects, and this statement can thus be considered true.

Answer 39

Q39.1: B - Each of the three companies will be required to develop its own equipment.

Explanation: This can be verified by the information provided throughout the passage, but it can be specifically noted in the second paragraph, which states that each company will develop 'its own lunar landing'.

- **A: The three companies will be supported to develop a lunar lander.** There is nothing within the passage to suggest this. The emphasis is very much on how each company will develop a unique type of lunar lander itself.
- **C: The three companies will work collectively to build a lunar lander.** The passage informs us that each company will build its **own** lunar landing. This statement is, therefore, false.
- **D: Each of the three companies will launch its own rocket.** The passage asserts that Blue Origin's lunar landing is designed to launch aboard either the company's own rocket or the United Launch Alliance's Vulcan rocket, and it is therefore possible that this company will not launch its own rocket. We are also informed that Dynetics' lander is designed to launch aboard United Launch Alliance's Vulcan rocket, which indicates that this company will not launch its own rocket. This statement is, therefore, false.

Answer 39 (Continued)

Q39.2: C - each execute three actions.

Explanation: The third paragraph explains the three manoeuvres that the three landers are hoped to perform: transfer, descent, and ascent. We are told that Blue Origin's lander has three sections – one for each of these manoeuvres – while Dynetics' and SpaceX's landers will be a single structure that can perform all three of these manoeuvres. This statement is, therefore, supported by the information within the passage.

- **A: effect all of the basic requirements**. The passage does not mention any "basic requirements", and we cannot be entirely certain to what this statement alludes. We cannot categorically state that this statement is true.
- **B: avoid carrying out three actions.** This is false since the third paragraph explains the three manoeuvres that the three landers are hoped to perform.
- **D: perform various manoeuvres.** The passage states that the landers are envisaged to perform **three** manoeuvres. The word 'various' is not specific, but the passage provides us with a specific number: three. Hence, this statement is not true.

Q39.3: B - At least one of the three landers will be used.

Explanation: The final paragraph of the passage asserts that the intention is to launch one of the landers during the first mission. The same paragraph states that the other two landers could be used on subsequent missions. Since we are told that at least one of the three landers will be employed, this statement is always true.

- **A: Only one of the three landers will be used.** While the intention is to launch one of the landers during the first mission, the other two landers could be used on subsequent missions. This statement is not **always** true since it is possible that all three of the landers will be used.
- **C: Each of the three landers will be used simultaneously.** The passage states that one of the landers will be launched during the first mission, whilst the other two landers could be used on subsequent missions. While it is possible that the three landers might be used simultaneously at a later date, only one will be used initially. Hence, this statement is not **always** true.

Answer 39 (Continued)

- **D: There is potential that none of the three landers will be used.** This statement cannot be treated as always true since the intention is to launch one of the landers during the first mission. The passage does not imply that there is a possibility that none of the three landers will be used.

Q39.4: C - Can't Tell

Explanation: Although the passage does state that the mission 'aims to send astronauts back to the moon by 2024', it does not indicate if these astronauts have been to space previously. As such, it is not possible to tell if this statement is true or false.

Answer 40

Q40.1: A - The UK is the superior producer of offshore wind power globally.

Explanation: The second paragraph advises that 'the UK has the biggest offshore wind industry in the world'. This supports the assertion that the UK is the major producer of wind power across the globe.

- **B: The UK potentially houses the largest offshore wind industry in the world.** The second paragraph asserts that 'the UK has the biggest offshore wind industry in the world'. The passage does not indicate that the UK **potentially** houses the largest offshore wind industry in the world, and this statement is thus not true.
- **C: The major users of fossil fuels have now adapted to greener energy supplies.** While the passage informs us that Drax, the UK's biggest power plant, has switched to greener forms of energy, it does not give any information of other users of fossil fuels. Based on the information with which we are presented, we cannot be certain if the major users of fossil fuels have moved to greener energy.
- **D: Renewable energy will be the primary source of fuel for the UK in the year 2020.** Dr Simon Evans of *Carbon Brief* states that "there's a real chance that renewables will overtake fossil fuels in 2020 as a whole". Neither Dr Evans nor the passage confirms that renewable energy

Answer 40 (Continued)

will be the main source of power. This statement cannot be corroborated by the information with which we are provided.

Q40.2: B - Coal is the main industry that has been overshadowed by renewable sources.

Explanation: This statement is false as the fourth paragraph of the passage advises that, 'so far this year, renewables have generated more power than all fossil fuels put together'. We can therefore infer that coal is not the only fossil fuel that has been overtaken by renewable sources. The passage does not suggest that coal is the main industry that has been eclipsed, and this statement is incorrect.

- **A: The lockdown highlighted the dispensable nature of power stations.** The passage asserts that the National Grid responded to the drop in demand of electricity 'by taking power plants off the network'. Since the author does not illustrate any major detrimental impacts of this, we can deduce that power stations are not indispensable.
- **C: Nuclear power will potentially continue to make a contribution to energy supplies.** Based on the information with which we are provided, we cannot be certain if this is true or false. The fifth paragraph notes that nuclear accounted for approximately 18% of electricity supplied to the network this year, and the passage does not imply that it will not contribute to energy supplies in the future. We cannot confirm if this statement is true or false, and it cannot be selected as the correct answer option in this instance.
- **D: Renewable power was occasionally judged not to be cost effective.** This statement is supported by the information in the passage. The second paragraph describes how only a small amount of energy came from renewable sources ten years ago. The author notes that 'many people saw [this] as a costly distraction'. This suggests that it was considered an expensive idea.

Q40.3: A - True

Explanation: This statement can be considered true since, throughout the passage, the author details how renewable energy has steadily increased; the fourth paragraph highlights how renewables are now the main provider of energy in the UK. In the final paragraph of the passage, it is stated that 'the

Answer 40 (Continued)

remaining three coal plants in the UK will be shut down within five years' and, as such, 'the fuel that sparked the industrial revolution here in Britain almost two centuries ago will be a thing of the past'. Since the passage implies that coal might soon be an energy source of past generations, this statement can be deemed as true.

Q40.4: B - In one year, combined power from renewable sources exceeded power from fossil fuels by 60%.

Explanation: This can be inferred from the information provided in the final paragraph of the passage. The author notes that the total number of days in which combined power created by renewable sources exceeded combined power created by fossil fuels were 154, of which 91 occurred in 2019.Since 60% of 154 days is 91 days, this statement can be corroborated by the information within the passage.

- **A: It would seem that the major power plants will not be turned back on after the current lockdown.** This cannot be inferred from the information within the passage. The author suggests that the plants will be shut down within five years, but he/she does not imply that the closures will happen immediately after the current lockdown has ended.
- **C: Drax ceased the use of coal one decade ago.** This cannot be implied from the information provided. The passage does state that Drax was the biggest consumer of coal in the UK one decade ago, but it does not indicate when the company ceased the use of coal or, indeed, if it has completely stopped the use of coal.
- **D: Since the UK has the biggest offshore wind industry, the need for imports will gradually reduce.** This cannot be deduced from the details within the passage. The author notes reductions in other fuels, but he/she does not suggest that imports will also diminish.

Answer 41

Q41.1: B - The current conditions within the Arctic are potentially impacting on jetstreams.

Explanation: Speaking within the context of the jetstream, the fourth paragraph of the passage states that 'some scientists believe it's being affected by conditions in the Arctic'. As such, this statement is true as the passage places emphasis on the beliefs of **some** scientists, which suggests that the current conditions within the Arctic are **potentially** impacting on jetstreams.

- **A: The wildfires in Australia were indubitably the result of fluctuations in the Indian Ocean.** This cannot be confirmed as true. The passage notes that the wildfires in Australia were 'blamed' on the Indian dipole, but it does not give any firm evidence to corroborate this.
- **C: The removal of heat elements in the study will provide greater understanding of weather systems.** The penultimate paragraph of the passage explains that this action will 'offer a better understanding of British weather at least'. The words 'at least' imply that it might not provide an insight into **all** weather systems. Rather, it **might** provide an understanding of the **British** weather system. This statement thus cannot be verified by the information within the passage.
- **D: The increase in temperatures precedes the cloud levels rising.** Based on the information with which we are provided, we cannot confirm that this statement is true. Indeed, the author quotes Prof Palmer, who states that "we need to understand these processes better". The passage does not explicitly argue that the increase in temperatures precedes a rise in cloud levels.

Q41.2: A - Climate change is deemed the foremost cause for the recent weather anomalies.

Explanation: This statement cannot be supported by the information within the passage. The first paragraph states that, while '**some** place the blame [of unprecedented weather] on climate change', 'there's no strong evidence' of it. In addition, the passage does not outline evidence to support the belief that climate change is the major cause of recent unusual weather conditions.

- **B: The jetstream encircling the UK was the chief component in heightened temperatures.** This can be confirmed as true as the third paragraph advises that 'the jetstream was looped over the UK, holding the sunny weather in place'.

Answer 41 (Continued)

- **C: Greenhouse gases have the potential to cause a weather phenomenon.** The fourth paragraph notes that the unprecedented weather could be attributed to 'conditions in the Arctic, which is warming faster than anywhere on the planet, **because of** greenhouse gases'. Although the passage does not suggest that this has been evidenced, it implies that greenhouse gases have the **potential** to cause a weather phenomenon. This statement is, therefore, true.
- **D: The Atlantic storms were responsible for the amount of recent rainfall.** This statement is true as the author illustrates, in the third paragraph, the impact of the jetstreams locking in the Atlantic weather.

Q41.3: C - Can't Tell

Explanation: The passage outlines Prof Palmer's frustration that, while space receives much attention, we are not certain of what is happening to the climate of Earth. He implies that there is less consideration of the Earth's climate. However, we are not informed if there are discrepancies in the financial support provided. Based on the information within the passage, we cannot tell if this is true or false.

Q41.4: C - The Indian dipole has impacted on other occurrences.

Explanation: The fourth paragraph notes that the Indian dipole was 'blamed for the wildfires in Australia'. The passage thus infers that this has not been proven, and this statement can be considered as **possibly** true.

- **A: The use of space observations has assisted in the understanding of climate change.** The second paragraph of the passage notes that space observations have 'massively improved' our understanding of climate change. This statement is thus true (and not **possibly** true).
- **B: The impact of lower-level clouds will lead to cooler temperatures.** We are told that the clouds at low levels will cool the earth. Hence, this statement can certainly (and not **possibly**) be concluded from the passage.
- **D: There are some inadequacies in the current system of forecasting.** This is definitely corroborated by the information within the passage. The third paragraph notes the failure of the Met Office 'to predict the sudden leap to a dry spring', which highlights that the current system is not perfect.

Answer 42

Q42.1: B - Women are undervalued in the space industry.

Explanation: This statement is true as the first paragraph of the passage draws attention to the fact that females are depicted as 'holding trays of tea' and 'working in the 'back up team'. The final paragraph also refers to 'the women in those background shots' and highlights that, in the US, there are no women in astronaut training. Based on the information within the passage, it can be argued that women are undervalued in the space industry.

- **A: Women are underrepresented in the space industry.** Whilst women might not assume a pivotal role within the space industry, the passage notes that they are employed within it. It does not, however, provide the ratio of male to female employees. Based on the information with which we are provided, we cannot be certain if this statement is true.
- **C: Women are suppressed in the space industry.** Whilst the passage notes that women are not truly valued within the space industry, it does not provide any concrete evidence of acts of suppression. To confirm this statement as true, the passage would need to offer examples of women who have been blocked from succeeding in the industry.
- **D: Women are underestimated in the space industry.** This statement cannot be verified by the information with which we are provided. We are not given an example of a woman being misjudged or considered incapable of doing something that she can do.

Q42.2: C - were amazed at what they witnessed.

Explanation: The final paragraph notes that the women in NASA and the wives watching at home could not 'believe their eyes' when they saw a woman land on the moon. This confirms that they were amazed at what they witnessed, and this statement is thus true.

- **A: were disheartened at what they saw on the TV.** The final paragraph notes that the women in NASA and the wives watching at home could not 'believe their eyes' when they saw a woman land on the moon. As such, they were not 'disheartened' at what they saw on TV; their response was quite the opposite.
- **B: were delighted that they had finally been recognised.** While we might assume this to be true, it is not explicitly stated in the passage. We cannot confirm that this statement is true.

Answer 42 (Continued)

- **D: did not trust what was being shown on the TV.** Although the viewers were shocked, the passage does not support the idea that there was any element of mistrust. The author does not indicate that the viewers felt that the footage was fake.

Q42.3: D - America was desperate to put the second astronaut on the moon.

Explanation: The second paragraph notes that a moon base had become a priority for America. In addition, the third paragraph highlights the way in which America 'scrambled' to make arrangements to land on the moon. This statement can, therefore, be corroborated by the information within the passage.

- **A: The Soviet Union wanted to annoy America by sending a female astronaut to space.** The passage does not outline why the Soviet Union chose to send a female astronaut to space. Indeed, there might not have been any ulterior motive. We are not informed that this was a provocative manoeuvre, and this statement cannot be considered as true.
- **B: America was determined to put the first astronaut on the moon.** The passage only discusses America's determination to put the **second** astronaut on the moon. We cannot be certain that this statement is true.
- **C: The Soviet Union wanted to irritate America by sending a second astronaut to space.** This cannot be validated by the information with which we are provided. The author does not suggest that the second landing was carried out to infuriate the Americans.

Q42.4: B - relays the disbelief felt by many that a woman landed on the moon.

Explanation: The author details, in the final paragraph of the passage, the shock of those who watched the landing on TV by stating that they could not 'believe their eyes'. The author tells us that the viewers were in disbelief, and this statement is thus correct.

- **A: believes that women are employed by NASA to make tea.** While the author notes that women are seen holding trays of tea in NASA, he/ she does not state that they are employed purely to make tea. This statement is, therefore, not correct.

Answer 42 (Continued)

- **C: believes that women cannot be employed in the same capacity as men.** The author does not declare this. He/She does highlight that women seem to be pushed to the sidelines in this field, but he/she does not endorse this conceptualisation of an androcentric society.
- **D: disagrees with the way in which America treats women.** The passage does not discuss the way in which women are treated in America, and we cannot confirm that this statement is correct.

Answer 43

Q43.1: C - Can't Tell

Explanation: While the penultimate paragraph of the passage notes that cases of measles had risen by 300%, it does not confirm that this figure has been acquired through a study conducted by the WHO. We do not know from where this figure has been obtained, and we cannot be certain if this statement is true or false.

Q43.2: C - Can't Tell

Explanation: While the passage mentions that most of the cases of measles occurred in Orthodox Jewish communities in New York, we are not told how many people died of measles within these communities. We are unable to confirm if this statement is true or false.

Q43.3: B - False

Explanation: Montantes' mother maintained that all her children were vaccinated, and the first paragraph of the passage confirms that Catherine was vaccinated. We can therefore deduce that Catherine's siblings were vaccinated, along with Catherine, before she died. This statement is false.

Q43.4: B - False

Explanation: The passage claims that one or two people are killed for every one thousand infected. Therefore, if 10,000 people contract measles, it is estimated that between 10 and 20 people will die. It is not true that 20 people will definitely die, and this statement is false.

Answer 44

Q44.1: C - the country's preparedness for such events is admirable.

Explanation: The third paragraph explains how the ensuing tsunami from an earthquake that hit Chile in 2015 killed only 11 people. The passage infers that few people died because of the 'Chilean officials' advanced preparation and rapid response'. This statement can, therefore, be considered true.

- **A: the country witnessed the sixth strongest earthquake to ever be recorded.** While Chile did experience the sixth strongest earthquake to ever be recorded, it is the response to that earthquake (or, indeed, any earthquake) rather that its scale that proves useful to other countries. Hence, this is not the most suitable answer option.
- **B: less than a dozen people were killed when the country was hit by a tsunami.** While less than 12people were killed when a tsunami hit the country in 2015, it is the response to that earthquake (or, indeed, any earthquake) rather that its scale that proves useful to other countries. Hence, this is not the most suitable answer option.
- **D: officials are willing to share rapid response strategies.** This is not necessarily the reason for which other countries should look to Chile. The **success** of its rapid response strategies is why other countries should consider them; it would be unhelpful to adopt Chile's strategies if they were unsuccessful.

Q44.2: C - It was the first country to develop intricate plans after being hit by a deadly earthquake.

Explanation: This statement cannot be substantiated by the information provided in the passage. Although the plans are undoubtedly intricate, the passage does not suggest that Chile was the first country to do this.

- **A: It has the potential to augment healthcare globally.** The second paragraph states that copper 'is an ideal material for use in healthcare facilities' and that copper producers 'can improve global health by introducing affordable copper infrastructure into hospitals and other clinical settings around the world'. Since the passage tells us that Chile produces copper, this statement can be verified by the information with which we are provided.
- **B: It is reputed amongst astronomers.** This is confirmed at the end of the passage. We are told that La Serena is in close proximity to 'one of the world's best stargazing sites', which attracts astronomers from around the world.

Answer 44 (Continued)

- **D: It is not the poorest country in Latin America.** This is clearly supported by the opening words of the passage. We are informed that Chile is 'Latin America's richest country'.

Q44.3: C - Can't Tell

Explanation: Despite its reference to astronomy, the passage does not suggest that the author is (or is not) an astronomer. We cannot tell if this statement is true or false.

Q44.4: B - False

Explanation: The passage notes that La Serena is '**near** one of the world's best stargazing sites'. It is not a stargazing site itself. This statement is, therefore, false.

Answer 45

Q45.1:C - Can't Tell

Explanation: From the information provided within the passage, it is not possible to confirm this. The author states that he/she has spent 55 days in space over the course of five missions. However, there is nothing to suggest that any of the five missions did or did not include more than 14 consecutive days in space.

Q45.2: A - being in space can be profoundly mundane.

Explanation: The author notes that being in space is a mixture of 'the transcendently magical and the deeply prosaic'. These words highlight that, while it can be exciting, it can also be extremely boring and dull. This statement can thus be considered as true.

- **B: travelling to space is an insightful experience.** Although the author notes that the experience can be enchanting, he/she does not state that it is insightful. This statement cannot be supported by the information with which we are provided.

Answer 45 (Continued)

- **C: being in space is extremely productive.** Based on the information within the passage, we cannot be certain that this is true. The author does not give any support for this statement.
- **D: going to space is not something that everyone can experience.** While we might assume that this is true, there is nothing within the passage to support it. As such, it is impossible to confirm that this is a view of the author.

Q45.3: C - Can't Tell

Explanation: While the author points out certain negative aspects of travelling in space, he/she does not suggest that he/she is (or is not) bored of it. We cannot be certain if this statement is true or false.

Q45.4: D - There are drawbacks to travelling to space.

Explanation: The author outlines the negative aspects of travelling in space in the initial paragraph of the passage; he/she describes how the experience can be 'crowded, noisy, and occasionally uncomfortable'. This statement is, therefore, true.

- **A: The author is not short.** The author states that, upon learning that one grows in space, he/she thought "Oh cool, I'll be tall". This infers that the author is short, and this statement is thus false.
- **B: Travelling to space is not challenging.** The author describes the challenges of travelling to space, highlighting that it is not glamourous and that it can be overcrowded, noisy and uncomfortable. Therefore, this statement is false.
- **C: It is difficult to pinpoint how space travel makes one feel.** Based on the information within the passage, this statement is false. The author is able to describe how space travel makes him/her feel, choosing words such as 'surreal' and 'breathtaking'. He/She even compares the experience to the film *Wizard of Oz*; the words "we're not in Kansas anymore, Toto" emphasise the feeling of being in a strange world. This statement is, therefore, false.

Answer 46

Q46.1: C - Can't Tell

Explanation: We are told that the survey found that approximately 16.6% of 16 to 20-year-olds ate fast food at least twice a day. However, the passage does not provide any information to confirm the number of 16 to 20-year-olds who are considered overweight. Therefore, we cannot tell if this statement is true or false.

Q46.2: B - 20%

Explanation: This can be found in the third paragraph of the passage, which notes that the average adult has six meat free days each month. This totals 20% of the average month (six out of 30 or 31 days).

Q46.3: C - Can't Tell

Explanation: The final paragraph of the passage states that 'social media was identified as a contributing factor in the obesity epidemic'. However, it does not specify that the **negative** impact of social media is contributing to the obesity crisis. Indeed, we are told that individuals post photos of meals that they cook or the food that they eat in restaurants on social media; this does not necessarily imply negativity. We thus cannot tell if this statement is true or false.

Q46.4: D - People should not necessarily cease to eat meat.

Explanation: This statement can be supported by the information within the passage. The passage quotes the director of BBC Good Food, Christine Hayes, who states that meat can still be enjoyed when it is balanced with 'some meat-free dishes'. The passage does not suggest that people should stop eating meat completely, and this statement is correct.

- **A: The author believes that young people consume too much fast food.** While the passage details the amount of fast food that young people consume, it does not suggest that the author does (or does not) consider this excessive. We cannot tell if this statement is true or false, and we thus cannot select it as the correct answer option.
- **B: In the UK, the number of vegetarians outweighs the number of meat-eaters.** Based on the information with which we are provided, we

Answer 46 (Continued)

we cannot be certain if this is true. The passage does state that 'the **typical** adult now eats meat at least twice a day', but we are not given any concrete statistics to confirm how many people in the UK are non-vegetarians. As such, we cannot confirm that this statement is true.

- **C: Young people often post pictures of their food on social media.** The information within the passage does not support the idea that young people **often** post pictures of their food on social media. We are told that 40% of people aged between 21 and 34 years had posted **a photo** of a meal they had cooked on social media, whilst one third had posted **a photo** of a meal they had eaten in a restaurant. The frequency of their posts is not highlighted. In fact, the words '**a** photo' suggests that they did this only once. This statement thus cannot be verified by the information within the passage.

Answer 47

Q47.1: C - Can't Tell

Explanation: The first paragraph highlights how the device will need a substantial amount of energy in order to function. The same paragraph also notes that providers have been asked to submit low carbon options. However, the passage does not advise if this will be feasible, and it is not possible to tell if the new supercomputer will itself have an environmental impact.

Q47.2: C - The current device is presently costing £97m.

Explanation: The passage simply notes that there was a '£97m bill for the current supercomputer'. It does not confirm if that is the final cost to date, if this figure is set to increase, or if that was the cost when it was initially established. As such, we cannot confirm that the current device is **presently** costing £97m.

- **A: The implementation of the device will enable UK forecasters to be the most powerful analysts.** The author quotes the chief executive of the Met Office, who states 'we'll be streets ahead of anybody else'. This statement can thus be considered as true.
- **B: The device will allow researchers to better calculate temperature boosts.** Speaking within the context of rising temperatures, the fourth

Answer 47 (Continued)

- paragraph explains how the device will enable forecasters to 'add more detail to their projections'. This statement can thus be corroborated by the information within the passage.
- **D: The additional methods are providing substantial interpretations.** The third paragraph confirms that this statement is true. It claims that 'satellites, weather stations and buoys out in the ocean' provide more than 200 billion observations every day.

Q47.3: D - Its implementation will have widespread effects.

Explanation: The passage notes that the device could assist Environment Agency teams to deploy effective flood barriers, which would subsequently help areas that are at risk of flooding. The passage also asserts that the device might aid the National Grid to balance fluctuations in wind and solar power. This will have beneficial effects throughout the country, and this statement can be considered as true.

- **A: It will eliminate flooding.** The passage does not state that the device will eradicate flooding; it simply implies that the device could alleviate the impacts of flooding. It highlights the way in which the device will allow early warnings of potential flooding, and this statement is thus not true.
- **B: The surge in heat may be mitigated through correct usage of the device.** The passage does not suggest this. It merely indicates that the device will assist in projections of temperature.
- **C: It will effectively stabilise the use of natural resources.** Again, the passage does not confirm that this is true. It only advises that the device will be able to assist the National Grid to balance 'fluctuations in wind and solar power'; it does not state that the device **will** stabilise them. The device will not even out use of resources it will only be able to assist with that action.

Q47.4: C - The necessity for intense precision is critical to effectiveness.

Explanation: This conclusion can be drawn from the passage. The fifth paragraph highlights how rising temperatures can result in 'dangerous extremes of weather', which 'makes accuracy all the more important'. This supports the inference that, if weather extremes are anticipated effectively, other agencies will be able to provide 'mobile flood barriers or help the National

Answer 47 (Continued)

Grid balancing fluctuations in wind and solar power'. Based on the information within the passage, we can deduce that effective forecasts need to be precise.

- **A: The device will potentially need financial support from private companies.** The author does not make any suggestion to support this conclusion. While the passage does refer to the cost of the device, there is no information to indicate from where the funding will come.
- **B: The device will play a significant role in achieving the emissions target of 2050.** Again, this is not a conclusion that can be drawn from the information within the passage. The author mentions the UK's target of net zero emissions by 2050, but he/she does not suggest the role that the device will play in achieving this.
- **D: The protection of peat bogs will have a considerable impact on emissions targets and the fuelling of this device.** While the final paragraph of the passage does pay attention to the preservation of peat bogs, it does not detail their impact on the emissions targets.

Answer 48

Q48.1: A - The word 'vaccine' existed before the end of the eighteenth century.

Explanation: The passage states that the word 'vaccine' was created from the Latin term 'vacca' in 1798. Hence, this statement is true.

- **B: Jenner allowed his critics to deter his enthusiasm.** We are told that, despite being 'widely ridiculed', Jenner persisted in his research. He was 'undaunted'. This statement is, therefore, false.
- **C: No children under the age of one year were actively involved in the testing process.** The passage asserts that Jenner experimented on his own 11-month-old son. This statement is thus false.
- **D: Jenner enlisted the help of adults to test his hypothesis.** The passage talks of children only, and we cannot be certain if Jenner tested his hypothesis on adults. We cannot say that this statement is definitely true.

Answer 48 (Continued)

Q48.2: C - was far too radical.

Explanation: The passage asserts that 'Jenner was told that his ideas were too revolutionary'. In addition, critics said that injecting material from a diseased animal into a human was 'repulsive andungodly'. This statement can, therefore, be corroborated by the information within the passage.

- **A: was unlikely to be viable.** Whilst Jenner's experimentation was met with criticism, the passage does not suggest that his theory was ever considered unfeasible.
- **B: was supported by sufficient evidence.** The passage states that, after submitting a paper that described his experiment, he was told that he needed more proof. This statement is, therefore, false.
- **C: was ideally positioned to establish a cure for the smallpox.** Although this was fundamentally true, the passage does not confirm that Jenner was told this. This statement is thus false.

Q48.3: B - mocked for his research.

Explanation: This statement can be considered as true since we are told that a satirical cartoon depicted individuals who had been vaccinated with cow's heads. This supports the idea that Jenner was mocked for his research.

- **A: viciously attacked for his research.** While Jenner's research was unpopular and ridiculed, we are not informed that he was 'viciously attacked'. This statement cannot be supported by the information within the passage.
- **C: accepted for his research practices.** We are told that the advantages of vaccination eventually became recognised and vaccination became widespread, which resulted in Jenner becoming famous. However, the passage does not confirm that his methods were ever **accepted**. Indeed, we are informed that critics saw his practice as 'repulsive and ungodly'. Therefore, this statement cannot be verified by the information within the passage.
- **D: not appreciated for his research.** The passage states that the advantages of vaccination eventually became recognised and vaccination became widespread, which resulted in Jenner becoming famous. This statement is, therefore, false.

Answer 48 (Continued)

Q48.4: D - Many children were saved by dint of Jenner's experiments.

Explanation: Based on the information within the passage, we can deduce that Jenner's experiments were successful and enabled vaccines to be developed. Hence, the passage suggests that children were saved **because of** his experiments, and this statement is true.

- **A: Many children continued to die as a result of Jenner's experiments.** The passage asserts that the advantages of vaccination eventually became recognised, and vaccination became widespread. This highlights that Jenner's experiments were successful; it does not suggest that children died **as a result of** these experiments. This statement cannot be supported by the information within the passage.
- **B: Many children were saved despite Jenner's experiments.** Based on the information within the passage, we can deduce that Jenner's experiments were successful and enabled vaccines to be developed. Hence, the passage does not suggest that children were saved **despite** Jenner's experiments. Rather, they were saved **because of** his experiments.
- **C: Many children continued to die despite Jenner's experiments.** Based on the information within the passage, we can deduce that Jenner's experiments were successful and enabled vaccines to be developed. Hence, the passage does not suggest that children continued to die **despite** Jenner's experiments. Rather, they were saved **because of** his experiments.

Answer 49

Q49.1: B - rather than posts that endorse a particular item.

Explanation: The fourth paragraph explains how Emily Canham often promotes various services and merchandise. However, the fifth paragraph explains how she now feels it is more important to listen to her followers rather than promote a specific item. As such, this statement is correct.

- **A: rather than posts that promote her products.** The fourth paragraph explains how Emily Canham often promotes various services and merchandise. However, we are not told that she promotes (or even produces) her own products. We cannot be certain that this statement is true.

Answer 49 (Continued)

- **C: rather than posts that discuss topical issues.** The passage does not give any indication that Emily Canham has ever used her Instagram account to discuss current affairs. Based on the information with which we are provided, we cannot confirm that this is true.
- **D: rather than posts that encourage purchases.** The fourth paragraph highlights how Emily Canham often promotes various services and merchandise. However, the fifth paragraph explains how she currently feels it is more important to listen to her followers than promote a specific item. This statement is thus incorrect.

Q49.2: B - Those who work in the fashion industry are facing job losses.

Explanation: The passage begins by explaining how the current pandemic has led to individuals not taking summer holidays. As a result, they are not purchasing summer clothes. We are told that more than 80% of transactions are made in store, and we can therefore deduce that the fact that people are not purchasing clothes will have an impact on the number of people required to work in stores. Additionally, due to the low sales, many brands have stopped advertising. This might also point to job losses. Based on the information with which we are provided, we can infer that this statement is true.

- **A: The way in which the British public shops will change as a result of coronavirus.** The passage does not give any indication that, when the pandemic ends, customers will not return to the physical shopping experience. Based on the information in the passage, this statement cannot be confirmed as true.
- **C: Many retailers have stopped advertising because they do not have the money to fund it.** While we are told that some brands have suspended advertising, we are not informed that this is due to financial constraints. In fact, we might assume that advertising has been suspended since people are not interested in buying summer clothes. We therefore cannot be certain that this statement is true.
- **D: Emily Canham's business has survived because she has more than 700,000 followers on Instagram.** Whilst she does have more than 700,000 followers on Instagram, the passage does not suggest that this is the reason for her continued success. Rather, we might infer that she has maintained her success by adapting to the current situation. Based on the information with which we are provided, we cannot tell if this is true or false. We therefore cannot select it as the correct answer option.

Answer 49 (Continued)

Q49.3: C - Can't Tell

Explanation: Although the passage does refer to the summer season, it does not indicate that this will (or will not) be the only fashion season affected by coronavirus. As such, we cannot tell if this statement is true or false.

Q49.4: C - Can't Tell

Explanation: While the passage states that this is 'a real existential crisis for the fashion industry', we cannot be certain that it is unique. We therefore cannot tell if this statement is true or false.

Answer 50

Q50.1: B - Some of those on board the *Titanic* were from France.

Explanation: The first paragraph states that the *Titanic* stopped in Cherbourg in France. We realise that passengers embarked in Cherbourg, since we are told that the city's dock was too small to accommodate the *Titanic* and passengers had to be transported to the ship. We can deduce that some of these passengers would have lived in France, and this statement is correct.

- **A: The *Titanic* was considered the largest ship of its time.** The first paragraph of the passage asserts that the *Titanic* was **one** of the largest ships at that time. However, it was not necessarily **the** largest ship of its time.
- **C: Fewer than half of those on board the *Titanic* were passengers.** The passage notes that the ship contained 2,200 people of whom 1,300 were passengers. Hence, more than half of those aboard were passengers.
- **D: The *Titanic* was quite close to reaching its final destination.** The passage does not provide any information to suggest how close the ship was from its final destination. Based on the information within the passage, we cannot be certain if this is true or false.

Answer 50 (Continued)

Q50.2: C - Can't Tell

Explanation: While the passage explains that, on the evening of 10th April, the *Titanic* stopped in France, we are not told when or from where it first set sail. You might know that the ship first departed from the UK; you might therefore presume that it would have set sail on the same day it reached France (10th April). However, we are not provided with this information, and we cannot be certain that the ship began its journey on 10th April.

Q50.3: C - the *New Yorker* strayed into its path.

Explanation: The passage describes how suction from the *Titanic* dragged the docked *New Yorker* into its path. This statement is, therefore, true.

- **A: the *New Yorker* nearly strayed into its path.** This statement suggests that the ship **almost** strayed into the path of the *Titanic*. However, the passage describes how suction from the *Titanic* **did** drag the docked *New Yorker* into its path. This statement is, therefore, false.
- **B: it strayed into the path of the *New Yorker*.** The passage describes how suction from the *Titanic* dragged the docked *New Yorker* into its path. This statement implies that it was the *Titanic* that strayed into the path of the *New Yorker*, which is incorrect.
- **D: it almost strayed into the path of the *New Yorker*.** This statement is not true. We are told that suction from the *Titanic* dragged the docked *New Yorker* into its path. This statement implies that it was the *Titanic* that strayed into the path of the *New Yorker*, which is incorrect.

Q50.4: B - The passengers' messages took precedence over their safety.

Explanation: The passage states that Phillips and Briderelayed passengers' messages. We are told that Phillips had admonished the crew of the *Californian* for 'interrupting him' whilst he was handling passengers' messages (the *Californian*, which was nearby, had sent word that it had stopped after becoming surrounded by ice). This indicates that Phillips' priority was to relay passenger messages, and this ultimately took precedence over their safety. This statement can be supported by the information within the passage.

- **A: The *Titanic* should not have been steered towards an area that had icebergs.** This statement cannot be corroborated by the information within the passage. We are not told why the ship was near an area that had icebergs or whether it should have been there.

Answer 50 (Continued)

- **C: Altering the ship's speed would have changed what happened next.** The passage advises that, when the *Titanic* began to approach an area known to have icebergs, the ship's speed was not altered. However, we are not told why this was done or what would have happened had the ship's speed been changed. This statement is not supported by the information within the passage.
- **D: Human error led to the sinking of the *Titanic*.** The passage does not corroborate this statement. It does not mention that human error led to the sinking of the ship, and this cannot be selected as the correct answer option.

Answer 51

Q51.1: C - Can't Tell

Explanation: While the final paragraph explains the reasons for which this opinion is held by many millennials, we cannot be certain that the author agrees with it. There is nothing within the passage to either confirm or deny that this is also his/her viewpoint and that he/she agrees with the statement. As such, the correct answer is 'can't tell'.

Q51.2: B - Numerous babies who were born in Britain after the War ended had the opportunity to grow up in a better world.

Explanation: This statement can be considered as true since the passage explains, in the first paragraph, that the new generation had the opportunity to 'grow up with faith in a better tomorrow'. The author also notes how 'it could only get better', which further supports the fact that this statement can be corroborated by the information within the passage.

- **A: Several women who had a baby after the War ended brought hope to the people of Britain.** This cannot be verified by the information within the passage since we are not told that the birth of these children brought hope to others in Britain. The author only refers to those who belonged to the generation itself.
- **C: The analogy of turning on a light in a dark room is often used to describe this period.** The author uses the analogy of 'floodlights', but floodlights are not used inside rooms. This statement is thus not wholly accurate, and it cannot be selected as the correct answer option.

Answer 51 (Continued)

- **D: Many people wanted their children to grow up in a more hopeful world.** Whilst we might presume that this is true, it is not corroborated by the information within the passage. Indeed, the passage focuses on the opinions and behaviours of the baby boomers themselves.

Q51.3: A - They have very outdated morals and traditions.

Explanation: Based on the information within the passage, this trait cannot be associated with baby boomers. Indeed, the author emphasises how they were the ones who defied and changed 'Victorian puritanism, censorship, class snobbery and inhibitions of the establishment'. These actions contradict the attributes mentioned in this statement.

- **B: They took several opportunities for granted.** The final paragraph of the passage explains how the benefits that the baby boomers 'took for granted' have been denied to subsequent generations. This statement can thus be supported by the information within the passage.
- **C: They created problems with which the future generations had to deal, and this has ultimately damaged their future.** This can also be substantiated by the information in the final paragraph of the passage, which states that baby boomers 'were – and are – accused of sabotaging [their] children's future, hoarding power and money while expecting those with the least to foot the potentially hefty bills'. This highlights how future generations must now deal with the issues caused by baby boomers and how this has 'sabotaged' their future.
- **D: They are hungry for power and tend to hoard it.** This trait is noted in the final paragraph of the passage, which asserts that baby boomers are accused of 'hoarding power'. This statement can thus be supported by the information within the passage.

Q51.4: C - Can't Tell

Explanation: We know that the author is a baby boomer since he/she uses the pronoun 'we' (for example, in the phrase 'we baby boomers'). The passage states that baby boomers were 'born between 1946 and the mid-60s', but it does not, at any point, confirm the decade in which the author was born. It is therefore not possible to confirm if this statement is true or false.

Answer 52

Q52.1: C - Personality tests do not reflect the person's true ability to carry out a particular job.

Explanation: The third paragraph notes how, according to critics, this type of test does not 'predict anything meaningful about job or life performance'. This supports the statement that personality tests do not provide a sound indication of an individual's ability to carry out a specific job. This statement is thus the correct answer option.

- **A: Personality tests are often inaccurate and do not reflect the person's true self.** The passage does not cite this as a reason for which personality tests are condemned by critics. The passage infers that personality tests are not valid and not meaningful; it does not explicitly state that they are inaccurate.
- **B: Personality tests can be expensive, and several employees cannot afford to purchase them.** The passage does not discuss the overall cost of personality tests or assert that employees are required to pay for them. This statement cannot be supported by the information within the passage.
- **D: Personality tests often do not accurately predict an individual's life performance.** Once again, this is not cited as a reason for which personality tests are condemned by critics. The passage argues that personality tests do not 'predict anything **meaningful** about job or life performance'; it does not state that they are inaccurate.

Q52.2: D - An individual's ability to manage physical and emotional pain.

Explanation: The second paragraph of the passage maintains that personality tends to be defined in terms of five basic traits: openness to experience; conscientiousness; extraversion; agreeableness; and neuroticism. The ability to manage physical and emotional pain is not included here, and this answer option is thus correct.

- **A: An individual's willingness to experience new things.** The passage claims that one of the five basic traits of personality is 'openness to experience'. Therefore, an individual's willingness to experience new things is considered part of his/her personality.
- **B: An individual's disposition to care for and look after others.** The passage asserts that another of the five basic traits of personality is 'agreeableness'. Therefore, an individual's disposition to care for and look after others is considered part of his/her personality.

Answer 52

- **C: An individual's likeliness to experience anxiety and fear.** The passage maintains that one of the five basic traits of personality is 'neuroticism'. Therefore, an individual's likeliness to experience anxiety and fear is considered part of his/her personality.

Q52.3: C - Can't Tell

Explanation: While the first paragraph of the passage notes that personality can change over time, it also states that 'one's core characteristics tend to remain steady over a lifetime'. This seems to corroborate the first part of this statement. The passage asserts that personality is 'a mix of inborn dispositions and inclinations along with environmental factors and experiences'. We are told that, while an individual's personality is influenced by his/her instincts, other external aspects also play a role. However, the passage neither supports nor disproves the idea that the **majority** of our personality derives from our genetics and our instincts. For this reason, we cannot tell if this statement is true or false.

Q52.4: B - False

Explanation: The passage states that Hippocrates and the ancient Greeks 'defined **four** basic temperaments'. This statement is, therefore, false.

Answer 53

Q53.1: C - Can't Tell

Explanation: It is not possible to confirm if the **author** believes that understanding how a teenager's brain functions is key to making living with him/her more manageable. The second paragraph of the passage tells us that Frances Jensen undoubtedly feels that knowing what is happening inside a teenager's brain makes him/her easier to live with. However, we cannot be certain if the author also holds this view.

Answer 53 (Continued)

Q53.2: B - The way in which their brain is connected means that they are unable to plan effectively.

Explanation: This is confirmed in the final paragraph of the passage, which explicitly relates tidiness to planning. It states that 'tidiness needs a sophisticated level of cognitive control' and 'the way the teenage brain is connected means that their planning is not very good'. In addition, the final sentence of the passage advises how teenagers are untidy as they do not allow themselves sufficient time to clean up; the passage suggests that this is an issue of time management. This statement can thus be corroborated by the information within the passage.

- **A: Tidiness requires a higher level of cognitive control which several teens do not develop until they become adults.** The passage does not state that tidiness needs a **higher** level of cognitive control but, rather, a **sophisticated** level. Additionally, the passage does not advise that certain teens do not reach this level before adulthood. This statement thus cannot be supported by the information within the passage.
- **C: The brain is coated in myelin, which is formed over a prolonged period of time.** This statement is not correct: the passage notes that only parts of the brain – synapses – are covered with myelin.
- **D: Cleaning is not considered as a priority for teens as they deem other tasks more important.** The final sentence of the passage advises how teenagers are untidy as they do not allow themselves sufficient time to clean up. The passage suggests that it is an issue of time management; it does not necessarily imply that teenagers find tidying up unimportant. This statement is, therefore, not supported by the information within the passage.

Q53.3: A - True

Explanation: The second paragraph of the passage explains Jensen's thought that 'we expect a little bit more out of adolescents than we should'. This clearly supports the statement and, as such, it can be considered true.

Q53.4: C - Can't Tell

Explanation: Based on the information with which we are provided, it is not

Answer 53 (Continued)

possible to confirm if this statement is true or false. The first paragraph of the passage states that Frances Jensen is a 'University of Pennsylvania neurologist', but it does not assert that she is **from** the state of Pennsylvania.

Answer 54

Q54.1: B - False

Explanation: The first paragraph of the passage states that 'ash dieback could cost the UK economy billions of pounds', whilst the final paragraph asserts that 'a recent estimate suggested that ash dieback would cost the UK economy £15bn'. Yet, the passage does not indicate that this would trigger a recession. The term 'recession' denotes a major decline in economic activity; it tends to occur after a widespread decline in spending. We can therefore assume that this statement is false.

Q54.2: B - it was prudent to investigate its growth.

Explanation: The passage details how researchers examined the progress of the disease in an area within north-eastern France. They monitored the initial stages of its spread during 2012 (two years after the disease was first identified there) and reassessed the same area between 2016 and 2018 to see how the disease had established itself. As such, this statement can be considered as true; researchers realised that it was prudent to investigate how the disease was growing.

- **A: it was impossible to scrutinise the early spread.** The passage does not confirm that this is true. We are told that researchers monitored the initial stages of its spread in an area of France during 2012, which was two years after the disease was first identified there. However, we are not told why it took two years to investigate it, and we cannot be certain that it was **impossible** to examine the early spread of the disease. Indeed, there are many factors that might have prevented this. The passage also discusses the fact that the disease first arrived in Britain in March 2012 and that, by October 2012, it had spread to the wild. However, the passage does not inform us of whether it was (or was not) possible to examine the early spread of the

Answer 54 (Continued)

disease. This statement cannot be corroborated by the information within the passage.

- **C: it became apparent that its spread was due to the lack of documentation in the area.** We are not provided with any information to suggest that this is true or false, and we cannot select it as the correct answer option in this instance.
- **D: it transpired that the fungus had been predominant for some time beforehand.** The passage does not confirm if the disease had been present before it was first identified. We thus cannot be certain if this statement is true.

Q54.3: A - The disease was apparent outside of the UK prior to its discovery within the country.

Explanation: The passage advises that the disease arrived in the UK in March 2012. It also explains that researchers started to investigate the progress of the disease in an area of France in 2012, which was approximately two years after the disease was first identified there. We can thus deduce that the disease was found in a country outside the UK two years before it was discovered within the UK, and this statement is correct.

- **B: The initial occurrence of the disease in Britain was not identified in a garden centre.** The passage asserts that the disease first arrived in the UK in 2012, 'when it was found on some ash trees in a nursery'. This statement is thus false; the disease was first found in a garden centre.
- **C: The spread of the disease was maintained within a British nursery for several months.** There is nothing within the passage to indicate that the disease was maintained within the nursery. The passage merely states that it was not discovered in the wild until later that year. We cannot be certain that this statement is correct.
- **D: All trees in a British nursery were affected by the disease.** The passage states that the disease was identified on **some** ash trees in a nursery, which does not imply that **all** ash trees in the nursery were affected. We might also assume that there were other types of trees in the nursery; the passage does not explain what happened to them. This statement cannot be supported by the information within the passage.

Answer 54 (Continued)

Q54.4: B - The financial impact of the disease will extend beyond anything tangible.

Explanation: This statement can be corroborated by the information within the passage. We are told that the financial impact will be significant, and the passage suggests that dealing with the dead trees will have a financial effect. We can thus deduce that the financial impact will extend beyond any physical impact.

- **A: The spread of the disease had been expected by tree enthusiasts.** The passage explains how tree enthusiasts' 'worst fears were realised' when the disease was found in a woodland in Norfolk. We therefore understand that tree enthusiasts **feared** the spread of the disease, but we are not told that they necessarily **expected** it. This statement is thus not supported by the information within the passage.
- **C: There will not be a substantial impact on the amount of carbon in the air.** The final paragraph of the passage explicitly states that there will be a loss of the benefits provided by trees through water and air purification and 'locking in carbon from the atmosphere'. As such, this statement is untrue.
- **D: The clearing up operation will need to consider alternative means of water purification.** Whilst the passage suggests that there will be an impact on water purification, it does not give any indication that alternative methods need to be established in conjunction with the process of clearing up the dead and dying trees. The statement is, therefore, not true.

Answer 55

Q55.1: C - Can't Tell

Explanation: Although the passage states that the hornets destroy honeybees and feed their bodies to their young, it does not maintain that this is the creatures' only source of sustenance. As such, we cannot tell if this statement is true or false.

Answer 55 (Continued)

Q55.2: A - The hornets have had the most detrimental impact on honeybees.

Explanation: The passage does assert that the hornets have had a huge impact on honeybees. However, it does not confirm that they are responsible for the greatest hardship that the creature has ever endured. In addition, the final paragraph concludes that 'populations of honeybees and other pollinators in the US were already under pressure'. As such, this statement cannot be corroborated by the information within the passage.

- **B: The hornets possess the capability of destroying human life.** The first paragraph of the passage states that multiple stings can be lethal to humans. Hence, this statement can be supported by the information within the passage.
- **C: The hornets are substantial in mass in comparison to similar species.** We are told that the hornets are 'shockingly large' and 'roughly the size of a matchbox'. We can thus deduce that the size of the creatures is significant in comparison to other similar species, and this statement can be supported by the information within the passage.
- **D: The hornets develop territories over two seasons.** The penultimate paragraph states that the hornets build their habitats in the summer and the autumn. This statement can therefore be validated by the information with which we are provided.

Q55.3: D - Murder hornets have evolved into a species that no longer circumvents humans.

Explanation: Although the passage details that the hornets' stings can be deadly to humans, we are told that the creatures tend to avoid people. As such, this statement is untrue.

- **A: The Asian giant hornets have maintained their presence in Asia.** The passage tells us that, in Asia, as many as 50 people die each year from the creatures' stings. Hence, this statement can be supported by the information with which we are provided.
- **B: Murder hornets may potentially decimate a hive in a comparatively short period of time.** The author describes how the hornets have the ability to 'destroy a honeybee hive in a matter of hours'. As such, this statement can be corroborated by the information within the passage.

Answer 55 (Continued)

- **C: The worker hornets do not initiate habitat creation prior to the arrival of the queens.** This statement can be validated by the details within the passage. The author explains that the life cycle of a hornet begins in April as this is when the queens come out of hibernation. It is only at this point that the hornets start to feed and find places in which to build their nests. The author continues that the creatures build their habitats in the summer and autumn (which is after the arrival of the queen in the spring). As such, this statement is true.

Q55.4: A - undertake a method to ultimately eliminate this species.

Explanation: The final paragraph of the passage states that the scientists intend to 'detect and eradicate the species'. This statement can thus be considered as true.

- **B: pursue action to trap the hornets who kill honeybees.** The final paragraph of the passage asserts that the queen hornets will be trapped. Yet, we are told that the worker hornets are the ones who are 'sent to find food' and consequently decapitate honeybees. The queen hornets do not kill honeybees; this is the role of the worker hornets. This statement is thus false.
- **C: take whatever methods are required to reduce the species.** This statement cannot be considered true for two reasons. Firstly, the scientists have a controlled plan to try to eradicate the hornets. Secondly, the scientists intend to completely eradicate the species; they do not aim to simply reduce the numbers.
- **D: undertake research to trap and eliminate the hornets.** The passage explains how a plan has already been formulated to try to eliminate the species. It does not suggest that the scientists need to undertake research first; it infers that this has already been done. This statement is, therefore, false.

Answer 56

Q56.1: B - The exigence for fossil energies appears to have stimulated a decrease in emissions.

Explanation: The second paragraph of the passage highlights how the demand for fossil fuels in India has been decreasing for some time. However, this statement suggests that the urgent need or necessity for fossil fuels has led to a decrease in emissions. The passage infers that it is the increase in demand for sources of **renewable energy** that has promoted a decrease in emissions. This statement thus cannot be corroborated by the information within the passage.

- **A: Analysis detects a substantial emission reduction with the passage of time.** We are told that a study conducted by *Carbon Brief* indicates that India's emissions growth trend started to reverse in March. It also maintains that India's carbon dioxide emissions 'are likely to have fallen by 30% in April'. That the words 'likely to have' are used implies that emissions are expected to continue to reduce with time. This statement can thus be verified by the information within the passage.
- **C: The mining industry has observed a steady decline in demand.** The passage states that, while the use of coal to generate power decreased in March and the first three weeks of April, the demand for the rock was weakening even before India was put into lockdown. This statement can thus be supported by the information within the passage.
- **D: The pressure for more resourceful supplies has progressively intensified.** On several occasions, the passage illustrates how the demand for fossil fuels has been steadily decreasing and the preference for renewable energy sources has been increasing. This statement is thus verified by the information within the passage.

Q56.2: B - fashioned a minor, but noteworthy, bearing on emissions.

Explanation: This statement can be corroborated by the information within the final paragraph of the passage. The author notes that, in the economic year that ended in March 2020, deliveries of coal decreased by approximately 2%. He/She claims that this is 'a small but significant reduction'; these words support this statement.

- **A: transpired following an upsurge in demand for sustainable sources.** Whilst the passage does maintain that there has been an increase

Answer 56 (Continued)

in demand for sustainable sources of energy, the author states that this has 'weakened the demand for fossil fuels'. He/She does not explicate that there has been an **upsurge** in the demand for sustainable energy. Rather, we can infer that it has been gradual. This statement is thus not corroborated by the information within the passage.

- **C: occurred following the unparalleled and abrupt limitations.** The author highlights how India's demand for coal had already started to decline before coronavirus took hold; it was not triggered by this unprecedented situation. This statement is thus false.
- **D: been the least influential factor in the recent revision of emissions.** The passage suggests quite the opposite. It states that 'virtually all of the drop-off in power demand has been borne by coal-fired generators' and that this has caused the 'dramatic' reduction in emissions. We can infer that the decline in the demand for coal has proved an influential factor in the recent reduction of emissions, and this statement cannot be corroborated by the information within the passage.

Q56.3: B - The unparalleled constraints imposed upon the country recently have sent its emission tendencies backwards.

Explanation: While we are informed that India's emissions have not fallen purely as a result of the country's lockdown (since the country's emissions had started to decline before the current restrictions were put in place), the second paragraph of the passage states that the lockdown 'finally tipped the country's 37-year emissions growth trend into reverse'. These words substantiate this statement.

- **A: When the current restrictions are revoked, it is plausible that emissions will return.** There is nothing within the passage to support this. In addition, we are told that India's emissions have not fallen purely as a result of the country's lockdown. Rather, the demand for fossil fuels had been weakening for some time, and the country's emissions had started to decline before the current restrictions were put in place. This statement cannot be verified by the information within the passage.
- **C: There has not been any significant increase in demand for substitutes of non-renewable energy.** The second paragraph details how competition from renewable sources of energy has weakened the

Answer 56 (Continued)

demand for non-renewable forms of energy. We can therefore deduce that there has been an increase in demand for substitutes of non-renewable energy, and this statement is thus untrue.

- **D: The previous forty years have witnessed a consistent decline in demand for non-renewable sources of energy.** While we are informed that India's emissions had started to decline before coronavirus, the passage does not suggest that the demand for non-renewable energy has been steadily declining for the last 40 years. In addition, the passage mentions the country's '37-year emissions growth trend'. This indicates that its emissions have continued to increase during the previous 37 years, which can, in turn, be attributed to non-renewable forms of energy. This statement cannot be corroborated by the information within the passage.

Q56.4: A - Their growing popularity had been evident for some time.

Explanation: The passage explicates that competition from renewable sources of energy was present before the coronavirus hit the country. It also highlights how coal deliveries decreased by approximately 2% during the economic year ending March 2020. We can thus infer that the preference for renewable sources of energy is not new, which supports this statement.

- **B: The present methods will decline at a rapid pace.** While the passage does suggest that the use of non-renewable energy will decrease, it does not indicate the pace at which this will happen. As such, we cannot be certain that this statement is true.
- **C: The generators will be affected and become superfluous.** The passage does not mention generators. As such, we cannot tell if this statement is true or false.
- **D: It has taken over forty years for the effects of emissions to be recognised.** Once again, the passage does not provide any information to support or disprove this statement.

Answer 57

Q57.1: B - There is sufficient evidence to establish a conclusive timeline of events.

Explanation: The passage highlights how radiocarbon dating of charcoal and bone, as well as tsunami deposits from the Indian Ocean, have established when the event happened. This statement can therefore be corroborated by the information within the passage.

- **A: There was a small window of opportunity that would have allowed many of the inhabitants to escape.** The first paragraph suggests that, since the bones were found intact and there was no indication of war or illness, the villagers 'had drowned and were buried in the shattered remains of their homes'. This supports the belief that there had been no time for the inhabitants to escape, and this statement cannot be considered as true.
- **C: The tsunami followed an almost identical pattern to a contemporary episode.** The final paragraph of the passage equates the tsunami that occurred a millennium ago with the tsunami that occurred in 2004.However, it does not state that the two events were **almost identical**. This statement thus cannot be corroborated by the information within the passage.
- **D: The inhabitants were self-sufficient prior to the point of the tsunami.** The passage does not affirm that this village was attached to any other village or town. As such, we might deduce that the inhabitants were self-sufficient. However, we are not provided with enough information to suggest that this is true or false, and we cannot select it as the correct answer option here.

Q57.2: B - The village was a thriving dwelling close to the shoreline.

Explanation: The second paragraph details the finding of matter from the Indian Ocean, which was quite close to the location. This supports the fact that the village was near to the shoreline. The passage notes that the bones discovered belonged to both adults and children and that the researchers 'kept finding more human bones'. This highlights that the village had a substantial population that consisted of a mixture of age groups. If the village were in decline, it arguably would not have been as populated. This statement can, therefore, be corroborated by the information within the passage.

Answer 57 (Continued)

- **A: The numbers found suggest the impact was somewhat mitigated.** The second paragraph of the passage states that, 'wherever the researchers dug, they kept finding more human bones'. This suggests that a significant number of people died, which does not support the idea that the impact of the tsunami was mitigated in any manner.
- **C: The magnitude of the disaster would never be comparable with future incidents.** The final paragraph of the passage asserts that the tsunami that occurred one thousand years ago was 'similar in scale and intensity to the 2004 tsunami'. These words thus refute this statement.
- **D: The village had lain undiscovered for many thousands of years.** The information in the final paragraph of the passage confirms that the tsunami occurred 'a millennium ago'. Hence, the village could have lain undiscovered for a maximum of one thousand years and not for **many thousands** of years.

Q57.3: C - It would appear plausible that the inhabitants succumbed by the influx of water.

Explanation: The first paragraph of the passage suggests that the villagers drowned and that there were no indications of illness or conflict. This statement can thus be corroborated by the information within the passage.

- **A: The inhabitants do not appear to have been killed within their own homes.** The first paragraph of the passage hints that the villagers 'had drowned and were buried in the shattered remains of their homes'. Therefore, this statement is false.
- **B: There was sufficient time for evacuation, which allowed some residents to escape.** As above, the passage explain show the villagers 'had drowned and were buried in the shattered remains of their homes'. This supports the belief that there had been no time for evacuation. Of course, we cannot be entirely certain that this is false since the passage does not confirm that no one managed to escape. However, based on the information within the passage, we cannot select this statement as the correct answer option here.
- **D: The discoveries initially intimated victims of genocide.** The passage is conclusive in stating this is not true. It indicates that 'war and disease didn't seem to account for the village's sudden demise' and that 'no cut marks or signs of illness were on any of the bones'. Hence, this statement cannot be confirmed as true.

Answer 57 (Continued)

Q57.4: C - The intensity was of an analogous ilk to a later manifestation.

Explanation: The final paragraph of the passage asserts that the tsunami that occurred one thousand years ago was 'similar in scale and intensity to the 2004 tsunami'. These words thus corroborate this statement.

- **A: It appears to have established a pattern of transpiring at distinctive interludes.** The passage speaks of two occurrences only. As such, there is insufficient evidence to support this statement.
- **B: The ferocity caused the inhabitants to be eradicated gradually.** The passage implies that the inhabitants had become trapped and drowned quickly within their own homes. The number of bones discovered suggests that the village was wiped out quickly and not **gradually**. This statement can therefore be considered as false.
- **D: The impact might have been mitigated by lower water levels and changes in the climate.** There is nothing within the passage to suggest that this is true or false. As such, we cannot select it as the correct answer option here.

Answer 58

Q58.1: C - were comparable to specimens in other Neanderthal territories.

Explanation: The final paragraph of the passage details the resemblance between the recent discoveries and bones found at later sites thought to have been occupied by Neanderthals. This statement can thus be supported by the information within the passage.

- **A: were all entirely human in origin and directly linked.** The final paragraph states that the discoveries were 'broadly human'. It does not confirm that the fragments found were certainly or entirely human. This statement cannot be verified by the information within the passage.
- **B: were entirely indistinguishable from previous excavations.** The passage offers clear opposition to this statement as it advises that the bones 'resemble examples found at later sites'. (This refers to sites that can be dated to a later era and not to later excavations.)
- **D: exposed a strong likelihood that feral animals co-existed in that era.** There is nothing within the passage to suggest that feral animals

Answer 58 (Continued)

did (or did not) co-exist with Neanderthalsat that time. The passage does make reference to 'pendants made from cave bear teeth', but it does not infer that feral animals co-existed with Neanderthals.

Q58.2: B - Modern-day humans indubitably cohabited with alternative species.

Explanation: The author indicates several times that modern-day humans and Neanderthals interacted. The second paragraph states that Neanderthals disappeared 'shortly after modern humans appeared on the scene', which indicates that they did cohabit. In addition, the final paragraph notes that 'the two groups interacted sufficiently for modern humans to influence Neanderthal behaviour'. We can therefore deduce that the author **agrees** with this statement.

- **A: Neanderthals are direct ancestors of the modern-day human race.** While the author implies that Neanderthals and modern humans lived together for a period of time, he/she does not suggest that modern humans are descendants of Neanderthals. The author does not corroborate this statement.
- **C: The advance of modern humans boosted the extermination of their cohorts.** The passage states that there are clues towards the impact of modern humans on the extinction of Neanderthals, but it does not provide conclusive evidence to support this. We cannot be certain that the author agrees with this statement.
- **D: Modern humans directly descended from another species due to cohabitation.** Once again, there is nothing within the passage to propose that the modern human descended from another species. Therefore, this cannot be confirmed as an opinion of the author.

Q58.3: A - The modern human potentially influenced the conduct of the other group.

Explanation: This can be corroborated by the final sentence of the passage. We are told that the groups might have interacted to such a level to enable 'modern humans to influence Neanderthal behaviour'.

- **B: The two groups undoubtedly mingled for an extensive period before any superiority emerged.** The information within the passage does not support the fact that the two groups interacted for an **extensive** period of time. Rather, the author describes how Neanderthals vanished 'shortly after' modern humans emerged.

Answer 58 (Continued)

- **C: The interaction between species led to a catastrophic impact on both of them.** This cannot be corroborated by the information within the passage. The author does imply that there was an impact on Neanderthals since the emergence of modern humans led to their distinction. However, the author does not evidence an impact on modern humans.
- **D: The potential for earlier habitations is conclusive.** The first paragraph of the passage states that recent tests **suggest** that Homo sapiens inhabited Europe up to 2,000 years before what was previously thought. The passage does not confirm that this is true.

Q58.4: C - Anatomical discoveries broadly interlinked both species.

Explanation: The passage asserts that the bone and tooth samples were sufficiently connected to advocate the co-habitation of the two species before one took precedence. The final paragraph explains how recent discoveries can be connected to discoveries at sites confirmed to date to a later time. It also states that the evidence implies that 'the two groups interacted sufficiently for modern humans to influence Neanderthal behaviour'. This statement can thus be supported by the information within the passage.

- **A: There is clear proof that interaction indubitably led to the extinction of the weaker species.** While the author does imply this, he/she does not provide any concrete evidence to confirm that it is true.
- **B: The artefacts detected were identical to those associated with modern humans.** The passage advises that the objects '**resembled**' (and were not identical to) those found at later sites. This statement thus cannot be corroborated by the information within the passage.
- **D: There is conclusive evidence of the intermingling of numerous life types.** While the author does imply this, he/she does not provide any concrete evidence to confirm that it is true.

Answer 59

Q59.1: C - They have an intense aim to enhance the economy at the earliest opportunity.

Explanation: The passage explains how energy companies have put in place plans to create jobs in order to aid the economic recovery of the country. It advocates that companies are keen to 'help the UK emerge from the worst economic downturn in 300 years'. This statement can thus be supported by the information within the passage.

- **A: They have bowed to ecological mandates.** Although the companies are keen to base actions on sustainable investments, the passage implies that they have voluntarily initiated this. The passage does not suggest that the companies have been forced to do so, and this statement cannot be corroborated by the information within the passage.
- **B: They have forecast an opportunity to expand their local workforce.** Whilst the author states that SSE's and Equinor's plans will 'support a local supply chain industry', he/she does not confirm that their workforces will expand or that locals will be employed. Based on the information with which we are provided, we cannot be certain that this is true.
- **D: They will provide a systematic approach to promoting renewable energy.** The passage seems to suggest that the companies are supporting the targets set by the government. It does not confirm if this approach is promoted by the companies themselves or if they are being guided by government legislation and, as such, if this is a one-off provision. We thus cannot be sure if this statement is true.

Q59.2: D - They are looking to capitalise in an area of longevity and suitability.

Explanation: The passage advocates that the companies have undertaken analysis to consider the suitability and viability of the locations. The final paragraph states how 'Equinor and SSE Renewables picked the Port of Tyne to host the operations hub through a competitive tendering process', which illustrates how the most suitable location has been chosen. This statement can, therefore, be supported by the information within the passage.

- **A: They are keen to use environmental and funding opportunities to promote their businesses.** The passage does not give any information

Answer 59 (Continued)

to support the idea that funding opportunities are available to these companies. Hence, this statement cannot be verified by the information within the passage.

- **B: They are seizing the prospect of capturing a global market in a cost-effective location.** While the passage alludes to the development of 'offshore wind development 'and 'a surge in demand from windfarm developers', it does not make reference to the economy of the area or suggest cost effectiveness of this area of the market. As such, this statement cannot be corroborated by the information within the passage.
- **C: They are keen to invest in deprived areas with high unemployment.** The passage does not suggest that this is the intention of the companies. In addition, it does not indicate that the areas in which the companies wish to invest are deprived areas with high unemployment. Hence, we cannot confirm that this statement is true.

Q59.3: A - The companies are dedicated to paying urgent attention to ecological requirements.

Explanation: The passage is underpinned by the fact that the companies are committed to providing clean energy. This is mentioned on several occasions. This statement can thus be supported by the information within the passage.

- **B: The locations are those in which the workforce will be obtained at a reduced cost.** There is nothing within the passage to suggest that this is true.
- **C: The triumph of renewable power is now leading to increased competition.** Whilst we might assume that this is true, the passage does not provide any information to corroborate it.
- **D: There is an inference that the project is subject to a lift in the economy.** The passage suggests the exact opposite of this statement. We are told that the project is underwritten by the desire to lift the economy; the project is not dependent on the recovery of the economy.

Q59.4: B - The project is in receipt of support from government sources.

Explanation: This is borne out by the details of comments made by the government's business secretary, who not only supports the impact on the

Answer 59 (Continued)

country's economic recovery but also the contribution to the target emissions objective. This statement can thus be considered as true.

- **A: The employment opportunities will be offered to those who can easily commute.** While this might seem a plausible conclusion, the passage does not suggest that this is correct.
- **C: The proposal is subject to the successful implementation in additional locations.** The passage does highlight alternative locations for further projects, but it does not infer that this project will be compared to or influenced by any other. This statement cannot be deemed as true.
- **D: The potential of suitable personnel was the determining factor in selecting the location.** The passage neither supports nor disproves this statement. Based on the information with which we are provided, we cannot confirm that it is true.

Answer 60

Q60.1: C - earlier timeframes appear to have been superseded.

Explanation: The final paragraph of the passage states that, while scientists had predicted that such a drought would begin in approximately 2030, the recent study evidences that the drought has already arrived. This statement can therefore be supported by the information within the passage.

- **A: the lack of comparative data has negated the trustworthiness of the research.** The passage does admit that the severity of the droughts that have occurred within this decade compared to historic drought is unknown. However, it does not suggest that this will contradict the validity of this research. This statement cannot be corroborated by the information within the passage.
- **B: contributing personnel did not have the essential wealth of expertise.** The passage neither corroborates nor disproves this statement, and we cannot confirm if it is true or false.
- **D: the impact on resources may be paused with expediate action.** The author does not, at any time, broach this issue. We thus cannot confirm if this statement is true or false.

Answer 60 (Continued)

Q60.2: C - the analysis has detailed the impact on climate change progression.

Explanation: The second paragraph highlights how a reduction in water levels at the mouth of the Missouri was 'due to rising temperatures linked to climate change'. The passage explicitly relates rising temperatures and reduced snowfall to climate change, and this statement can thus be concluded from the information within the passage.

- **A: snowfall diminution would not appear to corroborate climate effects.** The second paragraph of the passage explicitly states that climate change has 'reduced the amount of snowfall in the Rocky Mountains in Montana and North Dakota'. This statement is, therefore, false.
- **B: the researchers are only proficient in the scale of drought in one location.** This statement is contradicted by the information within the passage. The author explains that the researchers are 'familiar with drought of this magnitude in the dry Southwest' and that they were 'surprised to find it in the Midwest'. This illustrates how the researchers now have knowledge of drought of this scale in more than one location. This statement is thus untrue.
- **D: the details in the report display contrasting worldwide impacts.** The passage focuses on the areas within the region of the Missouri River. It does not discuss other areas of the world, and this statement cannot be supported by the information with which we are provided.

Q60.3: A - It will have a bearing on aquatic species and, subsequently, their food successions.

Explanation: There is clear evidence within the passage to support the fact that a protracted lack of rainfall will impact on marine life. The final paragraph states that prolonged drought 'harms marine life that must cope with lower water levels'; it is possible that they might not be able to adapt to lower water levels. The passage claims that this will, in turn, affect 'animals such as waterfowl that rely on fish to survive'. This statement can thus be corroborated by the information within the passage.

- **B: It will increase the amount of commercial travel within the area.** While the final paragraph of the passage notes that prolonged

Answer 60 (Continued)

drought can 'slow commercial traffic in rivers', we are not told that the amount of commercial traffic within the area will increase. Based on the information with which we are provided, we cannot confirm that this statement is true.

- **C: It will instigate a replication of the Dust Bowl.** The author states, in the first paragraph of the passage, that the recent drought has left the Upper Missouri River Basin 'even more parched than during the disastrous Dust Bowl of the 1930s'. We can thus assume that this period of prolonged drought is likely to have a **greater** (rather than an equivalent) impact than that of the Dust Bowl.
- **D: It will dramatically reduce water directed for specific uses.** While the passage details how water is used for various functions, it does not indicate that certain sources of water are **directed** for specific purposes or that these sources will be **dramatically reduced**. This statement thus cannot be verified by the information with which we are provided.

Q60.4: B - The severity of the drought would appear to be unparalleled.

Explanation: The author states, in the first paragraph of the passage, that the recent drought has left the Upper Missouri River Basin 'even more parched than during the disastrous Dust Bowl of the 1930s'. We can thus assume that the severity of this drought is **greater** than any previous drought, and this statement can be supported by the information within the passage.

- **A: Experts had forecast the effect and ensured solutions were initiated.** This statement is contradicted by the information within the passage for two reasons. Firstly, whilst experts had anticipated this drought, they had predicted that it would arrive in 2030. Secondly, we are not told that any solutions were put in place or activated.
- **C: Water from elevations had potentially begun to diminish fifty years ago.** The passage does not confirm that this is true. It states that 'runoff from the mountains to the Upper Missouri started decreasing in the 1950s'. However, we do not know when this passage was written, and we cannot be certain if the 1950s were 50 years ago.
- **D: It is improbable that species will endure reduced water levels.** The passage does suggest that the drought will have an impact on various animals, but it does not categorically state they will not survive if water levels are low. Rather, it asserts that they 'must cope with lower

Answer 60 (Continued)

water levels'. Based on the information with which we are provided, we cannot be certain that animals will not endure reduced water levels.

Answer 61

Q61.1: A - There are no specifics to accurately establish when the offspring were slaughtered.

Explanation: While the passage states that the family was killed on 17th July 1918, it asserts that 'no bodies were immediately found' and highlights that the dowager empress 'doubted the news of her family's death'. We are also told that 'even the executioners' later accounts were so muddled as to invite speculation'. It thus appears that there has been some doubt whether the children were killed on this date. In addition, the passage discusses how there has been a long-standing debate as to whether all of the children were killed or whether Anastasia survived. As such, it cannot be accurately confirmed when the children were killed or, indeed, if they were all killed. This statement can thus be corroborated by the information within the passage.

- **B: Numerous affiliates of the household absconded safely.** We are told that the dowager empress had managed to find refuge in Crimea, but we cannot be certain that she lived in the same household as the Tsar, his wife, and their children. Moreover, the passage does not indicate if other members of the household were able to flee. This statement thus cannot be verified by the information within the passage.
- **C: The slayings instigated the initiation of the collapse of the realm.** The first sentence of the passage asserts that the Tsar 'Nicholas II abdicated the throne on March 15, 1917'. As such, the assassinations did not mark the end of his sovereignty or initiate the collapse of his empire; he had already rescinded the throne. This statement thus cannot be supported by the information within this passage.
- **D: The precise setting of their initial incarceration has been uncovered.** The passage states that the family was 'taken captive and **eventually** moved to a house in the Ural Mountains'. We can thus deduce that the site of their **initial** incarceration was not the Ural

Answer 61 (Continued)

Mountains. The passage does not inform us of the place in which they were initially imprisoned, and we cannot be certain if this statement is true or false.

Q61.2: C - The incident afforded a platform for fabricated identity claims.

Explanation: The second paragraph of the passage outlines how 'imposters sprang up all over the world in the ensuing decades'. This conclusion can thus be confirmed by the information within the passage.

- **A: Despite the subsequent pandemonium, specific timings can be speculated.** The passage does not suggest that a conclusive timeline of events can be established. The author explains how even the accounts of the executioners were 'so muddled' that they encouraged speculation of what happened.
- **B: The extent of the charred relics permanently eradicated identification.** Even though the remains had been burned, DNA evidence was used to confirm that the bodies found in the 1970s belonged to the Tsar, his wife, and three of their daughters. This statement is thus false.
- **D: The Tsar elected to abdicate in the anticipation of curtailing the insurgency.** While the first sentence of the passage informs us that the Tsar abdicated, the passage does not provide any information to support the reason for which he did so. As such, we cannot select this as the correct answer option here.

Q61.3: D - considers there is still no conclusive evidence of the fate of Anastasia.

Explanation: This can be concluded from the information within the passage. The final paragraph states that 'Anastasia's remains **were likely** one of the bodies that had been found earlier'. That the words 'were likely' are used implies that there is still no conclusive evidence of what happened to Anastasia.

- **A: persists in the conviction that the princess escaped the massacre.** There is nothing within the passage to indicate that the author holds this belief. Rather, it seems that he/she supports the opinion that the fate of Anastasia has still not been proven.
- **B: deems that further investigations are still required.** The author does not advocate that further investigations are required. This statement

Answer 61 (Continued)

cannot be corroborated by the information with which we are provided.

- **C: intimates that there was a politically motivated concealment of evidence.** There is nothing within the passage to suggest that the author believes this. This statement cannot be supported by the information within the passage.

Q61.4: A - Anastasia's body was unquestionably one of the previous cadavers discovered.

Explanation: The final paragraph states that 'Anastasia's remains were **likely** one of the bodies that had been found earlier'. That the words 'were likely' are used refutes this statement. The passage does not claim that Anastasia's body was **unquestionably** one of the bodies found previously.

- **B: It is probable that the widow of the preceding Tsar evaded the annihilation.** The first paragraph claims that the dowager empress (who was the widow of the preceding Tsar) had fled to Crimea and 'doubted the news of her family's death'. Therefore, this statement is true.
- **C: The assassins themselves provided capricious reports.** This can be supported by the information in the first paragraph of the passage, which states that 'even the executioners' later accounts were so muddled as to invite speculation'.
- **D: Some pretenders have neither been established nor refuted.** The author explains, in the second paragraph, how imposters appeared over the following years. Although many were disregarded, it was neither proved nor disproved that Anna Anderson was Anastasia. This statement is thus true.

Answer 62

Q62.1: B - the rising was efficacious in terms of what was sought to be accomplished.

Explanation: The final paragraph of the passage affirms that 'the rising achieved everything that the organisers thought it would'. This statement can thus be corroborated by the information within the passage.

- **A: the overall sacrifice overshadowed the advances made.** While the passage highlights the sacrifice that was made by the protestors (450 people were killed and 2,614 were injured), it does not state that this overshadowed the achievements of the event. This statement thus cannot be supported by the information with which we are provided.
- **C: the organisers had been assured of victory through the means used.** The passage does not suggest that this statement is true. Indeed, the final paragraph states that 'they did not expect it to win power'. This indicates that the organisers were not confident of victory.
- **D: it had been a strategic incident intended to provide a symbol of contempt.** Whilst the event was symbolic, it was not necessarily strategic. Indeed, the fourth paragraph describes the confusion caused by conflicting orders. This statement cannot be wholly supported by the information within the passage.

Q62.2: A - The insurgents had devised a response for the counter offensive.

Explanation: The passage does not provide any information to support this statement. While it details how the shipment of arms had been captured three days before the event, it does not indicate that compensations had been made for this. Additionally, the conflicting orders from the leading insurgents caused confusion. We can thus assume that minimal preparations had been established to counteract the opposition from the British, and this statement is not supported by the information within the passage.

- **B: The directives disseminated resulted in orders being misconstrued.** This can be verified by the information in the fourth paragraph of the passage, which details how 'confusion was caused by conflicting orders sent out to the Irish volunteers'.
- **C: The Irish population acquired an understanding of the aim of the incident.** Dr McGarry's comments, which are noted in the final paragraph of the passage, corroborate this. He states that the incident had 'transformed public opinion', which implies that the Irish population understood the reasons for the rebellion.

Answer 62 (Continued)

- **D: The British troops had not been fully prepared.** The passage describes how there were 400 troops and approximately 1,000 insurgents. This supports the fact that the British were not sufficiently prepared, and this statement is thus true.

Q62.3: B - The military did not deem there was any tangible threat from the rebels.

Explanation: This statement can be substantiated by the information within the second paragraph of the passage. We are told that there were far fewer British troops than insurgents. The fact that the British had not sent adequate manpower supports the idea that they did not feel there was a tangible threat from the rebels.

- **A: The insurgence would have succeeded had there been a greater number of volunteers.** Whilst we might assume that this would have been helpful, it cannot be supported by the information within the passage. In addition, the final paragraph affirms that 'the rising achieved everything that the organisers thought it would', which suggests that the insurgents **did** succeed. This statement cannot be corroborated by the information within the passage.
- **C: The rebels were wholly conscious that the rising would not be efficacious.** The passage does not imply that the volunteers were totally convinced that the event would be unsuccessful. While they might not have expected to win power, they aimed to transform public opinion, and the passage does not state that the organisers believed this definitely would not happen.
- **D: The rebels had not predicted the antagonism of the general public.** There are no indications in the passage to support this statement. The passage claims that the event changed public opinion and the rebels gained support; it does not hint that the rebels were met with antagonism from the public.

Q62.4: B - the event heralded the commencement of Irish independence.

Explanation: The author does not dispute Dr McGarry's comments that the event had 'derailed Home Rule' and created 'public support for republicanism'. If the author did not agree that the event had triggered the commencement of Irish independence, he/she would have arguably dismissed these comments. We can thus deduce that the author agrees with this statement.

Answer 62 (Continued)

- **A: the insurgence had an adverse impact on public attitudes.** The author includes, in the final paragraph of the passage, the thoughts of Dr McGarry, who maintains that the Easter Rising 'transformed public opinion by winning public support'. The author thus suggests that the insurgence had a positive (and not an adverse) impact on the attitudes of the public, and this statement is false.
- **C: the surrender was viewed as a treachery of the aims of the rebels.** While it is plausible that some might have been unhappy with the surrender, the author neither supports nor refutes this opinion. He/She does indicate, however, that the aim of the event had been achieved (despite the surrender). This statement cannot be corroborated by the information within the passage.
- **D: the mayhem between the superiors was the decisive cause for failure.** The author does highlight that the conflicting orders caused confusion, but he/she does not suggest that this was the reason for any failure. In addition, we are told that 'the rising achieved everything that the organisers thought it would', which insinuates that it did not fail. This statement is, therefore, untrue.

Answer 63

Q63.1: C - The introduction of animal or human cells can produce a similar consequence.

Explanation: The third paragraph of the passage corroborates this statement. We are told that 'if mouse stem cells in a primed state are added to a mouse blastocyst, many of the embryos end up dying, just as when human stem cells are added'. We can thus deduce that the introduction of animal or human cells can produce a similar effect.

- **A: The experiments will generate organs for those necessitating urgent transplants.** The passage does not confirm this. It merely highlights that it might be an important step towards discovering ways to grow organs outside of the body. However, it does not explicitly assert that this will be possible.
- **B: Subsequent research will necessitate investigation into the brain cells.** The passage does not give any consideration to the further investigation of brain cells. This statement cannot be supported by the information within the passage.

Answer 63 (Continued)

- **D: The cells utilised were attained from those needing transplants.** While the passage does state that human cells were used in this experiment, it does not suggest that they were taken from individuals who needed an organ transplant. Based on the information with which we are provided, we cannot be certain that this is true.

Q63.2: A - The studies will enrich transplant development research.

Explanation: The penultimate paragraph implies that these experiments will prove valuable to further research. Whilst the ethical issues surrounding such research are highlighted, the experiments are still considered an 'essential step towards finding ways to grow organs outside bodies'. Based on the information with which we are provided, we can deduce that these studies will enhance future research in the field of transplantation. This statement is, therefore, true.

- **B: The studies are of minimal use to furthering human transplants.** The penultimate paragraph implies that these experiments will prove valuable to further research in the field of transplantation. Whilst the ethical issues surrounding such research are mentioned, these experiments are still considered an 'essential step towards finding ways to grow organs outside bodies'. This statement is, therefore, false.
- **C: The results, to date, will be sufficient to make the process feasible.** We cannot draw this conclusion from the passage. Indeed, the penultimate paragraph details how this experiment is an important **step**. It does not state that the current results are **sufficient** to make the process immediately viable.
- **D: The use of small animals will not provide sufficient analysis.** This cannot be concluded from the information that we are given. In fact, we are told that mice (which can be considered as small animals) provide adequate analysis. The passage suggests that further investigations are required, but it does not advocate that the use of small animals is unhelpful. This statement is thus untrue.

Q63.3: C - This research will serve to enhance their development in animals.

Explanation: The penultimate paragraph states that 'growing human organs in animals could be an essential step towards finding ways to grow organs outside

Answer 63 (Continued)

bodies'. We can thus infer that the use of animals in such studies can aid the development of human organs. As such, this research will help to enhance the development of human organs in animals, and this statement can be supported by the information within the passage.

- **A: The results will provide an indisputable solution to their production.** The passage highlights that these results raise several issues, both medical and ethical. It explicates the need to 'decide on what can and cannot be done in this area'. We realise that any solution found might be challenged, and this statement is thus false.
- **B: This type of research requires a team that is significant in size.** While the passage alludes to 'Feng's team', we are not told of how many people that team comprised. Hence, we cannot be certain of the team required for this type of research, and we cannot confirm if this statement is true or false.
- **D: They will need to be suitably matched to the cells used.** There is nothing within the passage to support this thought. The passage does not suggest that this had been considered, and we thus cannot be certain that it is true.

Q63.4: D - Organs have the potential to be dominated by animal characteristics.

Explanation: The passage does not provide any information to support this statement. Therefore, it cannot be corroborated by the passage.

- **A: The team has considered several ethical ramifications.** The final paragraph of the passage states how a decision of the ethics committee helped this research to be successful, which demonstrates that ethical consequences were contemplated. In addition, the penultimate paragraph suggests that other ethical issues need to be discussed. This highlights that the ethical ramifications of this research have been considered.
- **B: The importance of the results for future research is immeasurable.** The passage illustrates the importance of the recent results, but it also recognises the need for further research. It advocates that this research has provided an immensely valuable basis for further experimentation, and this statement can be considered as true.

Answer 63 (Continued)

- **C: The human cells interacted with numerous tissues in the embryo.** This statement is supported by the information within the second paragraph in which the author describes the interaction of the human cells with the mouse embryo's eye, liver, and red blood cells. This statement is this true.

Answer 64

Q64.1: D - the document will encompass a constructive conservational component.

Explanation: This can be confirmed by the final paragraph of the passage, which states that 'the draft also includes a goal to plant three billion trees in the EU by 2030, to help absorb carbon dioxide from the atmosphere and make cities greener'. This will add a positive conservational element to the proposal.

- **A: a reduction in the use of chemical pesticides will stop the decline of pollinators.** While the opening sentence of the passage claims that 'the European Commission is seeking to halve the use of chemical pesticides by 2030 to halt the decline of pollinators', the passage does not state that a reduction **will definitely stop** it. Rather, the passage implies that a reduction in the use of pesticides **might help** the situation. Based on the information with which we are provided, we cannot be certain that it **will stop** it.
- **B: the potential for adverse consequences is immense.** The passage does discuss the consequences of a ban on pesticides, but it does not outline the extent of such consequences. We therefore cannot be certain that they will be **immense**. The passage states that a widespread ban 'could cause crop yields to fall', which implies that this is a **possible** consequence rather than a definite outcome.
- **C: the legislature will be approved with negligible obstruction.** The passage asserts that the plan is 'likely to draw criticism both from those urging a phase-out of the substances and from farmers who say crop yields will suffer'. We can therefore assume that there will be reasonably significant obstacles to overcome in order to implement the legislation, and this statement can be considered as false.

Answer 64 (Continued)

Q64.2: C - The influence of previous sanctions has been established as effective.

Explanation: The passage affirms that, while the EU banned the outdoor use of neonicotinoid insecticides in 2018, the number of bees continues to decline. We can assume that previous sanctions have not been wholly effective. After all, if they had been, there might not be a need to introduce further measures. This statement thus cannot be deduced from the information within the passage.

- **A: The outlined article is not restricted to debating insecticides.** Whilst the passage does describe how the document is centred on the use of insecticides, it also highlights how intentions to plant trees will be included. This statement is, therefore, true.
- **B: Reduction of selected pesticides has previously been initiated.** There is clear support for this statement in paragraph five of the passage, which claims that the outdoor use of neonicotinoid insecticides was implemented in 2018.
- **D: There is a visible inclination that the annihilation of insects is increasing.** The fourth paragraph of the passage corroborates this statement since it highlights how 'beekeepers in western Europe have reported a fall in the number of bees and colony losses over the last 15 years'. This statement can thus be deduced from the information within the passage.

Q64.3: C - The specifics of enforcing the reduction in usage have not been distributed.

Explanation: The passage highlights that the plan is currently a 'working document' which has not yet been adopted and is still 'subject to change'. Based on the information within the passage, we can assume that the specific details have not yet been circulated since they have not yet been finalised. This statement is thus true.

- **A: There has been a proactive initiative amongst the major stakeholders to tackle the issue.** The passage indicates that Bayer aims to reduce the environmental impact of pesticides. However, it does not provide any evidence to suggest that companies have been proactive in tackling the issue to date. It seems to imply that they are awaiting the document, and this statement cannot be supported by the information within the passage.

Answer 64 (Continued)

- **B: Effective regulations have already been initiated to challenge the impacts of pesticides.** The passage asserts that, while the EU banned the outdoor use of neonicotinoid insecticides in 2018, the number of bees continues to decline. We can therefore assume that previous sanctions have not been wholly effective.
- **D: The Commission has measured the bearing on crop production.** The fifth paragraph of the passage illustrates how 'some farming groups have said a wide ban on pesticides could cause crop yields to fall and have urged the Commission to assess the impact of the measures before fixing binding targets'. The fact that certain groups have **urged** the Commission to **assess** the impact of these measures on crop production indicates that it has not yet evaluated this. This statement is thus false.

Q64.4: B - decreases are putative, but attainment targets must be pragmatic.

Explanation: Based on the information within the passage, we can conclude that legislation to decrease the use of pesticides is now in progress. We can also deduce that there is a request for attainable targets: the fifth paragraph details how certain farming groups have 'urged the Commission to assess the impact of the measures before fixing binding targets'. This statement can thus be corroborated by the information within the passage.

- **A: the exclusion of insecticide will intensify the bee population.** The passage does not offer any information to substantiate this. Indeed, it is plausible that various other factors are causing the bee population to decline. The removal of certain pesticides will arguably contribute towards an increase in the number of bees, but we cannot be certain that it will **intensify** the population.
- **C: decreasing pesticide usage will deliver a negligible impact.** Whilst the passage suggests that the removal of pesticides will help to increase the bee population, it does not state that it will be the ultimate solution. On the other hand, the passage does not indicate that a decrease in the use of pesticides will only have a **negligible** impact. Based on the information with which we are provided, we cannot be certain if this statement is correct.
- **D: a widespread prohibition will have a bearing on other industries.** The passage does affirm that a widespread ban on pesticides

Answer 64 (Continued)

will potentially affect crop yields. However, it does not mention the potential impacts on other industries. Therefore, we cannot confirm that this statement is true.

Answer 65

Q65.1: B - Brown initiated a proactive attack on international climate change.

Explanation: The passage highlights how Brown oversaw the world's first Climate Change Act. It also details how he announced an agreement to tackle climate change in 2005. It is evident that he assumed a proactive role in the fight against climate change, and this statement can thus be corroborated by the information within the passage.

- **A: Brown was accountable for the protracting recession within the UK.** While the passage states that 'the greatest challenge he faced in office was the worldwide financial crisis and the following recession', it does not indicate that Brown was responsible for prolonging the recession. This statement cannot be supported by the information within the passage.
- **C: Brown instigated an initiative for the legal challenges in the health sector.** While we are told that Brown oversaw the implementation of 'a legally-enforceable right to early cancer screening and treatment', we are not informed that his initiative extended to the whole of the health sector. This statement cannot be corroborated by the information within the passage.
- **D: Brown became the longest serving Chancellor of the Exchequer.** The passage maintains that Brown 'was Chancellor of the Exchequer during the longest ever period of economic growth'; it does not state that he was the longest serving Chancellor of the Exchequer. This statement is thus false.

Q65.2: C - Brown was impeded by damage to his eye which deteriorated during his ministry.

Explanation: This statement is incorrect for two reasons. Firstly, while the passage does confirm that Brown sustained an injury to his eye whilst at university,

Answer 65 (Continued)

it does not suggest that this affected his competence in any manner. Secondly, we are not told that the effects of this injury worsened during his time in office. This statement is thus not supported by the information within the passage.

- **A: Brown was instrumental in bringing the war in Iraq to a conclusion.** The passage explains how the war in Iraq started under the previous prime minister, but it ended under Brown when forces were withdrawn from Iraq. Based on the information within the passage, we can assume that, as the prime minister, Brown did play an influential role in bringing the war to an end. This statement is thus true.
- **B: Brown was keen to support the sharing of power in Ireland.** The final paragraph of the passage details Brown's aim to negotiate the devolution of certain powers in Northern Ireland. It seems that he allowed Northern Ireland to control certain issues and his own government to control others. This statement can thus be considered as true.
- **D: Brown endeavoured to implement improved financial regulations.** The passage highlights that Brown 'pledged to improve financial supervision and regulations'. This statement can thus be deemed true.

Q65.3: B - Brown was extremely driven in addressing global debts.

Explanation: This conclusion can be drawn from the passage since it explicates Brown's 'passion for global justice' and his announcement of an agreement to support the world's poorest countries. The passage states that he negotiated to cancel the debts of the world's poorest nations and to triple the development budget.

- **A: Brown was practical in addressing inequality in class structure.** Whilst this might be surmised from his policies, the passage does not provide any information that supports this statement.
- **C: Brown took charge of eradicating the influences of the fiscal institutes.** The passage details how Brown implemented measures to control and manage the financial institutions. It does not, however, claim that he had any desire to **eradicate** them. Based on the information with which we are provided, we cannot be certain that this statement is true.

Answer 65 (Continued)

- **D: Brown augmented financial pressure with his overseas aid strategy.** We might assume that the cancellation of debts and the increase in overseas budgets would cause some financial burden. However, the passage does not confirm if this is true or false, and we cannot select it as the correct answer option here.

Q65.4: C - Brown was a powerful influence in initiating the war with Iraq.

Explanation: The passage does not outline Brown's role in the initiation of the war with Iraq. Based on the information with which we are provided, we cannot confirm that this statement is true.

- **A: Brown prevented further financial indiscretions through regulation.** This statement can be supported by the information in the fifth paragraph of the passage, which describes Brown's attempt to 'improve financial supervision and regulation'. We can assume that this would have prevented any further indiscretions of the financial institutes, and this statement is thus true.
- **B: Brown enhanced local policing and security throughout the country.** This is supported by the information in the third paragraph of the passage, which advises that Brown oversaw 'the introduction of neighbourhood policing in every area'.
- **D: Brown exhibited an exceptional moral compass in relation to poorer states.** The passage asserts that Brown aimed to eradicate the debt of poorer countries and increased the support given to them, which confirms that this statement is true.

Answer 66

Q66.1: B - The incident was not a vibrant validation of British defiance.

Explanation: This statement is refuted by the fact that the first paragraph asserts that the event was 'an act of stubborn defiance' by Britain. The use of positive words throughout the passage, such as 'pride' and 'victory', further support the fact that this statement is untrue.

- **A: There had been a contentious turnaround.** That the event was considered 'contentious' is supported by the information within the

Answer 66 (Continued)

second paragraph of the passage, which states that 'the British retreat to Dunkirk was controversial'. This statement can thus be deemed true.

- **C: The utilisation of small vessels was not instigated from experience.** Whilst the first paragraph asserts that small boats 'were essential to the operation's success', we are not told if this strategy had been used previously. Therefore, we cannot be certain if this statement is true or false. It cannot be selected as the correct answer option in this instance.
- **D: The directives of the German army contributed to the accomplishment.** The third paragraph of the passage describes how 'German errors, particularly the halt order, allowed the escape to happen'. This statement can therefore be supported by the information within the passage.

Q66.2: B - The event was the result of a tremendous mistake of planning.

Explanation: The second paragraph of the passage highlights how the evacuation was successful due to the Allies being 'in a desperate situation'. The 'poor planning, intelligence, leadership, and communications' implies that the troops were able to be withdrawn to safety. This statement can, therefore, be corroborated by the information within the passage.

- **A: A significant percentage of British troops were repatriated to safety.** The passage details that 338,226 troops and other personnel were evacuated from the beaches of northern France. Yet, it does not state that this included a **significant** percentage of British troops who were in France. In addition, it does not confirm that they arrived safely at their destination.
- **C: The mission was successful solely due to the smaller ships.** The first paragraph asserts that small boats 'were essential to the operation's success'. Nevertheless, there is nothing to indicate that the success of the operation was **solely** due to these boats. We are not told if other boats and vehicles were used, and we cannot be certain that this statement is correct.
- **D: There were negligible casualties in all of the military services.** While the passage does not provide the exact number of casualties, the third paragraph details how the RAF, the British navy and the French navy 'sustained huge losses'. This refutes the suggestion that there were **negligible** casualties. In addition, whilst the passage discusses

Answer 66 (Continued)

these three military services, we are not told if other military services were involved in the event. Hence, we cannot be certain if **all** of the military services are discussed here.

Q66.3: A - The incident succeeded against a backdrop of imminent disaster.

Explanation: The first paragraph of the passage notes that the evacuation 'was a victory snatched from the jaws of defeat', which illustrate show, at that time of the successful evacuations, there was a strong possibility that the British would be defeated. This statement can thus be supported by the information within the passage.

- **B: The RAF was ultimately accountable for the defeat.** The passage affirms that the RAF was 'criticised for failing to cover the troops on the beach adequately', which refutes the idea that it was accountable for the victory. The passage does not provide sufficient evidence to verify this statement since it only highlights the criticism towards the RAF.
- **C: The salvage operation encompassed army personnel and nationals.** While we might assume that the smaller boats were provided by non-military people, the passage does not state that citizens were actively involved in the event. This statement cannot be corroborated by the information within the passage.
- **D: There were enormous casualties within the German army.** The passage does not give any indication of the number of individuals within the German army who died or were injured. This statement cannot be supported by the information within the passage.

Q66.4: A - the mission was, in essence, an accomplishment due to its impact on British moral.

Explanation: Although the need to evacuate might be viewed as a defeat, the author describes it as 'one of the proudest moments' of the War. The passage suggests that the impact of the event on British moral was immense due to 'the pride that the British people felt after the successful rescue of the country's men'. This statement can, therefore, be supported by the information within the passage.

Answer 66 (Continued)

- **B: the mission was exceptionally well orchestrated.** The passage does not confirm that this is true. In fact, it claims that the RAF was 'criticised for failing to cover the troops on the beach adequately', and it highlights the 'huge losses' suffered by the British and French navies. We might therefore assume that it was not **exceptionally** well orchestrated.
- **C: the use of the shorelines was needed due to the obliteration of the quayside.** The passage does not give any indication that this was the reason for the use of the shorelines, and we cannot be certain that this statement is correct.
- **D: the project has overshadowed more positive exercises.** The final paragraph of the passage indicates how other rescue missions have been outshone by Dunkirk. However, we are not told that these missions were **more positive** than Dunkirk. Therefore, we cannot be certain that this statement is correct.

Answer 67

Q67.1: A - De Valera may be considered one of the major influences in Irish politics during his time as leader.

Explanation: The information throughout the passage appears to support this statement. The passage claims that de Valera had 'the most formative influence on the development of the new state'. In addition, the fact that he was re-elected as the President of Ireland in 1966 also demonstrates how his influence had not diminished over time.

- **B: De Valera's attempt to collaborate with America had little impact on the success of independence.** While de Valera was unsuccessful in gaining America's recognition of the Irish Republic, he did raise $5 million in funds during his time in the country. The passage implies that this money helped to finance his objective since, upon his return to Ireland, 'he at once gave new impetus and cohesion to the Sinn Féin government'. Based on the information with which we are provided, we cannot say that his attempt to collaborate with America had **little** impact on Irish Independence, and this statement is not correct.

Answer 67 (Continued)

- **C: De Valera appeared to face a moral dilemma with the terms of the Treaty.** The passage does not suggest that this is true. Although de Valera chose 'not to lead the Irish delegation which negotiated the Treaty', the passage does not indicate that this was due to a moral dilemma that he faced. We are told that he went on to oppose the treaty and fuel opposition to it but, once again, the passage does not imply that this was based on his morals.
- **D: De Valera resolved to instigate civil war in the country.** While we are told that de Valera's 'attempts to his attempts to mobilise opposition to [the Treaty] made a civil war more likely', the passage does not state that he actively sought to instigate a civil war. This statement cannot be supported by the information within the passage.

Q67.2: A - De Valera's incarceration assisted his profile.

Explanation: The second paragraph of the passage informs us that de Valera's imprisonment 'enhanced his credibility with republicans'. This statement can, therefore, be supported by the information within the passage.

- **B: De Valera had exercised sound judgement in abstaining from discussions in London.** We are told how de Valera was criticised for his decision to not lead the Irish delegation which negotiated the Treaty and how he needed to defend the fact that he had remained in Dublin. Since his decision seemed to divide opinions, it cannot be considered as an exercise of **sound** judgement, and this statement is not supported by the information in the passage.
- **C: De Valera founded a new party following his altercation with his former faction.** Whilst de Valera did form a new party, the passage does not detail the reason for this. We cannot be certain if this statement is true or false, and it cannot be selected as the correct answer option in this instance.
- **D: De Valera's personal qualities were the foundations of his success.** Although it is credible to assume that de Valera's personal qualities assisted his success, the passage does not state this. In fact, we are told of his '**inflammatory** speeches'. The passage does not provide any specific details of his personal attributes, and this answer option cannot be selected in this instance.

Answer 67 (Continued)

Q67.3: A - De Valera's decision to maintain neutrality during the conflict was the reason for the party losing power.

Explanation: While we are told that de Valera aimed to maintain neutrality in the Second World War, the passage does not indicate that this was unpopular or that it had any bearing on the fact that his party lost power between 1948 and 1957. In addition, de Valera did not lose power until 1948, which was four years after the end of the War. This statement cannot be supported by the information with which we are provided.

- **B: De Valera was active in the movement for Irish independence.** The passage outlines how de Valera travelled to America in an attempt to gain support for the Irish Republic and how he 'gave new impetus and cohesion to the Sinn Féin government'. We are also told that he sought to weaken links with Britain. This statement can thus be verified by the information within the passage.
- **C: De Valera was disposed to provocative outpourings.** This statement can be supported by the initial paragraph of the passage, which alludes to de Valera's 'inflammatory speeches'.
- **D: De Valera played a pivotal role in founding the autonomous country and its first government.** The passage highlights how de Valera was heavily involved in the country's government throughout the crucial time that followed the achievement of independence. The party that he formed himself, as well as the establishment of a newspaper, contributed to the development and enhancement of an independent state. It appears that he was not only involved in the fight for an independent country, but he was also one of the leading figures in establishing the new government. This statement can, therefore, be corroborated by the information within the passage.

Q67.4: A - retired from politics through age not choice.

Explanation: This can be inferred from the information at the end of the passage. The fact that he was 90 years of age when he retired suggests that it was his age (and possibly health factors associated with age) that prompted him to leave. This answer option is the most appropriate one in this instance.

- **B: was a symbol of diplomacy and negotiation.** There is no clear inference that de Valera was an icon of these traits. Rather, the passage details his often antagonistic speeches.

Answer 67 (Continued)

- **C: operated primarily for his own significance.** The passage does not appear to suggest that de Valera's intentions were for his own benefit. Rather, it highlights how he operated for the success of the new independent state. This statement cannot be supported by the information within the passage.
- **D: was solely responsible for the economic development of the country.** There is no doubt that de Valera played an extremely important role in developing the country and stimulating 'economic self-sufficiency'. However, the passage does not assert that this was **solely** due to de Valera. This statement cannot be selected as the correct answer option in this instance.

Answer 68

Q68.1: C - The utilisation of carbon dating has transformed archaeological investigations.

Explanation: The first paragraph of the passage highlights how the use of carbon dating has given archaeologists a revised timescale which pre-dates previous suggestions. It has, therefore, proved extremely valuable and has transformed archaeological investigations. This statement can, therefore, be considered as true.

- **A: The preceding explorations had not been conducted effectively.** Whilst the findings from the previous explorations are now deemed to be inaccurate, there is nothing to indicate they were not carried out correctly. The development of technology has enabled a more in-depth analysis to be undertaken; the original investigations seemed correct using what was available at that time. This statement can thus be considered as false.
- **B: These discoveries enhance those already documented.** While the previous findings are important, the time scales provided were incorrect. As such, the previous discoveries now have minimal relevance. This statement can be considered as untrue.
- **D: Present constraints have impeded the promotion of all excavations.** The author notes the impact of present restrictions but only in relation to visitors to the site. The passage does not suggest that

Answer 68 (Continued)

constraints have caused any negative impact on the researchers' fieldwork, and this statement cannot be considered as true.

Q68.2: A - The site has the potential to become recognised as a world heritage site.

Explanation: While the passage states that the site is of 'historic importance' and of 'huge significance', there is no indication that it may be awarded world heritage status. This statement thus cannot be corroborated by the information within the passage.

- **B: The excavation has indicated that this was a major and central point.** This can be supported using the information in paragraph two. The author suggests that, at its most important point, the habitation might have 'rivalled the largest known post-Roman settlements in Europe'.
- **C: The periods established formerly now appear to be somewhat inappropriate.** This is evident quite early in the passage. The author details that the site was considered to date back to the Bronze or Iron Age but, following carbon dating, it was suggested to be Pictish, which is a much earlier era.
- **D: This area has been the subject of analysis for a significant period of time.** The second paragraph of the passage affirms that extensive fieldwork has been conducted in the area **since 2011**. While we are not told when this passage was written, the final paragraph mentions the restrictions that were imposed on the UK in March 2020 due to the coronavirus pandemic. It seems that the passage was written after March 2020 since the leader of Aberdeenshire Council is hopeful that visitors will start to come to the site 'once restrictions start to be lifted'. As such, this statement can be considered as true.

Q68.3: B - there will be a need to regulate visitors to ensure that the site is not endangered.

Explanation: Although the site is currently not open to visitors, the passage does not suggest that, when it does open, there will be any restrictions. The final paragraph advises that visitors from 'far and wide' will be welcomed. It does not outline the need for any specific protective measures or regulations, and we cannot confirm that this statement embodies the thoughts of the author.

Answer 68 (Continued)

- **A: the precursor to this dig proved erroneous.** The author is quite clear in stating that the previous investigation provided inaccurate details. This statement is, therefore, supported by the thoughts of the author.
- **C: it will necessitate considerable investigation to collaborate findings.** Although the researchers have already discovered much information, the author implies that there is still a great deal left to be understood. Further investigation will enable more details of the site to be uncovered, and we can thus confirm that the author agrees with this statement.
- **D: there has been some discord as previous data appears incorrect.** The author demonstrates how the importance of this site had previously been overlooked due to erroneous data. The third paragraph explains that samples were taken from the site simply to place other discoveries in a wider context; it seems that this discovery was made almost by chance. Previous data had incorrectly attributed the site to a different era and had made the area seem unimportant. Based on the information within the passage, the author appears to agree with this statement.

Q68.4: C - Can't Tell

Explanation: The passage suggests that there is the potential for the site to have held one of the largest populations in Europe. However, it does not confirm that it was one of the most populous areas **worldwide**. We cannot be certain if this statement is true or false.

Answer 69

Q69.1: D - The link between childhood influences and subsequent behaviour is not deliberated sufficiently.

Explanation: The passage begins by stating that there is insufficient emphasis on the importance of teaching morals during childhood. The writer frequently uses the verb 'should', highlighting the fact that the link between childhood influences and subsequent behaviour ought to be considered. In addition, the

Answer 69 (Continued)

third paragraph notes the influence of certain groups on young people, once again stressing that this association **should** be considered. This statement is, therefore, corroborated by the information within the passage.

- **A: The stimulus of the household at a future period cannot overturn mindsets.** The writer explains that, although major stressful life events may be encountered, these serve to strengthen attitudes. In addition, paragraph four details how these events 'can reinforce one's moral code'. Therefore, if the mindset of good morals has been established during an individual's most formative years, any provocations later in life would not lead to a lessening of these. Based on the information within the passage, this statement is false.
- **B: The greatest period for felonious actions is in adolescence.** This statement cannot be supported by the information within the passage. While the writer claims that adolescence is a period during which one develops morally, he/she does not confirm that it is the time in which most criminal actions are undertaken.
- **C: Antisocial behaviours will always diminish significantly in the latter years of an individual's life.** Although the passage discusses the effect of antisocial behaviour on young people, it does not suggest that misconduct will reduce with time. Rather, the general inference is that such behaviours are instilled and will form lifelong attitudes. This statement cannot be corroborated by the information within the passage.

Q69.2: A - The absence of strong guidance during childhood is not rescindable.

Explanation: The emphasis throughout this passage is that an individual's younger years are the most impressive and formative. The passage proposes that childhood through to adolescence is a critical time, suggesting that development is formed from childhood and extends to 'later childhood and adolescence'. As such, we can infer that, even if an individual does not have strong guidance during childhood, this can be revoked in the years between later childhood and adolescence. The statement's suggestion that an absence of strong guidance during childhood is 'not rescindable' thus cannot be deemed accurate.

- **B: A strong moral compass instilled from birth is impractical.** There is nothing within the passage to either insinuate or confirm this.

Answer 69 (Continued)

Therefore, we cannot be certain if the writer supports or challenges this statement, and it cannot be selected as the correct answer option.

- **C: The effects of influences may dissipate when not consistent.** The writer states that, 'if environments that foster moral development are not prolonged and sustained across several years, the effect on moral behaviour may be short lived'. We realise that, if positive environments that help to instil values in individuals are not constant, a person's moral behaviour can be affected. This statement can therefore be supported by the information that the writer provides.
- **D: The effect of peer pressure has been shown to be significant.** This statement can be corroborated by the information within the passage. The writer asserts, in paragraph three, that the opinions of peers are 'likely to affect how the young person feels'. We can easily comprehend that peer pressure is influential, and this answer option cannot be selected here.

Q69.3: A - The promotion of the association between morality and misconduct.

Explanation: The whole passage is centred around the significance of the link between moral attitudes and subsequent antisocial behaviours. The second paragraph explains the writer's assertion that moral education should be considered in a similar way to other educational themes. Based on the information within the passage, it seems sensible to consider that, if the link between morality and misconduct is highlighted, the case for the establishment of the compulsory teaching of morals would be promoted. This statement is thus the correct answer option.

- **B: The accentuation of the limitations of parental abilities.** The passage does not explicitly suggest that accentuating the limitations of the abilities of certain parents will strengthen the case for the establishment of the compulsory teaching of morals. This answer option is not the most appropriate one in this instance.
- **C: The indication that educational establishments are the solitary source of influence.** The passage does not infer this any point; the emphasis is very much on the various sources of influence. This statement is, therefore, false.
- **D: The indication that life supporting subjects are more beneficial than academic focuses.** The writer does not, at any time, indicate this.

Answer 69 (Continued)

Therefore, we cannot select it as the correct answer option here.

Q69.4: C - is convinced that instilling an understanding of behaviours at an impressionable age is vital to combatting issues.

Explanation: That this is the belief of the writer is corroborated throughout the passage. There search data is used to highlight how behaviour may be displayed from 'as young as three' and to suggest that, the sooner good morals and behaviour are taught, the more ingrained they become. He/She stresses the link between 'moral emotions and offending behaviour in young people'. Additionally, the comment that 'students absorb positive moral behaviours when surrounded with just and fair role models, rules, and interactions' enables us to conclude that this statement supports the view of the writer.

- **A: considers that a moral compass determines cognitive behaviours.** The writer does not, at any point, discuss cognitive behaviours. The passage focuses on moral behaviours and the ensuing crime-related actions linked to them, and this statement cannot be selected as the correct answer option in this instance.
- **B: deems that class structure has an influence on moral attitudes.** The passage does not insinuate that personal circumstances may have a bearing on the moral views of children. This statement cannot, therefore, be considered an opinion of the writer.
- **D: intimates that behaviours are proven to be repetitive through subsequent generations.** There is little within the passage to support this. The writer does state that parents are influential, but he/she does not provide any further evidence to confirm this. We thus cannot be certain that the writer holds this opinion.

Answer 70

Q70.1: B - Supplementary studies will be vital to authenticate the impact on alternative species.

Explanation: This conclusion may be drawn from the final paragraph of the passage, which details how additional investigations will be needed to ascertain the impact of the findings on adult coral. The current research has been carried

Answer 70 (Continued)

out on larvae. We are also told that the additional investigations will include a variety of coral species, extending the scope of the research beyond the species used in the recent study. This statement can, therefore, be corroborated by the information within the passage.

- **A: The investigations have conclusively proved that corals endure heated seawater.** This statement is incorrect. The studies have actually shown that the increase in ocean temperatures is causing the corals to lose their colour and 'gradually starve to death'.
- **C: Algae are the solitary resource of defence for the coral reefs.** Algae are not a form of defence for the coral reefs but, rather, they are providers of food. They feed the coral; they do not defend it. This statement is thus false.
- **D: At this time, research is not sufficient to corroborate the discoveries.** Although the passage states that further research is required, it is needed to assess the impact on adult coral. The current research is sufficient to prove the discovery that the coral 'with the heat-resistant algae remained healthy'. This statement is, therefore, incorrect.

Q70.2: A - the absence of colour signifies the imminent demise of the coral.

Explanation: This is stated in the third paragraph of the passage. The author explains how, when the corals lose colour, they take on a bleached appearance and, with time, they will starve and die. This happens when seas become too warm. This statement can, therefore, be deduced from the information in the passage.

- **B: global warming will ultimately result in the extinction of corals.** Although it would be logical to assume that this is true, the passage does not explicitly state this. Additionally, there is no mention of global warming in this context.
- **C: there appears to be a systematic cycle of the occurrence of bleaching.** While the passage states that the Great Barrier Reef has suffered its'third mass bleaching event in five years', it does not suggest that this is a systematic occurrence that can be accurately anticipated. This statement cannot be verified by the information within the passage.

Answer 70 (Continued)

- **D: the emergence of shorter, cooler seasons has impacted on the coral reefs.** The passage does not discuss the lengths of the seasons or the impact of the cooler parts of the year. This statement cannot be supported by the information within the passage.

Q70.3: B - The effects may be counteracted through the cultivation of algae that can withstand extreme warmth.

Explanation: This statement can be corroborated by the information in the passage. The passage claims that the research has, and will continue to, offset the consequences of heat by developing heat-resistant algae. The passage infers that the impact of warm waters may be overturned using algae.

- **A: The effects of the warmer waters may potentially be overturned.** The passage only discusses the effects of warmer waters on coral. Warmer waters arguably have far reaching consequences, and there is insufficient evidence within the passage to suggest that all impacts may be reversed.
- **C: The true impact of warmer waters has emerged in the preceding five years.** The only reference to a five-year period is in the second paragraph in which the author highlights the three bleaching events that have occurred in five years. The passage does not affirm that the effects were not noticed prior to this time, and this statement cannot be corroborated by the information with which we are provided.
- **D: It will be comparatively straightforward to increase tolerance points.** The final paragraph of the passage states that further research is required, but it does not suggest how straight forward this will be. We therefore cannot confirm that this statement is true.

Q70.4: B - The solution will be equally appropriate for developed and undeveloped coral.

Explanation: The information within the passage does not support this statement. The research to date has been conducted on larvae, and there is now the need for further investigation to ascertain the impact on adult coral. At this point, the solution cannot be assumed to be suitable for both young and developed coral.

Answer 70 (Continued)

- **A: If emissions are not reduced, artificial fortification should be considered.** The passage outlines how, if the effects of warmer waters are not reduced soon, artificial methods may be vital to save the coral reefs. This statement is, therefore, true.
- **C: The research has substantiated indications that the corals may be conserved.** Although more research needs to be undertaken, the indications are that the reefs may be conserved if all types of coral are assisted. The results are noted as 'promising' and, as such, this research may save the extinction of the corals. This statement is, therefore, true.
- **D: Further research will be vital for sufficient progress to be made.** This statement is supported by the information in the passage. The author indicates the need for additional research to assess the effect of the algae on adult coral; it has presently only considered the impact on larvae.

Answer 71

Q71.1: B - Best's reputation transcended the football domain.

Explanation: While the passage notes that George Best was one of the greatest players in history, it suggests that his reputation went well beyond the football arena. The passage describes how he became the subject of newspaper attention and that eventually his behaviours 'off the field' became more high profile than his footballing accomplishments. He was as well known for his 'squandered talent as for his undeniable brilliance'. Based on the information within the passage, this statement can be regarded as true.

- **A: Best was the most renowned signing that Manchester United has taken.** Whilst it cannot be contradicted that he was a magnificent player, the passage does not indicate that he was the **most renowned** individual to ever play for the club. This statement cannot be verified by the information within the passage.
- **C: Best did not fall prey to the burden of the media interest.** Based on the information within the passage, this cannot be considered true. As detailed in the third paragraph, the media interest 'also helped foster a drinking problem'. The passage hints that the weight of the media interest had an impact on him.

Answer 71 (Continued)

- **D: Best was construed as priority for transplant.** Although the passage notes that Best underwent a liver transplant, it does not suggest, at any point, that he was given priority. This statement cannot be verified by the information within the passage.

Q71.2: D - Best contradicted every skill he emanated through his dependences.

Explanation: The author indicates this several times in the passage. Whilst his skill as a footballer is not debated, Best's drinking problem would, ultimately, 'prove to be his undoing'. The passage highlights how, even after moving to lesser football teams, his 'drinking continued to affect his play'. In the final paragraph, the author describes how Best wasted his talent due to his love of alcohol. This statement can, therefore, be corroborated by the information in the passage.

- **A: Best exposed an innate aptitude that was enhanced through tuition.** This statement is not supported by the information within the passage. Indeed, we are told that he was considered a 'genius' when he was first discovered; this was before he received any formal tuition. The passage does not necessarily propose that his talent was enhanced through tuition, and we cannot select this as the correct answer option in this instance.
- **B: The impact of prominence led Best to reliance on outside stimuli.** Although the passage does highlight that Best's fame contributed to his dependence on alcohol, it does not mention other 'outside stimuli'. This statement is thus not the most appropriate answer option in this instance.
- **C: Best's departure from football was in limited glaring contrast to his initial days.** This statement contradicts the information in the passage. When Best first became famous, he was considered an 'immediate sensation'. Yet, the passage suggests that, by the time he had stopped playing football, he was considered someone who had wasted his talent. This statement thus cannot be supported by the information within the passage.

Answer 71 (Continued)

Q71.3: A - Best was the stimulus for press attention amongst football players.

Explanation: Although Best was 'the first of many footballers' who attracted media attention, the passage does not affirm that he was **the** impetus for this interest. Therefore, this statement cannot be supported by the information within the passage.

- **B: Best failed to invigorate his career within substitute clubs.** Best appears to have tried very hard to stimulate his career by playing for 'lesser teams' in several countries. The passage advises, in the final paragraph, that he was unable to achieve this. This statement can thus be corroborated by the information within the passage.
- **C: Best was the initial footballer to attract the attention of the newspapers.** Although he was not the stimulus for press interest, he was noted as 'the first of many footballers' to attract the attention of the media. This statement can, therefore, be considered as true.
- **D: Best wasted his abilities due to his lack of self-discipline.** This can be corroborated by the information within the passage. We are told that, while Best was an exceptional player, he had a drinking problem that 'would prove to be his undoing'. Due to the fact that he was unable to discipline himself sufficiently, he 'was unable to overcome his alcoholism'.

Q71.4: A - Best was a victim of his own success.

Explanation: This is the undoubted underlying opinion of the passage. Best was an unknown schoolboy who, at a young age, was recommended to and subsequently joined a famous football team. His continued success played a role in the way in which he behaved, and his 'playboy' image seems to have contributed to his eventual downfall. This statement is, therefore, the correct answer option.

- **B: Best was refused adequate support to address his demons.** There is nothing contained in the passage to support this statement. Therefore, we cannot be certain that it is correct.
- **C: Best was too immature to handle the experiences he encountered.** Although the passage notes that he shot to fame at a young age, the passage does not infer that Best was too immature to handle the situation. We cannot be certain that this statement is true.

Answer 71 (Continued)

- **D: Best continually entertained unwelcome attention from the tabloids.** There is nothing within the passage to suggest that he invited or encouraged the unwarranted press attention. It is not possible to suggest that he actively incited attention, and this statement cannot be considered as true.

Answer 72

Q72.1: D - there has been a palpable lack of perception of the impact.

Explanation: The penultimate paragraph of the passage implies that individuals might not be aware of the dangers of THMs. It states that Friends of the Irish Environment 'has called for customers to be informed of any exceedances in their water supply so that they can act to protect themselves'. It has said that 'consumers with supplies over the World Health Organisation levels can use simple charcoal filters to ensure that THMs are removed. They will not do this, however, unless they are made aware of the danger'. These words indicate that consumers are possibly unaware of THMs and their associated dangers. This statement is thus supported by the information within the passage.

- **A: the measures previously undertaken have been satisfactory.** The third paragraph states that, 'although some progress has been made, Ireland has not been complying with the rules since December 2003'. This statement thus cannot be verified by the information within the passage.
- **B: the consequences of the contamination have been unheeded.** The passage does not necessarily state that the consequences have been **ignored**. It implies that consumers are possibly unaware of THMs and their associated dangers. This statement is, therefore, false.
- **C: there has been a nonchalant attitude to the issues.** Whilst the passage highlights that little has been done to address the issue, this seems to be due to a lack of awareness. The passage does not necessarily state that people have adopted a relaxed attitude, and this statement cannot be corroborated by the information within the passage.

Answer 72 (Continued)

Q72.2: A - Whilst advances have been made, the country has long been non-compliant.

Explanation: The second paragraph of the passage advises that progress to address the problem has not been sufficient, but these words suggest that some advances have been made. The same paragraph also notes that Ireland has 'been in breach of the directive since 2003', which corroborates the second part of this statement, emphasising how the country has not been compliant with measures to aid the problem. This statement can, therefore, be verified by the information within the passage.

- **B: The foremost source of the contamination is the removal of farming waste.** The passage does not support this statement. It highlights several reasons for the contamination, but it does not explicitly suggest that farming waste is the **main** source.
- **C: Subsequent research provides undeniable evidence of the impact on the unborn.** The third paragraph of the passage notes the impact of high THM levels on the unborn. However, we are not provided with enough information to confirm that **undeniable** evidence of this has been offered. As such, this statement cannot be supported by the information within the passage.
- **D: The issue has been exacerbated by homeowners not adhering to directives.** We might assume that household waste is a contributing factor to the issue. However, there is nothing within the passage to support the idea that homeowners have not adhered to directives and that this has exacerbated the problem. The passage does not suggest that householders hold (or do not hold) responsibility, and this answer option cannot be selected as the correct one in this instance.

Q72.3: D - The foremost contamination is occurring in water consumption.

Explanation: The statement cannot be considered accurate as the passage outlines several ways in which the infected water may prove harmful. While drinking contaminated water can cause THMs to become ingested, we are also told that they can be inhaled in the bath and shower or from steam when washing clothes and dishes. Drinking water is not the **foremost** source of contamination, and this statement cannot be corroborated by the information in the passage.

Answer 72 (Continued)

- **A: The issues are being supervised by suitable consultants.** The fifth paragraph of the passage alludes to the involvement of the Friends of the Irish Environment. This statement can thus be considered accurate.
- **B: Compliant decontamination levels will not be compromised.** The final paragraph of the passage details how compliance with THM standards may be achieved 'without compromising disinfection'. Therefore, this statement can be deemed accurate.
- **C: Individual households might have been proactive if they had been directed accordingly.** We can ascertain the accuracy of this statement as the passage notes the request for 'consumers to be informed'. It can be deduced that, if consumers had been advised accordingly, they would have been able to 'act to protect themselves'.

Q72.4: C - The introduction of legislation which must be adhered to.

Explanation: This can be confirmed as the most likely factor to cause the implementation of measures. The passage highlights how previous advisory procedures had not been adhered to for many years, but it seems that the four-month deadline might push the appropriate personnel to initiate effective actions and solve the problem.

- **A: An enhanced awareness and ensuing demand for action.** The passage does not suggest that this is the most likely stimulus for the introduction of measures. This statement cannot be selected as the correct answer option in this instance.
- **B: The effect on wellbeing if preparations are not initiated.** The passage does not suggest that this is the most likely stimulus for the introduction of measures since it does not discuss future research in the field or strategies to enhance public awareness. This statement cannot be selected as the correct answer option in this instance.
- **D: The adverse bearing on water companies' revenues.** The passage does not imply that this is a cause for the introduction of measures. This statement cannot be selected as the correct answer option in this instance.

Answer 73

Q73.1: B - Despite the steps that have already been taken in this field, further work is required.

Explanation: The passage states that 'we have seen extraordinary advances both in technological development and the openness of drivers to using automated vehicles', which supports the first part of this statement and implies that steps have been taken in this field. The passage also indicates that advances will continue to emerge in the future. It states that smart motorways will interact with drivers for the moment, but it claims that 'ultimately this data will be transferred directly to vehicles, which will then respond appropriately'. This highlights how further work in this field is still needed. This statement is, therefore, supported by the information within the passage.

- **A: The programmes will safeguard the vehicle in unknown situations.** The passage does not provide sufficient information to support this statement. As such, we cannot select it as the correct answer option in this instance.
- **C: The trials have scrutinised both data and basic concepts.** Once again, the passage does not offer sufficient information to corroborate this statement. It does not provide the details of trials or the examination of data, and it cannot be selected as the correct answer option here.
- **D: A blended approach that uses all technologies has been essential for the implementation of the technology.** The passage does not offer sufficient information to support this statement. Therefore, it cannot be chosen as the correct answer option in this instance.

Q73.2: B - Driverless vehicles should be able to negotiate narrow lanes and roundabouts.

Explanation: The fourth paragraph of the passage affirms that roundabouts and narrow country lanes are not 'a big deal'. While these obstacles have the potential to create danger, the passage implies that driverless vehicles will be able to navigate them in future. This statement is thus correct.

- **A: There is the potential for major impediments if the technology fails.** While we might assume this to be true, the passage does not detail what could happen if the technology were to fail. It is plausible that a system will be put in place to prevent major incidents, but we

Answer 73 (Continued)

cannot be certain. Based on the information with which we are provided, this statement cannot be considered as true.

- **C: The automobile will be meticulously regulated to safeguard safety.** The passage does not confirm if this is true or false, and we cannot select it as the correct answer option in this instance.
- **D: The vehicle will be equipped with an opportunity for passenger intervention.** Although the final paragraph of the passage mentions that the driver might receive a text message, we are not told that the driver will be able to intervene. This information is not contained in the passage, and this answer option cannot be selected here.

Q73.3: B - The driverless car will interrelate effectively with human behaviours.

Explanation: This statement cannot be deduced from the information within the passage. For example, it does not suggest that driverless cars will be able to anticipate the movements of pedestrians or the conduct of other road users.

- **A: It is essential for the car to perform complex manoeuvres.** The fourth paragraph of the passage advocates that various manoeuvres will need to be mastered by the technology. We are told that mini roundabouts must 'be fully comprehended by the driverless tech, as do school runs and zebra crossings, bumps in the road and narrow country lanes'. This statement can thus be considered as true.
- **C: The smart motorway network will be the principal and most suitable location for such vehicles.** The third paragraph of the passage explains that smart motorways will be where 'driverless vehicles are most likely to appear first'. This statement can thus be corroborated by the information within the passage.
- **D: The initiation of this category of vehicle is now preordained.** We are told that 'the AA believes driverless vehicles may be a common sight on UK roads in a matter of years'. It can thus be argued that this type of vehicle is destined to be available soon, and this statement is supported by the information within the passage.

Answer 73 (Continued)

Q73.4: A - there are still numerous deliberations required before implementation.

Explanation: The passage suggests that driverless vehicles need to learn to cope with mini roundabouts, school runs, zebra crossings, bumps in the road and narrow country lanes. The words 'for the immediate future' are used within the passage, implying that there are further factors to consider before the vehicle can be fully implemented. This statement is thus correct.

- **B: the perception of the driver is that this will be immensely advantageous.** The passage does not evidence the thoughts of drivers. As such, we cannot draw this conclusion from the information we are given.
- **C: the person within the vehicle will continue to maintain control.** The passage neither supports nor refutes this statement. The passage states that the driver 'may get a text to help plan a next move', but it does not mention the control that the driver will (or will not) have. This statement cannot be corroborated by the information within the passage.
- **D: there will be a colossal environmental impact of a constructive quality.** The passage does not allude to the environmental impact of this type of vehicle. Therefore, we cannot select this statement as the correct answer option in this instance.

Answer 74

Q74.1: B - Thatcher followed a strategy of eliminating much of the provisions of the welfare state.

Explanation: The fourth paragraph of the passage states that Thatcher's government 'followed a radical programme' which aimed to 'reduce the role of government and increase individual self-reliance'. It suggests that she intended to eliminate the provisions of the state and encourage people to become independent and self-reliant. This statement can therefore be corroborated by the information within the passage.

- **A: Thatcher was one of the most unpopular of all prime ministers.** The passage does not confirm that Thatcher was the one of the country's

Answer 74 (Continued)

most unpopular prime ministers. Based on the information with which we are provided, we cannot confirm that this statement is true.

- **C: Thatcher faced issues with almost all government policies.** The passage implies that some of Thatcher's policies were unpopular; we are told that Sir Geoffrey Howe resigned in protest at her attitude towards Europe. However, the passage does not suggest that **almost all** of her policies were met with discontent. This statement cannot be corroborated by the information within the passage.
- **D: Thatcher had immense experience prior to becoming leader.** The passage does highlight her previous experience, but we cannot be certain that it was **immense**. Based on the information that we are given, we cannot confirm that this statement is true.

Q74.2: C - Thatcher had considered entering the legal profession.

Explanation: The second paragraph of the passage notes that, before she was elected as a Conservative MP, Thatcher 'read for the Bar'. This implies that she had intended to enter the legal profession, and this statement can thus be supported by the information within the passage.

- **A: Thatcher rapidly lessened the proportion of unemployment.** While the passage asserts that unemployment was very high during Thatcher's first two years in office, it does not indicate whether she managed to change this. We cannot select this statement as the correct answer option in this instance.
- **B: Thatcher achieved the backing of those primarily opposing her.** The passage does not advocate that Thatcher gained the support of those who initially opposed her. Based on the information with which we are provided, we cannot be certain that this statement is true.
- **D: Thatcher found immense support from all areas after having declared a war.** While the passage notes that Thatcher 'added to her reputation by leading the country to war against Argentina', it does not indicate that this granted her unequivocal support from **all** areas. In addition, the passage does not confirm if her declaration of war changed her reputation for the better or for the worse. This statement cannot be corroborated by the information within the passage.

Answer 74 (Continued)

Q74.3: C - Thatcher's altercation with a minister ultimately dictated her demise.

Explanation: This statement can be corroborated by the information within the passage. The penultimate paragraph highlights how the resignation speech of Thatcher's Foreign Secretary, Sir Geoffrey Howe, 'brought about events which were to lead to [Thatcher's] exit from 10 Downing Street later that month'. We can thus deduce that her dispute with this minister ultimately led to her departure from the role of prime minister.

- **A: A causative reason for Thatcher's success in the election was the lack of a credible opponent.** The passage states that Thatcher's win in the 1983 election was aided by a 'divided opposition'. However, it does not indicate that the opposition party lacked a **credible** leader. Based on the information with which we are provided, this statement cannot be confirmed as true.
- **B: Thatcher delivered her policies through promoting her supporters to leading positions.** While the third paragraph asserts that Thatcher 'brought more of her supporters into the Cabinet', it does not confirm that she promoted them to positions of leadership. This statement cannot be verified by the information within the passage.
- **D: Thatcher's decision to resign was imposed on her.** The final paragraph of the passage maintains that Thatcher was 'eventually persuaded not to go forward to the second ballot'. It can therefore be argued that **she** ultimately decided to resign, and this statement cannot be supported by the information within the passage.

Q74.4: A - True

Explanation: The passage describes how Sir Geoffrey Howe's resignation speech 'brought about events which were to lead to [Thatcher's] exit from 10 Downing Street later that month'. We can thus deduce that he was the stimulus for John Major's uptake of the position as prime minister.

Answer 75

Q75.1: D - The patronage of the authorities will be critical to ensure attainment of new technologies.

Explanation: There is nothing within the passage to support this statement. Whilst it notes the importance of the governments, it does not categorically affirm that it is their sponsorship that will be vital to the achievement of advances.

- **A: Internal frictions within administrations may ultimately hamper success.** This can be supported by the information in the third paragraph, which states that the 'politics of a given country' can affect how developments are made and who initiates them.
- **B: The determining factor is often the safety of the citizen.** This statement is corroborated in the final paragraph of the passage in which the author states that 'strong regulation is playing a part'.
- **C: Governments will be the determining factor on who advances biometrics.** This statement is verified by the information in the third paragraph of the passage, which explains that a country's government will affect 'how [biometrics are] developed and by whom'.

Q75.2: A - Dictatorial countries will have decisive regulation over the advances of technologies.

Explanation: The fourth paragraph corroborates this statement as it quotes Dr Benjamin: "An authoritarian state might be more closely involved in its development". This refers to the development of technologies and highlights how countries with a dictatorial government will face increased controls. This answer option is thus the correct one in this instance.

- **B: The appointment of a patent will result in enormous costs.** The passage refers to patent protection, but it does not give any indication of the cost incurred. This statement thus cannot be verified by the information in the passage.
- **C: The safeguarding of human rights will have an adverse effect.** The final paragraph of the passage highlights the importance of 'protecting people's rights'. The passage does not imply that the protection of human rights would have a negative impact on any new technologies, and this statement cannot be supported by the information within the passage.
- **D: Data protection legislation will play a pivotal role.** The passage

Answer 75 (Continued)

does not suggest that data protection legislation will assume a crucial role. It does indicate the impact of General Data Protection Regulation in Europe, but it simply notes that this might slow the process.

Q75.3: A - judges that success will be seen earlier where there are limited regulatory systems.

Explanation: The second paragraph highlights how developers working in a country with a 'weak regulatory oversight' are able to introduce technology faster than those in countries that enforce more stringent regulations. This statement is, therefore, true.

- **B: believes that regulation and advisory standards do not have to negate advances.** There is nothing within the passage to suggest that the author supports this. He/She simply implies that guidelines will have a bearing on the speed of approval.
- **C: deems it vital that all necessary data privacy measures are in place.** Whilst the author supports the protection of people's rights, the passage does not state that the implementation of data privacy measures is **vital**. The passage also implies that data protection considerations should not impede progress. This statement is, therefore, untrue.
- **D: estimates that it is important to address the standards of the outcomes.** This statement is not correct as the author does not **estimate** that regulation is important. Rather, the author clearly states that 'strong regulations play a part'. This infers that he/she is determined that they should be addressed, and this statement is thus incorrect.

Q75.4: C - Can't Tell

Explanation: Although the passage discusses the advances in various parts of the world, the author does not specifically suggest that there is a global incentive. It is difficult to ascertain from the passage if these advances relate to all countries, and we thus cannot tell if this statement is true or false.

Decision Making

Answer 1

C – Finn

Name	Music Genre
Reign	Blues
Finn	Jazz
Sloan	Rock
Chord	Pop

We know that Reign does not like rock music, does not host jazz nights, and never attends any pop concerts. Hence, Reign likes the blues through elimination.

Finn does not like rock music. He also accompanies Sloan and their friend to pop concerts. Given that Reign likes the blues, Finn must enjoy jazz music.

Sloan accompanies Finn and their friend to pop concerts. Hence, Sloan likes rock music, and Chord likes pop music.

Answer 2

D – 6,000

We know that the shop offers six doughnuts to anyone equal to or taller than 150cm and 12 doughnuts to anyone shorter than 150cm.

If all those equal to or taller than 150cm accept the free doughnuts, then, on average, each will be given 1 X 6 = six doughnuts. If half of those shorter than 150cm accept the free doughnuts, then, on average, each will be given 0.5 X 12 = six doughnuts. Therefore, we know that the total number of free doughnuts given will be 6 X 1000 = 6000, regardless of the number of people in each group.

Answer 3

Q3.1 **NO.** It does not specify that Xin is in the year group in question.

Q3.2 **NO.** Not everyone in C1 is Malaysian.

Q3.3 **NO.** The remaining seven students in C1 may also be international students.

Q3.4 **NO.** It does not specify that all students in C2 originate from Hong Kong.

Q3.5 **YES.** Eshen is Malaysian and is part of the year group in question. All Malaysian students from that year group have been placed in C1.

Answer 4

A. YES. Teachers find children to be better at addition and subtraction during Mathematics classes when they bring money to school.
The argument is that, by encouraging children to bring money to school, they will learn to count change and gain a sense of responsibility. The fact that teachers find children to be better in Mathematics classes proves that dealing with loose change enables children to improve their addition and subtraction skills.

B. YES. Children carry fewer bags to school when they don't bring lunch.
Although this is a by-product of bringing money to school, the question has nothing to do with bringing fewer bags.

C. NO. Parents think that children are not disciplined enough to look after money.
The main argument for encouraging children to bring money to school is to teach them a sense of responsibility, but the thought of the parents that children are not disciplined enough means that they cannot bring money to school.

D. NO. School hawkers would rather not accept coins and/or cash.
The statement does not make reference to school hawkers.

Answer 5

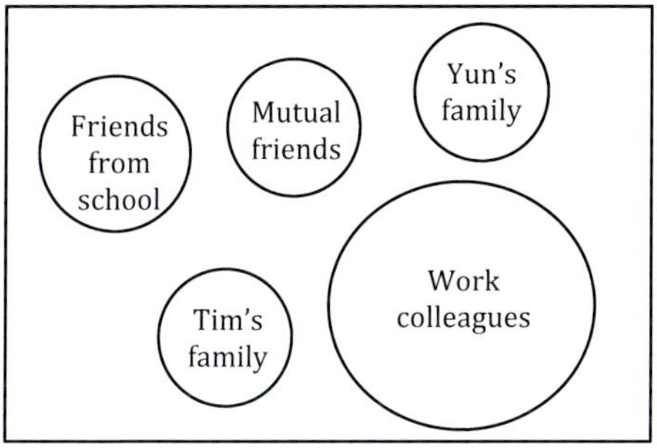

Since Yun's family is sat furthest from Tim's family, Yun's family must be E. We know that the seating area for mutual friends is equidistant to the seating area for work colleagues as it is from the seating area for their friends from school. Hence, table D is for mutual friends, and tables B and C are remaining. Since table B was not allocated to their friends from school, table B must be for work colleagues.

B – Work colleagues

Answer 6

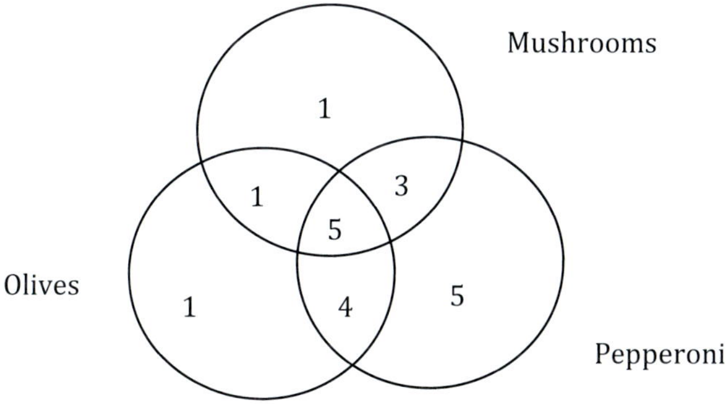

C – First, eliminate the diagrams that represent the incorrect total number of pizzas, thus remove option A. Option D does not represent eight pizzas with two toppings. Only option C represents 17 pizzas that are topped with pepperoni.

Answer 7

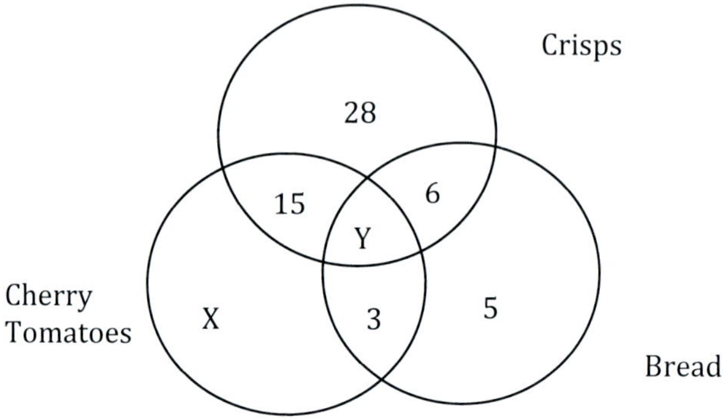

X and Y are the two unknowns. However, we know that:
X + Y + 3 + 5 + 6 + 15 + 28 = 60, so X + Y = 60 – 57 = 3.
Therefore, the number of mice that snatched the cherry tomatoes altogether is X + Y + 3 + 15 = 3 + 18 = 21 **(B).**

Answer 8

A – Hayley is the fifth child of the family.

Knowing that Matthias is two years older than Marvel, Ella must be in the middle of the two. As Venice is the youngest, this leaves Anlene, Maddox and Hayley.

Since Anlene and Maddox are five years apart, this means that the remaining four siblings were born between the two of them. Given the fact that each brother has a sister who is one year older than them, Anlene must be the eldest, and Hayley must be one year older than Maddox.

Therefore, we can place the siblings in the following order: Anlene, Matthias, Ella, Marvel, Hayley, Maddox, and Venice.

Answer 9

Q9.1 **NO.** There is the possibility that the three slices that were dropped were all cheesecake slices. As such, the remaining number of cheesecake slices would be equal to the number of durian cake slices.

Q9.2 **YES.** If two slices of carrot cake and one slice of cheesecake were dropped, there would be five slices of each remaining.

Q9.3 **NO.** If three slices of carrot cake were dropped, there would still be four slices remaining. There are three slices of durian cake, and so there cannot be equal slices of each type of cake.

Q9.4 **YES.** There is the possibility that three slices of carrot cake were dropped, leaving four slices of carrot cake and three slices of durian cake.

Q9.5 **NO.** There is the possibility that all three slices of durian cake fell.

Answer 10

B. YES. It will encourage doctors to put patients on fewer medications and will encourage healthier living.
This is the strongest argument as it addresses the key part of the question on excessive prescriptions.

A. YES. The NHS can use the extra income to fund budget cuts.
Although this could be a by-product of charging for medications, the question has nothing to do with where the additional income could be spent.

C. NO. Non-working and needy elderly patients will be most affected.
This statement, although true, does not answer the question.

D. NO. Requiring patients to pay for their medications may trigger strikes against the NHS.
This is a possible outcome, but it is not the strongest argument.

Answer 11

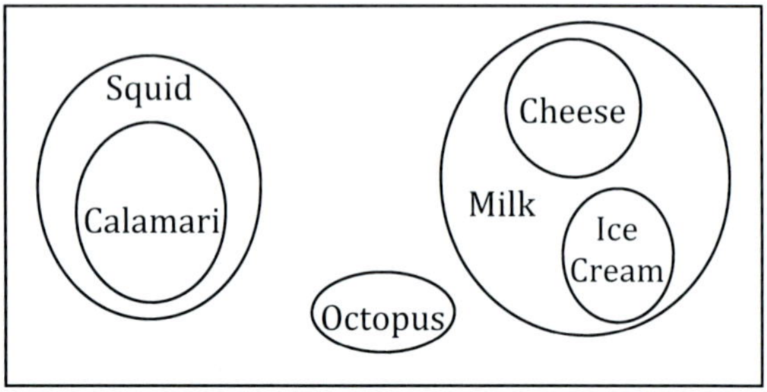

A Euler diagram is used to represent existing relationships in the real world.

D – Cheese and ice cream are a subset of milk. Calamari is a subset of squid. That leaves octopus as a lone sector.

Answer 12

C – Amarit

Since Henry and Lupita prefer sauce as a side, we know that they did not chose peas.

Huang does not like any food that is green. Hence, Amarit must have chosen peas.

Answer 13

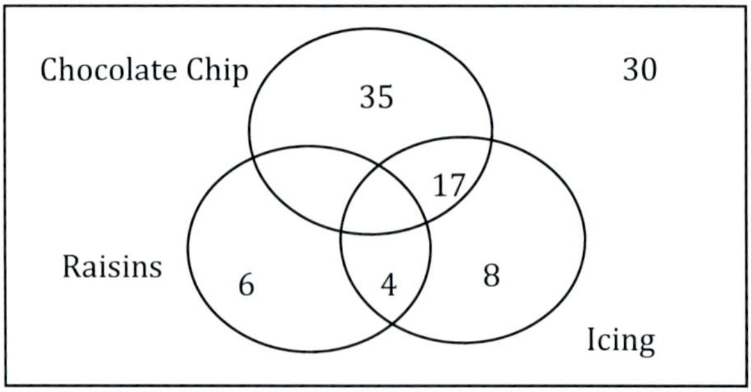

B – This answer option correctly identifies the total number of cookies that contain chocolate chips (52), icing (29) and raisins (10).

Answer 14

B – Mr Phillips teaches Mathematics too.

This is the only true statement.

Drama is taught by Mr Phillips and Miss Holiday.

English is taught by Mrs Ball and Miss Holiday.

Mathematics is taught by Mr Phillips and Mrs Ball.

Answer 15

C – Only 38 items meet Vanessa's preferences.

Answer 16

Q16.1 **YES.** If one registrar carries the crash call bleep and the consultant does not, this means that the remaining two crash call bleeps are carried by two junior doctors.

Q16.2 **NO.** Generally, consultants do not carry a crash call bleep, regardless of whether they are sick.

Q16.3 **NO.** The passage states that only one registrar carries the crash call bleep. We should not assume that the other registrar is not carrying a crash call bleep because he/she has called in sick. There is the possibility that both registrars are present and still only one carries the crash call bleep.

Q16.4 **NO.** The passage does not state the number of staff present. Therefore, this statement cannot be conclusive of the situation as not enough information has been given.

Q16.5 **YES.** This is true. The passage states that the crash call bleep is only divided among members of the on-call team.

Answer 17

A – 0%

If Brandon's uncle has cystic fibrosis and his father does not, Brandon's father has a 50% chance of being a carrier. Since Brandon's mother doesn't carry the gene, Brandon has a 0% chance of having cystic fibrosis.

Answer 18

Month	Winner	Flavour
February	Pathma	Winter Melon
May	**B – Arun**	Assam
June	Baskie	Oolong
August	Ashley	Taro

We know that Arun won the lucky draw three months after Pathma. Therefore, the months of May and August were the only possible months in which Arun could have won. We know that Ashley was the last winner, meaning she won in August. Hence, Arun won in May.

Answer 19

C. NO. This will mean that migrants will be unable to use the NHS. They might then present with complications and in emergency situations at a later date.
This will place greater pressure on the NHS to cope in these situations.

A. YES. This will reduce the number of migrants seeking opportunities in the UK. Therefore, this will ensure that there are more jobs and university spaces for residents. This statement is not the strongest argument since it does not directly address the NHS.

B. YES. Not all migrants pay tax, especially students.
Although this may be true, it does not address the NHS.

D. NO. This will affect lower-income families and their future in the UK. This may be a challenge faced, but the argument does not address the NHS.

Answer 20

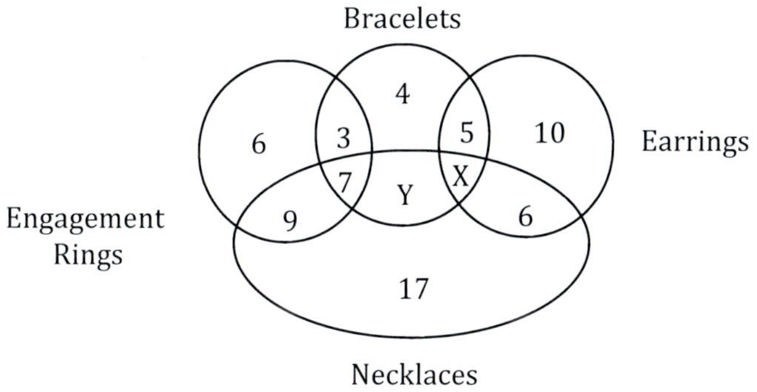

A. The total number of households with necklaces is: 17 + 7 + 6 + 9 + X + Y, so 39 + X + Y. In comparison to earrings, 10 + 5 + 6 + X, so 21 + X. Therefore, the statement is true.

B. There are no households that own all four types of jewelry. This can be determined from the diagram. Therefore, the statement is false.

C. The total number of households with bracelets is: 4 + 3 + 7 + 5 + X + Y, so 19 + X + Y. The total number of households with necklaces is: 39 + X + Y. As X and Y are both positive integers, this statement is false.

D. There are 37 households with only one type of jewelry.

Answer 21

Q21.1 **NO.** We know that Harold is from the pond. Since no frogs from the pond like rain, we know that Harold does not like rain. We know that green frogs like rain. So if a frog does not like rain, it cannot be a green frog.

Q21.2 **YES.** Frogs with red eyes are rare. Small frogs are common. If the frog is rare, it cannot be a small frog. Hence, frogs with red eyes are not small frogs.

Q21.3 **YES.** Harold is from the pond, and he does not like rain. Frogs who do not have red eyes are green. Since Harold is not a green frog, he has red eyes. Frogs who have red eyes are not small. Thus, Harold is not a small frog.

Q21.4 **YES.** None of the frogs in the pond like rain. So if a frog likes rain, it cannot be from the pond.

Q21.5 **NO.** Frogs with red eyes are rare, so frogs that are common do not have red eyes and, therefore, must be green.

Answer 22

D – Matsuri has a medium-sized black suitcase.

There are only three medium-sized suitcases, so if one is white, the other two must be black. All cabin-sized suitcases are grey. Therefore, Enoki could not have had a black cabin-sized suitcase.

Answer 23

B. YES. Exams are a good indicator of knowledge and understanding.
Exams are a good indicator of the knowledge and understanding of each student. This will help teachers to guide students when they enter secondary school.

A. YES. It is a good way to rank students across the nation.
This is a likely outcome, but it does not address the main issue regarding entering secondary school.

C. NO. This will apply enormous pressure on young students and can be very stressful.
This may be a valid argument, but it is not relevant to determine secondary school entrance.

D. NO. Secondary schools will be ranked based on performance so that top-ranked students can get into the best schools.
This will put weaker students at a disadvantage since they will be unable to access the best schools.

Answer 24

Circle = x   Triangle = y   Square = z

x = 3y   z + 2y = 2x

z = 2(3y) – 2y, so z = 4y or y = 1/4z. Hence, x = 3/4z

4x = 3z (**C – Square**)

Answer 25

Small glass of wine (125ml, ABV 12%)	1.5 units	Pint of lager/beer/ cider (473ml, ABV 5.2%)	3 units
Can of lager/beer/cider (440ml, ABV 5.5%)	2 units	Alcopop (275ml, ABV 5.5%)	1.5 units
Single small shot of vodka (25ml, ABV 40%)	1 unit	Large glass of wine (250ml, ABV 12%)	3 units

From the information provided, we know the total amount of alcohol consumed in a week by Judith (10 x 1, so 10 units), Cindy (1.5 x 7, so 10.5 units), Garrett (14 x 3, so 42 units), and Sally (3 x 1, so 3 units).

C. Cindy has a higher alcohol intake than Judith.

A. Sally does not have the greatest alcohol intake in the group.

B. Garrett has exceeded the recommendation of 14 units per week.

D. Judith consumes a total of 10 units a week.

Answer 26

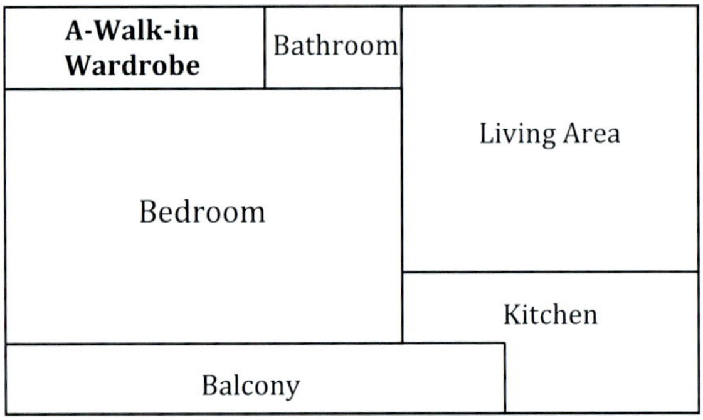

We know that the balcony is the longest and narrowest area, so C is the balcony. From the kitchen, you can see the view from the balcony, so D is the kitchen. The kitchen is the furthest away from the walk-in wardrobe to prevent the clothes from smelling. Hence, A is the walk-in wardrobe. This is coinciding with the statement that the bathroom (F) is located in between the living area (E) and the walk-in wardrobe (A).

Answer 27

B. YES. Healthier carbohydrates contain more fibre, vitamins and minerals.
This is the strongest statement. Increasing healthier options from food providers encourages healthier living among consumers.

A. YES. It will encourage greater production of healthier carbohydrates.
The point is not to increase the production of healthier carbohydrates but to create an incentive. However, this statement does not address healthier options.

C. NO. Healthier carbohydrates are less popular and may affect local businesses. Although this may be true, it does not address the main question regarding healthier living among consumers.

D. NO. Healthier carbohydrates will generate more waste.
This point is irrelevant and redundant.

Answer 28

Q28.1 **NO.** Any obese person who does not have diabetes could potentially be a doctor.

Q28.2 **YES.** There is a possibility that some obese people could be doctors.

Q28.3 **YES.** No doctor has diabetes. Therefore, diabetics cannot be doctors.

Q28.4 **NO.** This cannot be definitively concluded.

Q28.5 **YES.** Although obesity is mentioned here, it does not change the fact that diabetics cannot be doctors. Diabetes, rather than obesity, is the determining factor here.

Answer 29

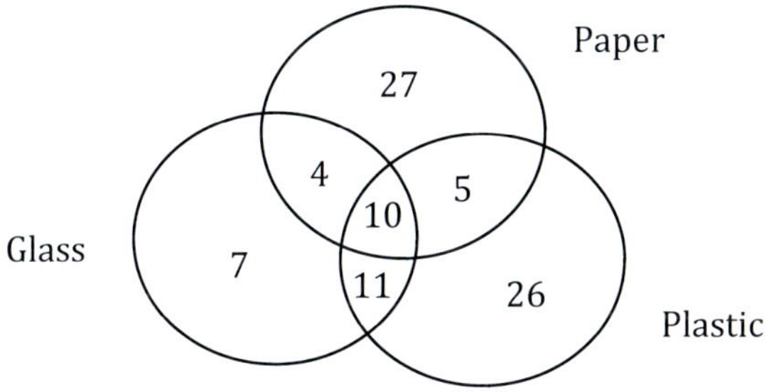

The easiest approach is to use a Venn diagram.

We know that 27 people from the Venn diagram do not recycle glass and plastic. However, we must consider those who do not recycle at all. We know that, from the Venn diagram, 27 + 4 + 10 + 5 + 11 + 26 + 7 = 90, so 100 – 90 = 10.

Therefore, the number of households that do not recycle either glass or plastic is 10 + 27 = 37.

B – 37

Answer 30

Buzz	Woolos	Gwent	Manor
RM103	RM48	RM95	RM40

C – Gwent spent RM95 on her activity.

We know that Manor spent the least amount of money. Therefore, Manor spent RM40. We know that Woolos spent RM8 more than Manor, so Woolos spent RM48. Buzz spent RM8 more than Gwent, and so Buzz spent RM103 and Gwent spent RM95.

Answer 31

A – Only 60 people had turkey, potatoes and gravy but not pudding and stuffing at the Christmas dinner buffet.

Answer 32

A – Rose is the heaviest.

The order from lightest to heaviest is Lily, Petal, Bea and Rose.

Lily is lighter than Petal and Rose.

Bea is heavier than Petal.

Rose is, therefore, the heaviest.

Answer 33

Tickets	Friday	Saturday	Sunday
Standing	41	60	70
Seating	24	19	22

A – Standing tickets made (70 x £40) £2,800, while seating tickets made (22 x £70) £1,540. Therefore, standing tickets made more revenue than seating tickets.

B. There were (24 + 19 + 22) 65 seating tickets sold, while there were (41 + 60 +70) 171 standing tickets sold. There were more sales of standing tickets than seating tickets.

C. There is no evidence to support this. Therefore, this statement is false.

D. On Friday, (41 + 24) 65 tickets were sold. On Saturday, (60 + 19) 79 tickets were sold. Therefore, Saturday sold more tickets than Friday.

Answer 34

A. YES. This will encourage people with learning disabilities to work and to be independent.
Regarding self-development among people with learning disabilities, having a job will cultivate interpersonal skills such as discipline, independence and a sense of responsibility.

B. YES. Large food companies will gain publicity for social inclusion.
This may be a possible outcome, but it does not address the key point.

C. NO. People with learning disabilities are more vulnerable to criticism in the workplace.
Although this point is reasonable, it does not mean that people with learning disabilities should not be allowed to work.

D. NO. Impatient customers are more likely to avoid these food companies which may subsequently affect businesses.
This may well be a consequence, but the question focuses on creating opportunities for people with learning disabilities.

Answer 35

Q35.1 **NO.** There is the possibility that all those who eat potatoes also eat rice. Hence, the correct proportion would be five out of 10 students.

Q35.2 **YES.** The minimum number of students who eat neither potatoes nor pasta is two out of 10.

Q35.3 **NO.** There is the possibility that no one eats all three carbohydrates, as two out of the 10 students eat neither potatoes nor pasta.

Q35.4 **NO.** There is the possibility that all those who eat pasta also eat rice. This means that three out of the 10 students eat both, three out of the 10 students eat rice and not pasta, and four out of the 10 students eat neither. It would be true if at least one out of the 10 students ate neither pasta nor rice.

Q35.5 **YES.** There cannot be more than three out of the 10 students who eat all three carbohydrates.

Answer 36

△ = a ○ = b □ = c ♡ = d

From the diagram, we can deduce the following equations.
3a + 2b = 2c ————————-1
d + b = 2a ————————- 2
3d = 2c + b ————————- 3

3 rearranged: 2c = 3d – b
1 - 3 ——3a = 3d – 3b, so simplified a = d – b ——- 4
2 + 4 ——3a = 2d, a = 2/3d————————5

d + b = 4/3d
b = 1/3d————6

2c = 3d – 1/3d
c = 4/3d——————-7

To solve the diagram,
a + c = ?
a + c = 2/3d + 4/3d, so the correct answer is 2d ♡♡
(Option **A**)

To substitute in the other shapes, we would get either: 6 circles, 3 triangles or 1.5 squares.

Answer 37

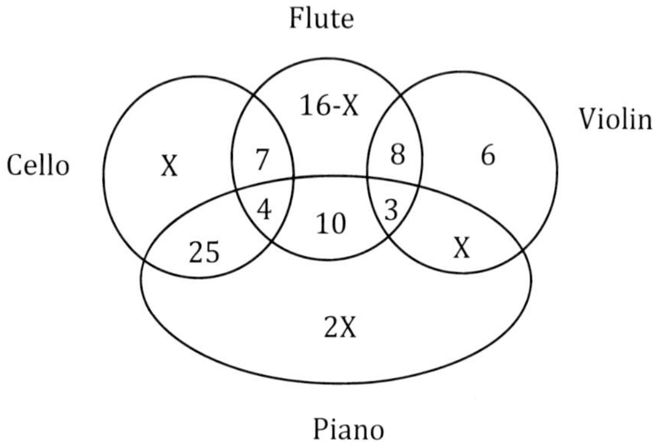

First, you need to find the value of X. X + 25 + 4 + 7 + 16 – X + 10 + 8 + 3 + X + 6 + 2X = 100, so X = 7. Therefore, you can deduce that the number of children playing the violin, flute, cello and piano is 24, 41, 43, and 63, respectively.

B. The total number of children who play the piano (63) is less than the total number of children who play both the cello and the violin (67).

A. The total number of children who play three musical instruments is seven.

C. The number of children who play only the violin is six, while the number of children who play only the cello is seven.

D. The number of children who play both the cello and the piano is 29. The number of children who play the flute is 41. Hence, this statement is false.

Answer 38

Results	UK	Non-UK / EU	International
Offered	250	33	20
Waitlisted	169	7	430
Rejected	2570	100	1377

To answer this question, you would need to work through the answers using a method of elimination and some quick calculation.

D – Overall, 12% of applicants were rejected.

A. The total number of applicants this year was 4,956.
B. The percentage of UK students who received an offer was eight times greater than the percentage of international students who received an offer.
C. There were more UK applicants (2,989) than international and non-UK applicants combined (1,967).

Answer 39

B – completes the equation. Each bar is counted as one. The sequence is as follows:

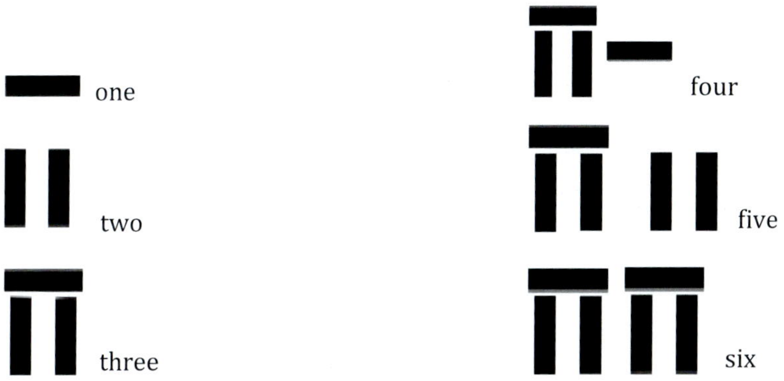

Answer 40

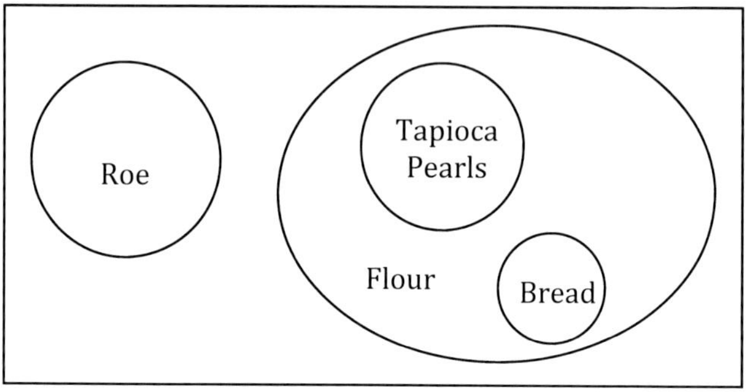

Decision Making

D – Tapioca pearls and bread are both made with flour.

Answer 41

D – 1/9

Since 10 of the 30 songs are by Band R, the probability that any one song will be by that band is 10/30 = 1/3. The probability that the next two songs are by Band R is equal to the product of two probabilities, where each probability is that the next song is by Band R: (1/3) X (1/3) = 1/9. They are independent events.

Answer 42

B – Thirty-two pieces of A5 paper can completely fit into an A0 piece of paper.

Two A5 pieces of paper make up one A4 piece of paper.
Two A4 pieces of paper make up one A3 piece of paper.
Two A3 pieces of paper make up one A2 piece of paper.
Two A2 pieces of paper make up one A1 piece of paper.
Two A1 pieces of paper make up one A0 piece of paper.

The area of an A2 piece of paper is equivalent to eight pieces of A5 paper.

An A1 piece of paper is eight times larger than an A4 piece of paper.

The area of an A0 piece of paper can accommodate eight pieces of A3 paper.

Answer 43

D – 403 patients who tested positive for COVID-19 had both diarrhoea and vomiting.

Answer 44

Calculate the respective areas.

$P = 2X^2$

$Q = 8X^2$

$R = 18X^2$

$S = 32X^2$

D – Q + Q + Q + P + P + P + P = S

Answer 45

Q45.1 **YES.** He is the only one in the family who doesn't like Tteokbokki.

Q45.2 **YES.** This is a possibility.

Q45.3 **NO.** There is a possibility that he has more than two family members. Therefore, it is not a must that he likes Bibimbap.

Q45.4 **YES.** This is a possibility.

Q45.5 **NO.** We do not know this for certain. For example, Logan may not like both Bibimbap and Tteokbokki.

Answer 46

C – There is a six out of sixteen chance that the tree has only one dominant trait.

Dihybrid cross is a cross between two different lines/genes that differ in two observed traits. The traits follow a ratio of 9:3:3:1.

9/16: Two dominant traits (pink flower and sweet fruit)

3/16 x 2 : One dominant trait (either pink flower or sweet fruit)

1/16: Two recessive traits (purple flower and sour fruit)

Answer 47

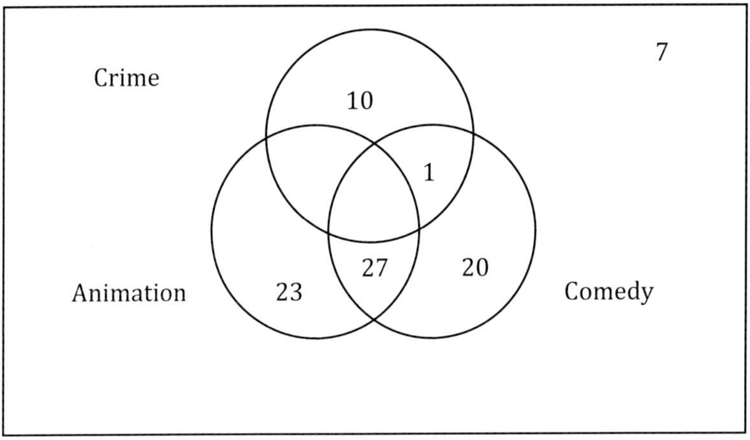

C – Correct Answer

We know that only one person enjoys crime and comedy. Hence, answers B and D are incorrect. The total number of people in A is 89. Hence, C is the correct answer. The numbers in diagram C also represent the information given.

Answer 48

D – 0

There are 28 patients, 15 of whom are male and 13 of whom are female.

There are seven staff members. There are five more females than males on the ward. If all seven of the staff members are female, this would meet the criteria. Therefore, the answer is 0.

Answer 49

A - More students took part in ice skating than those who did not.

Total number of students represented by the diagram is 19 + 18 + 16 + 22 + 10 + 8 + 14 + 13 = 120.

- 22 participated in gymnastics, ballet and ice skating
- 16 participated in ice skating and gymnastics
- 10 participated in ballet and ice skating
- 8 participated in gymnastics and ballet
- 59 participated in gymnastics
- 67 participated in ice skating
- 54 participated in ballet

A. More students took part in ice skating (67) than those who did not (120 – 67 = 53).

B. 32 students took part in neither gymnastics nor ice skating.

C. Fewer students participated in ballet (54) than ice skating (67).

D. There are more students who did either ice skating, ballet or gymnastics (102) than those who did not (18).

Answer 50

D – 80

If the probability of drawing a £20 note is 1 in 25 chances, and there are five £20 notes in the box, the total number of notes in the box is 25 x 5 = 125. 125 – 40 – 5 = 80.

Answer 51

C – 2

Pre-school	Total children	Equal to or above 5 years	Under 5 years
A	12	6	6
B	24	16	8
C	8	0	8
D	6	6	0

We know that B has 24 children, A has 12, C has eight, and D has six.
A has six children under five years and six children equal to or above five years.
B has 16 children equal to or above five years. Therefore, eight children are under five years.
Hence, C has eight children under five years and 0 children equal to or above five years; D has 0 children under five years and six children equal to or above five years.
Only two pre-schools (C and D) have children only in one age group (either equal to or above five years or under five years).

Answer 52

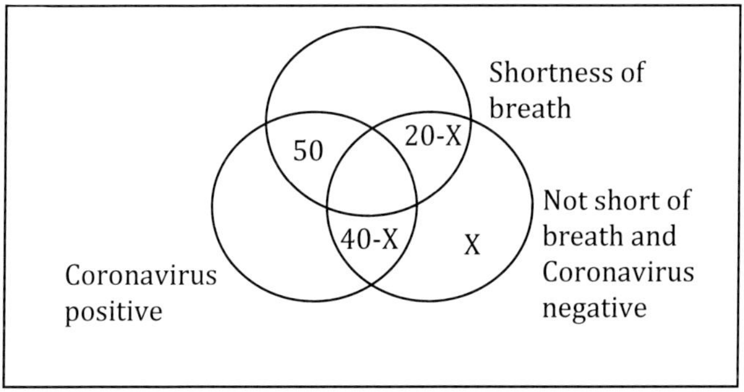

Use a Venn diagram to answer this question.

We know that the total number of patients is 100.

100 = 50 + 20 – X + 40 – X + X

X = 10 (B)

Answer 53

B – More than half of those equal to or taller than 170cm work in professions other than patissiers and entremetiers.

The total number of those equal to or taller than 170cm is (2 + 8 + 11) 21. The number of those equal to or taller than 170cm who do not work as patissiers and entremetiers is 11, so more than half the total number of those equal to or taller than 170cm work in professions other than patissiers and entremetiers.

A. In total, 10 + 6 + 8 + 2 + 14 = 40. The number of people shorter than 170cm and entremetiers only is 10. Ten out of 40 = 25%.

C. Two of the poissonniers equal to or taller than 170cm are entremetiers.

D. Fourteen chefs work with both pastry and vegetables. Six are shorter than 170cm, and the ratio is 3/7 not 4/7.

Answer 54

We know that F is the reception desk. Therefore, Khalid's and Amore's offices are either A or E. Min Ju's and Malachi's offices are either B or D. C is the coffee room.

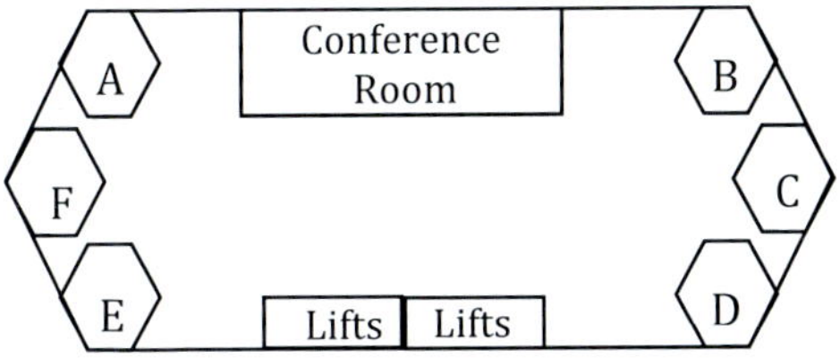

1st possibility

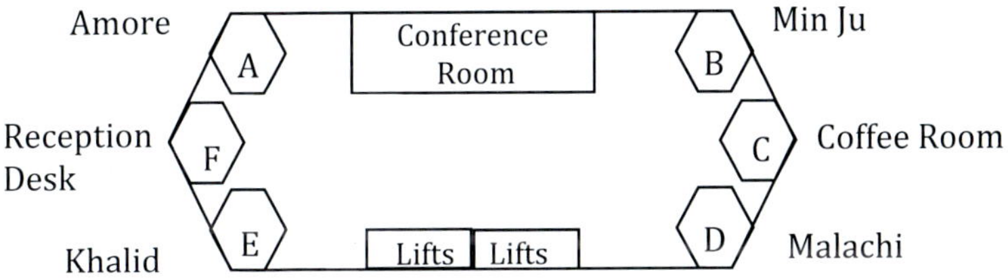

2nd possibility

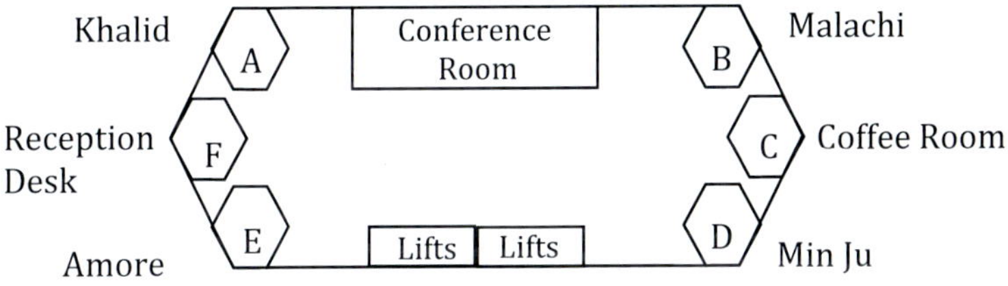

A. The conference room is the closest to either Min Ju's and Amore's offices (1st possibility) or Khalid's and Malachi's offices (2nd possibility).

B. The coffee room is directly opposite the reception desk.

C. If A is Amore's office, then D represents Malachi's office.

Therefore, if Andrew exits the lift and turns right, he will see Malachi's office, the coffee room, and Min Ju's office. **(D)**

Answer 55

Q55.1 **YES.** This is a possibility because all impressionist portraits are treasures and so, if something is not treasurable, it cannot be an impressionist portrait.

Q55.2 **YES.** This is a possibility because all impressionist portraits are treasures. Since this painting is an impressionist portrait, it can be concluded that some treasurable impressionist portraits are paintings.

Q55.3 **NO.** This may not always be true because only this drawing is treasurable; we are not told about all paintings.

Q55.4 **YES.** This is a possibility because we are told this painting is an impressionist portrait and all impressionist portraits are treasures. Therefore, some paintings are treasures.

Q55.5 **NO.** This may not always be a possibility because only this painting is an impressionist portrait; we are not told about all paintings.

Answer 56

D – Brown rice, albacore, tamago.

A → 150 + 3690 + 265 = ¥4105
B → 456 + 3285 + 333 = ¥4074
C → 305 + 3543 + 188 = ¥4036
D → 304 + 3330 + 300 = ¥3934

Answer 57

C – The solution in V is hypotonic.

Solution in T is hypertonic, causing the chilli to shrink and weigh less.
Solution in U is isotonic, causing the weight of the chilli to remain the same.
Solution in V is hypotonic, causing the chilli to swell and weigh more.

Answer 58

Annalise → 20 x 12mg = 240mg
Oliver → (4 x 16.6mg) + (10 x 15.4mg) = 220.4mg
Aafaaq's grandfather → 4 x 50.89mg = 203.56mg
Gigi → 2 x 144mg = 288mg
Schmitz → 2 x 144mg - 288mg

A – Aafaaq's grandfather smokes the least amount of nicotine in a day.

Answer 59

B – F

F represents students who travel via a combination of MRT, walking and bus.

Answer 60

A. YES. This will reduce the number of people violating lockdown measures and hopefully reduce the number of affected cases.

This argument best represents the statement as it addresses reducing the further spread of the Coronavirus and reducing the number of people violating lockdown measures.

B. YES. This will help reduce the number of admissions to hospital. Although this is a by-product, it does not address the statement directly.

C. NO. Due to non-essential workers lacking income, this will affect the poorer population largely. Although this is a possible side effect, it does not address the main issues highlighted.

D. NO. Administering fines will not prevent others from violating the rules. This point does not acknowledge the main issue of preventing the further spread of the Coronavirus.

Answer 61

The total number of gifts received by Class 6 at St. Thomas' School is:
20 x 3.3 = 66.
We know that 8 x 4 = 32 and 7 x 3 = 21. 66 – 32 – 21 = 13.
If Melessa is X, Shu Min is 2X, Nia is 2X, Jee Nee is 2X, and Julin is 6X.
13 = X + 2X + 2X + 2X + 6X
X = 1

Therefore, Julin received six gifts. (B)

Answer 62

B – 2

If you add all the seashells together, you get a total of 60. If 25 seashells are removed, there are 35 seashells left in the bag. If the chance of drawing a purple seashell is now 2/5, then 14 of 35 seashells remaining must be purple. The original total number of purple seashells was 16. So, two purple seashells were removed.

Answer 63

C – 1 in 5525

The probability of getting three queens in a row is the product of the probabilities for each draw. For the first queen, that is 4 in 52 or 1 in 13; for the second, it is 3 in 51 or 1 in 17; and for the third, it is 2 in 50 or 1 in 25. So the overall probability is (1/13) x (1/17) x (1/25) = 1/5525.

Answer 64

Q64.1 **NO.** All receptionists speak Hangugeo and all those who speak Hangugeo love watching Korean dramas. Therefore, all receptionists love watching Korean dramas.

Q64.2 **NO.** People who love watching Korean dramas don't have to be receptionists. If they are not receptionists, then they can't work in famous hotels.

Q64.3 **NO.** "Only receptionists work in famous hotels" means that everyone who works a in famous hotel is a receptionist. It does not mean that all receptionists work in famous hotels. It is possible that some receptionists work in an unknown hotel.

Q64.4 **NO.** That would be true for all famous hotels (which are all painted gold), but an unknown gold hotel could have workers who speak any language.

Q64.5 **NO.** All receptionists love watching Korean dramas but not all who watch Korean dramas are receptionists.

Answer 65

To decode Mr Ri's message, first look at the example given.
The second word contains the 'time' to meet. The *number* hidden in the word represents the time in 24:00 hours.
The first word is the key to the message.
BANANA is a six-letter word indicating that the name of the location has six letters.
BANANA begins with the letter B, which is the second letter of the alphabet. Therefore, focus on the second letter of the following words after the second word. This reveals the location.

The message was:
BANANA-**TEN**TACLES-A**P**PLE-O**R**ANGE-R**A**SPBERRY-E**G**G GU**A**VA-M**E**LON
The soldiers met Mr Ri in Prague at 10:00 am.

The next code sent on Friday was:
CORN-NE**TWO**RK-LE**N**TILS-SP**I**NACH-SI**L**VERBEET-CH**E**RRY

The word CORN is a four-letter word indicating that the name of the location has four letters.
CORN begins with the letter C, indicating that the third letter of each word after the second word should be focused on to reveal the location.

Therefore, Mr Ri's soldiers will meet him in Nile at 02:00 am. (B)

Answer 66

To decipher the code, the important clues are in the third paragraph of the poem.

Focus on the last four lines of the poem.
"what is below men" is the word "calm"
"higher than honour" is the word "breaks"
"next to life" is either the word "your" or "will"
"above measure" is the word "pleasure"

The number of letters of each word make up the code:
Calm – 4
Breaks – 6
Your / Will – 4
Pleasure – 8

Since the clue tells you to go back in time, the answer is A: 8-4-6-4.

Quantitative Reasoning

Answer 1

Q1.1: **D. £441.30**
First, note that the family will be purchasing two adult tickets and one child ticket. The regular price of a ticket for the match they are watching is £117.

The VIP ticket for an adult would be 30% more: 1.30 x 117 = £152.10

The VIP ticket for children would be 152.10 - 15 = £137.10 at checkout.

Altogether, they will have to pay: (2 x 152.10) + 137.10 = £441.30

Q1.2: **B. £282.50**
Notice that the question asks how much they lost from their mistake. This means you can ignore how much extra money they spent on buying new tickets. Making any calculations based on the second sentence of the question will be a waste of precious time.

The couple spent money on two regular tickets and a delivery fee which amounts to: (2 x 140) + 2.50 = £282.50

Q1.3: **C. 1.93:1**
Let's look at this question in two cases and extract the important information we need.

Case 1: Watch with daughter - 1 adult ticket, 1 child ticket, Centre Court, Thursday
He will spend: 123 + (123 - 15) = £231

Case 2: Watch alone - 1 VIP adult ticket, No. 2 Court, Thursday
He will spend: 1.30 x 92 = £119.60

Ratio of Case 1 to Case 2: 231 / 119.6 = 1.93:1

Q1.4: **A. 7.5%**
Notice that the question says 'teenagers', which means the boys are above 12-years-old. The question does not specify if they're watching the match in a

Answer 1 (Continued)

stadium or from the grounds but, given that they are purchasing VIP tickets, we know that they are definitely watching the match in a stadium.

Collectively, the boys spent money on two VIP tickets and two discounted VIP tickets.
VIP tickets: 2 x 1.30 x 214 = £556.40
Discounted VIP tickets: 556.40 x 0.85 = £472.94
Total spent: 556.40 + 472.94 = £1,029.34

Since they divided the cost of the purchase equally, they each spent: 1,029.34 / 4 = £257.34

Original ticket price per person: 1.30 x 214 = £278.20

Percentage reduction: (278.20 - 257.34) / 278.20 x 100 = 7.5%

Answer 2

Q2.1: **E. £2,300**
Parker's annual income is 4 x £5,500 = £22,000. The payable annual income tax is: (0.05 x 10,000 + 0.15 x 12,000) = £2,300

Q2.2: **C. £38,000**
First, we work out Jake's annual payable income tax. He pays £500 a month, so that's 12 x 500 = £6,000 a year.

The simplest way to solve the question from here is to add two more columns to the table given. The solution is shown on the next page.

Answer 2 (Continued)

Taxable Income (£)	Tax Rate	Payable Income Tax per Bracket (£)	Cumulative Payable Income Tax (£)
Up to 10,000	5%	(0.05 x 10,000) = 500	500
10,000 - 25,000	15%	2,250	2,250 + 500 = 2,750
25,000 - 45,000	25%	5,000	2,750 + 5,000 = 7,750

From the table above, we know that Jake's annual income is beyond the 2nd bracket and is within the 3rd bracket as he only pays £6,000 annually.

Now, we have to work out how much tax he pays in the 3rd bracket: 6,000 - 2,750 = £3,250

Then we work out how much he earns from the 3rd bracket. We can simply do this by using algebra.
0.25x = 3,250
x = £13,000

This means Jake earns 25,000 + 13,000 = £38,000.

Q2.3: **£1,229**
To solve this question, simply extend the table that you worked on in Q2.2. However, for the new bracket, you would only have to apply 50% on £10,000 (60,000 - 50,000).

Answer 2 (Continued)

Taxable Income (£)	Tax Rate	Payable Income Tax per Bracket (£)	Cumulative Payable Income Tax (£)
45,000 - 50,000	40%	2,000	7,750 + 2,000 = 9,750
Over 50,000	50%	0.50 x 10,000 = 5,000	9,750 + 5,000 = 14,750

Therefore, Jennifer has to pay £14,750 per year. However, note that the question asks how much she has to pay per month. So it's important to divide £14,750 by 12, which will give you £1,229.

Q2.4: **B. 15%**
Given that Kelly earns £36,000, her annual income falls in the 3rd bracket. In the current year, she has to pay the maximum income tax of brackets 1 and 2 and 25% of the remaining in the 3rd bracket. That gives us 2,750 + (0.25 x 11,000) = £5,500.

In the following year, she has to pay 500 + (0.17 x 15,000) + (0.30 x 11,000) = £6,350.

The percentage increase in her pay would be (6,350 - 5,500) / 5,500 x 100 = 15%.

Answer 3

Q3.1: **E. 149.9g**
The volume of a cylinder is given by its area x height, which can be expressed as $\pi r^2 h$. Note that the question says the container is 28cm wide, which means its diameter is 28cm. Hence, its radius is 14cm.

Answer 3 (Continued)

r = 1.4dm
h = 5dm
(The dimensions are converted to dm for convenience as the question uses dm^3.)
Volume of the cylinder: 3.14 x 1.4 x 1.4 x 5 = $30.772dm^3$

Once you have the volume of the container, you can immediately multiply all the values in the question to get your answer without the need for any further conversion: 30.772 x 0.70 x 0.12 x 58 = 149.9g.

Q3.2: **B. 16,724cm^3**
We know that the volume of the container is $30.772dm^3$ and $1dm^3$ = 10cm x 10cm x 10cm = $1,000cm^3$. Therefore, the volume can also be expressed as $30,772cm^3$. Half of this volume is 30,772 / 2 = $15,386cm^3$, which is the volume of water poured into the container.

From the densities given, we can tell that, for each gram of water, $1cm^3$ of water gives us 1 / 0.92 = $1.09cm^3$ of ice. Since no water was lost or gained, the mass of water and the mass of ice remains the same. Therefore, the volume of ice after all the water freezes is 15,386 x 1.09 = $33,448cm^3$.

Q3.3: **C. 58.5%**
Original volume of water = $30.772dm^3$
Volume of water leaked in the hour: 5 x 60 x 60 = 18,000ml = $18dm^3$ Therefore, the percentage decrease of the water = 18 / 30.772 x 100 = 58.5%.

Q3.4: **B. 48.2%**
Original volume of water = $23dm^3$
Increase in water level after 1.5 hours = 0.2 x 1.5 x 60 = 18cm = 1.8dm

Note that this is an increase in the 1.8dm of the height of water in the cylinder. So we now have to find the increased volume of water. That would be 3.14 x 1.4 x 1.4 x 1.8 = $11.08dm^3$.

Hence, the percentage increase of the volume of water = 11.08 / 23 x 100 = 48.2%.

Answer 4

Q4.1: **A. £90.80**
Total funds raised: 45.60 + 61.10 + 24.00 + 56.80 + 39.50 = £227.00
Cancer Survivors take home two fifths of the total amount, so that makes it 2 / 5 x 227 = £90.80.

Q4.2: **C. £6.20**

Student	Number of songs	Amount of funds raised (£)	Amount of funds raised per song (£)
Rachel	5	45.60	45.60 / 5 = 9.12
Blaine	7	61.10	61.10 / 7 = 8.73
Kurt	3	24.00	24.00 / 3 = 8.00
Quinn	4	56.80	56.80 / 4 = 14.20
Jesse	4	39.50	39.50 / 4 = 9.88

The greatest and the smallest value calculated are £14.20 and £8.00, respectively. The difference between the two is £6.20.

Q4.3: **E. 25%**
From Q4.1, we know that Cancer Survivors initially received £90.80.
If the total amount of funds raised were divided equally, then Cancer Survivors would receive 227.00 / 2 = £113.50.
The percentage increase of their amount of funds received would be: (113.50 - 90.80) / 90.80 = 25%.

Q4.4: **E. £85.00**
If Sam had joined in, then there would be six students altogether. Hence, the total amount of funds received would be 52 x 6 = £312.

Sam managed to raise 312 - 227 = £85.00.

Answer 5

Q5.1: **C. 11**
Total number of hoops scored in the month of April: (7 x 8) + (9 x 12) + (6 x 15) + (8 x 10) = 334
Total number of days in April: 30 days
Mean number of hoops scored in each day: 334 / 30 = 11.133... = 11

Q5.2: **B. 52**
Total area available for stalls: 50 x 30 x (1 - 0.3) = 1,050m^2
Area of each stall: 5 x 4 = 20m^2
Maximum number of stalls that can fit the space: 1,050 / 20 = 52.5 = 52 (rounded down)

Q5.3: **E. 495**
Percentage who would prefer the first week of March: 100 - 34.5 = 65.5%
Total number of students in the school who would prefer the first week of March: 755 x 0.655 = 495

Q5.4: **D. 4,218**
Total megabytes that can be processed in 12 hours: 12 x 60 x 60 x (25 / 8) = 135,000
Maximum pictures that can be uploaded in 12 hours: 135,000 / 32 = 4,218.75 = 4,218 (rounded down)

Answer 6

Q6.1: **C. 0.03kg**
Mass of cumin in 250g of A: 250 x 0.3 = 75g
Mass of cumin in 100g of E: 100 x 0.45 = 45g
Mass difference between the two spices: 75 - 45 = 30g

30g is equivalent to 0.03kg.

Q6.2: **D. 32%**
As the question says that the spices are mixed in equal amounts, it can be assumed

Answer 6 (Continued)

that the spices are mixed in equal portions of 100 arbitrary units (a.u.). Hence, the numbers in the table can be directly worked with.

Total portion of turmeric: 49 + 15 + 55 + 70 + 30 = 219 a.u.
Portion of turmeric from Spice D: 70 a.u.
Percentage of turmeric from Spice D: 70 / 219 x 100 = 31.96% = 32% (rounded up)

Q6.3: **A. 16%**
The simplest way to approach this is to imagine having two 100 a.u. of Spice C mixed with three 100 a.u. of Spice D so that you do not have to worry about the percentages.

Given the above statement, it can be assumed that there are 500 a.u. of spices in the mixture.

The mass of turmeric in the final mixture is (2 x 55) + (3 x 70) = 320 a.u. Hence, the percentage of turmeric in the final mixture is 320 / 5 = 64%.

The proportion of turmeric in Spice C is 55%.

Hence, the percentage increase in percentage of turmeric is (64 - 55) / 55 x 100 = 16%.

Q6.4: **B. Cumin**
This question requires you to have a quick scan through the table to look for any possible links between two spices where one can be made into another. This involves looking for any two spices with the same ratio of any two ingredients.

The answer is cumin because the ratio of turmeric to coriander in A is similar to that in D, which is a 7:3 ratio. This means that one can be made into the other by manipulating the amount of cumin in it. However, given that D originally has less cumin compared to A, it is possible to make a mixture of A by adding cumin to D. Note that it will not be possible to make Spice D out of A as you will not be able to remove the cumin from the mixture.

Answer 7

Q7.1: **B. 3.9 hours**
Total hours spent in the gym: 7 + 7 + 5 + 6 + 3 + 4 + 4 + 2 + 0 + 1 = 39hrs
Total number of weeks: 10wks
Mean time spent in the gym each week: 39 / 10 = 3.9hrs

Q7.2: **D. 4th - 5th wk**
This question requires you to look at the downward slopes on the graph and identify which has the steepest gradient.

Q7.3: **C. 61%**
Mean of gym time in the first five weeks: (7 + 7 + 5 + 6 + 3) / 5 = 5.6hrs
Mean of gym time in the last five weeks: (4 + 4 + 2 + 0 + 1) / 5 = 2.2hrs
Percentage decrease in gym time: (5.6 - 2.2) / 5.6 x 100 = 61%

Q7.4: **B. 1.8 hours**
Mean of gym time per week for Neary: 4.8 - 3.9 = 0.9
Total hours spent in the gym in the term (i.e., 10 weeks) for Neary: 0.9 x 10 = 9hrs
Total time spent in each visit to the gym: 9 / 5 = 1.8hrs

Answer 8

Q8.1: **D. 30.2km**
45 minutes = 45 / 60 = 0.75hrs

Distance = Speed x Time
Distance = 25 x 0.75 = 18.75 miles = 18.75 x 1.609 = 30.2km

Q8.2: **C. 11.8**
Average speed = Total distance / Total time
Total time = 4 + 2 + 10 + 9 = 25mins = 25 x 60 = 1,500s

The total distance can be found by sketching a velocity against time graph and finding the area under the graph.

Answer 8 (Continued)

Total distance:
Part 1 – 0.5 x (4 / 60) x 40 = 1.33 miles
Part 2 – 40 x (10 / 60) = 6.67 miles
Part 3 – 0.5 x (9 / 60) x 40 = 3 miles

Total distance travelled: 1.33 + 6.67 + 3 = 11 miles = 11 x 1.609 x 1000 = 17,699m

Average speed: 17,699 / 1,500 = 11.8m/s

Q8.3: **B. 2.52**
Distance travelled in one minute = 1 / 60 x 80 = 1.33 miles = 1.33 x 1.609 x 1,000 = 2,145m
Number of laps that can be completed: 2,145 / 850 = 2.52

Q8.4: **D. 25mins**
Two thirds of the distance = 2/3 x 15 = 10 miles
Time taken, in mins, to travel 10 miles = 10 / 60 x 60 = 10mins

One third of the distance = 1/3 x 15 = 5 miles
Time taken, in mins, to travel 5 miles = 5 / 20 x 60 = 15mins

Total time taken: 10 + 15 = 25mins

Answer 9

Q9.1: **E. 166.6cm**
Total height of all the students in the class: (13 x 172.2) + (27 x 163.9) = 6,663.9cm
Mean height of students in the class: 6,663.9 / (13 + 27) = 166.6cm

Q9.2: **A. 181.4cm**
Total height of all the students in the class (including twins): 42 x 167.3 = 7,026.6cm

Answer 9 (Continued)

Total height of twins alone: 7,026.6 - 6,663.9 = 362.7cm
Height of each twin: 362.7 / 2 = 181.4cm

Q9.3: **B. 0.90%**
Total height of all the boys: 13 x 172.2 = 2,238.6cm
Total height of the boys excluding the tallest boy: 2,238.6 - 190.9 = 2,047.7cm
New mean height of the boys in the class: 2,047.7 / 12 = 170.6cm
Percentage reduction in mean height of boys: (172.2 - 170.6) / 172.2 x 100 = 0.90%

Q9.4: **B. 155.2cm**
Initial total height of all the girls: 163.9 x 27 = 4,425.3cm
New average height of girls (after the five girls left the class): 163.9 x 1.012 = 165.87cm
New total height of girls: 165.87 x (27 - 5) = 3,649.1cm
Total height of the five girls who left the class: 4,425.3 - 3,649.1 = 776.2cm
Mean height of the five girls who left the class: 776.2 / 5 = 155.2cm

Answer 10

Q10.1: **B. 101yrs**
Circumference = 113
πd = 113
d = 113 / 3.14 = 36.0 cm = 14.4 inches

Age in years = Diameter in inches (d) x Growth factor (k)
Age of given Dogwood tree = 14.4 x 7.0 = 101yrs

Q10.2: **C. Mode, mean, median**
Mean = (5+ 4 + 5 + 3.5 + 7 + 2 + 7.5 + 4.5) / 8 = 4.8125

To get the median, we have to arrange the numbers in ascending order: 2, 3.5, 4, 4.5, 5, 5, 7, 7.5. Given that there are eight terms, the median is the average of the 4th and 5th term. Hence, it would be (4.5 + 5) / 2 = 4.75.

Answer 10 (Continued)

The mode from the data is 5.0.

Hence, in descending order, the figures would be 5.0, 4.8125, 4.75, which would be: mode, mean, median.

Q10.3: **C. 36 inches**
1 foot = 12 inches
Initial diameter of both trees would be 24 inches.

Age in years (A) = Diameter in inches (d) x Growth factor (k)

Initially for Aspen, its age was A_a = 24 x 2 = 48yrs.
After 10 years, its diameter would be:
58 = d_a x 2
d_a = 29 inches

Initially for Sugar Maple, its age was A_s = 24 x 5 = 120yrs.
After 10 years, its diameter would be:
130 = d_s x 2
d_a = 65 inches

Difference in diameter would be: 65 - 29 = 36 inches.

Q10.4: **D. Green Ash**
The growth factor of a tree can be approximated by the slope (i.e. gradient) of a line of best fit that models the relationship between diameter and age.

The line of best fit should be visually estimated using a line of which half of the data points fall above it and the half of the data points fall below it.

Working that out, you should be able to deduce that the line of best fit has a gradient of approximately four. That should lead you to the answer Green Ash. The rest of the options are species of trees, of which growth factors will give results that are far off from the data shown in the scatter plot.

Answer 11

Q11.1: **B. 56,175**
Total percentage of RunningMan and Kickz: 16 + 5 = 21% = 0.21
Total RunningMan and Kickz shoes sold: 0.21 x 267,500 = 56,175

Q11.2: **E. £1,310,750**
Profit made from Presto shoes: 40 x 0.18 x 267,500 = £1,926,000
Profit made from Agile shoes: 55 x 0.22 x 267,500 = £3,236,750
The difference in the profit made: 3,236,750 - 1,926,000 = £1,310,750

Q11.3: **D. 4.7°**
Initial number of Sogdo shoes sold: 0.29 x 267,500 = 77,575
New percentage of Sogdo shoes after including 12,550 Sole Soul shoes in the pie chart: 77,575 / (267,500 + 12,550) x 100 = 27.7%
Decrease in percentage of Sogdo shoes = 29 - 27.7 = 1.3%
Decrease in angle size of sector = 0.013 x 360 = 4.7°

Q11.4: **A. £187**
Total RunningMan shoes sold: 0.16 x 267,500 = 42,800
Mean profit made per shoe: 8,000,000 / 42,800 = £187

Answer 12

Q12.1: **B. 1.4°C**
$\Delta Q = m \times c \times \Delta\theta$
$3000 = 0.5 \times 4{,}181 \times \Delta\theta$
$\Delta\theta = 1.4^{\circ}C$

Q12.2: **B. 0.94:1**
Given the equation $\Delta Q = m \times c \times \Delta\theta$ and that ΔQ and m are equal, we can deduce that $c \times \Delta\theta$ is constant for methanol and propanol.

Hence,
$c_m \times \Delta\theta_m = c_p \times \Delta\theta_p$
$\Delta\theta_m / \Delta\theta_p = \Delta\theta_m : \Delta\theta_p = c_p / c_m = 2{,}390 / 2{,}530 = 0.94:1$

Answer 12 (Continued)

Q12.3: **E. 0.458kg**
Given the equation $\Delta Q = m \times c \times \Delta\theta$ and that ΔQ and $\Delta\theta$ are equal, we can deduce that m x c is constant for sodium and potassium.

Hence,
$m_s \times c_s = m_p \times c_p$
$0.750 \times 1{,}214 = m_p \times 754$
$m_p = 1.21\text{kg}$

Difference between the two masses: 1.21 - 0.75 = 0.458kg

Q12.4: **C. 87.1**
Given the equation $\Delta Q = m \times c \times \Delta\theta$ and that ΔQ are equal, we can deduce that m x c x $\Delta\theta$ is constant for the unknown solid and gold.

Hence,
$m_{us} \times c_{us} \times \Delta\theta_{us} = m_g \times c_g \times \Delta\theta_g$

However, the question states that the mass of the unknown solid is 35% of that of the equivalent in gold. Thus, $m_{us} = 0.35m_g$. It also rises in temperature four times more than gold. Thus, $\Delta\theta_{us} = 4\Delta\theta_g$.

Substituting those values into the equation including $c_g = 122$,
$0.35m_g \times c_{us} \times 4\Delta\theta_g = m_g \times 122 \times \Delta\theta_g$
$c_{us} = 87.1$

Answer 13

Q13.1: **C. 7.6%**
Total students scoring straight As across all years: 91 + 112 + 70 + 95 + 145 + 102 + 82 + 110 + 110 = 917
Number of students scoring straight As in the lowest year: 70
Percentage of the total is the year with the least straight As: 70 / 917 x 100 = 7.6%

Answer 13 (Continued)

Q13.2: **D. 76.6%**
By looking at the graph, one can determine that the greatest increase between two consecutive years is the increase between 2012 and 2013.

Percentage increase between 2012 and 2013: (113 - 64) / 64 x 100 = 76.6%

Q13.3: **A. +34.1%**
By looking at the graph, one can determine that the smallest percentage increase between two consecutive years is the increase between 2016 and 2017.

Percentage change between 2016 and 2017 for School B: (110 - 82) / 82 x 100 = +34.1% ('+' because there was an increase in between the two years)

Q13.4: **D. School B has a higher average of straight A students across the nine years compared to School A.**

Total students scoring straight As across all years in School A: 91 + 112 + 70 + 95 + 145 + 102 + 82 + 110 + 110 = 917
Mean for School A: 917 / 9 = 101.9

Total students scoring straight As across all years in School B: 100 + 89 + 64 + 113 + 151 + 78 + 104 + 123 + 94 = 916
Mean for School B: 916 / 9 = 101.8

Option A is false because School A had only surpassed School B a total of five times across the nine years.
Option B is false because the smallest change in the number of straight A students in School B is 0, which is between years 2017 and 2018.
Option C is false because the greatest difference in the number of straight A students in both schools is 24, which is in year 2015.
Option E is false because, whilst the value 73 is correct, it was a decrease in the number of straight As and not an increase. This was between years 2014 and 2015.

Option D would have taken the most time to work out. Hence, it would be easier to select it as an answer by ruling out the rest of the statements.

Answer 14

Q14.1: **E. Transport**
Total profits made from each section:
Construction: 3.5 + 4.4 + 6.2 = 14.1
Oil & Gas: 4.2 + 6.2 + 8.0 = 18.4
Healthcare: 4.5 + 5.1 + 7.9 = 17.5
Transport: 4.0 + 6.3 + 6.6 = 16.9
Food & Beverage: 3.8 + 4.6 + 5.1 = 13.5

21% of the total profits overall: 0.21 x 80.4 = £16.9M

Hence, the answer is transport.

Alternatively, you could total up all the figures shown in the graph and multiply the total to get 16.9 right away. After that, if you study each private sector carefully, you will be able to easily rule out Construction, Oil & Gas, and Food & Beverage by doing a quick mental calculation of the sum of their whole numbers. A closer look at Healthcare and Transport will enable you to immediately tell that Transport totals up to 16.9.

Q14.2: **B. £35.1M**
Contracts ratio of profit to turnover: 3:17

Turnover of Oil & Gas in Thailand: 6.2 x 17/3 = £35.1M

Q14.3: **A. £8.8M**
Total profit across all areas other than F&B: 80.4 (as calculated in Q14.1) - 13.5 = £66.9M. This needs to be three quarters for the condition to be met. Therefore, profit across all sectors should be: 66.9 / (3/4) = £89.2M.

Actual profit from F&B: £13.5M
Target for F&B: 89.2 - 66.9 = £22.3M
Shortfall: 22.3 - 13.5 = £8.8M

Q14.4: **E. Transport**
Total profit across all areas other than F&B: £80.4M (as calculated in Q14.1)

Answer 14 (Continued)

Takeover offer price: 80.4 x 9 = £723.6M
Suggested offer price: 723.6 x 1.27 = £919M

Answer 15

Q15.1: **A. 9.74 Yuan**
£19.76 represents the conversion of 185 Yuan, inclusive of a 4% fee on the converted cost. To calculate the original cost of the pound, we will first let the original cost be denoted as C.

1.04C = 19.76
C = £19

We now know that £19 is equivalent to 185 Yuan. This means a pound would be 185 / 19 = 9.74 Yuan.

Q15.2: **C. 770**
Let p pounds be the cost of the 800 Yuan prepaid card. This implies that the exchange rate on a particular day is d/800 pound per Yuan. Suppose Sara's total purchases on the prepaid card were y Yuan. The value of y Yuan in pounds is y(d/800) pounds. If Sara spent the y Yuan on the traveller card instead, she would be charged 1.04y(d/800) pounds.

To answer the question about how much Yuan Sara must spend in order to make the prepaid card a cheaper option (in pounds) for the y Yuan, we can set up the inequality:
1.04y(d/800) > d

Removing the d on both sides,
1.04(y/800) > 1
y > 769.23

Hence, the least amount of Yuan Sara must spend for the prepaid card to be cheaper than the traveller card is 769.23 Yuan. Since the answers are all integers,

Answer 15 (Continued)

this means rounding has to occur. Given that the inequality states that $y > 769.23$, this means that the smallest acceptable integer must be 770.

Q15.3: **D. £352,941**

Let the original price of the property be C.
Price after first discount: 0.70 x C = 0.7C
Price after second discount: 0.7C x 0.85 = 0.595C

0.595C = 210,000
C = £352,941

Q15.4: **A. $m(p) = 7.5p - 15$**
A linear function that represents a relationship will be in the form of $m(p) = ap + b$, where a and b are constants and $m(p)$ is the monthly rental price, in pounds, of a property that was purchased with p thousands of pounds.

At this point, you can take whichever two ordered pairs of (p, m) from the table to substitute into the equation and find a and b. For this example, let's use (192, 1,425) and (210, 1,560).

Equation 1: $192a + b = 1{,}425$
Equation 2: $210a + b = 1{,}560$

E1 - E2:
$192a - 210a = 1{,}425 - 1{,}560$
$-18a = -135$
$a = 7.5$

Substitute $a = 7.5$ into E1,
$192(7.5) + b = 1{,}425$
$b = 1{,}425 - 1{,}440$
$b = -15$

Hence, the equation would be $m(p) = 7.5p - 15$.

Answer 16

Q16.1: **C. 1.37:1**
From the formula given, it can be deduced that the acceleration is represented by the gradient of the graph.

Since the question asks for the greatest acceleration of Camdyn and Elspeth, you can narrow your focus on the steepest slopes (i.e. greatest magnitude of gradient) on the graph. Alternatively, you could also find the biggest change in the velocity (as shown in the table) of each cyclist in a given second.

For Camdyn, the biggest change in velocity is between the 7th and 8th second. This would be an increase from velocities of 15.6 to 20.8, which is a difference of 5.2m/s. Hence, his acceleration in this second would be: 5.2 / 1 = 5.2m/s^2.

For Elspeth, the biggest change in velocity is between the 5th and 6th second. This would be an increase from velocities of 9.2 to 13.0, which is a difference of 3.8m/s. Hence, her acceleration in this second would be: 3.8 / 1 = 3.8m/s^2.

Ratio of Camdyn's to Elspeth's greatest acceleration: 5.2:3.8 = 1.37:1

Q16.2: **D. 4.75m**
Distance is a product of particular speed and time taken to travel at that speed. On a velocity-time graph, this can be calculated by taking the area under the graph.

As the table shows the velocity of the cyclists at each given second, you can imagine drawing vertical lines downwards from each marked coordinate on the graph. This will give you a triangle for the distance travelled in the first second. For the subsequent seconds, you will get trapeziums instead.

Now this may seem tedious, but there is a very simple way to approach it.

The formula to calculate the area of a trapezium is 1/2 x Base x Sum of both parallel sides. We know that the base for all the trapeziums would simply be a value of 1 as it represents 1s. The magnitude of both parallel sides, in this case, would be the magnitude of the velocities (i.e. the height of the imaginary vertical lines). So you will basically be finding the sum of the average velocities across each given second. E.g. between the 2nd and 3rd second, all you have to do

Answer 16 (Continued)

is take (2.0 + 3.5) / 2 = 2.75m. You can do this individually for the duration of each second and find its total sum at the end or you can use the simpler method below.

First, it is important to recognise a pattern in this sum.
The formula below is exactly what you would be doing if you adopt the method described above.
(a + b) / 2 + (b + c) / 2 + (c + d) / 2 + (d + e) / 2 + (e + f) / 2

This can be simplified to:
(a + 2b + 2c + 2d + 2e + f) / 2
OR
0.5a + b + c + d + e + 0.5f

With this simplified formula, you will be able to key in all the values in your calculator directly and get your answer in a shorter time. The only catch is that it requires you to multiple each middle value by 2 or to divide the first and the last term by 2 arithmetically.

Hence, for our cyclists, their distance travelled in the first five seconds is:

Camdyn: (0 + 1.6 + 4.0 + 7.0 + 10.6 + 7.3) / 2 = 15.25m
Elspeth: (0 + 2.4 + 6.4 + 9.0 + 13.0 + 9.2) / 2 = 20m
OR
Camdyn: 0 + 0.8 + 2.0 + 3.5 + 5.3 + 3.65= 15.25m
Elspeth: 0 + 1.2 + 3.2 + 4.5 + 6.5 + 4.6 = 20m

Difference in distance travelled: 20 - 15.25 = 4.75m

Q16.3: **A. 13.4%**
From the graph, we can tell that the nth second in this case would be the 6th second. The distance travelled after the 6th second (using the simplified method described in Q16.3) is: 6.5 + 14.9 + 17.5 + 20.3 + 23.6 = 71m.

Elspeth's acceleration at the 6th second was: (13.0 - 9.2) / 1 = 3.8m/s^2

If she had maintained her acceleration for the next three seconds, her velocity at the 9th second would be:

Answer 16 (Continued)

$a = (v_f - v_i) / \Delta t$
$3.8 = (v_f - 13.0) / 3$
$v_f = 24.4m/s$

Since she maintained her velocity after, 24.4m/s would be her speed at the 10th second as well.

If this was the case, her distance travelled could have been: [1/2 x 3 x (13.0 + 24.4)] + (24.4 x 1) = 80.5m

Hence, the percentage increase in her distance travelled would be: (80.5 - 71) / 71 x 100 = 13.4%

Q16.4: **E. 0.17mph**
Average velocity is given by the total displacement (in this case, it is equal to the total distance) divided by the total time of travel.

From Q16.2, we have the distance travelled for the first five seconds of both cyclists.
Camdyn: 15.25m
Elspeth: 20m

From Q16.3, we have the distance travelled by Elspeth from the 6th to the 10th second, which is 71m. Hence, we just have to find the distance travelled in between the 5th and 6th second. That would be: 1/2 x (9.2 + 13.0) x 1 = 11.1m.

Total distance travelled by Elspeth: 20 + 71 + 11.1 = 102.1m

Her average velocity: 102.1 / 10 = 10.21m/s

For Camdyn, distance travelled from the 5th second onwards: 3.65 + 11.5 + 15.6 + 20.8 + 23.6 + 12.45 = 87.6m
Total distance travelled by Camdyn: 15.25 + 87.6 = 102.85m
His average velocity: 102.85 / 10 = 10.285m/s = 10.285

Difference in mph: 10.285 - 10.21 = 0.075m/s = 0.075 / 1609 x 60 x 60 = 0.17mph

Answer 16 (Continued)

Her average velocity: 102.1 / 10 = 10.21m/s

For Camdyn,
Distance travelled from the 5th second onwards: 3.65 + 11.5 + 15.6 + 20.8 + 23.6 + 12.45 = 87.6m

Total distance travelled by Camdyn: 15.25 + 87.6 = 102.85m

His average velocity: 102.85 / 10 = 10.285m/s = 10.285

Difference in mph: 10.285 - 10.21 = 0.075m/s = 0.075 / 1609 x 60 x 60 = 0.17mph

Answer 17

Q17.1: **C. 1.05s**
Distance = Speed x Time
Time = Distance / Speed

Distance between moon and Planet X: 195.3 thousand miles = 195.3 x 1,000 x 1,609 = 314,237,700m

Time taken for light to travel: 314,237,700 / 3×10^8 = 1.05s

Q17.2: **C. 7,137**
Volume of sphere, $V = 4\pi r^3/3$

As $4\pi/3$ are constants, we can say that V is directly proportional to r^3.

Radius of the planet, r_X= 0.5 x 65,370 x 1,609 = 52,590,165m
Radius of the moon, r_m= 0.5 x 5,463 x 1,000 = 2,731,500m

Answer 17 (Continued)

$r_X / r_m = 52{,}590{,}165 / 2{,}731{,}500$
$r_X / r_m = 19.3$
$r_X = 19.3r_m$

Given the relationship between V and r^3,

$V_X / V_m = r_X^3 / r_m^3$
$V_X / V_m = (19.3r_m)^3 / r_m^3$
$V_X / V_m = 7{,}137r_m^3 / r_m^3$
$V_X = 7{,}137V_m$

Hence, we can conclude that the volume of Planet X is 7,137 times greater than the volume of the moon.

Q17.3: **C. 222**
The distance travelled by Planet X around the Sun is along the circumference of the orbit. That distance would be: $\pi d = \pi \times 9.44\text{x}10^8 = 9.44\text{x}10^8\pi$ miles

Speed (miles/s) = Distance (miles / Time (s))
Time = Distance / Speed
Time = $9.44\text{x}10^8 \times 3.14 / (680 / 1{,}609)$
Time = $7.01\text{x}10^9$s = $7.01\text{x}10^9 / 60 / 60 / 24 / 365$ = 222yrs

Q17.4: **B. 207**
Four fifths of a year expressed in hours: 4 / 5 x 365 x 24 = 7,008hrs

The moon orbits around the planet. Its movement is along an imaginary circle which has the planet at its centre. The radius of this circle is the distance between the centre of the moon and the centre of the planet.

Expressed as an equation, this would be:
Radius of imaginary circle = Radius of the moon + Radius of the planet + Distance between the surface of the moon and the planet

Radius of the planet: r_X= 65,370 / 2 = 32,685 miles
Radius of the moon: r_m= 5,463 x 1,000 / 1,609 = 3,395 miles
Distance between moon and Planet X: $1.953\text{x}10^5$ miles

Answer 17 (Continued)

Radius of orbit: 32,685 + 3,395 + $1.953 x 10^5$ = 231,380 miles
Circumference of orbit: $2\pi r$ = 2 x 3.14 x 231,380 = 1,453,066.4 miles

Orbital speed: Distance travelled / Time = 1,453,066.4 / 7,008 = 207mph

Answer 18

Q18.1: **D. Draco**

Name of Participant	Starting Weight	Mass (kg)	Ranking
Draco	50st 1lb	319.7	4
Rubeus	234lb	514.8	7
Neville	317kg	317	3
Fleur	45st	285.75	2
Myrtle	202kg	202	1
Quirinus	60st	381	6
Dolores	52st 2lb	334.6	5

The median of a series with seven terms with the 4th term. Hence, the answer is Draco.

Q18.2: **A. 1.2%**
If Neville reaches his target weight at the end of the programme, his weight would be: 317 x 0.80 = 253.6kg

If Dolores had the same weight as Neville at the end of the programme, that would mean she had a total loss in weight of: (334.6 - 253.6) / 334.6 x 100 = 24.2%.

Answer 18 (Continued)

As her target percentage weight loss was 23%, this means she had an extra loss of 1.2% beyond her target weight.

Q18.3: **E. 129**

Having lost only two sevenths of his 30% target, Rubeus' final weight would be: [1 - (2 / 7 x 0.30)] x 234 x 2.2 = 470.7kg.

Rubeus final BMI would be: 470.7 / 1.91^2 = 129

Q18.4: **C. Myrtle**

This question can be approached by making a smart guess. Looking at the masses of the participants, it is clear to see that Myrtle had the lowest starting weight. While she may also be the shortest, a quick calculation of 1.60^2 compared to 1.91^2 will make you realise that the height of the participants does not play a significant role in comparing their BMIs. Hence, looking at the weight alone, it would be safe to select Myrtle as the answer.

If you had to perform individual calculations, the table below shows the BMI of the participants for you to check your answers.

Name of Participant	Height (m)	Starting Weight	Mass	BMI
Draco	1.71	50st 1lb	319.7	109
Rubeus	1.91	234lb	514.8	141
Neville	1.77	317kg	317	101
Fleur	1.65	45st	285.75	105
Myrtle	1.60	202kg	202	78.9
Quirinus	1.80	60st	381	118
Dolores	1.78	52st 2lb	334.6	106

Answer 19

Q19.1: **D. 216**
Total staff hours on a weekday, excluding extra staff hours during peak times: (2200 - 0900) x 2 = 26hrs
Extra staff hours on a weekday: 5 (from total peak hours) x 2 = 10hrs
Hence, total staff hours on a weekday is 36hrs. Across five weekdays, that would be a total of 36 x 5 = 180hrs.

Total staff hours on a weekend, excluding extra staff hours during peak times: (1700 - 1000) x 2 = 14hrs
Extra staff hours on a weekday: 2 (from total peak hours) x 2 = 4hrs
Hence, total staff hours on a weekday is 18hrs. Across five weekdays, that would be a total of 18 x 2 = 36hrs.

Total staff hours: 180 + 36 = 216hrs

Q19.2: **A. 17.6oz**
500 / 28.4 x 1 = 17.6oz

Q19.3: **C. 67.5**
If the pearls gain 12.5% in weight during roasting and each cup requires 25g, the weight of unroasted pearls in each cup is: 25 / 1.125 = 22.2g.

Each bag from the supplier has 1.5kg, equivalent to 1,500g, of unroasted pearls. Hence, the number of cups that can be made from each bag is: 1500 / 22.2 = 67.5 cups

Q19.4: **C. 7**
To redeem a free cup, Ji-hye needs 5 x 32 = 160 points on her card as she needs 32 10p to make £3.20.
As she only buys one cup in each visit, she is only rewarded with 3 x 8 = 24 points per purchase.
Hence, she would only have enough points for a free cup after 160 / 24 = 6.67 = 7 (rounded up) purchases.

Answer 20

Q20.1: **D. Area X > Area Y; Perimeter X = Perimeter Y**
From the question, it can be deduced that Field X has sides of 70m. This means it has a perimeter of 70 x 4 = 280m.

Field Y has a length of 90m and a width of 50m. This means is has a perimeter of 280m and an area of 90 x 50 = 4,500m^2.

Q20.2: **D. £1.17M**
The plot of land is square, and each side is 100m. Hence, its area is 100^2 = 10,000m^2 = 2.47 acre = 1 hectare.

Price of plot on Blue land: 1/3 x 2.47 x 450k = £370.5k
Price of plot on Green land: 2/3 x 1 x 1.2M = £0.8M = £800k

Total price of plot: 370.5k + 800k = £1,170.5k = £1.17M.

Q20.3: **E. 697s**
Best record (converted to minutes and seconds): 184mins 18s
Total time taken for the first five rounds: 156mins 34s
Time to beat in sixth round: 184mins 18s - 156mins 34s = 27mins 44s

Time difference between 5th and 6th round: 39mins 21s - 27mins 44s = 11mins 37s

Q20.4: **C. 44.7**
If 1,789 photos account for 12% of the album space, the whole album has a total of 1,789 / 0.12 = 14,908 photos.

Size of photo album in GB: 14,908 x 3 x 0.001 = 44.7GB

Answer 21

Q21.1: **E. £2,497**
Total pairs of shoes purchased: (40 x 4) + 42 = 202 pairs
Total cost of shoes: 202 x 12 = £2,424
Shipping cost: £18
Cost of express delivery: £55

Grand total: 2,424 + 18 + 55 = £2,497

Q21.2: **B. £12,219**
Total shoes ordered: 60 + 600 = 660
Total cost of shoes alone: 660 x 10 = £6,660
Total cost for embroidery: 2 x 10 x [40 + (0.40 x 600)] = £5,600
Shipping cost for students (600 shoes): £7
Shipping cost for coaches (60 shoes): £12

Grand total of both orders: 6,600 + 5,600 + 7 + 12 = £12,219

Q21.3: **B. £17,101**
Total shoes ordered: 184 + 302 + 253 + 271 = 1,010
Total cost of shoes: 1,010 x 8 = £8,080
Total cost for embroidery: 1,010 x 10 = £10,100
Cost for express delivery: 10 x 1.25 = £12.50 (Note that the waiver for above a thousand units only applies to international orders)

Grand total (before discount): 8,080 + 10,100 + 12.50 = £18,192.50
Grand total (after discount): 0.94 x 18,192.50 = £17,100.95 = £17,101 (rounded off)

Q21.4: **E. 268**
The question does not give any obvious information of the origin of the school's alumni. It is easy to be assume that they are in Switzerland, but this is not the case. If you look at the second order, it says £17 for delivery charge. The question also clearly states that both orders were of standard delivery. Looking back at the question stem, the only shipping destination which costs £17 is Africa. This tells us that the school must be based in Africa.

Answer 21 (Continued)

First order:
Total number of shoes: 80 + 15 = 95
Total cost of shoes: 95 x 15 = £1,425
Total cost of embroidery: 80 x 10 = £800
Cost for delivery: £20

Total cost for first order: 1,425 + 800 + 20 = £2,245

Second order:
Let the total number of shoes be S.
For the price of each shoe, we know that, given the shipping cost is £17, the number of units ordered must be between 201-500. Hence, the price of each pair of shoes must be £12.
Total cost of shoes: £12S
Cost for delivery: £17

Since the overall total of both invoices is £5,298:
2,245 + 17 + 12S = 5,298
12S = 5,298 - 2,262
12S = 3,036
S = 253

We now know that the second order has 253 pairs of shoes without embroidery. However, the question asks for the total number of shoes without embroidery. Hence, that would be 253 + 15 = 268 shoes.

Answer 22

Q22.1: **C. 70%**
Total grams of maple syrup cakes consumed: 90 x 3 = 270g
Total salt intake: 270 x 0.7 / 100 = 1.89g
Percentage of RDA of salt consumed: 1.89 / 2.7 x 100 = 70%

Answer 22 (Continued)

Q22.2: **B. 2,006**
Total grams of lemon poppy cakes consumed: 3 x 55 =165g
Total energy from lemon poppy cakes: 165 x 601 / 100 = 991.65kcal

Total grams of Bailey's cakes consumed: 75 x 2 = 150g
Total energy from Bailey's cakes: 150 x 676 / 100 = 1,014kcal

Total energy consumption: 991.65 + 1,014 = 2,005.65 = 2,006kcal

Q22.3: **A. 19.2**
Total grams of half a packet of cherry almond cakes: 120 / 2 = 60
Total fat provided in half a packet: 60 x 32 / 100 = 19.2g

Q22.4: **D. 73.3%**
Total grams of eight packets of maple syrup cakes: 8 x 90 = 720g
Total fibre consumed: 720 x 1 / 100 = 7.2g
RDA of fibre: 27g
Percentage of fibre missed: (27 - 7.2) / 27 x 100 = 73.3%

Q22.5: **C. 225%**
Total grams of 14.5 packets of lemon poppy cakes: 14.5 x 55 = 797.5g
Total salt intake: 797.5 x 1.1 / 100 = 8.7725g
Excess salt intake expressed as a percentage: (8.7725 - 2.7) / 2.7 x 100 = 225%

Answer 23

Q23.1: **B. 9.5%**
Total of all animals in each zoo:
Quintal: 36 + 45 + 121 + 135 + 80 = 417
Tuin: 40 + 242 + 234 + 52 + 115 = 683
Jardins: 3 + 7 + 75 + 10 + 32 = 127
Parque: 56 + 84 + 78 + 44 + 24 = 286
Garten: 245 + 421 + 550 + 156 + 110 = 1,482

Answer 23 (Continued)

Total number of animals in all zoos: 417 + 683 + 127 + 286 + 1,482 = 2,995

Percentage of animals in Parque's: 286 / 2,995 x 100 = 9.5%

Q23.2: **B. 6%**
Original number of gorillas: 52
Total number of gorillas after increase: 52 x 1.34 = 69.68 = 70 (rounded off)
Total number of animals in Tuin's: 40 + 242 + 234 + 70 + 115 = 701
Percentage of lions in Tuin's: 40 / 701 x 100 = 6%

Q23.3: **C. 8:5**
Total number of elephants left in Garten's: 550 x (1 - 0.68) = 176
Total number of 'other' in Garten's: 110
The ratio of elephants to 'other' would be 176:110.
This can be simplified to be 8:5, after dividing 22 on both sides.

Q23.4: **C. 21%**
Original number of rhinoceros: 7
Total number of rhinoceros after increase: 7 + (7 x 2.25) = 22.75 = 23 (rounded off)
Increase in number of rhinoceros: 23 - 7 = 16
Hence, the decrease in the number of elephants must be 16 as well to keep the number of animals in the zoo the same.
This means that the percentage decrease of elephants would be: 16 / 75 x 100 = 21%

Answer 24

Q24.1: **B. 7.9%**
Total number of gold medals: 132 + 100 + 88 + 34 + 22 + 20 + 17 + 15 = 428
Percentage of gold medals won by Cheeseman: 34 / 428 x 100 = 7.9%

Answer 24 (Continued)

Q24.2: **B. 2nd**

This question is tricky and requires you to carefully interpret the numbers in the table. Bear in mind that the question stem states that the sport houses in the table shown are arranged in order of number of gold medals won.

First, you would need to identify the house that raised the least funds from the medals won. By looking at gold medals alone (which are the medals with the highest value), you might expect P. Ramlee (PR) to have the least funds raised as it has the least gold medals, but it is important to have a quick scan at Tunku Putra (TP) and Sirajuddin (S) as the number of medals won are within the same range.

A direct comparison between TP and S can be made as the number of bronze medals won by the two houses is the same. Whilst S may have won three gold medals more than TP, TP has won seven silver medals more than S. Since each gold medal is worth two silver medals, this would mean that S raised less funds than TP.

Next, you can compare S and PR. Using the same methods as above, you will realise that S raised less funds compared to PR. Hence, S is the house with the least funds raised`which, after calculation, should give you £700.

Now, you can calculate the amount of funds raised by Hamilton, which is (132 x 20) + (91 x 10) + (62 x 5) = £3,860. Half of that would be £1,930.

Thus, S would have 1,930 + 700 = £2,630 in total.

Wu Lien Teh (WLT) raised a total of: (100 x 20) + (50 x 10) + (70 x 5) = £2,850. With quick mental calculation, you should be able to roughly estimate that WLT raised more than £2,630.

Hargreaves raised a total of: (88 x 20) + (55 x 10) + (50 x 5) = £2,560. With quick mental calculation, you should be able to roughly estimate that Hargreaves raised less than £2,630.

You should not need to calculate how much Cheeseman raised as the house has significantly less medals than Hargreaves and WLT.

Answer 24 (Continued)

This puts S between WLT and Hargreaves. Hence, it comes in 2nd place. Bear in mind that Hamilton now only has £1,930 left so you do not have to worry about it either.

Q24.3: **D. 28.6%**
Total funds raised by PR from medals alone: (15 x 20) + (22 x 10) + (36 x 5) = £700
Increase funds raised from the PTA award: £200
Percentage increase in funds: 200 / 700 x 100 = 28.6%

Q24.4: **D. 100%**
Total gold medals won by national athletes in the three houses: (132 + 100 + 85) x 0.60 = 192
WLT's gold medals won by national athletes: 0.25 x 100 = 25
Hargreaves' gold medals won by national athletes: 0.40 x 88 = 35.2 = 35 (rounded off)
Hamilton's gold medals won by national athletes: 192 - 25 - 35 = 132

Hamilton won a total of 132 gold medals. Hence, it would be 100%.

Answer 25

Q25.1: **B. 20mg**
In 1% of solution, there is 1g in 100ml, which is equivalent to 1,000mg in 100ml.
In 2ml of 1% solution, there should be 1,000 / 100 x 2 = 20mg of drug.

Q25.2: **D. 0.025**
250micrograms/ml = 0.00025g/ml
Hence, in 100ml of the drug, there would be 0.00025 x 100 = 0.025%

Q25.3: **C. 0.5ml**
1 in 1000 = 1g in 1,000ml = 1,000mg/1,000ml = 1mg/1ml

Answer 25 (Continued)

Hence, 0.5mg is contained in 0.5ml of drug.

Q25.4: **E. 0.56**
Total dose of mebeverine in four weeks: 100 x 2 x 7 x 4 = 5,600mg
Volume of drug given: 5,600 / (50mg/5ml) = 560ml = 0.56l

Answer 26

Q26.1: **E. £1,463.97**
While making the calculations, do not forget to include the 20% discount for the products that have an order of more than 20kg. In Ellie's case, that would be for D2, D24 and D88.

Total cost of Ellie's order (excluding delivery fee): [(30 x 12.99) + (45 x 9.99) + (50 x 8.99)] x 0.80 + (12 x 15.99)+ (36 x 3) = £1,330.88
Total price to pay (including delivery): 1,330.88 x 1.10 = £1,463.97

Q26.2: **B. 547**
Let the number of durians used for the collection order be N.

Bear in mind that all his orders are above £20 so they all qualify for the 20% discount. This will be shown as 0.80 in the calculation.

Total spent on D series durians: [(300 x 9.99) + (360 x 12.99) + (300 x 8.99) + (270 x 10.99)] x 0.80 = £10,670.16
One third of this was delivered to him: 1/3 x 10,670.16 = £3,556.72
Two thirds were collected: 3,556.72 x 2 = £7,113.44

At this point, we have all the information we need for this collection order, that is: £(7,113.44 + 3N).

His delivery had Musang King durian as well. Hence, the total of his durian order (excluding delivery) is: (0.80 x 100 x 15.99) + 3,556.72 = £4,835.92. With delivery included, that would be 4,835.92 x 1.1 = £5,319.51.

Answer 26 (Continued)

Grand total = Collection total + Delivery total
14,073.95 = 7,113.44 + 3N + 5,319.51
3N = 1,641
N = 547

Q26.3: **A. -£35.35**
Cost price of the durians: 1.15 x 50 x (7.00 + 9.00 + 6.50 + 8.00) = £1,753.75
Selling price of the durians: 0.80 x 50 x (9.99 + 12.99 + 8.99 + 10.99) = £1,718.40

Since the selling price is lower than the cost price, a loss was made.
That loss costs: 1,718.40 – 1,753.75 = -£35.35

Q26.4: **D. £7.77; £8.88**
Let the price per kg for D88 and D101 be M and N, respectively.

	Price per kg	Monday (kg) Spent: £335.25	Tuesday (kg) Spent: 418.50
D24	12.99	10	10
D88	M	15	20
D101	N	10	15

She bought 10kg of D24 on both days, which cost her £129.90.

Equation 1:
335.25 = 129.9 + 15M + 10N
10N = 205.35 - 15M
N = 20.535 - 1.5M

Equation 2:
418.5 = 129.9 + 20M + 15N
15N = 288.6 - 20M

Answer 26 (Continued)

Substituting E1 into E2:
15(20.535 - 1.5M) = 288.6 - 20M
308.025 - 22.5M = 288.6 - 20M
2.5M = 19.425
M = 7.77

Substitute M = 7.77 into E1 and you will get N = 8.88. Hence, the answer is £7.77 and £8.88.

Answer 27

Q27.1: **B. £4.25**
If 1g is 0.04oz, then 1kg is 40oz.

Mass of butter in kg: 10.4 / 40 = 0.26kg
Cost of butter: (3.50 / 0.50) x 0.26 = £1.82

Mass of sugar in kg: 12.6 / 40 = 0.315kg
Cost of sugar: (4.55 / 3) x 0.315 = £0.48

Cost of eggs: (1.80 / 6) x 3 = £0.90

Mass of flour in kg: 11.0 / 40 = 0.275kg
Cost of flour: (3.80 / 1) x 0.275 = £1.05

Total cost of cake: 1.82 + 0.48 + 0.90 + 1.05 = £4.25

Q27.2: **D. 1.89kg**
With 1.65kg of flour, she is able to make 1.65 / 0.275 (mass of flour needed) = 6 cakes. This would require 6 x 0.315 = 1.89kg of sugar.

Q27.3: **A. 7**
This question requires a carefully planned and organised approach.

Answer 27 (Continued)

It is very common to fall into the trap and get the answer: 40.00 / 4.25 = 9.41 = 9 cakes (rounded down). However, having the figure 9 in mind would be a good start to approaching the answer.

First, draw a table to list out all the information you have been given. The two most important columns are 'Quantity of units to purchase' and 'Actual quantity of units purchased'. 'Actual quantity of units purchased' tells you the number of units that need to be purchased such that you have enough to make *n* number of cakes. It is simply a rounded up figure of the figure in 'Quantity of units to purchase'.

Assuming you were to make nine cakes:

Ingredient	Price per unit (£)	Size per unit (kg / pcs)	Amount needed per cake (kg / pcs)	Quantity of units to purchase	Actual quantity of units purchased	Total cost per ingredient (£)
Butter	3.50	0.5	0.26	9 x 0.26 / 0.5 = 4.68	5	5 x 3.50 = 17.50
Sugar	4.55	3	0.315	9 x 0.315 / 3 = 0.945	1	1 x 4.55 = 4.55
Eggs	1.80	6	3	9 x 3 / 6 = 4.5	5	5 x 1.80 = 9
Flour	3.80	1	0.275	9 x 0.275 / 1 = 2.475	3	3 x 3.80 = 11.40

If you total all of the cost of the ingredients above, it will come to £42.45. This is more than £40.00. Hence, it is impossible to make nine cakes with £40.00.

Hence, you have to reduce the number of cakes that can be made. Bear in mind that the main column that you are interested in at this point is the 'Actual quantity of units purchased'. This is because you would need to reduce the number of items purchased to keep within budget. You would need to achieve figures in

Answer 27 (Continued)

that column which will allow you to spend £2.45 less compared to the table above.

To save time, you can omit working on 'Sugar' as its quantity of units purchased is already 1. However, the table below still shows the working for completeness.

Assuming you were to make eight cakes:

Ingredient	Price per unit (£)	Size per unit (kg / pcs)	Amount needed per cake (kg / pcs)	Quantity of units to purchase	Actual quantity of units purchased	Total cost per ingredient (£)
Butter	3.50	0.5	0.26	8 x 0.26 / 0.5 = 4.16	5	5 x 3.50 = 17.50
Sugar	4.55	3	0.315	8 x 0.315 / 3 = 0.84	1	1 x 4.55 = 4.55
Eggs	1.80	6	3	8 x 3 / 6 = 4	4	4 x 1.80 = 7.20
Flour	3.80	1	0.275	8 x 0.275 / 1 = 2.20	3	3 x 3.80 = 11.40

As you only purchase less units of eggs, which is a difference of one unit (i.e. £1.80), this means that it is still impossible to make eight cakes with £40.00.

If you repeat the calculations once more for seven cakes, you will find that you would need to purchase one less unit of butter (i.e. £3.50) and one less unit of flour (i.e. £3.80). This means £40.00 is sufficient to make a maximum of seven cakes.

Q27.4: **D. +40p**
The difference in the cost of the cake would be due to the two changes stated in the question. That would be: [1.82 (original cost of butter) x 0.25] - [0.48 (original cost of sugar) x 1 / 8] = + £0.40. The '+' sign indicates that the new cost of the cake is 40p more than the original cost.

Answer 28

Q28.1: **C. 55mins**
Below shows a summary of Rachel's travel to work every day:
Home -> (5 mins walk) -> Underground -> Ferry -> (7 mins walk) -> Central Station -> (8 mins ride) -> Bus Stop -> (2 mins walk) -> Workplace

Rachel's walking time, as well as the underground, the ferry and the bus journeys, are all constant. However, the waiting times in between underground and ferry and at central station may vary. For her to save the most time, she should take the 7:29 am or 7:35 am underground. This is so that she can catch the ferry four minutes after leaving the underground stop. This leaves us with two options – to arrive by the ferry at 8:00 am or at 8:06 am. If she arrives at 8:00 am, she will walk and arrive at central station by 8:07 am, wait for two minutes, and catch the 8:09 am bus. If she arrives at 8:06 am, she will arrive at central station at 8:13 am, and she would have to wait for six minutes before catching the bus at 8:19 am.

Hence, Rachel should catch the 7:29 am underground if she wants to arrive at her workplace in the shortest time possible.

Her total travelling time, in minutes, would be: 5 (walk) + 12 (underground) + 4 (wait) + 15 (ferry) + 7 (walk) + 2 (wait) + 8 (bus) + 2 (walk) = 55mins

Q28.2: **B. 7:32 am**
Rachel's plan is to arrive at the office by 8:25 am. This means she has to be on the bus by 8:15 am. Hence, she has to catch the 8:09 am bus at central station. She would have to leave the ferry arrival terminal at 8:02 am, which works well for her if she takes the 7:45 am ferry. Since the taxi takes 13 minutes to arrive at the departure terminal, Rachel must leave her house by 7:32 am at the latest.

Q28.3: **D. -36.9%**
In a year, Rachel works a total of (40 x 5) + 20 = 220 days a year.

Each day, she spends 2(2.40 + 1.50 + 0.60) = £9 for round trip. (Bear in mind that the first line in the question stem states that she takes the same mode of transport to and from work every day.) In a year, she spends 9 x 220 = £1,980.

Answer 28 (Continued)

By purchasing the annual pass, Rachel saves 1,980 - 1,250 = £730.

Converting this into percentage: 730 / 1,980 x 100 = -36.9% ('-' because she is saving money compared to paying for individual journeys)

Q28.4: **A. 7:38 am**
27km = 27,000m
Time taken to drive to work: 27,000 / 20 = 1,350s = 22.5mins
If she has to arrive at work by 08:30 hours, she should leave her house by 8:30 am - 22.5 mins - 24 mins - 5 mins = 7:38 am.

Answer 29

Q29.1: **B. 480**
400kg of strawberry ice cream requires 400 x 0.12 = 48kg of extract.
Since only 10% of the strawberry produce can be used to make extract, this would require 48 / 0.10 = 480kg of strawberries.

Q29.2: **A. 744**
Take note that the question asks 'how much more' extract can be produced. This means the question is interested in the increase in extract production, not the overall extract production.

Increase in strawberry production per day: 0.40 x 600 = 240kg
Increase in extract production per day: 240 x 0.10 = 24kg
Increase in extract production in January: 24 x 31 = 744kg

Q29.3: **D. 29.5%**
Profit from strawberry produce: 300 x 2.35 = £705
Profit from strawberry ice cream: 300 x 0.10 / 0.12 x 4.00 = £1,000
Difference in profit made: 1,000 - 705 = £295
Percentage of added profit made from ice cream compared to produce: 295 / 1,000 x 100 = 29.5%

Answer 29 (Continued)

Q29.4: **E. £1.00**
If each jar is sold at 140% of the cost price, this would mean that the profit made per jar is 0.40 x 65 = 26p.

Extract required per jar of jam: 0.454 x 0.57 = 0.25878kg.
Every kilogram of strawberries can make 1 / 0.25878 = 3.86 jars of jam. Hence, every kilogram of strawberries can make 3.86 x 26 = £1.00 profit.

Answer 30

Q30.1: **B. *n* > 90**
The question begins by creating an inequality. The income from sales n duvets is $14n$.

For the company to profit, $14n$ must be greater than the cost of producing n duvets; therefore, the inequality $14n > 5n + 810$.

$14n > 5n + 810$
$9n > 810$
$n > 90$

Q30.2: **C. 5**
This question is tricky, and many might intuitively think that the answer is 4. However, that is incorrect.

To solve this question, you first have to identify the circumference of Coin A.

Let Coin A have radius r and Coin B have radius 4r. This means Coin A's radius is 2πr.

The trick lies in the distance travelled by Coin A. It is easy to jump to the conclusion that the distance travelled by Coin A is equal to the circumference of Coin B. However, that is not the case.

Answer 30 (Continued)

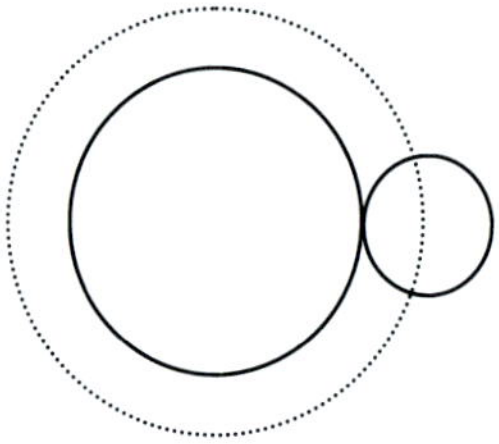

(Diagram above is only for illustration purposes. It is not drawn to scale.)

The distance travelled by Coin A during this course of action is shown by the dotted lines. When Coin A rolls itself around Coin B, the radius of the circular distance travelled by the coin is measured from the centre of both coins. Hence, the radius of the dotted circle is the sum of the radii of both circles: 4r + r = 5r.

Therefore:
Number of revolutions (n) x Circumference of Coin A = Circumference of dotted circle
$n \times 2\pi r = 2 \times \pi \times 5r$
$n = 5$

Q30.3: **B. 7x+1**

$$\frac{1}{(7x - 1)} = \frac{49x^2}{(7x - 1)} - P$$

$$P = \frac{49x^2}{(7x - 1)} - \frac{1}{(7x - 1)}$$

$$P = \frac{49x^2 - 1}{(7x - 1)}$$

$$P = \frac{(7x - 1)(7x + 1)}{(7x - 1)}$$

Answer 30 (Continued)

$P = 7x + 1$

This question requires the recognition of $49x^2 - 1$ as a difference of squares of factors.

Q30.4: **D. $12\sqrt{3} - 2\pi$**
This question deals with recognising that the regular hexagon can be divided into six equilateral triangles, in this case with equal sides of 2cm.

Performing Pythagorean Theorem to find the height (h) of each triangle,
$2^2 = h^2 + 1^1$
$h^2 = 4 - 1$
$h^2 = 3$
$h = \sqrt{3}$

Area of the regular hexagon: 6 x Area of equilateral triangles = $6 \times 1/2 \times \sqrt{3} \times 2 = 6\sqrt{3}cm^2$

Bear in mind that $6\sqrt{3}cm^2$ is the area of one side of the hexagonal earring.

To find the area of the hole in the centre:
Area of circle = $\pi r^2 = \pi \times 1^2 = \pi cm^2$

Hence, the area of coated gold on one side of the earring is $(6\sqrt{3} - \pi)cm^2$. This has to be multiplied by 2 as the earrings are coated on both sides; that would give: $(12\sqrt{3} - 2\pi)cm^2$.

Answer 31

Q31.1: **B. 1:250**
The length of the drawing is 20cm, which can also be expressed as 0.2m. Hence, the scale of the drawing is 0.2 / 50 = 1 / 250.

Answer 31 (Continued)

Q31.2: **B. 1,250 m^3**
First, it's best to get all the actual dimensions of the pool. This can be done using the scale you calculated in Q31.1.
Length: 50m; width: 25m (half of the length); depth: 2.5m (one tenth of the width)

We know that the only thing that changes is the depth of the pool on one side of its length, and the depth is decreased to one fifth of its original. Hence, the decrease in depth is 4 / 5 x 2.5 = 2.0m.

Volume of pool = 0.5 x 2.0 x 50 x 25 = 1,250m^3

Q31.3: **A. Lesser**
The perimeter of the original pool is 4 x (50 + 25 + 2.5) = 310m.
The surface area of the original pool is 2 x [(50 x 25) + (50 x 2.5) + (25 x 2.5)] = 2,875m^3.

If the surface area of the cubic pool is the same, then each face of the pool would have an area of 2,875 / 6 = 479.17. Hence, each edge would have a length of √479.17 = 21.89m.

Therefore, the new perimeter would be 21.89 x 6 = 131.34m, which is less than the original.

Q31.4: **B. 10 m**
The increase in the length of the pool doesn't affect its width and depth. Hence, all you'll have to do to solve this question is multiply 0.05 (to get the increment in the pool's length) and 4 (because there are 4 times the value of the length in its perimeter) to the original length of the pool.

Increase in perimeter of pool: 0.05 x 50 x 4 = 10m

Answer 32

Q32.1: **C. 2.52**

210mg is 5% of the recommended daily intake of potassium for adults. This means that the recommended daily intake of potassium for adults, which is 100%, is 210mg x 100 / 5 = 4,200mg. This is equivalent to 4.2g.

Since the recommended daily intake of potassium for teenagers if 40% less than that of adults, their recommended intake is 60% of 4.2g, which is 0.6 x 4.2 = 2.52g.

Q32.2: **E. 5/8**

Choconut provides 280 calories per cup.
Vanillow provides 240 calories in two thirds of a cup. This means a full cup has 240 / (2/3) = 360 calories.
The question states that a full cup of the mixture of the two cereals gives 310 calories.

From here on, the question can be solved using algebra.
Let x be the proportion of Choconut in the cup.

$280x + 360(1 - x) = 310$
$280x + 360 - 360x = 310$
$-80x = -50$
$x = 5/8$

Q32.3: **C. 0.252*m***

Each serving of Choconut provides 6% of the daily recommended intake of potassium for adults. This would be 210mg / 5 x 6 = 252mg of potassium in each serving. 252mg is equivalent to 0.252g.

Hence, if 0.252g of potassium is in each serving, this can be rewritten in an algebraic formula as $n = 0.252m$.

Q32.4: **A. 160**

A full cup of Vanillow has 240 / (2/3) = 360 calories. Hence, two full cups have 720 calories.

Answer 32 (Continued)

If this is equivalent to the amount of calories of a serving of Carameltz, which is three fourths of a cup, then one third of a cup with Carameltz would be 720 / (3/4) x 1/3 = 320 calories.

The calories due to fat is half of this value. Hence, its value is 160 calories.

Answer 33

Q33.1: **D. +10.21**
Change in energy used: [(0.14 + 0.20 + 0.33) x 43] - [(0.16 + 0.10 + 0.36) x 30] = 28.81 - 18.6 = +10.21MWh

Q33.2: **A. Library**
You should get the values in columns two and three in the table below.

Spaces	2000 (MWh)	2010 (MWh)	Difference in energy usage (MWh)
Classroom	10.8	14.19	3.39
Office	4.8	7.31	2.51
Library	6.6	6.88	0.26
Canteen	4.8	6.02	1.22
Sports Hall	3	8.6	5.6

You should not need to calculate the values in column four as, once you have obtained the values in columns two and three, it is obvious that the Library has the smallest change in energy usage.

Q33.3: **C. 4.5MWh**
Energy usage of classrooms in given year: 1.075 x 0.33 x 43 = 15.3MWh
Increase in usage compared to year 2000: 15.3 - (0.36 x 30) = 4.5MWh

Answer 33 (Continued)

Q33.4: **E.29.2%**
Energy used by classrooms in 2020: (1 - 0.16) x 0.33 x 43 = 11.9MWh
Energy used by all other spaces in 2020: (1 - 0.33) x 43 = 28.81MWh
Percentage of classroom usage compared to the total energy used: 11.9 / (11.9 + 28.81) x 100 = 29.2%

Answer 34

Q34.1: **B. Town II**
Rhys rides his bike at 20.5mph and arrives at his destination in 20 minutes, which is one third of an hour. Hence, he must have travelled 20.6 / 3 = 6.87 miles. This is equivalent to 6.87 x 1.6 = 11 km.

If he started at town IV and arrived at another town in 20 minutes, the only feasible option would be town II.

Q34.2: **A. 1.3:1**
Journey 1:
Distance from town VI to town IV: 9 + 7.5 = 16.5km
Average speed of travel: 16.5 / (45/ 60) = 22km/h

Journey 2:
Distance from town IV to town IX: 7.5 + 15.5 + 7 + 4.5 = 34.5km
Average speed of travel: 34.5 / [1 + (10 / 60)] = 29.6km/h

Ratio of Journey 2 to 1: 29.6 / 22 = 1.3:1

Q34.3: **B. 31%**
Distance from workplace (town III) to airport (town IX): 5 + 7.5 + 15.5 + 7 + 4.5 = 39.5km
Average speed of supposed travel: 39.5 / (45 / 60) = 52.7km/h

Distance from workplace (town III) to home (town VI) to airport (town IX): 39.5 + 9 + 9 = 57.5km

Answer 34 (Continued)

Time taken to travel: 7:15 - 1hr- 10mins - 5:15 = 50mins
Average speed of actual travel: 57.5 / (50 / 60) = 69km/h

Percentage increase in driving speed: (69 - 52.7) / 52.7 x 100 = 31%

Q34.4: **E. All are the same**
If you test out any of the towns by taking them as the start and end point, you will see a similar pattern. Routes I - II, II - III, III - IV and I- IV will always be one -way routes, and the rest will always be two-way routes, regardless of which town is the host.

Answer 35

Q35.1: **A. 40mg**
Dose given: 50mg / 5ml x 4 ml = 40mg

Q35.2: **E. 100µl**
First, convert 0.025g = 25mg.

25mg / (500mg/2ml) = 0.1ml = 100µl

Q35.3: **B. 0.072**
This question has a lot of unnecessary figures to trick you into thinking that they are important. The question is straightforward.

A 48kg patient who receives a drug which dose is 1.5mg/kg. Hence, the patient has to receive a dose of 1.5 x 48 = 72mg = 0.072g.

Q35.4: **D. 276mg**
This question is straightforward as well. Do not let long-winded questions trick you into thinking that the calculations have to be as complex as the text.

Dose to be given: 92 / 100 x 300 = 276mg

Answer 36

Q36.1: **C. £220**
Total cost of rent: 585 x 2 = £1,170
Deposit (D) + (5 x 190) = 1,170
D = 1,170 - 950
D = £220

Q36.2: **C. £300**
Let the rate per hours for the motorboat be M.
Cost of trip in December 2019: 250 + M + 50 (staff service) = £(300 + M)

In February, he goes on the canoe instead, and the cost of his trip in February 2020 is the same as that in December 2019.

Hence,
300 + M = 100 + [4 x (50 + 75)]
300 + M = 600
M = £300

Q36.3: **C. £262.50**
The question did not state if they had hired a member of staff in the first trip, but it stated that they 'decided to get a member of staff instead' during their second trip. Hence, it can be deduced that they did not hire a member of staff the first time around.

Cost of trip in February 2020: 100 + 75 = £125

As they returned a week later, it would mean that they returned on the 1st of March, which means that the prices of the rent had increased.

Cost of trip in March 2020: (100 x 1.15) + 2 x (75 x 1.15) + (2 x 50) = £387.50

Increase in cost: £387.50 - £125 = £262.50

Q36.4: **D. 21.4%**
Let the deposit of the yacht be D and its rate per hour be R.

Equation 1: 2,545 = D + 5R
Equation 2: 1,695 = D + 3R

Answer 36 (Continued)

E1 - E2:
2,545 - 1,695 = 5R - 3R
2R = 850
R = £425

Substitute R into E2,
1,695 = D + (3 x 425)
D = £420

Percentage increase in deposit of yacht compared to catamaran: (420 - 330) / 330 x 100 = 27.3%

Answer 37

Q37.1: **D. 71.7%**
The question asks for duration, but no figures are given for the speed of the plane. However, the question states that the plane flew at its usual speed. This means that there was no change in its speed, despite the change in distance travelled.

Since distance is a product of speed and time, the distance travelled is directly proportional to the duration of flight.

Supposed distance of travel: 8,915km
Actual distance of travel: 7,583 + 7,726 = 15,309km

Percentage increase in duration: (15,309 - 8,915) / 8,915 x 100 = 71.7%

Q37.2: **B. 1752**
Distance from Tokyo to Male: 7,583km
Average speed of travel: 550 x 1.6 = 880km/h
Duration of travel: 7,583 / 880 = 8.62hrs = 8hrs 37mins

13:15 in Tokyo is 09:15 in Male as Male is four hours behind Tokyo. This means the time of arrival would be: 09:15 + 8hrs 37mins = 17:52 hours.

Answer 37 (Continued)

Q37.3: **A. 83km/h**
Distance between Berlin and Rio: 10,013km
Initial average speed of flight: 10,013 / 18 = 556km/h

New duration of travel: (1 - 0.13) x 18 = 15.66hrs
New average speed of flight: 10,013 / 15.66 = 639km/h

Increase in average speed: 639 - 556 = 83km/h

Q37.4: **E. 0557 (+1)**
Looking at the distances of Male-Rio and Male-Tokyo, it can be deduced that Elsa will land in Tokyo before Anna lands in Rio. Since the question is interested in the earliest time in which they can contact one another, we can focus our calculations on Anna's flight.

Distance from Male to Rio: 12,933km
Duration of travel: 12,933 / (400 x 1.6) = 20.2hrs = 20hrs 12mins

Male is four hours behind Tokyo and Rio is 12 hours behind Tokyo. This means Rio is eight hours behind Male. Hence, the time in Rio during departure from Male was 1745 - 8hrs = 0945hrs.

Time in Rio at Anna's arrival: 0945 + 20hrs 12mins = 0557 hours (+1)

Answer 38

Q38.1: **B. 2.0 x 2.9**
Looking at the table, you will realise that the size of the paper decreased from A0 to A4, the height of a given paper is the width of its preceding paper, and the width of the given paper is half the height of the preceding paper. If the result of the halving is a number with a decimal, the number is rounded down to the nearest integer.

Answer 38 (Continued)

Hence, to calculate for A4, you have to obey the pattern and work out the dimensions carefully. The sizes of the papers, in mm, between A4 and A8 are shown below. It has been arranged such that it is easier if you read starting from A5 (at the bottom of the list).

A8: 52 x 74
A7: 74 x 105
A6: 105 x 148
A5: 148 x 210

A8: 52mm x 74mm = (52 / 25.4) x (74 / 25.4) = 2.0 x 2.9

Q38.2: **D. £21.50**
Cost of Jared's printing: (2 x 9.00) + 3.00 = £21
Cost of Chris' printing: 30.00 x (25 x 0.50) = £42.50

Difference in cost of printing: 42.50 - 21 = £21.50

Q38.3: **B. 44%**
Number of A4 papers that fit an A0 paper: (841 x 1189) / (210 x 297) = 16 copies

Cost of printing 16 individual A4 copies: 16 x 2.50 = £40

Cost of printing in A0: £22.50

Calculating discounts is similar to calculating percentage decrease: (40 - 22.50) / 40 x 100 = 44%

Q38.4: **D. 176**
The question does not specify on which type of paper George would like his printing to be. However, the question stem states that double-sided print is only available on uncoated paper.

The question also states that each page must be A4-sized and that the book will be secured through stapling as its backbone. This means the paper used has to be A3 as the paper will be folded at its centre to give two A4-sized pages.

Answer 38 (Continued)

Bear in mind that, if the booklet is eight pages but is printed on both sides, each booklet would have only four pieced of A3 paper.

The next question we have to ask is whether there is a way to reduce the cost price of each paper. Similar to Q38.3, George can use the free paper cutting service, and he can thus get his printing done on large pieces of paper instead. In this case, he can opt for A0 which, by calculation, would be able to fit eight A3 papers. This means the cost of a double sided A0 paper is equivalent to the cost of two booklets.

Cost of printing two booklets: 4.5 x 1.5 = £6.75

Maximum number of A0 papers that can be printed: 600 / 6.75 = 88.89 = 88 (rounded down)

From the 88 A0 papers, he can produce 88 x 2 = 176 booklets.

Answer 39

Q39.1: **D. 1.45x10^5**
Total of carbon dioxide produced: 577.9 + 464.1 + 372.7 + 299.3 + 240.4 + 193.0 + 155.0 + 124.5 + 100.0 + 80.3 = 2,607.2 tonnes

Average carbon dioxide produced per year: 2,607.2 / 10 = 260.72 tonnes = 1.45x10^{5}m^3

Q39.2: **B. 1.06**
You should not refer to a calendar while attempting the question as this would not be possible during the real test.

The year 2012 is a leap year, meaning that February had 29 days. The month had a total of four full weeks, plus an additional day. Since the question asks for the minimum average carbon dioxide produced per day, you should think about maximising the number of weekdays in your calculation. In this case, we

Answer 39 (Continued)

can take the extra day as a weekday, giving us 21 weekdays.

2012's total is 372.7 tonnes. In the month of February, 6% of this was produced. That would be 0.06 x 372.7 = 22.362 tonnes.

Likely minimum average carbon dioxide produced per day: 22.362 / 21 = 1.06 tonnes

Q39.3: **E. 6.4×10^4**
Total carbon dioxide produced from 2015 onwards: 193.0 + 155.0 + 124.5 + 100.0 + 80.3 = 652.8 tonnes
Had the filter not been installed, the factory would have produced extra carbon dioxide of volume 652.8 / 0.85 x 0.15 = 115.2 tonnes = 115.2 x 556 = $6.4 \times 10^4 m^3$.

Q39.4: **D. Reciprocal exponential decay**

This question may look complex, but it is quite straightforward.

The values in the table allow you to identify the trend of the numbers, which will enable you to work out the graph. Firstly, you would be able to tell that the values decrease over time. Options C and E can thus be ruled out immediately as they refer to the upward slopes of a curve.

Option A is incorrect because the gradient of the downward slope of a quadratic curve increases (i.e. becomes steeper) as it progresses. Given that the difference between consecutive years decreases, the gradient of the curve decreases (i.e. becomes less steep) instead.

Option B is incorrect because the difference between consecutive years is not constant. Hence, it cannot be a linear function.

Option D is correct. We can see that the difference between 2010 and 2011 is about 110 tonnes. In 2011 to 2012, the difference is about 100 tonnes. This difference decreases to about 20 tonnes in 2018 to 2019. The magnitude of the difference becomes smaller. Hence, the gradient of the graph decreases as it would in a reciprocal exponential decay curve.

Answer 40

Q40.1: **C. 169%**
The area of a triangle is given by 0.5 x base x height.

Given that the triangle in the question is an isosceles with sides *b* at its equal sides, the initial area of the triangle will be $0.5b^2$, which can also be denoted as *B*.
However, given that *b* has increased in length by 30% now, its new length will be 1.3*b*.
Hence, the new area of the triangle will be: $0.5 \times (1.3b)^2 = 0.845b^2$ which, for simpler terms, can also be written as $B \times 1.3^2 = 1.69B$.

From this, it can be deduced that the increase in the percentage of the area is $1.69B / B \times 100 = 169\%$.

Q40.2: **A. 39%**
The area of a circle is by πr^2 or $\pi d^2/4$, where r is its radius and d is its diameter.

The diameter is 60% greater in a larger pizza compared to a smaller pizza. This applies to its radius as well.

The area of the small pizza will be πr^2, which can also be denoted as *P*.
However, given that r has increased in radius by 60% now, its radius of the large pizza will be 1.6r.
Hence, the area of the large pizza will be: $\pi \times (1.6r)^2 = 2.56\pi r^2$ which, for simpler terms, can also be written as $P \times 1.6^2 = 2.56P$.

Percentage of large pizza that is small pizza: $P / 2.56P \times 100 = 39\%$

Answer 40 (Continued)

Q40.3: **C. 39%**
The volume of a cylinder is $\pi r^2 h$, where r is its radius and h is its height. That the question states that the diameter is equal to its height allows us to simplify the equation.

Given r = d/2 and d = h, the volume of the big cup can be rewritten as $\pi d^3/4$, which can also be denoted as *C*.
Given that the height and the diameter of the small cup is 15% less, its diameter can be given as 0.85d.
Hence, the volume of the small cup will be: $\pi \times (0.85d)^3 / 4 = 0.154\pi d^3$ which, for simpler terms, can also be written as $C \times 0.85^3 = 0.614C$.
Percentage decrease in the volume of the cup would be: $(C - 0.614C) / C \times 100 =$ 39%

Q40.4: **C. £40**
This question can be solved by working backwards. The first clue lies in the phrases 'spent two thirds of what was left by taking a cab home' and having '£7 left in his pocket' at the end of the day. This means that the £7 is one third of the amount he had before taking the cab. From this, it can be deduced that the cab ride was £14 and that £21 was remaining after purchasing the milkshake.

This means that he had £30 after purchasing the pizzas. If 3/4 of X is £30, then X original amount must be £40.

Answer 41

Q41.1: **A. 8:5**
AUD on 01.04.2020: 2.0388
USA on 01.04.2020: 1.2398

Ratio of AUD to USA: 2.0388:1.2398 = 1.6:1 (this is well approximated to 8:5)

Answer 41 (Continued)

Q41.2: **B. 21,051**
On 01.01.2020, £1 = 1.9674 NZD. Hence, £180,000 = 180,000 x 1.9674 = 354,132 NZD.

On 01.04.2020, the calculation has to be changed according to the NZD and EUR rate on that specific date. Hence, that makes it 354,132 / 2.0919 x 1.1316 = 191,565 EUR.

If he had converted the amount to EUR (£1 = 1.1812 EUR) directly in January, he would have got 180,000 x 1.1812 = 212,616 EUR.

He would have had extra EUR of: 212,616 - 191,565 = 21,051 EUR

Q41.3: **D. 31%**
In January, the rates for USD and CAD were 1.3251 and 1.7195, respectively. Their difference was 1.7195 - 1.3251 = 0.3944.
In April, the rates for USD and CAD were 1.2398 and 1.7556, respectively. Their difference was 1.7556 - 1.2398 = 0.5158.

The percentage change in April compared to January: (0.5158 - 0.3944) / 0.3944 x 100 = 30.8% (31% rounded off)

Q41.4: **C. AUD**
Note that the question says greatest percentage changes between the two points in time. Hence, it is logical to use the rate in January as your reference rate (the denominator in your calculation). You also need not worry about whether the rates have increased or decreased as the question is only interested in the greatest change in magnitude.

The percentage changes for each currency are:

USD: (1.3251 - 1.2398) / 1.3251 x 100 = 6.4%
EUR: (1.1812 - 1.1316) / 1.1812 x 100 = 4.2%
AUD: (2.0388 - 1.8883) / 1.8883 x 100 = 8.0%
CAD: (1.7556 - 1.7195) / 1.7195 x 100 = 2.1%
NZD: (2.0919 - 1.9674) / 1.9674 x 100 = 6.3%

Answer 41 (Continued)

An alternative and quicker way to solve this question would be to look at the graph and identify the currency that has the most obvious gap between its two bars. In this case, it would be AUD. From this, you calculate the percentage change for AUD and arrive at 8.0%. You can use this 8% as your reference in checking if there are any changes greater than this. For instance, you can start by checking the currency with the second most obvious gap, which would be NZD. To check this, simply take 1.9674 x 1.08. (1.08 because you are calculating how much the rate would be if there is an 8% increase on top of its current value.) This would give you 2.124 NZD, which is greater than the value given in the graph, that is, 2.0919. This means you can be sure that the percentage change for NZD must be less than 8%.

The next most obvious gap is USD's. However, this is a decrease. Hence, you will use 0.92 instead of 1.08. This will give you 0.92 x 1.3251 = 1.2191, which is much lower than the value given in the graph. This means the decrease in the exchange rate for USD must be less than 8%.

It's probably not worth checking for EUR and CAD as their respective gaps are (obviously) small and they are very unlikely to have a change of greater than 8%.

Q41.5: **E. £125,000**
We know that £7,500, in this case, is the 6% fee of the transaction. This means that 6% = 7,500. Hence, the value of the transaction is 7,500 / 0.06 = £125,000.

Answer 42

Q42.1: **E. 197.5ft**
Given that the regular bedrooms are square, the length and the width of the bedrooms are 3.3m. The length of the entire house is 7.0 + 3.3 + 3.3 = 13.6m. The width of the entire house is 6.7 + 9.8 = 16.5m. Even though the question asks you to exclude the exteriors, it does not actually make a difference to the perimeter. Hence, you can simply calculate the perimeter as 13.6 + 16.5 + 13.6 + 16.5 = 60.2m = 60.2 x 3.28 = 197.5ft.

Answer 42 (Continued)

Q42.2: **B. 1.8m**
The width of the regular bedrooms is 3.3m. There is a door between the hall and the regular bedrooms. Each door is 1.5m wide. Hence, for a door to still fit, the maximum width of the utility room is 3.3 - 1.5 = 1.8m.

Q42.3: **C. 2.7m**
316.83ft^2 = 316.83 / (3.28 x 3.28) = 29.45m^2

Imagine a horizontal line drawn as an extension of the longer portion of the wall of the bathroom. This divides the bedroom into two spaces.

To find the maximum length of the longer portion of the wall, the smaller area of the bedroom must be at its minimum. Hence, the bigger space must be at its maximum. The bigger space will have an area of (5.0 - 1.5) x 6.7 = 23.45m^2. This means the smaller space has an area of 29.45 - 23.45 = 6m^2. Its width must be 6 / 1.5 = 4m. (The minimum length of the wall with the narrower width is 1.5m as a door is placed there.) Hence, the length of the longer portion of the bathroom wall is 6.7 - 4 = 2.7m.

Q42.4: **D. 11.21cm^2**
The total width of the house is 16.5m. This would allow you to calculate the width of the porch: 16.5 - 5.0 - 3.3 = 8.2m = 820cm = 820 / 250 = 3.28cm (on the architect's blueprint). The length of the porch can be established from the length of the regular bedroom, which is 3.3m = 330cm = 330 / 250 = 1.32cm. The area of the porch on the blueprint is 3.28 x 1.32 = 4.3296cm^2.

The total length of the house is 13.6m. This allows you to calculate the length of the garage: 13.6 - 5.0 = 8.6m = 860cm = 860 / 250 = 3.44cm. The width of the garage is 5.0m = 500cm = 500 / 250 = 2cm. The area of the garage on the blueprint is 3.44 x 2 = 6.88cm^2.

Total exterior area = 4.3296 + 6.88 = 11.21cm^2

Q42.5: **D. £41,643.24**
From the question, we can tell that the dimensions of the bathrooms (and the utility room) is 1.8m by 3.5m. This is because it has been established that the length of the bathroom on the right side of the blueprint has a length of 3.5m.

Answer 42 (Continued)

Hence, the area of each bathroom is (1.8 x 3.28) x (3.5 x 3.28) = 67.78ft^2. Hence, two bathrooms would be 135.56ft^2. To floor this area with vinyl, it would cost 135.56 x 9.10 = £1,233.56.

The area of the master bedroom, the kitchen and the dining area combined is (13.2 x 3.28) x (5.0 x 3.28) - 67.78 = 642.27ft^2. To floor this area with marble, it would cost 642.27 x 26.50 = £17,020.27.

The area of the living room is (5.3 x 3.28) x (8.2 x 3.28) = 467.56ft^2. To floor this area with marble, it would cost 467.56ft^2 x 26.50 = £12,390.34.

The total area of the two bedrooms, the hall and the utility room is (3.3 x 3.28) x (13.6 x 3.28) - 67.78 = 415.06ft^2. To floor this area with marble, it would cost 415.06 x 26.50 = £10,999.07.

Hence, the total cost to floor the interior is 1,233.56 + 17,020.27 + 12,390.34 + 10,999.07 = £41,643.24.

Q42.6: **D. 49.54m^2**
Total area taken up by doors: (3 x 2.5) + [9 x (1.5 x 2.5)] = 41.25m^2
Total area taken up by windows: 5 x 1 = 5m^2

Since the height of the doors (i.e. 2.5m) is two thirds the height of the house, the house is 2.5 / (2 / 3) = 3.75m tall.

Once we have worked out the above, we can focus on the walls of the house. Bear in mind that the question refers to all the walls of the house. Thus, all you have to do is calculate the total length of the solid lines in the diagram and multiply the total by two as the walls have two sides.

From Q42.1, we know that the perimeter of the house is 60.2m. All that is left to do is calculate the solid lines in the house. Bear in mind that the question states that the dimensions of the bathroom are now 3.5m x 2.0m.

Total length of solid lines within the house: 3.5 + 2.0 + 8.2 + 5.0 + 3.3 + 3.3 + 7.0 + 7.0 + 2.0 + 3.3 = 44.6m.

Answer 42 (Continued)

In case you would like to check where the numbers above come from:

- 3.5 + 2.0 is the length and the width of the walls of the bathroom in the master bedroom.
- 8.2 is the width of the wall of the living room.
- 5.0 is the length of the wall of the 'kitchen and dining area' shared with the master bedroom.
- 3.3 + 3.3 is the length and width of the wall of the bedroom at the top right corner.
- 7.0 + 7.0 is the length of both sides of the hall.
- 2.0 is the width of the utility room shared with the bathroom.
- 3.3 is the width of the bedroom in the bottom right corner.

Total length of solid lines in the blueprint: 60.2 + 44.6 = 104.8m

Hence, the total area of the wall to be painted (taking into account the doors and windows): [(104.8 x 3.75) - 41.25 - 5] x 2 = 693.5m^2

Given that he finishes painting all the walls in 14 days, the average area covered per day would be 693.5 / 14 = 49.54m^2

Answer 43

Q43.1: **C. 2013**
Number of interviews expressed as a percentage of the number of applications:
2011: 3,524 / 13,583 x 100 = 25.94%
2012: 3,677 / 14,205 x 100 = 25.89%
2013: 4.002 / 17,366 x 100 = 23.04%
2014: 4,451 / 19,239 x 100 = 23.14%
2015: 4,153 / 22,011 x 100 = 18.87%

The calculations shown above are for you to check, should you have made five individual calculations as well. However, there is an alternative method to solving this question quickly. It requires you to interpret the numbers in the table and determine how the percentage of each individual year would rank against the rest.

Answer 43 (Continued)

For the sake of the explanation below, 'number of interviews' will be abbreviated to 'NIV' and 'number of applications' will be abbreviated to 'NAP'. Keep in mind that the question is looking for percentage of (NIV / NAP x 100). This means that, for the same NAP, a greater NIV would give a greater percentage. However, for the same NIV, a greater NAP would give a smaller percentage.

Looking at 2011 and 2012, the NIVs and NAPs in both years are similar, Hence, you can expect them to have similar percentages. Keep this in mind for now. Next, look at 2013. There is an estimated increase in NIV of about 300 between 2012 to 2013, but there is an estimated increase in NAP of 3,000. The larger increase in NAP compared to the increase in NIV would allow you to make a smart guess that 2013 would be placed below 2011 and 2012, if the years were ranked in descending order. The order we have now is 2011/ 2012, 2013.

Now, let's look at 2015. 2015 has an NIV that is roughly 150 greater than 2013's. However, it has an NAP that is greater by around 5,000. Again, the significantly larger increase in NAP compared to NIV would make you think that 2015 is ranked below 2013. The order we have now is 2011/2012, 2013, 2015.

Let's take a look at 2014. Compared to 2015, 2014 has a greater NIV and a lower NAP. Hence, you can be certain that 2014 is placed above 2015. Compared to 2013, 2014 has an NIV that's greater by about 450 and an NAP that's greater by about 2,000. Although 2,000 may sound about 4-5 times greater than 450, it's best to at least perform some calculation at this point to find whether 2014 is placed above or below 2013. If it is placed above 2013, then your answer would immediately be 2013. If it is placed below 2013, then your answer would be 2014.

Referring to the calculations performed earlier, you would find that they have similar percentages but that 2014's percentage is slightly greater than 2013's. Hence, the answer is 2013.

Q43.2: **A. 10.8%**
Percentage of all applicants who received an interview: 3,677 / 14,205 x 100 = 25.89%
Percentage of applicants who received an offer after interview: 555 / 3,677 x 100 = 15.09%

Answer 43 (Continued)

Difference in percentage: 25.89 - 15.09 = 10.8%

Q43.3: **B. 1.2%**
Rate of acceptance in 2011: 530 / 13,583 x 100 = 3.9%
Rate of acceptance in 2015: 610 / 22,011 x 100 = 2.7%

Difference in acceptance rates: 3.9 - 2.7 = 1.2%

Q43.4: **C. 2013 to 2014**
Since the question is only interested in the change in percentage, you need not worry about whether the numbers have increased or decreased.

Percentage change between the years:
2011 to 2012: (3,677 - 3,524) / 3,524 x 100 = 4.3%
2012 to 2013: (4,002 - 3,677) / 3,677 x 100 = 8.9%
2013 to 2014: (4,451 - 4,002) / 4,002 x 100 = 11.2%
2014 to 2015: (4,451 - 4,153) / 4,451) x 100 = 6.7%

Alternatively, you could make a smart guess. It would not be worth calculating for '2011 to 2012' as the raw difference is small on its own, which is approximately 150. The raw difference in '2012 to 2013', which is approximately 330, is worth noting as it is somewhat similar to the raw difference in '2013 to 2014', which is approximately 450. You could save yourself time from checking the percentage of '2014 to 2015' as the raw difference is similar to that of '2012 to 2013' but it has a greater denominator (4,153 vs 3,677) in the equation. Hence, it will definitely give you a smaller percentage than that of '2012 to 2013'. With this train of thought, you would then only need to perform two calculations for options B and C.

Answer 44

Q44.1: **B. £385.40**
Each driver was paid 40p per mile. Each car has travelled 896 miles. Hence, each driver should be paid: 0.40 x 896 = £358.40

Answer 44 (Continued)

Q44.2: **C. No**

Income

Total money contributed initially: 300 x 13 = £3,900

Expenses

Cost of bed-n-breakfast: 11.50 x 13 x 7 = £1,046.50
Cost of fuel: 0.40 x 896 x 3 = £1,075.20
Cost of meals: £2,206
Total expenses: 1,046.50 + 1,075.20 + 2,206 = £4,327.70

Their expenses exceeded their income.

Q44.3: **B. £32.90**

They exceeded by: 4,327.70 - 3,900 = £427.70 = 427.70 / 13 = £32.90

Q44.4: **C. £2.77**

Total cost of the tolls: 3 x 12 = £36 = 36 / 13 = £2.77 per person

Answer 45

Q45.1: **E. 216GB**

Barbossa has been using the service for seven years now. This means that he has received an extra 3GB of data and that he started with 12GB. In five years, he would gain an extra 3GB of data per month. That makes it 18GB per month. In a year, he would have 18 x 12 = 216GB.

Q45.2: **D. 8:5**

Swann has been using the service for four years, meaning she has gained an extra 2GB per month over this period. Hence, she started with 8GB per month.

In five years, Jones will gain an extra 2GB per month on top of what he has now, which is 6GB. That would make it 8GB after five years.

Ratio of Swann's GB to Jones' GB = 8:5

Answer 45 (Continued)

Q45.3: **E. 62.5%**
Sparrow has 9GB after using the service for three years. This means he must have started with 8GB initially.

If an individual uses the premium deal for 11 years, he/she would gain an extra 5GB per month.

The percentage increase in data: 5 / 8 x 100 = 62.5%

(Note that, to save time, you need not multiply the numbers with 12 to make it 'yearly' as they will eventually cancel each other out in the final step when you calculate the percentage increase.)

Q45.4: **E. 192**
423MB per day = 423 x 30 = 12,690MB per month = 12.69GB per month

The 'happy-three-friends' deal starts off with 5GB. The individual would need to reach a minimum of 13GB to match the data usage. This is an extra 8GB on top of the 5GB. To get an added 8GB, the individual has to use the plan for 8 x 2 = 16 years = 16 x 12 = 192 months.

Answer 46

Q46.1: **C. 2009**
Amount of money spent on buying houses in the UK = (Average no. of sales per calendar month x 12 months) x Average price of home

The formula above is the idealistic formula needed to approach the question. However, you can take a shortcut. First, you need not multiply 12 months as it is a constant for all calculations. You can also choose to omit the last four zeros (i.e. 0000) when doing your calculation as it will save you time and it will reduce your chances of making a mistake.

Answer 46 (Continued)

Amount of money spent each year (shortcut):
2007: 7 x 11 = 77
2008: 12 x 13 = 156
2009: 12 x 14 = 168
2010: 8 x 16 = 128
2011: 8 x 17 = 136

The year with the largest amount of money spent on houses is 2009.

Q46.2: **A. £70,800M**
To solve this question, simply use the values from Q46.1 and multiply them by 12, followed by adding the eight zeros. (Eight zeros because, in Q46.1, we removed four zeros from both the terms in the multiplication.)

From Q46.1,
2007: 77
2011: 136

Difference between the two years: (136 - 77) x 12 x 10^8 = £7.08x10^{10} = £70,800M

Q46.3: **C. 256%**
Percentage increase from 2007 to 2008: (120,000 - 70,000) / 70,000 x 100 = 71.4%

Assuming this were to continue for the next three years, the apparent price of an average house in 2011 would be 120,000 x (1.714)3 = £604,548

Percentage increase of the price of the house when compared to its actual price: (604,548 - 170,000) / 170,000 x 100 = 256%

Q46.4: **B. 23.8%**
For this question, once again, you can omit the four zeros in each term as they will be cancelled out when you calculate the percentage decrease.

Average monthly sale in 2009: 14 x 12 = 168
Average monthly sale in 2010: 16 x 8 = 128

Percentage decrease: (168 - 128) / 168 x 100 = 23.8%

Answer 46 (Continued)

Q46.5: **E. 6:7**
Average no. of sales per month in 2009: 120,000
Average price per home: 140,000

Ratio of monthly sales to price per home: 120,000:140,000 = 6:7 (divide both sides by 10,000 and then by 2)

Q46.6: **D. 2018**
If the average number of sales per year is 360,000, then the average number of sales per month would be 360,000 / 12 = 30,000.

Magnitude of decline in monthly sales between 2008 and 2009: 130,000 - 120,000 = 10,000

The number of monthly sales in 2009 is 120,000, and the end point given in the question is 30,000. The difference between the two is 90,000. Since the decline is 10,000 per year, it would take nine years after 2009 to reach 30,000. Hence, that would make it 2018.

Answer 47

Q47.1: **A. 19.5%**
Total phones sold in 2007: 54,267 + 42,566 + 40,066 = 136,899
Total phones sold in India: 42,566 + (2 / 3 x 40,066) = 26,710.7 (26,711 rounded off)
Percentage of phones sold in India: 26,711 / 136,899 x 100 = 19.5%

Q47.2: **B. 194M**
Total value of phones sold by Dianhua in 2009: 38,700 x 3,300 = 127,710,000 Yuan
Total value of phones sold by Oppa in China in 2009: 1 / 3 x 48,618 x 4,110 = 66,606,660 Yuan
Total value of phones sold in China in 2009: 127,710,000 + 66,606,660 = 194,316,660 Yuan = 194M Yuan

Answer 47 (Continued)

Q47.3: **E. 162M**
Total phones sold by Oppa across the five years: 38,262 + 40,066 + 36,100 + 48,618 + 47,662 = 210,708

Number of phones sold in China: 1 / 3 x 210,708 = 70,236
Total income from China: 70,236 x 4,110 = 288,669,960 Yuan

Number of phones sold in India: 2 / 3 x 210,708 = 140,472
Total income from India (expressed in Yuan): 140,472 x 39,500 / 10.6 = 523,456,981 Yuan

Total income of Oppa: 288,669,960 + 523,456,981 = 812,126,941 Yuan
Average income across the five years: 812,126,941 / 5 = 162,425,388 Yuan = 162M Yuan

Q47.4: **D. 15,665**
Total income of Oppa expressed in Rupees: 812,126,941 Yuan x 10.6 = 8,608,545,575 Rupees
Total income of Dianhua expressed in Rupees: (59,039 + 54,267 + 56,137 + 38,700 + 57,466) x 3,300 x 10.6 = 9,291,002,820 Rupees
Total income of Hailo expressed in Rupees: (56,193 + 42,566 + 58,046 + 50,937 + 48,874) x 26,300 = 6,749,000,800 Rupees

The company with the highest income is Dianhua. Its income is higher than Oppa by: 9,291,002,820 - 8,608,545,575 = 682,457,245 Rupees

The company asks for the least number of phones that Oppa needs to sell to match Dianhua's income. We know that Oppa sells phones in India and China in their local currencies. However, if we were to look at the value of the phone when it is sold in China, it would be 4,110 x 10.6 = 43,566 Rupees, which is a higher price than that in India (i.e. 39,500 Rupees). Hence, to sell the least number of phones possible, Oppa needs to sell more phones in China.

Given that Oppa needs 682,457,245 Rupees to equate to Dianhua, it needs to sell another 682,457,245 / 43,566 = 15,664.9 (15,665 rounded up) phones in China.

Answer 48

Q48.1: **B. £773M**
Number of staff in Medicine in 2018: 0.25 x 387,686 = 96,922
Total salary paid to all staff in Medicine per month: 96,922 x 102,438 / 12 = £827,374,653 = £827M

Q48.2: **D. 2018**
First, we calculate the number of employees in 2015. Let this unknown be N.

Since there was a 6% raise from 2015 to 2016, this means:
1.06 x N = 322,092
N = 303,860 employees in 2015

Now, we have the information we need to calculate the total salaries for GPs in each year. However, when working out your calculations, you can choose to omit the annual salary as it is a constant for all years. Hence, finding the number of GPs employed in each year would be sufficient.

2015: 0.37 x 303,860 = 112,428
2016: 0.33 x 322,092 = 106,290
2017: 0.32 x 346,993 = 111,038
2018: 0.29 x 387,686 = 112,429
2019: 0.25 x 449,708 = 112,427

The year with the greatest number of GPs (i.e. greatest amount paid to GPs) is 2018.

Q48.3: **C. 35%**
Number of employees in Surgery in 2016: 0.20 x 322,092 = 64,418

The figure above is equivalent to 12 + 15 = 27% of the employees in 2015. If 27% of the total employees in 2015 is 64,418, then the total number of employees in 2015 is 64,418 / 0.27 = 238,585.

Percentage increase in number of employees from 2015 to 2016 = (322,092 - 238,585) / 238,585 x 100 = 35%

Answer 48 (Continued)

Q48.4: **C. 24.8%**
First, establish that the average salary of an Admin and an 'Other' employee is £79,441 and £63,635. You can ignore the years stated in the question as there is no change in the average annual salary paid to employees across the years. You can also ignore having to calculate the monthly salary of these roles as they will be cancelled out when you calculate the percentage increase. These are distractors put in place to trick you into doing unnecessary calculations.

Percentage increase of Admin compared to Other: (79,441 - 63,635) / 63,635 x 100 = 24.8%

Q48.5: **D. 53,044**
Rate of increase in 2018-2019: (449,708 - 387,686) / 387,686 x 100 = 16% = 0.16

If this increase had begun in 2016, the apparent number of employees in 2019 would be 322,092 x $(1.16)^3$ = 502,752.

Compared to the actual number of employees in 2019, this would be an extra of 502,752 - 449,708 = 53,044.

Answer 49

Q49.1: **B. 154kg**
Volume of mix for each biscuit = 88 / 21 / 2 x 1.13 = 2.79cm^3 (Keep in mind that the biscuit is a hemisphere and the formula given is for a sphere.)
Mass of mix for each biscuit = Density of mix x Volume of mix for each biscuit = 2.79 x 6 = 16.73g

Each tray can hold 72 biscuits. There are 16 trays in a trolley, so each trolley can hold 16 x 72 = 1,152 biscuits. The bowl of biscuit mix fills eight trolleys, so it can supply 8 x 1,152 = 9,216 biscuits.

The mass of the mix is 9,216 x 16.73 = 154,184g = 154kg.

Answer 49 (Continued)

Q49.2: **A. £16,843**
Hourly rate for overtime: 8.20 x 1.25 = £10.25

Length of each shift: 5:00 pm - 9:00 am = 8 hours

Total pay per week for the factory worker: (4 x 8 x 8.20) + (6 x 10.25) = £323.90

Since there are 52 weeks in a year, he makes 323.90 x 52 = £16,843 a year.

Q49.3: **C. 875**
A full shift lasts for 8 hours, but the workers get to rest for an hour for lunch. That makes it 7 x 60 x 60 = 25,200 seconds of working.

A trolley can take up to 16 trays. This means it takes 16 x 9 = 144 seconds for a worker to fill a trolley.

Hence, a worker can fill up 25,200 / 144 = 175 trolleys in total. Five workers can fill up 175 x 5 = 875 trolleys in total.

Q49.4: **C. 11**
34 boxes = 34 x 22 = 748 biscuits

Each tray has 72 biscuits but, if 5% cannot be for sale, then only 72 x 0.95 = 68.4 (68 rounded off) biscuits can be for sale from each tray.

Hence,
68 x X = 748
X = 11

Answer 50

Q50.1: **B. 1**
Since the stars are mathematically similar, we need to find the ratio between the large star and the medium star.

Ratio: 3.5 / 2.1 = 5:3 (divide both sides by 0.7) = 1.67 (equivalent)

Hence, the height of the medium star would be 3.2 / (5 / 3) = 1.92cm

Q50.2: **D. 9.00cm^2**
Ratio from Q50.1: 5:3 or 1.67

Hence, the area factor in this case would be $(5 / 3)^2$ or 1.672 = 2.78.
Therefore, the area of the large star would be 3.24 x 2.78 = 9cm^2.

Q50.3: **E. 9.1mm**
Area scale factor = (Linear scale factor)^2

Hence, the linear scale factor in this question would be the square root of the area scale factor. That makes it $\sqrt{12.3906}$ = 3.52.

The width of the small star would be 3.2 / 3.52 = 0.91cm = 9.1mm.

Q50.4: **E. 448mm^2**
The bracelet has two small stars, and each small star has two sides. Hence, the total surface area of the small pendants is 1.12 x 2 x 2 = 4.48cm^2.

1cm = 10mm
1cm^2 = 100mm^2

Hence, 4.48cm^2 = 4.48 x 100 = 448mm^2

Answer 51

Q51.1: **A. Student**
Profit for each monthly plan = (Total number of customers - Customers who were unable to regulate their payments) x (Monthly retail price per customer - Average business cost per customer)

Student: (158,743 - 2,004) x (89.99 - 75.26) = £2,308,765.47
Basic Access: (202,718 - 1,696) x (199.99 - 122.12) = £15,653,583.14
Full Service: (186,846 - 2,348) x (259.99 - 215.71) = £8,169,571.44
Concession: (161,896 - 1,852) x (169.99 - 143.07) = £4,308,384.48
National Athlete: (54,921 - 883) x (159.99 - 137.54) = £1,213,153.10

'Student' membership contributed the second lowest profit to the club.

Q51.2: **C. 1.15%**
Total number of members: 158,743 + 202,718 + 186,846 + 161,896 + 54,921 = 765,124
Total number of members who were unable to regulate their payment: 2,004 + 1,696 + 2,348 + 1,852 + 883 = 8,783

Percentage of members unable to regulate payment: 8,783 / 765,124 x 100 = 1.15%

Q51.3: **D. 304%**
Profit made from each category (calculated in Q51.1):
Student: £2,308,765.47
Basic Access: £15,653,583.14
Full Service: £8,169,571.44
Concession: £4,308,384.48
National Athlete: £1,213,153.10

The two most profitable categories are Basic Access and Full Service. The total profit from the two categories is 15,653,583.14 + 8,169,571.44 = £23,823,154.58.

The total profit from the other three categories is 4,308,384.48 + 2,308,765.47 + 1,213,153.10 = £7,830,303.05.

Comparing the numbers in percentage: 23,823,154.58 / 7,830,303.05 x 100 = 304%

Answer 51 (Continued)

Q51.4: **C. £107,724k**
Total business cost for each category = Total number of customers x Average business cost per customer
Student: 158,743 x 75.26 = £11,946,998.18
Basic Access: 202,718 x 122.12 = 24,755,922.16
Full Service: 186,846 x 215.71 = £40,304,550.66
Concession: 161,896 x 143.07 = £23,162,460.72
National Athlete: 54,921 x 137.54 = £7,553,834.34

Total business cost = 11,946,998.18 + 24,755,922.16 + 40,304,550.66 + 23,162,460.72 + 7,553,834.34 = £107,723,766.16 (£107,724,000 rounded off to the nearest thousand)

Q51.5: **B. 13.6%**
Profit made from each category (calculated in Q51.1):
Student: £2,308,765.47
Basic Access: £15,653,583.14
Full Service: £8,169,571.44
Concession: £4,308,384.48
National Athlete: £1,213,153.10

The median is £4,308,384.48, from Concessions. The total profits made from all five categories: 15,653,583.14 + 8,169,571.44 + 4,308,384.48 + 2,308,765.47 + 1,213,153.10 = £31,653,457.63

Percentage of Concession category of total profits made: 4,308,384.48 / 31,653,457.63 x 100 = 13.6%

Answer 52

Q52.1: **C. 10**
Total Economic Index for Q2'11: 9 + 5.5 + 5 + 3.5 + 2.5 = 25.5
Total Economic Index for Q3'12: 9.5 + 7.5 + 6.5 + 6 + 6 = 35.5

Difference in Economic Index: 35.5 - 25.5 = 10

Answer 52 (Continued)

Q52.2: **E. 28.75**
Finding the midpoints between the marked points of Q4'11 and Q1'12,
Artemis: (3.5 + 5.5) / 2 = 4.5
Hephaestus: (8 + 9) / 2 = 8.5
Dionysus: (4.5 + 5) / 2 = 4.75
Heracles: (3.5 + 6) / 2 = 4.75
Leto: (6.5 + 6) / 2 = 6.25

Total of midpoints: 4.5 + 8.5 + 4.75 + 4.75 + 6.25 = 28.75

Q52.3: **D. Heracles**
Heracles only experienced a decline once in the two years.

Q52.4: **D. Q3'12**
Total Economic Index of all five companies for each quarter:
Q1'11: 23.5
Q2'11: 25.5
Q3'11: 28
Q4'11: 26
Q1'12: 31.5
Q2'12: 35.5
Q3'12: 35.5
Q4'12: 39

The quarters Q2'12 and Q3'12 both have the same total Economic Index.

Q52.5: **E. Leto**
This question can be approached without having to perform calculations for all of the companies.

First, we can be certain that Hephaestus is not the answer as it has an obvious overall declining trend. Secondly, from the graph, we can tell that Dionysus and Heracles have the same index in Q3 of 2012 but Dionysus has a greater index in Q2 of 2011. This means Heracles has had a greater increase in index compared to Dionysus. Next, we can compare Heracles and Artemis. Both their points at the two quarters are around the same range, and Artemis has a greater value than Heracles in both quarters. However, the gap between the two

Answer 52 (Continued)

is smaller in Q3 of 2012. This means that the increase in Heracles is greater than that in Artemis. Lastly, we look at the gap between Heracles and Leto. The space between the gaps is not as obvious. Unless you can tell the size of the gaps by looking at them, it would be wise to do some calculations at this point to be sure.

The increase for Heracles: 6 - 2.5 = 3.5
The increase for Leto: 9.5 - 5.5 = 4

Leto has a greater increase than Heracles. Hence, Leto is the answer.

Q52.6: **D. Hephaestus**
To answer this question, simply take the Economic Index value from Q1 of 2011 and subtract it from Q4 of 2012, or vice versa. However, you can eliminate some of the answers before doing any calculations.

Artemis and Heracles have the same start and end point. Hence, they both can't be the answer. Dionysus started with 1 arbitrary unit greater than Artemis/ Heracles and ended with the same gap. Hence, Dionysus can be eliminated as well. Now, you are left with Leto and Hephaestus. It is clear that the change in Economic Index for Hephaestus is 12 - 8 = 4. The change for Leto, however, is 9 - 4.5 = 4.5. Hence, Hephaestus is the company with the least change in Economic Index.

Q52.7: **C. 6.3**
Total Economic Index of all companies in Q1 of 2012: 5 + 5.5 + 6 + 6 + 9 = 31.5
Average Economic Index: 31.5 / 5 = 6.3

Q52.8: **A. 0**
From Q52.6, it has been established that Artemis, Heracles and Dionysus have the same magnitude of economic growth when comparing their Economic Index numbers in Q1'11 and Q4'12.

For this question, first, we can exclude Hephaestus as its economic value did not grow over the two years. Next, we can tell that the magnitude of economic growth of Leto is smaller than that of Artemis, Heracles and Dionysus as the gap between Leto and Dionysus has become smaller at the end of 2012 compared to the gap at the start of 2011. Now, let's look at the remaining three

Answer 52 (Continued)

companies. They have the same magnitude of change, but Dionysus has a greater Economic Index in Q1'11. This means that its percentage increase will be smaller than that of Artemis and Heracles as percentage increase is given by the 'magnitude of change divided by the original value'. Looking at the difference in economic growth, the answer is 0 as they both have the same growth.

Answer 53

Q53.1: **B. 53,625.36**
Cost of vacutainer bottle sets: 786 x 22.34 = £17,559.24
Cost of boxes of tourniquets: 54 x 12.54 = £677.16
Cost of otoscope specula packs: 1,961 x 13.28 = £26,042.08

Total cost (VAT included): (17,599.24 + 677.16 + 26,042.08) x 1.21 = £53,625.36

Q53.2: **E. 63.7%**
Unit price for winged infusion set for 1-10 units: 6.99 x 1.21 = £8.46
Unit price for winged infusion set for 10,001+ units: 2.54 x 1.21 = £3.07

Percentage decrease: (8.46 - 3.07) / 8.46 x 100 = 63.7%

You should not need to include the 21% VAT charge in this calculation as it will be cancelled off when calculating the percentage decrease. The solution above included it for completeness sake.

Q53.3: **D. £6,639.33**
Total cost of order (VAT excluded) = (1,384 x 7.03) + (836 x 10.27) + (11,053 x 13.36) = £165,983.32

Percentage difference in VAT charge = 25 - 21 = 4% = 0.04
Cost difference due to increase in VAT: 0.04 x 165,983.32 = £6,639.33

Answer 53 (Continued)

Q53.4: **D. 7,009**
Amount of money saved from reducing the number of otoscope specula packs: (7,368 x 13.28) - (459 x 15.86) = £90,567.30
One fourth of this amount would be 90,567.30 / 4 = £22,641.83

With this amount of money, you should now think of which price range of the winged infusion set is within your budget. You won't be able to purchase it at the price of £2.54 per unit because the minimum units to purchase would be 10,001, which will cost you a minimum of 10,001 x 2.54 = £25,402.54.

Hence, the best unit price you can get is £3.23. That will allow you to purchase 22,641.83 / 3.23 = 7,009.85 units (7,009 rounded down)

Q53.5: **D. 4.4:1**
Cost of 559 boxes of syringes (VAT included): 559 x 8.77 x 1.21 = £5,931.94
Cost of 89 boxes of tourniquet (VAT included): 89 x 12.54 x 1.21 = £1,350.43

Ratio of tourniquet to syringes: 5,391.94 / 1,350.43 = 4.4:1

You should not need to include the 21% VAT charge in this calculation as it will be cancelled off when calculating the ratio. The solution above included it for completeness sake.

Q53.6: **E. 677 units**
Cost of winged infusion sets (VAT included): 27,871.42 x 1.21 = £33,724.42
Cost of vacutainer bottle sets (VAT included): 52,024.68 - 33,724.42 = £18,300.26
Cost of vacutainer bottle sets (VAT excluded): 18,300.26 / 1.21 = £15,124.18

From this value, you can gauge the unit price at which the vacutainers were purchased. They could not have been purchased at £16.31 as the minimum cost would be 1,001 x 16.31 = £16,326.31. Hence, they must have been purchased at the price of £22.34. The quantity of units purchased would be 15,124.18 / 22.34 = 677 units

Answer 54

Q54.1: **C. 7,273**
Number of Elektronika shares that can be bought with £22,440 on 05.10.2011: 22,440 / 0.8 = 28,050 shares.
Number of Ieictreonaic shares that can be bought with £22,440 on 31.10.2011: 22,440 / 1.08 = 20,777.8 (20,777 rounded down) shares. [The value is rounded down because there was not enough money to purchase a full share unit to make it 20,778.]

Difference in share units: 28,050 - 20,777 = 7,273 units

Q54.2: **B. £3,456**
Price of Ceangal share on the respective dates:
05.10.2011: £1.98
15.10.2011: £1.50

Difference in price per share unit: 1.98 - 1.50 = £0.48

The number of shares sold were 7,200. Hence, there was a loss of 7,200 x 0.48 = £3,456

Q54.3: **D. £15,406**
Total made from selling 20,000 Phcheab shares on 15.10.2011: 20,000 x 1.7 = £34,000

The question states that he bought some share units from a company on 24.10.2011 and sold them on 31.10.2011 with a profit. This means the share must have increased in value over that period. From the graph, the only two shares that increased in value are Elektronika and Ceangal.

The increase in unit value for these shares are:
Elektronika: 0.93 / 0.64 = 1.45
Ceangal: 1.94 / 1.75 = 1.11

For him to have made the greatest profit possible, he must have purchased Elektronika. He made a profit of: (34,000 x 0.93 / 0.64) - 34,000 = £15,406.25 (£15,406 rounded off). £34,000 was subtracted because we are interested in the profit he made, not how much money he received from the sales of the share.

Answer 54 (Continued)

N.B. Division is used in the unit value increment calculation above instead of subtraction as you are interested in change in the value of the share based on its previous value. You will realise that the value you get when subtraction is used is inaccurate. An example will be shown below this solution.

If subtraction were to be used, the increase in unit value for these shares would be:
Elektronika: 0.93 - 0.64 = 0.29
Ceangal: 1.94 - 1.75 = 0.19

Elektronika has the greater increment from the values shown above. The profit made would be: 0.29 x 34,000 = £9,860. (Bear in mind that this is incorrect.)

Let's check our answer with a longer method.

The investor buys Elektronika on 24.10.2011 at 34,000 / 0.64 = 53,125 units.
He sells them on 31.10.2011 at 53,125 x 0.93 = £49,406.25.
He makes a profit of 49,406.25 - 34,000 = £15,406.25.
The investor buys Ceangal on 24.10.2011 at 34,000 / 1.75 = 19,428 units.
He sells them on 31.10.2011 at 19,428 x 1.94 = £37,690.32.
He makes a profit of 37,690.32 - 34,000 = £3,690.32.

This highlights that using division is the accurate way to solve the question.

Q54.4: **E. 27,795**
Number of Ieictreonaic shares bought on 05.10.2011: 27,000 / 1.41 = 19,148 units
Two thirds of the units were sold on 15.10.2011 for: (2 / 3 x 19,148) x 1.56 = £19,913.92

The money was used to purchase Elektronika shares on 31.10.2011: 19,913.92 / 0.93 = 21,412 units of Elektonika shares.

The investor still has one third of her shares in Ieictreonaic. That makes it: 1 / 3 x 19,148 = 6,383 units of Ieictreonaic shares.

The investor has a total of 21,412 + 6,383 = 27,795 units of shares.

Answer 55

Q55.1: **A. 27:16**
Number of students who qualified in Physics from Hubei: 150 / 100 x 72 = 108
Number of students who qualified in Further Mathematics from Yunnan: 125 / 100 x 51 = 63.75 (64 rounded off)

Ratio of students from Hubei to Yunnan: 108 / 64 = 27:16

Q55.2: **D. 75**
18 students from Xian qualified in Chemistry. Another 27 Chemistry finalists are needed to reach the national average.

Per 100 schools in Xian, 36 students would qualify for the finals. Hence, for 27 more students to qualify for the finals, there would have to be an extra: 27 / 36 x 100 = 75 schools participating.

Q55.3: **A. Yunnan**
Adding together the number of students qualified for finals in each subject per 100 schools:

Yunnan: 6 + 36 + 72 + 82 + 51 + 35 = 279
Jiangsu: 43 + 30 + 7 + 99 + 82 + 101 = 362
Xian: 11 + 18 + 36 + 78 + 9 + 54 = 206
Hubei: 28 + 72 + 82 + 57 + 34 + 7 = 280
Suzhou: 99 + 80 + 20 + 84 + 64 + 23 = 370

Next, adjust the numbers above to the actual number of students qualified for finals in each subject. You should not need to do this calculation separately. To save time, simply adjust the numbers as soon as you have found the sum.

Yunnan: 125 / 100 x 279 = 348.75 (349 rounded off)
Jiangsu: 25 / 100 x 362 = 90.5 (91 rounded off)
Xian: 50 / 100 x 206 = 103
Hubei: 150 / 100 x 280 = 420
Suzhou: 370

Arranging the above in ascending order: 91, 103, 349, 370, 420

The median is Yunnan.

Answer 55 (Continued)

Q55.4: **D. Hubei**
Adjusted number of finalists in Mathematics and General Knowledge combined:
Yunnan: (82 + 35) x 125 / 100 = 146.25 (146 rounded off)
Jiangsu: (99 + 101) x 25 / 100 = 50
Xian: (78 + 54) x 50 / 100 = 66
Hubei: (57 + 7) x 150 / 100 = 96
Suzhou: 84 + 23 = 107

Arranging the numbers in descending order: 146, 107, 96, 66, 50

The province with the second highest number of finalists in Mathematics and General Knowledge combined is Hubei.

Q55.5: **C. 111**
Hubei has 28 finalists per 100 schools.
Hence, to meet the national average of 31 finalists, it would need the following number of schools: 31 / 28 x 100 = 110.7 (111 rounded off)

Answer 56

Q56.1: **D. £29.40**
Cost to travel by car: 0.82 x 95 = £77.90
Cost for direct bus: £35
Cost for indirect bus: 42 x 0.70 = £29.40

Q56.2: **D. £116.85**
Cost to travel to New York: 0.82 x 95 = £77.90
Cost to travel back from New York (after splitting the cost): 77.90 / 2 = £38.95
Total cost of journey: 77.90 + 38.95 = £116.85

Answer 56 (Continued)

Q56.3: **D. £64.75**
Cost of one-way direct bus: £35
Cost of return: 35 x 0.85 = £29.75
Total cost: 35 + 29.75 = £64.75

Alternatively, you can shorten your calculation and use 35 x 1.85 = £64.75. (1.85 because 1 + 0.85; where 1 is the full cost of the trip to New York and 0.85 is the discounted portion of the return trip.)

Q56.4: **B. 4:30 pm; £165.30**
Maximum hours that can be spent while keeping the parking fee within £10:
10 / 1.50 = 6.67 = 6 hours (rounded down)
This means she must leave by: 10:30 am + 6hrs = 4:30 pm

Total cost of journey:
Parking fee: 6 x 1.50 = £9.50
Price of petrol for the round trip: 2 x 0.82 x 95 = £155.80
Total cost: 9.50 + 155.80 = £165.30

Answer 57

Q57.1: **C. 41.4%**
Total number of respondents: 63 + 51 + 38 = 152
Percentage of actors who deem 'Network' as necessary: 63 / 152 x 100 = 41.4%

Q57.2: **A. 9:13**
Number of actors who deem 'Risk-Taking' as important: 54
Number of actors who deem 'Education' as irrelevant: 78

Ratio of 'Risk-Taking' to 'Education': 54:78 = 9:13

Answer 57 (Continued)

Q57.3: **D. 8.9%**
There were 152 responses for each of the five qualities. This means that there were 152 x 5 = 760 responses altogether.
Total number of 'irrelevant' responses: 78 + 38 + 9 + 18 + 84 = 227
Total number of 'necessary' responses: 44 + 63 + 69 + 80 + 39 = 295
Difference in responses: 295 - 227 = 68
Percentage difference between the two: 68 / 760 x 100 = 8.9%

Q57.4: **B. Network**
Calculating the sum of 'necessary' and 'important' responses:
Education: 44 + 30 = 74
Network: 63 + 51 = 114
Determination: 69 + 74 = 143
Risk-Taking: 80 + 54 = 134
Multitalented: 39 + 29 = 68

Arranging the numbers in ascending order: 68, 74, 114, 134, 143

The answer is Network, with a total response of 114.

Alternatively, a quicker method would be to make a smart guess by working out sums with simple numbers. For example, take a look at the numbers in the tens place for all of the responses under 'necessary' and 'important'. You would be able to expect the total to be somewhere in the 70s, 110s, 130s, and 50s, for the qualities Education, Network, Risk-Taking and Multitalented, respectively. This immediately tells you that the one in the 110s will be the median. Hence, the answer is Network.

Answer 58

Q58.1: **A. Q1 2015**
You need not perform a calculation to get your answer. Simply work with the five options given to you since it will save you a lot of time.

Q1 2015: (31.5 - 9.8 - 5.4) x 1,000 / 121 = £134.71
Q2 2016: (39.7 - 12.5 - 8.1) x 1,000 / 158 = £120.89
Q3 2015: (33.6 - 10.5 - 6.1) x 1,000 / 147 = £115.65
Q1 2016: (36.5 - 10.9 - 7.0) x 1,000 / 163 = £114.11
Q2 2015: (33.8 - 10.7 - 6.6) x 1,000 / 125 = £132.00

The quarter with the highest revenue per customer is Q1 2015.

Note that, for the above calculations, you need not actually multiply 1,000 to get your answer as it is a constant for all calculations. This applies to some of the questions below as well.

Q58.2: **D. 4.42:1**
Profit made in Q4 2015: (34.5 - 11.0 - 6.8) x 1,000 = £16,700
Marketing spend: £3,780

Ratio of profit to marketing spend: 16,700 / 3,780 = 4.42:1

Q58.3: **A. -8.8%**
Fixed cost per customer in Q4 2015: 11.0 x 1,000 / 150 = £73.33
Fixed cost per customer in Q1 2016: 10.9 x 1,000 / 163 = £66.87

Percentage change: (73.33 - 66.87) / 73.33 x 100 = -8.8% ('-' because there is a decrease)

Q58.4: **D. Q2 2016**
Percentage increase in sales revenue for the following quarters compared to their previous quarter:
Q3 2015: (33.8 - 33.6) / 33.8 x 100 = -0.59%
Q4 2015: (34.5 - 33.6) / 33.6 x 100 = +2.67%
Q1 2016: (36.5 - 34.5) / 34.5 x 100 = +5.80%
Q2 2016: (39.7 - 36.5) / 36.5 x 100 = +8.77%
Q3 2016: (42.1 - 39.7) / 39.7 x 100 = +6.05%

Answer 58 (Continued)

The calculations on the previous page are shown for completeness. However, you do not need to spend time calculating the percentage change for options A. Q3 2015 and B. Q4 2015 as their change in sales revenue is small and is unlikely to give a percentage change of magnitude greater than the other options.

Q58.5: **B. £29.37**
Average transaction in the following quarters:
Q1 2015: 31.5 x 1,000 / 121 = £260.33
Q2 2015: 33.8 x 1,000 / 125 = £270.40
Q4 2016: 51.8 x 1,000 / 167 = £310.18

Percentage increase between Q1 and Q2 of 2015: (270.40 - 260.33) / 260.33 x 100 = +3.87%

If this percentage increase had remained constant for the next six quarters after Q2 2015, then Q4 2016 would be: 270.40 x 1.03876 = £339.55

Compared to the actual value, this would be greater by an amount of: 339.55 - 310.18 = £29.37

Answer 59

Q59.1: **E. 70,276**
Total number of deaths: 259 + 2,977 + 44,043 + 233,824 = 281,103
Average number of deaths: 281,103 / 4 = 70,275.75 (70,276 rounded off)

Q59.2: **C. March**
Number of new cases for each of the following months:-
January: 11,950 - 89 = 11,861
February: 86,604 - 11,950 = 74,654
March: 863,184 - 86,604 = 776,580
April: 3,301,083 - 863,184 = 2,437,899

Answer 59 (Continued)

Percentage increase in incidence:-
January: (11,861 - 89) / 89 x 100 = 13,227%
February: (74,654 - 11,861) / 11,861 x 100 = 529%
March: (776,580 - 74,654) / 74,654 x 100 = 940%
April: (2,437,899 - 776,580) / 776,580 x 100 = 213%

March is the month with the second highest percentage increase.

Q59.3: **C. 1,039,028**
Total number of cases = Total number of active cases + Total number of recovered cases + Total number of deaths
Total number of recovered cases = Total number of cases - Total number of active cases - Total number of deaths

Total number of deaths = 259 + 2,718 + 41,066 + 189,781 = 233,824

Total number of recovered cases = 3,301,083 - 2,028,231 - 233,824 = 1,039,028

Q59.4: **D. 412,131**
New cases
Number of new cases in Country X in March: (863,184 - 86,604) x 0.06 = 46,594.8 (46,595 rounded off)
Number of new cases in Country X in April: (3,301,083 - 863,184) x 0.06 = 146,273.94 (146,274 rounded off)

Percentage increase in new cases from March to April: (146,274 - 46,595) / 46,595 x 100 = 213.9%

Expected number of new cases at the end of May: 146,274 x 3.139 = 459,192.7 (459,193 rounded off) [3.139 was used instead of 2.139 because we have to account for the 100% that is 146,274. Meaning, 3.139 = 1 + 2.139]

Actual number of new cases at the end of May: 459,193 x 0.66 = 303,067.38 (303,067 rounded off)

Answer 59 (Continued)

Deaths

Number of deaths in Country X in March: 41,066 x 0.06 = 2,463.96 (2,464 rounded off)

Number of deaths in Country X in April: 189,781 x 0.06 = 11,386.86 (11,387 rounded off)

Percentage increase in new cases from March to April: (11,387 - 2,464) / 2,464 x 100 = 362.1%

Expected number of deaths at the end of May: 11,387 x 4.621 = 52,623.2 (52,623 rounded off)

Actual number of deaths at the end of May: 52,623 x 0.24 = 12,629.52 (12,630 rounded off)

Active Cases

Number of active cases in Country X at the end of April: 2,028,231 x 0.06 = 121,693.86 (121,694 rounded off)

Prevalence

Prevalence is the number of active cases at a specific point of time.

Prevalence at the end of May = Number of active cases at the end of April + Number of new cases in May - Number of deaths in May

Prevalence = 121,694 + 303,067 - 12,630 = 412,131

Answer 60

Q60.1: **A. Handtasche**

The calculations on the following page are for completeness sake, but you should not need to make calculations for all companies to solve this question.

Answer 60 (Continued)

Since the revenue is in millions (1,000,000) and the number of transactions is in thousands (1,000) for all the companies, you can omit these from your calculations as they are constants.

Handtasche: 17,720 / 457,920 = 0.0387
Bag Llaw: 13,015 / 684,302 = 0.0190
Handobaggu: 20,959 / 1,539,924 = 0.0136
Queens' Bags: 16,900 / 986,403 = 0.0171
Hendabega: 15,187 / 740,249 = 0.0205

From the above, we can conclude that Handtasche has the greatest revenue per transaction.

A quicker way to solve this question is to interpret the numbers directly from the table. Using any of the handbags as a starting reference, you should be able to roughly omit some of the choices before making any necessary calculations. For example, let's take Handtasche as the reference point.

Comparing Handatsche to Bag Llaw, Queens' Bags and Hendabega: It is impossible for any of these three companies to have a higher revenue per transaction then Handtasche because they generated less revenue whilst having more transactions.

Comparing Handtasche and Handobaggu: Handobaggu cannot have a higher revenue per transaction than Handtasche because, even though its revenue may be higher, its number of transactions is approximately three times more.

Q60.2: **B. 27:25**
Revenue per shop for Bag Llaw: 13,015M / 573 = £22,713,787
Revenue per shop for Hendabega: 15,187M / 721 = £21,063,800

Ratio of Bag Llaw to Hendabega: 22,713,787 / 21,063,800 = 1.078:1

27:25 is equivalent to 1.08:1, which is the closest option that will give you 1.078:1.

Answer 60 (Continued)

Q60.3: **D. 31**
Total number of employees: 25,087 + 23,344 + 15,314 + 20,906 + 17,690 = 102,341
Total number of shops: 610 + 573 + 489 + 945 + 721 = 3,338

Average number of employees per shop = 102,341 / 3,338 = 30.66 (31 rounded off)

Q60.4: **C. 45.2%**
Total revenue of Handobaggu and Queens' Bags: 20,959 + 16,900 = 37,859
Total revenue of all shops: 83,781

Percentage of revenue of Handobaggu and Queens' Bags of the total sum: 37,859 / 83,781 x 100 = 45.2%

Abstract Reasoning

TYPE I - Answer 1

Set A: None of the arrows point to the right. In the subsets where arrows are pointing down, the other objects are black and have mixed edges (straight and curved). In the subsets where arrows are pointing up, the other objects are grey and have straight edges. In the subsets where arrows point to the left, the other objects are white and have curved edges.

Set B: None of the arrows point to the left. In the subsets where arrows are pointing down, the remaining objects are white and have curved edges. In the subsets where arrows are pointing up, the remaining objects are black and have both curved and straight edges. In the subsets where arrows point to the right, the remaining objects are grey and have straight edges.

Subset 1.1 – Neither

Subset 1.2 – Set A

Subset 1.3 – Set A

Subset 1.4 – Neither

Subset 1.5 – Set B

TYPE I - Answer 2

This question works using an 'engine' method. The black circle moves across from left to right. If the first circle is black, the difference in the number of sides is 1. If the second circle is black, the difference in the number of sides is 2. If the third circle is black, the difference in the number of sides is 3.

Set A: If the remaining circles are grey, the object with the smaller number of sides is black. If the remaining circles are white, the object with the larger number of sides is black.

Set B: If the remaining circles are grey, the object with the larger number of sides is black. If the remaining circles are white, the object with the smaller number of sides is black.

TYPE I - Answer 2 (Continued)

Subset 2.1 – Neither

Subset 2.2 – Set B

Subset 2.3 – Neither

Subset 2.4 – Set B

Subset 2.5 – Set A

TYPE I - Answer 3

Set A: The letter corresponds to a number – A-1, B-2, C-3, D-4, etc. If the number that correlates with the letter is even, then there will be a larger number of objects with the same colour as the letter. If the number that correlates with the letter is odd, then there will be a smaller number of objects with the same colour as the letter. E.g. If the letter is B, the number that correlates with B is 2. The number 2 is an even number. If the letter B has a white font, there is a larger number of white-coloured objects in the frame.

Set B: The letter corresponds to a number – A-1, B-2, C-3, D-4, etc. If the number that correlates with the letter is even, then there will be a smaller number of objects with the same colour as the letter. If the number that correlates with the letter is odd, then there will be a larger number of objects with the same colour as the letter. E.g. If the letter is B, the number that correlates with B is 2. The number 2 is an even number. If the letter B has a white font, there is a smaller number of white-coloured objects in the frame.

Subset 3.1 – Set B

Subset 3.2 – Set A

Subset 3.3 – Neither

Subset 3.4 – Set A

Subset 3.5 – Neither

TYPE I - Answer 4

Set A: The shape that has a different number of sides to the others in the same frame is grey in colour.

Set B: The shape that has a different number of sides to the others in the same frame is white in colour.

Subset 4.1 – Neither

Subset 4.2 – Set B

Subset 4.3 – Neither

Subset 4.4 – Set A

Subset 4.5 – Neither

TYPE I - Answer 5

Set A: The vertices of the moon are pointing to one black circle and one white circle.

Set B: The vertices of the moon are pointing to two black circles.

Subset 5.1 – Set A

Subset 5.2 – Set B

Subset 5.3 – Neither

Subset 5.4 – Neither

Subset 5.5 – Set B

TYPE I - Answer 6

Set A: Has three objects each.

Set B: Has four objects each.

Subset 6.1 – Set B

Subset 6.2 – Neither

Subset 6.3 – Set A

Subset 6.4 – Set B

Subset 6.5 – Neither

TYPE I - Answer 7

Set A: Objects with one plane of symmetry are black.

Set B: Objects with one plane of symmetry are white.

Subset 7.1 – Neither

Subset 7.2 – Set A

Subset 7.3 – Set A

Subset 7.4 – Neither

Subset 7.5 – Set B

TYPE I - Answer 8

In each subset, there are four outer squares and four inner squares. The inner squares are smaller and are overlapping the centre part of the outer squares. To answer this question, focus on the colour of the inner squares.

Set A: The white inner squares are always diagonal to each other.

Set B: The black inner squares are always diagonal to each other.

Subset 8.1 – Neither

Subset 8.2 – Neither

Subset 8.3 – Set A

Subset 8.4 – Set B

Subset 8.5 – Set A

TYPE I - Answer 9

Set A: White dominoes have odd numbers on the top and even numbers on the bottom. Black dominoes have even numbers on the top and odd numbers on the bottom.

Set B: White dominoes have even numbers on the top and odd numbers on the bottom. Black dominoes have odd numbers on the top and even numbers on the bottom.

Subset 9.1 – Set A

Subset 9.2 – Neither

Subset 9.3 – Set B

Subset 9.4 – Neither

Subset 9.5 – Set B

TYPE I - Answer 10

Set A: A black circle is always diagonal to a white cross.

Set B: A white circle is always diagonal to a black cross.

Subset 10.1 – Neither

Subset 10.2 – Set A

Subset 10.3 – Set B

Subset 10.4 – Neither

Subset 10.5 – Neither

TYPE I - Answer 11

Set A: The number of black circles is odd.

Set B: The number of white circles is odd.

Subset 11.1 – Neither

Subset 11.2 – Set B

Subset 11.3 – Neither

Subset 11.4 – Neither

Subset 11.5 – Set A

TYPE I - Answer 12

Set A: If there is a black circle, there are three objects in total. If there is a white circle, there are four objects in total. If there is a grey circle, there are two objects in total.

Set B: If there is a black circle, there are two objects in total. If there is a white circle, there are three objects in total. If there is a grey circle, there are four objects in total.

Subset 12.1 – Neither

Subset 12.2 – Set B

Subset 12.3 – Set A

Subset 12.4 – Neither

Subset 12.5 – Neither

TYPE I - Answer 13

Set A: Black objects are in contact with each other.

Set B: White objects are in contact with each other.

Subset 13.1 – Set A

Subset 13.2 – Set B

Subset 13.3 – Set B

Subset 13.4 – Neither

Subset 13.5 – Neither

TYPE I - Answer 14

Set A: Each flower has four white petals.

Set B: Each flower has three white petals.

Subset 14.1 – Set A

Subset 14.2 – Set B

Subset 14.3 – Neither

Subset 14.4 – Neither

Subset 14.5 – Neither

TYPE I - Answer 15

Set A: If the domino is black, the top number is larger than the bottom number. If the domino is white, the top number is smaller than the bottom number.

Set B: If the domino is white, the top number is larger than the bottom number. If the domino is black, the top number is smaller than the bottom number.

Subset 15.1 – Set B

Subset 15.2 – Neither

Subset 15.3 – Neither

Subset 15.4 – Neither

Subset 15.5 – Set B

TYPE I - Answer 16

Set A: All of the shapes have curved sides.

Set B: All of the shapes have straight sides.

Subset 16.1 – Neither

Subset 16.2 – Set B

Subset 16.3 – Set A

Subset 16.4 – Neither

Subset 16.5 – Set A

TYPE I - Answer 17

Set A: The line of symmetry is horizontal throughout the set.

Set B: The line of symmetry is vertical throughout the set.

Subset 17.1 – Neither

Subset 17.2 – Set A

Subset 17.3 – Neither

Subset 17.4 – Set B

Subset 17.5 – Set B

TYPE I - Answer 18

Set A: There is only one black shape per box throughout the set.

Set B: There is only one grey shape per box throughout the set.

Subset 18.1 – Neither

Subset 18.2 – Set B

Subset 18.3 – Neither

Subset 18.4 – Set A

Subset 18.5 – Neither

TYPE I - Answer 19

Set A: For every grey shape, there are two black shapes.

Set B: For every grey shape, there is one black shape.

Subset 19.1 – Set B

Subset 19.2 – Set B

Subset 19.3 – Set A

Subset 19.4 – Neither

Subset 19.5 – Set A

TYPE I - Answer 20

The black and white circles are distractors.

Set A: Each subset has one black triangle and an additional shape that has straight sides.

Set B: Each subset has one black triangle and an additional shape that has curved sides.

Subset 20.1 – Set B

Subset 20.2 – Set B

Subset 20.3 – Set A

Subset 20.4 – Neither

Subset 20.5 – Set A

TYPE I - Answer 21

Set A: All shapes with curved sides are white.

Set B: All shapes with curved sides are black.

Subset 21.1 – Neither

Subset 21.2 – Neither

Subset 21.3 – Neither

Subset 21.4 – Set A

Subset 21.5 – Neither

TYPE I - Answer 22

Set A: For every triangle, there is a circle.

Set B: There is one more circle than the number of triangles.

Subset 22.1 – Neither

Subset 22.2 – Set A

Subset 22.3 – Set B

Subset 22.4 – Neither

Subset 22.5 – Set B

TYPE I - Answer 23

Set A: There are more black shapes than white shapes.

Set B: There are more white shapes than black shapes.

Subset 23.1 – Set A

Subset 23.2 – Neither

Subset 23.3 – Neither

Subset 23.4 – Set A

Subset 23.5 – Set B

TYPE I - Answer 24

Set A: The horizontal arrows are pointing to either the left or the right. Two arrows are 'cancelled out' if one is pointing to the right and the other to the left. There is one square for every arrow that isn't 'cancelled out'. The number of circles is not considered relevant.

Set B: The horizontal arrows are pointing to either the left or the right. Two arrows are 'cancelled out' if one is pointing to the right and the other to the left. There is one circle for every arrow that isn't 'cancelled out'. The number of squares is not considered relevant.

Subset 24.1 – Set A

Subset 24.2 – Set B

Subset 24.3 – Neither

Subset 24.4 – Neither

Subset 24.5 – Neither

TYPE I - Answer 25

Set A: The number of white shapes is always even, whilst the number of black shapes is always odd. The grey shapes are not considered relevant.

Set B: The number of white shapes is always even, whilst the number of grey shapes is always odd. The black shapes are not considered relevant.

Subset 25.1 – Set A

Subset 25.2 – Neither

Subset 25.3 – Set A

Subset 25.4 – Neither

Subset 25.5 – Neither

TYPE II - Answer 1

Answer: D

The black ball moves in a clockwise manner, increasing in distance from the previous by the length of the square (i.e. half, one, one and a half, two). The arrow turns anti-clockwise, 45 degrees each time. The grey arc block moves half the length of the square and forwards until it reaches the next corner and moves backwards.

TYPE II - Answer 2

Answer: B

The top right object decreases in number of edges by 1 (i.e. 4, 3, 2, 1, 0). The bottom left object increases in number of edges by 1 (i.e. 3, 4, 5, 6, 7). The sum of the number of edges in all boxes is seven, represented by either the arrow or heptagon in the centre. Box B completes the series.

TYPE II - Answer 3

Answer: A

There are two separate series in this question. The sticks represent points of intersection by addition of 4 (i.e. 6, 10, 14, 18, 22). The number of circles increases by 2 in each frame (i.e. 6, 8, 10, 12, 14).

TYPE II - Answer 4

Answer: C

The number of lines (both curved and straight) increases in each box using a prime number series: 2, 3, 5, 7, 11.

TYPE II - Answer 5

Answer: B

The series goes from top to bottom, left to right. All four boxes are read continuously in the series. Read the sequence by following the black raindrop from top to bottom, left to right. Spaces between each black raindrop increase in each sequence to the next black raindrop represented by either a white or grey raindrop (i.e. 1, 2, 3, 4, 5, 6, 7, 8, 9, 10). There is a grey raindrop after every black raindrop.

TYPE II - Answer 6

Answer: A

The shapes each represent a number that corresponds to the number of sides/ edges. A triangle – 3, a square – 4. Each frame has shapes that represent a palindromic number (e.g. first frame 313).

TYPE II - Answer 7

Answer: C

To answer this question, you have to read the white dominoes separately from the black dominoes. Once separated, focusing on the white dominoes, read diagonally from top to bottom then bottom to top for the first pattern (5 – 4 – 3 – 2 – 1). For the second pattern, begin from the bottom to top then top to bottom (2 – 4 – 6 – 4 – 2). Focusing on the black dominoes only, starting from the top and moving diagonally in a zig zag manner, the third pattern reads (6 –5 – 4 – 3 – 2). The last pattern reads (1 – 2 – 3 – 4 – 5). Hence, C is the figure that completes the series.

TYPE II - Answer 8

Answer: A

Focus on the music notes' heads individually. They all move in ascending order in the same increment between spaces and bars. The position of the tails act as a distractor.

TYPE II - Answer 9

Answer: A

This question deals with an increasing number of splits in each proceeding diagram. The number of splits given in the question is 0, 1, 2, 3. Imagine the lines as branches. You are looking at how many branches there are. The final number of branches is given by 2^n, where n is the number of splits.

To approach this question, you first need to be able to identify the starting point of each diagram.

First image: It doesn't matter where you start because the line doesn't split.

Second image: For this image, it also doesn't matter where you start, as long as you can identify that the line splits into two at one point. In essence, splitting only occurs once.

Third image: This image is a bit trickier. It is important to identify that the starting point of the line comes from the bottom left corner of the image. Following this line, you will realise that this line splits into two at one point, giving you two lines. These two lines split further into two lines each. Splitting occurs twice.

Fourth image: Again, for this image you have to identify the starting point of the line; it comes from the bottom of the image. It splits into two lines. Each of these two lines splits further into two lines each. And these two lines once again split further into two lines. Splitting occurs thrice.

TYPE II - Answer 10

Answer: D

To solve this question, the long hand and the short hand of the clock are pointing to numbers that you would normally read for the time. The long hand represents the numbers 15, 30, 45, 60, and the short hand represents the numbers 1, 2, 3, 4, 5, 6, 7, 8, 9, 10, 11, 12.

The multiplication of the two numbers represented by the short hand and the long hand gives you a number that will be used in this series.

In the first clock, 3 X 5 = 15. The second clock, 6 X 5 = 30. The third clock, 1 X 45 = 45. The fourth clock, 2 X 30 = 60. As you can see, the product of multiplication increases by 15 across the series. To complete the series, you have to look for the clock that will produce the number 75. Hence, the clock in D is 25 X 3 = 75.

TYPE II - Answer 11

Answer: B

Follow the grey square in a downward sequence manner. The circles are distractors.

TYPE II - Answer 12

Answer: C

The straight line oscillates in a pendulum-like manner. The grey circle is always diagonally opposite to the black square. The black square moves anti-clockwise, starting from three lengths of the square, to two lengths, to one length, and then stationary.

TYPE II - Answer 13

Answer: D

The sequence moves anti-clockwise as it lengthens. The sequence starts with a black square. The number of white squares increases each time, ending with a black square.

TYPE II - Answer 14

Answer: A

The black square moves one step in each sequence. The black square moves forwards first. Once it reaches the end, it moves backwards.
The black circle moves up and down in each sequence.
The number of edges of the remaining objects increases in the series.

TYPE II - Answer 15

Answer: B

The number of planes of symmetry increases across the series.

TYPE II - Answer 16

Answer: C

The squares at the three corners move to the next corner in a clockwise manner. For the line of small squares, focus on the black squares. The number of spaces between two small black squares across the series go by 1, 2, 3, 2, 1. The remaining small squares are white.

TYPE II - Answer 17

Answer: A

The top object is the result of the overlapped area from the previous sequence.

TYPE II - Answer 18

Answer: D

The number of edges of each object represents the movement of the long hand by 15 minutes. The short hand increases by the hour in each sequence. The other shapes are distractors.

TYPE II - Answer 19

Answer: C

Read from left to right, top to bottom, for each panel. Then focus on the colour of the compass. The arrows of the black compass rotate every 90 degrees clockwise in each black compass. The arrows of the white compass, rotate every 90 degrees anti-clockwise in each white compass.

TYPE II - Answer 20

Answer: C

The colour of the first circle represents the colour of the top object. The colour of the last circle represents the colour of the bottom object. The colour of the circles moves in a loop sequence: white – black – grey – white – black – grey – white – black – grey.

TYPE II - Answer 21

Answer: C

The total number of black circles is added to the next box. For example, the first box has five circles, of which one is black. Therefore, the next box has six circles in total (5 + 1 = 6 circles).
The third box will have 6 + 3 = 9 circles.
The fourth box will have 9 + 2 = 11 circles.
To complete the series, the box should have 11 + 3 = 14 circles.

TYPE II - Answer 22

Answer: C

In each box across the series, the white arrow rotates 90 degrees clockwise, the black arrow rotates 135 degrees anti-clockwise, and the grey arrow rotates 45 degrees clockwise.

TYPE II - Answer 23

Answer: D

In every new box, one grey circle is added, along with two black ones.

TYPE II - Answer 24

Answer: B

The diagonal line gradually gets longer, while the curve gradually gets shorter.

TYPE II - Answer 25

Answer: B

The number of black shapes increases in each box using a prime number series: 2, 3, 5, 7, 11.

TYPE II - Answer 26

Answer: D

The sum of the two previous boxes creates the amount in the next.

TYPE II - Answer 27

Answer: A

One circle is removed from each corner in an anti-clockwise manner.

TYPE II - Answer 28

Answer: D

Across the series, one additional grey shape is added, and one black shape is taken away, while the number of white shapes stays the same.

TYPE II - Answer 29

Answer: A

The number of sides of the larger shape increases by two between each frame. The number of sides of the smaller shape increases by one between each frame.

TYPE II - Answer 30

Answer: D

Each shape moves across the grid in a clockwise direction by one space in the second frame. In the third frame, each shape moves across the grid in a clockwise direction by two spaces. In the fourth frame, each shape moves across the grid in a clockwise direction by three spaces. To get the answer, each shape moves across the grid in a clockwise direction by four spaces.

TYPE III - Answer 1

Answer: D

The figure on the right is a mirror image of the figure on the left. To help visualise this, use a ruler to draw a line from the top left corner of the box down to the bottom right corner to act as a mirror.

TYPE III - Answer 2

Answer: D

Imagine looking at the shapes as objects in 3D. The top left square represents what you see from the top left of the stacked objects looking downwards and to the right. The bottom right square represents what you would see from the bottom right of the stacked objects looking upwards and to the left.

TYPE III - Answer 3

Answer: A

The letters in black font all have four right-angles in total, whereas the letters in white font have zero right-angles.

TYPE III - Answer 4

Answer: A

Let's say the 'bottom' side of the pentagon prism is the pentagon with the adjacent triangles attached to it in the frame. Focusing on the bottom pentagon, the black circle appears on a triangle that is joined to the pentagon's side rather than at its vertex. The circles have a gap in between them in one direction and two gaps in between them in the opposite direction. To answer the question, you have to treat the 'bottom' pentagon as the 'top' pentagon to find where the circles lie.

TYPE III - Answer 5

Answer: B

The black and grey circles always have an empty triangle between them in one direction.

TYPE III - Answer 6

Answer: B

The number of points of contact between a black circle and a white circle is represented in the number of turns in the curvy lines.

TYPE III - Answer 7

Answer: D

To answer this question, the arrows represent the number of degrees moving clockwise. The arrow pointing upwards is 0 degrees, downwards 180 degrees, right 90 degrees, left 270 degrees. The arrow in the box on the right shows the resulting direction (i.e. number of degrees) of the arrows in the box on the left.

TYPE III - Answer 8

Answer: C

To answer this question, draw a line between a black circle and a white circle within the same loop.

TYPE III - Answer 9

Answer: A

The square rotates 45 degrees clockwise. The white circle moves clockwise to the next corner of the square, whereas the triangle moves anti-clockwise. The black circle and the line are stationary following the rotation of the square.

TYPE III - Answer 10

Answer: C

The number of black circles represents the number of overlapped areas.

TYPE III - Answer 11

Answer: A

The blocks on the left represent the outline of the name of the shape on the right in words in lowercase letters.

circle 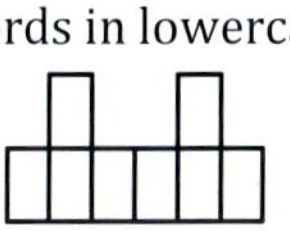

triangle 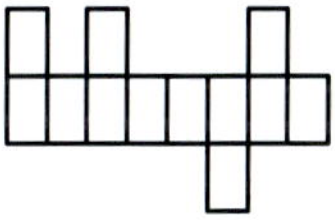

TYPE III - Answer 12

Answer: C

The number of black circles represents the number of objects.

TYPE III - Answer 13

Answer: B

The black circles represent the number of arrowheads. The white circles represent the number of arrowheads deducted by the number of intersections.

TYPE III - Answer 14

Answer: D

There are two types of bars in the series: a fine one and a broad one. Even though the bars are arranged differently, the number of broad bars is the same.

TYPE III - Answer 15

Answer: A

From top to bottom, the number of objects increases. In total, there are 15 objects.

TYPE III - Answer 16

Answer: A

The figure on the right has one less side than the figure on the left.

TYPE III - Answer 17

Answer: C

The figure on the right looks like the shape on the left that was 'cut out of' a rectangle.

TYPE III - Answer 18

Answer: D

The colour of each shape forms the colour of the outer shape in a clockwise manner. It also forms the colour of the inner shape in an anti-clockwise manner.

TYPE III - Answer 19

Answer: A

The number of sides in the shape is reduced by one and is rotated slightly. Two lines are placed alongside the edge of the new shape.

TYPE III - Answer 20

Answer: C

The shape increases in number of sides and the letter goes to the next vowel in the alphabet.

TYPE III - Answer 21

Answer: A

The corresponding box has one less black shape and one more grey shape, while the number of white shapes stays the same.

TYPE III - Answer 22

Answer: B

Each line is equal to one circle.

TYPE III - Answer 23

Answer: B

Every side of a shape in the box on the left is equal to one line in the box on the right.

TYPE III - Answer 24

Answer: C

Every black circle is equivalent to a triangle. Every white circle is equivalent to a diamond. Every grey circle is equivalent to a square.

TYPE III - Answer 25

Answer: C

The total number of sides of the shapes in the frame on the left is equivalent to the total number of circles in the frame on the right. The colour of the shapes in both frames is not relevant.

TYPE IV - Answer 1

Set A: Focus on the long hand. Lines of symmetry x 45 degrees (7.5 minutes) clockwise if black, anti-clockwise if white.

Set B: Focus on the long hand. Lines of symmetry x 45 degrees (7.5 minutes) clockwise if white, anti-clockwise if black.

Answer Set A: B
Answer Set B: D

TYPE IV - Answer 2

Set A: The arrows pointing up are represented by black circles. The arrows pointing down are represented by grey circles. The arrows pointing either left or right are represented by white circles. If any of the frames has more than one arrow pointing in the same direction, the respective circles are touching each other.

Set B: The arrows pointing up are represented by white circles. The arrows pointing down are represented by black circles. The arrows pointing either left or right are represented by grey circles. If any of the frames has more than one arrow pointing in the same direction, the respective circles are touching each other.

Answer Set A: C
Answer Set B: A

TYPE IV - Answer 3

Set A: In each subset, the numbers on the white domino represent two separate integers. The numbers on the black domino represent only one integer and are the result of the multiplication of the two integers on the white domino. For example, in the first frame 3 x 5 = 15.

TYPE IV - Answer 3 (Continued)

Set B: In each subset, the numbers on the white domino represent two separate integers. The numbers on the black domino represent one integer and are the result of the division of the two integers in the white domino. The integer on the left serves as the numerator, whereas the integer on the right serves as the denominator. For example, in the first frame 6 / 2 = 3.

Answer Set A: C
Answer Set B: A

TYPE IV - Answer 4

Set A: Shapes with 10 sides are black in colour. Shapes with five sides are white in colour.

Set B: Shapes with eight sides are white in colour. Shapes with four sides are black in colour.

Answer Set A: B
Answer Set B: D

TYPE IV - Answer 5

Set A: The number of overlapped areas is four.

Set B: The number of overlapped areas is five.

Answer Set A: C
Answer Set B: D

TYPE IV - Answer 6

Set A: The number of objects on the egg is 10.

Set B: The number of objects on the egg is 11.

Answer Set A: B
Answer Set B: A

TYPE IV - Answer 7

Set A: The main object, which is grey, starts from the middle (not always present). The object directly above and below, right and left of the object is black and diagonally is white.

Set B: The main object, which is black, starts from the middle (not always present). The object directly above and below, right and left of it is white and diagonally is grey.

Answer Set A: D
Answer Set B: C

TYPE IV - Answer 8

Set A: The objects complement each other.

Set B: The objects do not complement each other.

Answer Set A: D
Answer Set B: B

TYPE IV - Answer 9

The short hand represents the numbers (1, 2, 3, 4, 5, 6) and the long hand represents the numbers (5, 10, 15, 20, 25, 30, 35, 40, 45, 50, 55, 60).

Set A: The numbers represented by the short hand multiplied by those of the long hand gives a number that is divisible by three.

Set B: The numbers represented by the short hand multiplied by those of the long hand gives a number that is not divisible by three.

Answer Set A: C
Answer Set B: C

TYPE IV - Answer 10

Set A: Objects with both curved and straight edges are black.

Set B: Objects with both curved and straight edges are white.

Answer Set A: B
Answer Set B: C

TYPE IV - Answer 11

Set A: The number of dots is always even. The number of bars is always odd.

Set B: The number of dots is always odd. The number of bars is always even.

Answer Set A: A
Answer Set B: A

TYPE IV - Answer 12

Set A: All shapes are regular.

Set B: All shapes are irregular.

Answer Set A: B
Answer Set B: C

TYPE IV - Answer 13

Set A: The circle which is higher is black.

Set B: The circle which is lower is black.

Answer Set A: B
Answer Set B: C

TYPE IV - Answer 14

Set A: If there are only two of a certain shape, they are both black.

Set B: If there are only two of a certain shape, they are both white.

Answer Set A: D
Answer Set B: B

TYPE IV - Answer 15

Set A: One circle is adjacent or diagonal to another.

Set B: One diamond is adjacent or diagonal to another.

Answer Set A: D
Answer Set B: C

TYPE IV - Answer 16

Set A: There are three black shapes per box. However, these are all different shapes.

Set B: There are three black shapes per box, including two of the same shape.

Answer Set A: A
Answer Set B: D

TYPE IV - Answer 17

Set A: All irregular shapes are black. However, regular shapes can also be black.

Set B: All irregular shapes are grey. However, regular shapes can also be grey.

Answer Set A: D
Answer Set B: C

TYPE IV - Answer 18

Set A: There is no more than one black shape with straight edges per box.

Set B: There is no more than one grey shape with straight edges per box.

Answer Set A: C
Answer Set B: C

TYPE IV - Answer 19

Set A: The lightning bolt points towards the circle.

Set B: The lightning bolt points towards the cross.

Answer Set A: B
Answer Set B: B

TYPE IV - Answer 20

Set A: Each black triangle is equal to one curvy line with a shape at the end of it. Each white triangle is equal to one straight line with a shape at the end of it.

Set B: Each white triangle is equal to one curvy line with a shape at the end of it. Each black triangle is equal to one straight line with a shape at the end of it.

Answer Set A: B
Answer Set B: A

TYPE IV - Answer 21

Set A: Within each box, the number of white circles is one less than the number of sides that the large shape possesses. Likewise, within each box, the number of black circles is the same as the number of sides that the large shape possesses. The grey circles are not relevant.

Set B: Within each box, the number of white circles is two less than the number of sides that the large shape possesses. Likewise, the number of black circles is one less than the number of sides that the large shape possesses. The grey circles are relevant.

Answer Set A: B
Answer Set B: A

Situational Judgement

TYPE I - Answer 1

1.1: D – A very inappropriate thing to do

Explanation: You should never rush whilst completing discharge letters. As the discharge letter will be sent to the patient's GP upon discharge, it should be done correctly. A patient's discharge letter is the only document accessible to other healthcare professionals accessing the system to look up the patient's past medical history. Discharge letters also include the patient's current regular medications, and it is very important not to make mistakes.

1.2: D – A very inappropriate thing to do

Explanation: Even though it is 5:00 pm and Priya is running late, her patients' safety should always come first. Most of the time there is a reason for taking bloods from the patient for that day – whether it's discharge-dependent, a guide to your next management plan, or a way to monitor the patient's progress after starting/stopping/changing a medication or post/pre procedure. It is Priya's responsibility to check the blood results, if urgent, and not leave it to the next morning. If the bloods are routine, she could potentially leave them until the next morning, but only if she is very sure they are routine monitoring of a stable patient; this is, of course, on a case-by-case basis. In this case, it is very vague and should not be left until the morning.

If you've requested bloods to be taken or reviewed at a later time in the day, it is safe to hand it over to the on-call team for them to chase. However, note that they are doing a favour for you and there is a possibility of it being least prioritised on their on-call list. If the bloods are urgent, it is vital to make a note of this to the on-call team by either handing over the job face-to-face or, if there is a safe handover electronic system in place, making sure it is tagged as 'High Priority'.

1.3: B – Appropriate, but not ideal

Explanation: Although this is appropriate as it is Priya's responsibility as the day team doctor who knows the patients well, it is not ideal. Priya should prioritise her tasks and complete what's urgent first and routine last.

1.4: B – Appropriate, but not ideal

Explanation: Talking to Maura's supervisor, would mean that the situation is

TYPE I - Answer 1 (Continued)

handled and that patients are safe. However, Priya should not talk to another junior doctor's supervisor without addressing it with Maura first. You should always approach the person in discussion first before escalating it to a more senior doctor in the same team, and only to the on-call team last. (Junior doctor -> Senior House Officer -> Registrar -> Consultant -> On-call team).

TYPE I - Answer 2

2.1: D – A very inappropriate thing to do

Explanation: You should never start a patient-doctor relationship.

2.2: C – Inappropriate, but not awful

Explanation: Santana's actions are seen as inappropriate as she accepts his friend request. However, they are not awful as she politely rejects him.

2.3: C – Inappropriate, but not awful

Explanation: As the patient is still being cared for, this is not wholly inappropriate; the care of the patient has not been compromised. However, it is not ideal as the other junior doctor might have his/her own group of patients/tasks for which he/she is responsible. In addition, such measures should be put in place by a senior member of the team.

2.4: C – Inappropriate, but not awful

Explanation: Although you should never shame someone on social media, Santana anonymises the messages, and the patient cannot be identified.

2.5: D – A very inappropriate thing to do
Explanation: You should never humiliate a patient in front of your colleagues.

TYPE I - Answer 3

3.1: D – A very inappropriate thing to do

Explanation: As a doctor, you should always put your opinions aside and treat the patient. Stigmatising patients is frowned upon. However, in this case, Eoin passing the task onto his colleague may mean that the patient is still being looked after.

3.2: D – A very inappropriate thing to do

Explanation: Although the patient is safe as he still completes the task, you should never make a patient uncomfortable to be in your presence.

3.3: D – A very inappropriate thing to do

Explanation: You should never let your opinions put other patients at risk.

3.4: A – A very appropriate thing to do

Explanation: Double gloving will keep Eoin safe from any accidents, involving coming into contact with the patient's blood. Eoin is also completing the task efficiently.

3.5: B – Appropriate, but not ideal

Explanation: His fellow colleague is free, and Eoin expresses the urgency of the situation. Hence, the patient is not at risk. However, it is not ideal as Eoin's colleague may not know the patient as well as he does and may put himself at risk by not taking extra precautions.

TYPE I - Answer 4

4.1: D – A very inappropriate thing to do

Explanation: You should always speak directly to the patient. It is your duty to make your patient as comfortable as possible. In this scenario, there is a possibility that Mr Buggati is not allowing Leia to speak for herself out of fear that she may reveal something that he doesn't want revealed. It appears that Mr Buggati is very controlling, and there is a possibility that Leia is held against her own will. This is a safeguarding issue.

TYPE I - Answer 4 (Continued)

4.2: D – A very inappropriate thing to do

Explanation: If your patient doesn't speak English, it is your duty to provide a translator. Although this isn't common practice in real life, this is what you should do and what is expected of you.

4.3: A – A very appropriate thing to do

Explanation: Although this may enrage Mr Buggati, it is in the best interest of the patient, Leia. It is Jozsef's duty to act in the best interest of the patient.

4.4: A – A very appropriate thing to do

Explanation: Examining Leia in a different room with a chaperone gives Jozsef the opportunity to speak with her without Mr Buggati's presence. At the same time, Jozsef gives Leia the privacy needed for an intimate examination.

TYPE I - Answer 5

5.1: A – A very appropriate thing to do

Explanation: Kevin's actions are responsible and admirable here. Perhaps, Mr White has an unconscious bias towards Andrea and has unintentionally dismissed her presence. As a fellow colleague who is witnessing this, Kevin is doing the right thing by involving Andrea in conversations and sharing opportunities with her.

5.2: A – A very appropriate thing to do

Explanation: Kevin is addressing his concerns directly with Mr White.

TYPE I - Answer 5 (Continued)

5.3: C – Inappropriate, but not awful

Explanation: Although Andrea hasn't said anything, Kevin shouldn't assume that she is disinterested. Perhaps Andrea doesn't feel comfortable enough to voice her opinions.

5.4: C – Inappropriate, but not awful

Explanation: It is always best to speak to the person in question directly. Speaking to the consultant isn't favourable, but it also is not awful if Mr White changes his actions towards Andrea.

TYPE I - Answer 6

6.1: D – A very inappropriate thing to do

Explanation: Sakura is a medical student and doesn't know the patient well. It is not Sakura's duty to break the bad news on her own without the support of the team.

6.2: D – A very inappropriate thing to do

Explanation: You should never rush into breaking bad news, especially in this scenario where Mrs Johansson has just given birth.

6.3: A – A very appropriate thing to do

Explanation: This is the most ideal situation—to involve the medical team when breaking bad news.

6.4: D – A very inappropriate thing to do

Explanation: In this scenario, ignoring Jessica's request is inappropriate. However, this does not mean that Sakura should do what Jessica has asked; Mrs Johansson has just given birth and Sakura is a medical student.

TYPE I - Answer 7

7.1: D – A very inappropriate thing to do

Explanation: You should never bring patient-identifiable information home, unless you've received consent from specific individuals and it is saved on a password-protected hard drive.

7.2: A – A very appropriate thing to do

Explanation: This is the best way for Jonah to learn and still maintain patient confidentiality.

7.3: D – A very inappropriate thing to do

Explanation: Although he returns it the next day, it is still wrong for him to bring it home.

7.4: D – A very inappropriate thing to do

Explanation: You should never bring patient-identifiable information home, unless you've received consent from specific individuals and it is saved on a password-protected hard drive.

TYPE I - Answer 8

8.1: D – A very inappropriate thing to do

Explanation: James is on the ward as a medical student; he is not the main doctor or part of the team looking after Donna. Looking into her case notes and test results out of curiosity is an intrusion of her privacy. It is common decency to ask for permission to access a patient's case notes and test results.

8.2: D – A very inappropriate thing to do

Explanation: You should not look into GP records unless it is in the best interest of the patient or you have obtained consent from the patient for access.

TYPE I - Answer 8 (Continued)

8.3: B – Appropriate, but not ideal

Explanation: Speaking to the doctor/team who is looking after Donna for permission to speak to her is acceptable but not ideal.

8.4: D – A very inappropriate thing to do

Explanation: Sharing information about patients on social media, regardless of the severity and complexity of the case, is a very inappropriate thing to do.

8.5: D – A very inappropriate thing to do

Explanation: As a medical student, it is not James' duty to contact the patient's next of kin. Moreover, James is not part of the team who is looking after Donna. Donna's mother may not know about Donna's admission into hospital or that Donna is possibly sexually active. James should respect the patient's wishes and confidentiality by not calling her next of kin without her consent.

TYPE I - Answer 9

9.1: D – A very inappropriate thing to do

Explanation: You should never give out or confirm patient-identifiable information/case notes/updates over the telephone.

9.2: B – Appropriate, but not ideal

Explanation: Although this sounds ideal, Nikki must ensure that Parry is medically fit to speak to Fred by checking his wellbeing and state of mind with the nurse or the doctor in charge.

9.3: A – A very appropriate thing to do

Explanation: This is an ideal situation. Relatives/friends are allowed to visit during visiting times when the ward is less busy and not during ward rounds.

TYPE I - Answer 9 (Continued)

9.4: D – A very inappropriate thing to do

Explanation: It is inappropriate to provide patient information over the phone. However, it is very inappropriate to hang up the phone; Nikki must communicate with Fred in a professional manner.

9.5: D – A very inappropriate thing to do

Explanation: This is not an acute situation, and Nikki's colleague could be attending to something more serious. Nikki could suggest Fred calls back in a few minutes time as the attending doctor is currently occupied with another patient.

TYPE I - Answer 10

10.1: C – Inappropriate, but not awful

Explanation: It is always best to speak directly to the person in question. However, confronting and threatening to report Chidi is inappropriate.

10.2: A – A very appropriate thing to do

Explanation: This is the best case scenario. Being an understanding colleague is admirable.

10.3: C – Inappropriate, but not awful

Explanation: Going behind Chidi's back by reporting him before speaking to him first isn't ideal. However, if it helps provide support for Chidi's future placements, this will be in his favour.

10.4: C – Inappropriate, but not awful

Explanation: As a fellow colleague, Eleanor should at least try to understand why her placement partner isn't making the effort to join for house visits. It is also important to consider Chidi's wellbeing.

TYPE I - Answer 10 (Continued)

10.5: D – A very inappropriate thing to do

Explanation: You should never share humiliating events about your friends without their permission as you risk hurting their feelings and your friendship.

TYPE I - Answer 11

11.1: D – A very inappropriate thing to do

Explanation: You should never bring home patient-identifiable data unless it is on a password-protected pen drive and you have obtained consent/ethical approval to do so.

11.2: A – A very appropriate thing to do

Explanation: Emailing patient details using NHS-work email addresses is allowed.

11.3: C – Inappropriate, but not awful

Explanation: By saving the Excel sheet onto the NHS computer, you are not breaking patient confidentiality. However, someone else can gain access to the file.

11.4: D – A very inappropriate thing to do

Explanation: You should not email patient-identifiable information using your personal email.

TYPE I - Answer 12

12.1: D – A very inappropriate thing to do

Explanation: This is unacceptable behaviour. You should never shout at your fellow colleagues.

TYPE I - Answer 12 (Continued)

12.2: C – Inappropriate, but not awful

Explanation: Garrett admits he is in the wrong. He is willing to change. However, not telling his team is inappropriate.

12.3: D – A very inappropriate thing to do

Explanation: This is an example of communication failure. Angela will not feel comfortable to approach Garrett in the future, and this is a form of bullying.

12.4: A – A very appropriate thing to do

Explanation: This is a preferable situation: Garrett apologises and makes a change.

12.5: A – A very appropriate thing to do

Explanation: This is the most ideal situation: his team is aware of his mistakes, and he is willing to change.

TYPE I - Answer 13

13.1: D – A very inappropriate thing to do

Explanation: This is a very selfish act. The medical directorate will not be able to find a suitable substitute locum doctor at such short notice, which leaves patients at risk. Even though they are aware of her absence, she should never lie about being sick to get off work.

13.2 A – A very appropriate thing to do

Explanation: Although she has missed the conference, which is not ideal for her, she has acted in the manner that is in the best interest of the patients.

TYPE I - Answer 13 (Continued)

13.3 D – A very inappropriate thing to do

Explanation: This is an extremely selfish act. The medical directorate is unaware of Diana's absence and will not be able to find a suitable substitute locum doctor at such short notice, which leaves patients at risk.

13.4: B – Appropriate, but not ideal

Explanation: Patients are not at risk since Emma agrees to cover Diana's shift. However, this is not ideal as Emma must work an extra on-call shift. It has also placed Emma in a difficult position.

TYPE I - Answer 14

14.1: D – A very inappropriate thing to do

Explanation: It is very rude and unprofessional to interrupt any conversation. It is also extremely unprofessional and inappropriate to confront a patient.

14.2: C – Inappropriate, but not awful

Explanation: This is not very appropriate since Hana is a junior doctor. She must follow the hospital's protocols and discuss the matter with a senior member of the team before directly addressing the patient.

14.3: D – A very inappropriate thing to do

Explanation: It is very rude and unprofessional to interrupt any conversation. Hana must also remember that she is a junior doctor too.

14.4: D – A very inappropriate thing to do

Explanation: As part of the medical team, you should never share events/cases on social media, especially if the person is identifiable.

14.5: A – A very appropriate thing to do

Explanation: Checking on the wellbeing of your colleagues restores humanity.

TYPE I - Answer 15

15.1: D – A very inappropriate thing to do

Explanation: Requesting scans that need discussion with a radiologist normally takes about 30 minutes, depending on the availability of the onsite radiologist. Confronting without asking politely or trying to understand the situation first is frowned upon. Leaving a bad review for Tom is uncalled for as requesting the scans has a higher priority than teaching on the ward. It was out of Tom's control that he missed Caius' teaching.

15.2: D – A very inappropriate thing to do

Explanation: Reporting directly to the consultant without speaking to your fellow colleague first and trying to understand the situation is an example of communication failure.

15.3: A – A very appropriate thing to do

Explanation: This is the preferred situation. Asking politely and offering to help a colleague who is struggling to request radiology scans is a kind gesture. Caius' offer to repeat his teaching at a later date means that Tom won't miss out on the teaching, and this will give Tom an opportunity to provide Caius with feedback.

15.4: D – A very inappropriate thing to do

Explanation: This is very bad practice.

TYPE I - Answer 16

16.1: A – A very appropriate thing to do

Explanation: In the interest of patient safety, making an incident report is appropriate.

16.2: D – A very inappropriate thing to do

Explanation: This is blackmailing/bullying.

TYPE I - Answer 16 (Continued)

16.3: B – Appropriate, but not ideal

Explanation: Reporting to Henry's supervisor may result in Henry being more cautious about his prescriptions, thus ensuring patient safety. However, it is not ideal since it would be better to speak to Henry directly.

16.4: A – A very appropriate thing to do

Explanation: Even though the patient is asymptomatic, Henry should still apologise to the patient and admit his mistakes. An incident report should still be completed to avoid this happening again in the future.

TYPE I - Answer 17

17.1: A – A very appropriate thing to do

Explanation: This is the preferred scenario. By reporting to Occupational Health, Joloff is taking responsibility for his own mistakes and ensuring his own safety.

17.2: A – A very appropriate thing to do

Explanation: Joloff is taking full responsibility for his mistakes.

17.3: D – A very inappropriate thing to do

Explanation: You should not go through any patient's case notes without his/her consent.

17.4: D – A very inappropriate thing to do

Explanation: Joloff is not being responsible for his mistakes and is putting himself at risk of a blood-borne virus infection by not reporting to Occupational Health.

TYPE I - Answer 18

18.1: D – A very inappropriate thing to do

Explanation: You should never go behind your colleague's back and swap patients.

18.2: C – Inappropriate, but not awful

Explanation: Tom should explore Prakash's concerns further and address them with Morris.

18.3: A – A very appropriate thing to do

Explanation: This is the best case scenario because Tom takes the initiative to understand why Prakash is reluctant to have his procedure done by Morris.

18.4: B – Appropriate, but not ideal

Explanation: If a patient feels uncomfortable with his/her doctor, he/she will have to go back onto the waiting list for another doctor to see him/her. It isn't ideal, however, since the patient must now wait.

TYPE I - Answer 19

19.1: D – A very inappropriate thing to do

Explanation: Noah does not know what happened, whether Monet and Cyan were involved, and whether Mr Higgins is telling the truth. Noah should not force them to apologise without the correct knowledge. It is also inappropriate and unprofessional to confront someone.

19.2: A – A very appropriate thing to do

Explanation: This is the preferred scenario. Documentation is important.

19.3: B – Appropriate, but not ideal

Explanation: This is appropriate as the ward consultant is aware of Mr Higgins' concerns. However, it is not ideal as we don't know the indication of the testicular examination and who did it.

TYPE I - Answer 19 (Continued)

19.4: B – Appropriate, but not ideal

Explanation: Patients have the right to file a complaint if they feel that their dignity has been compromised. However, the incident needs to be investigated before it can be escalated and a complaint against the medical students can be filed. Noah needs to find out what truly happened first.

19.5: C – Inappropriate, but not awful

Explanation: While Noah can inform the Dean, he does not know what happened, whether Monet and Cyan were involved, and whether Mr Higgins is telling the truth. Noah needs to find out what truly happened first.

TYPE I - Answer 20

20.1: D – A very inappropriate thing to do

Explanation: It is best to speak to the person directly in a calm manner and privately.

20.2: D – A very inappropriate thing to do

Explanation: This is a form of bullying and gossiping.

20.3: A – A very appropriate thing to do

Explanation: This is the best way to approach Genevieve.

20.4: C – Inappropriate, but not awful

Explanation: It is inappropriate, but not awful, to ignore Genevieve's comments.

20.5: D – A very inappropriate thing to do

Explanation: This is a horrible thing to say and upon which to agree.

TYPE I - Answer 21

21.1: A – A very appropriate thing to do

Explanation: It is best to speak to the person in a calm manner and privately.

21.2: D – A very inappropriate thing to do

Explanation: It is Schofield's responsibility to break the news to Mr Burrows. He shouldn't ask the nurse to do it instead.

21.3: A – A very appropriate thing to do

Explanation: This is the best way to approach Mr Burrows.

21.4: D – A very inappropriate thing to do

Explanation: This is the worst case scenario. Mr Burrows will be furious to find out that he has been discharged from hospital without further explanation. This is irresponsible of Schofield.

TYPE I - Answer 22

22.1: B – Appropriate, but not ideal

Explanation: It is appropriate that Kellen tries to turn the tap off, but it doesn't address the already present pool of water in the corridor.

22.2: D – A very inappropriate thing to do

Explanation: This is a very irresponsible response. The pool of water is a hazard.

22.3: B – Appropriate, but not ideal

Explanation: Although this gives others a warning, it doesn't solve the problem.

TYPE I - Answer 22 (Continued)

22.4: A – A very appropriate thing to do

Explanation: Although he is late to the ward round, Kellen has acted responsibly.

TYPE I - Answer 23

23.1: C – Inappropriate, but not awful

Explanation: He may be too injured to work the shift. However, he shouldn't lie about what happened. He should also seek medical attention.

23.2: D – A very inappropriate thing to do

Explanation: He shouldn't lie about his injuries. This hinders the attending doctor from managing his injuries appropriately.

23.3: D – A very inappropriate thing to do

Explanation: His tweet is out of anger and provocative. Acting in this manner is unprofessional.

23.4: D – A very inappropriate thing to do

Explanation: Sao Feng is working the night shift. It is his responsibility to alert his team that he will be late.

23.5: D – A very inappropriate thing to do

Explanation: Two wrongs don't make a right. Shouting racial slurs in return reflects badly on Sao Feng.

TYPE I - Answer 24

24.1: D – A very inappropriate thing to do

Explanation: It is Jamaluddin's responsibility to stay at home if he still has ongoing symptoms.

24.2: D – A very inappropriate thing to do

Explanation: This is very irresponsible and unethical of Jamaluddin.

24.3: A – A very appropriate thing to do

Explanation: This is the best way to approach the situation.

24.4: D – A very inappropriate thing to do

Explanation: One should never self-medicate with antibiotics.

TYPE I - Answer 25

25.1: B – Appropriate, but not ideal

Explanation: Badrul is able to remain anonymous by reporting the video. However, this does not solve the problem. As the team does not know the cause of it, it is likely to recur.

25.2: D – A very inappropriate thing to do

Explanation: Confronting and shouting at your colleagues is unprofessional.

25.3: D – A very inappropriate thing to do

Explanation: This is an unethical and irresponsible response. Badrul should not publicly humiliate his fellow colleagues.

25.4: A – A very appropriate thing to do

Explanation: The best way is to speak to the group involved directly in a private setting.

TYPE I - Answer 26

26.1: D – A very inappropriate thing to do

Explanation: They should be honest and report the diamond ring. It is highly unethical to bring home items from the dissection room.

26.2: A – A very appropriate thing to do

Explanation: This is the best way to approach the situation as it demonstrates honesty. The supervisor is also the best person to whom to speak.

26.3: D – A very inappropriate thing to do

Explanation: This response is unethical and irresponsible. One should never bring items home from the dissection room, let alone sell them.

TYPE I - Answer 27

27.1: D – A very inappropriate thing to do

Explanation: Dove should not prioritise Ashton over other patients.

27.2: A – A very appropriate thing to do

Explanation: This is the responsible way to approach the situation. She should continue seeing patients according to the waiting list.

27.3: D – A very inappropriate thing to do

Explanation: Dove should not ask her colleague to prioritise Ashton over other patients.

27.4: D – A very inappropriate thing to do

Explanation: This breaches patient confidentiality.

TYPE I - Answer 28

28.1: A – A very appropriate thing to do

Explanation: It is best to speak to the person directly in a calm manner and privately. Rory also proceeds to ask for advice on how to improve.

28.2: D – A very inappropriate thing to do

Explanation: This is a form of bullying and gossiping.

28.3: D – A very inappropriate thing to do

Explanation: This is unprofessional of Rory.

28.4: A – A very appropriate thing to do

Explanation: By reflecting on her performance, Rory learns to understand and accept feedback constructively. It also allows her to improve on targeted interpersonal skills.

TYPE I - Answer 29

29.1: A – A very appropriate thing to do

Explanation: Making an effort to calm the baby is ideal. This will also calm the mother down and allow Seto to perform his task with minimal distraction.

29.2: D – A very inappropriate thing to do

Explanation: This is irresponsible of Seto. He should not handover the job just because it is inconvenient to him.

29.3: A – A very appropriate thing to do

Explanation: This is the best way to approach the situation.

TYPE I - Answer 29 (Continued)

29.4: D – A very inappropriate thing to do

Explanation: Although he completes the task, both the baby and mother are traumatised by the situation.

TYPE I - Answer 30

30.1: D – A very inappropriate thing to do

Explanation: This is unprofessional of Leia.

30.2: A – A very appropriate thing to do

Explanation: This is the best way to approach the situation.

30.3: D – A very inappropriate thing to do

Explanation: Framing her colleague is an outrageous thing to do. She should also not help a convict escape from jail.

30.4: D – A very inappropriate thing to do

Explanation: It is unethical and unprofessional of Leia to prescribe an overdose of insulin, despite stopping Immanuel escaping from prison.

TYPE I - Answer 31

31.1: B – Appropriate, but not ideal

Explanation: Dr Tancrady has a terrible history with the associated patient. If she is unable to treat the patient without emotional attachment, it is responsible of her to ask for help from her colleague. However, this is not ideal since her colleague now has an additional patient for whom to care.

TYPE I - Answer 31 (Continued)

31.2: D – A very inappropriate thing to do

Explanation: This is irresponsible and unethical of Dr Tancrady.

31.3: D – A very inappropriate thing to do

Explanation: This approach is outrageous. You should never investigate a patient's private details, let alone use them to blackmail him/her.

31.4: A – A very appropriate thing to do

Explanation: As a doctor, Dr Tancrady should treat all patients equally.

TYPE I - Answer 32

32.1: B – Appropriate, but not ideal

Explanation: It is appropriate that Sook Han politely rejects Lynn's offer. However, we do not know Lynn's past medical history. Reporting Lynn without further exploring the reasons why she takes the anxiolytic tablet is not ideal.

32.2: D – A very inappropriate thing to do

Explanation: Sook Han should not accept medications such as anxiolytic tablets from others without a prescription from her GP. Self-medicating is not good practice.

32.3: D – A very inappropriate thing to do

Explanation: It is possible that Lynn is addicted to the medication. However, for Sook Han to assume that this is the case without further questioning is a very inappropriate thing to do.

TYPE I - Answer 32 (Continued)

32.4: D – A very inappropriate thing to do

Explanation: It is bad practice to self-medicate with anxiolytic tablets. Common medications such as Paracetamol, Ibuprofen and Buscopan are acceptable tablets that can be used to self-medicate. These medications are usually available to buy over-the-counter (OTC) at a local pharmacy.

TYPE I - Answer 33

33.1: D – A very inappropriate thing to do

Explanation: Shouting at your colleagues is never the right thing to do. Even though Dr Winston is in the wrong, David should not retaliate by shouting and storming off the ward. Two wrongs don't make a right.

33.2: B – Appropriate, but not ideal

Explanation: Although it is David's right to file a complaint against Dr Winston, it is best for David to approach Dr Winston to try and iron things out in a calm and private manner first.

33.3: A – A very appropriate thing to do

Explanation: This is a sensible way for David to respond. It is good practice to deal with conflicts in a calm and polite manner.

33.4: D – A very inappropriate thing to do

Explanation: It is not healthy to hold grudges against fellow colleagues. Writing and publicising conflicts in a public newspaper article is frowned upon.

TYPE I - Answer 34

34.1: D – A very inappropriate thing to do

Explanation: This is a form of bribery. Annual reviews should be done in a professional setting.

34.2: C – Inappropriate, but not awful

Explanation: To a certain extent, this could be a form of bribery. However, recognising one's hard work in the form of a small gift is not awful.

34.3: A – A very appropriate thing to do

Explanation: Jeevaraja acknowledges that Mr Babatunde is performing his annual review and shows interest in looking forward to it.

34.4: D – A very inappropriate thing to do

Explanation: This is bad practice. You should never ask for another colleague's log in details to complete a review for yourself, regardless of how busy your colleague is.

TYPE I - Answer 35

35.1: A – A very appropriate thing to do

Explanation: Medical schools have strict etiquette with house visits. If medical students ever find themselves in a vulnerable and compromised situation, they should leave the situation immediately and report it.

35.2: D – A very inappropriate thing to do

Explanation: If, as a medical student on a house visit, you feel forced to do something with which you are uncomfortable, you should not follow through with it. The medical school is on your side, and there are legal firms such as the MDU (Medical Defence Union) and the MPS (Medical Protection Society) that support medical student claims.

TYPE I - Answer 35 (Continued)

35.3: A – A very appropriate thing to do

Explanation: Calling the police when you feel threatened during house visits is the appropriate thing to do.

TYPE I - Answer 36

36.1: D – A very inappropriate thing to do

Explanation: If you have witnessed an act of sexual abuse between staff or patients, you should report it.

36.2: D – A very inappropriate thing to do

Explanation: It is very inappropriate and highly unprofessional to confront and threaten someone.

36.3: D – A very inappropriate thing to do

Explanation: Although Quason asks his friends to keep the incident strictly confidential and they are his close friends, he has breached patient confidentiality, and this is not the appropriate manner in which to deal with the situation.

36.4: C – Inappropriate, but not awful

Explanation: This is inappropriate since one should not confront another individual. In addition, while Quason is correct to report Jean-Pierre to the staff manager, it is not his place to inform the police. This should be done by a senior member of the team.

TYPE I - Answer 37

37.1: B – Appropriate, but not ideal

Explanation: Although this is an appropriate way of trying to contact someone whom you suspect is a victim of domestic abuse, it is always best to approach the person privately.

37.2: D – A very inappropriate thing to do

Explanation: Charles should not assume that Slavic is the cause of Nadiah's bruises. Making a report hastily without further investigation is a very inappropriate thing to do.

37.3: A – A very appropriate thing to do

Explanation: This is the right thing to do. Charles first explores her bruises privately and then encourages her to make a report.

37.4: D – A very inappropriate thing to do

Explanation: There could be multiple reasons behind Nadiah's bruises. It is wrong of Charles to assume that this is the result of domestic abuse. It is very inappropriate to confront and threaten Slavic.

TYPE I - Answer 38

38.1: A – A very appropriate thing to do

Explanation: Approaching Asha and offering her a sanitary pad is a kind and helpful act.

38.2: D – A very inappropriate thing to do

Explanation: Speaking loudly will make Asha self-conscious and embarrassed.

TYPE I - Answer 38 (Continued)

38.3: D – A very inappropriate thing to do

Explanation: Asha may find that her privacy has been intruded by Sarah taking a photo of her blood-stained trousers without her permission.

38.4: D – A very inappropriate thing to do

Explanation: This is unacceptable behaviour from Sarah. It shows a lack of empathy, and it is a form of bullying.

TYPE I - Answer 39

39.1: C – Inappropriate, but not awful

Explanation: As the team leader, Timothy should be the one to break the news to Ruru and Mia if they are slacking in their work. This is inappropriate, but it is not awful if Henry approaching Ruru and Mia means that the work gets done.

39.2: B – Appropriate, but not ideal

Explanation: Timothy is taking the blame for the lack of commitment from his colleagues. This response is appropriate but not ideal as it does not solve the problem.

39.3: D – A very inappropriate thing to do

Explanation: This creates false gossip amongst colleagues, and it is unhealthy work ethic.

39.4: A – A very appropriate thing to do

Explanation: Calling for a group meeting to discuss everyone's progress is the appropriate thing to do.

TYPE I - Answer 40

40.1: D – A very inappropriate thing to do

Explanation: A doctor working on a visa should never violate the number of working hours allowed. This is illegal practice.

40.2: D – A very inappropriate thing to do

Explanation: This is unethical. One should never steal from the NHS, let alone sell stolen items online for one's own profit.

40.3: B – Appropriate, but not ideal

Explanation: Signing up for extra locum shifts whilst still keeping to the number of working hours allowed by his visa is appropriate. However, Harikrishna will have to sacrifice time spent with his family, which is not ideal.

40.4: D – A very inappropriate thing to do

Explanation: Although some procedures and services are offered privately in the NHS, doing so without the knowledge of the hospital's management team is a very inappropriate thing to do.

TYPE II - Answer 1

1.1: A – Very important

Explanation: For any patient who has had an unwitnessed fall, you should always consider the possibility that he/she has hit his/her head. You should do a full set of neurological observations to look for any signs that the patient may have a brain haemorrhage. This is very important to consider as it warrants further imaging of the head and changes your management plan.

1.2: C – Of minor importance

Explanation: The language barrier could be a challenge for the patient. Although he is being verbally abusive to the staff nurses, the patient's safety comes first which, in this instance, is to help him off the ground and into his bed. As a responsible doctor, Chiamaka should speak to the staff later about how they're feeling and if they need any remediation.

1.3: C – Of minor importance

Explanation: It is important to have a language translator on board when a patient does not speak English. However, in an acute situation, this would be at the bottom of your list of priorities. You should always rule out all possibilities of the patient hitting his/her head first, then get the patient into a position of safety, followed by calling for a translator.

1.4: A – Very important

Explanation: As a junior doctor, it is important to recognise your limitations and the need to call for senior help, especially if you're on the ward alone and when you're dealing with an acute situation.

1.5: B – Important

Explanation: Understanding the cause of the patient's fall is important to prevent other patients from falling. However, it is not Chiamaka's top priority at the moment.

TYPE II - Answer 2

2.1: D – Not important at all

Explanation: In a situation as such in which Gaël is not acting responsibly, it is important to put aside his reputation as a junior doctor. This is because patients would be at risk if he were to go to work the following morning in a drunken state.

2.2: A – Very important

Explanation: Being a responsible doctor and friend, Lyndon should consider the risk on the patients' safety if his colleague goes to work drunk.

2.3: C – Of minor importance

Explanation: Although Gaël's reasons are personal, a responsible thing to do is to take time off work if he is not emotionally stable.

2.4: D – Not important at all

Explanation: Although this is a recurrent habit of Gaël, Lyndon should act responsibly and raise the issue with his supervisor.

2.5: D – Not important at all

Explanation: This shouldn't be a reason for Lyndon to not notify Gaël's supervisor as his act of negligence shouldn't be at the expense of his team members.

2.6: D – Not important at all

Explanation: While Lyndon might be tired, he could simply send an email to Gaël's supervisor; this would take only a few minutes. It is the responsible thing to do as a colleague and a friend.

TYPE II - Answer 3

3.1: D – Not important at all

Explanation: You should always act in the best interest of the patient. In this case, the child is unable to speak for himself. The GP is most likely to have missed the bruise rather than ignored it. We all have a part to play.

3.2: A – Very important

Explanation: It is very important to raise his concerns with the GP if he thinks the bruise is a result of physical abuse.

3.3: D – Not important at all

Explanation: As the bruise is in such an odd location (neck and shoulder), it is unlikely to be self-inflicted. Whether the mother looks attentive or not, you should always keep a look out for signs of abuse in children as they are less likely to speak for themselves. You should never let a child leave your clinic if you suspect child abuse. Once he/she leaves, he/she is very unlikely to come back.

3.4: D – Not important at all

Explanation: The location of the bruise would suggest that it is not self-inflicted. Regardless, all bruises warrant further investigation and history-taking.

3.5: D – Not important at all

Explanation: It is wrong to assume that the GP had seen the bruise and dismissed it. GPs are human beings too - they sometimes make mistakes and miss signs. Never assume red flag signs were seen and dismissed.

TYPE II - Answer 4

4.1: D – Not important at all

Explanation: It is most likely that the consultant and Mustafa missed the notice that the patient is allergic to penicillin. As the prescriber, it is Ben Stew's duty to check the patient's medication allergy before prescribing any medication. It is everyone's duty to pick up prescribing errors and act on them.

4.2: D – Not important at all

Explanation: Mustafa has most likely made a mistake in prescribing a penicillin-based antibiotic. Regardless of how long Mustafa has been working on the ward, it is impossible to remember every patient's medication allergy.

4.3: D – Not important at all

Explanation: As soon as you've picked up that the antibiotic prescribed is not suitable for the patient, approach the doctor who prescribed it to ask for an alternative. It is imperative that the patient receives the right antibiotic. It'll only take you a couple of minutes to prescribe a different antibiotic.

4.4: D – Not important at all

Explanation: Yes, they may be upset with you interrupting, but they will thank you for highlighting the penicillin allergy. You should always act in the best interest of the patient.

4.5: D – Not important at all

Explanation: It is everyone's duty to act in the best interest of the patient.

TYPE II - Answer 5

5.1: C – Of minor importance

Explanation: Although it is not the best way to manage the situation, Killian has tried to approach Caru. Since this isn't helping, the next best step is to speak to her supervisor.

5.2: B – Important

Explanation: Caru needs extra support in order to treat patients effectively and efficiently. It is important to consider that there might be a reason for which Caru has not spoken to anyone about her difficulty.

5.3: A – Very important

Explanation: You should always put patients' care and safety first. If Killian has doubts that Caru's difficulty will affect her patients, then he has every right to speak to someone more senior about this.

5.4: D – Not important at all

Explanation: It is not Killian's responsibility to check and correct Caru's work, and he should not do this without her knowledge. It is important to remember that Killian is also a junior doctor, and it is not his role to correct Caru.

TYPE II - Answer 6

6.1: D – Not important at all

Explanation: You should never accept gifts from patients, regardless whether it is unknown to others. However, small gifts such as a 'thank you' card or chocolates to share with the team are acceptable.

6.2: D – Not important at all

Explanation: It is part of a doctor's duty to serve patients without expecting anything in return.

TYPE II - Answer 6 (Continued)

6.3: C – Of minor importance

Explanation: Although it may upset the patient, Laskna could suggest other ways for the patient to show appreciation (e.g., a card or donating to charity).

6.4: D – Not important at all

Explanation: Just because it is common practice does not mean you should do it.

TYPE II - Answer 7

7.1: D – Not important at all

Explanation: Benny isn't qualified to do a lumbar puncture. The most responsible thing to do in this situation is to call for a senior doctor on the team to perform the lumbar puncture.

7.2: D – Not important at all

Explanation: If all the doctors on the team, including Samuel, are busy, the next best person to contact would be the on-call doctor.

7.3: D – Not important at all

Explanation: Benny might have watched a lumbar puncture being performed, but he is definitely not competent enough to perform the procedure himself.

7.4: D – Not important at all

Explanation: Benny should act in the patient's best interest. It is not safe for him to do the lumbar puncture.

TYPE II - Answer 8

8.1: D – Not important at all

Explanation: It doesn't matter that no one else on the team has noticed Joffrey's late attendance to work. It is Aisling's responsibility as a colleague to act on it.

8.2: A – Very important

Explanation: Being late to placement is frowned upon.

8.3: C – Of minor importance

Explanation: Yes, Joffrey may be upset with Aisling, but it is in his best interest.

8.4: D – Not important at all

Explanation: Just because it is common practice does not mean that it is the right thing to do. Instead, Aisling should take the initiative to change the practice.

TYPE II - Answer 9

9.1: D – Not important at all

Explanation: You should always disclose a conflict of interest if you have a sibling/relative/close friend being interviewed by yourself/your team.

9.2: D – Not important at all

Explanation: Taeyang's previous rejections shouldn't prevent Yuzu from doing the right thing.

9.3: D – Not important at all

Explanation: It is a conflict of interest to interview students that year if your brother is applying to that university.

9.4: D – Not important at all

Explanation: Yuzu can help Taeyang prepare for his interview without staying on the panel.

TYPE II - Answer 10

10.1: D – Not important at all

Explanation: Milo's duty as a junior doctor is to not share patient-identifiable information over email. Therefore, it doesn't matter if no one else knows about the email. He shouldn't respond to it.

10.2: D – Not important at all

Explanation: It is not Milo's duty to place judgement over Habib's social history. It shouldn't change the way he responds in regards to patient confidentiality.

10.3: A – Very important

Explanation: That Milo feels threatened will influence how he behaves, and he must look after all of his patients. He should report the suspicious email to the hospital's IT department so that they can warn other staff about it and block the sender from sending future emails.

10.4: D – Not important at all

Explanation: The very reason that the sender has asked to not involve the police signifies that the sender is partaking in illegal activity. This shouldn't prevent Milo from contacting hospital security if he feels threatened.

10.5: D – Not important at all

Explanation: This shouldn't stop Milo from doing the right thing.

TYPE II - Answer 11

11.1: A – Very important

Explanation: The fact that Amornsri is struggling on the ward and has received multiple complaints from patients shows that she isn't doing her job well. Perhaps speaking to Amornsri first would be ideal. If necessary, Kurt could then speak to Amornsri's educational supervisor regarding ways to help her improve.

TYPE II - Answer 11 (Continued)

11.2: C – Of minor importance

Explanation: Yes, she may be upset initially. However, this shouldn't prevent Kurt from speaking to Amornsri's educational supervisor if that means Amornsri receives the additional support that she needs.

11.3: C – Of minor importance

Explanation: Amornsri may be going through an emotionally difficult time, but Kurt should still speak to her supervisor. It is also important to remember that Amornsri has been shouted at on the ward by a patient before.

11.4: D – Not important at all

Explanation: Kurt's feelings are not the focus here. Amornsri and the patients are most important.

11.5: D – Not important at all

Explanation: The length of time that Amornsri has worked on the ward is not important. What is important is that she needs help.

TYPE II - Answer 12

12.1: D – Not important at all

Explanation: This shouldn't stop Shelby from reaching out to the consultant. Patient care and safety are at risk because of Avery's mistakes.

12.2: D – Not important at all

Explanation: Even though no patients have been affected by Avery's mistakes, this shouldn't stop Shelby from rectifying the situation.

12.3: D – Not important at all

Explanation: Avery might be tired and trying hard, but the safety of the patients is ultimately compromised if she is making mistakes.

TYPE II - Answer 12 (Continued)

12.4: C – Of minor importance

Explanation: Yes, there is a possibility that the consultant will use this against Avery, but that shouldn't stop Shelby from highlighting it to the consultant if she feels Avery's mistakes will affect patient safety and care.

TYPE II - Answer 13

13.1: B – Important

Explanation: While samples do get lost in the system sometimes, Seren is confident that she took a crossmatch sample from Mr Groff. If she raises the concern with the blood bank, it is possible that they will look again and might be able to find it. That is the reason for which this is important.

13.2: A – Very important

Explanation: Mr Groff needs blood urgently. In emergency situations when a crossmatch hasn't been done, patients will receive O negative blood in the mean time. This has to be ordered from the blood bank.

13.3: D – Not important at all

Explanation: This shouldn't be taken into consideration when deciding what to do next. Mistakes do happen.

13.4: D – Not important at all

Explanation: There is a possibility of the consultant being frustrated. However, this shouldn't be taken into consideration in the process of ordering blood.

TYPE II - Answer 14

14.1: C – Of minor importance

Explanation: Codeine is a controlled drug, and doctors must be careful about the amount of tablets prescribed on discharge. In this scenario, the patient's request sounds genuine. If the patient needs a repeat prescription, the GP will reassess the need for Codeine.

14.2: B – Important

Explanation: If Mrs Dolby hasn't had any Codeine in the past three days, it shows that she perhaps doesn't require it. It is important to explain to patients that Codeine is a controlled drug and should not be prescribed as a regular medication, unless indicated. Since Mrs Dolby hasn't had Codeine in the last three days, it doesn't appear that she needs any at present. However, if her pain returns in the near future, she should approach her GP to review the need for Codeine.

14.3: D – Not important at all

Explanation: This shouldn't affect Zack's decision of whether to prescribe Codeine or not.

14.4: A – Very important

Explanation: Zack must explain to Mrs Dolby that, if the Codeine is for her husband's arthritis, he should seek advice from his GP.

TYPE II - Answer 15

15.1: D – Not important at all

Explanation: This shouldn't stop Bennett from telling the team what Crystal has confided in him. It is unsafe to discharge a patient if he/she is not back to his/her normal baseline.

TYPE II - Answer 15 (Continued)

15.2: A – Very important

Explanation: There is a possibility that Crystal might not know the severity of her condition and is putting herself at risk. Therefore, Bennett should break Crystal's promise as it is in her best interest.

15.3: C – Of minor importance

Explanation: Regardless of whether Crystal is adamant to leave the hospital, Bennett should let the team know that Crystal is still experiencing pain and is not back to her usual self.

15.4: D – Not important at all

Explanation: Yes, Crystal may be upset and lose confidence in Bennett but this should not be taken into consideration when deciding how to respond to the situation.

TYPE II - Answer 16

16.1: D – Not important at all

Explanation: It doesn't matter if she hasn't undergone her ALS training. The earlier chest compressions are started, the higher the chance of survival.

16.2: A – Very important

Explanation: There is no one else available to perform chest compressions at this moment.

16.3: B – Important

Explanation: Since Adele knows what to do in this situation, it is important that she starts chest compressions immediately.

TYPE II - Answer 16 (Continued)

16.4: C – Of minor importance

Explanation: It is of minor importance that the relative is asking for a doctor. The earlier chest compressions are started, the higher the chance of the patient surviving.

TYPE II - Answer 17

17.1: A – Very important

Explanation: It is very important to notify the DVLA about Melor's frequent epileptic history and especially the fact that she is still driving. She is putting others, and herself, in danger.

17.2: D – Not important at all

Explanation: This should not affect Aber's decision when deciding whether to report Melor's recent epileptic attacks to her supervisor or GP.

17.3: A – Very important

Explanation: Additional support will be very helpful for Melor.

17.4: D – Not important at all

Explanation: This should not stop Aber from reporting Melor's recent epileptic attacks to her supervisor or GP.

TYPE II - Answer 18

18.1: C – Of minor importance

Explanation: There might be a reason for which Mr Agarwal needs to adapt current guidelines. For example, certain guidelines might not be relevant in that particular community. Rebecca is correct to seek advice from Mr Agarwal regarding this, but she should not dismiss his competence.

TYPE II - Answer 18 (Continued)

18.2: D – Not important at all

Explanation: We all play a part in the healthcare system. Despite Rebecca being a medical student, both Rebecca and Mr Agarwal can learn from each other by having a simple discussion about Mr Agarwal's choice of treatment and current guidelines.

18.3: D – Not important at all

Explanation: This shouldn't prevent Rebecca from asking Mr Agarwal questions regarding his decisions on treatment plans.

18.4: D – Not important at all

Explanation: This shouldn't prevent Rebecca from asking Mr Agarwal questions regarding his medical advice.

TYPE II - Answer 19

19.1: D – Not important at all

Explanation: It is not good practice to promote private services in NHS clinics.

19.2: C – Of minor importance

Explanation: Although Mrs Wakowski gives good medical advice, she should not advertise her private services in an NHS setting.

19.3: C – Of minor importance

Explanation: There are ways to approach Mrs Wakowski about advertising her private practice in the NHS without affecting their professional relationship. However, this shouldn't stop Pamela from approaching Mrs Wakowski.

19.4: D – Not important at all

Explanation: It is not important that Mrs Wakowski is Pamela's educational supervisor; private practice shouldn't be encouraged.

TYPE II - Answer 20

20.1: D – Not important at all

Explanation: Just because it is common practice does not make it right. You should always wash your hands between seeing patients.

20.2: A – Very important

Explanation: It is very important to wash your hands between seeing patients, especially if the majority of patients are admitted with diarrhoea and vomiting. Patients are hosts of infections. Not washing your hands would mean transferring viruses from one patient to another.

20.3: D – Not important at all

Explanation: Hand washing will take less than a minute. This should not stop Samuel from doing it for fear of increased workload.

20.4: D – Not important at all

Explanation: Both Ponnuswammy and Samuel are in the wrong for not washing their hands and not wearing gloves when taking blood from patients.

20.5: D – Not important at all

Explanation: Samuel shouldn't use this as an excuse to not wash his hands.

TYPE II - Answer 21

21.1: A – Very important

Explanation: If someone else has stolen Adam's badge, he/she will have access to all the wards in the hospital, risking staff and patient safety.

21.2: A – Very important

Explanation: This is very dangerous. He should call IT and report a lost badge.

TYPE II - Answer 21 (Continued)

21.3: D – Not important at all

Explanation: Even though he managed to find his badge at home in the past, it should not prevent him from reporting a lost ID badge now.

21.4: C – Of minor importance

Explanation: He will be very lucky if an honest person found his badge and reported it. He should still report a missing badge himself.

21.5: D – Not important at all

Explanation: Even though it may be his last week working in the hospital, it is still his responsibility to report a missing ID badge.

TYPE II - Answer 22

22.1: C – Of minor importance

Explanation: Conway should make sure that he has all the information he needs before approaching the patient.

22.2: A – Very important

Explanation: As Conway was not involved in the MDT discussion and is unsure of the reasons behind the conclusion, he should gather all of the information he needs before approaching the patient.

22.3: A – Very important

Explanation: Conway should take note of the CT report in preparation for Mr Proctor's potential questions.

22.4: C – Of minor importance

Explanation: From a patient's point of view, Mr Proctor has been kept in the dark for quite some time. Conway should take this into consideration, but it is of minor importance.

TYPE II - Answer 23

23.1: D – Not important at all

Explanation: Smoking may be a coping mechanism for Mr Pring. However, Dr Katya should advise against it. There are other ways to cope with stress.

23.2: A – Very important

Explanation: This is a serious matter. Smoking will hinder Mr Pring's recovery. It is very important for Dr Katya to take this into consideration.

23.3: C – Of minor importance

Explanation: Despite exhausting all smoking cessation techniques, Dr Katya should still encourage Mr Pring to stop smoking. She could revisit some of the options previously offered.

23.4: D – Not important at all

Explanation: Patients do get frustrated sometimes. However, this shouldn't prevent Dr Katya from encouraging Mr Pring to stop smoking.

TYPE II - Answer 24

24.1: D – Not important at all

Explanation: It doesn't matter whether there is anyone around. She still shouldn't take hospital items home for self-use.

24.2: D – Not important at all

Explanation: Similar to the question above, she should not take home hospital items for self-use.

24.3: D – Not important at all

Explanation: It was unethical and unprofessional of Susan to do that, but that doesn't mean it is appropriate for Victoria to do the same.

TYPE II - Answer 24 (Continued)

24.4: D – Not important at all

Explanation: This should not cloud her judgement on what is right and wrong.

TYPE II - Answer 25

25.1: A – Very important

Explanation: The child is lost, afraid and vulnerable; he needs help. A crying child will also contribute to the chaotic environment that is already present in the Emergency Department.

25.2: A – Very important

Explanation: Yes, this is very important. The safety of the patient is Ara's utmost priority.

25.3: B – Important

Explanation: Although hospitals are usually well-secured locations, the Emergency Department is accessible by the public. The child cannot be left alone, especially as there seems to be a higher risk to children in this area.

25.4: D – Not important at all

Explanation: Even though it can be a challenge to speak to the child, she should still take action as his safety is at risk.

25.5: D – Not important at all

Explanation: Regardless of whether the child is related to the patient, he should not be in the patient's cubicle. This is because, if the child is related to the patient, it would be traumatising for him to watch his parent in pain and surrounded by lots of staff. On the other hand, if the child is unrelated to the patient, all the more it is wrong for the child to be in the patient's cubicle.

TYPE II - Answer 26

26.1: D – Not important at all

Explanation: If he is unsure of how to manage an acute patient, he should escalate and call for help.

26.2: D – Not important at all

Explanation: In an acute situation, this should be the last thing about which he should be concerned. The patient is his top priority.

26.3: A – Very important

Explanation: The patient being unresponsive should alert him to start doing basic examinations. Even though he may not remember the exact management, he should start doing a basic assessment of the patient (examining the patient's airway, breathing, chest, etc.). It is also quick and easy to look at the patient's notes to check for the patient's resuscitation status.

26.4: A – Very important

Explanation: Recognising one's own limitations is vital. If he doesn't recall anything from his ALS training, he should seek help immediately and carry out basic examinations whilst waiting for help to arrive.

TYPE II - Answer 27

27.1: A – Very important

Explanation: Whilst it is important to keep patients safe, it is also important to keep doctors safe too.

27.2: A – Very important

Explanation: This is a tricky situation. Emmett could quickly ask one of the staff members on the ward to look for an N95 mask from a different ward while he goes through the patient's case notes.

TYPE II - Answer 27 (Continued)

27.3: B – Important

Explanation: Although Emmett may be at high risk of developing severe COVID symptoms given his history, he has chosen to continue working. Healthcare workers have a choice to not work in a suspected COVID area if they feel they are at increased risk due to a medical condition such as asthma. However, it is important to consider this as the ward is not well stocked.

27.4: D – Not important at all

Explanation: This shouldn't be taken into consideration. Although he has recovered from Coronavirus, he is susceptible to a re-infection.

27.5: D – Not important at all

Explanation: This shouldn't be taken into consideration. Both his and the patient's safety are his top priorities.

TYPE II - Answer 28

28.1: C – Of minor importance

Explanation: If the family could provide a mobile phone for Selah, the ward staff will be able to use it for her to contact her family.

28.2: A – Very important

Explanation: As much as Marc would like to help patients, unfortunately lending Selah his phone is against recommended infection control guidelines.

28.3: C – Of minor importance

Explanation: As doctors, we understand and empathise that families are affected by strict isolation guidelines and are not able to visit loved ones in hospital. However, if the patient has his/her own mobile device, he/she will be able to use it to contact his/her family.

TYPE II - Answer 28 (Continued)

28.4: C – Of minor importance

Explanation: Similar to the answer in 28.3.

TYPE II - Answer 29

29.1: C – Of minor importance

Explanation: Llewellyn is in the middle of a high-risk operation. It would be unethical and irresponsible of him to leave the operation, even though his wife is about to deliver his firstborn son.

29.2: A – Very important

Explanation: It is very important to consider that he is in the middle of a high-risk operation. This is his current top priority.

29.3: A – Very important

Explanation: Acknowledging and understanding fellow team members' competencies is vital, especially when it comes to deciding whether they are able to complete operations unassisted.

29.4: C – Of minor importance

Explanation: On occasions, medical professionals must choose between work and family. It is a decision that is hard to make. Sometimes sacrifices have to be made.

TYPE II - Answer 30

30.1: D – Not important at all

Explanation: Although Badr and Kofi are competing for the same surgical training post, this shouldn't stop Badr from reporting Kofi.

30.2: D – Not important at all

Explanation: Kofi may be publicly embarrassed if Badr reports him, but Kofi should have anticipated the possibility of this occurring.

30.3: D – Not important at all

Explanation: This is not important at all. Badr should still do the right thing, regardless of whether he loses his long-term friendship with Kofi.

30.4: D – Not important at all

Explanation: Although Kofi saved Badr's daughter's life from a drowning incident a month ago, it should not stop Badr from reporting Kofi.

30.5: D – Not important at all

Explanation: This is an expected outcome for Kofi if he gets caught. However, he was willing to take the risk.

TYPE II - Answer 31

31.1: C – Of minor importance

Explanation: The patient has lost a lot of blood and requires immediate attention. In an ideal world, observing a procedure is not sufficient to allow one to perform it. However, this patient needs surgery now.

TYPE II - Answer 31 (Continued)

31.2: B – Important

Explanation: This is important to consider as the on-call consultant is arriving only in 40 minutes. It is imperative that Steve seeks help from someone more senior than him, perhaps the senior surgical registrar on-call.

31.3: C – Of minor importance

Explanation: It is good practice to be able to judge the urgency of an operation. However, he should not be the one performing the surgery as he is not trained to do so.

31.4: A – Very important

Explanation: This is an extremely important consideration. Given that Steve has never performed this procedure, he should not be the one performing it now. He should bleep the senior surgical registrar on-call.

TYPE II - Answer 32

32.1: B – Important

Explanation: It is important for Beatrice to consider the impact of Juan Manuel's paralysis on his life.

32.2: C – Of minor importance

Explanation: It is Beatrice's duty (do no harm) to not encourage Juan Manuel.

32.3: C – Of minor importance

Explanation: Beatrice may have exhausted all possible options to help Juan Manuel cope with his current disability. Beatrice could perhaps review the options available to help him.

TYPE II - Answer 32 (Continued)

32.4: A – Very important

Explanation: This is very important for Beatrice to consider. Juan Manuel is only 27 years old. Although things may seem frustrating now as Juan Manuel is still trying to adjust to his new "life", there is a possibility that he will accept his disability and start anew.

TYPE II - Answer 33

33.1: A – Very important

Explanation: If a decision is to be made by a child who is less than 16 years old, it is important to assess whether the child is Gillick competent by using the Fraser guidelines. Makiko is able to consider, understand and communicate the risks and side effects of the COCP to Nakupenda.

33.2: B – Important

Explanation: It is good practice to explore the age and persona of the patient's sexual partner. If Makiko's boyfriend was an adult in his 20s, further investigation should be made to the nature of their relationship and how they met.

33.3: C – Of minor importance

Explanation: It is good practice to involve parents, especially since Makiko and her boyfriend are sexually active. However, given that she is 15 years old and demonstrates maturity and Gillick competence, it is of minor importance.

33.4: A – Very important

Explanation: This is very important for Nakupenda to consider. Makiko is seeking help from Nakupenda for contraception. She has also expressed maturity and understanding of the risks and benefits of the COCP. Without the COCP, Makiko is at risk of an unwanted pregnancy, which may lead to more problems.

TYPE II - Answer 33 (Continued)

Fraser guidelines
The Fraser guidelines are used to assess if a patient below 16 years of age is competent to consent to treatment (Gillick competent), for example with respect to contraception.

The following points should be fulfilled:

- the young person understands the professional's advice.
- the young person cannot be persuaded to inform his/her parents or allow the professional to contact them on his/her behalf.
- the young person is likely to begin, or continue having, sexual intercourse with or without contraceptive treatment.
- unless the young person receives contraceptive treatment, physical or mental health, or both, is likely to suffer.
- the young person's best interests require him/her to receive advice or treatment with or without parental consent.

TYPE II - Answer 34

34.1: C – Of minor importance

Explanation: This is an emergency, and the child having a blood transfusion is life-saving. In this situation, it is of minor importance that he is a Jehovah's Witness.

34.2: A – Very important

Explanation: This is very important to consider. The child might die if he does not receive a blood transfusion immediately. Hence, it is a life-saving procedure.

34.3: D – Not important at all

Explanation: In a life-saving situation, it is not compulsory for the child or the parents to consent. The doctor also has the authority to overrule the parents in this situation; Imogen is able to administer a blood transfusion since it is in the patient's best interests.

TYPE II - Answer 34 (Continued)

34.4: A – Very important

Explanation: If the child is in an unconscious state, he is haemodynamically unstable. Hence, having the blood transfusion is a life-saving procedure.

TYPE II - Answer 35

35.1: A – Very important

Explanation: It is very important for Catrina to consider whether Mr Mason has the capacity to make a decision. If Mr Mason proves to not have capacity via the Mental Capacity Act, then Catrina will have to act in the patient's best interest. If Mr Mason is proven to have capacity, regardless of whether his decision is not considered acceptable, Catrina will need to respect Mr Mason's decision to not have surgery.

35.2: A – Very important

Explanation: Catrina does not have Mr Mason's consent to perform the surgery. If Mr Mason is deemed to have capacity, Catrina has to respect Mr Mason's decision, even though it is not in his best interest.

35.3: A – Very important

Explanation: It is Catrina's duty to ensure that Mr Mason understands the benefits of having surgery. This could involve a translator or using simple non-scientific terms.

35.4: D – Not important at all

Explanation: Patients sometimes make decisions with which doctors do not agree. However, if the patient is competent and is deemed to have capacity, his/her autonomy must be respected.

List of Sources Used in the Exercises in the Verbal Reasoning Section

The articles and literary passages used in this book are from the following academic, journalistic and online sources. They are thus copyrighted to the original source in its entirety. We gratefully acknowledge each and every source, and, once again, highlight that the original source retains the full copyright.

EXERCISE	NAME OF SOURCE	LINK
1	*Science Daily*	*https://www.sciencedaily.com/releases/2019/04/190424153711.htm*
2	*Coleg Gwent*	*https://www.coleggwent.ac.uk/learning/part-time*
3	*The BBC*	*https://www.bbc.co.uk/news/science-environment-52111309*
4	Charlotte Brontë	*Jane Eyre*
5	Leo Tolstoy	*Father Sergius*
6	*The Washington Post*	*https://www.washingtonpost.com/lifestyle/wellness/what-is-inulin-and-why-is-it-showing-up-in-so-many-food-products/2019/06/11/3ee3d4be-86ec-11e9-98c1-e945ae5db8fb_story.html?utm_term=.fc1d852ebdd4*
7	*The Irish Times*	*https://www.irishtimes.com/opinion/unshakeable-purpose-florencenightingale-the-woman-who-revolutionised-nursing-1.4249703*
8	*Science Daily*	*https://www.sciencedaily.com/releases/2020/04/200416135954.htm*
9	*Nobel Prize*	*https://www.nobelprize.org/prizes/medicine/1913/speedread/*
10	*Nature*	*https://www.nature.com/articles/d41586-019-02770-7*
11	*The BBC*	*https://www.bbc.co.uk/news/science-environment-49349566*

EXERCISE	NAME OF SOURCE	LINK
12	*The BBC*	*https://www.bbc.co.uk/news/world-48513108*
13	*The BBC*	*https://www.bbc.co.uk/news/science-environment-51861539*
14	*The BBC*	*http://www.bbc.co.uk/history/historic_figures/edward_vii_king.shtml/*
15	*The BBC*	*https://www.bbc.co.uk/news/uk-england-leicestershire-52847850*
16	Mary Alice Murray	*The Story of A Puppet*
17	*Civil Service Careers*	*https://www.civil-service-careers.gov.uk/departments/*
18	*CPS*	*https://www.cps.gov.uk/criminal-justice-system*
19	*TCBC*	*https://www.torfaen.gov.uk/en/EducationLearning/Extra-curricularActivities/DukeofEdinburghsAward/Duke-of-Edinburghs-Award.aspx*
20	*Wickes*	*https://www.wickes.co.uk/how-to-guides/bathrooms*
21	*Argos UK*	*https://www.argos.co.uk/*
22	*The BBC*	*https://www.bbc.co.uk/news/world-europe-52832801*
23	*Science Daily*	*https://www.sciencedaily.com/releases/2019/03/190307081029.htm*
24	*Britannica*	*https://www.britannica.com/event/Battle-of-Britain-European-history-1940*
25	*The Washington Post*	*https://www.washingtonpost.com/world/asia_pacific/india-moon-mission-set-to-launch-a-week-after-it-was-aborted/2019/07/22/d599087e-ac45-11e9-9411-a608f9d0c2d3_story.html?utm_term=.58ee00d64008*
26	*The Washington Post*	*https://www.washingtonpost.com/lifestyle/wellness/while-companies-push-sugary-beverages-parents-should-promote-water-heres-how/2019/06/14/b40faae4-87a8-11e9-a491-25df61c78dc4_story.html?utm_term=.84f26d5539be*
27	*Britannica*	*https://www.britannica.com/event/assassination-of-John-F-Kennedy*

EXERCISE	NAME OF SOURCE	LINK
28	*HISTORY.COM*	*https://www.history.com/topics/us-presidents/abraham-lincoln*
29	*The BBC*	*http://www.bbc.co.uk/history/historic_figures/da_vinci_leonardo.shtml*
30	*The BBC*	*https://www.bbc.co.uk/news/science-environment-52839678*
31	*The BBC*	*https://www.bbc.co.uk/news/50591261*
32	*GOV.UK*	*https://www.gov.uk/government/history/past-prime-ministers/harold-wilson*
33	*The BBC*	*https://www.bbc.co.uk/news/technology-51474115*
34	Lewis Carroll	*Alice's Adventures in Wonderland*
35	*The BBC*	*http://www.bbc.co.uk/history/historic_figures/albert_prince.shtml*
36	Jonathan Swift	*Gulliver's Travels*
37	*The BBC*	*https://www.bbc.co.uk/news/world-europe-48616174*
38	*The Irish Independent*	*https://www.independent.ie/life/health-wellbeing/the-science-of-laughter-and-how-to-harness-the-benefits-39081683.html*
39	*The New Scientist*	*https://www.newscientist.com/article/2242413-nasa-has-selected-three-lunar-landers-to-bring-humans-to-the-moon/*
40	*The BBC*	*https://www.bbc.co.uk/news/science-environment-52973089*
41	*The BBC*	*https://www.bbc.co.uk/news/science-environment-52921479*
42	*The New Scientist*	*https://www.newscientist.com/article/mg24532700-500-for-all-mankind-review-a-superb-alternative-history-of-the-space-race/*
43	*The Guardian*	*https://www.theguardian.com/society/2019/jul/10/vaccines-measles-outbreak-immune-system*
44	*The Guardian*	*https://www.theguardian.com/business/2017/jan/18/globalisation-world-trade-asia-global-poverty*

EXERCISE	NAME OF SOURCE	LINK
45	*Wired*	*https://www.wired.com/2014/11/marsha-ivins/*
46	*The BBC*	*https://www.bbc.co.uk/news/health-37511554*
47	*The BBC*	*https://www.bbc.co.uk/news/science-environment-51504002*
48	*The BBC*	*http://www.bbc.co.uk/history/historic_figures/jenner_edward.shtml*
49	*The BBC*	*https://www.bbc.co.uk/news/entertainment-arts-52394504*
50	*Britannica*	*https://www.britannica.com/topic/Titanic*
51	*The Guardian*	*https://www.theguardian.com/society/2018/apr/29/millennials-struggling-is-it-fault-of-baby-boomers-intergenerational-fairness*
52	*Psychology Today*	*https://www.psychologytoday.com/us/basics/personality*
53	*The Guardian*	*https://www.theguardian.com/lifeandstyle/2015/jan/25/secrets-of-the-teenage-brain*
54	*The BBC*	*https://www.bbc.co.uk/news/science-environment-52582304*
55	*The BBC*	*https://www.bbc.co.uk/news/52533585*
56	*The BBC*	*https://www.bbc.co.uk/news/world-asia-india-52614770*
57	*National Geographic*	*https://www.nationalgeographic.com/science/2020/05/1000-year-old-bones-oldest-known-east-africa-tsunami-victims/*
58	*The BBC*	*https://www.bbc.co.uk/news/science-environment-52614870*
59	*The Guardian*	*https://www.theguardian.com/environment/2020/may/13/green-energy-firms-on-track-to-deliver-multi-billion-pound-wind-farms*
60	*The Washington Post*	*https://www.washingtonpost.com/climate-environment/2020/05/11/missouri-river-drought-climate-change/*

EXERCISE	NAME OF SOURCE	LINK
61	*Britannica*	*https://www.britannica.com/story/did-duchess-anastasia-survive-her-familys-execution*
62	*The BBC*	*https://www.bbc.co.uk/news/uk-northern-ireland-35873316*
63	*The New Scientist*	*https://www.newscientist.com/article/2243348-algae-transplant-could-protect-coral-reefs-threatened-by-warming-seas*
64	*The Irish Independent*	*https://www.independent.ie/business/farming/tillage/eu-to-halve-pesticides-by-2030-to-protect-bees-biodiversity-draft-39208608.html*
65	*GOV.UK*	*https://www.gov.uk/government/history/past-prime-ministers/gordon-brown*
66	*The Conversation*	*https://theconversation.com/dunkirk-was-a-victory-for-morale-but-ultimately-a-humiliating-military-defeat-81195*
67	*The BBC*	*https://www.bbc.co.uk/history/british/easterrising/profiles/po06.shtml*
68	*The BBC*	*https://www.bbc.co.uk/news/uk-scotland-north-east-orkney-shetland-52660032*
69	*The Conversation*	*https://theconversation.com/why-young-people-commit-crime-and-how-moral-education-could-help-new-research-131855*
70	*The New Scientist*	*https://www.newscientist.com/article/2243348-algae-transplant-could-protect-coral-reefs-threatened-by-warming-seas/*
71	*Britannica*	*https://www.britannica.com/biography/George-Best*
72	*The Irish Independent*	*https://www.independent.ie/business/farming/forestry-enviro/environment/european-commission-give-ireland-four-months-to-solve-water-contamination-issue-affecting-180000-people-39208578.html*

EXERCISE	NAME OF SOURCE	LINK
73	*The Telegraph*	*https://www.telegraph.co.uk/cars/driving-smart/driverless-cars/?utm_campaign=tmgspk_plrbin_2847_AtpKbd7xhV0g&plr=1&utm_content=2847&utm_source=tmgspk&WT.mc_id=tmgspk_plrbin_2847_AtpKbd7xhV0g&utm_medium=plrbin&mvt=i&mvn=a41559bb0cca47feade807d0ba0878bd&mvp=NA-TELEDESK-11238861&mvl=Key-bin-advert_tmg_bin_1%20%5BWeb%20-%20Index%20-%20Sparkbrain1%5D*
74	*GOV.UK*	*https://www.gov.uk/government/history/past-prime-ministers/margaret-thatcher*
75	*The Times*	*https://www.thetimes.co.uk/static/future-authentication-biometrics-covid-facial-recognition-surveillance-raconteur/?utm_source=nativo*